ENGLISH RECUSANT LITERATURE
1558–1640

Selected and Edited by
D. M. ROGERS

Volume 306

ROBERT PERSONS
A Treatise of Three Conversions
(VOLUME THREE)
1604

ROBERT PERSONS
A Treatise of Three Conversions
(VOLUME THREE)
1604

The Scolar Press
1976

ISBN 0 85967 318 9

*Published and printed in Great Britain by
The Scolar Press Limited, 59-61 East Parade,
Ilkley, Yorkshire and
39 Great Russell Street,
London WC1*

1918735

NOTE

Reproduced (original size) from a copy in the library of Stonyhurst College, by permission of the Rector. The first and second volumes of this work are reproduced in English Recusant Literature volumes 304 and 305. The second part of this volume, *A review of ten publike disputations*, was also issued separately: see Allison and Rogers 638.

References: Allison and Rogers 640; STC 19416.

THE
THIRD PART

OF A TREATISE

Intituled
OF THREE CONVERSIONS
OF ENGLAND.

Conteyninge an examen of the Calendar or Catalogue of Proteſtant Saintes, Martyrs and Confeſſors, deuiſed by *Fox*, and prefixed before his huge Volume of Actes and Monuments: VVith a Paralel or Compariſon therof to the Catholike Roman Calendar, and Saintes therin conteyned.

THE LAST SIX MONETHES.

VVhervnto is annexed in the end, another ſeuerall Treatiſe, called: A re-view of ten publike Diſputations, or Conferences, held in England about matters of Religion, eſpecially about the Sacrament and Sacrifice of the Altar, vnder King Edward and Queene Mary.

By N. D.

❧❧❧

S. Aug. lib. 3. contra Parmen. cap. 6.
Sacrilegious ſchiſmatiks and impious heretiks, dare preſume vvhen they are puniſhed, to accompt the puniſhment of their fury for true martyrdomes.

Math. 25. Verſ. 32.
God ſhall ſeparate them a ſunder (at the day of iudgement) as the ſhepheard doth ſeparate the ſheep from goates.

Imprinted with licence, Anno Domini 1604:

The generall Contentes & Partes of the whole Treatise, intituled, of three Conuersions of England, published in three seuerall Tomes.

FIRST TOME.

THE *first Tome sheweth three Conuersions of our countrey from paganisme to Christian faith. The first vnder the Apostles in the first age after Christ. The second vnder* Pope Eleutherius, *in the second age. The third vnder* Pope Gregory the First *in the sixt age. And that the same Religion was truly* Catholike *and* Romaine, *and hath endured vnto our tyme. And that the Protestant Religion had neuer any beginning or progresse in England before these our dayes.*

SECOND TOME.

The *second Tome examineth the new* Calendar- Saints *sett downe by* Fox *in his Acts & Monuments for the first six Monethes of the yeare; And hath annexed vnto yt in the end by way of Appendix,* A defence of a certaine relation, *sent into England, concerninge a* Triall *made in the yeare* 1600. *betweene the Bishopp of* Eureux *and* Monsieur Plessis *in the presence of the* King of France *that now is, and his nobility, touchinge diuers falsityes obiected to the said* Plessis.

THIRD TOME.

The *third Tome discusseth the said* Calendar *of* Foxian Saints *for the second six Monethes of the yeare. And hath for his adioinder in the end,* A re-view of ten publike disputations, *held in* England *vnder* K. Edward *and* Q. Mary, *about diuers principall points of Religion.*

THE

THE
EPISTLE
DEDICATORY

*To the glorious Company of English
Sainctes in heauen.*

OVV cannot be ignorant
(moſt bleſſed Society) in-
ioying as yovv do, the happy preſence & viſion of your Lord
and Maiſter the lambe of God, in
vvhome, and by vvhome all things
are ſeene, and vvho is the light and
lanterne and ſunne yt ſelfe of that
your royall and celeſtiall Citty;
hovv that vpon this day tvvelue-
moneth, being our and your ſol-
lemne feſtiuall day of * *All-Sainčts*, 1. Non.
I conceaued a full purpoſe to dedi- anno
cate this vvhole vvorke (as then yt 1602.
vvas deſigned) vnto yovv the glorious Saints, and glorified ſpiritts of

　　　* 2　　　　our

our Ile of *Albion*, & this for the reasons vvhich heere againe I shall a little after, for the readers better instruction, in part repeat, hauinge at that tyme noted dovvne, & put in paper, the vvhole summe of my said Epistle dedicatory vnto yovv.

The first Tome of the Treatise of 3. conuersions conteyned in tvvo parts. But aftervvards the former tvvo parts of the said vvorke vvaxinge to the quantity of a seuerall tome I changed my purpose, thinkinge it better to direct the same vnto the Catholiks of our Countrey, for diuers reasons and respects expressed in my Epistle directed vnto them, and prefixed before the said first Tome: so as there remained this third part onlie more properlie indeed belonginge vnto yovv, for that it conteineth the examen of a nevv Calendar of nevv English Saints latelie made and published

in

in print, vvho pretend by help
of their nevv fangled factious pa-
trons, to intrude into your roomes
and places.

And for that this part alfo grevv
fo faft vnder my hands, as it vvas
thought meet to be reparted into
tvvo feuerall Tomes or Volumes;
the one vvas adiudged fitteft to be
offered to our Englifh Proteftants,
the other to yovv Englifh Saints,
though vpon farre different and
diftant reafons peculiar to your feuerall eftates & conditions; yet one
great reafon vvas common to you
both that is to fay, the common iniurie offered to each of you by this
nevv affociation thruft vpon you
by *Iohn Fox*, I meane, vpon Proteftants on earth, and vpon yovv in
heauen, though vpon them by in-
ducemēt & confent of their ovvne
vvills for that they are content

* 3   to

to be matched vvith ſuch companions: but vpon yovv by intruſion
and violence, vvho haue euer de-
teſted ſuch hereticall mates. And
for that I haue ſpoken ſufficiently
in the Epiſtle dedicatory of my ſecond Tome, concerning the ſhame
and diſhonour, vvhich accrueth to
Proteſtants by this coniunction, I
ſhall novv ſpeake of your iniury
only, vvhich is ſo much the greater,
and more intolerable in all mens
ſight, by hovv much more high &
ſacred is your ſtate, and your heauenly mynds repugnant to theirs.

For firſt vvhat greater iniury can
there be offered tovvards vvights
of your vvorthineſſe, then that
vvheras yovv haue byn ſeaſed novv
for ſo many yeares and ages togeather, of that immortall ioy and
bliſſe, vvhich yovv poſſeſſe in the
ſight and company of our Sauiour;
and

and the fame being beleeued, ac-
knovvledged, and publifhed vpon
earth by the teftimony of his vniuerfall Church & Kingdome, in all
her hiftoryes, martyrologes and Ecclefiafticall Calendars; vvhat thing
(I fay) or attempt may be thought
or efteemed, more violent vvrong-
full, or iniurious, then novv to be
difpoffeffed therof, and driuen out
in a certaine manner, by this incur-
fion of Foxian Saints into our Englifh Calendar, vvherin not fo much
as one of your order, that is to fay,
of our Englifh, Brittifh, or Scottifh
Saints, hath byn fuffered to keepe
his roome, or permitted to hould
his place, but all vvithout differéce
remoued and fhutt out from that
Ecclefiafticall fenate of his, though
fome fevv of other contreyes he
doth lett ftand as he found them in
our Calendar, vvherby doth ap-

The firft great iniury offered to Englifh Saints.

* 4   peare

peare the speciall stomake that vvas, and is against yovv and your honour in particular. And this for the first point.

The next iniury offered yovv is somevvhat greater then this: for if in your places he had aduaunced to the honour of Saints Martyrs and Confessors, some, more eminent in meritt of vertue and sanctitie then your selues; such is your perfection of humility, and entire loue of truth and iustice in the most perfect state vvhich novv yovv possesse as no cause of offence could grovv to yovv or others therby: But the base exchanges he maketh of yovv, and for yovv in this behalfe, are indeed more intollerable, then the iniurie yt selfe of strikinge your names out of his Calendar; vvherin I referre me to that vvhich hath byn often noted before

before in this kind, by comparinge the tvvo Calendars togeather, and by confrontinge page vvith page, day vvith day, and fainct vvith fainct in euery moneth both of thes and the former fix monethes, vvherin yovv fhall find, that for a mayne multitude of moft venerable and learned Bifhopps, Fathers, and Doctors, glorious Martyrs, moft admirable Confeffors, holy Virgins, Eremites, Anachorites, and religious retyred Saints abandoninge the vvorld, and follovvinge Chrift after the ftraiteft manner of life, expreffed in our Calendar, all vvhich did agree both exactlie in one faith and Religion, though in different ftate of life, each one fought to glorifie his Sauiour in the higheft degree: yovv fhall find (I fay) that for all thefe, and in their places Fox
and

and his fellovves haue brought in and canonized a rablement of moſt contemptible people, partly Engliſh, and partly of other nations dravven togeather from all Tribunalls of Iuſtice, vvhere they haue byn puniſhed for their vvickedneſſe, & particularly for their diſagreeinge in Religion, aſvvell from vs, as amonge themſelues, being vvillfully giuen to ſects and obſtinate fancyes of their ovvne braines both men and vveomen, as by reading of this hiſtory is euident; and yovv (moſt glorious Saints) in heauen cannot but moane and lament ſuch madneſſe of your contreymen, ſo farre forth, as your preſent happy ſtate may be capable of compaſſion tovvards the ridiculous folly of ſuch attempts.

There remaineth the third and greateſt iniury of all, though not
indeed

indeed concerninge so much yovv
and your particular honours, as the
honour of your Lord and Maister, The third
vvho taught yovv both by his do- & grea-
                                   teſt iniu-
ctrine, & example of conuerſation, ry.
the true vvayes of life and ſanctity,
vvherby you aſcended to the ſame:
vvhich vvayes theſe men haue
ſought to diſgrace and diſauthorize
as much as in them lay, by aduan-
cinge to this title and ſtile of Saints,
ſuch men as tooke the quite contrary courſe to that of yours, & oppoſite to all Saints that euer vvent
before yovv.

For vvheras the firſt ſtepp to ſanctity in yovv, vvas vnion and moſt
exact conformity in faith, as before
vve haue ſhevved theſe men haue
pleaſed to make their choyſe of
nyne or ten different condemned
ſects for their Catalogue of Saints,
as in the * narration of the firſt ſix * *Supra*
                                        cap. 3.
                                  monethes

monethes vve haue declared. And
then conformablie to this ſuite
they paſſe on to the reſt of ould
Chriſtian vertues ; that vvheras for
example many of yovv tooke the
heauenlie vvay of virginitie, chaſti-
tie, and continencie ; fevv or none
of theſe nevv Saints haue allovved
of that vvay , noe one of them
lightlie ſo much as profeſſinge the
firſt , and for the ſecond , their
cheefeſt pillars haue impugned,
they being Apoſtata prieſts, mõks,
and friars that for loue of the fleſh
broke their vovves made to almighty God of religious chaſtity.
Faſtinge alſo , vvatchinge , large
prayer, hayr-cloth , lyinge on the
ground, and other ſuch chaſtiſmẽts
of the body for conſeruation and
encreaſe of ſpiritt , vvere ordinarie
vvayes in yovv , to arriue vvhere
yovv novv raigne : vvhich vvayes
                                         are

are ſo contemned by theſe nevv
Saints, as they diſdayne to heare
them ſo much as named.

VVhat ſhould I ſpeake of large &
aboundant almeſdeeds, building of
churches, monaſteryes, hoſpitalles,
colledges, ſchooles, bridges, high-
vvaies, and other publike benefitts,
and moſt honourable monuméts,
vvhervvith none of theſe nevv later
Saints vvould euer lightlie trouble
themſelues or eſteeme them as any
path tovvards paradiſe, but profeſſed rather that they vvould enter by
only·faith, hovv deuoid ſoeuer they
vvere of all theſe other furnitures of
good-vvorks: So as this nevv vvay
to ſanctity being once found out, or
deuiſed by them; the ould vvayes of
good life taught by Chriſt, & all his
Saints after him, are not only di-
ſhounoured, but reiected alſo therby. And this is the higheſt kind of
iniury

iniury in deed that both yovv and
your Maifter our Sauiour do receaue at thefe mens hands.

The con-
clufion
and au-
thors pe-
tition. VVherfore to conclude this my
dedicatorie Epiftle or prefentation
of this fmall vvorke againft your
aduerfaryes (moft glorious Saints
& celeftiall fpiritts)I do moft humbly befeech yovv by that inflamed
loue & charity,vvhervvith I knovv
yovv are indued in that heauenlie
citty by the fruition of your euerlaftinge creator and redeemer, to accept in good part, this fmall oblation of myne as proceedinge from
the higheft degree of all venerable
and dutifull affection tovvards you
and your eftate, and to protect the
author & offerer vvith the mighty
fhield of your holie prayers and in-
terceffion for him that in fome part
at leaft he may follovv and imitate
your happy fteps in the feruice of
your

your King and Maister, and therby
ariue finallie to that euerlasting fe-
licitie vvhich you possesse. Second-
lie to respect your deare countrey
afflicted in this age vvith multipli-
citie & infelicitie, of sects, schismes,
and heresies, the heauiest scourge
that possiblie could fall vpon her;
vvherin notvvithstandinge by the
great and singular mercie of our Sauiour and your intercession, there
haue not failed manie vvorthie
schollers and children of yours to
stand most constantlie in this con-
fraction, euen to the sheddinge of
their last bloud in defence of the
pietie, & puritie of Catholike faith
& Religion, vvhome in like manner I comend to the continuance
of your protection, as also I do most
earnestlie the reduction of those
that are yet aduersaryes, and out of
the vvay, depriued of true light, and
de-

deceaued vvith the falſe ſhevv of pretended *reformation* and verball holines in theſe nevv Saints by their ſolifidian Iuſtification, deuoid of all true ſanctity both of faith and vvorks, and of all good exerciſes of Chriſtian piety, as in this hiſtory I doubt not, but vvill aboundantly appeare. And ſo I end, moſt humbly and dutifully takinge my leaue of yovv, vntill vve meete in that your heauenly Hieruſalem, vvhervnto I beſeech yovv to be perpetuall ayders and interceſſors for me. This firſt of Nouember 1603.

A TABLE

A TABLE OF THE

PARTICVLAR CONTENTS

and chapters of the vvhole treatise
of the Conuersions of England.

*The preface to the first Tome, vvherin diuers principall
points are handled: about iudgement in matters of
faith; and vvith how great care and sollicitude the
same ought to be considered of.*

THE FIRST PART,

Of this Treatise concerninge plantinge
and continuance of Catholike
Religion in England.

WHETHER *England, & Englishmen haue particular obligation to the Sea of* Rome *aboue other
nations, and of the first Conuersion of* Britans *to Christian Religion in tyme of the Apostles.* CHAP. I. **1.**

*An answere to certaine cauillations, lyes, & falsifica-
tions of* Syr Francis Hastings, *& his Maisters* Fox
and the Magdeburgians, *about the first preaching of
Christian faith in* Britany; *wherin is handled also the
controuersie of* Celebratinge Easter. CHAP. II. **2.**

*The former controuersie is handled more particular-
ly, how the* Grecian *custome of celebratinge Easter
day after the fashion of the* Iewes, *came first into the
British and Scottish Church, and how vntruly and wickedly* Iohn Fox *&* Iohn Bale *do behaue themselues
about this matter.* CHAP. III. **3.**

Of the second conuersion of Britany *vnder* K. Lucius *by* Pope Eleutherius, *and teachers sent from
Rome, about the yeare of Christ 180. and of the noto-* **4.**

* *

rious

*rious abſurd cauillatious of heretikes about the ſame
also.* CHAP. IV.

5. *Of another hereticall ſhifte about the former conuerſion of* Britany *vnder Pope* Eleutherius, *and
K.* Lucius, *as though the faith of Rome, that vvas
then, did not remayne now : vvhich is reproued by two
euident demonſtrations, againſt the inſtants giuen by*
Iohn Fox, *and* Syr Francis Haſtings, *the one demonſtration being negatiue, the other affirmatiue, and
firſt of the negatiue.* CHAP. V.

6. *It is proued by the ſecond kind of affirmatiue, or poſitiue arguments, that the points of Catholike doctrine
before denyed by* Fox, *and* Syr Francis, *vvere in vſe
in* Pope Eleutherius *his tyme, and in the ages immediatly followinge, and this by teſtimony of Proteſtant
vvryters themſelues.* CHAP. VI.

7. *The ſame argument is continued, and it is ſhewed
out of the* Magdeburgians *how they accuſe, and
abuſe the Fathers of the ſecond and third age, for holdinge vvith vs againſt them : vvherof is inferred,
that thoſe two ages vvere then alſo of our Religion.*
CHAP. VII.

8. *Of the third conuerſion of our Iland, and Engliſh
nation by* S. Auſten, *and his fellowes ſent from* Pope
Gregory *the firſt anno* Domini 596. *and of diuers
notorious hereticall ſhiftes, and impudencyes vſed to deface the ſaid two excellent men* S. Gregory, *and*
S. Auſten, *and the Religion brought into England by
them.* CHAP. VIII.

9. *That the* Roman Religion *brought into England
by* S. Auguſtine *vnder Pope* Gregory, *vvas the
very ſame, that vvas brought in before vnder* Pope
Eleutherius *by* Fugatius *and* Damianus, *and*
conti-

continued *afterward amonge the* Britans *vntill the comminge of* S. Auguſtine *to the Engliſh nation.* CHAP. IX.

The continuation of the ſame matter, vvherin is ſhewed by diuers proofes, and examples, that the Britans *before* S. Gregoryes *tyme, vvere of the ſame religion that he ſent into* England *by* S. Auguſtine, *to vvitt, of the* Romane. CHAP. X.   10.

The deduction of the aforeſaid Catholike Romane Religion planted in England *by* S. Auguſtine, *from his tyme vnto our dayes, and that from* K. Ethelbert *who firſt receaued the ſame, vnto* K. Henry *the eight, there vvas neuer any publike interruption of the ſaid religion in our land.* CHAP. XI.   11.

How the ſame Catholike Religion had continued, & perſeuered in England *duringe the tymes and raignes of* K. Henry *the eight, and his three children,* K. Edward, Q. Mary, *and* Q. Elizabeth, *notwithſtandinge all the troubles, chaunges, alterations, and tribulations that haue fallen out therabout, & that the ſame religion is like to continue to the worlds end, yf our ſinnes hinder it not.* CHAP. XII.   12.

THE SECOND PART,

For Searchinge of the Proteſtant Church and Religion.

OF *how great importance* Eccleſiaſticall *ſucceſſion is for triall of true Religion, and how ſectaryes haue ſought to fly the force therof, by ſaying that the Church is inuiſible: how fond a ſhift this is, and how fooliſhly* Fox *doth behaue himſelfe therin.* CHAP. I.   1.

* * 2   *The*

2.   *The particular examination of the difcent or fuccef-*
fion of Iohn Fox *his Church in* England, *or els where*
for the firft 300. *yeares after Chrift: to witt, vnto the*
tyme of the Emperour Conftantine, *and vvhether*
any fuch Church vvas extant then in the vvorld or no,
and in vvhome?   CHAP. II.

3.   *The profecution of the fame matter: to witt, of the*
difcent of the Catholike & Proteftant Church for other
300. *yeares, that is from* Pope Syluefter *and* Conftantine, *to* Pope Gregory, *and* Mauritius *the*
Emperour, *and vvhere* Iohn Fox *his Church lay hid*
in this tyme.   CHAP. III.

4.   *How matters paffed in the Chriftian Church both*
abroad, and at home in England *duringe the third fta-*
tion of tyme from Pope Gregory, *and* K. Ethelbert *of* Kent, *vnto* K. Egbert *our firft Monarch,*
conteyninge the fpace of 200. *yeares.*   CHAP. IV.

5.   *The fourth ftation or diuifion of tymes from* K. Egbert *vnto* William Conquerour *conteyninge the*
fpace of fome 290. *yeares. And how* Iohn Fox *his*
Church paffed in thefe dayes, and vvhether there vvere
any Pope Ioane, *or no?*   CHAP. V.

6.   *The narration of* English *Ecclefiaftical affaires du-*
ringe this fourth ftation or diftinction of tyme, is conti-
nued, and the abfurdityes of Iohn Fox *are difcouered.*
CHAP. VI.

7.   *The fifth Station of tyme conteyninge other* 300.
yeares from William Conquerour *vnto the tyme of*
Iohn Wickliffe, *vvherin is examined, vvhether the*
Cath. Roman *Church did perish in this tyme as* Fox
affirmeth. Heere is treated alfo of Pope Hilde-
brand, *and of* Mariage *of* Priefts. CHAP. VII.

8.   *There followeth a dreaminge imagination of* Iohn
Fox

Fox *contrary to yt selfe, about the fall of the Church of* Rome, *and risinge of Antichrist ; vvith the rest that remayneth of our Ecclesiasticall history from the Conquest to* Wickliffe. CHAP. VIII.

Of the tyme from Iohn Wickliffe, *vnto the beginninge of the raigne of* K. Henry *the* 8. *conteyninge about a hundred and fortie yeares, and how the Church of* Rome, *and* Fox *his Church passed in these tymes.* CHAP. IX.   9.

The most absurd & ridiculous succession of sectaryes appointed by Iohn Fox, *for the cōtinuance of his Church, from* Pope Innocentius 3. *downeward, vvhere also by this occasion is declared the true nature, and condition of lawfull Ecclesiasticall succession.* CHAP. X.   10.

The search of Iohn Fox *his Church is continued vnder the gouernment, and raigne of* K. Henry *the* 8. *and his children ; and yt is discussed what manner of Church* Iohn Fox *then had, or may be imagined to haue had.* CHAP. XI.   11.

Vvhether Iohn Fox *his Church hath had any place vnder* K. Edward, Q. Mary, *and her Maiestie that now raigneth: and how farre it hath bine admitted, or is admitted at this day.* CHAP. XII.   12.

The conclusion of both these former parts, togeather vvith a particular discourse of the notorious different proceeding of Catholiks & Protestants, in searching out the truth of matters in controuersie. CHAP. XIII.   13.

These Chapters are handled in
the first Tome.

THE THIRD PART,

Concerninge the examen of Iohn Fox his
Ecclefiafticall Calendar and Proteftant
Saints therein conteyned.

A Double Calendar, the one Catholike, the other
deuifed by Iohn Fox, for the peculiar Saints of
his Church.

A direction or inftruction to the difcreet and pious
Reader, how to vfe this double Calendar to his greateft
fpirituall comodity, and increafe of deuotion.

CHAPTERS.

1.   Of the Calendar of Iohn Fox his Martyrs, prefixed
before his Acts and Monuments; how abfurd a thinge yt
is, and different from the Catholike Calendar: and how
therin he doth imitate old heretiks, by fetting downe
malefactors for Martyrs of his fect, and defacinge other
that are true, and Cath. Martyrs indeed. CHAP. I.

2.   Of the particular caufes that moued the auncient
Chriftian Church to keep a Calendar of Saints-feafts,
and vvhat forts of honour fhe vfed towards them: and
that noe one point therof agreeth to Iohn Fox his
Church or Saints, by his owne confeffion. CHAP. II.

3.   A confideration of nyne feuerall fects, that haue principally troubled the Church of God for thefe laft 400.
years paft: to witt, from the yeare of Chrift 1200. vntill our tyme: And that all opinions and articles of beleefe, held by the Foxian Saints of this enfuinge Calendar different from the Catholike, may be reduced, to one
or more of thefe nyne fects, as their heads and origins.
CHAP. III.

VVhat

VVhat may be thought of Iohn Fox his Martyrs about ther forwardnesse in offeringe themselues to dy for their opinions: and vvhether yt may be called constancy or obstinacy? CHAP. IV. 4.

The suruey of euery moneth in particular; and first of Ianuary, *and of the Foxian Martyrs therin conteyned, the principall wherof are these rubricate sett forth in redd letters,* Iohn Wickliffe preacher, Syr Roger Acton Knight, *and* Iohn Philpot artificer. CHAP. V. 5.

Of the moneth of February, *and 26. Foxian Martyrs conteyned therin, wherof eyght are rubricate, or in redd colours, to witt:* Oldcastle, Onley, Luther, Rogers, Sanders, Hooper, Taylor *and* Farrar, *and the other 18. in blacke attyre, vvherof* Agnes Potten *and* Trunchfields vvife, *are the last.* CHAP. VI. 6.

Of the moneth of March, *and Foxian Saints and Martyrs therin conteyned, namely* Bilney *and* Cranmer, *that are the principall, vvith other accompaninge them.* CHAP. VII. 7.

Of the moneth of Aprill, *and of the Saints and Martyrs, which* Iohn Fox *assigneth therin to haue byn of his Religion; with a briefe examination both of their beliefe, liues, and deathes.* CHAP. VIII. 8.

The examination of the moneth of May, *and of the Martyrs & Confessors canonized therin by* Iohn Fox *for Saints of his Church, and so published in his Calendar.* CHAB. IX. 9.

The discussion of the moneth of Iune, *and what Martyrs and Confessors* Iohn Fox *doth place in the Catalogue and Calendar therof, as appertayninge to his triumphant Church.* CHAP. X. 10.

** 4.   These

These Chapters are conteyned in the second Tome, the rest that follow in this third.

11. The *discussion of the moneth of* Iuly, *wherin* Iohn Frith, *and* Iohn Bradford, *the first a marryed younge man, the second a minister, are cheife Cardinall and rubricate Martyrs, accordinge to* Fox *his Calendar.* CHAP. XI.

12. *Of the moneth of* August, *and what Martyrs and Confessors* Iohn Fox *setteth downe in the same to haue suffered for his Religion.* CHAP. XII.

13. *The moneth of* September, *and Foxian Saints therin conteyned; the number wherof is thirty and eight, beginninge with* Father Abraham *and endinge with* Iohn Fortune. CHAP. XIII.

14. *The moneth of* October *and view of Foxian Saints therin; wherin three are principall rubricate* Tyndall, Ridley *and* Latymer. CHAP. XIV.

15. *Of the Martyrs and Confessors of* Fox *his Church for the moneth of* Nouember, *both vnder* K. Henry *the 8. and* Q. Mary. CHAP. XV.

16. *Of the last moneth which is* December, *what Martyrs and Confessors it comprehendeth of* Fox *his Church; and that the number of Confessors therin is greater then of Martyrs, wherof* K. Edward *the sixt, is the last, and shutteth vp the moneth and whole Calendar.* CHAP. XVI.

17. *Eight seuerall obseruations & considerations about the premisses; wherin is considered what persons are left out, and what are put into* Fox *his Calendar: how they are canonized; of what spirit & agreement of Religion they were amonge themselues; whether they were lawfully punished or noe? and the like.* CHAP. XVII.

A briefe

A briefe Cenſure of Iohn Fox his wrytings, againſt which other two larger books are alſo ſaid to be in hand, the one in Latin, the other in Engliſh: And by occaſion heereof, the author giueth his iudgement why the hiſtory of England, ſo much deſired both by Catholiks and Proteſtants, cannot well be wrytten by eyther of them in theſe our dayes.   Chap. XVIII.   **18.**

A note of more then a hundred and twenty lyes vtte-red by Fox in leſſe then three leaues of his bookes of Acts and Monuments, and this is one kind only of perſidious dealing in falſifying the opinions of Catholikes, touching diuers cheefe points of their Religion. Chap. XIX.   **19.**

By occaſion of a falſe and ridiculous definition ſett downe by Fox of a Chriſtian man, according to the Popes Religion; there is examined the true deſcription of a Catholike and Proteſtant in our dayes, with the differences that enſue therof betwene them.   Chap. XX.   **20.**

A DOVBLE

A DOVBLE

CALENDAR.

The one Catholike, the other deuised by Iohn Fox, for the peculiar Saints of his Church.

In the first, are conteyned the names of those Saints, wherof the Roman Church doth celebrate the memoryes and festiuall dayes in her Calendar, as also those, which our English Calendar of the vse of Sarum *doth add of the particular Saints of our contrey. And where neither of these two Calendars hath any celebrity, or Saints feast, but only* Feria, *there is supplyed some one for that day, out of the Roman martyrologe.*

For which cause the letters c. r. in the said Catholike Calendar ensuinge, doe signifie *Calendarium* Romanum: c. s. *Calendarium* Sarum, and m. r. *Martyrologium Romanum.*

The second Calendar, is the same, word for word, which Fox *deuised and prefixed before his volume of Acts and Monuments, conteyninge the Catalogue of such his Martyrs and Confessors, as he presumed to be of his Church only, and not of ours, for that they were in some points of beliefe different, and for the same cause punished by ours, and so he maketh a Calendar of them apart, admittinge only some few of our Calendar, as you will see by the viewe.*

To both which sorts of Saints, there is added in eache Calendar a briefe note or explication what euery one was; which may serue for an epitome or summary of that, which is handled afterward more largly in the examen of euery moneth seuerally, and in the comparisons thervnto adioyned of both Calendars togeather.

The Moneth of Iuly.

Litt. ᴅñic.	Ann˜ Chr.	Dies menſ.	
ʒ	303	1	ᴍ.ʀ. SS. Iulij & Aaronis mart. *Theſe vvere tvvo holy men of the Brittiſh nation, that ſuffered death in England vvith S. Albane. Se* Gild. lib. de exid. Brit. *and* S. Bede lib. 1. cap. 7. geſt. Anglorum. *and others.*
A		2	ᴄ.ʀ. Viſitatio B. Mariæ duplex. *The celebration of this feaſt of the mother of God, in remembrance of her iorney into the mountaynes of Iudæa to viſit the mother of ſainct Iohn Baptiſt* Luc 1. *vvas inſtituted by the Church vpon the yeare of Chriſt* 1389. *to obtayne the rather by her interceſſion the takinge avvay of a certayne ſchiſme, vvhich ſoone after vvas obtayned. Se* Plat. *in the life of Pope Boniface the* 9. *& others.*
	1389		
b	350	3	ᴍ.ʀ. Heliodori Epiſcopi & Confeſſoris. *This vvas a holy Biſhopp of great learninge highly eſteemed by* S. Hierome, *vvho liued in his dayes, and to vvhome he vvrote a large epiſtle in the praiſe of ſolitary life, as alſo he dedicated to him the epitaph of the death of* Nepotianus, *making mention of him in like manner in many other places of his vvorks: as* ep. 2. ad Nepotianum & 37. ad Iulianum. *&c.*
ꜫ	306	4	ᴍ.ʀ. Theodori Epiſcopi & mart. *This man vvas of Libia in Africke and B. of a Citty named* Cyrene, *he vvas beaten to death vvith balls of lead for Chriſtian faith vnder Diocleſian, his tongue being firſt cutt of, that his complaint might not be heard. See the Greeke menaloge, the Roman Martyrologe, and others.*

ᴍ.ʀ.

The Moneth of Iuly.

Henry Voes &Iohn Eſch. mart. Theſe were two Apoſtata friars of Luthers owne order , to witt of the habitt of S. Auſten, though not of the Religiō being run out of their monaſtery for liberty;the former of them was not aboue 24. years old ; they were both burnt togeather at Bruxelis in the yeare 1523. Se *c.11.n.15.*

Iohn Frith Martyr. This was a yong marryed man of London, who being imbued with the ſpiritt of new doctrine in the beginninge of proteſtancy in England , went ouer the Sea to *Tyndall* in Flanders, and afterward returninge defended ſtrange opinions againſt the Biſhops,and went to the fire for the ſame, as yow may ſee in his ſtory at larg. *cap. 11. num.2.3.4.5.6. & deinceps.*

Andrevv Hevvit, & Antony Perſon mart. The firſt of theſe two , was a yong apprentiſe to a Taylor of London , ſome 2. yeares yonger then *Fryth*, who offered to dy for *Fryth* his opinions , though he knew not well what they were. The ſecond was a pariſh prieſt of *VVindeſore* who had deuiſed a new opinion about the bleſſed Sacrament , to vvitt, *that Chriſts body vvas the vvord of God, and the bread to be broken to the people*, and that this was the meaninge of thoſe words : *he tooke bread and brooke, &c.* See ibid. *num.16.17.18.*

Robert Teſivvood mart. This was a muſition of the Church of *lVindeſore* who was indighted and condemned vpon the ſtatute of 6. articles for ſpitefull raylinge ſpeaches againſt the bleſſed Sacrament of the Altar,& for pertakinge with *Antony Perſon*, in his new madd hereſie about the ſame. See *ibid. num.18.19.*

Henry

Litt. Dñic.	Ann⁹ Chr.	Dies menf.	The Catholike Calendar.　Iuly.
d	302	5	M. R. Zoæ mart. *This vvas a holy vvoman, vvife of S. Nicoſtratus the martyr, vvho geuinge herſelfe vvholy to deuotion, and being taken one day prayinge at S. Peters Altar, vvas for that cauſe beaten firſt by the perſecutors; and then hanged vp by the hayre on a tree, and choked vvith ſmoke of fire made vnder her. See her paſſion ſett forth by* Sur. tom.1. Ian.20. S. Bede *in his martyrologe, and others.*
e	86	6	M. R. Romuli Epiſcopi & mart. *This man vvas made Biſhopp of* Feſula *in Tuſcane by* S. Peter *the Apoſtle, and vvas martyred for Chriſtian Religion vnder Domitian the Emperor. See* Anton. part.1. tit.6. cap.26. Volater. *and others.*
f	755 705 664	7	M. R. SS. **Willibaldi** & Heddi Epiſcoporum & Confeſſ. & S. Ediiburgæ Virg. *All theſe three vvere Engliſh Sainɗs, & died in this moneth. The firſt was compagnion to* S. Bonifacius, *and firſt Biſhopp of the Citty of* Eyſtad *in* Germany. *The ſecond vvas Biſhop of the VVeſt-ſaxons. And the third vvas daughter of* Annas K. *of the* Eaſt-Angles. *See* Bed. lib.3. cap.5. & 8. & lib.4. cap.9. lib.5. cap.10. *and others.*
g	275	8	M. R. Quinquaginta militum mart. *Theſe vvere put to death vnder the Emperor* Aurelian *for confeſſion of their faith, in the hauen of* Rome. *They vvere conuerted by the preachinge of a holy vvoman called* S.Bonoſa. *See* Roman. Mart. *and* Dam. in vita Felicis PP. *and others.*

M. R.

Litt. Dñic.	Ann⁹ Chr.	Dies mens.	Fox his Calendar.　　Iuly.
d	1543	5	*Henry Filmer martyr.* This was alſo a towneſman of *VVindeſore* and an aſſociate of the former two in ſowing of hereſie, and raylinge at Catholike Religion in K. Henryes dayes for which he was condemned and burned togeather with them. They tippled ſo merely in the priſon and at the fire ſide, as Fox confeſſeth that ſome held they died dronke. See *ibid. num.* 19. 20.
e	1555	6	*Iohn Bradford Preacher martyr.* This man being borne at *Mancheſter* in Lancaſhire, was firſt a ſeruingman to *Syr Iohn Harrington* knight in K. Henryes dayes, but afterward being made a Proteſtant in K. *Edvvards* dayes became miniſter and preacher, being yet a lay man, and refuſing to be made Deacon by the orders then in force, as Fox confeſſeth being a preciſition, he was burned afterward in Q. Maryes tyme for Caluiniſme. See his ſtory at large. *cap.* 11. *nu.* 22. 23. 24. *& deinceps.*
f	1555	7	*Iohn Leafe martyr.* This was an apprentiſe to a tallow-chandelor in London, who being not able to wryte or read, yet afterward he anſwered ſo deſperately to the Biſhopps, as none like him. And when his hereticall articles were ſent to him to acknowledge, he being not able to ſubſcribe, pricked his fingar with a pin, and beſpotted the paper with bloud, ſendinge the ſame backe for his ſubſcription he was burned in Smithfield. See *ibid. num.* 27.
g	1555	8	*Margery Pulley* and *VVilliam Minge mart.* The firſt of theſe 2. was a poore woman of *Peppingbury* in Kent, burned for willfull ſtandinge in diuers hereſies. The ſecond was an Apoſtata prieſt impriſoned at *maidſtone,* and there died in priſon: Here Fox calleth him a Martyr, but in his Acts a Confeſſor only. See *ibid. nnm.* 28.

Richard

Litt. Ðñic.	Ann⁹ Chr.	Dies menſ.	
A	253	9	M. R. Anatoliæ virg. & mart. *This vvas a famous Chriſtiã virgin of the coũtrey of* Spoletum *in Italy, that did infinite miracles, & being caſt to a hideous ſerpent, vvas not hurt by the ſame, & ſo laſtly vvas pearced through vvith a ſvvord vnder the Emperor* Decius. *See of her* S. Bede *in* mart. & Pet. Diac. l. de vir. Illuſtr. *and others.*
♭	225	10	C. R. Septem fratrum mart. Semiduplex. *Theſe vvere 7. children of a holy vvoman of Rome named* Felicitas, *vvho vvas alſo martyred for Chriſtian faith; and theſe her children vvere all put to death on one day in* Rome *vnder* Antoninus *the Emperour, vvhoſe names are expreſſed in the Roman martyrologe.* S. Gregory *the firſt made a ſermon in their Church vpon their feſtiuall day.* Homil. 3. in Euangel. *and others.*
c	150	11.	C. R. Pij Papæ & mart. *This Pope vvas in the beginninge of the ſecond age after Chriſt, ſucceeded* S. Higinius, *and vvent before* S. Anicetus *both Popes and Martyrs. Of him doth vvryte* S. Iren. lib. 4. hiſt. c. 10. *he vvas put to death vnder the Emperor* Antoninus Pius, *as moſt authors do hold, though others ſay vnder* Marcus Aurelius Antoninus.
d	380	12	C. R. Naboris & Fælicis mart. *Theſe 2. bleſſed Martyrs vvere put to death at* Millaine *vnder* Maximinian *the Emperor. And* S. Paulinus *vvrytinge the life of* S. Ambroſe, *vvith vvhome he liued, teſtifieth the great deuotion of that people in viſytinge their bodyes and ſepulchers in thoſe dayes. See* S. Ambroſe lib. 7. in Lucam. cap. 13. & ep. ad Marcellin.
e	90	13	C. R. Anacleti PP. & mart. Semiduplex. *Of this bleſſed Pope & Martyr that vvas the third or fourth after* S. Peter, *and gaue his bloud for the confeſſion of Chriſtian faith vnder* Domitian *the Emperor, do make mention.* Iren. lib. 3. cap. 3. Euſeb. lib. 3. cap. 2. Optat. lib. 2. cont. Parmen. Aug. ep. 185. *and others.*

C. R.

Litt.	Ann⁹	Dies	Fox his Calendar.	Iuly.
Dñic.	Chr.	menf.		

A | 1555 | 9 | *Richard Hooke mart.* This was a certaine craftesman of *VVichefter* burned for new opinions in the 3. yeare of Q. Maryes raigne. Fox addeth no particulars; but that he was burned, *as a true vvitnes of the Lords truth.* See *ibid. num.* 28.

b | 1555 | 10 | *Iohn Bland preacher martyr.* This Bland vvas Minifter & Vicar of the Parifh of *Roluyndon* in Kent, who aunfwered roundly and flatly (faith Fox) the articles propofed vnto him; and fo finally fhewing himfelfe obftinate, he was burned with 3. other companions (the fourth relentinge) at Canterbury, the fame yeare 1555. See *cap.* 11. *num. ibid.*

c | 1555 | 11 | *Iohn Frankifhe* and *Humfrey Middleton mart.* Thefe are two of Bland the preachers companions, and were burned with him, though Fox giue them feuerall dayes, therby to extend his Calendar. The firft was a minifter the fecond an artificer, whofe difagreeinge aunfwers yow may fee *ibid. num.* 28.29.

d | 1555 | 12 | *Nicolas Sheterden mart.* This was another artificer companion to the former, but for that Fox faith he conquered *Doctor Harpesfield* and *Maifter Collyns* the B. Chaplin, in difputation, yea *Bifhop Gardner* himfelfe and others, he geueth him a feuerall feftiuall day, as alfo a large difcourfe of his Acts and Gefts in that difputation. See *ibid. num.* 29.

e | 1555 | 13 | *VVilliam Dighill* and *Dirick Caruer mart.* The firft of thefe was a craftefman burned in Kent. The fecond was a beere-brewer of the Parifh of *Brighthamfted* in the County of Suffex burned at *Levves*: both their opinions, and anfwers, as alfo their obftinacy therin yow may fee *ibid. num.* 30.

★★★   *Iohn*

Litt. Dñic.	Ann⁹ Chr.	Dies menſ.	The Catholike Calendar. Iuly.
f	1275	14	C. R. Bonauenturæ Episcopi & Cõfeſs. ſe-miduplex. *This vvas a great learned and holy man of S.Franciſ Order, as his vvorks doe teſti-fie , he vvas Cardinall and B. of Albane , and vvas canonized by Pope Sixtus 4. See of him S.Anton. p.3. tit.2. c.8. & 9. and others.*
g	308	15	M. R. Catulini Diac. & mart. *This man vvith diuers other companions of his, vvas put to death in the citty of Carthage in Africa. In vvhoſe praiſe S. Auſten made a large & learned ſermon as Poſsidonius vvryteth in his life cap. 9. He ſuffered vnder the Emperor Diocletian. And their reliques vvere kept vvith honour in the Church of S. Fauſtus. Of vvhich yovv may ſee Concil. Carthag. 6. & Concil. African. c.27. & Victor. l.2. de perſecut. Vandal. and others.*
A	253	16	M. R. Fauſti mart. *This ſame Fauſtus is he vvhoſe Church is mentioned in the precedēt day. He vvas nayled to a Croſſe vnder Decius the Emperor and continued 5. dayes vvith life, and at the end vvas ſhott through vvith arrovves: ſee the Greeke menaloge and Romanum marty-rologe. and others.*
b	398	17	C. R. Alexij Confeſſoris. *This vvas a noble young man of Rome, ſonne of a Senatour named Euphemianus, vvho being forced to marry, left his vvife vntouched,& ſtealing avvay by night, vvent as a pelgrim ouer the vvorld to viſitt holy places , and returninge vnknovvne after many yeares, vvas receyued in his ovvne Fathers houſe as a ſeruant and pilgrim, and neuer deſcryed vn-till after his death. See the Roman martyrologe and his Acts out of Metaphraſtes in Lippom. tom. 7. & Sur. tom. 4.*
c	125	18	C. R. Simphoroſæ cum 7. filijs mart. *This vvonderfull vvoman vvas of the Citty of Ty-bur by Rome vnder the Emperor Adriane; ſhe vvas the vvife of one Getulius that vvas mar-tyred for Chriſt , as ſhe alſo vvas vvith 7. chil-dren*

Litt.	Ann.	Dies	Fox his Calendar. Iuly.
Dñic.	Chr.	menf.	
f	1555	14	*Iohn Launder mart.* This Launder was a hufbandman of the Parifh of *Godftone* in the County of *Surrey* of 25. years ould, and burned at *Stenninge* in this yeare for obftinate defendinge diuers herefies , which yow may read *ibid.* num. 30.
g	1555	15	*Thomas Iuefon mart.* This was a carpenter of the Parifh of *Godftone* alfo , and was burned this yeare, and vpon this Moneth at Chichefter: He held amonge other opinions, *that his fynnes vvere not vvafhed avvay by Baptifme, but that his body only vvas vvafhed therby.* See *ibid.* num. 30. 31.
A	1555	16	*Nicolas Hall mart.* and *Iohn Alevvorthe Conf.* The firft of thefe 2. was a brickelayer of the Parifh of *Dartford* , who offered himfelfe to the fire for his opinions. The fecond was imprifoned for like caufe at *Reading*, and died in the fame prifon , for which caufe Fox giueth him the title of *Confeffor.* See *c.*11. *n.*30.31.32.
b	1556	17	*Iohn Careleffe confeffor.* This was a weauer of Couentry, that died in the Kings bench at London, being commytted thither for herefie , vpon the fourth yeare of Q. Maryes raigne , his opinions Iohn Fox fetteth not downe , fo as he might be of any fect whatfoeuer , for any thinge we know to the contrary. See *ibid.* num. 33.
c	1556	18	*Iulius Palmer , Iohn Huyn , and Atkins mart.* The firft of thefe 3. was a younge man of 24. yeares old, that hauinge byn put out of Magdalin Colledge in Oxford for libellinge againft the prefident, became a ghofpeller, and

★ ★ ★ 2   gott

Litt. Dñic.	Ann. Chr.	Dies menf.	The Catholike Calendar. Iuly.
			dren hauing paſſed firſt many ſorts of moſt cruell torments. See of her Mombrit tom. 2. & Pet. in catal. lib. 6. and others.
d	350	19	M. R. Macrinæ virginis. This holy virgin vvas ſyſter to the tvvo famous Doctors of the Church S. Baſill, and S. Gregory Niſſene, by vvhome ſhe vvas taught both to keepe the holy ſtate cf virginity, as alſo to exerciſe all other perfection of life. Of vvhoſe vvonderfull vertues the ſaid Greg. Niſſen vvryteth a large treatiſe ep. ad Olymp. and others.
c	242	20	C. R. Margaritæ virg. & mart. This bleſſed virgin ſuffered at Antioch in Aſia vnder the Emperor Decius, and diuers authors haue vvrytten her glorious paſſion at large, and amonge others Bapt. Mantuanus in verſe, as alſo Hieron. Vida B. of Albe. and others.
f	140	21	C. R. Praxedis virginis. This vvas one of the daughters of S. Pudens Senator of Rome, that firſt receyued S. Peter and S. Paul into his houſe, and ſyſter alſo to S. Pudentiana and S. Nouatus, and after a moſt holy life, gaue vp vvith like holynes her ſpiritt to our Sauiour. See the mart. of S. Bede and Mombr. tom. 2. de vitis Sanctorum. and others.
g	84	22	C. R. Mariæ Magdalenæ. duplex.
A	82	23	C. R. Apollinaris Epiſcopi & mart. Semiduplex. This bleſſed man vvas ordayned Biſhop by S. Peter the Apoſtle, and ſent to Rauenna in Italy, vvhere after many conflicts vvith the perſecutors of thoſe dayes, and many miracles vvrought by him, he vvas finally put to death vnder Veſpaſian the Emperor: See of him ſaint Gregory the great lib. 5. cp. 31. Venant. Fort. in Sacris Hym. Sur. tom. 4. and others.

C. R.

Litt.	Ann.	Dies	Fox his Calendar. Iuly.
Ðñic.	Chr.	menf.	
			gott vnto him *Guin* and *Atkins*, for his companions, he had his mothers curse for his euill behauiour, and soone after was burned, and so became a Martyr of Fox his Church. See *num. ibid.*
d	1556	19	*Catherine Cauches*, *Guillemine Gilbert*, and *Perotine Maſſy*, *vvith her child not one houre old, Martyrs.* Theſe 3. weomen were hanged and burned in *Garneſy* for theft and hereſy; the firſt was mother of the other two; and the laſt being a ſecret ſtrompett, not confeſſinge her ſelfe to be with child, the ſame brake forth of her belly and fell into the fire when ſhe was on the gallowes, but was borne dead: ſe their ſtory at large. *ib.n.34.35.36.&c.*
e	1556	20	*Thomas Dungate martyr.* This was a poore ſimple man burned at *Greenſteed* in Suſſex for obſtinacy in certayne new opinions about Religion, which yet Fox ſetteth not downe, but only ſaith, *that he ſuffered for righteouſnes ſake.* See *ibid. num.* 45.
f	1556	21	*Iohn Forman mart.* This *Foreman* was fellow to *Dungate*, and as vnlearned as he, and no leſſe obſtinate, for which cauſe he was burned with him at *Greenſteed*, vpon the 4. yeare of the raigne of Q. Mary. See *ibid num.*45.
g		22	Mary Magdalyn.
A	1556	23	*Symon Miller martyr.* This was a craftesman of *Linne* burned at Norwich: Fox telleth no particulars of him, but that he went vp and downe carryinge his confeſſion in his ſhoe, and asked the people, where he might go to communion, for which he was apprehended, and carryed to *Doctor Dunnings* the B. Chancelor. See *ibid. num.* 45.

***3   *Eliza-*

Litt. ꝺñic.	Ann⁹ Chr.	Dies menſ.	The Catholike Calendar. Iuly.
b	285	24	C. R. Vigilia. Chriſtinæ virg. & mart. *This admirable virgin being daughter of a pagan Iudge, that vvas feruent in Idolatry, & he perceauing that his said daughter not only vvas a Chriſtian, but had broken certaine golden Idolls of his, and giuen the money to the poore, caused her to paſſe an incredible number of torments of vvater, burning lyme, (serpents and the like, from all vvhich being deliuered by miracle, ſhe vvas finally martyred by many arrovves ſhott through her body.* See Vincent. in ſpec. lib. 12. cap. 86. Anton. p. 1. tit. 8. *and others.*
c	41	25	C. R. Iacobi Apoſtoli duplex.
d	1	26	C. R. Annæ matris B. Mariæ duplex. *Of this holy vvoman mother of the bl. Virgin do make mention many auncient Fathers, as S. Epiph. hær. 78. & 79. & in coment. de laud. Deipar. S. Ioan. Damaſc. l. 4. cap. 15. and the Emperor Emanuell in his conſtitution acknovvledged the same for a feſtiuall day in his tyme tit. de ferijs.*
e	301	27	C. R. Pantaleonis mart. *This vvas a famous phiſition in the perſecution vnder Maximinus the Emperor, vvho confeſſinge Chriſt moſt conſtantly, vvas by many torments put to death in Nicomedia, & his feſtiuall day vvas kept vvith celebrity preſently after in the Greeke Church, as appeareth by the forſaid Conſtitution of Emanuell the Emperor tit. de ferijs. and others.*
f	195 416	28	C. R. Victoris PP. & mart. & Innocentii PP. & Confeſſ. Semiduplex. *The firſt of these tvvo Popes ſucceeded Eleutherius, vvho conuerted the Britans vnder K. Lucius, and vvas martyred vnder the Emperor Seuerus, the other Innocentius liued a moſt holy life in S. Hierome and S. Auſtens tyme, of vvhose great ſanctity both of them do make mention. and others.*
g	84	29	C. R. Marthæ virginis. Semiduplex. *This vvas ſyſter of S. Mary Magdalen, and of Lazarus, vvho receaued our Sauiour into her house in* Bethania

Litt.	Ann.'	Dies	
b	1556	24	*Elizabeth Cooper mart.* This Elizabeth was a pewterers wife of Norwich, who hauinge firft recanted her new opinions, fell to them againe, cryinge out openly in the Church (faith Fox) that fhe reuoked her former recantation : fhe was burned with the forefaid *Miller* at Norwich. See *ibid. num.* 45.
c		25	Iames Apoftle.
d	1558	26	*Richard Yeoman martyr.* This *Yeoman* was an Apoftata Prieft, who being tempted with the flefh gatt him a woman, with whome he liued for a whole yeare fhutt vp in a chamber, fhe fpinninge, and he cardinge the wooll; he had many children by her, and at laft was burned at *Norvvich.* See *cap.* 11. *num.* 46 47.
e	1558	27	*VVilliam Pikes martyr.* This was a tanner burned at *Brainford* 7. myles from London, togeather with 5. other Craftefmen of like occupations, for fundry new opiniōs: all which Fox calleth the faithfull wittneffes of the Lords trew Teftament, as though the Lord had two Teftaments, the one trew the other falfe. See *ibid. num.* 48.49. & 59.
f	1558	28	*Stephen Cotten mart.* This was one of the former company of craftefmen and artificers taken at *Iflington* by London at their meetings in the fields, and was examined by D. Darbifhire Chauncelor to Bifhop *Bonner,* and finally being obftinate, he was condemned and burned likelife at *Brainford.* See *num. ibid.*
g	1558	29	*Iohn Slade* and *Stephen VVright mart.* Thefe were other two of the forefaid crew, who were fix in all, burned at Brainford; and albeit

* * * 4   they

| --- | --- | --- | --- |
			Bethania *ſhe liued & died moſt holily, after her* *departure from Iudea to* Marſeeles *and* Taraſcum *in* France. See Mombrit. to.2. *& others.*
A	253.	30	C.R. Abdon & Sennen mart. *Theſe vvere tvvo Chriſtian Perſians brought from thence in chaynes to* Rome *vnder* Decius *the Emperor, and there after many torments ſuffered for Chriſt, they vvere beheaded.* See Mart. Rom. Bed. & Mombrit. tom.1. Pet. in Catal. l.6. *& others.*
b	450	31	M.R. Germani Epiſc. & Conf. *This holy man being a Biſhopp in* France, *came tvviſe into Britany before Engliſhmen vvere Chriſtiãs, to reſyſt the* pelagians, *vvhich he did both by vvorks, and miracles, carryinge vvith him many reliques of Saints to that effeĉt, as vvryteth* S. Bede lib.1. hiſt.c.12. *and before him* Greg. Turon de glor. Confeſſ.c.41. Proſp. in chron. *and many other.*

The Moneth of Auguſt.

c	438	1	C.R. Petri ad vincula. duplex. *This memory or celebrity of the chaines vvhervvith* S. Peter *vvas bound, as vvell in* Hieruſalem *as* Rome, *vvas inſtituted about the yeare of Chriſt* 438. *vvhen the Empreſſe* Eudoxia *vviſe of* Theodoſius *the younger hauing gone in pilgrimage to* Hieruſalem, *had preſented vnto her the tvvo chaines, that* S. Peter *vvas tyed vvithall vnder* Herod, *vvherof there is mention* Aĉt. 12. *of vvhich ſhe retayned the one in* Conſtãtinople, *& ſent the other to* Rome *to* Eudoxia *her daughter, vviſe of* Valentinian *the Emperor: in memory of vvhich tvvo chaines, and the miracles done by them, vvere tvvo Churches erected, the one in* Conſtantinople, *the other in* Rome. See Sigebert in chron. an. 438. & 969. *and others.*
			C.R.

			they were burned all togeather vpon the 14. day of Iuly, yet Fox extendeth them to diuers for benefitt of his Calendar. See *cap.*11.*n.*49.
A	1558	30	*Robert Milles*, and *Robert Dines mart.* These were two other artificers of the former company, who had nothinge to say for themselues ; but to defie the Pope of Rome , and such other like raylinge speaches. See *ibidem num.* 49. *&* 50.
b	1558	31	*Thomas Brenbricke mart.* This fellow is called *Brenbridge* by Fox euery where in his Acts & Monuments, he was of the Diocesse of Winchester and condemned by *D. VVhite* Bishop of that Sea;he recanted at the fire, and wrote his recantation vpon ones shoulder, but yt was to late. See *ibid. num.*48.

Fox his Calendar, August.

The Moneth of August.

c	1527	1	*Leonard Keyser mart.* This was a poore obstinate Dutchman of *Bauaria* , burned at the towne of *Passauu* the 18. yeare of the raigne of K. Henry the eyght , he died for Lutheanisme , and for diuers particular fancyes of his owne , as for example.; that there vere three Confessions to be admitted , to witt Confession of faith , Confession of chaity, and Confession of counsell, but not of synnes by obligation. See *cap.* 12. *num.* 2.3.

Litt. Dñic.	Ann. Chr.	Dies menf.	The Catholike Calendar. Auguſt.
d	257	2	c. R. Stephani PP. & mart. *This vvas a moſt admirable man for his zeale and feruour in ſpreadinge abroad Chriſtian Religion ; he conuerted many great men & vveomen in the tyme of his Popedome, vvhich vvas but 7. yeares : he vvas finally beheaded in his ovvne ſeate, by the Emperor* Valerian *his officers. See the booke of* Dam. Rom. mart. The greeke menaloge, Metaphraſtes. *and others.*
e	420	3	c. R. Inuentio S. Stephani protomart. Semi-duplex. *Thu is the memory of that day vvhen by reuelation from God the body of* S. Stephen, *vvas found in* Hieruſalem *togeather vvith the bodyes of diuers other Saints, vvherby many miracles vvere done as* S. Auſten *recounteth lib.22. de ciuit. Dei. cap. 8. ferm. 31.32.33. & ep. 103. and other vvryters. It happened vnder* Honorius *the Emperor about* an. 420.
f	1223	4	c. R. Dominici confeſſoris. duplex. *This holy man vvas founder of the order of preachinge friars, vvhich had their name of him: yovu may ſee of his rare vertues and many miracles, and namely of 3. dead men rayſed to life by him, in* Sur. tom. 4. & S. Anton. p. 3. tit.23. cap.1.2.3. *and others.*
g	385 / 464	5	c. R. Dedicat. S. Mariæ ad Niues. duplex. *This memory is held of the Church builded and dedicated to the bleſſed Virgin by a ſpeciall reuelation from God ; and confirmed by a miracle of ſnovu fallen vpon this day, vvhen the heates are greateſt in* Rome, *in the place vvhere the Church vvas commaunded to be built vnder* Pope Liberius, *but more perfected aftervvard by Pope* Sixtus 3. See Dam. in vit. Sixti 3. Adriani PP. ep. ad Carolum Mag. *and others.*
A	33	6	c. R. Transfiguratio Domini. duplex. *This feſtiuall day vvas inſtituted by the Church in auncient tyme, in memory of that admirable trans-*

Litt.	Ann.	Dies	Fox his Calendar. August.
oñic.	Chr.	menſ.	
d	1555	2	*Iames Abbes martyr.* This was a poore begginge boy accuſed to the B. of Norwich for hereſie, which he hauing abiured, was diſmiſſed by him, with an almes alſo ; but after repentinge himſelfe (ſaith Fox) he returned to the Biſhopp, and diſputed both with him, and his Chaplyns, and finally being incorrigible was burned. See *ibid. num.* 4.
e	1555	3	*Iohn Denley gentleman martyr.* This *Denley* was of *Maidſtone* in Kent, and a great peruerter of people to hereſie in Q. Maryes dayes, he carryed alwayes about him his Confeſſion in wrytinge, full of phantaſticall opinions: in which he perſiſtinge obſtinately, was finally burned at Vxbridge. See his ſtory at large. *cap.* 12. *num.* 5. 6.
f	1555	4	*Iohn Nevuman mart.* This was a pewterer of the forſaid towne of *Maidſtone ,* and one of *Denleyes* ſchollers , who held the ſame opinions with him, & conquered in diſputation (yf we beleeue Fox) D. Thornton Suffragan of Kent, with diuers other learned men, and was finally burned with *Denley* at Vxbridge. See *ibid. num.* 5. 6. 7.
g	1555	5	*Patrick Patingham mart.* This was a craftes-man alſo of the ſame towne of Maidſtone, & another of the forſaid *Denleyes* ſchollers, defending all his opinions, as of a new Apoſtle, he was not burned at *Vxbridge* with *Denley* & *Nevuman,* but at *Saffron-VValden* in Eſſex. See *cap. ibid. num. ibid.*
A	1555	6	*VVilliam Coker martyr.* This was an artificer or labouringe man of Kent , which with fiue others, was brought before the forſaid *Doctor Thornton*

Litt. Dñic.	Ann. menſ.	Dies menſ.	Catholike Calendar. Auguſt.
			trnſfiguration *made by our Sauiour , on the* Mont Thabor , *before three of his diſciples.* Math. 7. Marc. 9. See *of this feaſt both the Latin and Greeke martyrologes , and the conſtitution of* Emanuel *the Emperor* tit. 7. cap. 1. & Tritem. lib. 2. cap. 36. *and others.*
b	366	7	c. R. Donati Epiſc. & mart. *This vvas a holy B. of the Citty of* Aretium *in Italy in the tyme of* Iulian *the Apoſtata: yovv may read of his miracles and vvonderfull life, amonge other authors* S. Greg. *the great* lib. 1. dial. c. 7. *vvhere he ſhevveth, that the officers of* Iulian, *hauinge broken a chalice in peeces, the ſame by his prayers vvas made vvhole againe.*
c	304	8	c. R. Cyriaci, Largi & Smaragdi mart. *Theſe vvere* 3. *noble men, that ſuffered martyrdome in* Rome *vnder* Diocletian *for Chriſtian faith , togeather vvith* 20. *more, on the ſame day, vvhoſe memory vvas ſo honoured among the Romans, as* S. Greg. *the great* l. 9. Regiſtr. ep. 22. *doth ſhevv that there vvas a Church in his dayes erected in* Rome *in honour of* S. Cyriacus. *And almoſt a* 100. *yeares before that againe, there is mention of the ſaid Church in the Acts of the ſecond Roman Synod vnder* Pope Symmachus. &c.
d	258	9	Vigilia. c. R. Romani mart. *This* Romanus *vvas a perſecutinge ſouldiar one of them that tooke* S. Laurence, *and hauing ſeene his conſtancy, vvas ſo much moued thervvith, as he deſired to be baptized by him , vvhich being done, preſently he vvas taken by the tormentors, & after much beatinge vvas beheaded. See the Acts of* S. Laurence *in the mart. of* S. Bede, Sur. to. 4. *and others.*
e	258	10	c. R. Laurentij mart. duplex. *This vvas that admirable* Roman Deacon *vvho ſeeinge* Pope Syxtus, *vvhome he vvas vvont to ſerue at maſſe, to be carryed to death by the ſouldiars of* Valerian

Litt. Dnic.	Ann. Chr.	Dies menf.	Fox his Calendar.　Auguſt.
			Thornton B. of Douer, D. Harpeſfield Arch-deacon of Canterbury, and other learned men in commiſſion, whome this ignorant obſti-nate heretike with his fellowes ſo contemned and reproached, as was intolerable, and in the end he was burned at Canterbury. See *ibidem num. 8.*
b	1555	7	VVilliam Hopper *martyr.* This was another of the ſame crew, who firſt (ſaith Fox) ſeemed to graunt the faith, and determination of the Catholike Church: but after calling himſelfe better to mynd, moſt conſtantly offered to dy for the contrary. This is Fox his *Encomyon* of him. See *ibid. num.* 8.9.10.
c	1555	8	*Henry Laurence martyr.* This is a third com-panion of thoſe Kentiſh labourers and craf-teſmen, who beſides his hereticall opinions, rayled alſo moſt ſpitefully againſt the iudges ſayinge : *Yee are all of Antichriſt, and him yee follovv:* See *ibid. num.* 9.10.
d	1555	9	*Richard Collier mart.* This is the fourth com-panion of the forſaid Canterbury combina-tion of obſtinate artificers ; he was of the towne of Aſhford, and more raſh, bold, and blaſphemous in auouching his opinions then any of the reſt : ſo as finally he was condem-ned and burned for the ſame at Canterbury, no perſuaſion auayling with him to the con-trary. See *cap. ibid. num. ibid.*
e	1555	10	VVilliam Steere *mart.* This was the fifth com-panion of the forſaid crew of Canterbury, who being an ignorant poore man was ſo in-ſolent notwithſtandinge in his anſwers, as ſhewed

Litt. Dñic.	Ann⁹ Chr.	Dies menf.	The Catholike Calendar. Auguſt.
			rian *the Emperor, cryed out (as S. Ambroſe and others do recount)* why do ye leaue me o fa- ther ; yow were neuer wont to offer ſacrifice without me your miniſter ; *and ſo at laſt he vvas burned on a hoate gridyron.* See S. Am- broſe lib. 1. offic. c.41. & l.2. c. 28. S. Auguſt. tract.27. in Ioan. & Serm.37.38. *and others.*
f	304	11	C. R. SS. Tiburtij & Suſannæ mart. *Theſe vvere both Romans and ſuffered vnder* Diocletian *the Emperor.* Tiburtius *vvas after many other tor- ments beheaded :* Suſanna *vvas a moſt noble virgin and neece to* Pope Caius , *put to death after the ſame manner.* See Sur. tom. 1. & 4. Greg. lib.9. Regiſtr. ep.22. *and others.*
g	1255	12	C. R. Claræ virginis. *This vvas a noble vvoman borne in* Aſſiſium *in the Dukedome of* Spole- tum *in Italy , vvho being ſtyrred vp by the ex- ample and holynes of* S. Francis , *borne in the ſame tovvne , did inſtitute a religious order of vveomen, vvith vvhome ſhe liued in moſt admi- rable ſanctity for many yeares ; ſhe vvas Cano- nized by* Pope Alexander *the* 4. *about the yeare of Chriſt* 1255. See Anton. p. 3. tit. 24. cap. 6. *and others.*
A	258	13	C. R. Hyppoliti & Caſſiani mart. *The firſt of theſe* 2. *vvas a noble Roman baptized by* S. Lau- rence, *vvho ſhevvinge himſelfe moſt conſtant in confeſſion of faith , vvas dravvne naked at a vvild horſe his tayle through great thicketts of thornes and bryers, vntill he vvas dead, and* 20. *more of his ovvne houſe vvere martyred vvith him.* Caſſianus *being a ſchoolemaſter, vvas de- liuered naked to his ſaid ſchollers to be ſlayne vvith their penknifes in the markett place of* Scilla *in* Rome. See Prudent. hym.11. Mombrit. to. 1. Sur. tom.4. *and others.*
b	347	14	Vigilia. M. R. Euſebij Confeſſoris. *This vvas a moſt Catholike Prieſt that ſtood againſt the* Arrians *in the tyme of* Conſtantius *the Empe- ror,*

Litt. Ðñic.	Ann⁹ Chr.	Dies menſ.	Fox his Calendar. August.
			ſhewed well the phrenſy of hereſy which poſſeſſed him, for being commanded by the iudge to anſwere to the articles laid againſt him, *he bidd him commaund his dogges, and not him,* adding further, *that Diske of Douer* (who was the Biſhopp) *had no authority ouer him.* See *cap.*12. *num.*10.
f	1555	11	*Richard VVright martyr.* This was the laſt of that Canterbury company of artificers, who being conuented before the foreſaid Biſhopp and other learned men in the publike conſiſtory, anſwered with like immodeſty & willfull obſtinacy, as the reſt, and ſo at length he was burned with them. See *ibid. num.* 8. & 9.
g	1555	12	*Elizabeth VVarne mart.* This was an Vpholſters wife in London, and ſo reſolute in her extrauagant opinions, as when ſhe was exhorted to be better inſtructed, ſhe anſwered (ſaith Fox) do what ye will, *for yf Chriſt vvas in error, then am I in error, and not othervviſe;* and with this aſſurance ſhe went to the fire. See *ibid. num.* 11. 16.
A	1555	13	*George Tankerfield mart.* This was a proud arrogant fellow, by occupation a cooke, who ioyninge with a painter as inſolent as himſelfe, vſed intollerable, and contemptuous words towards *B. Boner,* and being condemned, did communicate himſelfe before he went to the fire, with a loafe of bread and a pynt of Malmeſy, without help of a miniſter. See *ibid. num.* 11. 12. 13. 14. &c.
b	1555	14	*Robert Smith martyr.* This was the painter, companion of *Tankerfield; B. Boner* called one of them the ſpeaker of the houſe & the other the

ror, vvho being ſhutt vp in priſon continued 7.
monethes togeather in prayer, & he dying therin
vvas of ſuch fame for his holynes, *as not longe*
after he had a Church builded in honour of him
in Rome publikely, as appeareth by the firſt Ro-
man Synod vnder Pope Symmachus, *vvhich*
endureth vntill this day. See Mombrit. tom.1.
and others.

c   47   15   C. R. Aſſumptio B. Mariæ virg. *This is an an-*
cient feſtiuity in the Church of God in remem-
brance of the Aſſumption of the bleſſed Virgin
the Mother of God to euerlaſtinge ioy and glory
in the company of her bleſſed Sonne & Sauiour,
Of this feſtiuity do make mention S. Bede,
Vſuard, Ado, *and others in their martyrologes*
as alſo the Greeke menaloge, & the conſtitution
of Emanuell *the Emperor.* S. Greg. in Sacram.
Concil.Moguntin.ſub Carolo mag. & others.

d   308   16   M. R. Simpliciani Epiſc. & Confeſs. *This man*
vvas B. of Millayne, and of great holynes in the
tyme of S. Ambroſe and S. Auſten, betvveene
vvhome there vvas ſtrayte frendſhipp, as appea-
reth by Paulinus *in the life of S. Ambroſe and by*
diuers Epiſtles of S. Ambroſe vnto him, as alſo by
S. Auſten lib.4.Confeſs.cap.2.3. & 5. *vvho de-*
dicated diuers bookes vnto him.

e   274   17   M. R. Mamantis mart. *This Martyr being ta-*
ken by the perſecutors in his youth, vvas conti-
nued in affliction for Chriſtian faith for many
yeares togeather, vntill at length vnder Aure-
lianus the Emperor, he finiſhed his martyrdome
in Cæſarea *of Cappadocia, vvhoſe exceedinge*
praiſes are celebrated by S. Baſill, S. Greg. Nazianz. *and other Fathers.* S. Greg. *the great*
made a ſermon in his Church vpon his feſtiuall
day hom. 35.

f   330   18   M. R. Helenæ Conſtantini matris. *This vvas*
a lady bõrne in Britany, and mother to the fa-
mous Conſtantine the great; ſhe vvas zealous in
Chri-

			the controuller for their arrogancy in diſputinge and iangling, wherby they made themſelues Captaines and falſe guides to other poore men and weomen, that were priſoners with them, and depended vpon them; he was burned in Smithfield: See *ibid. num.*11.
ε	1555	15	*Stephen Harvvood mart.* This was one of the ſchollers and proſelites of the cooke and paynter aforeſaid, who followinge their obſtinacy and arrogancy in defending hereſies, was condemned with them by the B. of London, and burned at Stratford. See *cap. ibidem num. ibidem.*
d	1555	16	*Thomas Fuſt mart.* This was another of the ſame company by occupation a ſhomaker, who applauding to the anſwers of the cooke and paynter at length poſed the Biſhopp, by askinge him, *vvhere he found any greaſinge or annoynting in Gods booke?* By which yow may perceyue his ſkill: he was burned afterward at *vvare.* See *ibid. num.*11.12.15.
e	1555	17	*VVilliam Haile mart.* This *hayle* was an artificer borne in the towne of *Thorpe* in the County of Eſſex, & ſent vp priſoner to London by *Syr Nicolas Hare* , and other commiſſionars in company of the forſaid *Tankerfield* the Cooke, and *Smith* the paynter, by whoſe wholſome doctrine he cryed to the people; *Bevvare of the Idolater, and Antichriſt the B. of London.* See *ibid. num.*16.
f	1555	18	*Robert Samuel preacher mart.* This was an Apoſtata Prieſt., that being tempted of the fleſh tooke a woman in K. Edwards dayes, & ★★★★ would

			Chriſtian Religion & of great holynes of life, &
			all ancient authors do vvryte moſt honorably of
			her, and that finally ſhe died and vvas buryed in
			Rome. See Nicepo. lib.8. cap. 3. Euſeb. in vit.
			Conſtant. lib.3. cap. 41. Socrat. lib. 1. cap.12.
			Zozom. lib.2. cap.1. *and others.*
g	183	19	M. R. Iulij Senatoris mart. *This vvas a noble*
			man and ſenatour of Rome, vvho in the tyme of
			Commodus *the Emperor being accuſed of Chri-*
			ſtian Religion, and ſhevvinge himſelfe conſtant,
			vvas by the Emperors ovvne commandement
			beaten to death vvith cudgells for the ſame. See
			the Rom. martyrol. *and alſo* S. Bede, Vſuard.
			and others.
A	1153	20	c. R. Bernardi Abbatis duplex. *This vvas a*
			great renovvned man both for learning and ho-
			lynes of life, and many miracles vvhich he
			vvrought: He liued in France *in the tyme of* K.
			Henry *the 2. of* England *, to vvhome he vvrote*
			diuers Epiſtles. See *his life vvrytten in 5. books*
			by Godefridus Clareuallenſis, *and others.*
b	258	21	M. R. Cyriacæ Viduæ & mart. *This vvas a*
			holy vvyddovv of Rome, vvho giuinge herſelfe
			vvholy to pious vvorks of almes and buryinge of
			Martyrs bodyes, and the like, being apprehended
			for the ſame, vvas beaten ſo long vvith balles of
			lead, and ſcorpions, vntill ſhe gaue vp the ghoſt,
			vnder the Emperor Valerian. See Rom. mart.
			& Prudent. hym.11. *and others.*
c	276	22	c. R. Simphoriani mart. *This Martyr vvas put*
			to death in the head Citty of Burgundy *named*
			Auguſtodunum, *and ancient vvryters do make*
			moſt honorable mention of him and his mother
			that ran after him, vvhen he vvent to martyr-
			dome, cryinge: ſonne, ſonne, be myndfull of euer-
			laſtinge life, looke vp to heauen and remember
			vvho

Litt. Dñic.	Ann. Chr.	Dies menſ.	Fox his Calendar. Auguſt.
			would not forgoe her in Q. Maryes; he ſer- ued for miniſter at *Barnfield* in Suffolke, and was impriſoned for hereſie in Ipſwich, where his cheefe ſchollers were *Agnes Potten* , and *Ioane Truchfield*, of whome he had many vi- ſions as Fox affirmeth : He finally was bur- ned at the ſame towne: See *ibid.n.*17.18.19.20.
g	1556	19	*Ioane VVaſt* and *VVilliam Bongeor mart.* The firſt of theſe 2. was a poore woman of Darby borne blynd. The ſecond was a glaſier of *Colcheſter* , both of them being ignorant and willfull, ſtood reſolutely to their fancyes, and would by no meanes leaue the ſame, or be in- formed of the truth· See *ibid.num.*21.22.& 23.
A	1557	20.	*Robert Purcas mart.* This man is called *VVil- liam Purcas* by Fox in his Monuments · he was a fuller by occupation, & one of *Bongeor* his Companions at *Colcheſter* , with whome he was apprehended and condemned for the ſame hereſies, to witt, againſt the bleſſed Sa- crament, maſſe, & other points of Catholike Religion , and burned at the ſame place. See *ibid. num.* 23. 24.
b	1557	21	*Thomas Bennold martyr.* This was a tallow- chandelor of the former company of Col- cheſter , and ſtood in the ſame hereſies with them , who by no means could be remoued from the ſame, whervpon at length, all three were condemned , and burned togeather at Colcheſter the 5. yeare of Q. Maryes raigne. See *ibid. num.*23. & 26.
c	1557	22	*Agnes Siluerſide* aliàs *Smith mart.* This was an old poore woman infected with hereſie in the ſame towne of Colcheſter, who being called to aunſwere in company of the afore- ſaid artificers, would not ſeeme to be behind them in feruour of ſpiritt, & thervpon cryed out as a madd woman; *that ſhe loued no conſe-*

Litt.	Ann.	Dies	The Catholike Calendar. Auguſt.
Dñic.	Chr.	menſ.	*vvho raigneth there:* See Greg. Turon. lib. 2. hiſt. cap. 15. Venant. Fort. lib.7. *and others.*
d	140	23	Vigilia M. R. Eutichij Confeſs. *This man vvas the diſciple of S. Iohn Euangeliſt, by vvhome being ſent into diuers contreyes to preach Chriſtian Religion, and hauinge ſuffered diuers impriſonments, vvhippings, and torments of fire, and deliuered by miracle from the ſame, died at laſt quietly in his bedd.See the Greeke menaloge, and* Rom. mart. *and others.*
e	73	24	C. R. Bartholomei Apoſtoli. duplex.
f	1270	25	C.R. Ludouici Regis & Confeſſoris.*This vvas S. Levves, the 9. of that name K. of France, vvhoſe holy life, and conuerſation is vvrytten by many authors, as namely by* Gaufredus & S. Anton. p.3. tit.3. cap.1. *and others, he vvas canonized by Pope* Bonifacius *the 8.*
g	219	26	C. R. Zepherini PP. & mart. *This Pope vvas a Roman borne,and ruled that ſea 9. years during the perſecution of* Seuerus *the Emperor that died at Yorke in England, vvhoſe ſonne* Antoninus Caracalla *returninge to Rome, cauſed him to be put to death: See of him* Euſeb. lib.5.hiſt. cap.27. & lib.6. cap.15.Aug.ep.165. *and others.*
A	80	27	M. R. Rufi Epiſcopi & mart. *This vvas a great noble man ſonne of a ſenatour in* Rome, *conuerted and baptized vvithall his family by* S. Apollinaris B. *of* Rauenna *and aftervvard being made B. of* Capua,*vvas martyred for Chriſtian Religion. See the acts of* S.Apollin. in Sur.to.4. *and* Hier. Rubeus in hiſt.Rauen.l.1. *& others.*
b	432	28	C. R. Auguſtini Epiſcopi & Confeſſoris Eccl. Doctoris. duplex. *This vvas that famous Doctor of the Church, vvho of an heretike of the* Manichies

			cration, for that the bread vvas the vvorſe therby rather then better. See *num. ibid. cap. ibid.*
d	1557	23	*Ellen Evvringe* mart. This was wife to a Miller by Colcheſter, and of the foreſaid crew: ſhe anſwered (ſaith Fox) in effect as the other did, cleerly denyinge all lawes ſett forth by the Pope: *ſhe vvas ſomevvhat thicke* (quoth he) *of hearinge, yet quicke in vnderſtanding the Lords matters:* See *cap. ibid. num.* 23. & 26.
e		24	Bartholomew Apoſtle.
f	1557	25	*Elizabeth Felkes maid* mart. This was a ſeruingmayd in Colcheſter but ſo forward in the new ghoſpellinge ſpirit of thoſe dayes, as ſhe became a miſtreſſe in peruerting others, & being brought before the commiſſioners, behaued herſelfe moſt inſolently in ſpeaches, vrginge them to condemne her. See *ibid. num.* 23. 27. 28.
g	1557	26	*VVilliam Munt* mart. This was a huſbandman, that dwelt alſo neere to Colcheſter, who being apprehended togeather with his wife and daughter in law and ſent vp to London by the Earle of *Oxford* and the *Lord Darcy.* B. *Boner* vpon promiſe of amendment, lett them go againe, but growinge afterward worſe & more obſtinate then before, he was finally condemned and burned at *Colcheſter.* See *ibid. num.* 29. 30. 31.
A	1557	27	*Alice Munt* mart. This was wife to the foreſaid *VVilliam Munt* of Colcheſter, who being as forward in hereſie as her huſband, after her firſt diſmiſſion, was apprehended againe, with many other of the ſame crew vpon accuſation of the whole contrey, & ſo burned. See *cap. ibid. num. ibid.*
b	1557	28	*Roſe Allen maid* mart. This was daughter to the foreſaid *Alice Munt* of the age of 20. yeares, as Fox affirmeth, but of ſuch a ſpite-

★ ★ ★ ★ 3　　　　full

			Manichies *ſect, vvas conuerted and made a good Catholike by* S. Ambroſe *B. of* Millaine , *and after vvas the ouerthrovv of all heretiks of his tyme and before, vvhich his admirable vvorks do teſtifie. See* Poſſidon. *in his life and many* otherſ.
c	32	29	c. ʀ. Decollat. S. Ioan. Baptiſtæ. duplex. *Of this feaſt of the decollation of S. Iohn Baptiſt by* Herod, *mentioned* Math.14.Marc.6.Luc.9. *do vvryte both* S.Bede , Vſuardus , *and others in their martyrologes , as alſo the* Græeks *in their* menaloge, *and among other feaſts in the Conſtitution of* Emanuel *the* Emperor *tit. 7. cap. 1. apud* Theodor.Balſam. *and others.*
d	304	30	c. ʀ. Fælicis & Adaucti mart. *The firſt of theſe* 2. *vvas a Prieſt in* Rome, *vvho after many torments vnder* Diocletian *the* Emperor , *being led to death mett vvith one vnknovven , vvho ſaid he vvas deſirous to dy vvith him , vvhich the magiſtrats hearinge, beheaded him indeed vviih the other , and for that his name vvas not knovvne, he vvas called by Chriſtian people* Adauctus, & *a monaſtery vvas erected in* Rome *in honour of them both, as yovv may ſee in* Damaſus *in the life of Pope* Iohn *the firſt. an.*552.
e	651	31	м.ʀ. Aidanus Epiſc. & Confeſs. *This man vvas B. of* Lindisferne *in the Kingdome of the Northumbers , and vvas of moſt admirable life in the* Engliſh *primitiue Church , vvhoſe ſoule* S. Bede *ſaith that* S. Cuthbert *then being but a ſheppard , ſeing one day to be carryed vp to heauen by the hands of Angells , vvas conuerted therby to a religious life. See* S. Bede.lib.3. hiſt. cap.3.5.14. & in vit.Cuthberti c.4. *and others.*
			The

			full hereticall ſpiritt, as is incredible in à wench of thoſe years : ſee her arrogant and contumelious ſpeaches. *cap*.12. *num*.32.
c	1557	29	*Iohn Iohnſon mart.* This was a labourer one of the former crew of Colcheſter a diſciple of *VVilliam Munt*, who did approue and applaud his anſwers in all things, & finally was condemned and burned with him, vpon this moneth and yeare of Chriſt 1557. See *ibidem num.* 29.
d	1557	30	*George Eagles mart.* This Eagles was by his craft a Taylour, called otherwayes *Trudgo-uer-the-vvorld* for that he was a famous wanderer, walking vp and downe from countrey to countrey, and inſtillinge his new opinions to as many as he could, and therwithall ſedition and treaſon alſo, againſt the ſtate, for which he was indighted, condemned, hanged and quartered, and his quarters ſett vp at 4. ſeuerall townes, to witt, *Colcheſter, Harvvich, Chelemsford* and *S. Rouſes.* See *ibid. num.* 33. 34. 35. & 36.
e	1557	31	*One Friar & the ſaid George Eagles ſiſter mart.* Of theſe 2. Martyrs we haue no further narration but theſe words of Fox : About the ſame tyme, one named Friar, with a woman accompaginge him, who was the ſyſter of George Eagles, in like cauſe of righteouſnes ſuffered like martyrdome. But what this friar or woman was, or what was their righteouſnes, we read not. See *ibid. num*.33.

****4

The

The Moneth of September.

| f | 480 | 1 |

c. R. Aegidij Abbatis. *This man vvas borne in Athens of Greece, and of royall lynage, vvho forsakinge the vvorld, and geuinge all his goods to the poore vvent to hide himselfe in France, vvhere he liued many yeares in a vvildernes neere to the citty of Arles, and vvas maintayned only by the milke of a do, that at certaine tymes by Gods appointment came vnto him; vvhich do being one day chafed vvith the hounds of* King Clodoueus, *ran to this sainct for fuccour, and therby he vvas found out, and intreated by the said K. to take vpon him the gouerment of a monastery, vvhich in that place he vvould build.* See Vincent. in fpec. lib. 23. cap. 139. Anton. p. 2. tit.13. cap.6. and others.

| g | 379 | 2 |

M. R. Iufti Epifcopi & Confefs. *This vvas the 13. B. of* Lions *in France famous for his vertue and learninge, and vvas fent legate for the vvhole cleargy of that countrey to the Councell of* Aquileia *in the tyme of* Gratian *the Emperor, vvho returninge from that Councell, left his Bifhopricke and vvent to liue an eremiticall life in the vvildernes of Aegipt, vvhere he vvrought many miracles, and died a great fainct.* See his Acts *in* Sur. to.5. & Ado *in his cronicle an.*379. and others.

| A | 120 | 3 |

M. R. Serapiæ Virg. & mart. *This vvas a noble young Virgin of Rome, vvho profeffing Chriftian Religion and virginity vnder Adrian the Emperor, fhe vvas firft deliuered to 2. lafciuious young men to abufe her, but fhe by Gods help ouercomminge them, vvas caft into a fire, and deliuered from thence alfo vvithout hurt, vvhervpon fhe vvas firft beaten vvith cudgells and after beheaded.* See the mart. of Bede, Vfuard, Ado and others, *as alfo* Sur. to.5.

M. R.

The Moneth of September

f	1428	1	*Father Abraham mart.* This was an old poore ſimple man of Colcheſter burned for Lollardiſme and Wickliffianiſme in the tyme of K. Henry the ſixth, almoſt 200. yeares paſt. his particular opinions are not knowne nor recyted by Fox, for which he was a Martyr. See *cap.13. num.2.3.*
g	1428	2	*VVilliam VVhite Prieſt martyr.* This was an Apoſtata Prieſt that vpon *VVickliffes* doctrine, gaue ouer his Prieſthood (ſaith Fox) and tooke vnto him a godly young woman, named *Ioane* : for which he being apprehended by order of *Henry Chichely* Archbiſhopp of *Canterbury* abiured, but for relapſe was burned at *Norvvich* afterward, vnder the aforeſaid K. Henry the ſixth. See *ibid. num.2. 4. 5. 6.*
A	1428	3	*Iohn VVaddon Prieſt marty,.* This was another Wickliffian Prieſt, like vnto *VVilliam VVhite* before mentioned, whoſe articles ſaith Iohn Fox, were not vnlike to thoſe of the other, but yet what they were in particular, or what opinions he held in Religion, is not ſett downe, but yf they were the comon Wickliffian opinions, yow may read them afterwards *cap13.* See *ibid. num.2. & 6.*

VVilliam

Litt.	Ann.	Dies	The Catholike Calendar. **September.**
Dñic.	Chr.	menf.	
b	150	4	M.R. Marcelli mart. *This vvas a principall man of the City of* Cabvlon *in France, vvho being inuyted by the prefident of that countrey, named* Prifcus, *to a banquet, & vvhen he favv prophane idolatrous meate come in, he detefted the fame, for vvhich he vvas put into ground vp to the middle, and the reft left naked vvas abufed and tormented by all kind of cruelty for 3. dayes togeather, notvvithftandinge vvhich he neuer ceafed to finge praifes to God: this his martyrdome happened vnder* Antoninus *the Emperor. See the Roman Martyrologe, as alfo* S. Bede, Vfuard, *and* Sur. to. 5. *and others.*
c	98	5	M.R. Victorini Epifcopi & mart. *This vvas B. of a tovvne called* Amiternum *in Italy, vvho being fent into Banifhment vnder the Empsrour* Nerua, *vvas aftervvard by a cruell iudge hanged vp three dayes by the feete, vvith his head dovvnevvard for the Confeffion of Chrift, and fo he died. See the Acts of* S. Nereus *and* Archileus *in* Sur. tom.3. die 12. Maij. *and others.*
d	98	6	M.R. Onefiphori Epifcopi & mart. *This vvas fcholler to* S. Paul; *of vvhome he maketh mention in his fecond Epiftle to* Timothy, *in the firft and fourth Chapter: he vvas B. of* Colophon, *and goinge about to preach vvas taken by the Emperors prefident, and moft cruelly beaten, and torne in peeces vvith vvyld horfes. See* Mart. Rom. Bed. Adon. & alios, *and the Greeke menalogé vpon the* 28. *of* Aprill.
e	303	7	M.R. Ioannis mart. *This vvas a great noble man of the Citty of* Nicomedia, *vvho vvhen the tvvo perfecutinge Emperors* Diocletian *and* Maximinian *vvere prefent in the fame citty, & had fett vp cruell Edicts againft Chriftians, he tore them dovvne, as rebellious againft Chrift, vvhervpon he vvas tormented vnto death by all kind of moft exquifite torments: See* Eufeb. l.8. hift. c.5. Niceph. l.7. c.5. *and others.*

C. R.

Litt.	Ann.	Dies	Fox his Calendar. September.
Dñic.	Chr.	menſ.	
b	1552	4	*VVilliam Gardener*, and *VVilliam Allen martyr*. The former of theſe two, was a young factor to a marchant of Briſtow, named *Pagett*, who was burned in *Lisbone* of Portugall for a moſt deſperate fact, of ſnatching the bleſſed Sacrament out of the Prince Cardinalls hands of Portugall in a ſollemne maſſe, at the marriage of the K. ſonne in K. Edward the ſixth
	1555		his dayes. The ſecond named Allen was a ſimple labouringe man of *VValſingham*, burned vnder Q. Mary for obſtinacy in certayne Caluinian opinions. See *ibid.* 8.9.10.11.13.14.
c	1555	5	*Thomas Cobb* and *Roger Coo martyrs*. The former named *Cobb* was a bucher, and *Coo* was a Sherman. Yow may ſee both by their diſputations with the Biſhop of *Norvvich*, and his Chancelor, and their ſtrange victory ouer them, as alſo their inſolency, pride, and obſtinacy, as Fox recounteth the ſtory. *ibidem num.* 13.14.15.16.
d	1555	6	*VVilliam Andrevv* and *Iohn VVade confeſſors*. Theſe 2. Confeſſors died, the firſt in Newgate, the ſecond in the Kings bench, being laid in for Proteſtant Religion as Fox affirmeth; the firſt of them was a Carpenter, the ſecond a crafteſman of another occupation: See *ibid. num.* 13.
e	1555	7	*Thomas Leyes confeſſor*. This was an artificer, companion of *Iohn VVade*, and fallinge ſicke in the ſame priſon with him, they were permitted to go forth vnto their frends houſes in London, where afterward dyinge, they are heere canonized both of them, as yow ſee by Iohn Fox for Confeſſors of his Church. See *ibid. num.* 13.

George

Litt.	Ann.	Dies	The Catholike Calendar. September.
Dñic.	menf.	menf.	
f	Ante chriſtum. 15 *428	8	c. R. Natiuitas B. Mariæ Virg. duplex. *This feſtiuity of celebratinge by annuall memory the byrth of the bleſſed Virgin vvas inſtituted after the Councell of * Epheſus, vvherin the ſupreme title of* Mother of God *vvas giuen vnto her againſt Neſtorius the heretike, though not in all places at one tyme. See* S. Bernard. Serm. 4. Sup. Salu. Reg. *and* S. Ioan. Damaſc. orat. de natiu. Dei Geneer. *and both the* Rom. *and* Greeke *menaloge.*
g	304	9	c. R. Gorgonij mart. *This vvas a noble man in great honour and fauour vvith* Diocletian *the Emperor; he one day in his preſence confeſſing to be a Chriſtian at the* City *of* Nicomedia, *he commaunded him preſently to be hanged vp by the feete and beaten vvith vvhippes, and then his ſkyn to be pulled of his backe and belly, and the fleſh to be rubbed vvith ſalt, and then to be layd on an hoate gridyron; all vvhich he hauing paſt, ended his life by ſtranglynge. See* Euſeb. lib. 8. cap. 6. Niceph. lib. 7. cap. 5. *and others.*
A	1306	10	M. R. Nicolai confeſſoris. *This vvas a religious man of the order of* S. Auſten *of a* City *in* Italy *called* Tolentinum, *vvho lead a very holy life more then* 300. *years gone, and aftervvard vvas by Pope* Eugenius *canonized vpon the yeare of Chriſt* 1446. *he died* anno 1306. *See* S. Anton. p. 3. tit. 22. cap. 11. *and* Sur tom. 5. *and others.*
b	257	11	c. R. Proti & Hiacinthi mart. *Theſe vvere 2. Eunuches that did ſerue the noble Virgin* Eugenia *in* Alexandria *of* Egipt, *vvho vvayting vpon her aftervvard to* Rome *in the time of* Galienus *the Emperor, vvhere ſhe vvas put to death alſo for Chriſtian Religion vpon the* 23. *of December: theſe* 2. *her faithfull ſeruants vvere martyred by all kind of tormēts in like manner, in vvhoſe memory there vvas a Church erected in* Rome *ſoone after. See* Dam. in vit. PP. Symmachi. *& others.* M. R.

Litt. Dñic.	Ann. Chr.	Dies mensf.	Fox his Calendar. September.
f	1555	8	*George Catmer martyr.* This was an artificer burned at Canterbury vpon the third yeare of Q Maryes raigne, togeather with 4.others his companions, no leſſe willfull and obſtinate then himſelfe; yow may ſee his fond anſwers. *cap.13. num.17.18.19.*
g	1555	9	*Robert Streater martyr.* This was another artificer of the ſame of *Canterbury* with *Catmer*, of whome Fox wryteth little but only that he denyed ſtoutly diuers articles of our Religion, but with how much reaſon or ground he had ſo to do, is eaſy to gheſſe. See *ibid. num.17.*
A	1555	10	*Antony Burvvard mart.* Of this *Burvvard* alſo another companion of the former fellowſhip of Canterbury craftſmen Fox wryteth little in particular, but that he was as foreward to dy, as the reſt, and would not yeld a iote in his conceyued phantaſyes. See *cap.ibid.nu.ib.*
b	1555	11	*George Bradbridge & Iames Tutty mart.* Theſe two made vp the former number of artificer martyrs aforſaid burned at Canterbury. Their anſwers were much a like in raylinge and defyinge confeſſion, maſſe, the reall preſence and other ſuch like articles, which they ignorant men vnderſtood not. See *ibid. num.17.*

Thomas

c	300	12	M. R. Antonini Epifcopi & mart. *This good Bishop flyinge out of Italy into the eaſt parts, vnder the cruell perfecution of Diocletian, vvas taken aftervvard by the gentills at maffe, & ſlaine by the Altar-ſide. See his acts* tom. 6. Lippom. Sur. tom. 5. *and others.*
d	219	13	M. R. Philippi mart. *This vvas the Father of the forſaid* Eugenia *vvho being Gouernour of Egypt, left his office vnder* Caracalla *the Imperor, for that he vvas a Chriſtian, and could not vvith fafe confcience execute the Emperors lavves made againſt them, for vvhich cauſe his Succeſſour* Terentius *cauſed him to be beheaded. See the* Rom. mart. *and that of* S. Bede, Vſuard, *and others.*
e	628	14	C. R. Exaltatio S. Crucis. duplex. *This feſtiuall day is kept in memory of the recoueringe backe the Croſſe of our Sauiour out of* Perſia, *by* Heraclius *the Emperor after the victory of* Cofrhoes *King of* Perſia, *vvhich happened vpon the yeare* 628. *albeit the like feaſt of exaltation of the Croſſe vvas vſed amonge the Greeks, before this victory happened, as appeareth in the life of* S. Chryſoſtome *and other ancient Fathers: See alſo* Lippom. tom. 7.
f	90	15	C. R. Nicomedis mart. *This vvas a holy Prieſt of* Rome *vnder* Domitian *the Emperor, vvho being commaunded to facrifice vnto Idolls aunſvvered: I do not vſe to facrifice but to one God only, vvhich is omnipotent, for vvhich he vvas tormented to death; he had foone after an auncient Church erected in honor of him in* Rome, *vvherof there is mention in the firſt* Roman *Councell vnder Pope* Symmachus. *See* Sur. tó. 3. 12. Maij. *and others.*
g	980	16	C. S. Edithæ Virginis. *This Virgin vvas an Englifhvvoman, and daughter of the excellent* K. Edgar, *and fyſter to* K. Edward *the martyr after*

Litt. Dñic.	Anñ Chr.	Dies mensf.	Fox his Calendar. September.
c	1555	12	*Thomas Hayvvard* and *Iohn Gorevvay or Gorey mart.* Thefe 2. were men of like quality to the former burned at Canterbury, Fox fetteth not downe for what articles they died, but prefumeth them to haue byn of his Religion, becaufe they were punifhed by vs: they were burned at Lychfield. See *ibid. num.*17.18.
d	1555	13	*Robert Glouer mart.* This man was of Manchefter, and being called before the Bifhopp of Lichfied for the common Zwinglian and Caluinian herefies of thofe dayes, he behaued himfelfe moft infolently, and befides this, wrote many feditious and fpitefull letters abroad to peruert others. Wherof fee at large *cap. ibid. num.*18.19,20.21.22.23.
e	1555	14	*Cornelius Bungay mart.* This was a Capper of *Couentry*, who after great paines and labour taken with him for his conuerfion, by the Bifhop and other learned men, he remayninge obftinate and infolent, was burned in the fame towne, togeather with the forenamed *Glouer.* See the cappers herefies, pride & arrogancy. *ibid. num.*18.19.20.
f	1556	15	*Edvvard Sharpe mart.* This was a poore artificer, or feruinge man burned at Briftow, togeather with another youth that was a carpenter, vpon the fourth yeare of the raigne of Q. Mary. Fox fetteth downe no articles of their beleefe, but only faith that they died moft glorioufly, to the terror of the wicked and comfort of the good, &c. See *cap. ibid. num. ibid.*
g	1556	16	*Iohn Hart,* and *Thomas Rauenfdale mart.* The firft of thefe two was a fhomaker, and the fecond was a Curtiar, burned togeather at *Maifield*

Litt. Dñic.	Ann⁹ Chr.	Dies menf.	The Catholike Calendar. September.
			after vvhofe death diuers of the nobility and people vvould haue crovvned her *Queene* before Etheldred her brotherin-lavv , but fhe refufinge all vvorldly preferment made herfelfe a nunne , in the monaftery of Wilton and there both liued and died moft holyly. See her excellent life in Policron. lib. 6. cap. 7. and Sur. tom. 5. and othsrs.
A	172	17	M. R. Iuftini prefbyteri & mart. *This vvas a holy Prieft of Rome vvho vvas moft famous for his conftancy in Chriftian Religion, duringe the perfecutions of* Valerianus *and* Galienus *, he vvas prefent at the death of* S. Laurence *and* Pope Sixtus *, and gathered vp their facred reliques and after vvas put to death himfelfe vnder the Emperor* Claudius . *See the Acts of* S. Laurence *, and vvryters therof* Rom. mart. *and others.*
b	300	18	M. R. Ferreoli mart. *This vvas a Tribune or Coronell, vnder the Emperor* Diocletian, *of great zeale in Chriftian Religion, for vvhich he being apprehended at* Vienna *in* France, *and caft into a darke dungeon, all the gates vvere opened in the night & all his chaines broken vvith a cleere light appearinge and guidinge him forth , but being after taken againe, he vvas beheaded. See of him* Venant. Fortun. lib. 7. Sydon. Apollinar. lib.7. Epift. 1. *and others.*
c	320	19	C.R. Ianuarij Epifcopi & Sociorum mart. *This man vvas B. of* Beneuentum *in* Italy *, but he vvas put to death at* Puteolis *faft by* Naples *vvith diuers others of his Church vnder* Diocletian ; *his head and bloud are kept at this day in feuerall places at* Naples. *and vpon his feaft are brought togeather vvith follemne proceffion , at vvhich meeting the bloud that is dry before, doth miraculoufly vvax moift and cleere to the admiration of all them , that behould the fame publikely. See* Sur. to. 5. Mombrit. to. 2. *and others.* C. R.

			Maiſield in Suſſex for pertinacity in diuers hereticall opinions , which they had choſen to defend ; Fox wryteth alſo of them , that they died glorioufly in the iuſt quarrell of Chriſts ghoſpell, but this ghoſpell ſtretcheth farre with Fox. See *cap.*13. *num.*25.26.
ꬠ	1556	17	*Iohn Horne and another vvoman martyrs.* This *Horne* was a poore fellow of the towne of *VVolton-vnder-hedge* in Gloceſterſhire : The woman Fox declareth not what ſhe was, nor what acquaintance ſhe had with *Horne*; but that ioyning togeather in defence of certaine hereticall opinions (which yet Fox declareth not what they were) they were burned, in the ſame place togeather. See *ibid. num.*25.
b	1556	18	*Iohn Kurd* and *Cecily Ormes mart.* The firſt of theſe two was a ſhomaker of the Pariſh of *Shirſham* in *Northamptonſhire* and burned in Southampton; the other was a ſimple woman of Norwich, but ſo obſtinate, as ſhe diſputed with the Biſhopps Chancelor , rayled and ſcoulded extreemely , and could not be kept from the fire. See *ibid.num.*26.27.30,
c	1557	19	*Rafe Allerton,Richard Roth,&* Ioyce Levves *m.* Of theſe 3. the firſt was a Taylour burned at *Iſlington*, he was a great Preacher & Captaine to all the reſt, hauing had many long & large diſputations with B. Bonner. and his learned Aſſiſtents. *Roth* was an artificer burned with him at the ſame place. And *Ioyce Levves* was wife of one *Thomas Levves* of *Manceter*, who preſented her to the B. of Couentry for her exceſſiue vnquiet ſpirite of hereſie. See *ibid. num.*26.27.28.
			✶ ✶ ✶ ✶ ✶ *Iames*

Litt.	Ann'	Dies	The Catholike Calendar. **September.**

Litt. Dñic.	Ann' Chr.	Dies menf.	The Catholike Calendar. **September.**
d	120	20	C. R. Vigilia. Euſtachij & Sociorum mart. *S. Euſtachius vvas before his baptiſme called* Placidus, *and vvas a famous vvarryer & great Captayne vnder* Titus & Veſpaſian *Emperors, at the ouerthrovv of Hieruſalem, but after-vvard being made a Chriſtian, he vvas appre-hended for the ſame vnder Adrian the Emperor tegeather vvith his vvife and 2. Children, and all foure vvere caſt to lyons, but not being tou-ched by them, they vvere put into a braſen bull vvith fire vnder them, and ſo ended their mar-tyrdome. See* Niceph. lib. 3. hiſt. cap. 19. Sur. tom. 5. *and others.*
e	90	21	C. R. Mathæi Apoſtoli. duplex.
f	303	22	C. R. Mauritii & Sociorum mart. *S. Maurice vvas Captaine of a legion of ſouldiars vnder Maximinian the Emperor, called the* Theban *legion, all vvhich reſuſinge to ſacrifice to Idols, vvere after many torments by the ſaid Emperors commandement, put cruelly to death at* Sedu-nium *in France. See* Sur. tom. 5. Mombrit. to. 2. Venant. Fort. lib. 2. *and others.*
g	68.	23	C. R. Lini Papæ & mart. Et comm. S. Theclæ virg. & mart. *The firſt of theſe 2. vvas Pope of Rome next after S. Peter (as ſaith* Iren. l. 3. c. 3. *and* Euſeb. l. 3. c. 12.) *and martyred aftervvard vnder* Nero. *The ſecond vvhich is* Thecla, *being a diſciple of S. Paul, after incredible variety of torments ſuffered, both of fire, beaſts, beatinge, and other like, died at laſt quietly in her bedd, and all auncient Fathers do vvryte vvonderfull praiſes of her. See* S. Gregor. Nazianz. exhor-tat. ad virginit. *and others.*
70			
A	110	24	M. R. Audochij presbyteri & ſociorum mart. *This Prieſt vvas borne in Aſia, and ſent from thence vvith tvvo companions* Thirſis & Fœlix *by S. Policarpe to preach Chriſtian doctrine in France, vvho vvere taken at* Auſtum *in Bur-gundy,*

Litt. Dñic.	Ann. Chr.	Dies menf.	Fox his Calendar. September.
d	1557	20	*Iames Auſtovv and Margery his vvife mart.* Theſe 2. were burned alſo at Iſlington togeather with *Allerton* the Taylor, who was their cheefe Doctor in hereſie, they behaued themſelues very obſtinatly, eſpecially the wife, of whome Fox ſaith, *that they vvere as found in matters of faith, and anſvvered as truly, as euer any did, eſpecially the vvoman to vvhome the Lord had giuen the greater knovvledge, &c.* See *ibid. num.*26.29.33.
e		21	Mathew Apoſtle.
f	1557	22	*Agnes Bongeor mart.* This was a moſt willfull woman of Colcheſter, who being accuſed of hereſie and of many blaſphemous and ſpitefull ſpeaches againſt diuers points of Catholike Religion, and of her peruerſe opinions therin, ſhe perſiſted obſtinate, and being repriued after the burninge of ſome others to the intent to ſaue her, ſhe would in noe wiſe conſent thervnto. See *ibid. num.*34.
g	1557	23	*Margaret Thurſtan mart.* This was a companion of the former *Agnes Bongeor* no leſſe malepart, arrogant, and willfull then ſhe, who being put in pride and vanity that ſhe ſhould be an elect Martyr and Confeſſor of Chriſt, & ſo glorious to poſterity vnder that title, ran willfully to the fire, and was burned at Colcheſter, the fifth yeare of Q. Maryes raigne. See *cap.ibid. num.ibid.*
A	1557	24	*Iohn VVarner mart.* This VVarner was burned alſo at Colcheſter with three other companions, that enſue after vpon ſeuerall dayes for ſo doth Fox thinke conuenient to honour them, though they were all burned on one

★ ★ ★ ★ ★ 2   day;

Litt. Ðñic.	Ann. Chr.	Dies menf.	The Catholike Calendar. September.
			gundy, and there vvhipped and hanged vp by the hands, & caſt into the fire, but could not be burned. And ſo at laſt they vvere beheaded. See the Rom. mart. Beda, Vſuard, Pet. in Catal.lib.8. cap.16. and others.
b	300	25	M. R. Firmini Epiſcopi & mart. This vvas the firſt B. of Amians in France, vvho in the perſecution of Diocletian after many torments ſuffered vvas beheaded by comaundement of the preſident Rictiouarus. See the Rom. mart. as alſo that of S.Bede, Vſuard, and Democar.l. 1. de Sacrific. Miſſæ. and others.
c	302	26	c. R. Cypriani & Iuſtinæ mart. This S. Cyprian is not that famous Doctor and Martyr, that vvas B. of Carthage, but another borne at Antioch, vvho firſt vvas a Magitian, before he vvas a Chriſtian, and vvas conuerted by the holy perſuaſions of the Virgin Iuſtina, vvhcme by Magicke art, he vvould haue dravvne to his luſt. Both of them ſuffered glorious martyrdome aftervvard vnder Diocletian at Nicomedia. See Sur. tom.5. Lippom. tom.6. and others.
d	301	27	c. R. Coſinæ & Damiani mart. Semiduplex. Theſe vvere 2. brethren famous phiſitions in the Citty of Aegea in Arabia, vvho being called before Lycias preſident of that countrey for being Chriſtians, and they ſtandinge conſtantly to the ſame, vvere firſt beaten vvith vvhipps and after bound and caſt into the ſea, vvhence being miraculouſly deliuered, they vvere tyed to a ſtake and fire put to them, but it vvould not touch them, vvhervpon at length they vvere beheaded. See Bede, Vſuard, Ioan. Diac. in vit. S. Gregor. lib.1. cap.1. Rom. mart. and others.
e	225	28	M. R. Priuati mart. This vvas a Roman, vvho being afflicted (as Iob vvas) vvith a leproſy ouer all his body, vvas miraculouſly healed by S. Calixtus Pope the firſt of that name, vvherat the Emperor Alexander Seuerus talinge diſdayne, that

			day, he wryteth no particular neither of him nor his fellowes, but only ſaith in generall, that they ſuffered *for the true teſtimony of righteouſnes.* See *ibid. num.*35.
b	1557	25	*Chriſtian Grouer mart.* This was one of the forſaid companions of VVarner burnèd with him vpon this moneth and yeare at Colcheſter: Fox ſaith that he wanted the records, & therfore could ſett downe nothinge particular of her, more, then that ſhe died for the true teſtimony of righteouſnes. See *ibid.n.*35.
c	1557	26	*Thomas Athoth mart.* This was another companion of VVarner, one that had forſaken his prieſthood, and taken vnto himſelfe a mate, and was become a new ghoſpeller, and being obſtinate therin, was condemned by *B.Chriſtophorſon* of Chicheſter, and burned with the reſt at Colcheſter. See *ibid. num.*35.
d	1555	27	*Iohn Aſhdone mart.* This was the fourth companion of the forſaid Crew of Colcheſter, Fox deliuereth only their names, and conſequently we know not of what ſect they might be in particular, or what priuate opinions or hereſies they might hold. See *ibidem num.* 35.
e	1555	28	*Thomas Spurdance martyr.* This was a ſeruant (as Fox ſaith) to Q. Mary, and being accuſed of hereſie by certayne of his fellowes; as namely *Iohn Hammon* and *George Lavvſon,* he was apprehended and ſent priſoner to Bury.

Litt. Dnic.	Ann⁹ Chr.	Dies menſ.	The Catholike Calendar. September.
			that the *Chriſtian Biſhopps ſhould vvorke miracles cauſed him to be beaten to death vvith balles of lead, and the Pope alſo that healed him.* See tom. 7. Sur. *and the* Acts *of* S. Calixtus Rom. mart. *and others.*
f	495	29	c. R. Dedicatio S. Michaëlis Archang. dupl.
g	420	30	c. R. Hieronymi presbyteri & confeſs. Eccl. Doct. duplex. *This is that renovvned Doctor and Father of Gods Church, borne in* Dalmatic *vnder Conſtantius the Emperor, baptized, brought vp in learning & made Prieſt in Rome, but died in* Bethlem, *vvhere he liued many yeares vvith admirable holynes. Of him ſee at large his life vvrytten by* Marianus Victorius B. of Reati, *gathered out of his ovvne vvorks and others.*

<hr>

The Catholike Calendar. October.

The Moneth of October.

A	545	1	c. R. Remigij Epiſcopi & confeſs. *This vvas* B. of Rhemes *in France vvhich Church he gouerned more them* 70. *yeares vvith great holynes of life, he conuerted and baptizea* Clodoueus *the firſt Chriſtian K. of the french nation.* See of him Concil. Mogunt. cap. 36. Greg. Turon. lib. 8. cap. 21. hiſt. Franc. Sigeb. in chron. *and others.*
b	1287	2	c. s. Thomæ Herefordenſis Epiſc. & confeſs. duplex. *This vvas an Engliſhman borne of noble parentage, vvho after ſtudy in* Oxford, Paris *and other places, vvas firſt made Chancelor of* Oxford, *and then of the vvhole realme vnder K.* Henry *the third, and vpon the yeare* 1275. *vvas choſen B. of Hereford, and goinge aftervvard to* Rome,

			and there , after fome tyme remaynïnge ftil obftinate in his opinions, he was burned. See *ibid. num.* 36.
f		29	Michell Archangell.
g	1557	30	*Iohn Fortune martyr.* Of this fainct; being the laft in this Moneth of September , Iohn Fox wryteth, that he was by occupation a black-fmyth ; *in ſpiritt zealous and ardent ; in ſcriptures ready; in Chriſtes cauſe ſtout & valiant, and in his anſvvers maruelous, &c.* Yow may fee his difputations with the Bifhopps and Doctors, fomewhat at large, and his fingular arrogancy , *and maruelous anſvvers* therin, *ibid. num.*36.37.38.39.40.

Fox his Calendar.　October.

The Moneth of October.

A	1534	1	*Bartholet Millan mart.* This was a frenchman burned in Paris in the yeare 1534. which was the 25. of the raigne of K. Henry the 8. partly for herefie, and partly for fedition efpecially for hauinge caft abroad and fett vp diuers blafphemous bills and libells againft fundry points of Chriftian Religion in feuerall places of that citty. See *cap.*14. *num* 2.3.
b	1534	2	*Iohn de Burge a rich marchant martyr.* This was companion to the forefaid Bartholett, conuicted of the fame fedition and herefie and burned with him in Paris for the fame eaufe. Fox doth not fett downe what their particular opinions were ; fo as they might be of what fect foeuer for any thinge that

✶✶✶✶✶ 4　　　　he

			Rome , in his returne died in Italy , and aboue 100. yeares after vpon proofe of his excellent life and miracles vvas canonized vnder Pope Iohn the 22. in the yeare 1413. See his life in Sur. to.5. Pol. Virg. Weſtmon. and others.
c	695	3	M.R. Heualdorum fratrum mart. *Theſe vvere 2. Engliſh Prieſts (as S.Bed.doth recoũt) that in feruour of our primatiue Engliſh Church vvent firſt into Ireland to gaine ſoules, & then into Saxony vvhere they vvere ſlaine by pagans vpon this day for confeſſion of Chriſtian religion; their bodyes brought to* Colen *by* K. Pepin *of France, are honoured there vntill this day, & many miracles vvrought by the ſame. See S.Bede l.5.hiſt. c.11.Math.* Weſt.*an.*695.*Sig.in chr. and others.*
d	1226	4	C.R. Franciſci Confeſſoris. *duplex. This holy man vvas founder of the order vvho of his name are called* Franciſcans ; *he vvas borne at Aſſiſium in Italy, gaue all avvay that he had to the poore,vvas of admirable ſanctity, vvrought many miracles and vvas canonized by Pope* Greg. *the* 9. *an.*1228. *See S.Bonauent. in his life, and S.Anton. p.3. tit.22. c.10. and others.*
e	296	5	M.R. Charitinæ virg.& mart. *This vvas a holy V.rgin,vvho vnder Diocletian th' Emperor being accuſed to be a Chriſtian,& confeſſing conſtantly the ſame,vvas caſt firſt into the fire,& then into the Sea,from both vvhich being deliuered miraculoſly, her teeth vvere beaten out of her head, and her hands and feete cut of, and ſo ſhe gaue vp the ghoſt in prayer.See the* Greeke menaloge *and the* Rom. mart. *and others.*
f	1101	6	M.R. Brunonis conf. *This vvas a man of great ſanctity in the prouince of Calabria in Italy, vvho aboue 500. yeres gone vvas author of the order of Carthuſiãs,vvhich ſince that tyme hath brought forth ſo many holy men. His admirable life,rare virtues and many miracles, are vvrytten by diuers authors vvhich you may ſe related in Sur.to.5. and diuers others.* C.R.

Litt. Dñic.	Ann. Chr.	Dies mens	Fox his Calendar.
			he sheweth to the contrary. See *ibidem num.* 2. & 3.
c	1534	3	*The receyuer of Naunts mart.* This was another fellow of that company burned in Paris with the former two, whose name yt seemed that Fox knew not, as neyther his Acts or Gests, and yet persuadeth himselfe assuredly that he was of his Church and Religion. See *cap. ibid. num. ibid.*
d	1534	4	*Henry Poile martyr.* This was a fourth companion of the former seditious and hereticall crew, that set vp blasphemous bills and libells in Paris concerninge matters of Religion, he was burned with his foresaid company. See *ibidem.*
e	1534	5	*Catelle a schoole-maistres martyr.* This was a buisy syster of the former hereticall congregation in Paris, who was burned with the foresaid company at Paris, and whome Fox presumeth to haue bin a Saint of his Church, though he knew not what opinions she held. See *ibid.*
f	1534	6	*Stephen de la Forge marchant mart.* This was the sixt & last brother of the forsaid Parisian combination, who albeit they were burned all in one day, yet do their festiuall memoryes occupy 6. seuerall dayes in Fox his Calendar, as yow see, for lake of better furniture to stuffe them with all. See *ibid. n. 2. & 3.* William

g	336	7	c. R. Marci PP. & confeſs. *This Pope vvas a Roman borne, and ſucceded S. Siluefter in tyme of Conſtantine the great: and albeit he kept the ſeat but 3. monethes; yet vvas his holynes of life ſo great , that ſoone after there vvere diuers Churches erected in his memory as appeareth by the firſt Councell held in Rome vnder Pope Symmachus. See* Dam. in vit. Nicolai PP. & ep. Adrian. PP. ad Carol. mag. *and others.*
A	1	8	M. R. Symeonis Senis confeſſoris. *This holy old man vvas he that teoke our Sauiour Chriſt in his armes and pronounced him to be the Meſſias, vvhen he vvas yet in his ſvvadlinge cloth s Luc* 2. *The memory of his holy departure is celebrated both in the Latyn and Greeke Church, though the Grecians keep his feaſt on the firſt of this moneth, as appeareth by their menaloge.*
b	99	9	c. R. Dionyſij , Ruſtici , & Eleutherij mart. ſemiduplex. *This* Dionyſius *vvas he , vvho being a iudge in Athens of the Tribunall named* Areopagus, *vvas conuerted by S. Paul, and after comminge to Rome vvas ſent by Pope Clement, ſucceſſor of S. Peter to preach in France, togeather vvith* 2. *companions* Ruſticus *a Prieſt and* Eleutherius *a Deacon , all vvhich vvere martyred at Paris by* Feſcennius *gouernour of that countrey for the Emperor* Traianus. *See* Hincmarus B. *of Rhemes* ep. ad Carolum Caluum, & Sur. tom. 5. *and others.*
c	644	10	M. R. Paulini Epiſc. & conf. *This man vvas ſent from Rome by S. Greg. the great vnto S. Auſten our Apoſtle in England to aſſiſt him; and by him (ſaith S. Bede) the holy Pope ſent all things neceſſary for the Altars & ſacrifice of the maſſe, as chalices, veſtements, and the like. He vvas B. of Yorke, & conuerted K. Edwyn & the Northumbers to the Chriſtiã faith & died* an. Dñi. 644. Se S. Bed. l.1. hiſt. c. 19. & l.2. c. 9.12. *at large. and others.* M. R.

Litt. Dnic.	Ann. Chr.	Dies mens.	Fox his Calendar. October.
g	1536	7	**William Tyndall** martyr. This was first a Prieſt in K. Henry the 8. his dayes, and being refuſed of B. Tonſtall to be his chaplin, tooke a wife, and made diuorce with Catholike Religion. He tranſlated much of the Bible into Engliſh, and that moſt falſely and corruptly as K. Henry and his parlament declared, he was burned in Flanders at the towne of Filford for diuers hereſies. See *cap.* 14. *num.* 4. 5. 6. 7. *& deinceps.*
A	1537	8	*VVilliam Layton* mart. This was an Apoſtata monke, who forſakinge his order and habitt ioyned himſelfe to a woman, and after that became ſo lewd in ſcoffinge ſpeaches againſt diuers points of Catholike Religion, as K. Henry himſelfe commaunded him to be burned for the ſame. See *ibid. num.* 13.
b	1537	9	*Puttedevv,* and *Iohn Lambert* mart. The firſt of theſe 2. was an obſcure fellow, whoſe proper name Fox knew not, nor what he held in Religion, but only that he was burned about this tyme in *Suffolke.* *Lambert* was of much more fame, being condemned by K. Henry himſelfe, and by Cranmer and Cromwell in a ſolemne iudgement for Zwinglianiſme, & burned in Smithfield. See *ibid. num.* 13. 20. 21. *& deinceps.*
	*1538		
c	1538	10	*Colyns* and *Coubridge* martyrs. The firſt of theſe 2. Fox confeſſeth to haue byn a madman, & to haue held vp a dogg in the Church to be adored in deriſion of the bleſſed Sacrament. *Coubridge* he granteth beſides all other blaſphemyes, to haue denyed the name of Chriſt expreſsly. See *ibid. num.* 34. 35. 32.

Peter

Litt. Dñic.	Annu. menſ.	Dies menſ.	The Catholike Calendar. October.
d	326	11	M.R. Sarmatæ mart. *This vvas a holy monke of Egipt diſciple of S.Antony , and famous both for his learning and ſanctity of life, as S. Hierome teſtifieth , and vvas ſlaine for the confeſſion of Chriſt by the Saracens in the monaſtery founded by S.Antony himſelfe. See S.Hierome in chron. an.22.* Conſtant. Imp. *and others.*
e	732	12	M. R. Wilfridi Epiſc. & confeſs. *This vvas a holy man of the Engliſh nation B. of Yorke , and tvviſe driuen out of his Biſhopricke by violence vvhich occaſion God vſed (as in the diſperſion of th'Apoſtles)to the conuerſion of the Southangles, vvhome he conuerted from paganiſme , as alſo the Ile of Wight. See S. Bede at large of his life and geſts lib.3. cap.28. lib.4.cap.12.lib.5. c.20. and others.*
f	90	13	M.R.Carpi Epiſcopi & Confeſſoris. *This vvas one of S. Paul the Apoſtle his ſchollers , made by him B.of Troas in* Aſia Minor: *he vvas a man of great holynes of life, and his feaſt is celebrated both by the Greeke and Latyn Church : but the Grecians hold him to be one of the 72. diſciples choſen by Chriſt. See* S. Paul.2.Tim.4.*and* Dionyſius Areopag. ep.8. *and others.*
g	225	14	c. R. Calixti PP. & matt. Semiduplex. *This Pope vvas a Roman borne , and of great holynes vnder the vvicked Emperors* Macrinus, *and* Heliogabolus: *he builded that famous Cemitery of* Calixtus *vvhere infinite Martyrs reliques vvere kept, and himſelfe finally being taken, and kept vvithout meate for certaine dayes, & beaten vvith vvhippes,vvas at laſt throvvne out of a vvyndovv headlonge into a deepe priuy, and ſo ended his martyrdome. See* Sur. to.7.Mombrit. to.2. *and others.*
A	740	15	M.R. Teclæ Abbatiſſæ. *This holy vvoman vvas called out of England by* S.VVinfride *aftervvard called* Boniface Archbiſhop of Mentz & Apoſtle of

Litt.	Ann.	Dies	Fox his Calendar. October.
Dñic.	Chr.	menf.	
d	1539	11	*Peter a German martyr.* The surname of this Peter was not knowne vnto Fox, nor is his life or faith fett downe by him, though *Alanus Copus* do shew, that he denyed Christ to haue taken flesh of the blessed Virgin, and that Fox confessed the same in his former edition. See *cap.14. num.14.*
e	1536	12	*Lancelot, Iohn a painter, & Giles German martyrs.* These 3. were burned in S.Giles field vnder K. Henry the eyght, vpon the yeare of Christ 1539. for certayne opinions, which eyther Fox knew not, or would not fett downe: some suspition there is that they were Anabaptists, wherof yow may see more at large. *ibid. num, 15.16.*
f	1539	13	*Robert Barnes mart.* This was an Augustine friar of *Cambridge,* who becomming an Apostata, first recanted and abiured his heresies, but after returned to them againe, ran ouer the sea to Luther in Germany, whose opinions he defended afterwards against both Catholiks and Caluinists vnto the death: he was afterwards taken, and burned in Smithfield in England. See *ibid. num.17.18.*
g	1539	14	*Thomas Gerrard mart.* This was a Priest companion to Barnes but yet opposite to him, in the article of the reall presence, and other Lutheran atticles, for that he was an earnest Zwinglian, and was burned for the same in company of Friar *Barnes* as yow may see *ibid. num.17.18. & deinceps.*
A	1539	15	*VVilliam Hierome martyr.* This was another Priest of the same crew burned in the same fire also with *Barnes* and *Gerrard* vnder King Henry

Litt. Dñic.	Ann⁰ Chr.	Dies menſ.	
			of Germanye vvho hauinge conuerted that nation to Chriſt, and being deſired by the Chriſtian vveomen therof to inſtitute amonge them ſome nunryes of religious diſcipline and regular life, he called out of England, being an Engliſhman himſelfe, this Tecla, *vvith diuers other vveomen of great vertue and holynes as* Cunigildes, Bergita, Cunitrudes, Lioba, Walburga, & *others. See the life of* S. Boniface apud Sur. 5. Iunij. Mart. Roman. *and others.*
b	787	16	M. R. Lulli Epiſcopi & confeſſoris. *This Biſhop being borne in England of a noble houſe, and Coſyn to* S. Boniface B. of Mentz, *vvas called ouer by him into Germany, and after good experience of religious life vvas made Prieſt by him, and at length appointed ſucceſſor in his Biſhopricke, vvhich he held for* 32. *yeares after him, vvith great demonſtration of ſanctity and miracles vvrought by him, as both all German and other hiſtoriographers do record. See the life of* S. Boniface, *as alſo* Vincent in Spec. lib. 23. c. 137. Tritem. lib. 3. de vir. Illuſtr. c. 193. *and others.*
c	131	17	M. R. Heronis Epiſcopi & mart. *This vvas a famous holy man B. of Antioch ſcholler of Saint Ignatius, to vvhome he vvrote his* 13. *epiſtle, and he vvrote another in like manner to* S. Ignatius *after his martyrdome deſyringe his prayers, himſelfe alſo being ſoone after martyred for the ſame. See* Euſeb. lib. 3. hiſt. cap. 30. Niceph. lib. 3. cap. 15. & Baron. in Annal. ann. 110. & 131. *and others.*
d	90	18	C. R., Lucæ Euangeliſtæ. duplex.
e	750	19	C. S. Frideſuidæ Virginis. duplex. *This Virgin vvas of the Citty of Oxford, and daughter of a noble man named* Didan; *and vvhen as ſhe vvas ſollicited by another principall noble man called* Algarus, *to yeld vnto his luſt, ſhe reſyſtinge the ſame, eſcaped miraculouſly his violence he being on the ſuddayne ſtroken blynd by God for offering* the

Litt. Ðñic.	Ann⁹ Chr.	Dies menſ.	Fox his Calendar. October.
			Henry the eyght, for holdinge Zwinglius his opinions about the Sacrament of the Altar. They agreed not in opinions concerninge their beleefe, and yet Fox maketh them Martyrs of one Church: and albeit they were burned all three in one day, yet he alloweth them three ſeuerall dayes for their ſolemnity. See *cap. ibid. num. ibid.*
b	1555	16	*VVilliam VVolſey mart.* This was a labouringe man of *VViſbich* who being infected with hereſies, & called before the commiſſionars for the ſame, behaued himſelfe ſo inſolently and contumeliouſly towards them in contemptuous and blaſphemous ſpeaches, as was intolerable; he was a Zwinglian in his opinions, and for the ſame was burned. See *cap. 14. num. 37.38.*
c	1555	17	*Robert Pyggot martyr.* This was a paynter of the ſame towne of *VViſbich*, and a companion to *VVolſey*, the one of them ſtyrringe vp the other to anſwere proudly and reproachfully to *Doctor Shaxton* ſuffragan to the B. of Ely, and other commiſſionars authorized to examine them: they were both burned at Ely for Sacramentary opinions, & conſequently were heretiks vnto Luther himſelfe. See *cap. ib. n. ib.*
d		18	*Luke Euangeliſt.*
e	1555	19	Nicolas Ridley Biſhopp martyr. This man was a Prieſt borne in Northampton ſhire, brought vp at *Nevvcaſile*, and firſt was made Chaplyn to K. Henry the 8. of whoſe Religion he was during the Kings life: he made him B. of Rocheſter; but after ioyninge with Cranmer in K. Edwards dayes to promote Zwin-

Litt. Ðñic.	Ann⁹ Chr.	Dies menf.	The Catholike Calendar. October.
			the same. See Pol. virg. lib. 5. hift. Math. Pa- rifiens. Molan. in addit. ad Vfuard. mart. Rom. aud others.
f	366	20	M. R. Artemij mart. *This vvas a noble man of* *high authority vnder Conftantine the great,* *being prefiaent ouer fix prouinces in Egipt , a-* *gainft vvhome Iulian the Apoftata bearing en-* *uy for his zeale to Chriftian religion caufed him* *to be putt to death by greuous torments.* See Theodoret. lib. 3. hift. cap. 17. Niceph. lib. 10. cap. 35. *and others.*
g	389	21	C. R. Hilarionis Abbatis, Et com. S. Vrfulæ & Sor. mart. *Of the holy Abbot Hilarion, his* *rare life, and miracles, and of his goinge to fee* *S. Antony in the deferts of Aegipt , S. Hierome* *& others do vvryte largely. As for S. Vrfula and* *her fellovves, they vvere Brittan Virgins about* *an eleuen thoufand ; accordinge to the common* *account of all authors. They vvere fhipped in* *great Britany to paffe ouer into little Britany in* *France, there to haue byn marryed to others of* *that nation, but being driuen by tempeft dovvne* *to the Mouth of Rhene neere vnto the Citty of* *Colen , they vvere flaine by the Hunnes and* *others enemyes of Chriftian faith , for defence* *therof and defence of their chaftity.* See Gauf. Monumet. lib. 5. cap. 15. Weft. an. 392. *and* *many others.*
A*	389	22	M. R. Cordulæ virg. & mart. *This vvas a prin-* *cipall Virgin one of S. Vrfula her companions,* *vvho being terrified vvith the fpectacle of the* *cruell death of her fellovves, hid herfelfe, but the* *next day repentinge her ovvne frailty, came and* *offered*

			Zwinglianifme , he gat by that meanes the Bifhopricke of London by depriuation of *B. Bonner*, and was afterward in Q. Maryes raigne burned for herefie and treafon. See his ftory at large. *c.14.n* 40.41.42.43.*& deinceps.*
f	1555	20	Hugh Latimer Bifhop martyr. This man was borne in *Lecefterfhire*, ftuddied at Cambridge, was an earneft Catholike ; but by fhryuinge of *Thomas Bilney* (faith Fox) he was conuerted to fauour Proteftants religion, which yet he abiured many tymes afterward , and was made B. of Worcefter in K. Henryes dayes, and after depriued for his euill demaynour and neuer could be reftored by K. Edward: He was at laft burned at Oxford togeather with the forfaid Ridley : See *ibid.num.*44.45. *& deinceps*
g	1555	21	*Iohn VVebb gentilman*, and *George Roper mart.* Thefe were 2. fimple contreymen burned at Canterbury vnder Q. Maryes raigne: Their articles (faith Fox)were the common articles miniftred in thofe dayes , to witt, againft Zwinglianifme & Caluinifme ; their anfwers were infolents fond, & obftinate, as of ignorant deceyued men. See *ibid. num.*61.
A	1555	22	*Gregory Parke mart.* This was a third companion of the former two burned at Canterbury, no leffe vnlearned and ignorant then they, nor yet leffe obftinate and arrogant in his aunfwers ; they went with fuch fond ★★★★★ rafhnes

Litt. Ðñic.	Ann' Chr.	Dies menf.	The Catholike Calendar. October.
			offered herselfe vvillingly to martyrdome; See S.Vrsula her life in Sur.to. 5. and diuers others.
b	366	23	M. R. Theodori presbyteri & mart. This vvas a Prieſt of Siuill in Spaine vvho in tyme of Iulian the Apoſtata ſhevvinge himſelfe conſtant in Chriſtian religion vvas after many torments of rackinge, and burninge his ſides by tearinge his fleſh vvith hoat yrons, beheaded. See Zozom. lib.5. cap.7. Mart. Rom. and others.
c	620	24	M. R. Maglorij Epiſc. & Confeſs. This Maglorius vvas a Brittan borne, and a monke, but goinge ouer to preach Chriſtian religion in the leſſer Brittany of France, vvas there made B. vvhich after he left againe for deſire of retyring himſelfe to an Eremits life, vvherin he ſhined vvith rare holynes and vvorkinge of miracles alſo. See Trit. lib. 3. de vir. Illuſtr. cap. 50. & lib.4. cap.27. and others.
d	260	25	C. R. Chriſanthi & Dariæ mart. Theſe vvere 2. noble Romans man and vvife, vvho giuinge themſelues vvholy to deuotion, and gatheringe togeather of Martyrs reliques, vvere taken and put to ſtraunge torments, and at laſt vvere putt into the ground vp to the head and ſhoulders, and ſo ſtoned to death. See Gregor. Turon.lib. de glor. mart. c.38.and Sur.to.5. and others.
e	120	26	C. R. Euariſti Papæ & mart. This holy Pope liued in the firſt age ſoone after the Apoſtles, he vvas a Grecian borne, and illuſtrated much the Church of God by his life and martyrdome. See of his ſucceſſion Iren. lib. 3. cap.3. Euſeb. lib.3. cap.18. and others.
f	292	27	M. R. Vigilia. Vincentij mart. This man ſuffered at Abula in Spaine vnder Diocletian the Emperor, by commandement of Dacianus the preſident of that Countrey. He is another different from that Vincentius the famous Deacon martyred

			rafhnes to the fire, as one of them gaue a greake fkipp when he came vnto yt. See *cap. ibid. num. ibid.*
b	1449	23	*Adam VVallace mart.* This was a poore fimple Scottifhman (as Fox affirmeth) condemned & burned in *Edenburrough*, during the raigne of K. Henry the fixth, to witt vpon the yeare 1449. He held certayne Wickliffian and Lollards opinions, as yow may fee *ibid.num.62.*
e	1555	24	*Marke Burges*, and *VVilliam Hooker mart.* Of thefe two, *Marke Burges* was a fhipman burned in *Lifbone* for Zwinglian opinions : and *VVilliam Hooker* was his fhippboy killed with ftones (yf we may beleeue Fox) vpon the fame yeare at *Siuill* in Spaine, by the youthes of that citty for the fame caufe. See *ibid.n.63.*
d	1556	25	*Simpfon Prieft, Beuerich Friar,* and *Dauy Stratton gentilman martyrs.* Thefe three Martyrs are only found in Fox his Calendar, but not in his Acts and Monuments : fo as we find neither their Acts or Cefts, or articles of beleefe, nor where, nor why they were burned, albeit yt may be ghefled at, yf the yeare of their burninge be true which he noteth, to witt 1556. See *cap.4. num.64.*
e	1556	26	*Keyler Black friar, Norman Gorley Vicar* of *Dolor martyrs.* Thefe alfo being fellowes of the former, are not found in any of Fox his tables ; fo as we haue only their bare names in his Calendar with their Canonization for Martyrs. See *ibid.*
f	1556	27	*A Black Canon vvith 4. others martyrs.* Thefe fiue in like manner are not found but only in this place of the Calendar. And heere yow fee how Iohn Fox fcrapeth togeather only bare names of vnknowen Martyrs to fill vp his

Litt. Dñic.	Ann. Chr.	Dies mēnſ.	The Catholike Calendar. October.
			martyred vnder the ſame Dacianus *in the Citty of* Saragozza. *See* Vaſæus *in* chron. *and others.*
g A	64 240	28 29	c. r. Simonis & Iudæ Apoſtolorum. duplex. m. r. Narciſci Epiſcopi & Confeſs. *This vvas a very holy man, and the thirtith Biſhopp of the Citty of* Hieruſalem: *he lyued vntill he vvas an hundred & ſixtene yeares of age, and vvas highly commended by the auncient Fathers for his rare life and miracles. See* Euſeb. lib.4. cap.19. *and* Niceph. lib.5. cap.9. *and others.*
b	240	30	m. r. Eutropiæ virg. & mart. *This vvas a Virgin of* Alexandria, *vvho vnder* Decius *the Emperor, goinge to viſitt Martyrs in priſon vvas taken for the ſame, and put to exquiſite torments vntill ſhe gaue vp the ghoſt. See the* Greeke Menaloge, *and* Roman Martyrologe, Sur. tom.5. *and diuers others.*
c	293	31	m. r. Vigilia. Quinctini mart. *This vvas a noble Cittizen of* Rome, *of the order of Senatours, vvho vnder* Maximinian *the Emperor vvas putt to death in* France *for Chriſtian Religion at the Citty novv called of his name* S. Quinctaines: *his body vvas reueyled by an* Angell *50. yeares after his death, and found vncorrupt, and many miracles vvrought therby. See* Greg. Turon. lib. de glor. mart. cap. 72. & 73. Sur. tom. 5. *and others.*

The Catholike Calendar. Nouember.

The Moneth of Nouember.

Litt. Dñic.	Ann. Chr.	Dies mēnſ.	
d e	180	1 2	c. r. Feſtum omnium Sanctorum. duplex. c. r. Commemoratio omnium fidelium defunctorum. duplex. *This pious office to pray yearly,*

			Calendar : for neither is there *blacke* or *llue* canon found in his Acts and Monuments, and much lesse the other foure companions by him vnnamed. See *ibid. num.*64.
g A	1556	28 29	Simon and Iude. *Three died in prison at Chichester confessors.* Here yow see , that as before we had Martyrs , so haue we now Confessors without name, for that they died in Chichester prison: But for many causes they might be put there, and consequently , they are very doubtfull Confessors , and very fitt for Iohn Fox his Catalogue. See *ibid. num.*65.
b	1556	30	*Mother Seaman confessor.* This was an old poore woman of Norwich, who though she died at home in her bed, yet for that she had byn pratlinge about new opinions , and had byn called before the comissionars for the same, she is canonized for a Confessor by Iohn Fox. See *ibid.*
c	1556	31	*Mother Bemiet confessor.* This was another poore woman also of Norwich companion to the aforesaid *Mother Seaman*, with whome she had byn examined, but dismissed, and so died in her owne house as Iohn Fox confesseth. And with her he endeth the Moneth of October. See *ibid. num.*65.

The Moneth of Nouember.

d		1	The feast of all Sainctes.
e	1541	2	*Richard Mekinges martyr.* This was a poore boy of London, burned in Smithfield vnder

★★★★★★3   K. Henry

			yearly vpon a certaine day for all ſoules depar-

yearly vpon a certaine day for all ſoules depar-ted, hath bin an auncient cuſtome amongſt Chriſtians in the Catholike Church: Ex maiorum traditione (ſaith Tertullian in the ſecond age after Chriſt) pro defunctis annua die facimus. VVe do by tradition of our anceſtors yearely offer vp ſacrifices for the dead. lib. de coron. mil. *and the like hath* Greg. Nazianzen. orat. in fun. Ceſarij frat. *and others, though this particular day vvas inſtituted aftervvard. See* Sigeb. an. 998, *and others.*

998

f | **664** | **3**

c. s. **Winifridæ** virg. & mart. duplex. *This Virgin being of the Britiſh bloud, vvas beheaded by* Cradocus *ſonne of* K. Alane *of North-Wales for that ſhe vvould not yeld to the violence of his concupiſcence; in place of vvhich martyrdome ſpronge vp miraculouſly a vvell vvhich indureth to this day, by the name of* S. Winifrides *well Her reliques vvere kept in the Church of Shrevvſhury vvith great honour. See* Robert. Salop. *that vvrote her life,* Sur. to. 6. Molan. Mart. Rom. *and others.*

g | **296** | **4**

c. r. Vitalis & Agricolæ mart. *Theſe tvvo vvere apprehended in the Citty of Bonony in Italy vnder Diocletian the Emperor for ſpreading Chriſtian doctrine,* Vitalis *vvas boundman vnto* Agricola, *but made his fellovv by martyrdome: yea preferred before him in the Calendar, for that he ſuffered more tormëts then the other. Of them both* S. Ambroſe *vvryteth at large* lib. de exhort. ad virgin. *and* S. Paulinus *Biſhop of* Nola, natal. 9. Greg. Turon. lib. 2. cap. 16. *and others.*

A | **8** | **5**

m. r. Zachariæ & Elizabeth. *Theſe vvere the holy parents of* S. Iohn Baptiſt, *highly comm n-ded for their holynes in the goſpell* Luc. 1. *See alſo* S. Epiphanius *of their rare life and vertues* lib. de vit. Prophet. cap. 23. *and others.*

M. R.

Litt.	Ann°	Dies	Fox his Calendar. November.
dñic.	Chr.	menf.	
			K. Henry the eyght , vpon the ftatute of fix articles, he denyed the reall prefence, and faid at the fire fide , that Friar *Barnes* had taught him that opinion , but Fox faith that could not be fo ; for that *Barnes* was neuer of that opinion himfelfe. See *cap*.15. *num*.1.2.3.
f	1541	3	*Richard Spencer martyr*. This was an Apoftata Prieft of *Sarifbury*, that had taken a woman, and with her left his vocation of Priefthood (faith Fox) & became a player of Enterludes, & further then this fell to deny the reall prefence in the Sacrament, & fo was condemned and burned in the fame citty vpon the ftatute of fix articles. See *ibid. num.*2.3.
g	1541	4	*Andrevv Hevvit mart*. This was a comedian, one of the fellow-players of *Spencer* the marryed Prieft ; he was condemned and burned with him in Salifbury the fame yeare & day: as yow may fee *cap. ibid. num. ibid.*
A	1541	5	*Iohn Porter mart*. This was an Apprentife that died in Newgate in K. Henryes dayes, he was put in prifon vpon the Statute of fix articles ; he had (faith Fox) an audible voyce and read the Bible in Englifh to fuch as reforted to him , which was then lawfull, but he was accufed for makinge falfe commentaryes theron: See *ibid. num.*4.

★ ★ ★ ★ ★ 4   *Thomas*

b	559	6	M. R. Leonardi confeſ. *This vvas a holy man of Aquitany in France, vvho being ſcholler to S.Remigius B. of Rhemes, & inſtructed by him in all kind of ſanctity of life, retyred himſelfe into his countrey, & liued in a deſert, & vvrought many miracles both before and after his death.* See Sur.to.6.Trit.l.3.de vir.Ill.c.29.and others.
c	736	7	M. R. Willebrordi Epiſcopi & Confeſſoris. *This vvas an Engliſhman, borne in Yorkeſhire, vvho in the zeale of our primitiue Church going forth of England to preach Chriſtian religion to the gentills of forraine nations, as many other did, he conuerted very many of the Friſians and Danes, and vvas ordayned B. of Vtright in Friſeland, and his name* Willebrord *changed into* Clement, ſee Bed. l.5.hiſt. cap. ☞ Tritem. lib.3. de vir. Illuſtr. cap.137. and others.
d	295	8	C. R. Sanctorum quatuor Coronatorum mart. *Theſe vvere 4. brethren put to death in Rome vnder Diocletian, vvhoſe names being then not kuovvne; their reliques vvere kept, & Churches builded to them vnder the title of foure crovvnd brethren, as may appeare by* S. Gregor. lib.4. regiſt. indict. 13. cap. 44. *aftervvard their names vvere reueyled to be* Seuerus, Seuerianus, Carpophorus, *and* Victorinus. *See* Bed. Vſuard, Rom.mart. and others.
e	298	9	C. R. Dedicat. Baſilicæ Saluatoris. duplex. Et commem. S. Theodori mart. *Of the firſt, to vvitt the dedication of the lateran Church in Rome to* S. Iohn Baptiſt *in honour of our Sauiour, ſee* Pet. Damianus, *and others alleaged by* Baronius *in his notes to the* Rom. Martyrol. *vpon this day.* S. Theod. *vvas a Chriſtian ſouldiar put to death in* Amaſæa *of the countrey of* Pontus *by exquiſite tormēts, vnder Maximinian the Emperor, in vvhich Chriſt appeared vnto him & comforted him extraordinarily.* Se Metaphr. 27. Feb. & 26. Nou. & Sur. to. 3. and others.

C. R.

Litt.	Ann.	Dies	Fox his Calendar. Nouember.
Ðñïc.	Chr.	menſ.	
b	1542	6	*Thomas Bernard mart.* This was an artificer of Lincolne, who in the dayes of the same K. Henry was apprehended and examined by *B. Longland* of that Dioceſſe, and ſhewinge himſelfe very inſolent and obſtinate in certayne hereticall opinions was burned in the ſame citty. See *ibid. num.4. & 5.*
c	1542	7	*Iames Morton mart.* This was another poore fellow of the ſame towne of Lincolne, companion of the forſaid *Bernard* and burned with him (ſaith Fox) for hauinge *S. Iames* epiſtle in Engliſh: but this is refuted *cap. ibid. num. ibid.*
d	1546	8	*George VVſchart mart.* This was a Scottiſh-man condemned of ſedition and hereſie in Scotland vpon the yeare 1546. which was the laſt of K. Henryes raigne of England, and the fifth of Q. Mary of Scotland. He behaued himſelfe moſt contemptuouſly & ſeditiouſly in his publike arraignment. and was burned at *S.* Andrewes. See his deſcription and ſtory. *ibid. num.6.7.8.9.*
e	1546	9	*Iohn Kerby martyr.* This was a poore labouringe man of *Ipſich* wholy vnlearned, yet being once peruerted by the perſuaſion of ſome of Zwinglius his ſect, he was ſo willfull therein, and in denyinge the reall preſence in the bleſſed Sacrament, as no reaſon or perſuaſion to the contrary would ſerue, but that he would needs to the fire, and there how inſolently he behaued himſelfe, yow may ſee *cap.15. num.11.12.*

Roger

Litt. Dnic.	Ann. Chr.	Dies mensf.	The Catholike Calendar. Nouember.
f	253	10	c. R. Tryphonis Respicij & Nimphæ mart. *The first of these three conuerted vnto Christ the other two; for that being put to torments for confession of his faith, his constancy vvas such, as he conuerted first Respicius the Emperor Decius his Tribune, and aftervvard Nimpha a Virgin, both vvhich vvere for the same martyred vvith him. See the Greeke menaloge* 1. Feb. Procop. l.1. de ædif. Iustin. Imp. *of the famous Church erected in honour of S.Tryphon in Constantinople and others.*
g	397	11	c.R. Martini Episcopi & Confessoris duplex. *This is that renovvned S. Martin B. of Tovvars in France, though borne in Hungary of heathen parents, and at* 10. *yeares old vvas called by God to be a Christian against their vvilles, and aftervvard liued a most holy life, of vvhome all antiquity do vvryte most honorably, as* Sulpitius Seuerus *in his life,* S. Paulinus B. of Nola, Greg. Turon. *and others.*
A	350	12	c. R. Martini Papæ & mart. Semiduplex. *This Pope vvas borne in Italy, & seate in the Roman Sea vnder Constans the Emperor of Constantinople, vvho being infected vvith Arrianisme vvas offended vvith him for that he condemned one* Paulus *an hereticall patriarch of Constantinople, and caused him to be apprehended in Rome sent into Banishment to an Iland of* Mare Aegeum, *vvhere he died vvith misery. See* Sur. tom.6. *and many others.*
b	437	13	M. R. Arcadij & Sociorum mart. *VVith this* Arcadius *vvere put to death by exquisite torments in Spaine three others named* Paschasius, Probus, & Eutychianus *vnder* Gensericus K. *of the Vandalls, for that they vvould not yeld to Arrian heresie. See an excellent Fpistle of* Antoninus B. *of Constantinople in those dayes vnto* Arcadius *exhorting him to Constancy. & others.*
c		14	M. R. Laurentij Episcopi & Confessoris. *This vvas*

f	1546	10	*Roger Clark martyr.* This was a labourer alfo of the towne of Bury and fellow to the former Kirby, whofe difciple he feemed to be for that he followed him in all things, and confequently holding his herefies alfo about the bleffed Sacrament, was condemned and burned at the fame towne of Bury. See *ibid.*
g	1531	11	*Richard Bayfield aliâs Somerfam mart.* This was an Apoftata monke of the forfaid towne of Bury, whofe office being, to receaue pilgrims that came by that monaftery, he fell acquainted with two bricklayers of London, by whome he was inftructed in the new doctrine, tooke a woman, caft of his coule, and became a booke-feller, & at length was burned at the fame place. See *ibid. num.*13.14.
A	1556	12	*Iohn Clark Confeffor.* This was a labouringe man of Kent, who being apprehended, and examined vpon new opinions was committed to the Caftle of Canterbury, and there died, and by that meanes came to be regiftred by Fox for a Confeffor, togeather with 4. other companions which do enfue. See *ibid. num.* 15.
b	1556	13	*Dunftan Chittiden confeffor.* This was another poore man of the former company imprifoned at Canterbury, and though they agreed not in their anfwers, *but vpon ignorant fimplicity* (faith Fox) *fwarued a little in the number of Sacraments:* yet were they fo refolute and willfull to go to the fire, as nothing could ftay them. See *ibid. num.*15.
c	1556	14	*VVilliam Fofter confeffor.* This was another of them

			vvas a holy B. of Dublyn in Ireland, vvhoſe excellent life aud acts yovv may ſee ſett dovvne at large in Sur. tom. 6. vpon this day. He vvas Canonized by Pope Honorius 3. in the 10.yeare of his Popedome, vvhich vvas of Chriſt 1214.
d	561	15	c. s. Machuti Epiſcopi & Confeſſor. duplex. *This vvas a holy man of the Brittiſh nation, vvho vvas othervvaiſe called* Meclouius *before the Conuerſion of the Engliſh nation by S. Auſten: He vvas of rare life for vertue, and vvrought diuers miracles, and vvent into leſſer Brittany, vvhere he vvas made B. and died finally in France, his life is vvrytten by* Sigebert, *in* Sur. to.6. *and in his chron. an.*561. Tritem. de vir. Illuſtr. lib.3. cap.35. *and others.*
e	1240	16	c. s. Edmundi Epiſcopi & Confeſſ. duplex. *This man vvas Archbiſhop of Canterbury, vvho after a holy life, ſeing the liberty of his Church to be greatly infringed, & many diſorders grovv vvhich he could not remedy, choſe rather to go into voluntary baniſhmët, & ſo retyred himſelfe to a religious life in a monaſtery in France by* Sueſſon, *and ſix years after his death vvas canonized by* Innocentius 4. *to vvitt* an. 1546. See Math. Paris *hoc an.* Pol. Virg. lib. 16. *and others.*
f	1200	17	c. s. Hugonis Epiſcopi & Confeſſor. duplex. *This holy man vvas by nation a Burgundian of the order of Carthuſians, vvho through the fame of his learninge and holynes of life, being called into England by K.* Henry *the ſecond, vvas made firſt prior of a monaſtery of his order at* Wydam, *and then B. of Lincolme, vvherin he liued and died very holily; and 20. years after his death to vvitt* 1220. *he vvas canonized by Pope* Honorius 3. See Math. Paris. Silueſter Giraldus Sur.to.6. *and others.*

C. R.

Litt. nñic.	Ann. Chr.	Dies menf.	Fox his Calendar. Nouember.
			them that died in the forefaid Caftle of Canterbury vnder Q. Mary, or rather he was Captaine of all the reft, though none more ignorant then he: he faid yt was as good to carry the gallowes about in proceffion for them whofe Fathers were hanged, as to carry the croffe in memory of Chrifts paffion. See *ibid. num.*15. *&* 16.
d	1556	15	*Alice Potkins confeffor.* This was the wife of a poore craftefman, but fo malepart in new doctrines, and fo proud therwith, that being asked by the commiffionars of her age, aunfwered, that accordinge to her old byrth fhe had 49. years, but accordinge to her new byrth fhe was but of one yeare old. See *cap. ibid. num. ibid.*
e	1556	16	*Iohn Archer confeffor.* This was the laft of the former crew of Canterbury Caftle Confeffors, by occupation a weauer, and in his opinions he profeffed to hold with the others; for fome of them (faith Fox) graunted but one Sacrament, *vvhich is Chrift hanginge on the Croffe.* See *ibid.*
f	1557	17	*Iohn Hooke martyr.* Of this man Iohn Fox wryteth no more, but that he read, that in this prefent 1556. was burned one *Iohn Hooke* a true wittneffe of the Lords truth at *Chefter. &c.* but what this truth was, and how truly *Hooke* did wittneffe the fame he fheweth not in particular. See *ibid. num.*17.

Litt.	Ann̄	Dies	
ðñic·	Chr.	menſ.	
g	325	18	c. ʀ. Dedicat. Baſilicarum Petri & Pauli. duplex. *This is the memory of that day, vvhen Conſtantine the great 300. yeares after Chriſt, did lay the foundation of 2. famous Churches of S. Peter and S. Paul in Rome, conſecrated by* Pope Silueſter, *but longe before this, euen from the ſaid Apoſtles martyrdoms, their bodyes vvere honoured vvith great concourſe of Chriſtian people, as yovv may ſee in* Euſeb. lib. 2. hiſt. cap. 24. *and others.*
A	236	19	c. ʀ. Pontiani PP. & mart. *This Pope vvas a Roman borne, and gouerned that Sea vnder the Emperor* Alexander Seuerus, *by vvhome he vvas taken and caſt into the Iland of* Sardinia *vvhich in thoſe dayes vvas very barbarous, and of an vnvvholſome ayre, vvherein after many miſeryes ſuffered, he died. See* Dam. *in his life* Niceph. lib. 5. hiſt. cap. 26. *and others.*
b	870	20	c. s. Edmundi Regis & mart. duplex. *This vvas K. of the eaſt Angles to vvitt Norfolke, Suffolke, and ſome parts adioyninge, he vvas martyred for Confeſſion of Chriſtian faith by* Hinguar *a Daniſh King, that intred that contrey by violence: aftervvard he had a goodly Church and monaſtery erected vnto him at a tovvne called of his name* S. Edmonds- bury. *See* Abbo Floriacens. *in his life.* Sur. tom. 6. Stow. *and others.*
c	598	21	m. ʀ. Columbani Abbatis. *This vvas a renovvned monke of* Scotland *vvho vvas the founder of many monaſteryes, and after a longe religious life made a bleſſed end aboue* 1000. *years gone. Many authors do vvryte of him, as* Sigeb. in chron. an. 598. Vincent. in ſpec. l. 23. c. 4. Trit. de vir. Illuſt. l. 2. c. 5. *and others.*
d	226	22	c. ʀ. Ceciliæ virg. & mart. Semiduplex. *This vvas a noble Virgin of Rome, vvho being eſpouſed vnto* Valerianus *a heathen, brought both him & his brother* Tiburtius *to be Chriſtians, and*

Litt.	Ann⁹	Dies	Fox his Calendar. Nouember.
Dñic.	Chr.	menſ.	
g	1557	18	*Iohn Hallingdale martyr.* This was a ſimple ignorant fellow burned in Smithfield, who ſtood vpon this point principally, that ſuch as were condemned in theſe dayes for heretiks were true Saints; which yow may ſee how he proueth out of the Apocalips, *ibidem num·17·18.*
A	1557	19	*VVilliam Sparrovv mart.* This was companion of the forſaid *Hallingdale*, and burned with him in Smithfield; he was a ſeller, and ſpreader of ſeditious ballads, and once before had recanted and ſubmitted himſelfe to the B. of London, but now fallinge into relapſe, and ſtandinge therin obſtinatly was burned. See *ibid. num.17.18.19.*
b	1557	20	*Ricard Gibſon mart.* This was the third companion burned alſo in Smithfield with *Hallingdale* and *Sparrovv*, but that he was much more arrogant then any of them both, refuſing to anſwere to ſuch articles, as were propoſed vnto him by the B. rather propoſinge other to him againe about Antichriſt, and the beaſt in the reuelation, the whore of Babylon and the like. See *ibid. num.17.20.*
c	1558	21	*Alexander Gouch mart.* This was a weauer of ſhredded Couerletts, who vſing to the houſe of one Alice Driuer at *Groſborrovv* in Suffolke, was ſo peruerted by her, with new opinions of thoſe dayes, as he was content to go to the fire for the ſame; he was taken in a haygulſe with the ſaid *Alice.* See *ibid.nu.21.*
d	1558	22	*Alice Driuer martyr.* This was the doctrix of the forſaid weauer, who was ſo malepart and contumelious before the iudges, as firſt her eares were cutt of, for callinge Q. Mary *Iezabell,*

Litt. Ðńic.	Ann⁹ Chr.	Dies menſ.	The Catholike Calendar. Nouember.
			and to ſuffer martyrdome vvith her for Confeſ-ſion of Chriſtian faith togeather vvith Pope Vr-banus, vvho baptized them. See their admirable hiſtory in Sur. tom. 6. Lippom. tom. 5. *and others.*
e	103	23	c. ʀ. Clementis Papæ & mart. Semiduplex. *This Pope vvas of the Roman nobility, an aůcient ſcholler of S. Peter and S. Paul, and ſate in the Sea of Rome, in the third place aftɛr S. Peter; he vvas caſt into the Iland of* Lycia *by the Emperor* Traian *to geather vvith many other Chriſtians, for Confɛſſion of Chriſtian faith; and in the ɛnd vvas throvvne into the Sea vvith an auchor at his necke. See the* Roman Mart. Dam. *in his life*, Lippom. tom. 5. *and others.*
f	294	24	c. ʀ. Chryſogoni mart. *Thiſ vvas a noble man of Rome, vnder Diocletian, vvho after the loſſe of all his goods, ɛnd tvvo yeares impriſonment, vvas ſent for by the Emperor to be brought bound to* Aquileia, *vvhere he vvas, thinkinge by fayre meɛnes and promiſes to dravv him to deny Chriſt, but vvhen he could not, he cauſed him to be beheaded. See* Sur. tom. 6. Mombrit. tom. 1. Niceph. lib. 14. *and others.*
g	302	25	c. ʀ. Catharinæ virg. & mart. duplex. *This vvas a noble Virgin of* Alexandria *in* Egipt, *greatly renovvned both for her nobility, rare learning and conſtancy in Chriſtian religion, for vvhich after many torments, ſhe vvas beheaded ɛy commandement of* Maximinus *the Emperor. See her ſtory in* Sur. to. 6. Metaphraſt. Lippom. to. 5. Rom. mart. *and others.*
A	313	26	c. ʀ. Petri Alexandrini Epiſcopi & mart. *This vvas that renovvned B. of Alexandria in Egipt, vvho firſt of all did excommunicaɩe* Arrius *the Archheretike being a Prieſt of his Church for mouinge nevv opinions againſt the diuinity of Chriſt: vnto vvhome, vvhen he vvas in priſon and*

			zabell , and after many diſputations with diuers learned men, ſhe would needs burne for her new doctrine. See *ibid. num.* 22.23.24.25. *& deinceps.*
e	1558	23	*Philip Humfrey mart.* This was a ſimple poore man burned at Bury vpon the laſt yeare of Q. Maryes raigne, togeather with two Brethren *Iohn* and *Henry Dauy* : Fox ſetteth not downe any of their opinions , but ſaith that they ſuffered for the true teſtimony of Ieſus Chriſt: See *cap.* 15 *.num.* 30.
f	1558	24	*Iohn Dauy* and *Henry Dauy mart.* Theſe were the 2. brethren companions of *Humfrey* named by Fox in the precedent day, and burned with him at Bury, but for that we know not their opinions for which they were burned, we can determine nothinge of their ſanctity. See *ibid.*
g	1558	25	*Iohn Cornforth martyr.* This was an artificer of VVortham in Kent , who with 4. others 2. men and 2. weomen were burned at Canterbury for new opinions , not aboue ſix dayes (ſaith Fox) before the death of Q. Mary, their phantaſticall aſſertions yow may ſee ſett downe in part out of Fox togeather with their obſtinacy therin. *ibid. num,* 31.
A	1558	26	*Chriſtophor Brovvne martyr.* This vvas a huſbandman of *Maydſtone* in Kent, and companion to the foreſaid Cornforth and burned alſo with him for the ſame peruerſity of opinions : They held that opinion of Luther againſt Caluyniſts , that Chriſts body was ✱✱✱✱✱✱✱ preſent,

Litt. Dñic.	Ann. Chr.	Dies mens.	The Catholike Calendar. Nouember.
			and condemned to dy by *Maximinus Emperor*, *and some Priests came vnto him to intreat for* *Arrius, Christ appeared, and bidd him neuer to* *receyue him into his Church againe.* See Ruffi- nus lib. 1. hist. cap. 14. Athan. orat. 2. cont. Arr. Euseb. lib. 7. cap. vlt. *and others.*
b	428	27	M. R. Iacobi intercisi mart. *This is a renouu-* *ned martyr of* Persia *vvho being a Christian,* *and hauinge by the persuasion and allurements of* K. Isdegald *denyed his faith , tooke such repen-* *tance therof , that he vvent vnto the King and* *recalled that Act, vvhervpon he vvas dravvne* *in peeces vvith horses.* See Niceph. lib.14. c.20. Sur. to. 6. & 7. *and others.*
c	298	28	M. R. Rufi mart. *This Rufus being a young man* *of the Roman nobility vvas conuerted to Chri-* *stian faith by* S. Chrysogonus, *of vvhome vve* *spake a little before, togeather vvith his vvhole* *family, vvherof* Diocletian the Emperor *being* *aduertised , caused them all to be put to death:* See the Rom. mart. Pet. in catal. lib.10. c.120. *and others.*
d	309	29	C. R. Vigilia. Suturnini & Sisinij mart. *Of* *these tvvo, the first vvas an old man, the second* *vvas a Deacon , and both of them put to death* *by many torments vnder* Maximinian *the Em-* *peror at Rome, in via* salaria, *vvhere there vvas* *a memorable Church erected in their honour.* See their acts in Sur. tom. 1. *and the acts of* S. Marcellus. *and others.*
e	62	30	C. R. Andreæ Apostoli. duplex.

The

			Fox his Calendar. Nouember.
			present in the Sacrament of the Altar *only in the vfe, &c.* See *ibid. num.*31.32.
b	1558	27	*Iohn Hurft mart.* **This** was the third confort of the forfaid crew, he was inhabitant of *Afhford* in Kent, and burned at Canterbury, with the fotefaid *Cornforth* and *Brovvne*, with whome he concurred in their herefies, and obftinacy for defence of the fame. See *cap.*15. *num.* 31.
c	1558	28	*Alice Snoth mart.* **This** was a younge woman of the fame company burned at Canterbury with them for herefie fhe was extreeme willfull and arrogant, and when fhe came to the fire fide fhe fent for her Godfather and Godmothers, and recyted to them the common Creed, and asked them whether they had promifed any other thinge for her at her baptifme, and they anfwering no, fhe willed all to beare her wittnes therof, and fo fhe was burned. See *ibid, num.*33.34.35.
d	1558	29	*Katherine Knight martyr.* **This** was another fimple, wilfull and obftinate woman of the fame company, who tooke her felfe to be a prophetefe by readinge of fcriptures; fee her ftory *ibid. num.*33.
e		30	Andrew Apoftle.

*******2   The

The Moneth of December.

f	296	1	M. R. Olympiadis matt. *This vvas a man that had byn consull in Rome, and lyuinge at the citty of* Ameria *in Vmbria, vvas conuerted by a blessed vvoman named* Firmina *to Christian faith, vvhich Diocletian the Emperor vnderstanding, caused him by many torments to be put to death in the same place. See the* Rom. mart. *and the register of that Church of* Ameria *and others.*
g	353	2	C. R. Bibianæ virg. & mart. *This vvas a Roman Virgin daughter to one* Faustus *and* Daphrosa *both Martyrs for Christian religion, vvhose example this Virgin imitatinge, gaue her life for confession of the same faith and religion vnder* Iulian the Apostata. *See* Pet. in catal. l.2. c.19. *the* Rom. mart. *and others.*
A	190	3	M. R. Lucij Regis. *This vvas the first Christian King, vvherof there is mention amonge the Britans, being conuerted by* S. Fugatius *and* Damianus *sent from Rome by Pope* Eleutherius, *about the yeare of Christ* 177. *as* Marianus Scotus *holdeth, vvherof See* Bed. lib.1.hist.c.4. *and others, as also the first part of this Treatise* Cap. 4.
b	1099	4	C. S. Osmundi Episcopi & Confess. duplex. *This vvas the second B. of* Salisbury *after the translation of that Bishoppricke from* Shirborne *to that place: he vvas a man of rare life, and first reduced the order of seruice to the vse of* Sarum, *as* Polidor, *and others do recount, and died most holily an.* 1099. *and vvas Canonized by Pope* Calixtus. 3. *See* Pol. Virg. l. 9. hist. & lib. 23. Rom. mart. *and others.*

C. R.

The Moneth of December.

f	1534	1	*VVilliam Tracy eſquier confeſ.* This man was of *Todington* in Gloceſter-ſhire, who died in the 22 yeare of the raigne of K. Henry the 8. and being infected with hereſie, as was thought, made a phantaſticall teſtament, ſaying it imported not where his body was buryed, and that good works did not make a good man, &c. for which his body was taken vp & burned the next yeare after, and ſo made a Martyr of Fox his Calendar. See *cap.*16. *num.*4.5.
g	1545	2	*Peter Sapience mart.* This wiſe man, or man of wiſdome is only found in Fox his Calendar, whether by error or no I know not, but nothinge I find of him in his Acts and Monuments, neyther ſeemeth yt an Engliſh name, but that he was borrowed from abroad, yf there were any ſuch man at all. See *ibid. num.* 4.
A	1545	3	*George Bucker aliâs Damlippe mart.* This was a certayne Apoſtata Prieſt, hanged, drawne and quartered in *Calice* for treaſon againſt K. Henry the 8. in the laſt yeare, ſauing one, of his raigne, and was not burned at all, as Fox confeſſeth, and therby vniuſtly commeth he into this Calendar. See *ibid. num.*6,7.
b	1531	4	*An old man of Buckingham-ſhire mart.* Of this old man I find neyther name, nor geſts, nor place, nor his cauſe of martyring in Fox, but only by certayne gheſſes a farre of. See *ibid. num.* 8. 9.

c	531	5	c. R. Sabbæ Abbatis. *This vvas a holy Abbot in Palestina, vvhich both by sanctity of life and learninge did illustrate the Church of God much in his dayes, he is highly commended by all auncient vvryters, & died vvhen he vvas 94. yeres old vnder Iustinian th'Emperor. See Ioan. Diac. in the life of S. Greg. lib. 1. cap. 9. vvhere he talketh of S. Sabba his Church in those dayes in Rome. and others.*
d	320	6	c. R. Nicolai Episc. & Confess. Semiduplex. *This is that most renovvned B. of Myra in Lycia, vvho hauinge passed the persecution of Diocletian in Banishment, vvas recalled by Constantine the great to the Councell of Nice, vvhere he vvrought diuers miracles: See Niceph. lib. 3. hist. cap. 14. Lippom. tom. 5. Sur. tom. 6, and others.*
e	390	7	c. R. Ambrosij Episcopi & Confessoris Eccl. Doctoris. duplex. *This vvas that renovvned Father and Doctor of the Church B. of Millayne, vvho amonge other notable deeds conuerted S. Austen from the heresie of Maniches to Christian religion: and the festiuall memory of his departure is celebrated as vvell by the Grecians as by the Latyns: See their menaloge, and his life vvrytten by Paulinus, and others.*
f		8	c. R. Conceptio B. Mariæ. duplex. *This memory of the immaculate Conception of the Mother of God by the grace & povver of her sonne, that preserued her from all inquination of sinne, though yt vvere obserued in the Church both Greeke and Latyn of more auncient tyme; yet the publike celebration therof began first in the Church of England in the tyme of VVilliam Conqueror vpon priuate deuotion of some holy men, and vvas after admytted by the vvhole Church. See Baron. vpon the Rom. mart. die 8. Decemb. and others.*

M. R.

Litt. Dñic.	Ann Chr.	Dies mens.	Fox his Calendar. December.
c	1381	5	*Tvvo gray friars martyrs.* These mens names also, or sur-names, or any other particulars concerninge them, do I not find in Iohn Fox his Acts and Monuments, wherby I gather, that this moneth (his store of particular martyrs faylinge) he meaneth to furnish vp with generall names, as also with borrowed ghospellers from abroad; see *ibid. num.* 8.
d	1517	6	*Iohn Hilton* and *Iohn Coignes confessors.* This moneth being (as I said) sterile and barren of martyrs is furnished vp with Confessors by Fox; & these two heere mentioned were two artificers that had bin called to accoumpt for new opinions, but were not martyred for the same. See *ibid. num.*10.
e	1517	7	*Robert VVard confessor.* This was a third artificer called before the commissionars togeather with the former 2. about certayne heresies laid to his charge, which cause Iohn Fox thinketh sufficient to make him a Confessor and Sainct of his Calendar. *ibid. num.*10.
f	1522	8	*A Scholler of Abbouile mart.* Of this martyr also called as it seemeth from Abbouile in Picardy vpon the yeare of Christ 1522. & 13. of K. *Henryes* raigne as heere Fox noteth in his Calendar; I find nothinge afterward declared in his Acts and Monuments: so as he seemeth to be greatly strayned in finding out Saincts eyther forrayne or domesticall, to fill vp this moneth, whervpon he is forced also to lay hands on a Iew, vpon the next day followinge. See *cap.*16. *num. ibid.*

Litt. Dñic.	Annᵒ Chr.	Dies mensf.	The Catholike Calendar. **December.**
g	298	9	M. R. Leocadiæ virg. & mart. *This vvas a renovvned Virgin of the citty of* Toledo *in Spaine, vvhere she suffered martyrdome vnder* Diocletian *the Emperor, and had diuers Churches in old tyme erected vnto her, and sundry Councells of* Toledo *are kept in her Church.* See Vasæus in chron. Pet. de natal. in catal. lib.1. cap. 48. Marian. Sicul. l.5. Rerum Hispan. *and others.*
A	313	10	c. R. Melchiadis PP. & mart. *This Pope vvas borne in Africa, and sate in the Sea of Rome vnder* Maximinus *and* Licinius, *of vvhose persecution he vvas partaker, & therby called Martyr in the ancient Church, though aftervvard he died in his bed, vvhen Constantine had giuen peace to the Church. his successor vvas Pope Siluester.* See Dam. *in his life, and others.*
b	384	11	c. R. Damasi PP. & Confessor. Semiduplex. *This Pope vvas by nation a Spaniard, but of great learninge and rare life, vvho called togeather the councell of* Constantinople, *and condemned the heresie of* Eunomius *and* Macedonius *therin, as also he condemned the false Councell of* Arimine, *gathered against the Councell of* Nice *in fauour of the Arrians.* See Zozom. l.6. cap. 23. Niceph. in chron. S. Austen. ep. 165. *and others.*
	274	12	M. R. Synesij mart. *This man did serue the Church of Rome in tyme of* S. Syxtus Pope, *and* S. Laurence Deacon, *to vvhome this* Synesius *serued in the office of* Lector, *and being zealous to conuert pagans to Christian religion, he vvas accused therof to* Aurelianus *the Emperor, and by his commandement put to death. His festiuall day is also solemnely kept amonge the Grecians, as youu may see in their menaloge. And the* Rom. mart. *and others.*
d	299	13	c. R. Luciæ virg. & mart. duplex. *This vvas a Virgin of* Syracusa *in Sicily of very noble parentage,*

Litt. Dñic.	Ann. Chr.	Dies mensf.	Fox his Calendar. December.
g	1528	9	*A Ievv martyr.* This Iew(faith Fox) was firft a Chriftian, & then put to death for the fame by the Turks in Conftantinople, but whether the Iew were a Proteftant, whilft he was a Chriftian, & fo died for Proteftants religion, Fox telleth vs not: See *ibid. num.*10. *& 11.*
A	1515	10	*Richard Hunne mart.* This was a Marchant-taylor of London, who fome 2. or 3. yeares before the rifinge of Luthers doctrine, was put into the Lollards tower for Wickliffia-nifme, where fearinge the fentence that was likely to haue byn giuen againft him, he han-ged himfelfe as the magiftrats faid, and pro-ued. See the difcuffion of that matter *ibidem nnm.*12.13.14. *& deinceps.*
b	1531	11	*Iohn Tevvkfbury mart.* This was a leather-fel-ler of London who in the 22. yeare of the raigne of K. Henry the 8. defended certayne herefies moft arrogantly before *Tonftall* then B. of London: as for example, *that euery man is Lord of vvhatfoeuer another hath : that the Ievves put Chrift to death vvith good intent, & zeale,* and other fuch like. See *ibid. n.*20.21.22.
c	1555	12	*Iames Gore* and *VVilliam VVifeman confeffors.* Thefe were two other Confeffors, the firft a poore man that died in prifon at Colchefter, the other a *Cloth-vvorker* of London, that died in the Lollards tower, both of them faith Fox for the right and truth of Gods worde. but no more in particular. See *ibidem num.* 23.
d	1557	13	Iohn Philpot preacher martyr. This rubri-~~cate martyr was~~ borne in *Hampfhire* after-ward.

rentage, vvho refuſinge to marry in reſpect of the vovv of virginity vvhich ſhe had made, vvas accuſed to Paſcaſius preſident of that countrey vnder Diocletian, vvho after many torments vſed tovvards her, vvhich ſhe miraculouſly endured, he cauſed her to be beheaded. See her ſtory at large in Sur. tom.6. Sigeb. lib. de vir. illuſtr. cap.172. and others.

c   **138**   **14**

M.R. Spiridionis Epiſcopi & Confeſſoris. *This vvas B. of Cyprus in the tyme of Maximinus the perſecutinge Emperor, and of Conſtantine the good Emperor that follovved him; by the firſt he had his right eye pulled out, togeather vvith many others Confeſſors: by the ſecond he vvas much honoured & called to the Councell of Nice, vvhere among other things, he conuerted a heathen philoſopher by diſputation.* See of him Euſeb. lib.10. hiſt. cap.3. Socr. lib.1. cap. 8. Zozom. lib.1. cap.11. *and others.*

f   **450**   **15**

M.R. Valeriani Epiſcopi & mart. *This vvas a B. in Africa in S. Auſtens tyme vnder* Genſericus *the Arrian K. vvho being of* 80. *yeares old, vvas commanded by him, to giue him his Church Veſſells, vvhich he denyinge to do vvas caſt into the fields vvith commaundement that no man vnder paine of death ſhould ſuccour him, and ſo he died for hungar and cold.* See Vict. Vticens. l.1.de Perſecut. Vandal. Mart. Rom. *and others.*

g   **402**   **16**

M.R. SS. Virginum Africanarum mart. *Theſe vvere a great number of Catholike young vveomen and virgins, vvhich in Africa vnder* Hunnericus *an Arrian K. of the Vandals ſuffered death by intolerable torments of burning of their breaſts, and the like, for that they vvould not admitt the Arrian hereſie, nor yet falſely accuſe Catholike Biſhopps to haue abuſed their bodyes.* See Victor. Vticens. lib.1.de Perſecut. Vandal. Mart. Rom. *and others.*

M. R.

Litt. Ðñic.	Ann. Chr.	Dies menf.	Fox his Calendar. December.
			ward came to be Archdeacon of Winchester, and after that againe fallinge into new opinions in K. Edwards, dayes he was called to accompt for the fame vnder Q. Mary, and many meanes vfed to recall him, which not takinge place, he was at laſt burned in Smithfield. See his ſtory *cap.*16. *num.* 24. 25. 26. *& deinceps.*
e	1557	14	*Iohn Rough preacher mart.* This *Rough* was a Dominican friar in Scotland, who runninge from thence into England in the beginninge of K. Edwards dayes, when free liberty was giuen to all ſorts of apoſtataes to reſort thither, he tooke a woman named *Kate* vnder the name of wife; but in Q. Maryes dayes after diuers examinations and conuictions of hereſies, he was bnrned in Smithfield. he was alſo miniſter of the ſecret Congregation of Proteſtants in thoſe dayes in London. See *ibid. num.* 31.
f	1557	15	*Margaret Meringe martyr.* This was a poore pratlinge woman of London, excommunicated out of the foreſaid Proteſtant congregation by Friar *Rough* the miniſter therof, for her euill demaynor., as Fox confeſſeth, but yet for that ſhe was burned herſelfe alſo afterward for her obſtinate ſtanding in hereſie, Fox is content to take her in for a martyr. See *ibid. num.* 32.
g	1557	16	*Thomas Tiler* and *Mathevv VVhither confeſſor.* Why theſe 2. men are made Confeſſors by Fox I know not; nor do I find any thinge of them in his acts, but yt is probable, that they were in ſome trouble for the new ghoſpell in thoſe dayes, and a very ſmall matter in that kind is ſufficient for Fox to canonize Confeſſors: See *ibid. num.* 33.

Iohn

Litt. Dñic.	Ann. Chr.	Dies mensf.	The Catholike Calendar. December.

A — 87 — 17

M. R. Lazari Episc. & confessoris. *This vvas that* Lazarus *brother of* S. Mary Magdalen *and* Martha, *vvhome our Sauiour raised from death to life* Ioan. 11. *vvho aftervvard vvith his tvvo sisters flyinge the persecution of the Ievves, came to* Marseeles *in France, and there vvas made Bishopp, and both liued and died in great holynes. See the acts of* S. Mary Magdalyn, S. Martha, S. Maximinus; *the Greeke menaloge, and* Rom. mart. *and others.*

b — 252 — 18

M. R. Gratiani Episcopi & Confess. *This vvas the first B. of* Towars *in France, ordayned by* S. Fabianus *Pope of Rome vpon the yeare of* Christ 251. *he vvrought many miracles in his life, and vvas a man of admirable vertue. Of vvhose acts yovv may see at large.* Greg. Turon. *his successor in the same sea* lib. 1. de gest. Franc. cap. 3. & lib. 10. cap. 31. *and others.*

c — 253 — 19

M. R. Nemesij mart. *This man being a souldiar in* Alexandria *of* Aegipt, *and knovvne to be a Christian, vvas first accused of theft, but being quitt for that, and diuers other souldiars condemned, he vvas accused presently for religion, vvhich he confessinge :* Aemilianus *the Iudge gaue sentence, that he should be put to death vvith th'other theeues, but first be beaten tvvise as much as any of them. he suffered vnder Decius the Emperor. See* Euseb. lib. 6. cap. 34. *and the Epistle of* S. Dionys. Alexand. *vvherein his martyrdome is recounted,* Rom. mart. *and others.*

d — 340 — 20

Vigilia. M. R. Philogonij Episc. & Confess. *This man vvas B. of Antioch, and hauinge byn a famous lavvyer before, vvas aftervvard a zealous defender of Catholike religion against* Arrius, *vvho vvas vvont to call this* Philogonius *his principall aduersary as saith* Epiphan. hær.

Litt. Ðñic.	Ann⁹ Chr.	Dies menſ.	Fox his Calendar. December.
A	1550	17	*Iohn Dale confeſſor.* This was a husbandman of the towne of Hadley in Suffolne, who hauinge byn inſolent, and rayled extreemely in the Church openly vpon *Maiſter Neuill* his paſtor, and this in tyme of diuine ſeruice, he was put for the ſame into the cage, and afterward ſent to priſon at Bury, where he died. See *ibid. num.*33.
b	1550	18	*VVilliam Plaine*, *Elizabeth Lawſon* and *Iohn Glouer confeſſors.* Of theſe 3. Confeſſors, the firſt was a buſy fellow of London, who in K. Henryes dayes had byn putt into the towar for carryinge of letters to one *Doctor Crome*, As Fox affirmeth; the ſecond was an vnquiett woman impriſoned at *Bredfield* in Suffolke. The third was impriſoned at *Lichfield*; but yet all three died in liberty and in their beds. See *ibid. num.*34.
c	1526	19	*Nicolas Burton* and *Thomas Rhedonenſis Earle mart.* The firſt of theſe two was an Engliſh marchant burned at Siuill in Spaine for Caluinian opinions, vpon the fifth yeare of Q. Elizabethes raigne. The ſecond *Rhedonenſis* was no Earle, but a french Carmelite friar of whome we haue treated before the 10. day of February, and he is put twiſe into this Calendar of Fox. See *cap.*16. *num.*35.36.
	1436		
d	1497	20	*Picus Mirandula confeſſor.* This was a younge noble man of Italy of rare learning in the laſt age ſauinge one, and moſt Catholike in Religion ſo as Fox doth him exceeding great iniury and diſhonour to putt him in heere amongſt ſuch a rabble of burned heretiks, whome

			hær. *69.* S. Chryfoftome *did preach in his Church vpon his feftiuall day , vvhich fermon is yet extant* to.3. Operum. *See alfo* S. Hierome, Niceph. *and others.*
e	75	21	c. R. Thomæ Apoftoli. duplex.
f	253	22	M. R. Chæremonis Epifcopi & Soc. mart. *Thefe are very aũcient Martyrs,vvho in the perfecution of Decius , as* S. Dionyf. Alexandrin. *that vvas an eye-vvitnes teftifieth , vvere driuen out of Alexandria into a vvilderneſſe in great number , vvherof fome vvere deuoured vvith beafts, others died vvith hunger and cold, others vvere flaine by theeues & barbarous heathens. See their vvhole ftory in* Eufeb. lib. 6. hift. c.34. *taken out of* S. Dionyf. Mart. Rom. *and others.*
g	254	23	M.R. Victoriæ virg. & mart. *This vvas a noble Roman Virgin , vvho againft her vvill , being efpoufed vnto* Eugenius *a pagan , vvould not marry , vvhervpon ſhe being accufed for Chriftian Religion, and that ſhe had dravvne many other young vvoomen to the fame purpofe of virginity vvithin the Citty of Rome, ſhe vvas putt to many torments, and finally paſſed thorovv vvith a fvvord. See the* Rom. Mart. *and* S. Adelmus lib. de laud. virg. Pet. in catal. lib.1. cap.83. *and others.*
A	253	24	Vigilia. M. R. Quadraginta virginũm mart. *Thefe 40. Virgins vvere put to dcath togeather in the Citty of Antioch in the forfaid perfecution of* Decius *but by different torments , fome fuffering more, fome leſſe. See the mart. of* S. Bede. Vfuard. Ado. Vandelbert Pet. in catal. lib. 1. cap. 89.
b	25	25	c. R. Natiuitas Domini noftri I E S V Chrifti. duplex.
c	27	26	c. R. Stephani Protomartyris. duplex.
d	28	27	c. R. Ioannis Apoftoli & Euangelistæ. dupl.
e	29	28	c. R. SS. Innocentium mart. duplex.

			whome he from his hart did moſt earneſtly deteſt. See *cap.16. num.*37.38.39. *& deinceps.*
e		21	Thomas Apoſtle.
f	1513	22	*Eraſmus Roterodamus confeſſor.* The like iniury and violence is done heere to Eraſmus in putting him into his Calendar amongſt Lutherans and Zuinglians (whome in his life he deteſted) as was before to *Picus Mirandula,* though not ſo great, for that by his indiſcreet and raſh wrytings he gaue occaſion to the ſaid heretiks to build on him diuers opinions, which he greeuouſly afterward repented. See *ibid. num.* 41.42.43. *& deinceps.*
g	1549	23	*Martyn Bucer confeſſor.* This man was by lynage a Iew, by profeſſion a Dominican friar, who leauing his habitt tooke a woman after the example of *Luther,* whoſe ſcholler he was, though afterward he left his doctrine and followed *Zuinglius,* but repented and returned; yet after that againe he brake from him once more and taught Zuinglianiſme in England, and died ſo doubtfully, as diuers thinke that he died in Iudaiſme. See *ibid. num.* 58.59. 60. *& deinceps.*
A	1551	24	*Paulus Phagius confeſſor.* This was a German Prieſt companion to *Bucer* for his iorney into England in K. Edwards dayes, they both hauing byn expelled from *Straſburge* a little before for ſeditious preachers: he died in England: ſee *ibid. num.* 67. 68.
b		25	Natiuity of our Lord.
c		26	Stephen mart.
d		27	Iohn Euangeliſt.
e		28	Childermaſſe.

Philipp

Litt. Dñic.	Ann° Chr.	Dies menf.	The Catholike Calendar. **December.**
f	1172	29	c.ʀ. Thomæ Cantuariensis Episcopi & mart. Semiduplex. *This excellent man of most holy life and constancy S.* Thomas Becket *Archbishopp of* Canterbury, *vvas slaine in his ovvne Church by a conspiracy of vvicked men, vvithout commission or order of Iustice. Of vvhose rare miracles vvrought at his tombe after his death; as also of his most excellent vertues vvhile he liued many learned men do vvryte vvho liued vviih him, as* Herbert *aftervvard Cardinall,* Ioan. Salisburgens. *B. of* Carnotum *in* France: William *and* Benedict, *tvvo Abbotts of* Canterbury *and others.*
g	290	30	m. ʀ. Sabini Episcopi & Soc. mart. *This man vvas B. of* Spoletum *in* Italy, *and vvas put to death for Christian religion by many torments, vnder* Maximianus *the Emperor, togeather vvith* Exuperantius *&* Marcellus *his deacons, and* Venustianus *the president of that countrey, vvhome he had conuerted togeather vvith his vvife and children, all vvhich vvere martyred togeather. See* Pet. in catal. lib.2. cap.19. Paul. Diac. de gestis Lombard. lib.1.c.5. *and others.*
A	335	31	c.ʀ. Siluestri PP. & Confessoris. duplex. *This Pope vvas he, that baptized* Constantine *the great, confirmed the Councell of* Nice, *and did many other most excellent things, as appereth in the history of his life vvrytten by many authors, vvhich yovv may read gathered togeather in* Sur. tom.6. & Lippom. tom.5. *and others.*

The end of the Cath. Calendar.

In the

Litt. Dñic.	Ann' Chr.	Dies mensf.	Fox his Calendar. December.
f	1559	29	*Philipp Melanchthon confeffor.* This was one of the fifirst and cheefeft fchollers of Luther, and one that moft fet forth and fpread his doctrine at the beginninge , being himfelfe but 22. years old , when firft he began to interprete *S.Paules* Epiftles contrary to the old interpretation of the Fathers: afterward he became doubtfull and various, and his faluation is doubted of by thofe of his owne fect and others. See *cap.16. num.72.73.74. & deinceps.*
g	1562	30	*Peter Martyr confeffor.* This was an Italian Friar , who runninge from thence, and makinge the ordinary entrance to the new ghofpell by taking a woman (as did alfo *Bernardinus Ochinus* another Friar of Italy) came both with their faid weomen into England in the beginninge of K. Edwards dayes to plant the ghofpell: Albeit Peter Martyr was doubtfull at that tyme what Religion to beleeue or teach. See *ibid. num. 90.91.92. & deinceps.*
A	1553	31	King Edward the fixt Confeffor. This was the fonne of K. Henry the 8. and the firft K. of England that euer was numbred amongft Proteftants fince yt was firft a Kingdome, yf yet this may iuftly be fo numbred, feeing he was but 9. yeares old , when he tooke the crowne, and not fully 16. when he died. Both he and his Father were infinitely abufed by the change of Religion, and perhaps himfelfe may better be called a Martyr then a Confeffor , feing yt was the caufe of his ruine. See *ibid. 97. 98: 99. vfque ad finem.*

The end of Fox his Calendar.

****

THE SVMME
OF ALL SAINTS NA-
MED IN BOTH CALENDARS.

In the Catholike Calendar.

The number of all mentioned 1704. wherof are Popes Martyrs 27. Popes Confessors 8. Bishops Martyrs 37. Bishops Confessors 63. Virgins Martyrs 76. (besides the 11000. slayne with *S. Vrsula*) Virgins Confessors 11. Kinges and Queens Martyrs 3. K. and Q. Confessors 8. Other holy men and weomen Martyrs 3429. other men and weomen Confessors 42.

All these were of one faith and Religion agereable to the Roman at this day.

In the Foxian Calendar.

The number of all mentioned 456. Bishops-pseudomartyrs 5. Bishops Confessors 1. Virgin martyrs 000. mayd-martyrs 3. Kinges and Queenes Martyss and Confessors 1. Other men and weomen Martyrs 393. other men and weomen Confessors 53.

These vvrre of diuers sects and opinions , and contrary in many points the one to the other. As for example:

Waldensians & Albigensians 13. Lollards & Wickliffians 36. Hussits & Lutherans 78.
Zuin-

Zuinglians and Calninifts 268. Anabaptifts,
Puritans, and doubtfull of what fect 59.
Againe of thefe vvere.

Husbandmen, weauers, fawyers, fhoma-
kers, curryers, fmithes and other fuch like
occupations 282. poore weomen and fpinfters 64. Apoftata monkes & friars 25. Apoftata priefts 38. Minifters 10. puplike malefactors and condemned by the lawes for
fuch 19.

The greateft difputers of this ranke againft the Ca-
tholike Bifhops and learned men vvere:

MEN.

George Tankerfield a cooke. *Auguft.* 13.
Iohn Maundrell a cowheard. *March* 27.
Richard Crafhfield a young artificer. *May* 28.
Raphe Allerton a taylour. *Septem.* 19.
Iohn Fortune in black-fmith. *Sept.* 30.
Richard Woodman an Iron-maker. *Iun.* 23.

VVEOMEN.

Ellen Ewring a Millers wife. *Aug.* 23.
Ioane Lafhford a marryed maide. *Ian* 18.
Ifabel Fofter a Cutlers wife. *Ianuar.* 17.
Anne Alebright a poorewoman of Canter-
bury. *Ian.* 19.
Alice Potkins Spinfter. *Nouemb.* 15.
Alice Driue a famous doctrix. *Nou.* 22.

To the gentle Reader.

Besides the faults escaped in the printinge, we praie the, gentell Reader, to correct these also, which chaunced in the wrytinge.

In the first part in the addition to the Catholikes *pag.*3. for S. Ambrose added. *Read.* a deuout Bishopp added.

Pag. 155. *linea* 2. for Ioannes Diaconus that liued with him. *Read.* whoe liued not long after him.

In the third part and first six moneths *pag.*16. *linea* 22. for Dioscorus an hereticall Bishopp of the same Sea.*Read.*an hereticall Bishop of Alexandria.*pag.*90. *linea* 4. wee saw all that tyme. *Read.* we saw at that tyme.*pag.*108. *linea* 19.cannot to be well. *Read.* cannot be well.

In the third part and last six moneths *pag.* 27. *linea vltima.* for declared by many. *Read.* declared by them by many.*pag.*119. for and simple life.*Read.* and single life *pag.* 132. *linea* 3. sometimes abdinge certayne. *Read.* addinge certayne *pag.* 187. *linea* 11. two names. *Read.* two nauies. *pag.* 190. *linea* 16. which such taunts. *Read.* with such. *pag.*249. dung-former one. *Read.* dung-farmer one.

A N

AN OBSERVATION

TO THE READER

About the multitude of Foxian Martyrs,

Which in the former Calendar are recorded to haue suffered death, and other punishments for their opinions.

IT may be (gentle Reader) and so commonly it falleth out in the best natures, that thou wilt haue a certayne horror of mynd, to see vnder one vew so many burned for their opinions in Religion, as in this Calendar, hath byn laid before thee; and to some yt may seeme perhaps great rigor & cruelty (and so Fox endeauoureth euery where to make yt appeare) and to others this cogitation may offer yt selfe, that at least wayes these men and weomen, that haue offered their liues so willingly for defence of their Religion, had some great inward testimony of the truth therof. But for the first, whether yt was necessary iustice, and no cruelty to punish such willfull and malignant people; yow shall see yt proued perspicuously in the 17. Chapter of this booke, by the testimony also and practise of protestants themselues, wherof I haue thought good to sett downe some examples in this place.

Two points to be considered.

And for the second point, to witt, that this willinge or rather willfull sufferinge death in sectaryes for their particular opinions, is not to be called Constancy, but rather pertinacity, and no good proofe at all of the

A   *truth*

truth of that, for vvhich they ſuffered: yow ſhall ſee diſcuſſed at large in the 4. Chapter of this booke, as alſo ſomewhat in the firſt, vvhere diuers examples are ſhewed of ancient heretiks, that profeſſed this kind of Conſtancy, or rather audacity, much more to vtter appearance then Catholike Martyrs did. And yet further for thy better inſtruction heerin, I thought good to ſett downe a briefe note of ſundry heretiks, condemned and put to death in our countrey, different from the Proteſtants Religion; yea condemned and executed for the moſt part by Proteſtants themſelues: So as heerby thou maiſt ſee, that neyther only Proteſtant Sectaryes do offer themſelues to go to the fire, nor only the Catholike Clergy and Magiſtrate hath, or doth exerciſe ſuch puniſhment vpon them. And finally I haue thought good alſo, to lay before thee heere at the beginninge certayne ſentences of holy Fathers concerninge this matter, vvherby thou maiſt the better be directed to iudge of all the reſt, that enſueth throughout the vvhole booke.

A NOTE

A NOTE
OF SVNDRY HERETIKS
AND SECTARIES,
Different in opinions both from Catholikes and Protestants of our dayes,

VVho offered themselues to death for the defence of their said opinions.

IN the yeare of Christ 1162. and eight yeare of *K. Henry* the second his raigne, thirty heretiks that were commonly called Publicans, with their Captayne *Gerrard* entred into England, were disputed withall in *Oxford*, and for that they would not yeld in their fond and blasphemous opinions, (denyinge among other points, *Baptisme, Matrimony, and the Lords Supper*) they were condemned to death, wherat they did singe; *blessed are yow, vvhen men reuile and hate yow for truthes sake, &c.* as both *Nubergensis* and others do relate: and that being thrust out finally of all houses, and depriued of help, they died for cold and hunger, holding themselues for elect Martyrs of Christ.

Vpon the yeare of Christ 1222. and sixt of the raigne of *K. Henry* the 3. was burned in Oxford a Deacon, who had circuncised himselfe and made himselfe a Iew, *vvhere miserablie*

A 2   be

Stow pag. 262. he ended his life (faith Stow) which is a token that he repented not, but thought he died for a very good caufe.

Vpon the fame yeare alfo, a young man that would not come to any Church, nor be partaker of any Sacrament, but faid that he was Chrift, and for proofe therof fhewed wounds in his hands, feete and fides, and a woman that called herfelfe the mother of Chrift was of his profeſsion alfo, and both of them died obftinately, holdinge themfelues for true Martyrs of Chrift.

Chriſt-heretike.
Stow ibid.
Mother-Chriſt heretike.

Vpon the yeare of Chrift 1535. and 27. of the raigne of K. Henry the 8. the 25. of May, were condemned at S. Paules Church in London 25. heretiks. *They held* (faith Stow) firſt, *that in Chriſt are not two natures*; fecondly, *that Chriſt tooke neither flesh nor bloud of the virgin Mary*; thirdly, *that children borne of infidells ſhalbe ſaued vvithout baptifme*; fourthly, *that the Sacrament of Chriſts body, is but bread only*; fifthly, *that vvhoſoeuer ſinneth vvittingly after baptifme, cannot be ſaued*. Fourtene of them ftood ftiffely in their herefies, & were burned, two in Smithfield, the reft in other Cittyes.

Eutichian and Monophifitian heretiks.
Stow pag. 965.

Anno Domini 1538. and 30. of the forfaid K. Henryes raigne, were condemned 4. Anabaptifts the 24. of *Nouember*, for denyinge that children ought to be baptized of neceſsity, or yf they were, then, that they muft be rebaptized againe when they came to age; and other fuch abfurdityes of fectaryes in thofe dayes.

Anabaptift heretiks.
Stow pag. 273

The

The same yeare also, and vpon the 29. of *Nouember* (not many dayes after the burninge of *Iohn Lambert* for denyinge the *reall presence*) there were condemned and burned in Smith-field two other: to witt, a Dutch-man and Dutch-woman that held the same, and other Sacramentary opinions with *Lambert*, but yet mingled with the forsaid Anabaptisme; and thought themselues iolly Martyrs in going to the fire for defence therof; & in that cause contemned whatsoeuer persuasions, eyther Catholiks or Protestants could vse vnto them in those dayes, against their opinions.

Mixt heretikes.

Stovv ibid.

In the yeare of Christ 1540. and 32. of the forsaid K. Henry, were burned in the high way beyond *Southwarke* towards *Newton*, the 29. of Aprill, one called *Maudeuill*, another *Collyns* with a third companion; All which stood stiffely in certaine particular opinions of their owne, denyinge with the old hereliks called *Dimarits* and others, *that Christ tooke flesh of the blessed Virgin, and that there ought to be any publike Magistrats.*

Dimarite heretiks. Epiph. li. 3. cont. har.

Stovv pag. 976.

Vpon the yeare of Christ 1549. and third of K. Edward the sixt, the 27. day of Aprill, B. Cranmer, and other his assistants condemned to death certayne Anabaptists, to the number of 5. or 6. wherof some of them recanted, and bare fagotts at *Paules Crosse, Colchester* and other places.

Anabaptists.

Stovv pag. 1005.

In the yeare of Christ 1550. being the 4. of the forsaid K. Edwards raigne, vpon the 2. of May, went resolutely to the fire *Ioane Knell.*

A 3   alias

Ioane of
Kent.

aliàs *Bourcher*, comonly called *Ioane* of *Kent*, for
defence of her opinion *against the flesh of Christ*,
which she held with such assurance of her
saluation, as iestinge at the Protestants said,
she died for a peece of flesh as Anne Ascue had done
a little before *for a peece of bread*. She was condemned, and burned in Smithfield by *B. Cranmer* and his fellowes. *And at her burninge* (saith
Stow) *preached at the stake Doctor Story to haue
conuerted her, but she not regardinge his doctrine, said
he lyed like a,* &c.

Stovv pag.
1021.

Vpon the yeare of Christ 1551. and fifth of *K.
Edward* the sixt, was condemned in London
by the forsaid Bishops of that tyme, one *George
Paris* a Dutch-man, for holdinge *that Christ was
not God, nor equall to his Father*: and being obstinate, nor yelding any thing to the persuasion
of the said Bishops and other learned men, he
was burned aliue in Smithfield, persuadinge
himselfe, that he did offer vp a liuely sweet sacrifice to almighty God for his true Religion.

Arrian
heretike.

Stovv pag.
1022.

Vpon the yeare of Christ 1573. and 15. of
Q. Elizabeth the 4. day of Nouember, *Peter
Burchett* a gentleman of the *middle-temple* was
vpon the point to haue byn condemned to
the fire, by *Edwyn* B. of *London* sollemly in *Paules Church*, for diuers hereticall opinions that he
held, for which he had byn burned, yf by diuers learned men (saith *Stow*) he had not with
great paines byn persuaded to renounce: and
yf he had died, he would haue taken himselfe
for a great Saint; he was after hanged for kil-
linge his keeper.

Peter Bur-
chett an
heretike.
Stovv pag.
1157.

In the

In the yeare of Chriſt 1575. and 17. of the forſaid Q. Elizabeth her raigne, the third of April, were condemned 27. heretiks, by the B. of London and his aſſiſtants, for holdinge with the old Catharits and other heretiks, *that yt was not lawfull for a Chriſtian man to take an oath, and that no Chriſtian may be a magiſtrate, or beare the ſword,* and the like: wherof 4. only did recant, and bare fagotts at *Paules Croſſe* in ſigne of burninge, yf they had perſeuered obſtinately in the ſame opinions.

Catharite or puritan heretiks.

Stovv pag. 1160..

Vpon the ſame yeare, and vnder the ſame Q. the 12. of May, an eleuen perſons were condemned to death in the Conſiſtory of Paules, for like Anabaptiſticall opinions; and after great paines taken with them (ſaith *Stow*) one woman only was conuerted of that number, the reſt remayninge obſtinate, notwithſtanding all the Proteſtant perſuaſions that could be vſed.

Anabaptiſts.

Stovv pag. 1162.

Item the 12. day of Iune, the ſame yeare, fiue perſons were condemned in Paules Church, by the Biſhops and Clergy, for the ſect of *Family of loue*, who eſcaped death by recantinge that hereſie, and by deteſtinge the author therof H. N. at a ſermon at Paules Croſſe, who otherwiſe had byn burned.

Sectaryes of the family of loue.

Stovv ibid.

The very ſame yeare alſo, and 22. day of Iuly, two Dutch-men Anabaptiſts were burned in Smithfield, for obſtinate ſtandinge in their opinions, *vvho died* (ſaith Stow) *in great horror and cryinge*; but yet would not yeld an ynch in their opinions.

Anabaptiſts.

Stovv ibid.

Vpon the yeare of Chriſt 1583. and 26. of the forſaid Q. Elizabeths raigne, the 17. day of September *Iohn Lewes* (ſaith Stow) who named himſelfe *Abdoyt*, an obſtinate heretike denyinge the godhead of Chriſt, and holdinge diuers other deteſtable hereſies (much like to his predeceſſor *Mathew Hammond*) was burned at *Norwich.* So ſaith *Stow* : and yow muſt not doubt, but that he went as reſolutely to the fiar for his opinions, as any of Fox his martyrs did whatſoeuer.

Arrian martyrs.

Stow pag. 1189.

In the yeare of Chriſt 1589. and 31. of the ſame Q. raigne, one *Francis Kett* a maiſter of art, borne (ſaith Stow) at *VVymmondham* in *Norfolke*, was condemned by *Edmond* B. of *Norwich*, for holdinge diuers deteſtable opinions againſt Chriſt our Sauiour, and was burned neere to the citty of *Norwich, &c.* Neither muſt yow imagine, that he went to the fiar with leſſe courage or reſolution, then the former, or any of Foxes martyrs, whome he highly recomendeth for that point of haſty going to the fiar.

Heretiks impugninge Chriſt.

Stow pag. 1283.

Vpon the yeare of Chriſt 1591. and 33. of Q. Elizabeth, was hanged in Cheapſide the 16. day of Iuly, *VVilliam Hackett* of *Owndall* in *Northamptonſhire* yeoman for holding & preaching himſelfe to be Chriſt, & ſtood thervnto, vnto the very death, threatning puniſhment to his perſecutors, when he came to his kingdome in the next life. And ſo much of Sectaryes of different faith from Fox and his people, puniſhed and put to death in England.

Chriſt-heretike.

Stow pag. 1289.

And

And vnto this number of domesticall examples, might be added diuers others, punished by Proteſtants in like ſort abroad, as for example *Michaell Seruetus* a Spaniard, burned in *Geneua* by *Caluyns* approbation & procurement, for that *he denyed three perſons in God, and 2. diſtinct natures in Chriſt.* And *Valentinus Gentilis* a Neapolitan Schoole-maiſter, burned by the Proteſtants of *Berna* amongſt the Switzers, for renewinge *Arrianiſme,* and the hereſie of the *Trinitarians* in this our age. And the ſtoryes are wrytten and allowed by *Caluyn* & *Beza* themſelues, and one thinge is to be ſpecially remembred, in all theſe ſectaryes, that euery one of them pleaded ſcriptures reſolutely for himſelfe and his opinions.

And yet no Proteſtant can ſay, but that theſe men were heretiks, and ſo do we ſay alſo; and the Catholike Church would haue done no leſſe by them, then the Proteſtant Magiſtrate did, yf they had byn in her power. And yf I would diſtribute theſe men into ſeuerall dayes for their feſtiuity, as Fox doth his Martyrs, though they were hanged or burned many togeather vpon one day and in different countreyes, theſe being as yow ſee allmoſt a hundred and thirty in number, would make the third part and more of a new Calendar of Martyrs after Fox his faſhion, that agree neyther with him nor vs. And therby the diſcreet reader may diſcerne, that yt is not inough for men or weomen to dy reſolutely for their opinions, therby to proue them-

Michell Seruetus. Valētinus Gentilis. Calu.lib. de ſupplicio Serueti. Et Melanchon. loc. com. Manlij. cap. Ecleſia. Beza. lib. de hæret. à ciuili magiſtratu puniendæ.

themselues martyrs, but they muſt be tryed
by the iuſtneſſe of their cauſe, ſeing that, as
wiſely ſaith *S. Cyprian, non pœna, ſed cauſa facit
martyrem,* yt is not the puniſhment, but the
cauſe that maketh a martyr; and ſo I doubt
not, but the wiſer ſort of Proteſtants will ſay
alſo; but who ſhalbe iugde? herein lyeth
the difference betweene vs: for Fox will ſay
the ſcriptures; but we aske further, who ſhall
iudge of the ſcriptures, and true meaninge
therof? for that euery one of theſe ſectaryes
alleaged ſcriptures aboundantly as before
hath byn ſaid, and ſo did old heretiks alſo, that
offered themſelues no leſſe reſolutely to death
for their opinions, then theſe men do now.
We ſay that the Catholike, and knowne viſible Chriſtian Church of euery age muſt be
iudge, who alleage ſcriptures rightly, and in
their true ſenſe, and who do not; and conſequently who are true martyrs, and who are
not, who are heretiks or Catholiks, and who
are not, wherof doth enſue, that whoſoeuer
obeyeth not this Church, but impugneth her,
or departeth from her, cannot be a martyr;
nor ſaued by ſufferinge death for any opinion
or doctrine whatſoeuer. To which effect,
yow may read the ſentences of holy Fathers
that do enſue.

Cypr. ep. 41. ad Corn.

A NOTE

A NOTE

OF CERTAINE ANCIENT

FATHERS SENTENCES,

About sufferinges of heretikes for their opinions;

Declaringe the same to be no martyrdomes, yf they be not allowed by the Catholike knowne Church of euery age.

S. Cyprian lib. Simplicitate Prælat. siue de Eccl. vnitate.

WHOSOEVER *is separated from the Church, and ioyneth himselfe to an adulteresse conuenticle, is separated also from the promises of the Church, nor euer shall he come to enioy the rewards therof yf he leaue her; he is an alien, a prophane person, an enemy, he cannot haue God for his Father, that hath not the Church for his Mother: yea though he should be slayne for the confession of Chrifts name, yet can he not be saued,* macula ista nec sanguine abluitur, *this crime of separatinge himselfe from the Church, cannot be vvashed away vvith bloud:* inexpiabilis culpa nec passione purgatur, *yt is a fault vnexpiable, nor can yt be purged by death yt selfe.*

An heretike or schismatike out of the Church cannot be saued though he should dy for Chrift.

The same S. Cyprian in the same booke.

He cannot become a martyr, vvho is not a member of the Church, neyther can they euer come to Chrifts Kingdome, vvho do forsake his spouse vvhich is there to raigne. Though tyed to stakes they burne in flames, and be con-

He cannot be a martyr that is not a member of the Church,

be consumed vvith fiar, though throwen to vvild beasts they be by them deuoured, non erit fidei corona, sed pæna perfidiæ, *such suffering shall not be any crowne of their faith, but a punishment of their perfidiousnes. It shall not be a glorious vpshott of their religious vertue, but a death desperate: vvell may such a one be killed, but crowned he cannot be.*

The same S. Cyprian in another place of the same booke.

He that is slaine for Christ out of the vnity of the Church is damned.

May he be thought to be with Christ, who is against his Priests? nay rather he who separateth himselfe from the clergy & the society therof, doth beare armes against the Church, & repugne against the ordinance of almighty God: & consequently if he be put to death, being out of the Church, he cannot attayne vnto the rewards, which are due only vnto the Church. There is but one God, one Christ, and one Church, one faith, and one flocke, which by the glue of concord, is conioyned to make one entyre body. VVhatsoeuer is separated from the roote or mother Church, cannot be a part, eyther liue, or breath, but hath lost the very substance of all life and safety.

S. Augustine lib. 1. de serm. Dñi. in monte. cap. 9.

An heretike hath no revvard for his sufferings.

It is not fruitfull to suffer persecution howsoeuer, but to suffer it for Christs cause, not only vvillingly, but also ioyfully: for many heretiks deceyuinge soules vnder the name of Christians, do suffer much, but therfore they are excluded from their reward, because it was not only said, blessed be they, which suffer persecution, *but presently it was added,* for iustice: *vvhich iustice cannot be found, vvhere there is not true faith, &c.*

The

The fame S. Aug. tract. 6. in Euang. Ioan.

Heretikes do fometymes bragg (namely the Dona-
tifts) that they do giue much almes to the poore and do
fuffer much, but this is not for Chrift but for Donatus
their firft founder, &c. Looke for vvhome thou fufferest
quia foràs miffus es, ideo mifer es, *for that thou*
art caft forth from the vnion of the Church, therfore
art thou miferable, vvhatfoeuer thou doeft or fufferest
otherwife: heare the Apoftle fayinge of himfelfe: yf I
fhould giue all that I haue to the poore, and
deliuer my body to the fiar without charity,
I am nothinge, &c.

And againe in his booke de Patient. cap. 26.

If any man being in Schifme, herefie, or out of the
Church fhould fuffer tribulations, torments, fiar and
death yt felfe, rather then he vvould deny Chrift, yt
vvere laudable in him, and no vvayes to be reprehended,
and may help perhaps to make his damnation the more
tolerable, then yf he had denyed Chrift: but yt cannot
faue him; the Apoftle faying, that yf I giue my body to fiar, &c. yt will not profitt me, *that is to*
fay, yt vvill not profitt me to Saluation, though yt may
profitt to a more tollerable damnation.

S. Chryfoftome hom. 11. in Epift. ad Ephef.

And albeit vve fhould do innumerable good vvorkes,
yet fhall vve be punifhed no leffe, yf vve breake the inte-
grity of Chrifts Church, then vvere thofe that violated
his owne body, vvhile he vvas vpon earth. There vvas a
certayne holy man (to vvitt S. Cyprian) that faid a
thinge vvhich to fome may feeme boldneffe, but yet he
fayd

Schifme heresy, & fedition cannot be vvashed avvay vvith the bloud of martyrdome.

said yt: to vvitt, that this sinne cannot be vvashed a way vvith the bloud of martyrdome : Dico & obteftor Ecclefiam fcindere non minus effe peccatum, quàm in hærefim incidere. *I do say and proteft, that to cutt and diuide the Church of God (by schifme or fedition) is no leffe damnable a sinne, then to fall into herefie.*

S. Pacianus Epift. 2. ad Sympron. Nouat.

VVhy no heretike out of the Church can be crovvned.

Though Nouatianus suffered somwhat, yet vvas he not put to death: and though he had byn put to death, yet should he not be crowned. Yow vvill aske me vvhy? I anfvvere, for that he had not the peace of the Church, neyther vvas in concord vvith her, but vvas cut of from that mother, vvhose portion he muft needs be that vvill be a martyr. Harken to the Apoftle. If I should (faith he) haue all faith, so that I could re-mooue montaynes, and haue not charity, I am nothinge; And yf I should diftribute all my goods to be meate for poore; and yf I should deliuer my body so that I burne, and haue not charity, yt doth profitt me nothinge.

S. Aug. lib. 4. de baptif. cont. Donatift. c. 17.

Neyther baptifme nor martyrdome profiteth an heretike.

Neither is baptifme profitable to an heretike being out of the Church, nor yet yf for the confeffion of Chrift he should be put to death, for that he is conuinced to vvant charity, vvherof the Apoftle faith, though I should deliuer my body, so that I burne, and haue not charity, yt doth profitt me nothing.

The fame S. Anguft. epift. 204. ad Donat. presb. Donatift.

Yf thou be out of the Church, and feparated from the knott

knott of vnity and band of charity, thou shalt be punished vvith eternall paines, although thou shouldest be
burned quicke for the name of Christ. And the same
hath Saint Augustine againe in many other places of
his vvorks.

Burninge aliue for Christ saueth not a Sectarye.

S. Fulgentius lib. de fide ad Pet. Diac. cap. 29.

Do thou most firmely hould, and no vvayes doubt, that
vvhatsoeuer heretike or Schismatike, though he be baptized in the name of the Father, the Sonne, and the
holy Ghost, yf he be not a member of the Catholike
Church, though he giue neuer so much almes; nay though
he shed his bloud for the name of Christ, notwithstandinge he cannot in any case be saued. For vnto him who
houldeth not the vnity of the Catholike Church, neyther
can baptisme, nor almes, though neuer so copiously dealt,
no nor death yt selfe suffered for Christ, be auayleable
vnto euerlastinge saluation.

Heretiks and schismatiks damned though they dye for Christ.

S. August. lib. 2. against Petilian the Donatist. cap. 98.

VVhat glory is it, yf for your offences yow be iustly
punished, so as neyther in this vvorld yow haue temporall comfort, nor in the vvorld to come shall haue life
euerlastinge; but heere haue the anguishes of vnhappy
men, and there hell fire prepared for heretiks.

Heretiks punished in this life, and the next.

The same Father in Concio. de gest. cum Emerito.

Yf vnto an heretike being out of the Church of
Christ, yt should be said by an enemy of Christ, offer vp
Frankencense vnto my Idols, and adore my Gods, and
he not adoringe them should be put to death by the said
enemy

An heretike dying against idolatry cannot be saued.

enemy of Chrisſt; vvell may he ſhed his bloud, but crow-
ned he cannot be.

Idem lib. 1. contra Gaudent. cap. 33.

For him that dieth for a fa-ctiō there is no ſal-uation.

He vvho for the verity and vnity of Chrisſt, doth not only looſe his liuelyhood, but his life alſo, he hath truly faith, he hath truly hope, he hath truly charity, he hath truly God almighty; but vvhoſoeuer for the part of Donatus vvould looſe but a threed of his cloke, he ſheweth himſelfe to haue no vvitt in his head.

S. Gregory lib. 2. Regiſtr. Epiſt. 36.

That not paine, but the cauſe maketh a Martyr.

Yow muſt vnderſtand (as S. Cyprian ſaith)that not paine, but the cauſe maketh a Martyr : vvhich being ſo, yt is very abſurd for yow to glory of that perſe-cution, vvhich yow ſay yow ſuffer, yt being a thing moſt certayne , that therby yow cannot attayne to any hea-uenly reward. Let then the integrity of true faith bring yow backe now at length to your mother the Church, by vvhome yow had firſt your Chriſtianity.

The Concluſion and Collection vpon the Premiſſes.

1.   By all theſe authorityes is ſeene; Firſt , that here-tiks of vvhat ſect or faction ſoeuer, dyinge for de-fence of their particular opinions, dy not for Chriſt, but

2.   for the founders of their Sects. Secondly, that albeit they ſhould dye expreſſely for Chriſt, yet canne they not

3.   be ſaued. Thirdly, that yf they ſhould be martyred by infidell perſecutors for refuſinge to yeld to Idolatry, yet

4.   muſt they be damned. Fourthly , that the caſe of Schiſmatiks , and of ſuch as diuyde the Churches vnity

is all

is all one, albeit otherwise they be of neuer so good life.
Fiftly, that the reason of all this is, for that they be out   5.
of the vnion of the Catholike Church, which Church
must iudge of all. Sixtly, *that the Church vnderstood*   6.
by these Fathers, was no inuisible or hidden Church, but
knowne to all the world in euery age, wherof the Ro-
maine was a chiefe member, out of which, and against
which, Fox his Martyrs died, as did also the other old
heretiks heere ment, or mentioned by these Fathers.

An other animaduersion about the Sto-
ry of Foxian Martyrs that ensueth
throughout euery Moneth.

To preuent all occasions of Cauill (gentle
reader) to him that will seeke to wrangle,
I do heere fore-signify first, that I do not pro-   1.
secute in my narration all particulars that Fox
setteth downe of his Martyrs and Confessors, for that had byn to wryte as large a volume, as he hath done. Secondly, I do not   2.
lay forth such praises of them as he dilateth
euery where, with all his art of Oratory
skill; and this partly for that I do not beleeue
them (findinge him so false in other narrations, as I haue done) partly also for that
though some of them had morall vertues, yet
were they neyther eminent nor extraordinary, as will appeare by the view of this our
history: and whatsoeuer they were or might
haue byn; yet they being sectaryes, and out of
the Church, could receyue no auayle by them
            B   towards

3.

towards *Saluation*, as by the former doctrine of the Fathers yow haue ſeene. Thirdly then, whatſoeuer I haue heere wrytten of them, I haue taken yt commonly out of Fox himſelfe, or of ſome other good author, whoſe words I do euer recyte, as alſo the place and page where they are to be found, which Fox often doth not. So that whatſoeuer I haue omitted, or left out touchinge them, I haue done yt of purpoſe for breuity ſake, and vpon good cauſes; and what I haue wrytten and affirmed, I haue done yt with all truth and fidelity, and ſo will he find that ſhall read my narration, and conferre it with Fox himſelfe; and this animaduerſion being premiſed, lett any heretike cauill or wrangle that liſteth, his arguments are anſwered before he beginne.

THE

THE CONTINVATION
AND CONNEXION

Of this second volume of Foxian Saintes with the other sett forth before:

And what principall partes or pointes
the former conteyned.

IN the end of my former booke (good *Christian rea-*
der) conteyninge the *first six Monethes of Iohn Fox*
his Calendar, I did aduertise yow (*yf yow do remem-*
ber or haue read the same) that the said booke growinge
into further length , than at the beginninge vvas expe-
cted, I vvas forced to diuide yt into two little volumes,
therby to make yt more manuall and portable , but yet
for that both of them indeed do make but one booke , as
I thought yt not amisse in the end of the former to for-
warne thee breefly , what was to be conteyned in this
later : so now least the one may chance to come to thy
hands vvith out the other , yt shall not be perhaps from
the purpose, heere to lay downe in few vvords by vvay
of preambles, the summe of the former subiect , and
principall parts therof , togeather vvith their cohe-
rence and connexion vvith this, for so shalt thou see and
behould in a short vew the comprehension of all.

OF THE PREFACE,
INTITVLED:
A direction for the vse of the tvvo Calendars.

FIRST *of all then after the briefe dubble* Calendar *prefixed in the former volume of* Catholike *and* Foxian Saints *of the first six Monethes, and a certayne* antidotum *adioyned thervnto, against the admiration of such boldnes in going to the fire for maintenance of heresies, as* Fox *would stirre vp, by the example of so great a multitude of his Martyrs: (all which is recorded againe in this volume) there followeth* in the former, A certayne direction or instruction to the discreet and pious reader, how to vse the said dubble Calendar *(of* Catholike *and* Foxian Saints*)* to his greatest spirituall commodity and increase of deuotion, *which in effect consisteth in this; that vvheras by the very vew and manifest opposition of the said two Calendars, the one against the other, yt is euident that the one conteyneth a most noble ranke of holy seruants of* Christ*, venerable for their antiquity, renowned for their sanctity, illustrious for their miracles, and the most of them famous also for science and learninge : the other a poore rabble of later phantasticall people proud, vvillfull, and obstinate in their particular opinions, and contrary to the former, in most of the forsaid points of commendation ; and that the sectaryes of our dayes for promotinge of these new vpstarts, had gone about to disgrace, and detract*

The difference of Saints of the Cath. and Protestant Calendar.

from

from those ould standars in Christ Church: this I say
being so; yt seemed to the vvryter, that the best direction vvhich in such an affaire could be giuen, vvas to
contemne the one, and make more accompt, than
euer, of the other, especially by honouringe them vvith
that reuerence, vvhich is due, to so speciall frends and
seruants of almighty God, vvith vvhome they are now
in glory; and further for our owne good, to call vpon
them vvith earnest and frequent deuotion, to be our
helpers and intercessors vvith their Lord and Maister Christ Iesus, as vve haue need in this miserable and daungerous vvorld, for arryuinge to them,
and obtayninge their happy society for all eternity
to come.

And albeit for their greater disgrace, the heretiks of our tyme, haue qualified this recourse and inuo-
cation of ours to them, by the most odious name of
superstition, and Idolatry (vvhich euidently is refuted
in the very beginninge of the said direction, by
shewinge the lymitts and differences, that are betweene
prayinge to God and prayinge to Saints): yet must
vve not therfore giue ouer, but rather for that cause
be more earnest and diligent in that kind of Catholike and true Christian deuotion, partly to conuert therby (I meane by the feruerous intercession of all holy
Saints) the enemyes and heretiks themselues, yf yt be
possible, from the fury of their contumelious raylinge
spiritt; partly also, to make recompence for that
omission, vvhich in this behalfe hath byn vsed in
many parts of the vvorld these later yeares, vpon
the clamors and outcryes of these sectaryes against
the same: vvhich clamors hauinge byn examined,
and found to be vayne, and to haue proceeded

VVhy vve
ought to
encrease
our deuo-
tion in
prayinge
to Saints.

B 3   only

only of enuy, indeuotion, ignorance and impiety; the best vvay seemeth to be for vs, to double our said deuotion in prayinge to them.

This was the counsell and direction giuen in that place to him, that would withdraw his soule from these wearisome contentions raysed by heretiks of our dayes, to the quiett vse and possession of deuotion and piety, vvhich our Catholike and happy forefathers enioyed before these vvranglings beganne. And for greater encouragement and example heerin, yt vvas thought good to lay forth somewhat of the holy practise and exercise of the most eminent Saints, and blessed Fathers of Gods Church in this behalfe, that is to say, not so much their bookes and vvrytings about this matter (for that vvere ouerlonge, and almost infinite) but vvhat is extant of their doings in this kind of deuotion: to vvitt, vvhat manner of prayers they vsed to make in their dayes to Saints desceased, vvithout feare or doubt of Idolatry, or other offence of God therin, and vvithout reprehension or mislikinge of any good man or vvoman, learned or vnlearned, or of the Church of God in those dayes; to vvhich effect is alleaged the continuall discent, (though very breisely) of all ages, both before the cominge of Christ, among the Iewes, as also since; and namely of the Patriarks, Prophetts, and most holy men of the hebrewe Church, and the like of the Christian, as the examples there alleaged both of Greeke and Latyn ancient Fathers, for the space of a thousand yeares after Christ, doth declare: vvhich being done, yt is inferred to be considered, how much more secure yt is in the sight of a discreet man, to follow the example & foote steppes of such ould, ancient, and expert guides in points of religion that cöcerne our soules; then these new late vpstart

Doctors,

The auncient Fathers deuotion in prayinge to Saints.

*Doctors, that brabble to the contrary, and are vvholy
deuoyde of all deuotion in themselues ; and vvith this in
effect endeth that direction.: now followeth a short
abridgment of the Chapters conteyned in the former volume.*

OF THE FIRST CHAPTER,
That treateth of the nature of an
Ecclesiasticall Calendar, & vpon
vvhat cause it vvas inuented, and
put into vse first in the Church
of Christ.

I N *this Chapter, after declaration of the words* Martyrologe *and* Calendar, *and vvhy they vvere instituted in the Christian Church , vvho vvere the authors, and to vvhat end and effect , and other such like
points : discouery is made of diuers hereticall practises
vsed by ancient sectaryes against Catholike Saints, and
Martyrs in euery age , and this commonly vpon enuy of
the honour done vnto them in the said Church; of which
practises the first was, to seeke by all meanes to disgrace,
and corrupt their true historyes; and the second to oppose their owne false Martyrs against them , and preferre their vvorthynesse before them . VVhich two
practises vvith some other of like nature, are shewed to
haue byn put in vre egregiously by* Iohn Fox, *in this his
volume of* Acts *and* Monuments, *many examples being
alleaged for proofe therof, as vvhere he corrupteth the
historyes of* S. Boniface, *Archbishopp of* Mentz, *and*
B 4   *of*

of S. Edward *the Martyr*, S. Elphegus, S. Thomas of Canterbury *and other English Martyrs, and
in the second vvhere by name he preferreth his* Tho-

Foxin epist. ad doct. Lector.

mas Cranmer, before six hundred Thomas
Becketts, *compareth his* Nicolas Ridley, with
any S. Nicolas that euer was, *and aduanceth his*
Latymer, Hooper, Marsh, Simpson, *and other
like companions*, before the highest and greatest
Saints of the Roman Calendar whatsoeuer,
as there more particularly, and largely is handled.

OF THE SECOND CHAPTER,

That shevveth the seuerall causes
of honour done to Saintes in the
Catholike Church, & that none
of them agree to Foxian Saints.

*I*N *this Chapter fiue causes in particular are assigned,
why the ancient Fathers did in ould tyme keepe an-
nuall memory of Saints and Martyrs in their Churches,
& Ecclesiasticall tables or martyrologes; the first, therby
to yeld to the said Martyrs, and to Christ by them (by
whose grace and power they were made Martyrs) due*

1.

2.

*honour and memory for their heroicall actions: the se-
cond, to be made pertakers of their meritts by vvay of
association and communion of Saints: the third, to be
holpen by their prayers and intercessions ioyned with
ours, which includeth also our prayers vnto them: the
fourth, to stirre vp others to their imitation by the high
opinion, which the Church sheweth therin to haue of*

3.

4.

mar-

martyrdome : the fift, to confirme therby alſo the certainty of our faith, ſeing ſo many wittneſſes one after
another, to dy in, and for one, and the ſelfe ſame faith
and beleeſe. All which fiue cauſes are ſeuerally and di-
ſtinctly proued out of the ſayings & wrytings of ancient
Fathers ; and then againe yt is declared that none of
theſe cauſes could rightly mooue Fox to wryte his martyrologe or Calendar of new Saints. For as for the firſt
three points of celebration of their feaſts, aſſociation of
their meritts, and interceſſion by their prayers, the Proteſtant doctrine admitteth them not. And for the laſt
two, which are imitation of their life and doctrine, and
confirmation of Proteſtant faith by them and their
example ; though in words Fox may ſeeme perchance to
pretend ſomewhat ; yet in truth he cannot, for that ſuch
are his Martyrs ſett downe in this Calendar (as after
yow ſhall ſee) that neither in faith, works, Religion or
liſe, he may preſume to adhere abſolutely vnto them, &
much leſſe take them for examples to imitate, their
faithes, opinions and beleeſes being different : for that
ſome were Waldenſians, ſome Albigenſians, ſome
Lollards, ſome Lutherans, ſome Zwinglians,
and ſome of other ſects, as the enſuinge hiſtory will declare. Their liues and actions alſo in moſt of them, are
ſhewed to haue byn ſuch, as no way can grace the new
ghoſpell to imitate the ſame. And finally yt is diſcuſſed
what manner of honour, reuerence or memory is vſed
towards Catholike Saints in the ſacrifice of the maſſe, or
celebration of holy miſteryes, and that Fox his owne fellowes do not in earneſt hold his Calendred people for
true Saints, as out of their wrytings is declared.

OF THE THIRD CHAPTER,

Concerninge nine feuerall fectes in Religion, vvhervnto all Fox his Sainctes may be reduced.

I N *this Chapter, for more fuller declaration of the difagreement, and diuifion which is betweene Fox his Saints in points of Religion (vvhome yet he maketh all to be breethren of one Church) are feit downe niue feuerall fects, fpronge vp againft the Roman Church at fundry tymes, and in diftinct places, and vpon different occafions vvithin the fpace of thefe laft* 400. *yeares: The names of the fects and fectaryes are :* Waldenfians, Albigenfians, Wickliffians, Lollards, Lutherans, Anabaptifts, Swinglians, Caluinifts *and* Puritans, *vvhofe beginnings and progreffe, authors and occafions, agreements and differences of opinions are breefly declared, togeather, vvith the particular articles vvhich euery fect hath eyther peculiar to yt felfe, or common vvith fome other, but yet all oppofite to the Catholike Church. By confideration of which articles, and other circumftances, and by comparing them vvith the anfwers, fpeaches and propofitions of Fox his Saints in their examinations, it vvill be eafy to iudge, of vvhat fect euery Saint vvas, and for vvhat opinions or fancyes of their owne, he or fhee offered themfelues to dy. And for that thefe particularityes are many, this Chapter groweth to be longer then the reft, but yt is worth the readinge, for the inftruction of the carefull reader, and the variety is fuch, as vvill not eafily vveary him in peruſinge yt ouer.*

O F

OF THE FOVRTH CHAPTER,

VVhat may be thought of the for-
vvardnesse of Fox his Saintes, in
offeringe themselues so readily
to dye for their opinions.

THIS *Chapter is prefixed immediatly before the
entrance to the examen of the first six monethes,
comprehended in the former volume, therby to informe
the Readers iudgment somewhat about the obstinacy,
and temerity of hereticall spirits, in running to the fyre
for defence of their opinions, which are their owne
Idolls; and besids that which is laid forth before, both out
of the examples of most vvicked and notorious heretiks,
condemned and punished as vvell by Protestant as Catholike Magistrats, for extrauagant opinions held for
heresies by them both sides, as also out of the sentences
and declarations of holy Fathers there sett downe, concerning the damnable deathes of such willfull hereticall
people; Besides all this (I say) yt was thought conuenient*
to add *this seuerall Chapter in like manner, wherin
first of all is declared, how that pertinacity & obstinacy
is an essentiall part or propriety of heresy, without which
heresy cannot be heresy, but only error, and that this
pertinacity was in all ould heretiks, is, & wilbe in those
that be present or to come; and that in particular, they
had this property by testimony of the ancient Fathers,
that they held euer their owne punishments to be perse-
cutions and martyrdomes: vvhich being declared by*

*Pertinaci-
ty essen-
tiall to
heresie.*

many

*many and sundry testimonyes of antiquity, the same
points are examined also in Fox his Martyrs, who finally are found to haue byn of the very same spiritt, and
consequently do deserue to haue the same iudgment
made of them, touching this point of hereticall obstinacy,
which the ancient Fathers made of those ould heretiks,
and with this preuention and preparation is the entry
made to treate of each moneth in particular.*

OF TH' EXAMEN
OF THE FIRST SIX
MONETHES,
Conteyned in six seuerall
Chapters.

AFTER *the former 4. Chapters, as
inductions to the principall matters of Foxian Martyrs heere to be
handled, there followeth, in the precedent volume the discussion and vew of
the first six Monethes,* Ianuary, February, March, Aprill, May, *and*
Iune, *with the particular historyes
breefely touched of all such new Martyrs,*

Infra cap.
17. &
deinceps.

tyrs, and Confeſſors, as Fox hath thought vvorthy of this his new Ca-lendar, albeit (as in ſome other places I thinke I haue noted,) there be diuers other ſanctified by him, vvith large diſcourſes in ſundry places of his vvorke, vvhome yet I find not in his Calendar, as namely Q. Anne Bullen, Crom-vvell, Q. Catherine Parre, Q. Iane, *the* Duke & Dutcheſſe *of* Suffolke, *the* Duke *of* Somerſet, Iuſtice Hales *that drowned himſelfe, and diuers other like vvorthyes of his Religion, vvhoſe ſtoryes notwithſtandinge* I do *not take vpon me to handle in particular, for that my purpoſe is, to examine only his Calendar & Calendred Saints, vvherof I ſhall giue yow heere a ſhort taſt only in generall, for the firſt ſix Monethes that go in the former vo-lumes.*

IANVARY.

IANVARY.

THE Moneth of Ianuary beginneth with *Iohn VVickliffe*, and hath 28. dayes repleni-shed with Foxian Martyrs, the other three being left only to three feasts that were in our Romayne Calendar before, which are the *Circumcision, Epiphany,* and *Conuersion of S. Paul*; all the other are made to giue place to his new Martyrs, wherof three are sett forth in great read letters, as Cardinall-martyrs more emynent then the rest: to witt, the aforesaid *Iohn VVickliffe*, whome he calleth *Preacher-martyr*, though he died in his bedd, and was neuer martyred (as Fox himselfe elswhere confesseth) *Syr Roger Acton* intituled in the Calendar *Knight-martyr, who was drawne, hanged, and buryed* vnder the gallowes (faith Stow) *in S. Gyles field, vnder K. Henry the 5. for treason, and open rebellion.* The third is *Iohn Philpott* Martyr, a poore ignorant artificer, burned in *Canterbury* for Caluinisme vnder *Q. Mary*, in the yeare 1557. and I take yt to be an error, in that this *Philpott* is sett downe in the place of the other *Iohn Philpott* Preacher-martyr burned at *London*, whose festiuall day is vpon the 13. of *December*, as in this booke afterwards you shall see; And therfore his history is differred vnto that place.

The residue of this moneth sett downe in blacke letters, are more ordinary people for their titles, but no lesse notorious for their boldnesse in answeringe, as *Tudson* an apprentice,

Stovv anno Domini 1414.

tice, VVent a fherman, *Browne* a labourer, and foure or fiue moft infolét weomen, *Ioane Lashford*, *Agnes Snoth*, *Anne Alebright*, and *Ioane Catmer* whofe immodeft behauiour, and infolent anfwers do well fhew of what fpiritt they were. And fo much in generall for this Moneth.

FEBRVARY.

THE fecond Moneth of *February* is more fertile of rubricate Martyrs, then *Ianuary*, for that yt hath 8. in number, two Wickliffians, *Syr Iohn Oldcaftle* a Ruffian-knight as all England knoweth, & commonly brought in by comediants on their ftages: he was put to death for robberyes and rebellion vnder the forefaid *K. Henry* the fifth and *Syr Roger Onely* Prieft-martyr, condemned for coniuringe and wichcraft vnder *K. Henry* the fixt. The third is *Martyn Luther* confeffor, that ftands alone in the middeft of this moneth, as vmpyre betweene the other two ranks: to witt, the former two, and fiue other that do enfue, which are *Iohn Rogers* and *Laurence Saunders* Preachermartyrs, *Iohn Hooper* and *Robert Farrar*, Bifhopmartyrs, and *Rowland Taylor* Doctor-martyr. Of which number fome were Lutherans in Religion, as *Doctor Taylor* and *Farrar*, fome were Caluinifts, as the reft, whofe ftoryes are particularly handled in this moneth: and after thefe the moft eminent perfons in this tragicall comedy, are *Iohn Claydon* a Wickliffian

Ann. 1418.

Ann. 1441.

Curriar,

Curriar, that made his owne fonne a Prieſt,
and gaue him authority to ſay maſſe, at his
mothers vpſitting from Childbirth; *Iohn Ziſca*
a Bohemian Rebell, and moſt cruell tyrant
and murderer of innocent people ; the lady
Eleanor Cobham, condemned of ſorcery and
wichcraft, with intention to haue murdered
K. Henry the 6. *Agnes Potten* and *Trunchfields* wife
of Ipſwich named by Fox *Matron-Martyrs*, the
one a ſhomaker, the other a beere-brewers
wife, both of them greate diſputers as in their
liues and hiſtoryes is to be ſeene.

MARCH.

THE Moneth of March hath two rubricate Martyrs only , *Thomas Bilney* and *Thomas Cranmer*, both Prieſts; the one was burned
vnder *K. Henry* the 8. for certayne new opinions which once he had held , but after recanted them before his death , and ſo died a
Catholike ; the other was Archbiſhopp of
Canterbury , and condemned vnder *Q. Mary*
both of treaſon , and hereſie ; and though he
recanted alſo ; yet was he burned for relapſe,
as in his ſtory appeareth. The remnant of this
Moneth were ſome Wickliffians, as *Taylor,
Veſcelus, Veſſallianus* who denyed in like manner the proceeding of the holy Ghoſt from the
ſecõd perſon in Trinity, with other like hereſies: Other were Lutherans, as *Sutphen, Huglene,
Fleßidius, Clabaccus* and *Hamelton* all ſtrangers.
But the cheefe Captaynes of the Caluinian
crew

crew of this Moneth , (I meane of artificers)
were three: to witt, *Spicer* the Mason, *Cober-
ley* the Taylor, and *Maundrell* the cowheard,
which *Maundrell* was the Maister and guyde
of all the rest, and disputed for them, with
cryinge out in the Church, that Purgatory
was the *Popes Pinfold*, and that wodden Images
vvere good to rost a shoulder of Mutton, and other
like speaches proportionable to these, and to
his profession.

APRILL.

THE Moneth of Aprill hath no rubricate
Martyr at all, sett downe by Iohn Fox,
which yet is maruayle that he esteemeth none
of his Saints in this Moneth worthy of that
title, especially seeing in the very first ranke
of them vnder K. Henry, was burned *Maister
Iames Baynam* gentleman-martyr of *Glocestershire*, who had married *Symon Fish* his wife, that
made the *Supplication of beggars*, answered by
Syr Thomas More, of which *Baynam* Fox recounteth a strange miracle, *that being burned in the fire,
he felt no more payne, then yf he had byn in a bedd of
downe.* Which miracle yf Fox held for true, yt
seemeth that he might deserue a redd garment in his Calendar; but it is like, that he
lost this prerogatiue, by being a Lutheran in
the article of the *reall presence*, though in other
points he was much against him, as also
against Iohn Fox, yf yt be true that he granted to the Papists, as himselfe saith, these articles

C

*Ann.*1532.

Fox *pag.*
939.

ticles, followinge, firſt *that a man making a vowe
cannot breake the ſame without deadly ſinne.* 2. *that
a Prieſt promiſinge to liue chaſt, may not marry a wife.*
3. *that Luther did naught in marryinge a Nunne; and
other ſuch like points.* In reſpect wherof, though
Fox graunt him to be a Martyr, yet no *Cardi-
nall-martyr.* There is alſo in this Moneth *George
Marſh* Preacher-martyr, who for his valiant
acts deſcribed by Fox, might haue deſerued
the place of a rubricate Saint, had not his
doubtfullnes perhaps about the *reall preſence*
excluded him. But eſpecially I maruayle of
VVilliam Flower Miniſter-martyr, who by the
particular induction of the holy Ghoſt (as Fox
is content we ſhould beleeue) being an Apoſtata monke, wounded greeuouſly a Catholike Prieſt with his woodknife in *S. Margarets*
Church at *VVeſtminſter*, and was executed afterward for the ſame, and for his hereſie. And
finally there is in this Moneth, the martyrdome of *VVilliam Tymmes* Deacon, who might
ſeeme by his anſwere, to deſerue the place of
another *S. Stephen* or *S. Laurence,* amonge Fox
his Martyrs, but only *that he denyed all preſence of
Chriſt in the Sacramēt, both & corporall ſpirituall, &c.*
Wherby he ſeemeth to agree neyther with
Lutherans nor Caluiniſts, for that the one do
graunt corporally, the other at leaſt ſpiritually, Chriſt to be preſent.

Fox pag.
1711.

MAY.

M A Y.

T H E Moneth of May hath three rubrica-
ted Martyrs in Fox his Calendar: to witt,
Iohn Huſſe , *Hieronimus Sauonarola* and *Iohn Card-
maker* ; the firſt was a Bohemian Prieſt and
burned at the Councell of *Conſtance*, almoſt
200. years gone, and in many points he was
farre different from Iohn Fox his Religion.
The ſecond was a Catholike and religious
man of *Florence* in Italy, of *S. Dominiks* order, &
no Proteſtant at all, nor euer held any one article that is knowne of Proteſtant Religion,
as both *Guicciardine*, *Tarcognota*, and other forraine authors do teſtifie. The third was an
Engliſh Apoſtata friar of *S. Francis* order, who
takinge a woman became a Miniſter,and was
burned vnder Q. *Mary* for diuers hereſies,
though in the matter of the Sacrament, he
ſeemed little or nothing to diſagree from the
Catholiks. And theſe are the cheefe Martyrs
of this Moneth;though there be diuers others
alſo of markable quality, as namely *Robert
King* , *Robert Debnan* and *Nicolas Marsh* induced
by the ſpirit of God(as Fox iudgeth) to robbe
and ſpoile the Church of *Douer-court* in *Kent*,
for which they were hanged in chaynes by
cōmandement of *K. Henry* the 8.There are alſo
Hugh Lauerocke & *Iohn Aprice* Martyrs, the one a
cripple, the other a blind man , moſt inſolent
in their blaſphemous anſwers , as in Fox is to
be ſeene, with diuers others of like diſpoſitiō.

*Güiccard.
lib. 1. hiſt.
fol. 99.*
*Tarcogn.
part. 2,
hiſt.*

Fox *pag*
940.

C 2 IVNE.

IVNE.

THE laſt of theſe firſt ſix Monethes is Iune which hath but one rubricate Martyr, & this vpon the firſt day therof, named *Ierome* of *Prage*, condemned alſo in the forſaid Councell of *Conſtance* as was *Iohn Huſſe*. This *Hierome* was a lay-man of the vniuerſity of *Prage* in *Bohemia*, and ioyninge with *Iohn Huſſe* that was a Prieſt, had cauſed much ſedition in the ſame vniuer-ſity, before he fell into hereſie, but much more afterwards; Wherupon he being taken in the towne of *Hirſau* was ſent by the Duke therof, to the Councell of *Conſtance*, and there was ac-cuſed, & condemned of diuers notorious he-reſies, which though once he abiured, yet af-ter fallinge into the ſame againe he was bur-ned. The ſecond Martyr of this moneth is *Anne Aſkue*, burned vnder K. *Henry* the 8. for denying the reall preſence, and ſome other articles of Cath. faith, albeit ſhe recáted twiſe her forſaid opinions about the bleſſed Sacrament, but fell againe into relapſe, and ſo was burned. And after theſe two, which lead the firſt ranke, there follow almoſt 70. other Foxian Mar-tyrs and Confeſſors, which are more, then in any other Moneth beſides. But the chiefe diſputers amonge theſe artificers were two by name, *Edmund Allen* a myller, and *Richard VVoodman* an Iron-maker, who by ſcriptures conquered all that ſtood againſt them, yf yow will beleeue Iohn Fox his narration of their Acts and Geſts, as more largely may be ſeene

in

in their hiſtoryes. And this ſhalbe ſufficient
for a briefe abridgment of theſe ſix monethes.

OF THE APPENDIX

AND TREATISE

adioyned thervnto, about the
triall of Pleſſis Mornay.

WHEN *the firſt volume vvas brought by the
print to this place, yt ſeemed to haue growne to
ſo great a bulke, that all the reſt which vvas to
follow for complement of the whole matter, could not
conueniently be contayned therin; and therfore by a certayne* Appendix *the parts that remayned for this ſecond volume being breifely declared, an end vvas put to
the other, but yet notwithſtandinge, for that yt ſeemed
capable of ſome more ſheets of paper, yt was iudged not
amiſſe, to adioyne thervnto, a certayne defence of a relation wrytten ſome three yeares paſt, of a triall made
before the moſt. Chriſtian King of* France *about ſundry points of Religion, betweene* Monſieur Peron
B. of Eureux, *and* Monſieur Pleſsis Mornay
gouernour of the towne, and countrey of Saumur *in*
France, *a cheeſe learned Proteſtant, highly eſteemed by
them, vvhich triall vvas made principally, to conuict the
ſaid* Pleſsis *of manifold falſifications, vſed in his booke
againſt Catholike Religion, and namely in one againſt
the maſſe, then newly vvritten. Of vvhich falſifications,* 4000. *vvere promiſed to be conuinced by the ſaid
Biſhopp;* 800. *vvere gathered out, and brought to the*

place

place of triall 500. *offered to be exhibited prefently:* 60. *vvere giuen him to beginne withall for one day,* 19. *were chofen out by* Pleſſis *himfelfe as moft defenfible,* *and* 9. *vvere examined the firſt day, and found all fal-* *fified on* Pleſſis *behalfe.*

And for that the faid Pleſſis *fled prefently the com-* *batt , and refufinge afterward to returne to the fame* *tryall , fett forth in place therof a falfe narration and* Iuſtification *of himfelfe, and flaunder of others; and one* Mathew Sutcliffe *an* Englifh- miniſter, *did the fame* *in* England *for defence of the faid* Pleſſis *and his* *doings : yt feemed not amiſſe in the end of the former* *volume to place this new* Treatife *about the faid* French Triall, *addinge fuch other matters thervnto, as* *I perfuade my felfe vvill be both profitable and pleafant* *to him that fhall pervfe the fame. And this fhall fuffice* *for the order, method, and connexion of thefe two vo-* *lumes togeather makinge in effect but one booke : fo as* *the former endinge vvith the* Moneth of Iune , *that* *made the tenth* Chapter , *this beginneth vvith* Iuly *comprehendinge the eleuenth.*

THE

THE
INTRODVCTION
TO THE HISTORY
OF THE SIX ENSVINGE
MONETHES,

With some brief directions for the profitable reading therof.

A S the continuation before sett downe of these later six monethes, with the former six sett forth in another booke, doth shew their connexion and coherence togeather, and that all indeed is but one history, and should haue gone in one volume, yf the bignesse would haue permitted yt: so are there certayne aduertissements common to them all, wherof some are sett downe in the former booke, and some reserued as speciall for this place. In the former are those two Chapters, that go before the said monethes, to witt the third and fourth, wherof the third conteyneth a Declaratio of nine seuerall sects sprong vp within these last 400. yeares, wherunto all Fox his Calendar-Saincts may be reduced. The fourth comprehendeth the pertinacity and inflexible obstinacy of hereticall heads, when once they fall into that humour, *wherof you shall see no lesse notable examples in these later monethes, then in the precedent: For better consideration wherof, I haue thought good to adioyne these fevv particular directions following.*

C 4
The

*The first is, that after the Fathers sentences well pon-
dered and weighed,which before we haue alleaged,con-
cerninge the damnable end of those that dy out of the
Church for their particular opinions,the reader do consider also and peruse that,which we haue written afterward in the* Reuew of ten disputations, *but especially the second and third Chapters therof , vvhere the
grounds are layd downe of three principle articles , for
vvhich most of Fox his Martyrs vvent to the fire, vvhich
are the* Reall-presence, Transubstantiation,
and sacrifice of the masse. *For vvhen he shall haue
seene and pondered vvith some attention , how many
great and vveighty grounds, both of Scriptures,Fathers,
Councells,Antiquity,Continuance,Consent of Nations,
Miracles , Sanctity , VVisdome, Learning, and other
such motiues, vvhich these articles haue for arguments
of their infallible truth : and on the other side shall see
a company of ignorant and vnlearned people , artificers , craftesmen , spinsters, and other poore vveomen,
stand so resolutely vpon the contrary assertions , as yf
these Catholike articles had no ground at all ; yea to
raile, reuile, blaspheme, contemne, and scoffe at them,
as yf they vvere new fictions, or old-wyues tales , and
thervpon most resolutely to go to the fire , and aduenture both body and soule euerlastingly theron; yt
must needs mooue a man much both to maruayle and
compassion.*

The second direction may be to read ouer the 17.
Chapter of this booke, intituled of obseruations,
*before he read the history it selfe of these monethes; for
that therby he shalbe able much better to iudge , and
make reflexion vpon diuers points heere handled, especially yf he marke vvell and consider* the fifth obseruation;

uation; *vvhich is*, that such as hould the Sacramentary doctrine against the reall-presence, (*vvhich are the farre greatest part of Fox his Martyrs*) cannot be saued, but by the damnation of many other of his Saints in the same Calendar, *but especially of Lutherans*, *as both* Luther *himselfe and all his followers do hold and testify in all their books, speaches, sentences, iudgments, protestations, acts and vvrytings as there is to be seene.*

Thirdly yt may serue also for no euill direction to a iudicious man, in readinge ouer this history, to consider among these people that stood so resolutely in their opinions, *concerning these articles of the Sacrament, what great variety & diuersity they had therin among themselues, and yet all went to the fire for that*, *which each man listed to defend. I will name yow some examples out of thes last six monethes only, which yow may read ouer more largely and particularly in the story yt selfe. First all the pure Zuinglians do hould euery where, that there is nothing in the Sacrament, but* a bare signe of Christ his body, *and as the words of* Iohn Webb, George Roper, *and* Gregory Parke *are, recyted and allowed by Fox*; yt is nothing but only a remembrance of Christs body. *But the pure Caluinists, as* Ridley, Bradford, *and all their fellowes do affirme*; that Christ is truly, and wholy in the Sacrament, but spiritually, and as present to faith as bread to the senses, *as yow may read in their historyes.* Doctor Barnes, Taylor, Farrar, *& other purely following the doctrine of* Luther, *hold, that* Christs body *is really and substantially in the* Sacrament, togeather with bread, *as yow may see by their examinations*, *arraignments, and* Confessions:

Third direction.

Octob. 21. & 22.
anno 1555.
Octob. 19.
anno 1555.
Iulij 6.
anno 1555.

fions: But Iohn Fox, *and his faithfull people that fol-*

Fox pag.
1529. & 3.
August.

low him exactly , do hold *(as himselfe professeth)* that Chrift, is neyther corporally nor fpiritually in the Sacrament. *So as heere now yow haue* 4. *oppofite vvayes , and yet none true or Catholike, the one , that yt is a bare figne and remembrance only, the other , that yt is Chrifts true corporall body and bread togeather : the third , that Chrift is there fpiritually and not corporally ; the fourth, that neyther fpiritually nor corporally. And then from thefe fountaynes fpring other opinions , as incompatible as thefe , and yet muft euery one be defended, by death of the defender.*

Nouemb.
25.26.27.
& 28.

Iohn Corn-forth, Katherine Knight, *and foure more of their conforts in the moneth of Nouem-ber held, that* Chrifts body was only in the Sacrament, when yt was receyued, *and not otherwayes ; fo as yt did come and go , and was now there, and now not there , and more they held, as* Fox *relateth,* that a temporall vifible thinge was receyued with yt, *but they explicate not what.* Iohn Clarke *labouring-man, and* Alice Potkyns *fpinfter and foure more with them defended to death, in the*

* die 12.13.
14. &c.

fame moneth of ✶ Nouember *,* that there was but one Sacrament only, *and that this was* Chrifts body hanginge on the croffe. Patricke Pa-

August. 3.
4. 5.

tingham, Iohn Newman *the pewterer, & other of that company held ftoutly, & died vpon it,* that Chrift is no otherwife in the Sacramēt, then as he is, where two or three be gathered togeather in his name : *So as where two or three are gathered togeather in his name , there is* Chrifts body *as much as in the Sacrament or Communion.* But Iohn Bland A-

Iulij 10.

poftata-prieft and Minifter vvent yet further, and
burned

burned for the same: that Chrifts body is no otherwife in the Sacrament, then in euery other good body, *whether he ioyne himfelfe with others in Chrifts name or no: So as wherfoeuer yow find a good body, there is Chrifts body as much as in the Sacrament.*

William Tyndall *called by* Fox *and* Bale, the Apoftle of England, *held*, that yt was indifferent to beleeue, whether Chrifts body were in the Sacrament or no. *But* Iohn Frith *his scholler went further*, *and offered himfelfe to death rather then to yeld*, that yt was a matter of fayth to beleeue the prefence or abfence of Chrifts body in the Sacrament. Antony Perfon *the Apoftata prieft of* Windefore, *with* Teftwod *the mufition, and other* Windefore-men, *paffed on yet further, affirming that the words of Chrift*, this is my body that is broken for yow, *was meant of the breaking of Gods word vnto the people: So as wholy thefe fellowes feeme to haue taken away and euacuated the inftitution of the Sacrament;* but Iohn Cowbridg *paffed them all*, *who faid*, that the Sacrament was a fraud and deceyt; *and that the words of Chrift:* This is my body which fhalbe geuen for yow, *hath this fenfe;* This is my body, that fhall deceyue yow. *And yet is this good fellow with all the reft that heere are named, celebrated by* Iohn Fox *for a martyr of his Calendar. And feing that all thefe dozen & more opinions are found in the brethren of one profeffion, within the compaffe of thefe fix laft monethes, and euery one of them held themfelues replenifhed with the fpiritt of God, and thervpon died confidently for defence of the fame opinions, yow may eafily*

Octob. 6.

Iulij 2.

Iulij 5.

Oct. 10.

easily imagine what a company they are. And this may serue for the third direction.

4 . directiõ.　　The fourth and last shall be, that yow consider, that all this which heere is wrytten in the examen of these monethes, is taken only or principally out of Fox himselfe, who may be presumed to haue written the opinions, speaches, and answers of his good sainctes in the best manner for their honors and creditt. And yf such absurdities be found notwithstanding registred by himselfe; vve may imagine what we should find, yf we had the true records and registers of the Bishopps and other Ecclesiasticall iudges, before whome the examinations were made, and by whose order they were iudicially enrolled and registred. And this shall suffice for an induction to the history of these last six monethes.

THE

THE
DISCVSSION OF THE
MONETH OF IVLY.

VVherin Iohn Frith *and* Iohn Bradford, *the first a married yonge man, the second a Minister, are chiefe Cardinall and rubricate martyrs, according to Fox his Calendar.*

CHAPTER XI.

OF the dayes of this moneth which are 31. in number, Iohn Fox hath left two only to our ould Saincts, to witt, the 22. to *S. Mary Magdalen*, and the 25. to *S. Iames* the Apostle; all the other dayes he distributeth only to his owne Saincts and Martyrs, eyther vnder *K. Henry* the eight or *Q. Mary*, for that ancienter then these he alleageth none in this moneth; but of these two ranks he chooseth out two seuerall Captaines, as heads & guides of the rest, to witt, *Iohn Frith*, of those that liued and died vnder *K. Henry* the eight, and *Iohn Bradford* of the other vnder *Q. Mary*, wherfore of these two we must treat first of all according to our former custome, but yet as briefly as may be, for that this Treatise groweth longer then was expected at the beginning.

2. First then Iohn Frith being a yonge man borne in London, and brought vp afterward in Cambridge, & there made bacheler of art, was transferred thence with diuers others (as

Io. Frith and his story anno 1533.

Fox

Fox and Bale do affirme) vnto the Colledg
of *Chrifts-Church* in *Oxford*, newly erected by
Cardinall VVolfey, and *this not fo much for loue of
learning and vertue* (faith Fox) *as for pomp and
vayne glory*, fo charitably do thefe men cenfure
their founders and benefactors; & this tranflation of *Frith* and his fellowes from Cam-
bridg to Oxford, feemeth to haue byn about
the yeare 1527. at what tyme *Frith* might be
fome 18. or 19. yeares ould, for that he was but
26. when he was burned; and 3. he fpent in
trauayle with his wife, and other three in prifon before his burning. The occafion therof,
was, that he comming acquaynted with *VVilliam Tyndall* a marryed Prieft, that was a forward new ghofpeller in thofe dayes, though
not refolued to follow the fect eyther of *Luther* or *Swinglius*, as afterward yow fhall fee,
he was by him perfuaded to take the fame
courfe, *being of great pregnancy of vvytt, and forward both in the Latyn and Greeke tongue*, as Fox

Fox pag.
941.

faith; And friar *Bale* accordinge to his wanton
vayne of fpeech, addeth further in his com-

Bal.Cent.5.
Script.Brit.

mendation, that he was *elegantißimus forma &
ingenio iuuenis*, a moft elegant yong man both
in bewty and witt, accordinge to which ele-
gancy, he tooke vnto him a yong wife in
thofe his yong yeares, and went ouer into
Flanders after the forfaid *VVilliam Tyndall*, of

VVilliam
Tindall
Maifter to
Fryth.

whome we fhall talke more largely in his fea-
ftiuall day vpon the fixt of October, (for he is
alfo a Foxian Martyr) and by the faid *Tyndall*,
Fryth was inftructed in Flanders, and from
                                    thence

thence fent into England againe, no otherwife (faith Iohn Bale) then Paul did imploy *Bal. ibid.*
Tymothy, *in miniſterij ſocium adoptans* adopting
him into the aſlociation of his myniſtery:
Whervpon *Fryth* leauing his yong wife with
Tyndall, he aduentured to go into England
after two yeares he had byn in Flanders.
Fox faith that his comminge into England ,,
was, to gett fome exhibition of the Prior of ,,
Readinge, and to carry the faid Prior ouer *Sea* ,,
with him (wherof is inferred that he had ,,
hope to peruert him) but being at *Readinge* ,,
(faith Fox) yt happened that he was there ta- *Fox pag.*
942.
ken for a vagabond and fett in the ſtocks, and
after that againe fleetinge from one place to ,,
another, and often changinge both his gar- ,,
ments and place of abode, yet could he be ,,
no where in fafety, fo that at laſt being trayte- ,,
rously taken, he was fent to the Towar of ,,
London, where he had many conflicts with ,,
the Biſhops, but eſpecially in wrytinge with ,,
Syr Thomas More, then Chancelor of England. ,,
3. Thus farre wryteth Fox of the returne of
Iohn Fryth from Flanders, and of his committinge to the Towar, which was of likelyhood vpon fome matter of ſtate allſo befides
his Religion, (for otherwife he ſhould not
haue byn commytted to the towar) as namely
perhaps his practizinge with the faid Prior of
Readinge, to make him an Apoſtata, as his Maiſter Tyndall was, and befides to cary him out
of the land. But now what a fitt match, eyther for difputinge or wrytinge this marryed
yong

yong man *Frith* might be, to haue conflicts
with the most learnedst Bishops of England,
as Fox heere affirmeth, & afterward expoundeth them to be the Bishopps of *Canterbury,*
VVinchester, London, Lincolne and *Rochester*, as also
to contend in wrytinge with *Syr Thomas More,*
B. Fisher, and *Doctor Rastall* by name, (as a little
after Iohn Fox doth bragg that he did) how
fitt a match (I say) this was *Frith* being not yet
aboue 23. yeares old, as also marryed and dis-
continued from his studyes, euery man of
meane iudgment will consider. But this is the
vanity, pride & presumption of heresie, which
that yow may the better perceyue, we shall
passe to this yong mans doctrine, and points
of Religion which he defended against the
forsaid learned men, and for which he would
needs dy, and therby yow will easily remember, what hath byn wrytten before in the
fourth Chapter of this Treatise, about such
willfull and obstinate people. I shall sett the
matter downe in Foxes owne words, or
those of *Frith* himselfe, as they ly in Fox his
narration.

4.   The whole effect of *Frythes* disputarion
with his aduersaryes (saith Fox) consisteth
especially in these 4. points about the Sacrament of the Lords supper. First, *that the matter*
of the Sacrament is no necessary article of faith vnder
paine of damnation. This was *Frith* his first article, fitt as yow see for a yong man of his age,
being a peculiar new point of hereticall doctrine proper to himselfe, and held perhaps
by

Fox *pag.*
942.
The pecu-
liar do-
ctrine of
Frith a-
bout the
Sacrament.

by no other sectary of our age except *Tyndall*
his Maister, from whome he had yt, as after
shalbe shewed;yet doth Fox highly commend
the man in this point, saying of him; *that he*
maintayning this quarrell of the Sacramēt of the Lords   Fox pag.
supper no lesse godly then learnedly, and so as no man in   943. col. 1.
a manner had done yt more learnedly and pithily before   num. 60.
him, &c. But let vs heare out the matter fur-   ,,
ther, how Iohn Frith vnderstood and defen-   Fox his
ded this his new doctrine and paradox; *that*   foolish
the beleefe or not beleefe of Christs reall presence in the   bragg of
Sacrament, is not a necessary article of faith, he wry-   faith.
teth in a certayne epistle to his frends recor-
ded by Iohn Fox, about his examinations by
the Bishops, thus:

5. They examined me (saith he) touchinge   Fox *ibid.*
the Sacrament of the Altar, whether yt was   ,,
the very body of Christ or noe? I answered,   ,,
that I thought yt was both Christes body,and   ,,
our body, &c. (Marke another deuise, and   ,,
peculiar point of doctrine in this yong Do-   ,,
ctor.) But let vs go forward. Well (said they)   ,,
dost thou not thinke, that his naturall body,   ,,
flesh, bloud, and bone is really conteyned vn-   ,,
der the Sacrament,and there present without   ,,
all figure or similitude? No, said I, I do not so   ,,
thinke, notwithstandinge I would not, that   ,,
any should accompt, that I make my sayinge,   ,,
which is the negatiue,any article of faith. For   No article
euen as I say that yow ought not to make any   of faith to
necessary article of your part,which is the af-   beleeue or
firmatiue;so I say againe,that we make no ne-   reall pre-
cessary article of faith of our part, but leaue yt   sence, ac-
                                                    cording to
                                                    Frith.

D   indif-

,, indifferent for all men to iudge therin as God
,, shall open their harts, &c. Lo heere this *ele-*
gant yong mans deep diuinity, diuifed of his
owne head, and neuer held I thinke by any
Catholike or heretike before him;to witt that
yt is no neceffary article of faith,to beleeue,or
not beleeue whether Chrift be really prefent
in the Sacrament or no; though the matter be
expreffely fett downe in the fcripture,and the
beleefe therof moft earneftly commended by
all ancient Fathers to Chriftian people ; and
yet was this *yong man* fo refolute in this his
owne fancy,as he would needs dy for defence
of this his diuifed doctrine. For heare him I
pray yow, how he aunfwereth an obiection
againft this :

Fox *pag.*
944.

6.   Heere peraduenture (faith he)many will
maruaile, that for fo much as the matter tou-
,, chinge the fubftance of the Sacrament being
,, feparate from the articles of faith, & bynding
,, no man of necefsity vnto faluation or damna-
,, tion, whether he beleeue yt or not, but rather
,, may be left indifferently vnto all men, freely
,, to iudge, eyther on the one part or on the
An obie-
ction of
Io. Frith
made
againft
himfelfe
and foo-
lishly anf-
vvered.
other, &c. What then is the caufe, why I
would therfore fo willingly fuffer death? The
caufe why I dy, is this, for that I cannot agree
with the diuynes & other head prelates, that
yt fhould be neceffarily determined to be an
article of faith, *that the fubftance of bread and wyne*
,, *is changed into the body and bloud of our Sauiour Iefus*
,, *Chrift*, the forme and fhape only not being
,, changed, which thinge yfyt were moft true
(as

(as they shall neuer be able to proue yt by any „
authority of the scripture or Doctors) yet shall „
they not so bring to passe, that that doctrine, „
were yt neuer so true, should be holden for a „
necessary article of faith, for there are many „
things both in the scriptures and other places, „
which we are not bound of necessity to be- „
leeue, as an article of faith; so ys yt true, that „
I was a prisoner and in bands when I wrote „
these things, and yet for all that I will not „
hould yt for an article of faith, for that yow „
may without danger of damnation, either be- „
leeue yt, or thinke the contrary. Thus he. „

7. And I haue alleaged this place more at large, that yow may perceaue therby the wisdome and learning of this rare and excellent diuine of Iohn Fox, who holdeth that neyther the matter of the reall presence, nor of Transubstantiation, though yt were neuer so true or sett downe in scriptures, is any article of faith, or necessarily to be beleeued vnder paine of damnation; which yf yt be so, then may we beleeue so much of scriptures as we list, and leaue the rest; seing according to this doctrine, it is not sufficient to make any thing an article of faith, or necessarily to be beleeued, for that yt is putt downe in scripture: which is most absurd and contrary to their owne doctrine, which make only scripture the cannon of beleefe. And as for his foolish comparison, that himselfe was truly in prison when he wrote these things, and yet that yt is no article of beleefe, yt is so impious and ri-

diculous as euery man feeth, in that he will
compare his fayings with fcripture, and Fox

Fox pag.
944.

himfelfe being a fhamed therof, maketh this
wife note in the margent: *this is to be weighed
vvith the tyme, vvhen Frith vvrote*; as who would
fay, that the difference of tymes may make
differences alfo of beleefes, or that matters ne-
ceflary to be beleeued in one tyme, are not fo,
at another tyme, and that *Frith* might compare humaine faith with diuine faith in King
Henryes dayes, though we may not now.
And thefe be Iohn Fox his ordinary com-
ments, for excufinge the abfurdityes of his
Saints in their fpeaches and doctrine.

8.   But to returne to *Frith*; after he had faid,
as yow haue heard, adding further for his excufe in this indifferency in doctrine, that one
caufe therof was, for that he would not be
preiudiciall by any affirmatiue of his, in this
point of the Sacrament, to the *Germans* and
Heluetians, to witt eyther thofe that tooke Luthers part for the reall prefence, or thofe that
held with *Oecolampadius* againft the fame, he

Fox ibid.

concludeth thus: *VVhich things ftandinge in this
cafe, I fuppofe there is no man of any vpright confcience,*

The caufe
vvhy Frith
vvould go
to the fiar.

vvhich vvill not allow the reafon of my death, &c. So
wrote he, and then fubfcribed in thefe words:
*I Frith thus do thinke, and as I thinke fo haue I faid,
wrytten, taught, and affirmed, and in my books
haue publifhed.* Vnder which fubfcription Fox
wryteth thus: *And when by no meanes he could be
perfuaded to recant thefe articles, neyther be brought*

Ibidem.

to beleeue, that this Sacrament is an article of faith,
                                                    he

he *vvas condemned by the Bishopp of London* , &c.

9.   Heere now we haue the whole caufe of
Iohn Frith, for which he would needs dy, vttered in his owne words, and whether this
were obftinacy or conftancy is not hard to
iudge. Fox confeffeth as now you haue heard,
that all means were vfed to recall him from
thefe opinions, and the Bifhopps fentence yt
felfe affirmeth the fame in many words, and
no leffe then 4. Bifhopps trauayled with him
to that end : and after his condemnation Fox
confeffeth moreouer, that they fent againe to
K. Henry to know his pleafure the fame day
he was burned, before they would fend him
to the fire ; all which being true, iudge yow
with what face Iohn Fox doth fo greuoufly
complayne in another place, * *of the lamentable*
death, and cruell handlinge of Iohn Frith fo learned and
excellent a yong man, &c. So he: and there is no
fhame in thefe mens wrytings or doings.

Fox pag.
955. col. 1.
num. 64.

* *pag. 948.*
col. 1. n. 18.

10.   The very truth is, that this yong man
being marryed, and fcarce 20. yeares old,
when he tooke vpon him by pride to be a patriarke or Satrapa amonge the new ghofpellers, as hath byn faid, and going forth of England, and turninge againe for aduancement
therof, was put into fuch a humor of vayne
glory, as he was ready to dy in the fire for any
thinge, efpecially being pricked thervnto exceedingly by his Maifter *Tyndall*, who partly
vpon the heate of herefie, and partly, as fome
men feeme to gather vpon his owne letters, to
retayne with himfelfe *Frithes* yonge wife (as

after yow ſhall ſee) ſtirred him vp exceedingly
by his ſaid letters, when he was in the Towar, to make him go to the fire. Some of
his ſpeaches yow ſhall heare recorded by Fox
himſelfe.

Tyndalls
vehement
incitements of
Frith to
go to the
fire for de-
fence of
his opi-
nions.

11. Sticke (ſaith Tyndall) at neceſſary things,
and remember the blaſphemyes of the enemyes of Chriſt, ſayinge they find none, but
that will abiure rather then ſuffer the extre-
mity; moreouer the death of them that come
againe after they haue once denied, though yt
be accepted with God and all that beleeue;
yet is yt not glorious, *&c.* And againe in the
ſame epiſtle: *God ſhall ſett out his truth by yow won-*
derfully, and worke for yow aboue all that your hart
can imagin; yea *and yow are not yet dead, though the*
hypocrits haue ſworne your death: Vna ſalus victis nul-
lam ſperare ſalutem, &c. Yt ſhall make God to

Fox *pag.*
986.

carry yow through thicke and thynne for his
truthes ſake, in ſpite of all the enemyes of his
truth, *&c.* Let not the perſuaſions of worldly
wiſdome beare rule in your hart, no though
they be your frends that counſell yow; Let
Bilney be a warninge to yow; let not their vi-
zards beguile your eyes; let not your body
faint, *&c.* Two haue ſuffered in *Antwerp in die*
Sancta Crucis, vnto the great glory of the ghoſpell; 4. at *Bruſſells* in Flanders; at *Roane* in
France they perſecute, and at *Paris* are 5. Doctors taken for the ghoſpell, ſo yow are not
alone, *&c.* Thus wrote *VVilliam Tyndall* vnto
Iohn Frith to ſtirre him vp to the fire in England, and laſt of all he addeth this perſuaſion:

Syr

Chap.11.
Friths
vvife con-
tent he
fhould be
burned.
pag. 987.

Syr your vvife is well content vvith the vvill of God, and vvould not for her fake haue the 'glory of God hindered, &c.

VVilliam Tyndall.

12. Vpon thefe and other like perfuafions tooke *Frith* the refolution before mentioned, to dy for opinions neuer held perhaps before him, by any fect or fort of men whatfoeuer: yet wryteth Iohn Fox thus of his condemnation: *VVhen no reafon* (faith he) *vvould preuayle againft the force and cruelty of his furious foes, he vvas condemned vpon the yeare of our Lord* 1533. But *Iohn Bale* addeth further: *Circundatus à pinguibus tauris Bafán, Londinenfi, Lincolnienfi, Vuintonienfi Epifcopis, & alijs antichrifti miniftris, Londini damnatur ad ignes conftantißimus Chrifti teftis, & exuritur. die* 4. *Iulij. Anno ætatis fuæ* 26. He being inuironed with ,, the fatt Bulles of *Bafan*, to witt the Bifhopps ,, of *London, Lincolne, VVinchefter*, and other mi- ,, nifters of antichrift, this moft conftant witt- ,, neffe of Chrift was condemned to the fire at ,, London, and was burned the fourth day of ,, Iuly 1533. and the 26. yeare of his age, vnder ,, K. Henry the eyght.

The fha-
meleffe
cenfure of
Fox and
Bale about
Frithes
condem-
nation.
Fox *pag. ibid.*
*Bal.Cent.*5.
fcript. Brit.

13. Thus do they wryte of him ; and yow may imagine with what truth or reafon, confidering his obftinacy and peruerfity. And yet one thinge would I haue yow to note more, which is, that notwithftandinge this yonge man *Frith* was fo refolute as yow haue heard, to dye, rather then to confeffe, that the reall prefence of Chrift was in the Sacrament, or

that

Io. Frith offereth to be a Lutheran about the reall presence, vvith a condition that vve vvill yeld somvvhat to him also.

Fox pag. 943. col. 1. num. 86.

that the beleeuing therof, yea or noe, was any article of faith, *yet offered he to Syr Thomas More* (faith Fox) *to admitt the opinion of Luther and friar Barnes for the said reall presence, so that the other would graunt that yt was not to be vvorshipped*; and this doth Fox testifie of him, cytinge for yt a Treatise wrytten by *Frith* and intituled: *The exile of Barnes against More,* and then Fox addeth further in the prayse of this conformity of *Frith: VVhich vvords* (faith he) *of this most meeke Martyr in Christ, yf they would take place in the seditions, diuisions & factions of these our dayes, with great ease and little labour men might be brought to vnity in this controuersie,* &c,

14. Behould heere the stability of Iohn Frith in his beleefe, and the wisdome of Iohn Fox in relatinge and approuinge the same, Frith hauing denyed before to beleeue the reall presence, and offered also to dy for the same, yet now is contented to admitt yt, yf we would yeld to take away all worshipp from yt; so as though he should graunt it to be the very true body, and bloud of our Sauior Christ, as both we and Luther do hould, togeather with his diuinity, which is inseparable; yet doth he not thinke yt worth the worshippinge; yea Fox that sheweth himselfe so earnest a Caluinist euery where, and so eager an enimy to the said reall presence, as in this his volume of Acts and Monuments appeareth, yet now is he content to prayse *Frith* for offeringe to yeld thervnto, and to confesse the true presence of Christ in the Sacrament, so we would graunt

not

not to honour or worshipp him therin; a most
fond and impious demaund. For yf Christ be
truly and really there, as he was vpon earth,
or is now in heauen, why should we not
worshipp him as well in the one place, as in
the other.

15.   Add thus much of these mens phrensie.
Now lett vs see of the rest that were burned
vnder K. Henry in this moneth with *Iohn
Frith*, and drawne heere, into Fox his Calendar to make vp the number of Saints, which
are six, and the first two in ranke are fetched
from Brussells in Flanders, where they were *Fox pag.* 798.
burned for Lutheranisme vpon the yeare
1523. to witt, six yeares after the beginninge
of Luthers doctrine. The first of them was
called *Henry Voes*, the second *Iohn Eske* both of *Henry Voes Iohn Eske* Apostata friars.
them Apostata friars of Luthers owne order,
and the former but of 24. yeares of age, yf we
beleeue Fox, *and yet* (saith he) *they stood stoutly to
yt, euen to the fiar yt selfe*; to witt, against Iohn
Fox his Religion, concerninge the reall presence, and diuers other points, and protesting
at their deathes, *that Luther had taught them nothing, but as Christ taught his disciples, vvhen he vvas
on earth.* Which Fox I hope will not confesse,
though he praise them neuer so much for
their stout standinge, and dyinge in the same.
These are riddles which are hard to solue, and
so I leaue both Fox and them.

16.   The third of this halfe dozen was *Andrew
Hewytt* a yonge man of 24. yeares apprentise
to a Taylor of London, named *VVarren* in
VVatling-

Andrew
Hevvyt an
apprentife
Taylor
holdeth as
Io. Frith
doth.

VVatlingstreet who being infected with herefy
at the fame tyme, that *Iohn Frith* was in the
tower, and fomewhat famous throughout
London for his difputing and writing againft
the Lord Chancelor, and the forfaid Bifhops
of Canterbury, *VVinchefter, Lincolne, London, and
Rochefter*, the apprentice thought yt a matter
of great glory, to hold with the faid *Frith* in his
opinions (they being neere of an age) yea and
to burne alfo with him for the fame, though
yet he knew not well (as appeareth) what his
opinions were; *for being called before the forfaid
Bishops and demaunded* (faith Fox) *vvhat he thought
as touchinge the Sacrament of the laft Supper? he*

Fox pag.
945. col. 2.
num. 17.

*anfwered; I beleeue as Iohn Frith doth. Then faid one
of the Bishops vnto him; doft thou not beleeue, that yt is
really the body of Chrift borne of the Virgin Mary? So,
faith he, do not I beleeue. And vvhy not, faith the Bifhopp? Becaufe* (faith he) *Chrift demaunded me not
to giue creditt rafhely to all men which fay*; behold
heere is Chrift and there is Chrift, for many
falfe Prophetts fhall arife vp faith the Lord.
Then certayne of the Bishoppes fmyled at him, &c.

17. Thus relateth Fox, and mifliketh much
that the Bifhopps fhould fmyle at fo graue an
anfwere. But who doth not fee how fond
and ridiculous an anfwere this of the yonge
Taylor was, efpecially before fo graue and
learned men, that for fo much as yt was for-
told, *that fome falfe Prophetts fhould arife, and fay
heere is Chrift, and there is Chrift*; ergo he would
not beleeue the reall prefence in the Sacrament, taught by the fcriptures & declared by
the

the Church: Which point notwithstandinge yow haue heard before, that *Iohn Frith* himselfe offered to beleeue, yf we would take away all worship from the same, so consonant be thes men to them selues. But let vs go forward. It followeth in Fox. *Then the Bishop asked Andrew Hewyt yf he would forsake his opinions; wherunto he answered, that he would do as Frith did, wherupō he was sent to the prison to Frith, & afterward they were caried together to the fiar.* So he, and addeth presently *the Bishops vsed* (saith he) *many persuasiōs to allure this good man from the truth to follow them, but he manfully persisting in the truth would not recant.* So Fox of this yong Taylors faith & cōfessiō, which yet depended (as yow see) vpon another mans direction, and conseqnently, whether this were pryde and pertinacy in him or noe, so obstinately to offer himselfe to death for the same, I leaue to euery discreet mans iudgment to consider. And so much of him.

Hevvyt vvill recāt yf Frith vvill.

Fox pag. ibid.

18.   There follow the last three of this ranke burned vnder K. Henry the 8. who are *Antony Parson, Robert Testwood, & Henry Filmer,* all *VVindesor* men: the first a Parish Priest, the second a musition of the Church, the third an artificer of the towne, all condemned and burned for malitious speaches and blasphemous doctrine against the blessed Sacrament of the Altar, and other articles. Thy were condemned vpon the statute of six articles, by a Iury in *VVindesore* in the yeare of Christ 1543. as Fox setteth yt downe in his Calendar, and their most vild, despitefull & raylinge speeches are to be seene

Antony Parson. Robert Testvvood. Henry Filmer. burned at VVindesore. 1543.

in

in their endightements, regiſtred by Fox himſelfe, and are not fitt to be repeated here. And beſides, this *Antony* the Apoſtata prieſt ſaid to the Biſhop and other iudges; *yow are not only theeues but murderers, &c.* And then he paſſed ſo farre againſt the inſtitution it ſelfe of the bleſſed Sacrament, that he ſeemed to take yt wholy away, and to euacuate Chriſts ordinance therin, for thus wryteth Fox of him:

Fox pag. iiii. col. 2. num. 26.

After he had preached and commended the ſcripture, callinge yt the vvord of God, he ſaid as followeth: This is the word, this is the bread, this is the body of Chriſt, &c. And further he ſaid: *That Chriſt ſittinge with his diſciples tooke bread, bleſſed and broke yt, and gaue yt to his diſciples ſayinge, take and eat yt, This is my body; and vvhat is this to vs, but to take the ſcripture of God, and breake yt to the people.*

The moſt blaſphemous hereſie of Antony Perſons.

19.   Thus farre Fox out of *Antony Perſons* indightement, wherby yow ſee, that he maketh the inſtitution of the Sacrament, nothing els, *but a commandement to preach, and breake the vvord to the people,* which is a moſt impious and blaſphemous hereſie, euacuatinge the whole inſtitution of the Venerable Sacrament; and yet this infamous hereſie did the madman offer to defend by the ſcriptures, and to dye for yt alſo, as he did: For thus wryteth Iohn Fox of his finall anſwere to the iudges: *To this* (ſaith he) *Antony anſwered and ſaid, I vvilbe tryed by God, and his holy vvord, and by the true Church of Chriſt, vvhether this be hereſie or noe, vvherof yow haue endighted me this day:* So as Antony denyed not this doctrine for which he was endighted, but only

only denyed that it was herefie. And this may
be another fect now different from all others:
to witt, as well from *Lutherans, Zwinglians, Ca-*
rolftadians, Oecolampadians, and Caluinifts recyted
before in the third Chapter about this controuerfie; as from all others; For that this
man, as yow fee, farre differeth from them all,
and hath a new diuife, of his owne interpreting the meaning of thofe words, *This is my bo-*
dy, in a different fenfe from all others hitherto: to witt, that the meaning is: *This fcripture is*
my body broken vnto yow; For which diuife notwithftandinge he went to the fire, and fo did
the other two that were burned with him,
I meane the fingar and the townefman of
VVindefore. Which three Martyrs, when they
came to the fire fide, the potts did walke fo
merily amonge them, the one drinkinge and
pledginge another, as Fox confefleth, that
men faid they died dronken, *vvhen as they vvere*
(faith he) *no otherwife drunke*; *then the Apoftles*
were, when the people faid they were full of new vvyne.
But yet by Fox his leaue, he muft confefle that
there was a great differéce in this his defence,
and that other of *S. Peter* when he defended
thofe firft Chriftians. For that *S. Peter* excufed the matter fayinge, that they could not be
drunke, for that they had not drunken that
day at all; which yet Fox his Martyrs had
done very liberally, both in the prifon before
they came out, and alfo at the fire fide, as
himfelfe confefleth.

20. And yt is to be remembred, that Fox in
his

VVindfor
martyrs
tipplinge
at the fire.

Fox pag.
1113.

Act. 2.

his former editions had adioyned a fourth companion to this crew of VVindefore Martyrs: to witt, *Iohn Marbecke* organ-player of that Church, and had fett downe diuers particulars of his death, as namely how merily he went to the fire; but *Marbecke* being found many yeares afterward to be aliue, and Fox called vpon & iefted at for the fame by diuers wryters, and amongft the reft by *Alanus Copius*, who cyteth his owne words out of his Latyn Acts and Monuments, he was forced in this his laft edition to excufe yt, but how trow yow? Truly with the modefty and humility which fuch men are wont to do. Yow fhall heare how he beginneth. *Be yt knowen* (faith he) *protefted, denounced and notified, to all and fingular fuch carpers, wranglers, exclamers, deprauers, with the whole brood of whifperers, raylers, quarrell pickers, corner-creepers, fault-finders and fpider-catchers, &c.* This was his exordium, and therby yow may fee the grauity of the man. But after this preface, the fubftance of his defence is that he was deceaued; and the like defence muft he make in many other fuch particulars, wherin he fetteth downe one thinge for another, and men martyred for men aliue; which defence yet, when yt is fincerely vfed, I for my part am very eafy to accept, for that I know hiftoriographers may haue many falfe informations. And fo yf yow marke, yow fhall fcarce euer find me to vrge this point againft Fox of falfe relatinge one thinge for another, for that yt may be more an other mans fault then his, albeit

Iohn Marbecke orgã-player of VVindefore a liue Martyr.

Alan. Cop. dial. 6. pag. 697.

Fox pag. XII4.

albeit his alfo in fome degree, for not being
more wary and diligent; but my cheefe complaint againft him is of willfull error, which
he could not choofe but know to be falfe
when he wrote them, wherof yow haue a
great number in this booke & others, which
lyes cannot any wayes be excufed, wherof
yow fhall fee aboue 120. in one Chapter af- *Cap. 15.*
terward, taken out of leffe then three leaues
of his Acts and Monuments, and therby
perceaue the creditt that may be gyuen to
Iohn Fox his narrations, and this may fuffice
for the tyme of K. Henry.

Of Foxian Martyrs and Confeffors in this moneth vnder Qu. Mary. §. 2.

21.   The fectaryes that were punifhed vnder
Q.Mary, may be diuided into three rankes according to the tyme fet downe by Fox, wherin they weare punifhed: to witt, the yeare of
Chrift 1555. 1556. and 1558. (for of 1557. he
hath none): Of the firft ranke there are 15. of
the fecond 12. and of the third 8. And of all
thefe is the Captaine and ringleader *Iohn Brad-*
ford preacher-martyr, whofe feftiuall day of martyrdome is afigned by Fox vpon the fixt day
of Iuly, of the forfaid yeare 1555. and he endeauoureth fo highly to honour this his renowned Martyr and Preacher, as he beftoweth
aboue a hundred columnes in fettinge forth
his Actes and Gefts, but we fhall briefly tell
yow what he was, & how he liued and died,
                                                    and

and for what caufe; and that fhalbe fufficient
for difcreett men, that are not ledd by thefe
fooleryes of Fox his vaine oftentation.

22.   Iohn Bradford then, accordinge to Fox
his owne relation, being borne at *Manchefter* in
Lancafhire was firft a feruingman vnto *Syr*
Iohn Harrington knight, but afterward in K. Edward his dayes leauing him and his feruice, he
being made a Proteftant, went to ftudy in
Cambridge, with defire to enter into the miniftery, where he ftudied, and pleafed all men
fo well, that within one whole yeare (faith
Iohn Fox) after he had bin there, the vniuerfity did giue him the degree of *Maifter of art*, &c.
So he, and by this youe may vnderftand his
deep learninge, for that prefently vpon this
he was perfuaded by Friar *Martyn Bucer* (with
whome he was very familiar) to become a
Preacher; vnto which perfuafion when *Brad-*
ford anfwered, that he was vnable through
want of learninge, *Bucer* (faith Fox) *vvas vvont*
to reply: yf thou haue not fine manchyet bread, yet giue
the poore people barly bread, &c.

23.   To this counfell Bradford obeyed, and
began to breake his barly bread, (if it were fo
good) vnto the people, and for that he was yet
a meere lay man, and could not preach without fome Ecclefiafticall order and degree, accordinge to the lawes of England then in
force; *Doctor Ridley* (faith Fox) *that vvorthy Bifhop*
of London, called him to take the degree of deaco, accor-
dinge to the order, that then was in the Church of Eng-
land: but for that this order was not vvithout fome fuch
                                                            abufe

Fox *pag.*
1456.
The ftory
of Iohn
Bradford
proteftant
preacher
burned
vnder Qu.
Mary.

„

Fox *ibid.* ¶

Bradfords
barly
bread.

Fox *ibid.*

abuse, as to the which Bradford would not consent, the Bishopp then was content to order him then deacon, vvithout any abuse euen as he desired. Lo heere Bradford a precision, and a famous preacher vpon one yeares study only, and yet Fox must giue vs leaue not to beleeue him, in that he saith *Bishop Ridley* was content to yeld to order him deacon, accordinge to the fashion that himselfe desired, and not according to the Ecclesiasticall English lawes then in force, this being the fourth yeare of *K. Edward* his raigne.

Bradford a precisiō.

24. Yow may remember, how *Ridley* and *Cranmer* mortified *Hooper* B. of *Glocester* before, and forced him to take his degree of Bishopricke according to the Protestant law, and not to the Puritan, though both Dudley then Earle of Warwicke, and the King himselfe wrote in his fauour to the contrary, & consequently yt was not probable, that Ridley would so much humble himselfe to this newfangled Bradford, to order him after a peculiar new fashion, diuised by himselfe, and yf he did, he was a great dissembler to haue diuers fashions of makinge deacons, one accordinge to the lawe, and another according to fauour, and yt seemed they had great need of Preachers in those dayes, that would so hastily aduaunce to the pulpitt of Paules a man of so litle study, and learninge, as this Bradford may be presumed to haue bin with one yeares study in Cambridge only, after the life of a seruingman, and being yet but a deacon as may appeare by Fox, for that he neuer mentioneth

See before in Febr. die 23.

M. Ridley made Bradford Deacon after a nevv priuate fashion.

E   that

that he was made Minifter, but rather prefently vpon his deacon-fhipp taken after the new fafhion, he was made prebend, and preacher of S. Paules, *vvhere fharply* (faith Fox) *he opened and reproued finne, fweetly he preached Chrift crucifyed, pithily he impugned herefies, and errors, earneftly he perfuaded to good life, &c.* This is Fox his Rhetoricke in Bradfords exaltation.

Fox *ibid.*

25. But after three yeares preachinge K. Edward dyinge, and Q. Mary fucceedinge to the crowne, he was called to accompt for his doctrine, that he had fo fweetly & pithily preached, but efpecially for certayne feditious letters that he had wryten, and did wryte daylie abroad into all fhyres, exhorting men to conftancy, as he called yt, or rather to difobedience againft the Paftors, and Gouernors of the prefent Church of England; the firft occafion of his apprehenfion was, for that vpon the 13. day of Auguft in the firft yeare of the raigne of Q. Mary, Doctor Burne (afterward B. of Bath) preaching at Paules Croffe, had a naked dagger throwne at him by an heretike of the audience, and all the whole people allmoft fett in fedition and vprore, and for that Bradford was found to ftand neere to the preachers backe, expectinge (as was thought) fome fuch euent, to terrifie the Queene and counfell withall; he was accufed afterward as being priuy thervnto, efpecially for that he tooke vpon him to fpeake and pacifie the people for that prefent, therby to fhew his creditt, and authority with that crewe:

Bradford prefumed to be priuy to a very feditious act at Paules Croffe.

VVhome

VVhome (faith Fox) *as foone as the people fawe to be-*
ginne to fpeake vnto them, fo glad they were to heare
him, that they cried with a great fhout; Bradford, Brad-
ford, God faue they life Bradford, &c. So Fox, and
then addeth, that a little after as he was going
home, a gentleman of that crew meeting him
faid thefe words: *Ah Bradford, Bradford, thou haft*
faued him, that vvill helpe to burne the; I gaue the his
life: yf yt were not for thee, I would haue runne him
thorow vvith my fword, &c.

26. Thus wryteth Fox: wherby yow may
fee his creditt with that feditious company of
new ghofpellers, & with what fpiritt of mo-
deftie they began, & then Fox addeth further,
that Bradford was fent to the Towre vpon
thefe fufpitions, & afterward deliuered thence
to the Kings Bench in Southworke, and after
that againe he was fent to the counter in the
Poultrey, and in all thefe places for the fpace
of two yeares and more, he was moft gently,
and courteoufly handled, and fuffred both to
talke, write, fpeake, teach and preach, and oftentymes alfo to go abroad vntill yt was perceaued, what great hurt he did by his hereticall hypocrifie. *In vvhich places* (faith Fox) *for*
the tyme he did remayne prifoner, he preached twice a   The hurt-
day continually vnleffe ficknes hundred him; where al-   full liber-
fo the Sacrament was often miniftred, and fuch reforte   tie that
of good folks vvent daylie to his lecture, that commonly   Bradford
his chamber vvas vvell nigh filled therwith, &c. Thus   had to per-
farre Fox, and by this yow may vnderftand,   uert men
whether fuch ftrayttnes were vfed to hereti-   in prifon,
call prifoners in Q. Maryes dayes, as other-   Fox *ibid.*

where Fox would make vs beleeue; yt had
byn better for thousandes if greater vigilance
had byn vsed.

27.   But to say a word or two of the conferences had with this Bradford in prison both
before and after his condemnation, yow must
note, (and so doth Stow also in his story) that
diuers learned men, and some Bishops among
the rest, repayred to him in prison with desire
to saue him, yf yt had byn possible, and this
partly, for that he seemed to be.of a more softe
and myld nature, then many of his fellowes,
and partly for that his learninge in diuinity
being knowne to be very litle, as by the small
tyme of his study may appeare; yt was hoped
that by conference, he might haue byn reclaymed, and brought to see the truth, but the desperate humour of hereticall pride, selfeliking
and selfe persuasion had so preoccupyed his
mynd, and puffed him vp with vayne glory
and conceats of his owne assurance, in what
soeuer he said or imagined to be so, as there
was nothinge would enter contrarie to that.
3. or 4. appearances he made before the Chancelour, and other Bishops before his condemnation; and after the same may others went
to him, & had seuerall speaches with him in
prison, as namely *Doctor Harding, Doctor Harpsf-
field, Doctor VVeston,* two Spanish religious men,
the one *Alphonsus de Castro,* the other the Kings
Confessor, & besids these, two Bishops went
also in their turne, *Doctor Heath* Archbishopp
of Yorke, and *Doctor Day* Bishopp of Chichester;

*Stow anno
1555.Iulij 1.*

Diuers
confereces
had vvith
Bradford
before and
after his
condem-
nation.

ster; and all these conferences are sett out by Fox after his manner, makinge alwayes the speaches of Catholiks to be abrupt, baren, or impertinent, and to begin commonly with (why)though there be no neede of interrogation at all, as throughout his whole narration of examinations, and conferences, yow may see, and besides his narration of the matter in wrytinge, Iohn layeth foorth also the whole substance in seuerall printed tables to the viewe of the eye, and euer Bradford is made to be victor ouer the Bishops, and others that conferred with him, though his answers were neuer so simple, & absurd, wherof I shall note only some fewe in this place, out of this last talke with the Bishopps, wherby yow may make a ghesse of the rest, and what was in the man indeed, whome Fox so highly admireth and extolleth.

28. First then he recounteth the said two Bishops courteous repayre vnto him in the counter, after he was condemned, not vpon any commandement(as them selfes told him) but only vpon meere good will, and curtesie, & further Fox telleth how they would haue had Bradford sitt downe before them, which he refusinge, themselues stood also on foote, making him to be couered all the tyme of the conference. They beganne (saith Fox) with this question, *how he was so certaine of his saluation, and of his religion?* by which question we may perceaue, that Bradford did vse much to bragg of this singular assurance, that he had of the

Fox *pag.* 1467.

The repaire of the BB. of Yorke and Chicester to cōferre vvith Bradford.

E 3   right

right courfe he was in, which he faid *vvas fo
cleare and euident to him that there could be no more
doubt therof, then vvhether the funne did fhyne in a
fayre day*, for fo he had aunfwered fome fewe
daies before vnto Doctor Harpsfield, who af-

Fox pag. 1466.

kinge him (faith Fox) *vvhat yf yow be deceaued
Maifter Bradford?* he anfwered, *vvhat yf yow fhould
fay the funne did not fhyne now? vvhich did fhyne cleerly through the vvyndow*, fo as this man made yt as
cleare, that he was in the right way, as that
the Sunne fhined in a faire day, and this belike
was the caufe why the Bifhops beganne with
this queftion, *how he came to fo great a certainty*,
whervnto (faith Fox) he anfwered them thus,
*I am certayne of my faluation & religion by the Scrip-
tures*, but when they pofed him further, how
he could be fure of Scriptures themfelues, and
of their true meaning without the teftimony
of the Church; he had no other fhifte, but to
runne to the affurance of his owne fpirite, telling them, that albeit he receaued the knowledge of the Scriptures by the teftimony of

Ioan. 4.

the Church (as thofe of the Citty of Sichar
did the notice of Chrift by the woman from
the well), yet that when he once had them,
then could he vfe them well ynough, for vn-
derftanding them, and for fhew heerof, when
a litle after he had occafion to interprett fome

Bradfords affurance of his right cour-fe.

peeces of Scriptures, he did yt fo abfurdly as a
man myght well fee, how much myght be
buylded vpon the affurance of that his particular and priuat fpirite, as for example, among
other places, he tooke vpon him to proue by
                                                            Scripture

Scripture that the Pope was Antichrist, and
cited for yt only, those words of the Apostle
to the Thessalonians, *that Antichrist shall sitt in*
the Temple of God, &c. Which though it prooue
nothinge, as yow see, for that we deny not,
but that Antichrist when he commeth, shall
sitt in the Temple of God, yea, and pretende
to be God him selfe, (which no Popes euer
did or shall do); yet to Bradford the allegation
of this place seemed much to the purpose, and
to Iohn Fox, that admireth all which the
other vttered, it appeared so full a proofe, as he
maketh this note in the margent: *The Pope pro-*
ued to be Antichrist by Scriptures. But this proofe
(as yow see) standeth only vpon Bradfords
interpretation, which interpretation is not
only not conforme to any ancient Fathers exposition whatsoeuer, but is manifestly also
contrary to the text yt selfe, where immediatly before the words alleaged *that he shall sitt in*
the Temple of God; are these other wordes, *extol-*
letur supra omne quod dicitur Deus, aut quod colitur,
that Antichrist (when he cometh) shalbe ex-
tolled aboue all that is called God, or that is
worshipped for God, so as he shall not call
him Gods seruant (as the Pope doth) nor the
seruant of his seruantes but chiefe God himselfe, which no Pope, as is said, euer did or
will, and consequently these words cannot
possibly agree to the Pope, and yet forsooth
the spiritt of Bradford, that cannot erre or
be deceaued, doth expound yt so, and therby
yow see the certaynety of his spirit.

29. After this againe he went about to per-
swade the two Bishops, that he agreed with
them, and with their Church in substance of
faith and beliefe, and consequencly might be
saued with them, notwithstanding his deniall
of two articles, for which only he said he was
condemned: to witt, *Transubstantiation, and that
the euill men doe not receaue the body of Christ*, when
they communicat, which two articles Brad-

Bradford
holdeth
him selfe
to be of
the same
Church
vvith the
Bishops.

ford affirmed not to appertayne to the substance of faith, or foundation of Christ, & consequently that he was vniustly cast out of the
Church for them, for so much as he firmely
belieued all the articles of the creed with
them: wheruunto when the Bishops smylinge

Fox *ibid.*

replyed sayinge, *Yea? is this your diuinity? Bradford
answered, no*; *yt is Paules vvhich saith, that yf men*

1. Cor. 3.
vers. 12.

*hold the fundation Christ, though they buyld vpon him
strawe, and stubble, yet they shalbe saued*; So he,
wherby yow see that this great learned clarke
would proue by S. Paul, that both Protestāts,
and all other sectaries, that in words do professe to belieue all the Articles of the Creed
(though ech one in seuerall sense to himselfe)
shalbe saued together with Catholiks, & that
all these our contentions with them, & other
sectaryes are but strawe, and stubble, & touch
not the foundation of Christ at all. This was
his spiritt, and do yow thinke that this spiritt
could be deceaued, or will our English Protestants at this day, allow this spiritt', or ioyne
with Bradford in this paradox? I know they
will not, and would be ashamed to interpret
the

the place of S. Paul in that fenfe, for fo much
as yt is euident, that he meaneth of the ftraw
and ftubble of workes, and not doctrine, but
lett vs go forward.

30.   After the Bifhops had fmiled as hath byn
faid, he of Chichefter for refutation of this folly, alleaged againft him the authority and example of Martyn Luther, that did excommunicate Zwinglius, and his followers, for their
difference from him about the reall prefence,
and the place was read, where Luther doth
denounce them *hæreticos, & alienos ab Ecclefia Dei,*
heretiks, and aliens caft out from the Church
of God, and yet doth both Zwinglius, Oecolampadius, and the reft, profeffe to belieue the
articles of the Creed, as much as Luther or
Bradford did, wherto he anfwered; *My Lord,*
vvhat Luther wryteth, as yow much paffe not, no more
do I in this cafe; So he, adding notwithftanding
prefently, *and yet* (faith he) *do I thinke affuredly*
that they vvere, and are Gods children, and Saints with
him in heauen, to wit with Luther: vpon which
words as of great moment, Fox maketh this
note in the margét, *Maifter Bradford hangeth not*
vpon Luther, Zwinglius, or Oecolampadius, and yet ac-
compteth them good men; but heere I would afke
both Fox, and his holy Martyr Bradford (for
fo he entituleth him ouer all his pages) whether Martyn Luther, rayfed vp by God for fo
great a worke, as they hold, were not as fure
of his fpiritt, and right courfe therby as Bradford was of his? and yf they hold him (as heere
they fay) for *a child of God, and a Saint now vvith*
                                          him

Fox *pag.*
1468.
Bradford
careth
not vvhat
Luther
holdeth.

him in glory , how doth not Bradford paſſe much vvhat he vvrote *in this controuerſie of the reall preſence,* and yf he hold Zwinglius alſo, and Oecolampadius for Children of God, & fellow Saints vvith Luther in heauen , vvho vvere ſo contrary to him in doctrine vpon earth, and whome ſo earneſtly he cenſured *for heretiks and aliens caſt out from Chriſts trew Church;* then may all ſectaryes go to heauen togeather, and ſo may Catholiks and Proteſtants in like manner by Bradfords rule , for that each part profeſſeth to hold the articles of the Creed ; and yf this be ſo; then doth Bradford ſhew himſelfe a very ſimple fellow, that vvill burne for matters of ſo ſmall moment; heare vvhat he told the Biſhops , *Becauſe* (ſaith he) *I did deny Tranſubſtantiation , and the vvicked to receaue Chriſts body in the Sacrament , therfore am I condemned and excommunicate, &c.* But I vvould aske of him, yf he diſſented only in theſe two points from the Papiſts, & agreed in all other; & that theſe two did not touch the ſubſtance or foundation of Chriſts faith, as before he affirmed out of S. Paul; And yf Luther, Zwinglius , and Oecolampadius that had greater controuerſies betweene them , then theſe, could go notwithſtanding all three iointly to heauen, and be Saints togeather in Gods glory, as a litle before he affirmed; yf all this I ſay be true, then how great folly vvas yt in Bradford, to ſtand ſo obſtinatly vpon the deniall of theſe two articles that ſo litle imported him, **yea to go to the fire for the defence** , vvas he
                                                            no t

Bradford vvent to the fyre for a fancie of his ovvne.

not deceaued thinke yow in this ? or could this courſe be ſo certayne of ſaluation, as that the Sunne ſhined in a fayre day ? let Fox diſſolue this riddle yf he can; me thinketh that the folly is greater then that of Frith before, who would needs burne, rather then acknowlege that it was a neceſſary point to beleeue, or not beleeue that Chriſt is really in the Sacrament.

31. About vvhich point, for that yt vvas the principall in controuerſie at that tyme, yow will aſke me perhaps, that for ſo much as Bradford affirmeth heere ſo often, that he dyed for thes other two articles alone, vvhat did he thinke of the ſaid reall preſence ? yow ſhall heare him ſpeake himſelfe, and ſo may iudge therof; for yt is not cleare vnto me vvhat he thought of that point. For vvhen Doctor Harpſfield vpon the 26. of February conferred with him, and heard him repeat ſo often and confidently on the one ſyde, that he vvas no leſſe aſſured to go to heauen, then that the Sunne ſhined at midday, and further that he vvas no leſſe *certayne that his death ſhould be pleaſinge vnto the Lord*, (for ſo are his owne words), & on the other ſyde, that *he died only for thoſe two articles before named;* the Doctor ſaid vnto him. *Yow agree not with vs in the real preſence. &c.* Bradford: *How yow beleeue yow know, for my parte I confeſſe a preſence of whole Chriſt God & man;* And againe a little after, *I confeſſe a preſence, and a true preſence, but to the faith of the receauer;* And yet further in an other place to the Lord Chan-

Vvhat Bradford thought of the reall preſence.

Fox *pag.*
1463.
& 1466.

Chancelour, *I neuer denyed nor taught, but that to
faith, whole Chriſt, body and bloud was as preſent , as
bread & wyne to the due receauer,* by which places
ſome man vvould thinke that Bradford did
hold , that all faithfull men going to the communion, did receaue both bread and vvyne,
and the reall body and bloud of our Sauiour
withall according to Luthers opinion;yet according to his owne ſpeaches,and expoſitions
in other places, he ſeemeth rather to agree
with Caluyns fiction , in imagininge a reall
preſence by faith,and not a bare figure only or
type, as Zwinglius , and Oecolampadius did
hold ; but yet by other his ſpeaches againe,
which you haue heard vttered to the Biſhops,
he would not ſeeme to diſſent much in this
point of reall preſence from the Catholiks, yf
a man may take him at his word, in that he ſo
often repeateth , that they condemned him
only for denyinge two articles, to witt Tran-
ſubſtantiatiõ, & that euery man receaueth not
the body of Chriſt, wherby yt may ſeeme that
in all others points and namely the reall preſence he agreed with them : but in very deed
my opiniõ is,that the ſimple fellow knew not
well wherin he did agree, and wherin he did
diſſent from them in many points, & no maruaile, he hauinge byn a ſeruinge man ſo late
ThatBrad- before , and made firſt a Maiſter of art vpon
ford had one yeares ſtudy only, and then a preacher, &
no time to
be learned. in haſt miniſter, yf euer he were miniſter,ſo as
he had litle tyme to learne, and digeſt matters
of controuerſie well, and the moſt parte of his
two

two yeares imprifonment, was fpent in wrytinge longe letters to his Proteftant brethren,
and fifters abroad, wherin he tooke great delight, as may appeare by the large volume of
his epiftles fett downe by Fox, wherby as in a
glaffe, yow may fee the mans vayne glorious
fpirit, in dilatinge himfelfe in large difcourfes
and impertinent citations of Scriptures. But
to returne to his conference with the Bifhops,
do you thinke that he meant truly, & fincerely, when he faith, that he belieued all the articles of the Creed, as the Catholiks do? no
truly, for yf yow come to examine the matter
in particular, you fhall heardly find either him
or his fellowes, thorowly to agree with vs
in one & the fame beliefe of any one of thofe
articles, as learnedly yow may fee examined,
and proued by Maifter William Raynolds in
his booke intituled *Caluino-turcifmus*, vvhofe
particular butte and fcope is to fhew, that the
Proteftāts of our dayes haue peruerted all the
faid articles of the Creed, & do belieue no one
of them intyrely, without corruptiō or alteration, fpott of herefie or infidelity. And this he
declareth as a man that had byn a preacher of
that fyde, and had read all their books, and
knew all their fecrett driftes, and meanings.

32. And for example of this, yf yow would
haue asked Iohn Bradford how he belieued
that article, *Credo Ecclefiam Catholicam*, I beleeue
the Catholike Church, you fhould haue feene
him differ from vs prefently in the meaninge,
and vnderftandinge therof: for wheras we
toge-

together with the ancient Fathers, do inter-
prete that Catholike Church, to be the vniuersall visible Christian Church throughout
euery age, he will runne presently (as he
doth) to an obscure vnknowne Church, that

Hovv
Bradfords
Church
required
peculiar
eyes, or
spectacles
to be seene
vvith all.
Fox pag.
1468.

eyther is not visible at all, or requyreth a certayne kynd of peculiar eyes to see yt. For so
he answereth to the Bishops that obiected the
obscurity of his Church, *The fault* (saith he) *why
the Church is not seene of you, is not because the Church
is not visible, but because your eyes are not cleare ynough
to see yt.* Vpon which speach Fox maketh this
graue note in the margin. *The true Church is visible, and euer hath byn, but euery man hath not eyes to
see yt.* So Iohn, whose peculiar eyes or spectacles were needfull to spye out his Church.

33.   But now against this shifte of Bradford
& Fox, the Bishop of Yorke alleaged a cleere

Aug. cont.
epist. fun-
dam. c. 4.

place of *S. Augustine*, where he giuinge a rule,
how to know the true Catholike Church
,, against the heretiks and sectaryes of his tyme,
,, that ranne to their owne hidden Churches of
,, elect people, as Protestants do, saith, *Multa
,, sunt quæ in Ecclesiæ gremio me iustißimè tenent, tenet
,, consensio populorum, atque gentium, &c.* There are
,, many things which most iustly do hold me in
,, the lapp of the knowne Cath. Church: first
,, doth hold me the consent of people and na-
,, tions, that haue byn conuerted vnto yt, then
,, doth hold me the authority therof, begunne
,, with miracles, nourished with hope, increased
,, with charity, confirmed with antiquity: mo-
,, reouer doth hold me the succession of Priests,
euen

euen from the feate of Peter the Apoftle him- „
felfe, to whome our Lord after his refurre- „
ction, commended his fheepe to be gouerned „
vntill the prefent Bifhop that gouerneth that „
Sea, at this tyme, and laftly the very name of „
Catholike Church doth hold me, vvhich „
name not vvithout caufe, this only Church „
amonge fo many herefies hath fo peculiarly „
gotten to herfelfe, that vvheras all heretiks „
would gladly be called Catholiks, yet yf a „
ftraunger fhould come into any towne, and „
aske whether a man may go to a Catholike „
Church (to heare feruice) no heretike will „
dare to fhew eyther his Church, or his houfe „
for him to repayre vnto, &c.

34. Thus faith *S. Auguftine.* Now let vs heare Bradfords
fhifting
of the
vvords
of S. Au-
guftine.
Bradfords anfwere. My Lord (faith he) thefe
words of *S. Auguftine* make as much for me, as
for yow, although I might anfwere that all
thefe things yf they had byn fo firme, as yow
make them, might haue byn alleaged againft
Chrift & his Apoftles, for there was the law,
and the ceremonyes confented on by the
whole people, confirmed with miracles, antiquity, and continuall fucceffion of Bifhops
from *Aarons* tyme vntill that prefent. So he,
and do yow confider what accompt this fellow maketh of *S. Auguftines* proofe, againft the
heretiks of his tyme, and Fox alloweth this
euafion well by this note in his margent, *An-*
tiquity (faith he) *fucceßion of Priefts, the name Ca-* Fox ibid.
tholike, all this might be obiected againft Chrift and his
Apoftles by the Scribes and Pharifees. But I would
aske

aske both Fox and his Martyr, how the conuersion of Nations and Gentils heere mentioned, could agree to the Iewes Church that
dealt not with Gentils; as also the word *Catholike*, or vniuersall, seing that yt was but a
Church of that one seuerall nation only? I
world aske also, how the consent of all Nations, or their approbation of the Iewish Sinagoge; could with any reason be obiected
by the Scribes and Pharisees against Christ &
his Apostles? for so much as the Nations and
Gentils did not approue the Iewish Sinagoge,
nor entered into yt, as they did afterward into the Christian Church: and when Bradford
hath aunswered to these demaunds, then will
yow see how wyse a man he was, and whether he was as sure of his course, as that the
Sunne did shyne at noone tyde.

35.   But to go forward yet a litle further in
the examination of *S. Augustines* place, yow
must note the subiect that he handleth, & to
what end he brought the arguments, and
proofes, which was, to shew the differéce betweene Christian Churches (his question was
not with the Sinagoge) that is to say how, &
by what signes a man may discerne the true
Catholike Church, from the conuenticles of
heretiks, and albeit the place alleaged be directed particularly against the Manichyes
Church, yet doth the arguments hold against
all hereticall Sinagoges, *for that none of them
haue this generall consent of Nations, and succeßion of
Bishops, and other proprietyes heere alleaged*, wher-
                                                    fore

fore S. Auguſtine in the ſame place concludeth thus : *Iſta ergo* , &c. *Theſe moſt cleare bandes
therfore being ſo many , and ſo great , do hold me
in the Catholique Church , but with yow there is none
of theſe , but only promiſing that yow haue the truth,*
&c. ſo he. And to whatſoeuer particular congregation or Church of Sectaries theſe particulars ſhalbe applied, they will preſently trye
out the truth, and ſhew that yt can not be the
Catholique Church. Wherfore to returne to
our Caſe againe, the Archbiſhop preſſed him,
to anſwere to ſome particulars, ſaying , *But
what ſay yow to S. Auguſtine, where is your Church,
that hath the conſent of people and nations conuerted
vnto yt?* Bradford : *Euen all people and nations that
be Gods people, haue conſented with me , and I with
them in the doctrine of faith.* Do yow ſee this euaſi-
ſion? And might not the Manichies , Donatiſts , or any of other ſects haue anſwered the
ſame vnto *S. Auguſtine,* that all people, and nations that be of God (that is to ſay of their
owne ſect) haue côſented with them, & they
with them againe? And is not this a fooliſh
circle or euaſion? Who ſeeth not the vanitye
therof? & yet forſooth this man was as ſure &
certaine, that he could not be deceaued, as he
was that the Sunne could not chooſe but
ſhyne, when it did ſhyne, which kind of ſträge
confidence , or rather phreneticall preſumption Fox doth ſo highly commend, as he maketh this note in the margen : *Bold confidence,
and hope of Gods words and promiſe, ſeemeth ſtrange
among them which are not exerciſed in mortifica-*

F   *tion.*

tion. And by this you may iudge of them both.

36.   Wherfore to fay no more of this man or matter, he being found to be fo obstinate, and willfull, as no meanes of reafon would preuayle vvith him, he vvas finally burned in Smithfield: and there vvas burned vvith him at the fame tyme an apprentice of 19. yeares old named *Iohn Leafe*, that could neyther vvryte nor read; feruant to one Humfray Gaudy tallow Chandelour of the Parifh of Chrift Church in London, which ignorant yonge man, was fo forward and franticke in herefie, as being oftentymes called before the Bifhop of London, conferred, and difputed withall, could neuer be brought to yeald any one iote, but would defend his opinions to death. *The Bifhop* (faith Fox) *propounding the faid articles vnto him, as before, affayinge by all manner of wayes to reuoke him, found him the fame man ftill, &c.* And after other replyes made by the Bifhopp, mouinge him to returne to the vnity of the Church, he with a great courage of fpiritt (faith Fox) anfwered againe in thefe words: *My Lord yow call my opinion herefie, it is the true light of the vvord of God. And repeatinge againe the fame he profeffed, that he vvould neuer forfake his ftayed and vvell grounded opinion, vvhile the breath fhould be in his body, &c.* Thus wryteth Fox of his Tallow chandelour apprentice, but how grounded this boyes opinions could be, yt is eafy for euery difcreete man to iudge, confidering his learninge. Fox alfo addeth for his further prayfe and conftancy, that the Bifhop fending

Fox *pag.* 1447.

Iohn Leafe apprentice to a chandelour burned vvith Bradford.

Fox *ibid.*

to him his forefaid opinions and articles in
wrytinge (which were the ordinary Zwinglian opinions) he not being able to wryte
with pen, tooke out a pyn, and prickinge his
finger, befprinkled the whole paper which
bloud, fendinge the fame backe as fealed therwith to the Bifhop ; and by this yow may remember, vvhat vve haue vvrytten before in
the Chapter of hereticall pertinacity. Now
we fhall profecute the reft that follow in this
moneth.

An obfti-
nate defpe-
rate act of
a chădelors
boy.

Suprà c.4

37.   A dozen or 13. more do remayne of the
forefaid yeare 1555. vvherof the firft feauen
are thefe that follow, *Margery Pulley* vviddow
of the Parifh of Peppingbury in Kent, burned
at Tunbridge for vvillfull ftandinge in diuers
herefies; *VVilliam Minge* an Apoftata Prieft, that
being committed for diuers like offences, died
in prifon at Maydftone in Kent the fame
yeare, and for that caufe is regiftred for a Martyr by Fox in his Calendar, though in his
★ Acts and Monuments, he is content to accept him only for a Confeffor, *Richard Hooke*
Craftefman burned the next yeare after at
Chefter, as Fox wryteth in his ★ ftory, yet is he
placed in the Calendar vpon this yeare 1555.
and he telleth no more particulars of him, *but*
that he vvas burned as a true vvittneffe of the Lords
truth. To vvhich three may be adioyned 4.
other burned togeather at *Canterbury,* for like
caufes of vvillfull and phantafticall obftinacy
vpon the 12. of Iuly, to witt *Iohn Bland* Minifter, and Parfon of the Parifh of *Adifham* in

Margery
Pulley.

vvilliam
Minge an
apoftata
prieft.

★pag.1512.

Richard
Hooke.

★pag.1772.
col.2.n.843.

Kent, *Iohn Frankish* Vicar of the Parifh of *Rol-uingdon* in the fame county; *Humfrey Middleton* and *Nicolas Shetterden* artificers;all which being often examined vpon diuers articles, albeyt they agreed not in their anfwers,as appeareth by Fox himfelfe : yet vvould each one dye in whatfoeuer he tooke vpon him to defend or deny: *Seauen articles* (faith Fox) *being propounded vnto them,Iohn Frankish (the minifter) anfwered fom-vvhat doubtfully,Maifter Bland(the other minifter)anf-vvered flatly and roundly; Nicolas Shetterden, and Humfrey Middleton anfwered to the firft and fecond articles affirmatiuely. To the third, concerninge the Catholike Church, after a fort they graunted: To the fourth, fift, and fixt touchinge the reall prefence,* &c. *they refufed vtterly to anfwere : Middleton anfwered moreouer and confeffed, that he beleeued in his owne God, faying, I beleeue in my liuinge God, and no dead God,* &c. *Thackford* (their fifth companion) *re-lented, and vvas contente to take pennance,* &c.

38.   This is Fox his relation of their exami-nation and anfwers,yet doth he fet forth fuch triumph of *Nicolas Shetterden* artificer againft *Maifter Doctor Harpesfield* Archdeacon of Can-terbury, and *Maifter Colyns* the Commiffary in his difputatió with them, as that he faith that *Shetterden* concludeth vpon them by force of argument; *that they faid there was no god at all, or els no other god, but fuch as the heathen gods are, yea that there is no Chrift at all* : and other like bla-fphemyes and abfurdityes, as yow may fee in Fox his large relation of that difputation. And after that againe the fame *Shetterden* com-ming

Marginal notes (left column):

IohnBländ. I. Fräkish. Humfrey Middletõ. Nicolas Shetterdẽ.

Fox *pag.* 1521.

The varie-ty of here-ticall anf-vvering to th' articles propoun-ded.

Fox *ibid:*

Shetterdẽ the artifi-cer his conqueft againft learned men.

ming to difpute with *B. Gardner* of *VVinchefter*,
then Lord Chancelour and many other diuynes, he brought them into like ftraytes yf
we beleeue Fox, preffyng them with a text
of *Deuteronomy* in the fourth chapter, againft
painting God with a fhape, yet when the latyn Bible was brought, he could not fo much
as read the place; and yet forfooth did this
graue Doctor take vpon him both in fpeach
and letters, to fet downe his refolutions with
fuch prefumption, as yf he had byn the learnedeft man in the world, affuring both himfelfe & others, that he fhould be a great faint
in heauen, whervpon he wrote to his mother
the day before his death thefe words, as Fox
relateth them : *O my good mother, in that day God* Fox pag. 1523.
grant yow do fee my face vvith ioye, but deare mother
then beware of that Idolatry and blafpemous maffe, &c.
Oh giue ouer old cuftomes, and become new in the truth,
&c. And with this frenefie went the madd
fellow to the fire, wherin his face was burned
full black, but much more afterward with
the fire of hell yf he repented not, as it feemed
he did not, and confequently his mother was
like to take but fmall ioye in feeing his face yf
euer fhe faw him.

39. But as for his fellow Bland the Apoftata
Prieft, vvhich vvas the Captayne of this crue,
Fox fetteth downe fiue or fix examinations
of his, and in one of them being asked by the
Bifhop of Douer, whither after the words of
confecration, he belieued the body of Chrift
to be in the bleffed Sacrament, he aunfwered;

no:

Bland his
anſvvers
and opi-
nion a-
bout the
Sacramēt.

no: for that the Scriptures do not teach me (ſaith he)
that there ſhould remayne the fleſh of Chriſt *to eate, as
a man ſhould eate mans fleſh, &c.* Hereby yow
may perceaue how falſe a ladd this vvas, that
made his followers beleeue this to be our opinion, that Chriſt is ſo eaten in the Sacrament;
The ſame Bland alſo ſetteth downe (or Fox
for him) a certayne conference had betweene
him and one Maiſter Mills Prieſt of Chriſtes
Church in Canterbury, out of which conference he would ſeeme to drawe many abſurdityes againſt the ſaid Mills, which he amply-

Fox *pag.*
1518.

fieth, and Fox in his name both in the text &
margent of his booke, as to the ſimple and vnlearned reader may make ſome ſhewe of inconueniences graunted by the other, vvhich
in deed are none at all, but only do ſhewe the
cauillinge ſpiritt of the heretike vvhich may
vſe the ſame, or like ſcoffs againſt any other
article of Chriſtian Religion, yea againſt the
Incarnation of Chriſt, yf vve vvould follow
ſenſe only, and outward apparence of things;
vve ſhall examine his fooliſh arguments after

* in the
reuevv of
10.diſput.
*cap.*3. & 4.

in their * place, when we ſhall come to handle
the chiefe diſputations cōteyned in his booke
of Acts and Monuments.

40.   And finally vvhen he came to his laſt
anſwere a litle before his burninge, yt was demaunded him againe (ſaith Fox) *vvhether he belieued* Chriſt *to be in the Sacrament or no? VVhervnto
he anſwered and ſaid, that he belieued that* Chriſt *is in
the Sacrament, as he is in all other good bodyes,* &c.
By vvhich anſwere vve may ſee, vvhat man-

                                        ner

ner of presence he ascribed to Christ in the
Sacrament, and how different from that (at
least in sound of vvords) vvhich Bradford
professed before *of vvhole Chriſt, and true Chriſt to
be there, as preſent to faith, as bread and vvyne to the
ſenſe,* and such like speaches of others, all tendinge in deed to delude the simpler sorte, and
to euacuate the vvhole vertue of this diuine
Sacrament, in vvhich yf Christ be in no other
manner *then he is in euery good body,* vvhat priuiledge, I pray yow, or excellency may this venerable Sacrament be said to haue aboue other
things? then shall suffise to shew the vanity,
and impiety of these heretiks, vvhose ſtoryes
yow muſt remember are commonly recorded by Fox, as they vvere vvryten and sett
downe by their owne hands, and so much the
leſſe vvorthie of creditt, but only so farre
foorth, as they make againſt themſelues, and
no further.

41.   There remayne yet six more of this
yeare, *VVilliam Dighill, Diricke Caruer, Iohn
Launder, Thomas Iueſon, Nicolas Hall,* Martyrs, and *Iohn Alleworth* Confeſſor. Of the firſt
and laſt of theſe: to witt, *Dighill* and *Alleworth,*
Fox ſaith little or nothinge, but only that the
firſt was burned in *Kent* for profeſsing of the
ghoſpell, and the laſt died in priſon at *Reading*
for the ſame ghoſpell: but now yow know
that this Foxiā ghoſpell ſtretcheth very large,
and imbraceth many ſects and ſorts of men
& weomen, so as by this only that he calleth
them ghoſpellers, vve cannot know certainly

F 4   of

Blandes
ſingular
opinion
of Chriſts
being in
the Sacra-
ment.

VVilliam
Dighill.
Dirick
Caruer.
Iohn Laū-
der.
Thomas
Iueſon.
Nicolas
Hall.
Iohn Al-
levvorth.

of vvhat sect they were. Of the other 4. *Di-rick Caruer* was a beerebrewer of the Parish of *Brighthamsteed* in the County of *Sussex*, and vvas burned at *Lewes* for new opinions. *Iohn Launder* vvas a husbandman of the Parish of *Godstone* in the County of *Surrey*, burned at *Steninge*. *Thomas Iueson* was a carpenter of the Parish also of *Godstone*, burned at *Chichester*. *Nicolas Ball* was a bricklayer of the Parish of *Dartford*. All these learned company being brought before their Prelates and ordinaryes; they answered euery man as yt seemed best vnto them, but yet all with noueltyes and obstinacy therin. As for example, *Caruer* the beerbrewer answering to the articles proposed vnto them all, said; *concerninge the masse in Latyn,* (saith he) *there is no sa-crifice in the said masse; and there is no saluation for a Christian man therby, except yt should be said in the mother tongue, &c.* Item touchinge confession: *That yt is necessary to go to a good Priest for good coun-sell, but that the absolution of that Priest is nothinge profitable to mans saluation.* So said the beerbre-wer and offered to dy for yt, and yet yow see of how litle moment the points of his resolu-tion are.

42.   But *Launder* the husbandman, being about 25. yeares old answered, concerning the articles of the masse (saith Fox) *that yt is naught and abhominable, and directly against Gods vvord, and his holy Catholike Church, and that there is nothing said or vsed in yt good or profitable, For albeit the* Gloria in excelsis, *the* Creed, *the* Sanctus, *the* Agnus, *and other parts of the masse be of themselues good and* profi-

Fox pag.
1525.

The beer-brevvers resolutiõ.

Launder the hus-bandmans ansvvere.
Fox pag.
1526.

profitable : yet being vsed amonge other things that be
naught , they become naught also, &c. Thus that
yong husbandman resolued the case. *Thomas*
Iueson the carpenter, aunswered (saith Fox) to
the fourth article, that concerninge the Sacra-
crament of the Altar; *he beleeueth that yt is a very*
Idoll and detestable before God. Item, *that he hath*
not confessed nor heard masse at any tyme within seauen
years past. Item, *that auricular confession is not neces-*
sary to be made to a Priest, and that he cannot forgiue or
absolue from sinne. Item, that concerninge the
Sacrament of baptisme, *yt is a signe and token of*
Christ as circumcision vvas , and no otherwise , and he
beleeueth that his sinnes are not vvashed avvay therby,
but his body only vvashed, for his sinnes be vvashed away
only by Christs bloud, &c.

The Car-
penters
blasphe-
mous ans-
vvers.
Fox *pag.*
1527. &
1528.

VVicked
doctrine
côcerning
baptisme
and force
therof.

43. Thus relateth Fox of the Carpenters
aunswers, adding furthermore these vvords:
The said Iueson being earnestly trauayled vvithall to
recant, said in this vvise : I will not recant my opinions
for all the goods in London; yea yf there came an Angell
from heauen to teach me any other doctrine , then that
vvhich I am in now, I vvill not beleeue him; vvhich an-
sweere thus made, he vvas condemned, &c. Thus farre
he of his Carpenter Martyrs constancy : and
yet being ashamed somewhat at his blasphemous and Anabaptisticall opinion, about the
effect of baptisme, he maketh this note in the
margent, to temper the matter somewhat: *He*
meaneth not by the meere vertue of the element.
Which commentary is as foolish an euasion
of Fox, as the others opinion is impious. For
no man euer said, or immagined, that the element

Fox *pag.*
1528.

pag. eadem.

ment of water of yt selfe, could wash away
sinnes, but only by the vertue of Christs bloud
and passion applyed thervnto in baptisme.
And so this companion iumped full with the
Anabaptists to disgrace baptisme, and Fox
will needs be his fautor therin. And thus
much of his Martyrs in this yeare. For to prosecute all their absurdityes at large were a
thinge ouer tedious.

44.   In the next yeare following, which is
1556. Fox doth assigne some ten or eleuen

Fox pag.
1742.
Iohn Ca-
relesse.

Martyrs & Confessors more, wherof the first
was *Ionh Carelesse* a weauer of Couentry, that
died in the K. bench being committed thither
for heresy. Then followe there three other,
burned at *Neubery*, one *Iulius Palmer* a yongman of 24. yeares old, that had byn schoolma-
ster at *Reading*, togeather with two other fer-

Iohn
Gvvyn.
Thomas
Askyns.

uingmen companions of his, *Iohn Gwyn*, and
Thomas Askins, all three standing most obstinately in their opinions as euery man listed to
beleeue. The yong schoolmaister was putt out
a little before of *Magdelyn Colledg* in Oxford,
for seditious behauiour, and libelling against
the President; and he was of such good disposition, as going home to his mother, she hauing seene his manners, draue him out of her
house, and gaue him her curse, togeather with
Christs curse, whervpon I. Fox maketh this

pag. 1758.

note in the margent: *Mothers may giue their owne
curse but Gods curse they cānot giue, much lesse the Pope.*
And is not this, a wise note thinke yow. And
fit for I. Fox his braines, but let vs go forward.
                                             45. Next

45. Next to thefe three there enfue three other, or rather foure, martyred in the Ile of *Garnfey* vpon this yeare, to witt *Catherin Caw-ches,*the mother,and *Gillamine Gilbert,* and *Pero-tine Maffey,*her two daughters, with an infant not one houre old, that fell out of fhe faid *Pe-rotines* belly when fhe was burned. And vpon this ftory, doth Fox in his former editions & heere alfo make long difcourfes, & eager inue-ctiues:and fo do almoft all our Englifh pro-teftant writers ; and *Maifter Iewell* among the reft, both at Paules Croffe and in his bookes, thought good to playe the foole as others had donne before him in this argument, therby to make Catholiks hatefull in the beginning of the late Q. raigne. And I haue heard both *Maifter Toby Mathew* himfelfe, and diuers other preachers of moft fame, vfe all their rhetori-call inuectiues & exaggeratiõs vpon this fact, as a cruelty neuer heard of before, afcribing the fame to the perpetuall infamy of all Ca-tholiques and Catholique religion, as Fox doth heere: faying, *This is to be a fpectacle,wherin the vvhole vvorld may fee the Herodian cruelty of this gracelesse generation, of Catholike tormentors, ad per-petuam rei infamiam, &c.* So are his words:

Three vvo men han-ged and burned in Garnefey.

The excla-matiõs of Proteftãts about the 3.forfaid vveomen.

Fox *pag.* 1765.

46. But now, yf we come with moderation and temperate difcretion, to weigh the fub-ftance & circumftances of this ftory, we fhall find in this, as in infinite other matters that Fox and his fellowes haue little confcience in their fayinges, and wrytinges againft Ca-tholikes, and no regard of truth and fincerity

in

The mali-
tious en-
deauors of
Proteſtãts
to make
Catholiks
odious.
in the world, ſo they might make Catholike
Religion odious to the people. For firſt ſuppoſe, that in ſuch an out Iland, as *Garneſey* is,
vvhere the people are halfe French, and halfe
Engliſh, and many diſorderly and fearce, there
had happened in the execution of theſe three
weomē for the faults that after ſhalbe ſhewed,
ſome ſuch particular circumſtance, as that the
one of them hauing concealed her being with
child, and the ſame breaking forth in the fire,
ſome cruell harted fellow, takinge yt out and
ſeing yt dead, had caſt yt in againe (for Fox
himſelfe dareth not ſay yt was caſt in aliue)
vvhat is this to murder or Infanticide? (as by
him yt is called) or what appertayneth this to
the perpetuall infamy either of the Catholike
Clergy or Catholike Religion, or what is this
to the ſlaughter, murders, oppreſsions, and ef-
fuſion of bloud, which the new ghoſpellers
did vſe about this very tyme (when Fox firſt
of all publiſhed this ſtory), both in France,
Scotland, & other places? which yet, (though
a thouſand tymes more heynous then this,) he
would be loath to haue aſcribed to the perpetuall infamy of his ghoſpell. But now lett
vs come to examyne the fact yt ſelfe, according to Fox his owne Relation, and ſee what
truth ther is therin.

An examẽ
about the
fact of the
forſaid
three vveo
men in
Garneſey.
47. Firſt he graunteth that theſe three weomen, the mother and two daughters, were
put in priſon by the Iuſtices and Ciuill Magiſtrates of the Towne of *S. Peters* in Garneſey,
& an inuẽtory taken of their moueable goods
for

for accusation of theft and felony, made by
Nicolas Carey conſtable of the towne & others,
and this without intermedlinge of the Cleargy. And albeit Fox doth ſleightly in a word
or two, ſay that they were cleared afterward
by the teſtimony of their neighboures of the
ſuſpition of theſe things: yet doth he ſett
downe no authenticall record therof, as I preſume he would haue done, yf there had byn
any ſuch thinge, ſeing he alleageth other impertinent records of the forſaid towne for
other matters of leſſe moment, though againſt
himſelfe, as after ſhalbe ſhewed. And for that
he confeſſeth in this his narration, that they
were all three firſt hanged, or ſtrangled, (as he
calleth yt) and that the flame of fire made vnder them comminge to burne the ropes, they
fell downe into the flame, and therwith the
belly of *Perotine* breakinge, the dead child appeared; yt is euident, (I ſay) by this, that their
faults were not only hereſie, for then ſhould
they not haue byn hanged, as may appeare by
that which often hath byn repeated before, of
the hanginge and burning of *Syr Iohn Oldcaſtle,
Syr Roger Acton*, and their rebellious followers
in the field of *S. Gyles*, vpon the firſt yeare of
the raigne of K. Henry the fift: So as heerby
we haue, that theſe three weomen cannot be
pure Martyrs of Iohn Fox his Religion, eſpecially ſeing himſelfe confeſſeth and wryteth
in this place, that they offered to accomodate
themſelues in all things touchinge matters of
Religion, ſo they might haue eſcaped therby.

48. *They*

Thefe 3.
vveomen
martyrs
renounced
Fox'his
faith.

Fox *pag.*
*1764.col.*1.
num. 10.

Ibid. col. 2,
num. 18.

Hovv the
3. vveomē
vvere fent
to the Ec-
clefiafti-
call Magi-
ſtrate.

48.   *They being examined* (faith Fox) *of their faith,
concerning the ordinances of the Roman Church, made
their anſwere: that they vvould obey and keep the ordinances of the King and Queene, and the commaundements of the Church, notwithſtandinge that they had
ſaid and done the contrary in the tyme of K. Edward
the fixt,* &c. Which confeſsion of theirs is repeated againe afterward by Fox, when they
ſaid before the publike iudges, *that they vvould
entirely obey, obſerue, and keep the ordinances of the
King and Queene, as all good and true ſubiects are bound
to do,* &c. And this being true, I do not ſee by
what crooke Fox can draw them in to his
Calendar, or make them his Martyrs. But yet
ſeing he will needs haue them, lett vs leaue
them vnto him, and tell yow a word or two
what they were, and what falſhood he vſeth
in recountinge ther ſtory.

49.   The iuſtices hauing theſe weomen in
priſon for other faults, of felony and theft (as
hath byn ſaid) and vnſterſtanding by report
of their neighboures that they were heretikes
alſo ; ſent them to the Deane and Curates of
that Iland, to be examined in matters of their
faith, as the thing moſt reſpected by Catholike Magiſtrates. The Deanes name was *Syr
Iaques Amy*, who examining them togeather
with the reſt of the Cleargy, that were his aſſiſtants and in commiſsion with him, found
them by the depoſitiōs of many lawfull wittneſſes, to be heretiks, & to haue both ſpoken
and done many malitious things againſt the
Catholike faith, though themſelues for the
                                    preſent

present denyed that they were such, and offered all conformity as hath byn said. Whervpon the said Deane & his afsistants, without
giuing any iudiciall sentence vpon them, sent
them backe to the ciuill Magistrates againe
with informatiō, what they had found, as appeareth by the records of Fox sett downe in
this place in Latyn only, & for some causes, as
yow may imagine, not Englished by him, but
we shall do yt for him. It beginneth thus.

50. *Anno Domini* 1556. *die* 13. *mensis Iulij, &c.*
In the yeare of Christ 1556. the 13. day of Iuly,
an inquisition was made in the Church of
Saint Peter, in the port of this Iland, by vs the
Deane, *&c.* about points of the Catholike
faith, the sacraments of Baptisme, Confirmation, Pennance, Order, Matrimony, Eucharist, Extreme Vnction, efficacy of the Masse,
&c. Concerning *Katherine Cauches* & her two
daughters *Guillemine* and *Perotine, &c.* and hauing heard their deniall on the one side, and
the attestations and depositions of wittnesses
on the other side, and well considered the
same, according to the opinions of the Curats
and Vicars our afsistants in this Iland; we
haue found & do repute them to haue fallen
into the crime of heresy; wherfore we remitt
them backe againe to yow M. Bayliffe and
other your afsistants, as before we remitted
them, *&c.* Thus far the recorde. And heer-
vpon the said Bailiffe named *Elear Gosiline* called a Iury of 12. men, whose names Fox setteth downe out of the said records, who iudged

ged and condemned them to be ſtrangeled
and burned to aſhes; accordinge to which
ſentence they vvere executed vpon the day
and yeare aforeſaid.

51.   And here now I vvould aske any reaſonable man, vvhat fault the cleargy had in this
condemnation made by the Ciuil Magiſtrate,
or vvhat kind of Martyrs vvere theſe, ſeing
they denied openly Fox his Religion ſo often?
And thus much of all theſe three vveomen and
their comon cauſe, for which they vvere condemned and executed. Now let vs ſay a word
or two of Iohn Fox his little babe, put in his
Calendar for a tender Martyr, ſcarſe an houre
old, and baptized (as he ſaith) in his owne
bloud. But yf this babe had neuer life to any
mans knowledge, how was yt baptized in his
owne bloud? or yf the Bayliffe of *Garneſey*
ſeing yt taken out of the fire dead, did byd yt
to be caſt in againe, what cryme is this againſt
the Cleargy? Or yf *Perotine* the mother (as
preſently ſhalbe ſhewed) did conceale her
being vvith child, and vvould not vtter yt to
the Magiſtrate, who had ſo much fault as ſhee
her ſelfe? and conſequently ſhe vvas rather a
murderer then a Martyr.

52.   But (ſaith Fox) the ſaid Bayliffe, and
Iurers, togeather with the Deane & Cleargy
did ſubmitt themſelues afterward: to witt,
vpon the fifth yeare of Q. Elizabeth *anno Domini* 1562. vnto the Q. mercy, & had their pardons for this fact, vpon the complaint of *Mathew Cauches* brother to *Catherine Cawches,* and
                                                 vncle

vncle to the two daughters, as appeareth both
by his supplication, and the Queenes pardon
yet extant. Whexto I answere that yt is true,
accordinge as Fox setteth yt downe. But he
that will read the said memoriall and pardon
yt selfe, shall find first, that the said Ciuill and
Ecclesiasticall Magistrate submitted themselues, and the vvhole Iland vvith them, not
for this matter only, wherof they were accused by the said *Matthew*; but for many other
more greuous then this, as namely for the let- The cause
vvhy the
magistrats
of Garne-
sey sub-
mitted
them-
selues to
Q. Eliz.
anne 1562.
tinge goe of one *Nicolas Norman* a notorious
murderer, & for many other fellonyes, ryotts,
insolences, and other disorders laid against
them, and the vvhole Iland, for vvhich the
Queene did pardon them, and yt is not greatly to be maruayled at, at that tyme: to witt,
vpon the yeare 1562. which was six yeares after the forsaid three weomen were executed,
when as the said Catholike Magistrate were
terrified and persuaded by Protestants to submitt themselues, seing at that very tyme all
France, Scotland, and diuers other places vvere
in armes and combustion against Catholiks.
But yf we will see whether the Queene and
her commissionars did improue the iustice of
that fact, for the punishing of these weomen
accordinge to the lawes then in force: Lett vs
consider whether they restored the goods and
Chatells confiscated by that condemnation, as
Mathew Cawches in his memoriall had demaunded, and we shall find iust nothinge; which is
an argument, that they held their condemna-
G tion

tion for good and lawfull, though for more
assurance the poore Catholiks were persuaded
to submitt themselues. And so much of this.
Now to the particular of *Perotine* and her little
child Iohn Fox his babe.

53.   The learned and pious man Maister Doctor Hardinge, hauinge heard so much crying
out in the beginninge of Q. Elizab. raigne a-
bout this holy burned babe of *Perotine Cauches*,
and seing also, that not only simple and vulgar
people, but euen Maister Iewell himselfe, had
both at Paules Crosse, & in his bookes made
great stirre about this matter, the said Doctor
comminge ouer the seas, vsed means to informe himselfe of the truth of this fact in *Gar-
nesey*, and therby found (as in his reioynder he
testifieth) that this *Perotine* was indeed besides
her heresie a very strumpett, & for shame both
of her selfe, and of the new ghospell she professed, would not confesse to the iudges of her
being with child, nor demaund the benefitt of
the law allowed in that behalfe, for delayinge
of her death; and thervpon most iustly the said
Doctor Hardinge accuseth her both of whore-
dome, and of murderinge her owne child;
wherat Iohn Fox is most wonderfully troubled, and maketh the most fond and childish
discourses, therby to defend her, and the honour of his ghospell, that euer perhaps man
did, that was in his right witts. For first, when
Maister Doctor Hardinge chargeth him to bringe
out the Father of the child; he asketh, *how
be can do that? or how can any man point out the right*
                                                    Father

Perotine
the mo-
ther of
the babe
a strum-
pett.

Father (for so are his words) *eyther of his, or any other child?* and then he faith he will go as neere yt as he can, or as men may in such matters: and after seekinge vp and downe for this Father, he falleth vpon a certayne minifter named *Dauid Iores,* who he faith was marryed to *Perotine* in K. Edwards dayes, & confequently is like to be the Father, though he faith he will not affirme yt for certayne; and then he nameth another minifter called *Noel Regnet* a French man, that liued in *Saint Martyn Legrande* in London, when this ftory of Iohn Fox was wrytten, & affirmed that he marryed the faid minifter and *Perotine* togeather in K. *Edwards* dayes; fo as heere yow haue the teftimony now or affertions of 2. or 3. minifters togeather, to witt of *Dauid,* that was husband to *Perotine,* of *Noel* that marryed them, and of Iohn Fox that of his owne authotity doth legitimate the child, and yet neyther of them doth proue the matter directly, to witt that this babe of one houre old, was begotten by the firft minifter. Neyther do they proue that he liued in *Garnefey,* and had company with her at that tyme, during the raigne of Q. *Mary,* and yt is moft probable that he did not, both for that Fox dareth not affirme yt; and yf he had byn in *Garnefey* at that day, I do not fee how the minifter could haue efcaped punifhment alfo, when his ftrumpett was burned: fo as by tellinge vs only that fhe was marryed to this minifter, without fhewinge that he conuerfed with her, and fhe with no other, Fox maketh

Great adoe to feeke the babes father.

her

Perotine
had an
other huf-
bande be-
fides the
minifter.

her finne to be more greuous, to witt adultery (fhe hauing a husband) wheras before we
might haue imagined that yt had byn only
fimple fornication : though yet yt appeareth
that fhe had another husband alfo named
Maffey befides *Dauid* the minifter, of whome
fhe was called *Perotine Maffey*, (and fo Fox wryteth her in his ftory) as her fifter was named
Guillimine Gilbert by her husbád, & not *Cauches*
as their mother and father were, and her vncle
Mathew Cauches, of whome we fpake before.

54.   And this now being fo, as is verifyed by
Fox himfelfe in this place; I would aske the
poore fellow, whether the faid minifter *Dauid
Iores*, were her firft husband : to witt, before
Maffey, or no? and yf he were, then could not
the child be rightly afcribed to him, for that
fhe had a later husband aliue. But yf *Maffey*
were the former husband, and the minifter after him, then fhould fhe haue byn called *Perotine Iores* in her arraignement and condemnation, and not *Perotine Maffey* as fhe was, and is
called fo alfo by *Iohn Fox* himfelfe in all his ftory. And this much for the firft point of her
honefty. Now for the fecond about the murder of her child.

55.   In this point Fox accordinge to his fafhion maketh many longe and idle difcourfes,
the moft impertinent, that euer any man perhaps heard, alleaginge 7. or 8. foolifh coniecturall reafons, to proue that yf eyther *Perotine*
did, or fhould haue reueyled her being with
child to the Catholike Magiftrate at that time,
                                              before

before her execution yet would yt not haue
auailed her. Wherin notwithstáding I thinke
no man of sense or iudgment will beleeue
him, knowing the custome and order of our
lawes in such poynts. Wherfore we will not
stand to refute such childish coniectures, but
come to his conclusion. And for vpshott of
folly he maketh diuers large exhortations to
Maister Doctor Harding, to proceed with more
respect in his wrytings towards his martyrs
saincts, which yow shall heare in his owne
words, and therby iudge of the mans witt.
Briefly and finally (saith he) *whatsoeuer this woman*
was, she is now gone, &c. *To byte so bitterly against*
the dead is little honesty; Charity would haue iudged
the best;humanity would haue spared the dead; and yf
Doctor Harding could not affoard her his good word,yet
he might haue left her cause vnto the Lord, which shall
iudge both her and him. To praye for the dead he fin-
deth in his Masse, but to backbyte the dead, he' findeth
neyther in his Masse, Mattyns, nor euensong; and no
doubt but in his dirige and commendation of soules,he
comended many one lesse deseruing to be commended
then this woman. Let Catholike affection be sett a side,
and though the meritts of her cause deserued not his
commendation; yet did she neuer deserue such a Kyrie
eleyson, *after her departure, &c.* Thus farre Fox,
and by so graue an exhortation yow may
make a coniecture of the mans talent in this
kind.Now lett vs go forward.

56. Vnto these three Saincts of Garnesy,
Fox adioyneth foure others burned in this
moneth and yeare, two at *Greensteed* in Suffex,

Fox *pag.*
1768. *col.*1.

Fox his
foolish ex-
hortation
to M. D.
Harding.

and two at *Norwich*. The former two were *Thomas Dungate*, and *Iohn Foreman* poore men & obstinate, the other two were *Symon Milner* and *Elizabeth Cooper*. *Symon* was a Craftesman of *Norwich*, and *Elizabeth* was a peuterers wife of the same towne. Iohn Fox setteth downe no particulars at all of these first two, but only in generall, *that they gaue themselues to death for righteousnes sake*; and so meane we to be as briefe also leauinge them to the temporall fyre, which for their willfull obstinacy they suffered in this world, and to Gods eternall iudgment for the next. But for the second coople *Simon Milner* & *Elizabeth Cooper*, he sheweth that *Simon* being a simple fellow of *Lyn* in *Norfolke*, was so forward in spiritt, as he caryed about with him his confession of faith in his shewes, which appearinge one day out of one of his said shewes, he was taken thervpon, as also for that he inquired of the people where he might go to a communion. *Elizabeth* also was as forward as he, and so both burned together in the said towne of Norwich, for obstinate standinge in sundry heresies.

57.   In the next yeare following, Fox hath 8. Martyrs more, which with like breuity we shall runne ouer; their names are *Richard Teoman*, *VVilliam Pikes*, *Stephen Cotten*, *Iohn Slàde*, *Stephen VVight*, *Robert Mylls*, *Robert Dines*, and *Thomas Benbridge*. The first and the last were burned seuerally, and so we shall handle them apart, the other sixe vvere burned togeather, of whome we shall speake in the second place.

58. *Richard*

(margin, left:)
Thomas Dungate.
Iohn Foreman.
Symon Milner.
Elizabeth Cooper.

Fox *pag.* 1768.

58, *Richard Yeoman* vvas an Apostata Priest and had bin Curate to *Doctor Taylor* at Hadley, wherof we haue spoken ∗ before: he gott him selfe a wife in his old age, with whome, *he liued* (saith Fox) *more then a yeare togeather locked vp in a Chamber, by cardinge of vvooll, vvhich his vvife did spinne.* He had many children by her, & being brought to his aunswere, the summe therof was that he defied the Pope and all that appertayned vnto him, and so was condemned and burned at Norwich, the yeare aforesaid.

∗ *Mense Febr.* 25. Richard Yeoman an apostata priest burned at Norvvich an. 1558. Fox *pag.* 1855.

59. *Thomas Benbridge* was a gentleman saith Fox of the Diocesse of Winchester, and being called before Doctor White Bishopp of that Sea, he stood stoutly in defence of diuers new opinions, and some very singular and peculiar to himselfe, for defence wherof he went to the fire very vauntingly; and Iohn Fox describeth not only his words & countenance, but his braue Apparell also: to witt, of what stuffe his gowne was, to whome he gaue yt at the fire side, and that his ierkyn was layd on with gold lace *fayre and braue* (to vse Fox his words) which he presented to *Syr Richard Pepall* the high Sheriffe; *his capp of veluett he tooke* (saith he) *from his owne head, and threw yt away; then liftinge his mynd to the Lord made his prayers, &c.* And when *Doctor Seeton* exhorted him to recant, he said, *Away Babylonian, away.* But after feelinge the fire, he cryed I recant, and thrust the said fire from him; then he *subscribed to a recantation* (saith Fox) *vpon another mans backe, and thervpon vvas by the Sheriffe repriued,* but some dayes after

Thomas Benbrige burned at VVinchester.

Benbrige recanted but after vvas burned.

that he was appointed againe to be burned, and the Sheriffe was committed to prison for takinge him from the stake without commission. And this was the end of this gentleman Martyr *Benbrige* burned at Winchester vpon the 19. of Iuly 1558.

Six Craftesmen burned at Brainford *anno* 1558.

Fox *pag.* 1852.

60.   The last company of them that were burned in this moneth, and vpon this yeare, were the six named by me before, all burned at *Braynford* 7. myles from London, whome Fox calleth, *six faithfull vvittnesses of the Lords Testament.* The first of them as they stand in the Calender was *VVilliam Pikes,* or *Pikers* a tanner, and the other fiue of like occupations, to witt,

vvilliam Pikes. Stephen Cotten. Io. Slade. Stephen vvight. Robert Milles. Robert Dynes.

Stephen Cotten, Iohn Slade, Stephen VVight, Robert Mylles, and *Robert Dines.* Their Articles (saith Fox) were the same that were proposed to others before, to witt, 14. in number, & their answers thervnto, *were much the same, that other like Craftesmen had giuen before them,* especially those that had byn taken with them, namely one *Roger Holland* a Taylor, that commonly spake for all the rest, and to whose answers they much remitted themselues, though in some points also they added of their owne, euery one as yt came in his braine, and agreed only in certaine common things. As for example, being examined in the ninth & tenth articles about their meeting in the fields, and refusing to go to Cath. seruice, *Robert Mylles,*

Fox *ibid.*

Iohn Slade & *Stephen Cotten* answered (saith Fox) *that they do not allow the Popish seruice, because yt is against the truth, and in a strange language,* &c.

61. *Robert*

61. *Robert Dynes* and *William Pikes* would nether allow nor difalow the said Latyn feruice
(faith Fox) for that they vnderftood yt not,
and *Stephen Wight* would make no direct anfwere at all. And being further demaunded in
the article about the feruice booke, and religion vfed in K. Edwards dayes, *Robert Mylles,*
Iohn Slade & *Stephen Cotten* anfwered (faith Fox)
that concerning the bookes, fayth and religion fpecified
in this article, they do allow them fo farre forth, as
they agree with Gods word. Robert Dynes would
make no aunfwere thervnto, becaufe he
thought himfelf vnmeet to iudge therof. *Wil-*
liam Pikes doth not remember that he hath
mifliked of that feruice and Religion, *&c.*

The fry-
uolous
anfwers
of ignorāt
artificers.

„
„
„
Fox, pag.
1852.
„
„
„
„
„
„

62 .Thus farre Fox,and then addeth further,
that they being much vrged by *Maifter Doctor*
Thomas Darbifhire the Bifhopps Chancelor,that
they fhould agree among themfelues,& turne
from their priuate opinions to their mother
the holy Church, for that otherwife fentence
of condemnation muft be giuen againft them:
that all anfwered (faith he) *that they would not relent*
from any part therof, while they liued, &c. *And fo*
(faith he) *thefe good poore lambes being condemned*
the next day, and deliuered ouer to the fecular power,
went ioyfully to the ftake, &c. Thus he: and by
this yow may remember what we haue difcuffed before in the fourth Chapter of this
booke, about the fond, madd, and hereticall
obftinacy of Sectaryes. And fo much of this
moneth. The comparifon betweene this, and
the Catholike Catalogue of Saints in this

Fox ibid,

moneth

moneth will eafily appeare by that which we haue wrytten before. And by the view of the two Calendars themfelues; the principall perfonages of Fox his Religion in this moneth, (yf they be of his Religion) and thofe of moft learninge, are *Iohn Fryth*, *Iohn Bradford*, *Anthony Perfon*, *Iohn Bland*, all different in opinions about the Sacrament, as before yow haue heard; the chiefe difputers of leffe learninge were *Anthony Huet* the apprentice Tayler, *Iohn Leefe* the apprentice Chandelour, *Nicolas Shyterdon* laborour, and others of that callinge with the three honeft weomen of *Garnefey*, and their litle babe-martyr, as before yow haue heard.

The ende of *Iuly*.

O F

OF THE MONETH

OF AVGVST,

And what Martyrs and Confeßors
Iohn Fox ſetteth downe in the
ſame, to haue ſuffered for
his Religion.

Chap. XII.

I ADVERTISED thee (gentle **Reader**) before, that our author Iohn Fox deſyring to maketh vp a great number of Martyrs and Confeſſors of his Church, therby to fill his Calendar, he reſolued to draw them from all tymes, countreyes and places, and from all ſorts of Sectaryes whatſoeuer, within this two or three hundred yeares paſt. Wherfore for the better proſecution of this my examen throughout euery moneth, I thought beſt to diuide them ordinarily into three principall ranks. The firſt of ſuch as were puniſhed vnder the ancient Kings of England before K. Henry the 8. The ſecond of thoſe vnder the ſaid K. Henry. The third vnder Q. Mary.

2.　And for the firſt ranke, albeit there wanted not ſtore ſufficient for ſome of the firſt monethes, eſpecially whilſt the number endured of thoſe holy Wickliffian Rebell Martyrs, that cöſpired the death of K. Henry the 5.

Rebell-martyrs of S. Gyles field.

and

and were hanged & burned by him in *S. Giles
fields*, vpon the first yeare of his raigne as before
yow haue heard: vvhich Martyrs, Iohn Fox
hath sprinkled into diuers dayes of the foresaid monethes: yet afterward they faylinge,
we haue had only in the beginninge of euery
moneth, some few put to death in the tyme of
K. Henry the eyght, though not alwayes by
him, nor vnder him, but by other Princes in
other countreyes: And now that vayne also
seemeth to be well dryed vp, especially for this
moneth of August, where there is one only
sett downe vpon the first day therof, to witt

Leonard Keyser a Bauarian Priest, burned for Lutheranisme & some other fancyes of his owne,
vpon the yeare of Christ 1527. (vvhich vvas
the 18. of K. Henryes raigne) but in his Acts
& Monuments Fox saith, that he was put to
death vpon the yeare 1526. at *Passaw* in *Bauaria*
vpon the 16. day of August, though heere he
placeth his feastiuall day vpon the first of this
moneth.

3.   And albeit his opinions vvere such as
commonly Lutherans held in those dayes,
vvherby he could not be a trew member of
Fox his Churche, that disagreeth in many
principall articles from Lutherans; yet for
that he stoode obstinat in defence therof
against the Catholike faith, Fox vvill not lett
him goe, but perforce will haue him a Martyr of his Church, concludinge his story and
burninge with thes words: *This vvas the blessed
end of that good man, vvhich suffered for the testimony
of the*

Leonard
Keyser a
Bauarian
Priest.
Fox *pag.*
808.

Fox *ibid.*

of the truth, the 16. *day of August* 1526. And this is
all which he wryteth of any Martyr or Confeſſor of his in this moneth, before the tyme of
Q. Mary, vnder vvhome all the reſt that do
enſue were made Martyrs; And ſo we ſhall
recount them without any further diſtinction
of Princes raignes, or times for their ſuffering,
but only the diſtinctiõ of three ſeuerall yeares
wherin they were puniſhed vnder Q. Mary,
which are 1555. 56. and 57.

4. Firſt then for the yeare 1555. Iohn Fox
aſſigneth 18. Martyrs of his, wherof the for-
moſt is one *Iames Abbes* a poore yonge man, as
he ſaith, vvho firſt recanted his opinions before *Doctor Hopton* B. of *Norwich*, and was diſmiſſed with great charity, & an almes of money giuen him alſo, but afterward (ſaith Fox)
his conſcience greatly pricking him, he returned to the Biſhop, reſtored his almes, and ſaid
he would defend his former opinions: *VVhich
being done* (ſaith Fox) *the Biſhop vvith his Chaplyns
did labour a freſh to vvynne him, but in vayne, vvhervpon at length he vvas burned at Bury.* Fox doth not
tell what his opinions were, which he defended ſo ſtoutly againſt the Biſhop and his Chaplyns, but we may eaſily gheſſe, what a poore
begginge boy could ſay, diſpute, or defend in
ſuch a caſe, but by a Foxian miracle.

5. The next three that enſue are *Iohn Denley*
gentleman (as Fox calleth him) of *Maydſtone* in
Kent, and *Iohn Newman* pewterer of the ſame
towne, & *Patricke Pachingham* crafteſman burned at *Vxbridge*. The firſt two were taken, and
ſent

Iames
Abbes,
a poore
yongman.

„
„
Fox *ibid.*

Io. Den-
ley.
Io. Nevv-
man.
Patricke
Pachin-
gham.

sent vp to London by *Maifter Edmond Tyrell* ef-
quire and Iuftice of peace, he hauinge found
vpon them certayne papers of their new opinions, and many fcriptures fondly gathered
for proofe of the fame. One propofition of
theirs among diuers others, Iohn Fox fetteth
downe in thefe words: *Chrift is in the Sacra-*
ment, as he is vvhere two or three are gathered toge-
ther in his name. Which propofition Fox allowinge well, addeth this expofition vnto yt of
his owne. *The difference* (faith he) *of doctrine be-*
tweene the faithfull and the papifts, concerninge the
Sacrament is, that the papifts fay, that Chrift is corpo-
rally vnder, or in the formes of bread and vvyne, but
the faithfull fay, that Chrift is not there neyther corpo-
rally nor fpiritually. Loe Iohn Fox his interpretation and explication vvhat his faithfull
people do hold; but me thinketh he might
better haue called them the *faithleffe,* then the
faithfull in this behalfe, for heere they beleeue
nothinge, but rather vnbeleeue all. Befides
that, Fox playeth the Reynold in faying we
vfe the word *corporally,* and not *really,* or *fubftan-*
tially, which yet are the expreffe words of the
Councells of *Trent* & *Lateran* about that matter, and not *corporally* which in Foxes fenfe fi-
gnifieth properly a naturall bodyly prefence,
with ordinary locall dimenfions of quantity,
quality, *&c.* So as in no one thinge this our
Fox dealeth fincerely, but feeketh by all
fhiftes to make vs feeme to fpeake that which
we do not.

6.   I leaue to profecute any further the ab-
urdity

Fox pag.
1529.
Abfurd o-
pinions of
Fox & his
martyrs a-
bout the
Sacramēt.

Concil. Tri-
dent.feff.13.
cap.1. &
can.1.

furdity of *Denley*, and *Newmans* former propofition, allowed by Fox, vvho feemeth not to
vnderftand vvhat himfelfe or the other meaneth, affirminge that Chrift is prefent neither
corporally nor fpiritually, which is quite contrary to the beleefe both of *Luther, Caluyn,* and
other his owne Maifters, for that both thofe
fects do agree, that Chrift is eyther bodily or
fpiritually prefent; and none of them do go fo
farre in debacinge that Sacrament, as to fay
that Chrift, *is no otherwife there prefent, then when
two or three are gathered togeather in his name;*
which meeting might be as well called *Sacrament* of Chriftes prefence, as the *Supper,* yf *Den-
leyes* opinion were true, or Fox his approbation therof authenticall. But the one being as
fond, as the other is abfurd, I leaue them both
to the iudgement of the Reader.

Iohn Denley his abfurd opinion of the reall prefence in the Sacrament.

7.   It were ouer longe to fett downe thefe
mens large aunfwers, about 10. Articles obiected to them by the Bifhopp of London : I
meane of *Denley* and *Newman* his compagnion,
only I muft tell yow that Fox by enlarginge
fuch impertinent matter, aboue all meafure of
witt or reafon, hath brought his booke to the
bulke yow fee, almoft importable. But aboue
all, is it ridiculous, that after a long & fpeciall
combatt vvhich *Newman* the Pewterer, had
with *Maifter Doctor Thorneton* fuffragan of Kent,
and other learned men, at the towne of *Ten-
derden* about the Sacramēt of the Altar, (wherin Fox maketh him the victor, afcribinge
groffe ignorance to the faid examiners, and
                                    deepe

deep learning vnto the pewterer examined,)
in the end of all for an vpſhott and complete
triumph, he maketh the ſaid pewterer to putt

The peu-
terers lo-
gicall ar-
guments.

downe diuers arguments in logicall forme,
and namely one in the figure of *Cameſtres*, and
another in *Datiſi*, for conqueſt of the ſaid Doctors, which arguments are ſo fond and chil-
diſh, as I thinke not conuenient to ſpend paper in alleaginge them ; but yet finally they
would needs go all three to the fire, for defence of their opinions: *Denley* and *Newman* at
Vxbridge, & *Pachingham* at *Saffronwalden* in Eſſex,
and ther was an end of them, yf ſuch mens
puniſhments haue any end.

8.   Vnto theſe Iohn Fox adioyneth ſix more
burned at Canterbury in this yeare, examined
and condemned all togeather by the foreſaid
Doctor Richard Thorneton B. of Douer, *Doctor Nicolas Harpesfield* Archdeacon of Canterbury, &
others in comiſſion ; the names of the con-

Villiam
Coker.
Villiam
Hopper.
Henry
Laurence
Richard
Collier.
Richard
VVright.
VVilliam
Steere.

demned were *VVilliam Coker*, *VVilliam Hopper*,
Henry Laurence, *Richard Collyer*, *Richard VVright*,
and *VVilliam Steere*, all ignorant Crafteſmen of
Kent, but yet ſett in ſuch a ruffe with the
heate of new opinions in thoſe dayes ; as yt
vvas intollerable for their Prelates to deale
with them, ſo deſperate, inſolent, and contumelious were their anſwers, nor would they
be inſtructed or brought to any reaſon, or moderation about any opinions, which once they
had apprehended and determined to defend,
as by example of one or two yow ſhall heare.

9.   *Henry Laurence* (ſaith Fox) being exami-
                                                             ned

ned vpon the 16. of Iuly, denyed firſt auricular
Confeſsion; and then that he had not, nor
would not receyue the Sacramét; that yt was
an idoll, and no remembrance of Chriſts paſſion, and other ſuch like things. And at laſt,
ſaith Fox, being required to put to his hand in
ſubſcribinge to his anſwers, he wrote theſe
words vnder the bill of his examinations: *Yow*
are all of Antichriſt, and him yow follow, &c. *Richard*
Collyer, ſett downe his beliefe thus: *that after the*
vvords of conſecration there is not the reall and ſubſtan-
tiall body of Chriſt, but only bread, & wyne, & that it is
moſt abhominable and moſt deteſtable to beleeue other-
wiſe. Do yow ſee how reſolutly this Crafteſman determineth the matter? yet not only
Luther, but Caluyn alſo (as yow know) do
affirme yt to be abhominable *to hold yt only for*
bread, and vvyne. What will yow ſay to this
Martyr? Fox ſaith he was a bleſſed Saint, and
ſong pſalmes as ſoone as euer he was condemned, whervpon the Papiſts ſaid he died
madd: and ſo much of him.

10. *VVilliam Steere* another artificer of Aſh-
ford in Kent being examined, and required
by the Biſhopp, whoſe name (as yow haue
heard) was *Richard*, to aunſwere to the poſitions laid againſt him; *made anſwere* (ſaith Fox)
that he ſhould commaund his doggs and not him, and
further declared, that Dicke of Douer had no authority
to ſitt againſt him in iudgment, &c. And as touchinge the Sacrament of the Altar, he ſaid;
that he found yt not in the ſcriptures; and he told
the iudge further, that he vvas a bloody man, &c.

The obſti-
nacy of
diuers ig-
norant
people.

Fox *ibid.*

H   Wher-

Whervpon sentence was giuen againft them.
And thus (faith Fox) *thefe fix heauenly Martyrs and vvittneff-bearers of the truth , being condemned by the bloudy Suffragan, Archdeacon, and others, vvere burned at* Canterbury *at three feuerall ftakes, &c.* Thus pittifully wryteth he of his obftinate raylinge Craftefmen of Canterbury.

11.   Next after thefe doth he adioyne other fix for follemne Martyrs, condemned togeather by the Bifhop of London,after much trauaylinge with them in vaine to inftruct and conuert them. Their names are *George Tankerfield, Robert Smith, Stephen Harwood, Thomas Fush* and *VVilliam Hayle*, common ordinary artificers, and *Elizabeth VVarne* that had byn wife to one *Iohn VVarne* an vpholfter in London, burned before for like herefies in the moneth of May, as yow haue heard. The Captaynes and ringleaders of this daunce were the firft two, named *George Tankerfield* a cooke , and *Robert Smith* a painter; whofe infolent aunfwers and fpeaches to the faid Bifhopp , and other commiffionars at diuers times of their appearance before them, do fhew well their fpiritt. For that being often called before them, & gently required to anfwere to the articles laid againft them;they were fo malepart in their fpeaches, as the Bifhop called *Tankerfield, the fpeaker of the houfe,* and *Smith* the *Controller ,* for commonly he controlled all that was fpoken by others. Yow fhall heere fome of the conference vttered by the paynters owne penicell, as Fox putteth yt downe, I meane of *Smith ,* that
                                               wrote

George Tankerfield.
Robert Smith.
Stephen Harvvood.
Thomas Fush.
VVilliam Hayle.
Elizabeth VVarne.

wrote his owne combatt and victory, accordinge to the cuſtome of Fox his Actes and Monuments.

12. Vpon the 12. of Iuly (ſaith he) I vvas brought with my brethren into the conſiſtory, and my articles read before my L. Maior & the Sheriffes with all the aſſiſtants, where was ſpoken as folloveth:

Bonner. By my faith my Lord Maior, I haue ſhewed theſe people as much fauour, as any man liuinge might do, *&c.*

Smith. At this word, came I in, and taking him in the manner, ſaid my Lord, yt is wrytten yow muſt not ſweare.

Bonner. Ah Maiſter Controller are yow come? Lo my Lord Maior; this is *Maiſter Speaker* (pointinge to my brother *Tankerſield*) and this is *Maiſter Controller*, pointinge to me. Then he began to read my articles, and asked me, yf I ſaid not, as was wrytten, *&c.*

Smith. I anſwered no; and turninge to my L. Maior I ſaid: I require yow my L. Maior in Gods behalfe, vnto whome pertayneth your ſword, that I may heere anſwere all obiectiõs layd againſt me, and yf any thinge be approued hereſie, I will recant.

Maior. Whie *Smith* thou ſpeakeſt againſt the bleſſed Sacrament of the Altar.

Smith. I denied it to be any Sacrament,& do ſtand heere to make probatiõ of the ſame, *&c.*

Tankerſ. Then ſpake my Brother *Tankerſield*, & defended the probation of the things which they called hereſie.

Fox *pag.* 1534.
,,
,,
,,
,,

A dialogue betvvene the B. of London & the painter and cooke.

,,
,,
,,
,,
,,
,,
,,
,,
,,
,,
,,
,,
,,
,,
,,
,,

H 2   *Bonner.*

”   *Bonner.* By my troth, *Maiſter Speaker*, yow
”   ſhall preach at the ſtake.

”   *Smith.* Well ſworne, my Lord, yow keep
”   a good watch.   q V

”   *Bonner.* Well, *Maiſter Controller*, I am no
”   Sainct.

”   *Smith.* No, my Lord, nor yet good Bi-
”   ſhopp, &c.

The obſti-
nacy of
the pain-
ter and
cooke a-
gainſt the
Biſhops.

13. And thus vvent on theſe two learned
Doctors the cooke & the paynter, anſwering
moſt proudly and contumeliouſly in euery
point to the Biſhop, which yet I haue not ſett
downe altogether as their words lye in Fox,
for that their examinations and ſpeeches are
large, and full of cauelinge words, and among
the reſt the paynter denyed the force of water
in baptiſme, and ieſted at the Biſhop for eſtee-
minge yt ouer much, who at length after all
poſſible meanes vſed to perſuade them to
moderation, and to heare patiently the truth;
the painter anſwered: *My Lord to put yow out of*

Fox ibid.   *doubt becauſe I am weary, I will ſtrayne curteſy with
yow; I perceyue yow will not with your Doctors come to
me, and I am not determined to come to yow by Gods
grace, for I haue hardened my face againſt yow as hard
as braſſe.* Thus repotteth Fox of the painters
laſt ſpeaches. And no leſſe obſtinacy doth he
recompt in his fellow *Tankerfield* the Cooke;
who aunſwered (ſaith he) to the Biſhopp:

ibid. col. 2.   *I will not forſake my opinions, except yow my L. can
repell them by ſcriptures; and I care not for your diuinity, &c.* Thus the Cooke. And what would
yow do with ſuch people?

14. And

14.   And further more Fox writeth that after *Tankerfields* condemnation, a certaine learned schoolmaifter appartayning to *Syr Thomas
Pope* knight, then of the Counfell, dealt with
him about the controuerfy of the *Reall prefence*,
and other articles, vrging him much with
certayne authorityes & textes of the Fathers:
But (faith Fox) *as he vrged Tankerfield with autho-*
rity of the Doctors, wrefting them after his owne will,
fo on the otherfide Tankerfield aunfwered him mighti-
ly by the Scriptures, not wrefted after the mynd of any
man, but interpreted after the will of the Lord Iefu,
&c. Confider the folly of this goofely Fox, in
afcribing to his Cooke fo highe a talent of
mighty interpreting Scriptures after the will
of the Lord Iefus; where receaued the Cooke
fuch affuräce of expounding fcriptures thinke
yow? but yet do yow heare further of him, for
that his canonizer I. Fox relateth yet an other
heroycall act of him, faying; that he being in
the Inne of the Croffe Keyes at Saint Albans, „
preparing himfelfe to be burned, he demaun- „
ded of the winedrawer a pynt of malmefy, „
and a loafe to celebrate the communion to „
himfelfe before he died; which being brought
vnto him, he kneeled downe (faith Fox) and
read the Inftitution of the holy fupper by the
Lord Iefus out of the Euangelifts, and out of
S. Paul, and then receaued yt with thanks-gi-
uing, *&c.* So relateth Fox, & then faith of him „
further, that he hauing dronke vp the wine, &
eaten the bread, went to the place of execution
coragioufly, crying out vehemently, (as a man

bedlam

Fox pag.
1534. col. 2,
num. 84.

Tanker-
field his
cömunion
vvith a
pot of
Malmefy.

bedlam yow muſt thinke , or rauiſhed with
ſome ſudden fury) I *defy the vvhore of Babylon* ; I
Ibidem.   *defy the whore of Babylon;and vvith this* (ſaith Fox)
he ended his martyrdome , and fell a ſleep in the Lord,
&c. But ſuch a martyrdome,ſuch a ſleep:God
defende all good men from both.

15.   And thus much of theſe two Captaynes
of this crew:the reſt of their compagnions did
nothinge but applaud theſe mens ſayings and
doings, puttinge in now and then ſome blaſphemous and contumelious ſpeach alſo , to
ſhew therby their conformity of ſpiritt: as for
Thomas   example *Thomas Fuſh* the ſhomaker, being mo-
Fuſh ſho-   ued by the Biſhopp (ſaith Fox) to reuoke his
maker his   opinions, he anſwered: *No my Lord, for there is*
impudent
ſpeach.   *no truth that commeth out of your mouth , but all lyes:*
Fox *pag.*   *yea you condemne men , and vvill not heare the truth.*
1545.   *VVhere can yow find any anoynting or greaſing in Gods*
booke? I ſpeake nothing but the truth: yea I am certaine
that yt is the truth that I ſpeake, &c. Behold the
aſſurance that the ſhomaker had, that whatſoeuer he ſpake,*was truth*: and yet to heare him
lye ſo notably, that there is noe mention of
Leuit 4.7. any annoyntinge in Gods booke , (yf the old
16.   & new teſtament be Gods bookes) may teach
Deut. 1. 6.
7.   vs, that eyther the madd fellow knew not
1.*Reg.*9.10. what he ſaid, or cared not what he affirmed,
2. *Reg.* 11.
5.   true or falſe, ſo he ſaid ſomewhat, and named
Eccleſ. 45. Gods booke only. But lett vs heare his com-
Iac. 5.
panion.

vvilliam   16.   *VVilliam Hayle* alſo anſwered:(ſaith Fox)
Hayle.   *Ah good people beware of this Idolatry, and this Anti-*
Fox *ibid.*
chriſt the Biſhop of London. And finally *Elizabeth*
VVarne

VVarne the vpholsters wife, stood no lesse obstinate in her opinions, then the rest, for that
shee being earnestly exhorted (saith Fox) *to recant, she said: do what ye will, for yf Chrest vvas in error, then am I in error, and no otherwise, &c.* Behold this dame, that will equall herselfe with
Christ in certainty of her opinions, this somewhat passeth the shomaker, that could speake
nothinge *but truth.* What will yow say to this
people, was not this a maddinge moode or
moone that raigned in them? yet doth Fox
prayse them exceedingly for this their resolution, shewinge further, that they being all
condemned togeather, after many meanes
vsed to recall them (but in vayne) they were
sent to be burned in diuers parts of the
realme, for that no other end could be made
with them.

17. Next to this squadron of Craftesmen-
martyrs, Iohn Fox placeth a minister-martyr
and preacher named *Robert Samuell,* burned at
Ipswich in the same yeare. This fellow was
a Parish Priest, that had serued at *Barfold* in
Suffolke, and in K. Edwards dayes had taken a
woman vnder the name of his wife; but when
afterward in Q. Maryes raigne, order was taken (saith Fox) by the Queene, and published
by the commissionars, that all Priests that had
marryed in K. Edwards dayes, puttinge their
wyues from them, should be compelled to returne againe to their chastity, and simple life;
Maister Robert Samuell would not stand to this
decree, but vsed his wife still, whervpon he

Robert
Samuell
an Aposta-
ta Priest
become a
minister.

,,
,,
,,
,,
,,
,,
Fox *pag.*
1547.

,, was taken at home with his wife, put into
,, Ipſwich iayle, called before *Doctor Hopton* Bi-
,, ſhop of *Norwich*, and *Doctor Dunnings* his Chan-
,, celor, and by them examined and condem-
,, ned, *&c.*

18. This is the effect of Fox his narration
about *Samuell* the miniſter, who yet was a
Prieſt, as yow ſee; and yt is to be noted that all
marryed Prieſts are commonly called miniſters by Fox in his Calendar, as though their
hauinge wyues did vnprieſt them, and make
them true miniſters. Yow muſt remember al-

Febr. vlt. ſo, that we haue made mention of this Prieſt-
miniſter *Samuell* in the Story of *Agnes Potten* &
Ioane Trunchfield, the firſt wife of a beerebrewer, the other of a ſhomaker in Ipſwich,
principale diſciples of this *Robert Samuell*, of
whome he had viſions in his ſleepe, as namely
that he ſaw three ladders ſet vp towards heauen, of the which there was one ſomewhat
longer then the reſt, but at length became all

Fox pag. one, which viſion or dreame I. Fox expoun-
1547. deth in theſe words. *This vvas a forewarninge re-*

Certayne *ueyled vnto him, declaring vndoubtedly the martyrdome*
dreames *firſt of himſelfe, and then of tvvo honeſt vveomen, Agnes*
of Samuell *Potten, & Ioane Trunchfield vvho vvere brought forth,*
the mar-
ried prieſt. *and ſuffered in the ſame tovvne anone after,* &c.

19. This ſaith Fox: and then he vvryteth
another dreame of the ſaid *Samuell*, wherin he
ſeemed to ſee one ſtand before him cladd in
vvhite, and to ſay vnto him in his ſleepe:

Fox ibid, *Samuell, Samuell, be of good cheere. And finally* (ſaith
Fox) *as this godly Martyr vvas going to the fire, there*
came

came a certayne maid vnto him, which tooke him about the necke and kissed him ; vvho being marked by them that vvere present , vvas sought for the next day after to be had to prison , and burned , as the very party her-selfe informed me, being called Rose Nottingam , she being maruelously preserued by the prouidence of God, &c. Thus farre Fox , who sheweth himselfe very forward to beleeue any thinge neuer so stràge, of these his new Saints; but is altogea-ther incredulous of the miracles of Cath. Mar-tyrs neuer so ancient or authentically testified.

Rose Not-tingam kissed the minister as he vvēt to bur-ninge.

20. And as for that he telleth here of *Rose Nottingam* that kissed the minister in the street as he was going to burning , and was sought for the next day after to be had *to prison and burned,* seemeth a very improbable tale. For I would aske why she was not taken then pre-sently in the street , yf she kissed him so publi-kely? But I will not examine the probabili-tyes of Fox his miracles, especially of the last of all which he relateth of this his Samuell, by report (saith he) of them that were present: to witt , *that his body in burning did shine as bright and white, as new tryed siluer , in the eyes of them that stood by.* But these eyes are to be supposed to haue byn new ghospellers eyes yf any such were, & as ready to frame out vnto their ima-gination such a sight, as Fox is to beleeue and relate yt. For yf yow aske hundreds of others that stood by , none saw any such brightnes, but rather that he appeared both blacke and foule, vntill he was burned to ashes. And so much of him

An im-probable tale of Iohn Fox.

pag. 1547.

21. In

21. **In** the next place after this Apoſtata

Ioane
VVaſt the
blind vvo-
mar of
Darby.

Prieſt *Samuell*, there commeth in a blynd woman of *Darby* named *Ioane VVaſt*, woſe feſtiuall day of martyrdome is appointed heere
vpon the 19 day of this moneth. She was

Fox pag.
1771.

borne blynd in the towne of Darby (ſaith
Fox) her Father was a barber and ropema-

,, ker, and when ſhe was about 12. or 13. yeares
,, old, ſhe learned to knytt hoſen, and ſleues, and
,, as tyme ſerued ſhe would help her father to
,, turne ropes, and in no caſe would be idle: and
,, in K. Edwards dayes of bleſſed memory,
,, her father and mother being dead, ſhe by
,, hearing homylies and ſermons, became mar-
,, ueloully well affeċted to the religion then
,, taught, ſo as at length hauing by her labour
,, gott and ſaued ſo much money, as would buy
,, her a new Teſtament, ſhe cauſed one to be
,, procured for her; and with that ſhe repaired
,, to one *Iohn Hurte*, and ſometymes to one *Iohn*
,, *Pemberton* clarke of the pariſh, to read vnto her,

The blynd
vvomans
penny-
vvorth of
readinge
ſcripture.

and ſometymes ſhe would giue a penny or
two, as ſhe might ſpare, to ſuch perſons as
would not freely read vnto her, appointing
vnto them aforehand, how many chapters of

,, the new teſtament they ſhould read, or how
,, often they ſhould repeat one chapter vpon
,, a price, *&c.*

22. So relateth Fox of this blynd woman,
and that after ſhe being called before *Doċtor
Raph Bayne* B. of that Dioceſe, and *Doċtor Dra-
cott* his Chancelor, and other their aſſiſtants
and fellow Commiſſionars, ſhe was finally
condemned

condemned to be burned and executed in *Darby*, vpon great and singular obstinacy; we must imagine, for that otherwise I cannot see how so principall learned men, would haue agreed to the burninge of so miserable and ignorant a woman.

23. From *Darby* Iohn Fox steppeth to *Colchester*, vvhere he appointeth out sixe other martyrs of his, burned togeather in the same towne, 3. men, and 3. weomen. The men are *VVilliam Bongiar* glasier, *Thomas Bennold* tallow chandelor, and *Robert Purcas* (Fox calleth him *VVilliam* in his acts) by occupation a fuller. The vveomen are *Agnes Siluerside* vviddow spinster, *Helen Ewring* wife to *Iohn Ewring* myller, and *Elizabeth Fulkes* a seruing-mayde in Colchester of 20. yeares old. Of all which Fox writeth thus: Diuers examinations these good people had at sundry tymes, before diuers Iustices, Priests and officers, as *Maister Roper* Iustice, *Iohn Kingston* Comissary, *Iohn Boswell* Priest, and scribe to *B. Bonner*, and last of all, they were examined in *Mote-Hall* of Colchester vpon the 23. day of Iune by *Doctor Chadsey*, and the said *Iohn Kingston*, and other Priests, & of *Boswell* the scribe in the presence of the two Bayliffes of *Colchester*, &c.

24. Thus farre Fox: And furthermore he recounteth their resolute answers, wherin he gloryeth also, but yet confesseth that *Doctor Chadsey* amonge others, was so moued to compassion and pitty in hearinge the same, and consideringe their desperate vvillfullnes, as

the

VVilliam Bongiar.
Thomas Bennold
Robert Purcas.
Agnes Siluerside.
Helen Evvringe.
Elizabeth Fulkes.
Fox *pag.* 1821.
,,
,,
,,
,,
,,
,,
,,

The compassion of *D. Chadsey* towards obstinate people.

the teares trickled downe aboundantly ouer his cheekes, all the tyme the ſentence againſt them was in readinge. But nothinge vvould mooue them that vvere in moſt danger both of body and ſoule, ſo had the enemy of man-kynd blynded them with pride and preſump-tion of hereſie, and obdured their harts vvith pertinacity.

Fox pag.
1821. 25. *VVilliam Bongiar glaſyer* (ſaith Fox) *affirmed reſolutely, that the Sacrament of the Altar, was bread, is bread, and remayneth bread; and that for the Conſe-cration, yt is not the holyer, but rather the vvorſe, &c.* Conſider I pray yow what ſkill a glaſier could haue in this controuerſy, to aunſwere ſo reſo-lutely vpon his life and death both temporall and eternall. If he had read *S. Ambroſe* and *Ambroſ. lib. 1. de Sacr. c. 4.* would haue beleeued him, where he teacheth vs in his books *De Sacramentis* at large, that *Conſecratione,* &c. *by Conſecration, natures are chan-ged, and bread and vvyne turned into the true fleſh and bloud of Chriſt;* the poore glaſier perhaps would not haue byn ſo reſolute to the contrary. But now theſe miſerable ignorant people are drawne to their deſtructió, by the inchaunte-ment of a few heady Sectaryes, that make them beleeue, that vvhat ſo euer they ſay is Gods vvords. Yf they had appeared before *Martyn Luther*, as they did before thes other commiſsioners, what would he haue ſaid of them thinke yow? But let vs go forward with the reſt.

26. *Thomas Bennold* (ſaith Fox) tallow-chan-delor affirmed the like to *Bongiar*, but *VVilliam*

Purcas

Purcas the fuller said; *that vvhen he receaued the Sacrament, he receaued bread in a holy vse, that preacheth the remembrance of Chriſt.* Marke his phraſe. And this for the men. But the weomen were much more inſolent and obſtinate, as the faſhion is, eſpecially the yongeſt of them all, to witt, the Seruing-mayd *Elizabeth Fulkes* of 20. yeares old. For albeit Iohn Fox ſaith of *Agnes Siluerſide*, *that the good old vvoman anſivered them with ſuch ſound iudgement and boldnes,that yt reicyced the harts of many:* And then of *Helen Ewring* the myllers wife: *that albeit this good vvoman was ſomwhat thicke of hearinge; yet vvas ſhe quicke in vnderſtandinge the Lords matters, &c.* Yet doth he inſiſt moſt vpon *Elizabeth Fulkes* his yong mayden, as he calleth her, for that ſhe was much more malepart, then the other weomen, that were more aged, and this is proper alſo to hereſie, that the yongeſt and vveakeſt vvill preſume moſt, eſpecially in woman kynde: yow ſhall heare ſome of her behauiour out of Fox himſelfe.

27. *Elizabeth Fulkes* the yonge mayden (ſaith he) being examyned, whether ſhe beleeued the preſence of Chriſts body to be in the Sacrament ſubſtantially and really or no? ſhe anſwered; *that ſhe beleeued yt to be a ſubſtantiall lye, and a reall lye,* at which words the Prieſts and others chafed very much, *&c.* Thus Fox. And then he telleth further, that ſhe being asked, whether after conſecration, there remayned not the body of Chriſt, ſhe aunſwered: *that whatſoeuer man bleſſed vvithout Gods vvord, is curſed and*

and abhominable by the vvord. Then they examined her of confession, masse, authority of the
Pope, and the like, wherto she answered: *that
she did vtterly detest and abhorre all such trumpery from
the bottome of her hart, &c.* Then was she (saith
Fox)deliuered to her vncle *Holt* of Colchester,
to carry her home to his house,which he did,
and she might haue escaped but she would
not, but went backe to the Papists againe : to
witt, the comissionars , and findinge them at
the signe of the *white hart* in Colchester,she fell
to vtter defiance of them and their doctrine,
and so had in the end a papisticall reward, for
she was burned, *&c.*

The inso-
lent be-
hauiour of
Elizabeth
Fulks the
seruing-
mayd.

28.   Thus relateth Fox of his modest mayd
that defyed the wole world , and her lawfull
iudges. And of the same mayden Fox repor-
teth:*that when se came to the fyre, she put of her pet-
ticote,and taking the same into her hand , she threw yt
away from her, sayin g farewell all the world , farewell
fayth, farewell hope,a nd so taking the stake in her hand
said , welcome my loue ,* &c. Thus he of his mai-
den. And then of all six he concludeth in these
words : *Thus yelded vp they their soules and bodyes
into the Lords hands for the testimony of his truth. The
Lord graūt,that we may imitate them in the like quarrell, &c.* So he.The effect of which prayer had
byn well perhaps for Iohn Fox,& many hundred others deceyued by him since that ryme,
yf yt had lighted vpon him in those dayes of
Q. Mary, to witt, that he had byn burned
with this his mayden and her mates for like
quarrell, before he wrote this lying e and deceytfull

Fox *pag.*
1822.

Ibidem.

Fox his
censure of
their vvill-
full death.

ceytfull volume of his Acts and Monuments, for yt had byn lesse damnation in my opinion both to him and others. But for vs that be now aliue, God defend that euer we should fall into such fury or phrenesie of heresie, as to runne to the stake so headlong, as these ignorant distracted people did, for such a quarrell of defendinge their owne fancyes.

29. The last company burned vpon this moneth in the yeare 1557. were six more accordinge to Fox his relation, vvherof 4. vvere burned also at *Colchester*, and were of the former fraternity, of which we haue now spoken. Their names are *VVilliam Mont* husbandman, & *Alice* his wife, togeather with *Rose Allen* his said wiues daughter, & *Iohn Iohnson* another labourer of the same place. These & some 18. more being knowne to be very busy people, and to peruerte many of their neighboures in *Colchester* and round about, partly by contumelious and blasphemous speaches vsed dayly by them, aswell in words as wrytinge, against the doctrine & ceremonyes of the Catholike Church: as also by their examples in vsinge to meete in fields, & secrett houses, and to fly the said Church, they were vpon complaint made, apprehended by the *Earle of Oxford* the *L. Darcy, Maister Edmond Tyrrell*, and others in commission, and sent vp to London to be examined, where partly vpon compassion of such ignorant people, and partly vpon their submission and promise of amendment, they were dismissed & sent home againe without

any

VVilliam Mont.
Alice his vvife.
Rose Allen.
Iohn Iohnson.

any hurt (as Fox himſelfe confeſſeth), and conſequently the Catholiks were not ſo greedy of ſhedding bloud in thoſe dayes,as he euery where accuſeth them. But when theſe people came againe they proceeded farre more ſeditiouſly and inſolently then before, as may appeare by ſundry letters wrytten by *Syr Thomas Tye* pariſh prieſt of *Much-bentley*,and of his pariſhionars, as well to the foreſaid *Lord Darcy*, as alſo to B. *Bonner*. In the former letters they wryte thus:

The complaint of inſolent behauior of heretiks diſmiſſed.

30.   *By reaſon of three ſeditious perſons, VVilliam Mont and his vvife,and Roſe her daughter,who by their colourable ſubmiſſion vvere diſmiſt, and ſent downe from the B. of London. They ſince their comming, haue not only in their owne perſons ſhewed manifeſt tokens of diſobedience, but alſo moſt malitiouſly and ſeditiouſly haue ſeduced many, mockinge thoſe that frequent the Church, callinge them, Church-owles, and blaſphemouſly callinge the bleſſed Sacrament, a blind God,with diuers ſuch wicked blaſphemyes, &c.* And in the ſecond letters to Biſhop Bonner it is wrytten thus:

Fox pag. 1822.

Ibidem.

Synce the comminge downe of 24. *ranke heretiks*
,, diſmiſſed from yow, the deteſtable ſort of
,, ſchiſmatiks were neuer ſo bold, &c. They aſ-
,, ſemble togeather vpon the Sabboth day in the
,, tyme of diuine ſeruice, ſometymes in one
,, houſe, ſometymes in another, and there keep
,, their priuate conuenticles and ſchooles of he-
,, reſie. Your officers ſay, that the counſell ſent
,, them not home without great conſideration,
,, I pray God ſome of them proue not fauou-
,, rers of heretiks. The rebells are ſtout in the

towne

towne of *Colchester* ; the ministers of the
Church are hemmed at in the streets, and called knaues, the blessed Sacrament is blasphe-
med and rayled vpon in euery alehouse and
tauerne, prayer and fastinge is not regarded,
seditious talks and newes are ryfe both in the
towne and countrey, *&c.*

31. Thus wrote these Catholike men, whervpon this *VVilliam Mont*, with diuers of his
crew being apprehended againe, they vvere
carryed to Colchester Castle, and there examined, as yow haue heard of the former six.
There aunsweres vvere much like (saith Iohn Fox)
vnto the former; that is to say, rayling & blasphemous, as yow may assure your selfe, for that
VVilliam Mont, besides the denyinge of many
especially other articles of Cath. faith, the
diuell stirred him vp against the blessed Sacramēt of the Altar, which blasphemously he called *an abhominable Idoll.* And him followed both
Alice Mont his wife, and *Iohnson* the labourer.
But aboue all, as Iohn Fox delighteth euery
where in the malepart aunsvvers of his yonge
maydens ; so heere he bringeth in *Rose Allen* of
20. yeares old, daughter to the foresaid *Alice*,
for a singular example of forwardnes in his
ghospell.

32. Rose Allen mayde (saith he) of the age
of 20. yeares being examined of auricular
confession, goinge to the Church, hearinge
masse, seauen Sacraments, *&c.* she aunsvvered
stoutly, *that they stunke in the face of God, and that
she durst not haue to do vvith them for her life, neither*

*VVilliam
Mont his
blasphe-
my against
the B. Sa-
crament.*

*The im-
modest &
insolent
ansvvers
of Rose
Allen Fox
his maid.*

,,

I   *vvas*

Fox *pag.*
1522.

*vvas she any member of theirs, for that they vvere the
members of Antichrist, &c.* This was her first ans-

,, were, wherin yow fee more pride and info-
,, lency then in any of the reft. But being asked
,, further (faith he) what she could say of the
,, Sea of Rome, and Bishops therof; and whe-
,, ther she would obay the Bishopp therof? she
,, answered boldly, *that (she vvas none of his. And*
,, *as for his Sea* (quoth she) *yt is for crowes, Kytes,*
,, *owles and rauens to swym in, such as yow be*; for by
,, the grace of God I will not swymme in that
,, Sea while I liue, neither will I haue any thing
,, to do therwith. Thus aunfwered this wife
gyrle, not vnderftandinge what the *Sea of
Roome* was, or meant, but thinking yt had byn
a fea of water to fwymme in: and yet notwithftandinge would she needs dye, for defence of her knowledge and fancy therin, and
in other points of Religion. And Fox talking

Fox *ibid.*

of her condemnation, faith : *Then read they the
fentence of condemnation, and thus thefe poore condemned lambes vvere deliuered ouer to the hands of the fecular power.* So he. But lett any man confider
vvhether thefe kind of aunfwers vvere of
Iambes, or rather of wolues, Foxes, & Tigers,
proceedinge from an inraged mynd with fury
of herefie, againft their mother the Church.

33.   And now there remayne only 3. more
to make vp this moneth of Auguft: to witt,

George
Eagles, &
his fifter.

George Eagles, furnamed *Trudgeouer-the-world*,
whofe feaft is appointed vpon the 30. day
therof, ioyned with the feaft of one *Fryar*, and
the faid *George Eagles* fifter vpon the 31. And for
the

the laſt two, Fox only wryteth thus much:
that about the ſame tyme and moneth, one named Friar Friar and
vvith a vvoman accompanyinge him, vvho was the ſiſter hisvvomā.
of George Eagles, in the like cauſe of righteouſnes ſuf- Fox *pag.*
fered like martyrdome, by the vnrighteous Papiſts at 1825.
Rocheſter, &c. But what their opinions, articles,
or aunſwers were, and whether this fellow
were indeed a *Friar* or no, or only in name, or
whether this woman did accompany him in
trew or pretended wedlocke, or otherwiſe,
he ſaith no one word; for which cauſe, we
alſo ſhalbe ſilent heerin.

34. But as for the former, to witt *George* George
Eagles, yt appeareth by Fox his large narration Eagles
of him, that by occupation he was a Taylor, called
and thence made himſelfe a preacher, went *Trudgeouer*
vp and downe from countrey to countrey, to *the vvorld.*
make proſelites of his Religion, and to ſtitch
them to his Church; which vocation of his
Fox highly eſteemeth, for thus he wryteth
of him. *This George Eagles* is not to be neglected Fox *pag.*
for his baſe occupation, whome Chriſt called 1822.
thence to ſett forth his ghoſpell; rather we ,,
ought to glorifie God the more therby in his ,,
holynes, which in ſo blynd a tyme inſpired ,,
him with the gift of preaching, and conſtancy ,,
of ſuffering; who after a certaine tyme, that ,,
he had vſed the occupation of a taylor, being ,,
eloquent, and of good vtterance, gaue and ap= ,,
plied himſelfe to the profitt of Gods Church, ,,
&c. *And againe a little after.* He wandringe a- ,,
broad into diuers and farre countreyes, where ,,
he could fynd any of his brethren, he did there ,,
I 2   moſt

moſt earneſtly encorage , and comfort them, not tarrying in this towne or that, yet some- tymes abding certayne monethes togeather
,, as occaſion ſerued , lodging ſometymes in the
,, countrey , and ſometymes for feare , liuinge
,, in the fields and woods , who for his immo-
,, derate and vnreaſonable going abroad, was
,, called *Trudgeouer*, &c.

35.   Thus wryteth Fox of his martyr, but doth not tell vs therwith the ſeditious and treaſonable tricks , which this *Trudgeouer* did practiſe againſt the Q. Sate and realme in this his trudging vp an downe , for which he was condemned not of religion , but of treaſon, and executed for the ſame , by drawing, han- ging and quartering at the towne of *Chelemſ-* *ford* in Eſſex , without any one word mentio- ned vnto him for religion , that I haue heard or read. Fox ſetteth downe ſome words of his arraignment thus : *George Eagles, thou art en-* *dighted by the name of George Eagles, otherwiſe Trud-* *geouer-the world , for that thou dideſt ſuch a day make* *thy prayer, that god ſhould turne Q. Maryes hart, or els* *take her away.* This is all that yt pleaſed Fox to ſett downe of his endightment, for iuſtifiyng of his ſainct: but yet a little before in the ſame narration he wryteth thus : *The next day he was* *carried to London to the Biſhopp and the Councell , and* *there remayned a certayne tyme, and then was brought* *downe to Chelemsford to the Seſſions , and there was* *endyghred and accuſed of treaſon , becauſe he had aſ-* *ſembled companyes togeather,contrary to the lawes and* *ſtatutes of the realme in that caſe prouided, &c.*

36. Thus

36.   Thus he. and heerby we may fee, that *George Eagles* caufe was not religion, but manifeft treafon, though Fox make him heere a bleffed mattyr afwell in his Calendar, as alfo in the ftory of his Acts and Monuments. He telleth vs furthermore, that his foure quarters were fent to be hanged vp at foure feuerall townes, to witt, *Colchefter*, *Harwich*, *Chelemsford, and S. Roufes. His head* (faith he) *was fett vp at Chelemsford at the markett croffe vpon a long pole, and ftood till the wynd did blow yt downe, and lying certayne dayes in the ftreet was tombled about, vntill one caufed yt to be buried in the churchyard in the night, &c.* Fox doth not fay, whether he that buryed the relique of *Trudgeouer* was a Catholique or Proteftant, but well he fheweth that Proteftants do not honour the reliques of their faincts, in that they fuffered this their martyrs head to be tombled vp and downe fo many dayes in the ftreet, without fo much as taking yt vp. But fuch martyrs, fuch honour due vnto them.

37.   And one fpeciall Euloge, and worthy commendation I fynd in Fox himfelfe, giuen to this *Eagles* by the B. of *Rochefter* in Q. Maryes tyme, who reafoning with one *Allerton* a taylor and companion of this *Eagles*, faid to him in thefe words, as Fox relateth them: *VVere not yow a companion of George Eagles otherwife called Trudgeouer? My L of London telleth me, that yow are his fellow companion.* Allerton: *I know him very well, my Lord.* Bifhop: *By my faith I had him once before me, and then he was as drunke as an ape: for he*

I 3   *ftunke*

Trudge-ouer his quarters hanged vp in diuers places and his head cõtemned by the Proteftãts. *Ibidem.*

Fox *pag.* 1889.

Trudge-ouer a drunken martyr.

ſtunke ſo of drinke that I could not abide him, and ſo I ſent him away, &c. This teſtimony gaue the ſaid B. publikely. And albeit the taylor *Alberton* would ſeeme to deny the ſame, and ſay that *Trudgeouer* had not drunke any beere or wyne in long tyme before that; yet may a man eaſily conſider, how probable a thing this is; and whether the taylor that ſpake yt of a certayne animoſity, to contradict the Biſhop & defend the honour of his fellow taylor *Trudgeouer,* be more to be credited, then ſo honourable a perſonage as the Biſhopp of *Rocheſter* was, who affirmed yt of his owne knowledge in the preſence of many, that were preſent at the fact. And ſo much of this man and moneth. The compariſon betwene Fox his Calendar and ours, yow may eaſily make, by vew of that which before is ſpoken.

The ende of Auguſt.

T H E

THE MONETH

OF SEPTEMBRR,

and Foxian Saints therin conteyned;

The number wherof is thirty and eight;
beginninge with Father Abraham,
and ending with Iohn Fortune.

CHAP. XIII.

THE only dayes that are left in this moneth
to Catholike Saints , are the 21. to *S. Ma-*
thew the Apostle, and the 29. to *S. Michell* the
Archangell , which are both in rubricate letters in Iohn Fox his Calendar, as well as ours,
wherin we are somwhat beholden ynto him,
especially for the later : to witt, that he hath
left vs free the feast of *S. Michell* the Archangell , which is the feast also of all other Angells, to be celebrated with solemnity, wheras
otherwise he and his fellowes are wont to
obiect vnto vs the Religion of Angells, *&c.*
And this curtesy of his, is some recompence
for strykinge out in this moneth the feast of
the *Natiuity* of our *Blessed Lady,* mother of God,
(vvhich vve preferre before Angells) and do
celebrate her said feast vpon the eight day
therof, with great & ancient solemnity. And
seing he hath dealt so rigourouslye vvith

I 4   Christes

Chriftes mother herfelfe, as to put out her natiuity in the Calendar; we muft haue patience
with him for puttinge out other inferior
Saints alfo , as *S. Cornelius* Pope and Martyr,
S. Cyprian, S. Linus, S. Hierome and others ; yea
the feaft of the *Exaltation of Chriftes holy Croffe* yt
felfe, which in our Church is vpon the 14. of
this moneth , in memory of that day , vvhen
the faid Croffe with fo great honor was refto-
red by *Heraclius* the Emperor, from the poffef-
fion of the heathen Perfians vnto Chriftians
againe, as Ecclefiafticall hiftoryes do recount.
This memory (I fay) of the Croffe of our Sauiour, Iohn Fox hath thruft out, as well as the
reft, and in place therof, he hath fett vs foorth
in his Calendar *Cornelius Bungay* a capper of
Couentry. And on our Ladyes day, in fteed of
her *Natiuity*, is fett downe the feftiuall memory of *George Catmer,* a Cobler of *Hith* in Kent;
and for *Saint Hierome,* *Iohn Fortune* a prefumptuous heretical *Smith*, and other fuch like exchanges, which after yow fhall looke into
more particulariy by the vew.

Fox his
exchanges
of Saints.

2.   And firft of all is to be noted, that Fox
doth not place in the beginning of this moneth, any put to death vnder K. Henry the 8.
as hitherto he was wont, but only for the firft
three dayes fetteth downe three Lollards, or
Wickliffians burned vnder K. Henry the 6.
anno 1428. whofe names he faith he found in
a certaine old Regifter, wherof the greater
part could not be read. Thefe three are *Father
Abraham* a poore fimple old man of *Colchefter*,
                                   togeather

Father A-
braham.

togeather with *VVilliam VVhite*, and *Iohn VVad-*
don Apoſtata Prieſts, for whoſe apprehenſion
with diuers others ſuſpected of *hereſie and Lol-*
lardy (thoſe be the words of the comiſsion) he
cyteth the ſaid Kings letters to *Iohn Exceter* ke-
per of the Caſtle of Colcheſter, and others,
bearinge date the ſixt of Iuly and ſixt yeare
of his raigne. And yf we conſider the condition and circumſtances of that tyme, we ſhall
ſee yt was when Engliſh men were much occupied in French warres; by occaſion wherof,
the infection of Lollards & Wickliffians did
grow in diuers parts of England, but eſpecially in *Norſolke*, for ſo much ſignifie the ſaid
letters of the King, commandinge them to be
ſought out and puniſhed. And allbeyt moſt
of them, when they were apprehended, did
abiure publikely their opinions, wherof I ohn
Fox recordeth a catalogue of almoſt a hundred, that did the ſame, and therby eſcaped,
(whome notwithſtandinge he accounteth as
good members of his Church:) yet ſome few
of them were burned for relapſe afterward,
eſpecially theſe three here mentioned.

3.   And as for *F. Abraham*, we do not know
by Fox his relation heere what he was, otherwiſe then a poore man; or whether he were a
Iew, *Lollard* or *VVickliffian*, or why he was called *Father*, for that Fox his ſtory ſaith no more
of him, *but that Father Abraham of Colcheſter vvas*
burned for like opinions, that the tvvo Prieſts VVhite, &
VVaddon vvere. Now his articles might be like,
and yet farre different in ſubſtance from thoſe
of the

VVilliam
VVhite.
Iohn
VVaddon.

Henry the
ſixt his
letters for
apprehen-
dinge of
heretiks in
Norfolke.

Lollards
and VVic-
kliffians
abiure.

Fox pag.
609.

of the two Prieſts: but yf they were the true
articles of *Lollards* and *VVickliſſians*, we haue
treated therof before in the third Chapter of
this booke, where yow may ſee them ſett
downe at large.   Fox in this place talkinge of
the whole agreemēt of his *VVickliſſian* Saints,
as well thoſe that abiured as others, wryteth

Fox pag.
608.
thus: *I find* (ſaith he) *in the regiſters ſuch ſociety
and agreement of doctrine to haue byn amongſt them,
that almoſt in their aſſertions and articles there vvas no
difference.* Note I pray yow the word (*almoſt*)
concerninge their vnity; remember alſo that
in the margent of this place, Fox ſetteth
downe this note for their Antiquity againſt

Fox ibid.
B. *Bonner* by name. *Bonner* (ſaith he) *might ſee the
Church heere in this age, more then* 40. *yeares before
he vvas borne.* And is not this a great antiquity
(thinke yow) ioyned with their *almoſt vnity* in

Antiquity
and vnity
of VVic-
kliſſians.
thoſe dayes? But yf he would conferre their
opinions with thoſe of the Proteſtants of our
dayes; what vnity (thinke yow) ſhould he
find amonge them? yow may ſee them compared in the forſaid 3. Chapter of this booke.

4.   But as concerninge *Syr VVilliam VVhite* the
Prieſt (ſo named in the K. letters) by whome
yow may iudge of all the reſt, for that he was
their chiefe Captayne in thoſe dayes; Fox
vvryteth thus: *This VVilliam VVhite, being a fol-*

Fox pag.
199.
lower of Iohn VVickliffe, and a Prieſt not after the
„ common ſort, but as the ſcripture ſaith, *a mor-*

Eccl. 50.
ninge ſtarre in the middeſt of a cloud, &c. he gaue
„ ouer his Prieſthood and benefice, and tooke
„ vnto him a godly yonge vvoman to his vvife,
named

named *Ioane*, notwithstandinge he did not „
therfore ceafe, or leaue from his former office „
& duty, but continually laboured to the glory „
and praife of his fpoufe Chrift, by readinge, „
wrytinge and preachinge, &c. Whervpon he „
being attached at Canterbury vnder th'Arch-„
bifhop *Henry Chichefley*, in the yeare of our Lord „
1424. he there, for a certayne fpace ftoutly, and „
manly vvittneffed the truth vvhich he had „
preached, &c.

5. Thus Fox of his Martyr *VVhite*, and then
confeſsinge that he recanted and abiured publikely all his former opinions; yet that after a
tyme, being apprehended againe for relapfe
into the fame; *he vvas brought* (faith he) *before
VVilliam B. of Norwich, by vvhome he was conuict and
condemned of 30. articles, and there vvas burned in
Norwich, in the moneth of September anno 1424.* So
Fox. Which number of yeares notwithftandinge cannot agree, eyther vvith that vvhich
himfelfe fetteth downe in his Calendar, that
he vvas martyred vpon the yeare 1428. or
vvith that vvhich the Kings letters before
mentioned, for the apprehenfion of this *VVilliam VVhite* doth teftifie, naming the fixt yeare
of his raigne, vvhich vvas indeed the forefaid
yeare 1428. So as Fox neuer commonly is
found true or exact in his accompt of tyme, yf
yow compare one place with another.

6. And this is all in effect that he wryteth of
this *VVilliam VVhite* prieft, and his fellow *Iohn
VVaddon* like prieft to himfelfe, but only that
he addeth, that *Syr VVilliam VVhites* yonge wife

was

*Syr VVil-liam VVhite
vvith his
yong vvo-
man Ioane.*

Ibidem.

*Fox ibid.
col. 1.*

was fo kind to her husband, and fo forward & zealous in teaching, & preaching, as she would neuer leaue him, nor he her. *He going into Norfolke* (faith Fox) *with his said wife* Ioane, *and there occupying himselfe busely in teaching, he was at length apprehended,* &c. And againe. *VVhose said wife* Ioane *followinge her husbands footsteppes according to her power, teaching & sowing abroad the same doctrine, confirmed many men in gods truth,* &c. And finally Fox hauing told vs, how this *Syr VVilliam VVhitte* & his woman *Ioane* (for his wife she could not be, he hauing a follemne vow to the contrary) had their most aboad at the house of one *Thomas Moone* of *Ludney*, and from thence spread the ghospell; he addeth for a profe of his great holynes, these words : *That*

Fox *ibid.* *all the people had him in such reuerence, as they desyred him to pray for them, in so much that one* Margaret VVright *confessed, that yf any Saincts were to be prayed to, she would rather pray to him, then to any other,* &c.

Fox his manner of makinge a Priest-protestant vvith a vvench.   7.   All this relateth Fox of this Wickliffian abiured martyr, which I cannot fee why, or for what caufe or reafon he may be accompted for fo great a faint or of Iohn Fox his Church at all, but only for taking to himfelfe the yonge woman *Ioane* againft his vow of Chaftity; for in all other articles (or the moft part) he was oppofite and contrary. So as the making a good proteftant of a prieft, côfifteth by Fox, in taking a yonge woman when he groweth lafciuious. And fo much of him with his fellowes, burned vnder K. Henry the 6. And for that Fox his Calendar hath no other

of

of later date in this moneth, vntill he come to Zwinglians and Caluinifts burned vnder Q. Mary: vve fhall paffe to them, as they are fett downe in order.

8. But yet by the way we muft take one with vs, that was made martyr in K. Edward the fixth his dayes not in England, but an Englifhman, in *Lisbone* of Portugall, where he was burned for one of the moft defperate and wicked acts, that euer was heard of perhapps among Chriftian men, all circumftances confidered. His name was *VVilliam Gardner* of Briftow, a yonge feruant of one Pagett a marchant of that towne, & his factor for traffique in Portugall; he was not aboue 26. yeares of age (faith Fox) when he was fent thither, which yong age he noteth comonly for the more commendation of his martyrs, for that the yonger they are and of leffe witt, learning and iudgment, the more fitt to be ruled by the fpiritt of his new religion, which in many is *Spiritus vertiginis*, as yow fhall fee in this man.

9. His fact was, that he being come from England vnto *Lisbone*, vpon the yeare 1552. dronken with herefy, as many yong apprentices of profefsion were at that tyme, being towards the end of K. Edwards raigne, and finding the vfe of Catholike religion in great honour and celebrity there, according to the deuotion of that excellent Citty: this yonge Englifh profelite pricked on vvith pride, thought to make himfelfe famous by fome notable wicked attempt againft the fame, as
Eroftratus

The ftory of VVilliã Gardener burned for a defperate act in Lisbone.

Efai. 19.

Eroftratus in old tyme, by fettinge a fire the
temple of *Diana*; and to this effect feing one
day a great follemnity in Lisbone, at the marriage of the K. of Portugall his eldeft fonne,
to witt Prince Iohn, fonne of K. Iohn the 3.
vvith the daughter of Charles the Emperor,
the miferable vvretch gettinge into the
Church, and creeping neere to the high Altar,
vnefpied amongeft fo great a multitude of
Princes and people, as that day vvere prefent,
did, vvhileft maffe vvas a fayinge by *Prince
Henry* Cardinall (afterwards K. of Portugall)
rufh foddainly to the faid Altar, and ouerthrowinge the Chalice, tooke the Confecrated hoft, and moft impioufly trode yt vnder
his feete, in the prefence both of the K. Cleargy, and all other the nobility and people:
Wheruppon an vprore being made, he vvas
hurt, and like to haue byn flayne in the place,
but by the Kings cryinge (faith Fox) *to faue him*, he
vvas referued to further examination, and finally vvas burned.

10.   This vvas the heroicall act of this defperate yong marchant, vvhich Fox doth fo highly commend, as he maketh a longer preamble
in the rare praifes of this defperate apprentice,
then of any one of his Martyrs, to my remembrance, throughout the vvhole volume of
thefe his Acts and Monuments. And by this
euery man may iudge of his fpiritt. But let vs
heare his owne words: *VVilliam Gardener* (faith
he) is a man verily in my iudgement, not only
,, to be compared vvith the moft principall and
cheefe

Fox *pag.*
1241.

cheefe Martyrs of thefe our dayes; but alfo fuch a one, as the ancient Churches, in the tyme of the firft perfecutions, cannot fhew a more famous, vvhether vve do behould the force of his faith, his firme & ftedfaft conftancy, or the inuincible ftrength of his fpiritt, *&c.* ,,
Wherfore yf any praife or dignity amonge ,, men, as reafon is, be due vnto the Martyrs of ,, Chrift for their valiant Acts, this one man ,, among many, feemeth vvorthy to be renow- ,, ned and celebrated in the Church, vvith *Igna-* ,, *tius, Laurentius, Ciriacus, Crefcentius,* and *Gordia-* ,, *nus,* &c.

11. Thus vvryteth he, comparinge (as yow fee) this impious, madd, and furious yong ladd vvith thofe ancient holy Martyrs of Chrifts Church *S. Ignatius,* and the reft, as though they had byn of his Church, or their caufe like to that of *Gardener.* And yet yf yow remember, we haue fhewed before in this * Treatife, that * *Part.* 1? *cap.* *S. Ignatius* is reprehended by the Magdeburgians, for affirming the maffe to be a facrifice, and that the ftory of *S. Laurentius* vvrytten by *Prudentius* aboue **1200.** yeares gone, fetteth out fo cleerly the vvhole manner of Chriftian facrifice in thofe dayes, & the filuer and golden veffells vfed therin, for vvhich *S. Laurence* was called in queftion, by the couetuous Emperor; And yt is fo plainly defcribed, as we our felues can hardely deliuer the fame more cleerely now, then *Prudentius* did then. And how then may this defperate hereticke, that impugned the fame facrifice, by fo horrible and villanous
attempt,

attempt, be compared with thofe ancient holy Martyrs that defended the fame ? Or how
can this miferable forlorne companion, be
made equall with them in a caufe moft oppofite and contrary?

12.   Fox faith that he prayed much before he
tooke the matter in hand ; and fo did his three

*Sup.menf.
Maij.die 8.*

theeues alfo *King, Marsh* & *Debnam* (yf yow * remember) vvhen they vvent to robbe the
Church of *Douer-court* in K. Henryes dayes; &
fo did *Hackett, Arthington* & *Copinger* alfo, when
they refolued to make the faid *Hackett* Chrift,

See the
booke in-
tituled: *A
feduction of
Arthington
by Hacket,*
imprinted
at London
*anno Do-
mini* 1592.

and the other two Prophetts : Wherof yow
may fee a large particular relation fett forth by
Arthington himfelfe, after his pardon obtayned, and how earneftly they prayed alltogea-
ther that very morninge, when they were to
go forth & preach in the ftreets, *Hackett* lying
in his bedd, and leapinge out diuers tymes in
his fhirt (as the fpiritt came vpon him) to pray
with them at their bedds fides, and then returning to bedd againe: So as yt is not inough
to pray, but a man muft confider what he
prayeth, how and for what, and the Prophett

Pfal. 108.

faith of fome. *fiat oratio eorum in peccatum*, Let
their prayer turne into finne ; and fo did no
doubt the prayer of this defperate vvretch,
vvho prayed God to afsift him againft himfelfe, and the higheft honour done to him on
earth. And fo much of him.

13.   From the Story of *VVilliam Gardener* in K.
Edwards dayes, Iohn Fox paffeth to other 3.
Martyrs of his, burned vnder Q. Mary in the
yeare

yeare 1555. all simple ignorant men, but yet as willfull, as yf they had great learning for their foundation. The first was *William Allen* of Walsingham labouringe man; the second was *Thomas Cobb* of *Hauerhill* butcher; the third *Roger Coo* of *Melford* Sherman, to whome he adioyneth three Confessors also that died in prison: to witt *William Andrew* of Horsley carpenter, that died in *Newgate*, and *Thomas Ley* and *Iohn Wade* artificers, who sickening in prison, were carryed to their frends houses in London, and there died, and so were Confessors.

William Allen.
Thomas Cobb.
Roger Coo.
William Andrew.
Thomas Ley.
Io. Wade.

14. But to say somwhat of the forsaid three Martyrs, though Fox say but little, yet vttereth he so much as is sufficient to shew their foolish pertinacy euen to the death, & in matters, which they neyther vnderstood nor could haue other grounds to stand in, but their owne will. For of *Allen* the labourer, seruant to one *Iohn Houghton* of *Somerton*, Fox wryteth thus: That he being brought before the Bishopp, and asked the cause why he was in prison, answered: *for that he would not follow the Crosse in procession*: adding further, *that if he saw the King and Queene, and all other to follow the Crosse, yet he would not*; For which confession, lying Fox saith, that he was condemned, and sentence of death giuen against him. But how likely a tale this is, that for this only he should be condemned to death, euery man will easily consider, that hath reason, & knoweth the manner of Canonicall proceeding in that behalfe. And so much of him, for that Fox hath no more.

Fox pag.
1241.

K　15. But

15.   But about his two fellowes, *Cobb* the butcher, and *Coo* the sherman, Fox alleageth farre greater conflicts with the Bishops Chancelor, the victory alwayes remayning on Cobs and Coos side, & the other conquered. For thus is the Bishopp brought in to speake to *Coo* the sherman :

Fox pag. 1660.

    Bishop. Is not the holy Church to be beleeued ?

,,   *Coo.* Yes, yf it be grounded vpon the word
,, of God.

,,   Then said the *Bishopp* that he had charge of
,, *Coo* his soule.

,,   *Coo,* Haue ye so, my Lord, then yf yow go
,, to the diuell for your sinnes, where shall
,, I become ?

The reasoning of the *Bishopp* with *Coo* the sherman.

    Bishop. Will yow not beleeue as your Father did, was not he an honest man?

    Coo. It is wrytten, that after Christ hath suffered, there shall come a people with the
,, Prince, that shall destroy both people and san-
,, ctuary; I pray yow shew me whether this de-
,, struction was in my Fathers tyme or now?

,,   The *Bishopp* not aunsweringe this question,
,, asked him, whether he would obey the
,, Kings lawes?

,,   *Coo.* Yea as farre, as they agree with the
,, word of God, *&c.*

16.   And this is part of that wise conference which Fox setteth downe betwene the Bishopp, and the sherman, and concludeth the

Ibidem.

same abruptly, sayinge in the end: *This Roger Coo an aged Father, after his sundry troubles and conflicts*

flicts vvith his aduerſaryes, at length vvas committed to
to the fire at *Yerford* in *Suffolke* , vvhere he moſt bleſ-
ſedly ended his aged yeares. And the like conflict
he ſetteth downe, betvveene *Thomas Cobbe* the
butcher , and *Doctor Dunnings* Chancelor to the
Biſhop of Norwich about the bleſſed Sacrament, and reall preſence ; the butcher affirminge , *that he had not learned* (ſaith Fox) *in the*
ſcripture, that Chriſt ſhould be in the Sacrament, for
that Chriſt borne of the bleſſed Virgin was in heauen)
and he had read in the ſcriptures ; *that Chriſt*
did aſcend , and neuer deſcended ſynce . So ſaid the
Butcher , and offered himſelfe to the fyre for
yt at the towne of *Thetford,*this yeare 1555.and
this moneth of September . And this is all
vvhich in effect Iohn Fox hath of his two
martyrs *Cobb* and *Coo.*

The con-
ference of
Cobb the
butcher
vvith D.
Dünings.

Fox *pag.*
1550.

17. In the next place to theſe are brought in
by Fox ſeauen other martyrs , fiue burned at
*Canterbury,*and two at *Lichfield* in Staffordſhire.
The firſt 5. were *George Catmer, Robert Streater,*
*Antony Burward,George Bradbridg,*and *Iames Tutty,*
all ignorant vnlearned artificers , of whome
Fox himſelfe wryteth little or nothing , but
only that they ſtoutly denied diuers articles of
religion propoſed vnto them , as for example
Catmer ſaid: *Chriſt ſitteth in heauen at the right hand*
of God the father , and therfore I do not beleeue him to
be in the Sacrament of the Altar. A wiſe argument
no doubt , and by which he might proue alſo,
that Chriſt did not appeare to Saint Paul after
his Aſſenſion,which yet the Apoſtle himſelfe
affirmeth . And ſo did *Ananias* alſo , who was

George
Catmer.
Robert
Streater.
Antony
Burvvard.
George
Bradbridge
Iames
Tutty.
burned at
Canter-
bury.
Fox *pag.*
1552.

K 2   ſent

sent by Chrift to receaue and cure him saying:
Our Lord Ieſus Chriſt, that appeared vnto thee in the
way, hath ſent me hither. &c. But let vs goe forward. *George Bradbridge* (ſaith Fox) being demaunded after *Catmer* about Confeſsion, anſwered: *that he would not be confeſſed to a prieſt, for*
that the prieſt could not forgiue his owne ſynnes. Marke
the ſubſtantiall reaſon of this Foxian martyr.
Of the reſt he wryteth nothing at all, but only
doth regiſter the names of thoſe two burned
at *Lichfield, Thomas Hayward* and *Iohn Gory* without ſaing any thing at al what they did, what
articles were laid vnto them, or for what opinions they were burned.

18.   The laſt two martyrs placed by Fox in
this yeare 1555. are *Robert Glouer* gentleman, &
Cornelius Bungty the forſaid Capper of Couentry, burned both at one fyre in the ſame Citty,
for like opinions to the former, which were
the ordinary hereſyes of Zwinglians & Caluiniſts in thoſe dayes, ſauing that ſtill there
was ſome new tricke of each one to himſelfe;
as for example, the ſecond article of the Capper of Couétry was, as Fox ſetteth yt downe:
That by Baptiſme ſynnes are not waſhed away, becauſe
(ſaid he) *that waſhing of the fleſh purgeth the fleſh*
outwardly and not the ſoule. Which hereſy yow
know hath byn held by diuers of Fox his
Sainɗs before, and namely by *Launder* the
husbandman in the precedét moneth of ✶ Auguſt, and Fox did lett it paſſe for currant do-
ɗrine, helping it only with this impertinent
note in the margent; *that he meant that mans*
ſoule

Aɗ. 9.
1. *Cor.* 15.
2. *Cor.* 12.
Gal. 1.

Fox *ibid.*

Thomas
Hayvvard.
Io. Gory.

Robert
Glouer.
Cornelius
Bungay.

Fox *pag.*
1556.

✶ *num.* 30.
& 31.

soule is not washed by the only element of water, as though any man had euer doubted of that.

19. But heere now for his Capper, he deui-seth another shift, saying (when he cometh to recyte his answers to the articles obiected, wherof this of baptisme was the second) *that* Fox *ibid.* *he graunted first and after reuoked the same, &c.* But suppose yt were so, what sufficient ground haue I, or any man els to beleeue rather this his reuocation, then his former assertion? seing in the rest of the articles he stood stiffe, as before? As for example, the third was, *that there be in the Church only two Sacraments. To the* *Ibidem.* *third* (saith Fox) *he graunted, adding that in Scriptures, there be no more conteyned.* And how had the Capper(thinke yow)searched the scriptures for this matter? or how hansomely would he haue answered the manifold scriptures The dispu-tation of the capper of Couentry. that be alleaged for the other 5. Sacraments, yf they had byn brought against him? Yow may ghesse in part by that other article about Confession,which was obiected vnto him in these words : *that for these three yeares last past, the Capper had taught, argued and mayntened in Couentry, and Lichfield, and other places, that the priest* *Ibid.* 1556. *had no power to absolue any synner from his synnes, &c.* VVhich *he graunted* (saith Fox) *and euery part therof.* And this (for sooth) for that he said yt is not in the scripture ; and yet can nothing be more euidently sett downe in scripture, then these words of Christ many tymes repeated: *VVhose synnes ye remitt on earth, shalbe remitted in* Matth. 16. & 18. *heauen;and whose synnes yow retayne, shalbe retayned.* Ioan. 20.

K 3   Which

Which commiſſion *Saint Chryſoſtome* euery
where in his bookes *De Sacerdotio*, and all the

Chriſoſt.l.3.
de Sacerdot.
Hier. ep. 1.
ad Helio-
dorum.
Aug. l.50.
homiliarum
hom.49. &
50.
Hilar. can.
26. in
Math. &
alij.

reſt of the ancient Fathers in their works, do
apply to the authority of prieſts for abſoluing
ſynnes in thoſe, which be penitent and contrite for the ſame in the Catholike Church.
And yet will the Capper ſtand in yt moſt reſolutely, *that there is no ſuch authority at all giuen in
Scriptures vnto prieſts.* And Fox hauing heard all
the whole cauſe with much attention, giueth
ſentence in the end for the Capper againſt the
Biſhopp, ſaying: *Thus the forſaid Cornelius falſely*

Ibid. col. 1.

*condemned by the Biſhopp, ſuffered at the ſame ſtake
with the Chriſtian Martyr Maiſter Robert Glouer at
Couentry about the 20. of September, 1555.*

20. Thus wryteth he; & as for this Chriſtian
mártyr *Maiſter Robert Glouer*, he ſaith, that he
was a marryed man of the towne of *Manacheſter*,
and being brought before the ſaid B. of *Lichfield*, behaued himſelfe ſo inſolently in defence
of the vulgar hereſyes of thoſe dayes, as may

Th'exami-
nation &
condem-
nation of
Robert
Glouer.

be ſeene in his vanting relation, wrytten by
himſelfe; for comonly theſe new maiſters
wrote their owne acts and geſts with their
owne ſpiritt, and pen of pride: and yt may be
ſeene by the ſame narration, that this mans
cheefe feare was, when he was in priſon, leaſt
being ſicke, he might dy before his publike
anſwere, and ſo leeſe that blaſt of vayne glory
which he coueted before the people: *Becauſe*

Fox pag.
1593.

of my ſicknes (ſaith he to his wife) *I was troubled
by feare of death in impriſonment, before I ſhould come
to my anſwore, and ſo my death to be vnprofitable, &c.*

S2

So he. And to the end yow may perceaue in part, how well founded a diuyne this gentleman was, to offer himselfe to death againſt the Church of Chriſt, yow ſhall heare what ſubſtātiall reaſons he alleaged, in a large letter to his forſaid wife *Mary Glouer* to ſtyrre her vp therby againſt the ſaid Church, and to follow him in his folly and faction. *The Church of Chriſt* (ſaith he) *knoweth no other head but Ieſus Chriſt the* Fox *ibid.* *Sonne of God,but they* (meaning the Biſhops and all other Catholiks in Q. Mary dayes, as well in Englād as in other places) *haue refuſed Chriſt Ieſus* (for their head) *and choſen the man of ſynne, the ſonne of perdition,the dyuells deputy and lieſtenant, the Pope.* Behould his rayling ſpirit, and foolish argument; For yf it do follow, that Catholiks haue refuſed Chriſt Ieſus, for that they admitt the Biſhopp of Rome for his deputy vpon earth : then may yt as well be inferred, that the people of Ireland do refuſe the K. of England, when they receyue any lord or magiſtrate for his deputy in that Kingdome : and much more do the people of England refuſe Chriſt Ieſus, in that they admitted a woman to be his deputy in matters alſo Eccleſiaſticall. And this is his firſt argument. Lett vs ſee his ſecond :

21. *Againe* (ſaith he) *Chriſts Church,heareth, teacheth,and ruleth by his word,* &c. *their Church repelleth Gods word,and forceth all men to follow their tra-* *Ibidem.* *ditions.* &c. This reaſon is as good as the firſt. *Item* (ſaith he) *Chriſts Church dareth not to add or diminiſh , alter or change his bleſſed Teſtament : but*

K 4   they

they be not afraid to take away all that Christ instituted, & to go a whoring with their owne inuentions, &c.
This yow see, besides the feeblenes of the consequence, hath manifest lying & raylinge also.

The blas-
phemous
calumnia-
tions of
Glouer, to
his wife.

Item (saith he) The Church of Christ hath byn, is, and
shalbe, in all ages, vnder the Crosse persecuted, &c. But
these men persecute, murder and kill, &c. Item Christ
& his Church reserued the triall of their doctrine to the
word of God, and gaue the people leaue to iudge therof
by the same vvord: but this Church taketh away the
word from the people, and suffereth neyther the learned
nor vnlearned to examine, &c. Item, the Church of
God laboureth to resist and withstand the lustes, desyres,
and motiues of the world, flesh, and diuell: but these men
for the most part giue theselues ouer to all voluptuousnes,
&c. and by these & such like manifest probations, they
do declare themselues to be none of Christs Church, &c.
And yt shalbe good for yow, deare wife, oftentymes to
conferre & compare their proceedings, and doings with
the practise of those, whome the word of God doth teach,
to haue byn true members of the Church of God, and yt
shall worke in yow both knowledge, erudition & boldnes
to withstand, &c. Haue no fellowshipp with them, my
deare wife, nor with their doctrine & traditions, &c.

22.   This was the wicked and hereticall instruction of this *Glouer* to his wife, wherby
partly we may see his blasphemous spiritt in
raylinge, partly his impudency in affirminge

The con-
futation
of Glouers
Calum-
niations.

things most manifestly false; but principally
his malitious ignorance, in gatheringe these
notes of the Church (for so Iohn Fox saith
they be) vvhich for the most part do inferre
nothing at all to his purpose. His blasphemous
                                         raylinge

raylinge appeareth by his wicked words : his
impudency is most euident,in euery one of his
assertions,as namely, *that the Roman Church hath*
refused Christ; *in acknowledginge the Pope for his sub-* ,,
stitute; that she repelleth Gods word; that she ,,
hath taken away all that Christ instituted; ,,
that she doth not permitt eyther learned or ,,
vnlearned to examine matters of the scripture; ,,
that she giueth her self ouer to voluptuousnes, ,,
&c. All which be notorious impudent lyes, ,,
and shamelesse slaunders ; and so are proued ,,
when they come to the triall. ,,

23. And as for the third point of his ignorance, for asfigning these as proper and peculiar markes and notes for discerninge the true
Church, vvhich haue no further euidence in
deed in themselues, then euery sectary listeth
to apply them to his Church or against a Catholike, the thinge is most manifest. For what
blind conuenticle of Sectaryes was there euer
in the world,vnder the name of *Christians,*that
did not professe to hold Iesus Christ for their
head?And how do the Catholiks exclude him,
by acknowledginge only a substitute of his
vnder him in this world? What sect also will
not say, that he holdeth the Testament of
Christ wholy and vnchanged , and that his
aduersaryes do not? And as for trying of matters by the scriptures, doth not euery sect of
our tyme hold the same ? So as eyther this is
no note of the true Church, or els all sects are
true Churches. *The other note also of lyinge vnder*
*the Crosse of persecution,*hath it not agreed to Catholiks

The igno-
rance of
Glouer in
asfiginge
notes of
the
Churest.

tholiks vnder the late Queenes dayes, and in
K. Edwards raigne, as well as to the Proteftants in Q. Maries? how then is this a note of
the true Church, yf Catholiks be denyed to be
the true Church?

24.   And finally for the laft note, of refifting
the luftes, defires, and motiones of the world
and flefh, yf it be a fure marke to diftinguifh
betwene the true and falfe church; then haue
Fox his people loft the game already, I dare
affure my felfe by the iudgement of his owne
fellowes; for fo much as the difference betwene them and our men in ftraitneffe of life,
faftinge, prayinge, hayrcloth, fatisfaction, reftitution, pennance, difcipline, voluntary pouerty, vowing of chaftity and other like mortifications, is fo notorioufly knowne to the
world, as the Proteftants themfelues will not
deny the fame. And by this yow fee, what
manner of martyr this *Glouer* was, whome I
leaue with the capper, to try the matter in the
fire at Couentry, and (as I doubt) eternally afterward in another place.

25.   There followeth the next yeare after, to
witt 1556. in the beginning wherof I ohn Fox
giueth vs fix Martyrs in his Calendar, as burned for the ghofpell at diuers places vpon this
yeare and moneth. Wherof the firft two are
Iohn Hart fhomaker, and *Thomas Rauenfdale* cur-
rier, burned at *Mayfield* in Suffex: other two
were *Edward Sharpe* artificer, and a yonge man
namele e, by occupation a *Carpenter*, burned
at *Briftow*: And the third couple, were *Iohn*
                                                    Horne,

Ioh. Hart.
*Tho Ra-
uenfdale.*
*Edvvard
Sharpe.
& a yonge
man.
Io. Horne,
and his
vvoman.*

Horne, and a woman burned at *VVolton-vnder-hedge* in Gloſterſhire. Of all which halfe dozen, Fox relateth no opinions, articles, or anſwers at all, but only, *that they died moſt gloriouſly in a conſtant faith to the terror of the VVicked, and comfort of the godly; perſiſtinge in the iuſt quarrell of Chriſts ghoſpell, ioyfully yelding their liues, for teſtimony of the ſaid glorious ghoſpell, &c.* Which are glorious words, as yow ſee, of a vaynglorious fond fellow, that will needs chronicle theſe his cricketts with glory, wheras they were euery way indeed moſt contéptible wretches, and miſerable diſſected ſectaryes, not agreeing eyther with themſelues or others, and therby fitt to be iewells of Iohn Fox his treaſure; which by vs as raggs & rotten clouts are caſt out to the dunghill as they well deſerue yt.

Fox *pag.* 1772.

26. But now lett vs paſſe on, to the next yeare 1557. conteyning the third ranke of ſuch as were burned vnder Q. Mary, of whome Iohn Fox recounteth vs ſeauen burned neere togeather in tyme, though not altogeather in one place, to witt foure men and three weomen. The men were *Iohn Curd* ſhomaker burned at *Northampton*, *Raph Allerton* taylor, burned at Iſlington, and *Richard Roth* and *Iames Auſtow* burned at the ſame place. The weomen were *Cecily Ormes* burned at Norwich, *Ioyce Lewes* burned at Couentry, and *Margery Auſtow* wife to the ſaid *Iames Auſtow* at Iſlington. Of *Iohn Curde* the ſhomaker, there is nothinge els recorded by Fox, but that he was of the Pariſh of *Shirſham* in Northamptonſhire condemned

Io. Curd.
Raph Allerton.
Richard Roth.
Iames Auſtovv.
Cecily Ormes.
Ioyce Levves.
Margery Auſtovv.

pag. 1835.

by

by the Chancelor of the B. of *Peter-borrow*,
and that he had his pardon offered him when
he went to the fire, yf he would reuoke his
opinions; But of *Raph Allerton* the taylor, as of
a more principall man, who went vp and
downe the countrey readinge the new testament, to euery company of people whome he
found Idle, or easy to harken vnto him, Fox
maketh a farre longer difcourfe, and equalleth
him to many preachers of his religion in thofe
dayes:and albeit he had recanted once his opinions before, in tyme of a publike fermon at
Paules Croffe;yet he fell to them againe afterward which fuch vehemency, as he ftood in
difputation with B. Bonner (that before had
giuen him that pennance) which difputation
Fox fetteth downe at length, togeather with
other his combats with the faid Bifhop wrytten (as he faith) by the Taylors owne hand,
yea with his bloud for lacke of ynke, yf we
will beleeue him; though (as I faid) the difcourfes be very long to be writté with bloud;
But whether that be fo or noe; I can eafily
beleeue that they were wrytten by his owne
hand, for that they rellifh of his owne fpiritt,
to witt a proud Taylors fpiritt: which Taylor
by transformation of herefie, made himfelfe a
Doctor, and in that pride he bringeth in B.
Bonner in his wrytté relation with fuch contempt euery where,as ouercome and conquered by himfelfe in that conference ; as is ridiculous to reade. And firft for the moft part he
maketh him to beginne his fpeaches,fwearing
and

(marginal note) A proud Taylor made a Doctor by tranf-mutation of herefie.

and chafinge little to the purpofe; as for example, when Allerton had alleaged moft impertinently a place out of *Efdras*, to fignifie
therby a contumelious defcription of the Roman Church, he fetteth downe *B. Bonner* fpeaking to his Chaplyn *Maifter Morton* thus:

27. *B. Bonner.* Now by the bleffed Sacrament
Maifter Morton, he is the rankeft heretike that
euer came before me. How fay yow, haue
yow hard the like?

Morton. I thought what he was, my Lord,
at the firft, I:

Bonner. Now by all hallowes, thou fhalt be
brent with fiar for thy lyinge. Thou hour-
fone varlet, thou prickloufe thou, doft thou
find a prophecy of vs? Nay yow knaue, yt is of
yow that he fpeaketh of, *&c.* Is there any that
vnderftand this fcripture on this fafhion? Before God I thinke there is none in England
but thou.

Allerton. Yes my Lord, there are in England three religions.

Bonner. Saift thou fo? which be thofe three?

Allert. The firft is that which yow hold; the
fecond is cleane contrary to the fame; and the
third is a neuter.

Bonner. And of thefe three which art thou?

Allert. My Lord; I am of that, which is contrary to that which yow teach, *&c.*

Bonner. Ah Syr. Yow were heere with me
at *Fullam* once before, and had good cheere &
money in your purfe, when yow went away.
And by my faith, I had a fauour vnto thee, but

now

Fox *pag.*
1827.
,,
,,
,,
,,
,,
,,
,,
The con-
ference of
B. Bonner
vvith *Al-
lerton* the
Taylor.
,,
,,
,,
,,
,,
,,
,,
,,
,,
,,
,,
,,

,, now I see thou wilt be a naughty knaue still.
,, Why wilt thou take vpon thee to read scrip-
,, tures, and canst vnderstand neuer a word, *&c.*
28. Thus relateth Fox. And then passing from this talke to speake of the reall presence, he maketh the Deane to say, *that Allerton wilbe an honest man, and change his opinions.* Wherunto the Bishopp replyed : *O he is a glorious knaue, his painted tearmes shall no more deceyue me. Ah thou whorefone priklouse, doth not Christ say this is my body? and how darest thow deny these vvords?* And againe, when a certaine Lord there present said vnto the Bishop. *Be good vnto him, my Lord, he will be an honest man.* The Bishopp answered. *Before God how should I trust him, he hath once deceyued me already. But how say yow Syrra? After the words of confecration remaineth not there the very body of our Sauiour Iesus Christ, God and Man vnder the forme of bread ?*

,, *Allert.* Where fynd yow that my Lord
,, wrytten?

,, *Bon.* Lo Syr : why? did not Christ say, this
,, is my body?

The friuo-
lous aun-
svvers of
Allerton
the Tay-
lour.

Allert. I maruayle my Lord, why yow leaue out the beginning of this institution of the Supper of our Lord, for Christ said: Take ye, and eat ye. This is my body.

,, *Bon.* Why? then must thou needs say it is his
,, body.

,, *Allert.* I vtterly refuse to take the words of
,, our Sauiour so fantastically, as yow teach vs,
,, for then should we conspire with the *Nesto-*
,, *rians,* who said Christ had no body, but a fan-
tasticall

tasticall body , and therfore looke to yt for
Gods fake , and lett thefe words , *take ye, and
eat ye,* go before, *&c.* Thus prated that fanta-
 fticall fond Taylor, neyther knowning what
the *Neſtorians* held, nor how, nor why; nor can
any man of iudgement imagine , by what fe-
quele yt can be inferred , that by holding the
reall preſence of Chrifts true body in the Sacrament, we go about to make his faid body fan-
tafticall: No man (I fay) can imagine this, but
only the fancy of this taylour.

29. Thus notwitfanding goeth on that difputation , wherin Biſhop Bonner, and other
learned men about him, were blanked by the
Taylor , yf we beleeue himfelfe . And this
pride and arrogancy was fuch, both in him, &
his companions and fellow artificers, I meane
Roth , *Auſtow* , *and* *Curd* (wherof this was the
Captayne and common mouth) as in the end
the B. was forced to giue fentence againft
them. *Roth* and *Auſtow* faid litle , but were obftinate to defend, euen with their liues, euery
thing which this other prating companion
the taylour had pratled. But the three weomen were more infolent and malepart then
all the reft, and fo we muft fay a word or two
of them alfo.

30. *Ioyce Lewes* , was the wife of one *Thomas*
Lewes ot *Mancheſter* a difciple of *Robert Glouer*, of
whome we haue fpoken before. *Cecily Ormes*
was the wife of one *Edmund Ormes*, worfted-
weauer in *Norwich*. *Margery Auſtow* was the
wife of the forfaid *Iames Auſtow*. Thefe three
weomen

Ioyce
Levves.

Cecily
Ormes.

Margery
Auſtovv.

weomen cōming to be examined before their
Ordinaryes, behaued them felues as poffeffed
with fuch fpiritts of pride, prefumption, and
arrogancy, as herefie is wont to bringe forth.
Ioyce Lewes was prefented to the B. of Couentry by her owne husband, who feeing her
fo intemperately giuen to herefie, thought yt
his duty fo to do, for which Fox calleth him
a murderer, and then defcribeth he the beginning of their talke thus: *VVhen the B.* (faith he)
*reafoned vvith her, vvhy fhe vvould not come to the
maffe, and receaue the Sacrament of the holy Church?*
*She aunfwered, becaufe I find not thofe things in Gods
vvord*, &c. *The Bifhop replyed: yf thow vvilt beleeue
no more then is in fcripture, thou art in a damnable cafe.
At vvhich vvords, fhe vvas vvonderfully amazed, and
being moued by the fpiritt of God, told the Bifhopp, that
his vvords vvere vngodly and vvicked*, &c.

31.   So wryteth Fox and determineth as yow
fee, that this her immodeft aunfwere wherby
fhe reuiled the B. was by the motion of the
fpiritt of God. And fuch impious flattery as
this, caufed fuch fond and vaine people in
thofe dayes, to runne headlonge to the fire.
Whervnto when this miferable woman was
brought; *after fhe had prayd three feuerall tymes*
(faith Fox) and in that prayer defired God
,, moft inftatly, to abolifh the Idolatrous maffe,
,, and to deliuer this realme from papiftry, at the
,, end therof, the moft part of the people (faith
he) cryed *Amen*. Yea euen the Sheriffe that
ftood hard by her, ready to caft her into the
fire; and when fhe had thus prayed, fhe tooke
the

Fox pag.
1556.

Fox ibid.

Th'infolēt
behauiour
of Ioyce
Levves at
the fire.

the cupp into her hand, and said; I drinke to „
them all that vnfaynedly loue the ghospell, „
and wish for the abolishment of papiltry. Her „
frends dranke with her, & so did a great num- „
ber of the weomen of the towne, which were „
afterward put to open pennance for the same. „
Thus vvryteth Fox yf vve may beleeue him, „
and vvith this dronkennesse both in spiritt „
and body, vvent these miserable people to „
their end.

32.   *Cecily Ormes* and *Margery Austow*, vvere no
lesse vvillfull and obstinate then the former.
Cecily being examined about the reall presence; *She answered* (saith Fox) *that yt is bread,
and yf ye make yt any better, yt is vvorse, &c.* The
Chancelor told her, *she was an ignorant, vnlearned
and foolish vvoman, but she vvayinge not his vvords*
(saith Fox) *told him, that he should not be so desirous
to burne her sinfull flesh, as she vvould be content to giue
yt in so good a quarrell* ; & then Fox addeth these
words: *This Cecily Ormes was a very simple woman,
but yet zealous in the Lords cause, being borne in East
Derham, the daughter of one Thomas Haund taylor,
&c.* And finally goinge to her death she said:
*This I vvill not recant, but I recant vtterly from the
bottome of my hart the doings of the Pope of Rome, and
of all his Popish Priests and shauelinges, &c.* Lo with
what a modest spiritt this woman died.

33.   And the very like was seene in *Margery
Austow*, who being called before the Bishop togeather with her husband, as she had byn his
teacher and preacher at home; so would she
also needs be his speaker in that place, vvhich

The mad-
nesse of
Cecily
Ormes.

Fox pag.
1835.

Fox in like manner fignifieth, when he wryteth: That in matters of faith, thefe two his

Martyrs, *vvere as found, and anfwered as truly (God
be therfore praifed) as euer any did, efpecially the vvoman, to vvhome the Lord had giuen the greater knowledge, and more feruentneffe of fpiritt, &c.* By which
vvords of Fox yow may perceaue how the
vvorld vvent, and that the gray mare vvas the
better horfe, vvhich doth vvell appeare alfo
by her anfwers, they being moft arrogant and
infolent, as other fuch franticke weomen had
vfed before, and fo not worth the repeatinge
in this place.

34.   And to thefe yow may ioyne two other
honeft vveomen of like condition burned at
Colchefter in this yeare and moneth: *Agnes Bongier*, and *Margaret Thruftan* who were fo willfully fet to go to the fire, and did thirft fo after
yt, for the vayne glory vvhich they vvere put
into, vnder the title and name *of Elect Martyrs
and Confeffors of Chrift*: that albeit they vvere re-
pryued after the burninge of their fellowes,
yet by no meanes could they be ftayed from
obftinate purfuynge the fame, vvherby they
being feene by the Magiftrates to be reftleffe,
and neuer to ceafe from blafphemous fpeach
and continuall endeauors to corrupt others, a
vvryte vvas fent at length from London to
burne them both, this being the only laft refuge vvhich the Magiftrate had to refift greater inconueniences.

35.   There remayne now only fix of all this
moneth and yeare 1557. vvherof the firft foure

are

Fox *pag.*
1826.

Margery
Auftovv
her huf-
bāds Mai-
fter in
ghofpel-
linge.

Agnes
Bongier.
Magarett
Thruftan.

Fox *pag.*
1833.

are thefe accordinge to Iohn Fox his narration: *Iohn VVarner, Chriftian Grouer, Thomas Athoth*
Prieft and *Iohn Ashdone:* of all which Fox deliue-
reth vs only their names, and that they were
burned at *Colchefter* in Effex by *B. Chriftopher-*
fone, and his afsiftants, *for the true teftimony of*
righteoufnes. But how, or for what in particular, he faith he cannot tell, for that he vvanted
the records.

Io. VVar-
ner.
Chriftian
Grouer.
Thomas
Athoth.
Iohn Ash-
done.
Fox *pag.*
1836.

36. The laft two are *Thomas Spurdance* and
Iohn Fortune. Spurdance was a feruant of Q. Maryes, as Fox fayth, and being perceaued by his
fellowes, namely *Iohn Hammon* and *George Lo-*
fam to be infected with herefy and obftinate
therin, he was accufed by them, & fo apprehended & fent prifoner to *Bury*, and after diuers meanes vfed to recall him, he was burned in the fame place for the fame obftinacy,
in the moneth of Nouember, as Iohn Fox in
his Acts & Monuméts doth confeffe, though
in his Calendar he hath put him in the moneth of September vpon this day.

Thomas
Spurdáce.
Iohn For-
tune.

37. Of *Iohn Fortune* that fhutteth vp this moneth Fox wryteth thus : *This Iohn Fortune other-*
wife called Cutler of Hinklesham in Suffolke, was by
his occupation a blacke fmith : in fpiritt he was zealous
and ardent ; in the fcriptures ready ; in Chrifts caufe
ftout and valiant ; and in his anfwers maruelous. &c.
Thus wryteth Fox of that ghofpeling Smith,
and fetteth downe foure feuerall conferences
or difputations, which he had with the B. of
Norwich, wherin he fheweth thefe his *marue-*
lous anfwers, all wrytten, as he faith, with his

Fox *pag.*
1740.

A defcrip-
tion of
Fortune
the blacke
Smith.

owne hand ; for that this was a tricke as before yovv haue heard , of moſt of theſe nevv
bragging ghoſpellers, that when they had byn
at their examinations before the Biſhopps and
Comiſsionars they vvould alwayes at their
home cominge, vvryte their owne triumphes
vvith their owne hands, ſetting downe euery
thinge as yt pleaſed them beſt for their owne
glory , and for contentment of thoſe of their
faction abroad, as for example, the firſt words
of the firſt conference vvere theſe : as he relateth them.

Fox ibid.   38. Firſt *Doctor Parker* (ſaith he) asked me,
„ how I beleeued in the Catholike faith, and I
„ asked him againe vvhat faith he meant, eyther
„ that vvhich Stephen had, or the faith of them,
„ that putt Stephen to death, *&c.* Then the Bi-
„ ſhop asked me yf I did not beleeue the Catho-
The con- like Church? I ſaid I beleeued that Church,
ference & vvherof Chriſt is the head.
diſputatiō
of Fortune   *Biſhopp.* So do I beleeue alſo , but the Pope
the Smith is his Vicar vpon earth , and hath power to
vvith the forgiue ſynnes.
Biſhops &
Doctors.
„   *Fortune.* Then ſaid I, the Pope is but a man,
Pſal. 89. „ and the Prophet Dauid ſaid pſal. 89. *That no*
„ *man can deliuer his brother , nor make agremēt for him*
„ *to God,* &c.
„   Well ſaid the *Biſhop*, what ſayeſt thou to the
„ ceremonyes of the Church?
Math. 15.   *Fort.* I anſwered : *All things that are not plan-*
„ *ted by my heauenly father, ſhall be plucked vp by the*
„ *rootes,* &c.
„   *Biſhop.* They are good and godly.

Fort.

Fort. S. Paul called them, *vveake and beg-* *Gal.* 4.
garly, &c.   ,,

Bishop. How beleeueſt thou of the Sacra- ,,
ment of the Altar, doſt thou not beleeue that ,,
after the confecration, there is the reall ſub- ,,
ſtance of the body of Chriſt?   ,,

Fort. That is the greateſt plague that euer ,,
came to England.   ,,

Bishop. Why ſo?   ,,

Fort. Yf I vvere a Biſhop, I vvould be aſha- ,,
med to aske ſuch a queſtion : For a Biſhopp ,,
ſhould be apt to teach and not to learne, *&c.* ,,

39.   Behould heere the ſpiritt of this ghoſpellinge ſmith! he taketh vp the Biſhop for
askinge, *vvhy ſo?* and ſaith *that yf he vvere a Bi-*
ſhopp (vvherof no doubt he thought himſelfe
worthy) *he vvould be loath to aske vvhy ſo,*or learne
any thinge of any man. And this vvas the
humble diſpoſition, of men and vveomen of
that profeſsion in thoſe dayes. What became
of this man afterward, Fox ſaith,he knoweth
not, and yet doth he putt him downe in his
Calendar for a Martyr. *VVhether he vvere burned* *Pag.*1741.
(ſaith he) *or died in priſon, I cannot certainly find,*
but rather I ſuppoſe that he vvas burned. Certayne yt
is, howſoeuer he vvas made away, he neuer yelded, &c.
And in another place. *It is moſt certayne, that he* *Ibidem.*
neuer abiured nor recanted, howſoeuer yt pleaſed the
Lord by death to call him out of this vvorld.

40.   Thus vvryteth Fox of this his famous
Martyr, acertayninge vs of one thinge only,
to vvitt, that vvhatſoeuer opinion he held, or
vvhether he vvere burned or no, yet that he

neuer yelded or recanted. So as this obftinacy
and pertinacity, is the higheft commendation
amongeft Sectaryes, to ftand vvillfully to
vvhatfoeuer they apprehend ; and the more
ignorant and vnlearned, the more refolute
and immoueable are they in their fancyes,
once apprehended. And fo vvith this *Iohn For-*
tune vve vvill end Iohn Fox his Martyrs of
this moneth, togeather vvith their euill fortune in burninge for fo vnfortunate a caufe.
And as for the comparifon of both monethes
togeather, I remitt the reader to that vvhich
is fett downe in the beginninge of this examen, and to the columnes them-
felues of both Calendars
prefixed before
the fame.

The end of September.

THE

THE MONETH

OF OCTOBER,

and view of Foxian Sainctes therof;

VVherin three are principall rubricate,
Tyndall, Ridley, and
Latymer.

CHAP. XIV.

FOR three rubricate Sainćts of the Catho-like Calendar, which Fox hath thought good to spare and leaue standing, as he found them in this moneth, which are *Sainćt Luke* the Euangelist vpon the 18. day, and *Sainćt Symon* and *Iude* the Apostles vpon the 28. he hath taken vpon him to adorne other three of his owne with like dignity, to witt *VVilliam Tyndall* vpon the 7. day, *Nicolas Ridley* vpon the 19. and *Hugh Latymer* vpon the 20. intituling *Tyndall* also with the title of *Apostle of England.* Wherfore as he is Captayne and ringleader of all those, that were burned vnder K. Henry in this moneth (which make the number of some 14.) so are the other two, *Ridley* and *Latymer* cheiftaynes of the rest, that were put to death vnder *Q. Mary*, for which cause whe shall treate of them heere seuerally in two distinćt paragraphes.

L 4   of.

Of those, that were burned under K. Henry the 8. §. 1.

2. I haue aduertised often before, that Iohn Fox to make vp a great multitude of martyrs, and to fynd fraught, wherwith to furnish euery day of his Calendar, doth search out all corners of the world for Martyrs and Confessors, men & weomen imprisoned, burned, or otherwayes punished or put to death for any opinions whatsoeuer, so they be contrary to the Cathol. Roman faith: as for example,

in the first six dayes of this moneth of October, he setteth downe six distinct martyrs fetched out of France, & burned in Paris vnder K. *Francis* the first of that kyngdome, vpon the yeare of Christ 1534. and the 25. yeare of the raigne of our K. Henry the eight of England. Their names and titles are recorded by Fox in these words. *Bartolet Millon martyr; Iohn de Burge a rich marchāt martyr; the Receyuer of Nauntes martyr; Henry Poyle martyr; Catelle à schoolmaistres martyr; Stephen de la soarge martyr, &c.* Of all which six martyrs, Fox in his Acts & monuments wryteth only as followeth, & no more:

3. *These heere specified, were for certayne billes cast abroad, and sett vp, some against the Masse, and other absurdityes of the Pope, condemned and burned in Paris, anno Domini 1533. ex Ioanne Crispe, &c.* Wherby first we may perceaue that albeit there had byn no more against them, then heere is expressed

Marginal notes:

Hovv Fox bestirreth himselfe to find out Saints frō all partes.

Bartolet Millan. Iohn de Burge. Receauer of Naunt. Heary Poyle. Catelle. Stephen de la soarge. Fox *pag.* 819. *col.* 1. *num.* 70.

preſſed (which is vnlikely) yet were they ſeditious people , and not content to vſe their
hereſyes among themſelues , but preſumed
alſo to caſt libells abroad, and ſett vp billes of
blaſphemy & defiance againſt religion, in publike places, for which they might iuſtly be Six ſeditious
French
Saints.
puniſhed in reſpect of ſedition , though no
matter of hereſye had byn therin . Secondly
Fox telleth vs not , what was the ſentence
againſt them, nor what their opinions in particular were, which opiniōs might be as much
againſt him, and his doctrine, as againſt ours,
and ſo in all likelyhood they were in many
points : forſomuch as Caluiniſts they could
hardly be in thoſe dayes , when *Caluin* had
ſcarſe yet begon his ſect in *Geneua* , eſpecially
ſeeing that Fox aſsigneth their deathes ;vpon
the yeare 1533. though in his Calendar he
ſayth yt was a yeare later , to witt , 1534.
which was three yeares before *Caluin* was admitted for a Doctor in *Geneua* , whence he
was baniſhed two yeares after that agayne:
and returned not vntill *anno* 1541. as *Sutcliffe* in
his * *Suruey* ſayth , (yf it be his, or as other * *Cap.* 13
thinke Bancroft) & ſo much of theſe French *pag.* 21.
Martyrs.

4. Vpon the 7. day of this moneth is aſsigned the feſtiuall day of the martyrdome of
VVilliam Tyndall,whome Fox and Bale do honour (as hath byn ſaid) with the title of *Apoſtle
of England* , for that he was one of the firſt Engliſh prieſts, that ſhewed themſelues to fauour
Luthers doctrine, and by taking a woman
vnder

vnder coulour of his wife fell to Apostasy.
And because we haue spoké of him somwhat

¶ 2. *Iulij*. largely before in the story of * *Iohn Fryth* , that
was his scholler, we may be the breefer heere:
yet shall yow haue againe repeated so much,
as wilbe sufficient to know what a sainct he
was, and which was greater, eyther his Apo-
stleshippe or Apostasy.

The story
of VVilliã
Tyndall. 5. This *VVilliam Tyndall* then , aliàs *Hichins*,
according as Fox setteth downe his story,
was borne in the borders of *VVales*, studied at
Oxford , and there was made priest, and after
falling vpon some books of *Erasmus* , *friar Luther*, and other like wrytters, became to be in-
ueigled with the itch of new opinions and
carnall liberty, & therof being suspected, was
forced to retyre himselfe from that vniuersity of *Oxford* into the Contrey , and there to
be a schoolemaister, and after a certayne tyme
hauing thought better of the matter, & wan-
dred about the realme , resolued , (as it seemeth) to settle himselfe in Catholike Religion againe ; and to that end repayringe to

Fox *pag.*
981. London, made sute to *B. Tonstall* (then Bishop
of that place) to be his chaplyn, but was refused by him, vvhich Fox doth attribute to
Gods prouidence ; for that by this occasion

Tyndall
vvould
haue byn
B. Ton-
stalls cha-
plyn, but
vvas refu-
sed. (saith he) *he came to behould & mislike the pompe of
Prelates*; and so he determined to go beyond
the seas into *Saxony*, to conferre vvith *Martyn
Luther*, by vvhome he vvas fully persuaded to
be of his Religion, and to take a vvoman also,
as the other had done. Whervpon he returned

ned backe to *Antwerp* , and there he put himfelfe to ferue the Englifh marchants as their
clarke, and vvas maintayned by them for diuers yeares , in vvhich tyme he vvrote fundry
hereticall books accordinge to the currant
veyne of thofe tymes ; the former of them fauouringe of Lutheranifme, the later tendinge
to Zwinglianifme, or rather to an indifferency betwene both , as after yow fhall fee more
particularly : for which caufe Fox in his narration of him, noteth diuers times in the margent thefe vvords: *Tyndall bearinge vvith the*
tyme, &c.

Fox *pag.*
983. col. 1.
num. 24.

6.　He tranflated alfo the new Teftament,
and diuers books of the old, into Englifh, by
the help of one *Myles Couerdale* another marryed Prieft, as alfo by the counfell and fpeciall
conference vvith *Iohn Frith,* notwithftandinge
the faid *Frith* at that day, by Fox his accompt,
could not be full 20. yeares old (as by our former narration of him may appeare) and confequently a man may eafily iudge, vvhat a
Counfelor *Frith* cold be in thofe dayes for fuch
a bufynes , but all was then frefh nouelty and
forwardnes therin , and vvhofoeuer fhewed
himfelfe moft rafh , and prefuminge vpon his
owne particular fpiritt, he was thought to
haue moft of Gods fpiritt, & to be moft Euangelicall: vpon which ground, young *Frith* was
not only taken for a counfelour in the tranflation of the Bible , but fent into England to
fruetifie there as an Apoftolicall man , and to
make the vvay for others : *Euangelicus homo,* &
Iefu

172   *The Examen of Iohn Fox his*

Bal cent. 5.
script. Brit.

& Iesu Christi Apostolus Gulielmus Tindallus (faith
Bale) *hunc Ioannem Frithum, non aliter, quàm Ti-
motheum Paulus, in ministerij socium adoptans; horta-
batur, &c.* The Euangelicall man and Apostle
,, of Christ *VVilliam Tyndall*, adopting *Iohn Frith*
,, in the society of ministery, no otherwise then
,, *Paul* did *Tymothy*, exhorted him (at his sending
,, into England) to be constant, *&c.* Which exhortations of *Tyndall* persuadinge *Frith* to go to

✢ *2. Iulij.* the fire for his opinions, yow haue heard ✢ before, in the story and life of the said *Frith*, and
how that finally after many other persuasions,
one was, that *Frithes* wife left in keeping with
Tyndall, was content also that he should be
burned, for his Religion, yf he felt himselfe
called therynto ; for so Fox relateth the matter out of *Tyndalls* letter to *Frith* himselfe , say-

Fox pag.
987. col. 1.
num. 14.

inge as yow haue heard before : *Syr, your vvife
is vvell content vvith the vvill of God, and vvould not for
her sake haue the glory of God hyndred.* Tyndalls

Frithes
vvife indu-
ced by
Tyndall to
allovv of
her hus-
bands
goinge to
the fire.

meaninge is that *Frithes* vvife and he vvere
agreed, and would not haue him to stay his
martyrdome for their sakes, to which effect he
vseth very many other exhortations, as we
haue related before in Frithes story. By which
incitations, togeather vvith infinite vayne
prayses giuen vnto him aboue all measure or
proportion, eyther of his age or learninge, he
put the miserable yonge man into such a
veigne of pride and ambition of some glorious death , as nothinge could vvithhold
him, but that he vvould thrust himselfe into the fire vpon the vanity and folly , as indeed

deed he did. And so much for his death.

7. But now lett vs see, what counsell Tyndall giueth him about matter of doctrine and articles of faith: Thus he beginneth, wryting vnto him vnder the name and figure of Iacob. *Dearly beloued brother Iacob, &c. Keep yow alow by the ground, auoydinge high questions, that passe comon capacity, but expound the law truly, and open the veyle of Moyses to condemne all flesh, &c.* then *shall your preachinge be vvith power, and not as the doctrine of Hipocrites, &c.* This is his beginning in a very high stile as yow see, to so yong a ladd, importinge great misteryes : but yow shall heere what ensueth, & by the way yow must note, that both heere and before by the word *hipocrites*, this seditious marryed Priest meaneth the Bishopps and Prelates of the Catholike Church, as Christ did the Scribes and Pharasees; and therby yow see his pride and malice. But harken how he goeth forward.

Fox pag. 987.

Tyndalls direction to Frith for matter of doctrine.

8. *Sacraments* (saith he) *vvithout significations refuse; yf they put significations to them, receaue them, yf yow see yt may help, though yt be not necessary.* This doctrine also is obscure, and vnderstood (I trow) by few ; and Fox noteth againe in the margent. *Maister Tyndall heere beareth vvith tyme*; and then it followeth in the same epistle: *Of the presence of Christs body in the Sacrament, meddle as little as yow can, that there appeare no diuision amonge vs: Barnes vvilbe hoate against yow : the Saxons be sore on the affirmatiue, vvhether constant or obstinate I omitt yt to God. Philipp Melanchthon is said to be vvith the French King : there be in Antwerp, that*

Fox ibid.

About the Sacramentary controuersie.

say they faw him come into Paris vvith 150. *horfes*; *yf* *Ibidem.* *the French men receaue the vvord of God, he vvill plant the affirmatiue in them*, *&c.* Thus vvryteth he, ftandinge in great doubt and vncertainty, as yow fee, what word of God would be placed in France; for yf the affirmatiue about the *Reall prefence*, which *Melanchthon* was to preach, were not the truth; then what word of God was yt, that planted vntruth in fo weighty a matter; but yow fhall heare this good fellow Atheift, vvhat reckoninge he made of the thinge.

Ibidem. 9. *I vvould haue* (faith he) *the right vfe preached, and the prefence to be an indifferent thing, till the matter might be reafoned in peace at leafure of both parts, &c.* So faith he. And will yow fo Syr? How much do yow differ from the ancient Fathers, that held this matter for one of the higheft mifteryes of all our beleefe? and how can yt be an indifferent thinge (except with Politiques and Atheifts) to beleeue the hoft after confecration to be a peece of bread, or true Chrift God and man himfelfe? But there enfue precepts how Frith muft dally in the matter. *If yow be required* (faith he) *fhew the* *Ibidem.* *phrafes of the fcripture, and lett them talke vvhat they vvill,* &c. *Yow perceaue my mynd; howbeit yf God fhew yow otherwife, yt is free for yow to do as he moueth yow,* &c.

10. Heere yow fee a great humility in *Tyndall*, that hauinge fett downe the opinion of all the learned men of Saxony, and amonge them of *Doctor Luther* himfelfe, who florifhed

in

in thefe dayes, and of *Doctor Barnes*, and *Doctor Melanchthon* in the affirmatiue part for the reall prefence, and his owne alfo for the indifferency therof; yet all is fubmitted finally to the particular fpiritt of this ladd *Frith*: fo as *yf God fhew him otherwife* (that is to fay yf his owne fpiritt tell him otherwife) and different from that which he had fhewed to all thefe other Doctors before: then yt is free for Frith to thinke or do, as he lift; and fo he did; for he died for a point, which none of them perhaps euer thought of, or imagined that a man would dye for, as in his ftory yow haue feene. And it is to be noted, that once againe Iohn Fox wryteth in his margent vpon thefe laft words of Tyndall; *Heere Maifter Tyndall againe beareth with the tyme*, which is the third tyme that Fox aduertifeth this of him, by a fpeciall note, which is no great figne of his conftancy, yf yow confider yt well.

Tyndall a times-mā by Fox his teftimony.

11. Wherfore to draw to an end, yow fee by this little, what manner of Apoftle Tyndall was, that had not the doctrine of his Apoftlefhipp certayne, but ftammered and ftaggered, liuing in indifferency of beleefe, and putting doubts into mens heads, therby to draw them to diffidency and infidelity. In which kind of Apoftafy, *Tyndall* did more hurt (as may appeare by *Syr Thomas Mores* books, and other mens wrytings againft him) in thofe firft beginnings of herefy in our countrey, then many others heretiks togeather, efpecially by his falfe and deceytfull tranflation of the Scriptures

ptures into Englith, and with his corrupt notes and wicked commentaries theron. Which
K. Henry the 8. well confidering, though for
many yeares he had permitted the fame, and
fome other Englith tranflations: yet vpon the
34. veare of his raigne, which was of Chrift
1543. he hauinge caufed diligent fearch to be
made of the faid falfhood, did forbid *Tyndalls*
tranflation by name, in an act of parlament
made vpon the forfayd yeare in thefe words:

Statut.
Henr. 8.
an. 34. & 35
sius regni.
cap. 1.

12.   *And therfore be yt enacted, ordayned and efta-*
blifhed by our faid foueraigne Lord the King, the Lords
fpirituall and temporall, and the comons in this prefent
Parlament affembled; and by the authority therof; that
all manner of books of the old and new Teftament in

Tyndalls
Tranflatiõ
cõdemned
by parla-
ment for
falfe and
corrupt.

Englifh, being of the crafty, falfe, and vntrue tranfla-
tion of Tyndall, be cleerly and vtterly abolifhed, &c.
This act was made about 7. yeares after *Tyn-*
dalls burning, which happened vpon the yeare
of Chrift 1537. at a towne called *Filford-Caftle*
in Flanders, 3. yeares after *Frithes* burning in
Smithfield. And yt is thought that K. Henry
the eigth procured the fame with the Emperor and his officers, and would haue done as
much himfelfe for him in Englãd, yf he could
haue gotten the man into his fingers, for that
he held him not only for an heretike, but for
wicked alfo & feditious. And fo much of him.

13.   After Tyndall there enfue diuers others,
VVilliam
Layton, an
Apoftata
monke.]
Iohn Put-
tedevv.
put to death in diuers parts of the realme vnder K. Henry in this moneth, as namely *VVil-*
liam Layton and *Iohn Puttedew* of Suffolke. The
firft an apoftata monke of the towne of *Aye*,
the

the second, an obscurre fellow, that Fox seemeth not otherwise to know, but only that he
was burned about those parts of Suffolke in
the yeare 1537. and that they were discouered
and apprehended vpon certaine scoffing opprobrious words, vttered about some points
of Catholike religion, though yet of what religion or sect themselues were, he knoweth
not, and yet will he needs haue them Saincts
and Martyrs of his Church. And the very like
doth he with two other, *Colyns* and *Cowbridge*,
whome he confesseth to haue byn madd, and
one also of them to haue denyed Christ, as a
little after we shall shew more largely.

14.   And by the same madnes he putteth in
also for a martyr vpon the 11. day of this moneth, one *Peter a Germaine*, of whome I fynd
nothing at all related in his Acts and monuments; though *Alanus Copus* in his Dialogues,
doth affirme, that the said *Peter the German* denyed Christ *to haue taken flesh of his mother, the
blessed virgin*, and that Fox confessed the same
in his former edition, though now in his last
I find no such thing in him, nor of this Peter,
but only his name continued for a Martyr in
his Calendar vpon the day aforsaid; but of his
Acts and Gests nothing; which is also a tricke
now and then vsed by our Fox, to canonize
men in his Calendar, and to say nothinge of
them afterward in his comentary. Which we
must passe ouer, and take in good part with
the rest.

15.   After the German Anabaptists, he placeth

Peter a Germaine

Alan. dial. 6. pag. 604.

Fox act. & mon. edit. 1. Lat. pag. 15 Angl. pag. 398.

ceth three other Martyrs of his made about
the same tyme, whose Religion notwithstanding he sheweth euidently that he knew not.
Yow shall heare all that he wryteth of them.

Fox *pag.*
1164.
Iohn a
painter.
Giles
German.

About the yeare (saith he) *of our Lord* 1539. *one Iohn
a paynter , and Giles German* were accused of heresie, and whilest they were in examyning at
London before the Bishopp and other iudges,
by chaunce there came in one of the K. ser-

,,
Lancelot.
mart.

uants, named *Lancelot,* who standinge by seemed by his countenáce and gesture to fauour
,, both the cause, and the poore mens frends,
,, whervpon he being apprehended was exami-
,, ned and condemned togeather with them, &
,, the next day at fiue of the clocke in the mor-
,, ninge was carryed with them into *S. Gyles* in
,, the field, and there burned, *&c.* This is Fox
his narration ; neyther hath he any more of
them, but only that he affirmeth for his con-

Ibidem.

clusion, *that they were blessed Martyrs of Christ Iesus,
that innocently suffered vvithin the tyme of K. Henryes
raigne for the testimony of Gods vvord and truth.* And
yet doth he not know (as yow see) what opinions they held, nor of what sect they were,
and accordinge to the tyme assigned by Fox
himselfe of 1539. or neere about, they might
be of that association in opinions, wherof *Iohn
Stow* writeth in the end of the yeare 1538 .

Stow anno
1538.

sayinge . *Vpon the* 24. *of Nouember, foure Anabaptists, three men and one vvoman, all Dutch, bare
fagotts at Paules Crosse , and vpon the* 20. *of the same
moneth, a man and a vvoman, Dutch Anabaptists also,
vvere burned in Smithfield, &c.* So as by this yow
see

fee vvhat opinions reigned in England at
that tyme.

16. But howfoeuer this bee, and whether
the *Painter*, and *Peter German*, and *Lancelot* the
Kings feruát were Anabaptifts or noe: fure yt
is, that Iohn Fox playeth the foole in making
them his Saints without knowinge their opinions, and no leffe in telling vs fo improbable
a tale, that one of the Kings feruants fhould
be apprehended only for his *countenance and ge-*
fture, and fo haftily condemned and executed,
as the very next morninge after his apprehenfion, he fhould be carryed to the fire without
makinge the King priuy therof; vvhich is
againft the whole procoffe of the cannon law,
which at that tyme they obferued, and againft
all reafon and common fenfe; feing that befides all examinations, proofes & conuictions
neceffary in matters of herefie, there muft be
a conuenient tyme giuen alfo to the party to
fee, whether he wilbe obftinate or noe, for fo
much as without obftinacy, there is no herefie
punifhable by law, as before we haue fhewed
in the fourth Chapter of this booke. And befides this alfo, after all is done by the examiners and iudges, there muft be a wryte gotten
out from the King *de comburendo hæretico*, before he can be executed. All which things put
togeather, to witt the apprehenfion, examination, conuiction, refpitt, condemnation, and
wryte of execution, yt is very vnlikely they
could be difpatched in one afternoone, efpecially againft one of the K. feruants, whome

An im-
probable
tale of
Iohn Fox

M 2   fo

so openly they would not dare to iniure; And therfore is Iohn Fox found to be a fond and fraudulent tatler of things without ground, iudgment or probability.

17.   Wherfore I will draw now to the last foure of his Martyrs vnder *K. Henry* the 8. in this moneth, wherof three, to witt *Robert Barnes* an *Augustine* friar, *Thomas Gerrard* and *VVilliam Hierome* Apostata Priests, were burned in Smithfield vpon the yeare of Christ 1540. as *Stow* and *Holinshed* haue in their chronicles, though Fox in his Calendar putteth the same vpon the yeare 1539. and in his Acts * and Monuments vpon the yeare 1541. and the fourth named *Iohn Lambert*, alias *Nicolsone* another Priest of the same quality, was burned in the foresaid place the next yeare before, being the 30. of the raigne of K. Henry.

18.   And first as concerninge *Friar Barnes*, we haue said somewhat of him before in the story of *Frith*, and he is famous by the bookes of *Syr Thomas More*, wrytten against him, and yt is the same man of whome yow haue heard *Tyndall* wryte before to *Frith*, inclyninge to deny the reall presence in the Sacrament, sayinge: *Barnes will be hoate against yow* ; to witt, for the reall presence, for that he was an earnest Lutheran : the other two burned with him, to witt, *Gerrard* and *Hierome* had passed somwhat further, and slydd into Zwinglianisme, so as these three burned togeather by K. Henry at one stake, were of different and opposite beleefes: Fox telleth long tales and maketh large discourses

Margin notes:
Robert Barnes.
Thomas Gerard.
VVilliam Hierome.

*Fox pag. 1095.

discourses of them all, and first of *Barnes*, he sheweth how he being a friar, and Prior of the Augustines in Cambridge, he began first to read there, *better learninge then before* to vse his words: *to vvitt, Terence, Plautus,* and *Cicero,* very graue authors for a man of his degree and callinge. And sheweth further, that *Barnes* had certayne secrett conferences about Luthers doctrine, at an Inne or Tauerne of that vniuersity, named the signe of the *vvhite horse,* which Tauerne for that cause (saith he) was commonly called in those dayes by the schollers, the *Inne* of *Germany*; which thinge being discouered, *Barnes* was taken and sent prisoner to London to *Cardinall VVolsey,* before whome he abiured publikely his new religion, *humbly kneelinge vpon his knees,* vvhervpon he vvas brought also soone after to Paules Church in a great sollemnity, and there bare a faggott for his pennance all the tyme of a sermon, and after that againe being fallen into a secrett relapse, he was sent to the monastery of Augustine friars in Northampton, whence he stole away by a notable coseninge tricke, leauinge his habitt behind him with a letter to the Maior of the towne, that he was in desperation to drowne himselfe in the riuer of the citty, where he requested the Maior to seeke him, and cause his body to be buryed, and that they should find letters of great importance about his necke, inclosed in a ball of wax, which the Maior beleeuinge sought 7. dayes in the riuer, while the other was runne away,

Barnes recanted.

Fox pag.
1088. col. 2,
num. 80.

A notable coseninge trike of Friar Barnes.

M 3   and

and vpon the Sea, paſſinge into Germany, where he liued with Luther, and other here-tiks vntill *Q. Anne Bullen* was crowned; at what tyme by fauour & vnder protection of ſome, heretically affected about the King, but eſpecially *Cromwell*, he returned into England: where yet ſome yeares after that againe, King Henry hauinge made the ſtatute of 6. articles againſt heretiks, before ſpoken of, cauſed aſwell this *Barnes*, as the other two *Gerrard* and *Hierome*, to be arrayned, condemned and burned vpon different articles of hereſie in thoſe dayes.

19.   And this is the breife ſtory of theſe three Foxian Martyrs, who though they died at one ſtake, and by the ſentence of one and the ſelfe ſame Kinge, as three Catholike * Prieſts alſo did, at the ſame tyme and place, for the Roman Religion: yet do I not ſee how theſe three Martyrs of Iohn Fox can be of one Church, for ſo much as friar *Barnes*, was ſo earneſt in auowinge the *reall preſence* in the Sacrament, as *Tyndall* teſtifieth: For denyall wherof, aſwell *Gerrard*, and *Hierome* on the other ſide, as alſo their fourth companion *Iohn Lambert*, went particularly to the fire; and yet all foure (as yow ſee) are made fellow Martyrs by Fox, though ſufferinge for oppoſite and contrary cauſes, and yow ſhall perceaue the ſame more particularly by the Story of *Lambert*, that now enſueth.

20.   This *Lambert* aliàs *Nicolſon* was a Prieſt of Norfolke, conuerted (as Fox ſaith) by *Tho-*

mas

*D. Abell.
Powell.
Fetherſtō.*

The ſtory of I. Lambert aliàs Nicolſon.

mas Bilney of whome yow haue * heard before, but he farre paſſed his maiſter, for that,
Bilney dying a Catholike , as we hould, or a
Lutheran in ſome points, as Fox will haue yt,
this man paſſed to be a Zwinglian, and reſolued to take a woman, of whome Fox wryteth
thus: *For as much as prieſts in thoſe dayes, could not be*
permitted to haue wiues, Lambert left his prieſthood,
and applyed himſelfe to the function of teachinge, in-
tending ſhortly after to be free of the groſſers and to
marry, &c. Lo how this groſſe prieſt, would

Fox pag.
1024.

leaue his prieſthood to be a groſſer, but the
reaſon is vrgent , for that forſooth he muſt
needs haue a wife; no one lightly of all Fox
his new eccleſiaſticall ſaincts, preſuming to
haue the gift of chaſtity or ſingle life. He beginneth Lambertes ſtory with this glorious
title following.

21.　*The hiſtory of the worthy martyr of God Iohn*
Lambert aliâs *Nicolſon , anno Domini* 1538. The

pag. 1005.

ſumme wherof is ; that this *Lambert* being a
prieſt fled out of England , was a great con-
federate of *VVilliam Tyndall & Frith* beyond the
ſeas, and after comming home againe, was
accuſed of Zwinglianiſme by one *Doctor Taylor*
(a man ſaith Fox *in thoſe dayes not farre diſagreing*
from the ghoſpell) vnto *Doctor Friar Barnes* of
whome we haue ſpoken before, which *Barnes*
(ſaith Fox) *although* he did otherwiſe fauour

Fox pag.
1024. col.2.

alſo the ghoſpell, notwithſtandinge ſeemed ,,
not greatly to fauour this cauſe, fearinge per- ,,
aduenture , that yt would bread ſome lett to ,,
the preachinge of the ghoſpell, yf ſuch *Sacra-* ,,

mentaries

,, mentaries fhould be fuffered : and there vpon
,, perfuaded Taylor by and by to putt vp the
,, matter to *Thomas Cranmer* Archbifhop of Can-
,, terbury, and fo he did, and the Archbifhop
,, fent for him, and brought him into the open

Cranmer
had not yt
fauored of
Zvvinglia-
nifme.

court, & forced him to defend his caufe openly, for the Archbifhop had not yet fauored the
doctrine of the *Sacrament, &c.* Thus wryteth
Fox of the beginning of *Lamberts* controuerfy,
altogeather moued, and profecuted by ghofpellers of other fects, as himfelfe afterwards
noteth, for that *Cromwell* alfo, and *Latimer* entred into the daunce, the later difputinge a-
gainft him, and the former giuinge fentence of
death, as after yow fhall heare.

22.   Now then *Lambert* being brought into
Cranmer the Archbifhops courte vpon accufation of Zwinglian herefie, againft the *bleffed
Sacrament,* and taking vpon him to defend the
fame in wrytinge, by ten feuerall arguments,
fuch as the *Sacramentaries* of thofe dayes were
wont to vfe, drawen out of fenfe, & humaine
reafon, againft faith (where of he wrote a long
difcourfe,) the matter came to be very famous
in the courte (as Fox noteth) and paffing alfo
to the hearinge of K. *Henry* that was a great
enemy to the *Sacramentary* herefie, and being
in like manner fignified vnto him, that *Lambert*
had made his appeale vnto his Maiefties tribunall, as fupreame head of the Church from
the faid Bifhops iurifdiction : the King refolued to heare the whole matter himfelfe, and
that in very folemne and publicke manner,
                                                                    both

both for his hatred to that herefie, as alfo for
that yt was the firft iudiciall act, that euer he
had exercifed publikely in his owne perfon,
touching matters of faith and religion, before
that day; wherefore callinge all his nobles af-
vvell temporall as Ecclefiafticall, vvith his
Iudges, Counfelors, and other officers togeather, appointed the day of difputation, wherein *Lamberts* caufe fhould be tried; and for that
he vnderftood that *Lambert* had giuen vpp the
forefaid ten reafons or arguments in vvriting,
drawen out of *Sacramentary* bookes againft the
reall prefence, to the Archbifhopp of Canterbury, he appointed ten feuerall Bifhopps to
confute thofe ten arguments, euery Bifhop a
feuerall argument; and to *Cranmer* was afsigned to confute the obiection about the impofsibility *of Chrifts being in tovv places at once,* that
being held for a principall bulwarke of his
herefie: to witt, that for fo much as Chrifts
body is a true naturall body, yt cannot be in
heauen & in the *Sacrament* at one time, as yow
fhall heare obiected often by them afterwards,
in the *reuiew of ten publike difputations* adioyned
to the * end of this booke, where yow fhall
fee euery *Sacramentary*, both man and women
lightly vrge this argument, as a matter of great
force on their fide, which hath none at all, and
B. *Cranmer* did fufficiently refute the fame before the King againft *Lambert,* euen by *Scripture*
yt felfe; though yet dealinge fomewhat tryf-
lingly therein, (as yt may appeare, by Fox his
narration) *Doctor Gardener* the Bifhop of *VVinchefter,*

VVhy the Kinge re-
folued to heare and iudge *Lambert* himfelfe.

* *Cap.* 3.
& 4.

chefter, was forced to helpe him out. But lett
vs heare Fox his owne relation of the matter
as in his owne words he fetteth it downe.

Fox pag.
1024.col.2,
num. 64.

23.   The Kinge (faith he) giuinge eaer more
willingely then prudently or godly (to euill
,, counfell) fent out a generall commifsion,
,, commaundinge all the nobles, and Bifhops of
,, his realme, to come with all fpeed to *London*,
,, where a great affembly of the nobility was
,, gathered from all parts of the realme, not
,, without much wonder & expectation in this
,, fo ftrange a cafe, all the feates and places were
,, full of men round about the fcaffold, & by &

The folemne
iudgment,
and condemnatiō
of *Lambert*
by the
Kinge.

by the *godly feruāt of Chrift*, *Lambert* was brought
in frō the prifon vvith a guard of armed men,
as a lambe to fight with many lyons, & placed
right ouer againft the Kings royall feate, fo
that now they tarried but for the Kings com-
,, ming to the place; at laft the K. himfelfe came
,, in as a iudge of that great controuerfie, with a
,, great guard clothed all in white, and couering
,, by that color and diffemblinge, feuerity of all
,, bloudy iudgement; on his right hand fate the
,, B. & behind him the famous lawyers clothed
,, all in purple accordinge to the manner, on the
,, left hand fate the peeres of the realme, the iu-
,, ftices, and other nobles in their order, behind
,, him fate the gentlemē of his priuy chāber, *&c.*
,, 24.   When the King was fett in his throne,
,, he beheld *Lambert* with a fterne countenance,
,, and then turning himfelfe to his Counfelors,
,, he called foorth *Doctor Day* Bifhop of *Chichefter*,
,, commaunding him to declare ynto the people
the

the cause of this present assembly and iudgement, *&c.* When he had made an end of his
Oration, the King standing vp vpon his feete,
and leaning vpon a cushion of white cloth of
tissue, turning himselfe towards *Lambert* with
his browes bent, said, *Ho good fellow what is thy
name?* Then the humble Lambe of Christ
humbly kneeling downe, said, my name is *Iohn
Nicolson* though of many I be called *Lambert.*
what said the Kinge, haue yow tow names?
I would not trust yow hauing two names,
though yow were my brother. O most noble
Prince (quoth *Lambert*) your Bishopps forced
me of necessity to change my name, and after
diuers prefaces and much talke to and fro, the
King commaunded him to goe to the matter,
and declare his minde and opinion, what he
thought as touching the *Sacrament of the Altar:*
then *Lambert* beginning to speake for himselfe
gaue God thankes, which had so inclined the
Kings harte, *&c.*

25. But the King with an angrye voice in-
terrupting his oration, said, I came not hither
to heare myne owne praises thus painted out
in myne owne presence, but briefly goe to the
matter, without any more circumstance: thus
he spake in Latyn. But *Lambert* being a bashed
at the Kings angry words, contrary to all
mens expectation, stayd a while consideringe
whither he might turne himselfe, in these
great strayts and extremityes, but the King
being hasty with anger and vehemency said,
*vvhy standest thou still, answere as touchinge the Sacra-
ment*

The K· combate vvith *Lambert.*

ment of the Altar? Whether doest thou say that yt is the body of Christ, or wilt deny it? and with that the King lifted vp his cappe. *Lambert.* I answere with S. *Augustine,* that it is the

,, body of Christ after a certayne manner. *King.*
,, Answere me neyther out of S. *Augustine,* ney-
,, ther by the authority of any other, but tell me
,, plainly whether thou saiest it is the body of
,, Christ or no? and these words the King spake
,, againe in Latin. *Lambert.* Then I deny it to be
,, the body of Christ. *King.* Marke well, for now
,, thou shalt be condemned euen by Christs
,, owne words. *Hoc est corpus meum.* Then he
,, commanded *Thomas Cranmer* Archbishop of
,, Canterbury to refute his assertion, *&c.*

26.   Thus writeth Fox of the beginning of this combat and disputation; though of the kings prosecution of his argument he saith no more, which *Hall* notwithstanding in his Cronicle, who was also a *Sacramentarie,* and present at the disputation, affirmeth most of all to haue vrged *Lambert* in that place, as presently yow shall heare him auouch: and as for

Cranmers argument, against Lambert. *Act.* 9.

Cranmers arguing against him, for confuting his first *Sacramentary* principle, *that Christs body cannot be in two places at once,* his said confutation was out of the acts of the Apostles, where Christ appeared to *Sainct Paul* in the way as he went to *Damascus,* whereby he proued, that Christs body might be in two places at once, for that he being in heauen, appeared also on earth at the same tyme, whereunto *Lambert* could not answere, but very rydiculously,

loufly, faying, *that Chrift did not appeare in deed,*
and really vnto Saint Paul, but that his voyce was heard
from heauen, which fhift when *Cranmer* went
about to refute out of another place of the
Acts of the Apoftles, where *Saint Paul* plainly
affirmeth, that Chrift appeared vnto him: but
yet femed to vrge the matter fomewhat cold-
ly: the Bifhopp of *VVinchefter* added a place or
two in confirmation, as 1. *Cor.* 9. *haue I not*
feene Chrift Iefus? and in the 15. chapter, & fame
epiftle: *He appeared vnto Cephas, &c. but laft of all*
vnto me: whereunto (faith Fox) *Lambert anfwered*
that he doubted nothing but that Chrift was feene, and
did appeare, but he did deny, that he was in two or in
diuerfe places according to the manner of his body.
which is a ridiculous anfwere yf yow marke
yt, & in fauour of his aduerfary: for when we
fay, that his body is in the *Sacrament* at diuerfe
places, we doe not fay that he is there after
the maner of his body, as yt was vpon earth,
or as it is now in heauen, but after another
manner, which we call *Sacramentally,* fo as this
is for vs: and fecondly when he graunteth that
Chrift did appeare really in diuerfe places
at once, and yet denyeth that he was in thofe
diuers places at once, wherin he appeared; it is
a contradiction in yt felfe, and therfore I maruaile not, that Fox doth fo rage and rayle at
B. Gardener for vrging *Lambert* fo much in this
place. *The Bifhopp of VVincefter* (faith he) *being*
drowned with malice againft this poore man, without
the Kinges commandement, obferuing no order, before
the Archbifhop had made and end, vnfhamefully kneeled
downe

Act. 26.

Fox *ibid.*

Fox *pag.* 1025. *col.* 2. *num.* 30.

*downe to take in hand the disputation , alleaging a place
out of the 12. chapter to the Corinthians,* &c.

27.   Thus Fox, and in the margent hath this
note, *the hasty impudencie of the Bishopp of VVinche-*
ster. And it is easie to see the reason of Fox his
choler against him, for pressing his martyr so
much, who became dumme at length & durst
to answere no thing, which Fox confesseth in
effect a litle after, to witt, *that Lambert in the end
became silent , and that he could not answere any fur-*
ther, yow shall heare his words & confession.

,, Then againe (saith he) the King and the Bis-
,, hopps raged against *Lambert,* insomuch as he
,, was not only forced to silence, but also might
,, haue bine driuen into a rage, yf his eares had
,, not bine acquainted which such taunts be-
,, fore and after. *And after this,* the other Bishops
,, euery one in his order being ten in number,
,, supplied the places of disputation, *&c.* so wry-
,, teth Fox: and a litle after he addeth theise
words : *Lambert in the meane tyme being compassed
with so many and great perplexities , vexed on the one
side with checkes and taunts , and pressed on the other
side with the authority and threats of the personages,
amazed with the maiestie of the place , and presence of
the King, wearyed with long standing, and brought into
dispaire that he should nothing profitt with speaking,
choose rather to hold his peace,* &c.

28.   Thus Fox for some excuse of his martyrs silence; when he was blanked; but *Edward
Hall* no lesse a *Sacramentarie* then Fox himselfe,
and one that was present at the disputation,
as may appeare by his speach writeth thus in
his

Lambert
brought
to be
dumme in
disputa-
tion.

his ſtory. This *Nicolſon* (aliâs *Lambert*) was a man named to be learned, but that day he vttered no ſuch learning, as he was of many ſuppoſed, that he both could and would haue done, but was exceeding fearfull & timorous. *&c.* Certaine of the Biſhopps miniſtred diuerſe arguments, but eſpecially the K. Maieſtie himſelfe did moſt diſpute with him, howbeit *Nicolſon* was not perſuaded, nor would reuoke, *&c.* So ſaith *Hall:* now let vs heare the reſidue that followeth in Fox, for his cõdemnation. Then ſaid the King vnto *Lambert:* What ſaiſt thow now after all theſe great labours taken for thee, and all the reaſons and inſtructions of theſe learned men? Art thou not yet ſatisfied? wilt thou liue or dye? what ſaiſt thou? thou haſt yet free choiſe. *Lambert. I yeald and ſubmitt my ſelfe to your clemencie.* Then ſaid the King, yf yow doe committ your ſelfe to my iudgement, then muſt yow dye, for I will not be a patron vnto heretiks, and by and by turninge himſelfe to *Cromwell* he ſaid; *Cromwell* read the ſentence of condemnatiõ againſt him, which he did out of a ſchedell, *&c.* Thus wryteth Fox, & preſently addeth theſe words about *Cromwell.*

29. This *Cromwell* was at that tyme the cheife friend of the ghoſpellers, & heere is much to be marueled at, to ſee how vnfortunatly yt came to paſſe in this matter, that *Sathan* did heere performe the condemnation of *Lambert* by no other miniſters then by ghoſpellers themſelues, *Taylor, Barnes, Cramner* and *Crom-*
                                        well,

well, &c. So he of his martyrs condemnation
by King *Henry* ; which King he maketh alfo
a ghofpeller as before yow haue heard, and
yet notwithftanding a bloudy perfecutor of
the fame ghofpell, for thus he wryteth a litle

Fox *ibid.*   after. Thus was (faith he) *Iohn Lambert*,in this
,, bloudy fefsions, iudged and condemned to
,, death by the King, vvhofe iudgement novv
,, remaineth vvith the Lord, againft that day,
,, when as before the tribunall feat of that great
,, Iudge, both princes, and fubiects fhall ftand,
,, and appeare not to iudge, but to be iudged, ac-
,, cording as they haue done and deferued, &c.

30.   Behold Iohn Fox his threat of damnation againft *King Henry* for condemning of
Lambert. His burning I let paffe, which Fox
fetteth out by a large pageant painting him in
the fyre, and theife vvords pafsing from his
mouth vp towardes heauen. *None but Chrift,
none but Chrift.* as though he had bine burned
for holding that fentence, or that *King Henry,
Cromwell, Cranmer, Latymer*, or other ghofpellers that vvere his iudges, vvould haue had
more Chrifts then one, or would be faued by
any other meanes then by Chrift. I leaue alfo
to recompt the moft foolifhe fabulous narration, or rather fiction of Fox, wherin he diui-
feth a certayne circuite which this *Nicolfon*
A notable   made that morninge, when he was to be bur-
lying tale   ned, tellinge vs, that he was brought out of
of Fox a-   the prifon at *Newgate* by eyght of the clocke in
bout Lam-   the morning, & being to be burned in Smith-
bert bur-   field, (which is hard by *Newgate* as yow know)
ning.   he

he tooke a contrary course, and crossed all
London to go to my *L. Cromwells* house (which
was in the *Augustine Friars* neere Bishopsgate)
and there being carryed into *Cromwells* inner
chamber, the said *Cromwell* asked him forgiuenes, for that which he had done against
him, and then they entred into such familiar
talke and conuersation, as *Lambert* seemed to
haue forgotten that he was to be burned that
day, till he was warned therof by others; and
that he was so pleasant and merry, as then also when he was admonished he would not
go to the fire, vntill he had first broken his
fast, with my Lords gentlemen. But heare
yt I pray yow, in Fox his owne words.

31. Vpon the day (saith he) that was appointed for this holy martyr of God to suffer, he
was brought out of the prison at eyght of the
clocke in the morning, vnto the house of the
L. *Cromwell* into his inner chamber, where, it
is reported of many, that *Cromwell* asked him
forgiuenes for that he had done, and there at
last *Lambert* being admonished that the houre
of death was at hand, he was greatly comfor-
ted and cheared, and being brought out of the
chamber into the hall, he saluted the gentlemen, & satt downe to breakefast with them,
shewinge no manner of sadnes or feare, and
when the breakefast was ended, he was carryed straightway to the place of execution in
Smithfield, to offer himselfe vnto the Lord a
sacrifice of sweet sauour, who is blessed in his
Saints for euer and euer.

Fox pag.
1028. col.2,
n.46.
,,
,,
The Lord
Cromvvel
said to
aske Lam-
bert for
gyuenes.
,,
,,
,,
,,
,,
,,
,,
,,

32.   This is Fox his moſt miraculous narration, and by this only, among fiue hundred other the like, in theſe his Acts and Monuments, let the reader iudge how much he is to be credited. For let any man of ſenſe or reaſon conſider what likelyhood heere is in this tale, that *Nicolſon* being condemned ſo ſolemnely by the King himſelfe, and ſo ſeuerely by his commandement put to excution afterward, *as no man* (to vſe Fox his words) *vvas ſo cruelly and pittifully handled as hee*; and comming forth from *Newgate* at eyght of the clocke in the morning in wynter, when all the people and nobility was gathered togeather in Smithfield to expect him, (and diuers no doubt of the counſell alſo) to ſee ſo ſollemne a ſpectacle, as the burninge of one, conuinced and condemned by the King himſelfe; let euery man imagine (I ſay) whether yt be likely or morally poſſible, that this condemned heretike, with a publike guard of iuſtice followinge him, and himſelfe goinge bound, as men are wont to do when they go to death, and apparayled alſo moſt contemptibly, as in ſuch caſe is accuſtomed: whether (I ſay) yt be likely that ſuch a perſon ſhould be permitted, to make a walkinge vagary throughout all London to Biſhoppſgate, and there to haue conference ſo familiarly with the *L. Cromwell*, in his inner chamber, who was at that tyme, the cheefeſt and higheſt magiſtrate vnder the King in England;or whether the *L.Cromwell* would haue vouchſafed or durſt to haue admitted any

ſuch

Ibidem.

such conference with an heretike goinge to
the fire, and condemned by the K. himselfe:
or whether yt be likely, that *Lambert*, who
shewed himselfe so fearfull at his disputation,
could now be so hardy, as to forgett that he
was to be burned that day, or would sitt
downe so familiarly to breakefast with my
Lords gentlemen, or that those gentlemen
would admitt him, or that he could eate his
armes being bound behind him: or that the
iustice and guard, that wayted vpon him,
would haue suffered such trifling out of tyme
in such a case: All these things (I say) are so improbable, as none but a Fox, or a foole would
haue written them. And so much be spoken of
this his *sweet sauouring Saint Martyr Iohn Lambert.*

33. There remayne only now for end of
those that were burned in this moneth, vnder
K. *Henry* the eyght two other, which are sett
downe vpon seuerall dayes in Fox his Calendar, in these words: *Colyns Martyr*, *Cowbridge*
Martyr and the former of the two he painteth
out pittifully in the fire togeather with a
dogge; and ouer his head he wryteth thus:
Collyns vvith his dogge burned : and then of the second thus: *The burninge of Cowbridge at Oxford
anno* 1538. About which two Martyrs, yow
must vnderstand, that Fox in his first edition
of his martyrologe, did sett forth their martyrdomes very pittifully described both in
Latyn and English, as of great Saints, beginninge his Latyn narration thus, as *Alanus Copus*
cyteth yt, (for I haue not the said edition by

Fox in his
first edit. in
Lat. anno
Christ. 1536
pag. 139.
& in edit.
prima An-
glie. anno
1539. pag.
570.
Alan. Cop
dial. 6. cap.
17. pa. 623.

me): *Me puero concrematus est Oxonij Coubrigius, &c.*
When I was a child, one *Coubridge* was burned
at Oxford, *mitis Christi ouicula,* a meeke sheep of
Christ, *Sanctus Christi seruulus,* a little holy seruant of Christ, *&c.* But since that tyme his
false and deceatfull narration being discouered, & laid open by the said *Alanus Copus,* or rather *Doctor Harpesfield,* the true author of those
learned dialogues, and the originall records
being cyted for the wicked opinions of both
these Foxian Martyrs, but especially 12. most
pestilent propositions of *Coubridge,* for which
he was condemned: Iohn Fox blushing therat, hath somewhat (as the sayinge is) pulled in
his hornes: and albeit of willfull obstinacy, he
would not put them out quite of his Calendar of Martyrs; yet is he forced to abate them
so much in this his last narration, as with farre
lesse shame might he haue left them out wholy: for thus he wryteth of them:

34.   *Colyns being besides his wits, seing a Priest hol-*
ding vp the host ouer his head, shewinge yt to the people;
he in like manner counterfettinge the Priest, tooke vp a
Fox pag.
1033. col. 1.
little dogg by the legges, and held him ouer his head,
shewinge him vnto the people; for which he was burned
in the yeare 1538. the same that Iohn Lambert was.
Thus he wryteth of *Colyns* and I would aske
Fox, yf this *Colyns* was besides his wytts, (as
he saith) how could he be a Martyr? and how
came he into his Calendar? Yow shall heare
the moderation, that Fox now in his later
edition, being chect by *Alanus Copus,* vseth,
about this his Saint and his dogge. *Although*
(saith

(saith he) *I do not heere recyte him as in the number of Gods professed Martyrs; yet neyther do I thinke him to be cleane sequestred from the Lords saued flocke and family, notwithstandinge that the Bishop of Rome his Church did condemne and burne him for an heretike, but rather do recount him therfore, as one belonginge to the holy company of Saints,* &c.

35. Consider heere (good Reader) how these things hang togeather. For in his Calendar Fox putteth him downe againe, as before, for a true martyr, assigning him his festiuall day, saiyng vpon the 10. of October, *Collyns martyr;* and yet in his story of Acts and monuments, he saith, as yow haue heard, *that he doth not recite him in the number of Gods professed martyrs.* How can this hang togeather, except yow will say, that Iohn Fox had some martyrs professed, & some vnprofessed or nouice-martyrs? And yf yt were so; yet me thinketh, that those, that are preferred to be Calendar-martyrs (such as *Collyns* and *Coubrige* are) ought to be professed martyrs. Marke also his cause and reason of making sainctes and martyrs, to witt, that *Collyns* therfore belongeth *to the holy company of sainctts, for that he was condemned by the B. of Rome, and his Church;* by which reason all malefactors, but especially *Anabaptists, Arrians* and other confessed heretiks, punished in Catholike countreyes, by authority of the said Church, may, by Fox his reason, belonge to the company of Protestant Saints. And so much of *Collyns* and his dogge celebrated by Fox for a madd Martyr.

36. But

36. But now lett vs passe to *Cowbridge*, Fox his second Martyr, placed by him vpon the same day in his Calendar : he beginneth his story thus: *VVith this forsaid Collyns may also be adioyned the burning of Cowbridge, vvho likewise being madd, and besides his right senses, vvas eyther the same or the next yeare after, condemned by Longland Bishop of Lincolne, and committed to the fire by him to be burned at Oxford. VVhat his articles and opinions vvere, vvherwith he vvas charged, yt needeth not heere to rehearse: For as he vvas then a man madde and destitute of sense and reason; so his vvords & sayings could not be found, &c.* Yea, Father Fox, and is yt so ? will yow runne out at that hole? how happeneth yt then, that yow made so long and pittifull a narration of him and his death in your former editions, calling him *the litle holy seruant of God, the meeke lambe of Christ,* and the like? how happeneth, that in this your last edition yow put him in againe for a Calendar-martyr, yf he were a madd man (as heere yow say) placing him on the tenth of this moneth, and striking out three renowned ancient Martyrs *Triphon, Respitius,* and *Nimpha,* to make him place ? Is not this more then madnesse in your selfe? Yow say it is needlesse to rehearse his opinions, but I thinke the contrary, and that yt shalbe well to recyte some of them at least, thereby to make your madnes and dishonest dealinge more notorious to the world: Thus then they stand in the publike register subscribed by his owne hand, and testified by many wittnesses, and that he vttered them not in madnesse,

Fox *pag.* 1033. The story of Cowbridge.

Fox ashamed to recyte his mad-martyrs opinions.

madnesse, but only in the maddnes and phrenesie of heresie, by which he being a lay man,
made himselfe a Prieſt by his owne ordination, ſaid maſſe and conſecrated, founding
himſelfe on the words of *S. Peter*, that *all Chriſtians are Prieſts*, & held beſides many opinions
of *VVickliffe* and *Huſſe*, and among many other
he held theſe ſingular of his owne, which do
enſue: taken out of the regiſter.

37. *Ego Gulielmus Coubrigius publicè aſſerui, &c.*
I *VVilliam Cowbridge* haue publikely affirmed,
that Prieſts are guilty of high treaſon, for de-
uidinge the hoſt into three parts.

    Item. That no man ought to chaſten or pu-
niſh his body by faſtinge.

    Item, that I would not confeſſe to any
Prieſt, except he would abſolue me, as I ſhould
appoint him.

    Item, that neyther the Apoſtles nor Euan-
geliſts, nor the foure Doĉtors of the Church,
haue opened the true way hitherto how ſyn-
ners ſhould be ſaued.

    Item, I haue affirmed, that Chriſt was not
the redeemer of the world, but rather the deceauer of the world.

    Item, that I haue held this name Chriſt, for
a filthy name, and haue ſcraped the ſame out
of my books, wherſoeuer I haue found yt.

    Item, I haue affirmed all thoſe, that beleeued
in the name of Chriſt, to be damned in hell.

    Item, I haue interpreted thoſe words of
Chriſt: *This is my body vvhich ſhalbe giuen for yow, in
this ſenſe;* This is my body which ſhall deceaue

yow,

*Alan. cap.
dial. 6.
pag 613.*
,,
,,
,,
,,
,,
,,
,,
,,
Cowv-
bridge his
blaſphe-
mous opi-
nions.
,,
,,
,,
,,
,,
,,
,,
,,
,,
,,
,,
,,

yow, or wherin yow shalbe deceaued or cir-
cumuented, &c.

38.   These and other like wicked propositions held this meeke lambe, and litle holy
Saint of Iohn Fox, for which he was condemned at the towne of *VVickam* by the B. of Lincolne; neyther could he by any perfuasion, eyther of him, or other learned men about him,
be reduced from these fancyes, vntill in the
very laft end, when being in the fire, he cryed
Iefus Chrift, Iefus Chrift, wherby fome were induced to thinke that he died repentant, as *Bilney* did before him. But howfoeuer this was,
yt is but a poore fhift of Iohn Fox, to fay, that
thefe his two Martyrs *Collyns* and *Cowbridge*
were madd; firft, for that it condemneth him
of more madnes (yf they were madd indeed)
to fill his Calendar with fuch madd-martyrs:
and fecondly, for that no fober men will euer
beleeue, that the B. of *Lincolne* (for example)
and other learned men of the vniuerfity of
Oxford, would euer haue taken fuch paines
at fundry tymes, both at *Oxford* and *VVickam*,
as by the publike regifter appeareth that they
did, to reduce *Cowbridge* from thefe errors, yf
they had held him for madd.

39.   But (as I faid before) his madneffe was
the madneffe of herefie, which is fo defperate
a phrenefie, where it entreth, as nothing can
How Cou
bridge
vvas madd
cure or moderate the fame, but that he that is
poffeffed with it, will dy for any thing that he
taketh to defend, wherof we haue heard fome
examples before, and I my felfe faw one, of
great

great admiration and compassion in a Scot-
tishmā at *Siuill* in Spaine, vpon the yeare 1595.
who being vnlearned, had taken so earnest an
apprehension, by readinge scriptures in his
owne language, of those words of Christ *No-*
lite iudicare, do yow not iudge : that he would
not yeld to the iudgement or condemnation
of any man; no nor yet of the diuell himselfe.
And albeit the Inquisitors of that place being
learned men of themselues, and diuers others
called by them to deale with him, did alleage
him many textes of scripture to shew, that
wicked men should be damned, and that *Iudas*
in particular was damned, and that heretiks
among others were sure to be damned, accordinge to the playne testimony of *S. Paul*, and
other such like demonstratiōs of damnation,
and that of the diuell there could be no doubt
at all, and consequently also men might iudge
them for damned; yet would he not yeld, but
rather dy, and be burned alyue (as after my departure thence he was) then graunt that we
may iudge the diuells to be damned. And albeit he was dealt withall continually to that
effect, for the space of two yeares togeather,
& his execution deferred, for this only cause,
to bringe him from this hereticall madnes, &
that diuers Inglishmen also laboured with
him in this tyme, to yeld and graunt that men
might iudge in some causes; yet all would not
serue, but that he would suffer death for that
foolish Anabaptisticall heresie, *that men may not*
iudge in any case. So that Iohn Fox may truly

The madd
obstinacy
of a Scot-
tishman
in Siuill
an.1595.
*Matth.*7.
*Luc.*6.

say

fay that thefe his two men were madd alfo,
but yt was hereticall madneffe, and confequently they were madd-martyrs indeed.
And thus much for them that were burned
vnder *K. Henry.*

Of thofe that were burned in this mo-
neth vnder *Qu. Mary.* §. 2.

40.   The firft two martyrs of Fox his Calendar, burned in this moneth for Zwinglian herefy during the tyme of Qu. Maryes raigne,
were *VVilliam VVolfey*, and *Robert Pigot* of *VVif-*
bich, the firft a labouring man, the fecond a
paynter, who were examined & condemned
after much treaty with them for their reduction, by *Doctor Shaxton* Suffragan to the Bifhop of *Ely*, and by *Doctor Fuller* his Chancelor,
& alfo by *Doctor Steward* and *Doctor Chriftopher-*
fon Deanes of *Ely* and *Norwich*, and other learned men in commiffion with them. The arrogancy of the two vnlearned Sectaryes is
fhewed by Fox himfelfe, for that he wryteth
how they called their iudges, *Scribes* and *Pha-*
rifees, and the like contumelious names; yet
the one of them to witt *VVolfey*, was offered
by *Doctor Fuller* (yf Fox fay true) to be lett go
free, yf he would haue accepted the fame, but
that he refufed yt. And the like curtefy was
vfed with the paynter alfo, but when nothing
would ferue, they were brought to iudgement, and being charged with diuers articles
of

VVilliam
VVolfey.
Robert
Pigot.

Fox pag.
1557.

of herefy; *the cheefeſt was* (ſaith Fox) about the Sacrament of the Altar, *VVheryuto their anſwere was, that the Sacrament of the Altar was an Idoll, and that the naturall body, and bloud of Chriſt was not really preſent in that Sacrament.* And to this opinion they ſaid they would ſticke. *Then Doctor Shaxton ſaid vnto them:* (this *Doctor Shaxton* had byn once Biſhop of *Saliſbury;* and had byn depriued with Latymer in K. Henryes dayes for ſuſpicion of herefy) *good brethren remember your ſelues, and become new men, for I my ſelfe was in this fond opinion once, that yow are now, but I am become a nevv man. Ah* (ſaid Wolſey the labouring man) *are yovv become a new man! VVoe be to thee thou wicked new man, for God ſhall iuſtly iudge thee.* &c.

41. Thus farre Fox; ſhewing further, that they were burned both togeather at *Ely,* and *that they were moſt holy and bleſſed martyrs,* But now conſider on the contrary ſide, the different ſentence of Luther, as credible a man as Fox is, who ſetteth downe this decree: *Hæreticos ſeriò cenſemus, & alienos ab Eccleſia Dei Zuinglianos & Sacramentarios omnes, qui negant Chriſti corpus & ſanguinem, ore carnali ſumi in venerabili Euchariſtia:* We do ſeriouſly cenſure for heretiks „ and caſt forth of the Church of God, all Zuin- „ glians & Sacramentaryes that deny the body „ and bloud of Chriſt to be receyued in the ve- „ nerable Sacrament, by our bodily mouth. And by this generall decree of *Martyn Luther,* ſo principall a new ghoſpeller of our tyme, and father of all the reſt, we may iudge not only of theſe Zuinglians martyrs, but of all other in

like

like manner, that were burned vnder Q. Mary, who commonly were condemned for denyall of this article of the *reall presence*, whome Luther also condemneth for heretiks, as yow see; So as whome Fox sanctifieth, Luther damneth, & which of the two shall we rather beleeue? See more of this matter afterward in the 17. chapter of this booke.

42.   There follow in the second place, two other Captaine rubricate martyrs *Nicolas Ridley* and *Hugh Latymer*, both of them sett downe for Bishop-martyrs vpon the 19. and 20. day of this moneth. And albeit much hath byn said of them before, vpon the festiuall dayes of *Cranmer, Hooper, Rogers*, and some other their companions; yet for that Fox doth place them specially in this moneth, we shall repeat heere some principall points againe.

Nicolas Ridley. Hugh Latymer.

43.   First then for *Nicolas Ridley*, he was borne in Northampton-shire, according to Fox, bred vp in Newcastle, studied at Cambridge, and there was made priest, trauayled ouer the sea to *Paris*, and returning againe became K. Henry the eight his Chaplyn, and by him was made Bishopp of Rochester, in which state he remained when the said King died, and was as forward to fauour the said K. proceedings and will in all things, and to burne heretiks while he liued, as was *Cranmer*, or any other Bishopp els: but when King Henry was dead, and his sonne Edward the child come to the crowne, considering with himselfe that the Protector *L. Seymer*, and other that bare

The story of Nicolas Ridley.

the

the fway, were enclyned to innouations in
religion, and that *Cranmer* partly by his owne
naturall leuity, and partly for the free vfe of
his woman, was fwaying alfo that way, *Ridley*
thought good, to take part & beare him company, both in that innouation and taking a
wife alfo, hoping therby to gett himfelfe a
better Bifhoprike through fauour of the tyme,
and by depriuacion of fome others, that were
more fcrupulous and conftant in Catholike
Religion then himfelfe, as namely *Doctor Bonner* and *Doctor Gardener*, Bifhopps of *London* and
VVinchefter, againft whome * *Cranmer* and he
procured themfelues to be made vifitours &
iudges, as before yow haue heard, and by the
help and accufations of *Hooper*, *Latymer* and
others, depriued them at length of the faid Bifhopricks; and *Ridley* gott for his reward
the Bifhopricke of London, for that yt firft
fell void before the other; which when he had
once obtayned, he thought good to ioyne
himfelfe in more ftraight league with the faid
Cranmer; and fo they two being vnited,
fwaying with the tyme, and fauouring herefy, ouerbare all the reft, yea kept downe alfo
diuerfe of their owne profefsion, that afpired
to rife, as namely *Rogers*, *Latymer*, yea *Hooper* alfo, for a tyme, though at laft he brake through
all obftacles by the power of his patron the
Earle of *VVarwicke*, and got two Bifhoppricks
togeather, and at once, as * before yow haue
hearde.

*In the fto-
ry of Cran-
mer. March.
23.*

Ridley
ioyneth
vvith Cra-
mer in
vvicked-
neffe and
treafon.

* *Febr. 13.*

44. But to goe forward, yt is further to be
noted

noted that this *Ridley* as well as *Cranmer*, followed firſt altogeather the fortune and fauour
of the Protector, but perceauing afterward
that he was inferior both in wildome, power
and courage to his antagoniſt *Dudley* the Earle
of *VVarwick*, afterward Duke of *Northumberland*, he left him, and ioyned with the other,
with whome both *Cranmer* and he ran hand
in hand, during all the tyme of his authority
& proſperitye, yea not refuſing to ioyne w ith

Ridleyes
ſermon at
Paules
Croſſe a-
gainſt the
ſucceſſion
of K. Hen-
ryes chil-
dren.

him alſo in that notable, wicked, and barbarous conſpiracie and treaſon, for the extirpa-
tion of all K. Henryes children, as appeareth
by the Acts and Regiſtres of that tyme, and
by a ſpeciall peſtiferous ſermon made by *Ridley* at Paules Croſſe, vpon the 16. of Iuly *anno*
1553. after K. *Edward* was dead : of which ſer-

Stow anno
1553. pag.
1035.

mon *Iohn Stow* writeth thus : *The ſixtenth of Iuly
being ſunday, Doctor Ridley B. of London, by comman-
demēt of the Councell, preached at Paules, where he vehemently perſuaded the people in the tittle of the Lady
Iane, late proclaimed Queene, and inueighed earneſtly
againſt the title of the Lady Marye,* &c.

45. But I would know heere what conſcience or reaſon, this intruded Biſhopp could
haue to inueigh againſt the title of *Queene Mary*, to whoſe ſucceſſion he had ſworne ſo ſolemnely not long before, vnder *King Henry* her
father? wherfore he being apprehended firſt
for this ſeditious and traiterous ſermon, and
conuicted therof, was aſwell for this, as for
diuerſe points of hereſy condemned, & finally
burned in *Oxford*. And this is the ſumme of the
life

life and death of *Nicolas Ridley*, of whome truely yt is ridiculous (as before also I noted in
the life of *Cranmer*) to see and consider what
adoe Iohn Fox maketh to commend him for
a singular rare man and pretious prelate, *a man
beutified* (saith he) *with such excellent qualities, so
ghostly inspired & godly learned, & now written doubt-
lesse in the booke of life, with the blessed saincts of the
Almightie, crowned and introned amongst the glorious
campany of martyrs,&c.* Thus he: as though *Ridley* had byn the first and highest saint: that
euer had byn Bishopp of *Rochester* or *London*
which nodoubt he was, yf herely be sanctity:
for he was the first that euer polluted those
two ancient and venerable Sees with that
poison, since the first planting of Christian religion among our English nation: but yf we
respect holines according to those old qualityes, which ancient Fathers were wont to
doe, especially in Bishopps, as *constancy* and *fortitude* in Catholike religion against innouations; much praying, fasting, continencie, gra-
titie, mortification of the body, large almes-
deeds, visiting prisons, building hospitals, education, and marriage of orphanes, and the like:
we shall finde *this ghostly inspired saint and godly
learned prelate* of Iohn Fox so bare, and naked
of all excellency of sanctity (euen by Fox his
owne narratiō of him) as by nowaies doe I see
how he can come to be so *inthroned, and gloriously
crowned a sainct*, but only by the absolute pon-
tificiall povver, and priuiledge of Iohn Fox,
who without proofe of merits may canonize
whome

Fox pag.
1559.

*Ridley the
first here-
ticall B of
Rochester
& London.*

Fox more
povve-
rable
then any
Pope.

whome he lifteth : which is a point, that no
Pope hitherto amõg vs, hath euer taken vpon
him to doe, or euer will.

46.   And as for the *ghoftly and godly learning,*
wherof he fpeaketh, I know not of what particular *ghoft* yt may proceed, but fure I am, that
the learning which he fhewed at his difputations in *Cambridge* vnder K. *Edward*, and in
his anfwerings at *Oxford* vnder Q. *Marie,* was
but very vulgar, and ordinary, as yow fhall fee
afterwards in a particular treatife, which I
meane to fet downe ★ of thofe difputations,
★ See in
the end of
this booke
though notvvithftanding yt be true , that
Crnmer and *Latymer,* vvho were ioyned with
him in the latter of thofe difputations , feemed to relie moft vpon this mans learning,
Fox pag.
1602.
or rather his craftie fhifting witt , as *Doctor
Brookes* Bifhopp of *Glocefter* declared , in his
laft exhortatiõ vnto them, before theire condemnation ; and we fhall fhew yt more particularly a litle after in *Latymers* ftory, and yt is
thought verely that if this man could haue bin
brought to haue feene and acknowledged
any parte of his error , the other two would
prefently haue yeelded in the whole, whervpon he was held guilty, not only of his owne
perdition, but of theirs alfo.

47.   And yet yf we confider the doubtfull
and vnconftant beginning of this miferable
man, to witt, how by litle and litle he came
into this *Sacramentarie* herefy for which principally he died, & to the obftinacy of the fame,
yt may feeme ftrange to them that doe not
know

know and confider what a dangerous and in-
curable inchantment herefy is, and how yt
fhutteth vp a mans eyes from all light of grace,
or reafon, when yt is once faftened on his
harte: For better confideration wherof in this
particular example, yow muft remember, firft,
that this *Nicolas Ridley,* duringe all *King Henryes*
time, was moft earneft againft the *Sacramenta-*
ryes with the faid King, as before hath byn noted, and in the beginninge of *K. Edwards* he
held the fame courfe for a tyme, as *Cranmer*
alfo did, concerninge the bleffed *Sacrament,*
though in other things he began to yeeld, as
is manifeft both by the firft ftatute, or Parlament fet foorth *anno* 1547. vnder that King in
fauour of the faid *Sacrament*; as alfo by the teftimony of *Doctor VVhite,* then Bifhop of *Lin-*
colne in his puolike fpeech to *Ridley* at *Oxford*
vpon the 30. of September 1555. when exhortinge him to returne from his new herefie, he
told him of two things, the one, that in a fermon preached at *Paules Croffe* vnder the fame
K. Edward, yow fpake (faith he) *as effectually and*
as Catholickly of that bleffed Sacrament, as any man
might haue done: the fecond that the faid *Ridley*
being fent at that tyme by the counfell to
winne the Bifhop of *VVinchefter Gardener,* to
theire bent in religion (wherevnto *Cranmer*
& he had frefhly applyed themfelues) he vfed
this perfuafion vnto him *that in other leffer points*
he might well yeeld & condefcend vnto them, fo he ftood
conftant in the Sacrament. The fpeech of *Bifhop*
VVhite is related thus by Fox: *I then being in my*

Q   *Lords*

(margin notes:)
The de-
grees of
Nicolas
Ridleyes
falling in-
to herefy,
and perti-
nacity
therin.

Fox *pag.*
1596.

Fox *ibid.*

Lords howse vnknowne (*as I suppose*) to yow after yow had talked with my Lord secretly, and were departed: my Lord immediatly declared certayne points of your talke, and meanes of your persuasion, and amonge other this was one, that yow should say: *Tush my Lord this matter of iustification is but a tryfle, lett vs not stick to condescend heerein vnto them, but for Gods loue, my Lord; stand stoutly in the verity of the Sacrament. For I see they vvill assault that also.*

The litle consciéce of Ridley in Religió.

48. Thus **B.** *VVhite* to *Ridley* himselfe; alleaging for his wittnes the L. Chancelour then liuinge; neyther could *Ridley* deny this speech but only excused yt, that yt was meant that he should stand stoutly against the Anabaptists that impugned the *Sacrament of the Altar*; but how simple an euasion this is, euery man may see: for that the Anabaptists doe no more impugne the *Sacrament*, then the *Zwinglians* doe, & yt agreeth nothinge to the rest of his speech concerning the counsell, that he should meane of Anabaptists. But this was *Ridleyes* inconstancy indeed, who went as that time did lead him, & as the fauour of these that were in gouernement drew him after them, & yow must note, that the foresaid Bishopp of *VVinchester* afterward Chancelour, vnto whome *Ridley* was sent by the counsell to persuade him to conformity, being imprisoned first of all for his not yeeldinge, and for a sermon preached at *VVhite-hall* in defence of the blessed Sacrament, vpon S. Peters day 1548. at what tyme

Stovv pag. 1005.

or very litle before may be gethered that *Ridley* made

made him this exhortation, to yeeld in other
points and to be constant in defence of the Sacrament; yet the very next yeare after, that is
to say 1549. and third of K. *Edwards* raigne, the
same *Ridley* defended publike conclusions
against the *reall presence, transubstantiation, & the
sacrifice of the masse in Cambridge*, as * afterward
more particularly shalbe declared, so as when
he once began to slide he rushed on a pace, &
it seemeth that the Lady Princesse Mary insinuated the same vnto him, in a certayne
speech of hers, which Fox relateth to haue
passed at her howse called *Hunsdon* in *Hartfor-
shire*, when he, as Bishopp of London, went to
visit her there vpon the yeare 1552. and 8. of
September, where shee told him first, how
shee had knowne him, when he was her Fathers chaplin, and remembred a certayne sermon of his at the marriage of the *Lady Clynton,
&c.* and when he requested that shee would
now heare him preach againe, she refused yt,
obiecting vnto him his inconstancy, yow shall
heare a reply or two betwene them.

49. *Bishop.* Madam I trust yow will not refuse Gods word.

Mary. I cannot tell what yow call Gods
word, for yt is not Gods word now, that was
Gods word in my Fathers dayes.

Bishop. Gods word is all one, in all tymes,
but hath byn better vnderstood, and practi-
sed in some age, then in others.

Mary. You durst not for your eares haue auouched that for Gods word in my Fathers daies.

O 2   Then

* See af-
tervvard in
the re-vevv
of 10. di-
sputations
Chap. 1.

Fox *pag.*
1270.

"
"
"
"
"

"
A speech
betvvene
the lady
Mary and
Ridley.
"
"

,, Then she asked him whether he were of
,, the counsell or no?he answered no:you might
,, well ynough (saith shee) as the counsell goeth
,, now adayes, and so she concluded (saith Fox)
,, in these words; my Lord for your gentlenes
,, to come and see me I thanke yow, but for
,, your offringe to preach before me, I thanke
,, yow neuer a whitt, *&c.* And this was the conceipt which that good Princes had of *Ridley*
for his inconstancy, yet Iohn Fox recompteth
an heroicall act of his, for reuenge of this contempt vsed towards him by the Lady Mary,
for being sent to the buttery to drinke, after
he had drunke (saith Fox) he paused a litle

Fox ibid.
A ridicu-
lous tale
brought
in by Fox.

while lookinge very sadly: and sodenly brake
out into these words; surely I haue done
amisse: why so (quoth *Syr Thomas VVharton* the
,, Ladyes steward? for I haue drunke (said he)
,, in that place where Gods word offered, hath
,, byn refused, where as yf I had remembred my
,, duety, I ought to haue departed immediatly,
,, & to haue shaked of the dust of my shooes for
,, a testimony against this howse; These words
were by the said B shopp spoken with such a
vehemency (saith Fox) that some of the hearers afterward confessed,that their haire stood
vp right on their heads.

50.   Thus Fox, & perhaps their heads being
newly powled, their hayre might stand vpright without miracle. And yt may be also
that the Bishop being thirsty vpon the former
conference with the Princesse, was content
to take his drinke first, and after to shew him-

felfe fory for takinge yt, when the thirft was paft, and therevpon infued the vehement fermon *of fhakinge of the duft of his fhooes*, after the wine was taken in; but how foeuer yt were, yow may heerby fee *Q. Maryes* iudgement, and eftimation of the man, as alfo her *fincere* conftancy in religion, againft thefe newfanglers innouations: And finally fhee comminge to the crowne the next yeare after, and findinge this *Ridley* both guilty of treafon for preaching againft her title, as alfo for obftinacy in herefy, fhe caufed him to be iudicioufly condemned of them both, and being pardoned for the one, was burned for the other at *Oxford* vpon the 19. of October 1555. And fo much of him.

51.   There followeth the narration of his fellow *Hugh Latymer*, whofe ftory hath this title in Fox: *The life, acts, and doings of Maifter Hugh Latymer the famous preacher and vvorthy Martyr of Chrift his ghoffell*: fo glorious titles giueth Fox, to his burned fectaryes when he lifteth, though otherwife they be in themfelues and for their deferts neuer fo contemptible, as in deed this *Latymer* was amongeft all wife and fober men, in refpect both of his fmall learninge, but efpecially of his moft feditious and turbulent manners and behauiour, ioyned with fcoffes & fcurrility of fpeech in all occafions, as fhall appeare by that which enfueth. Firft (faith Fox) this *Hugh Latymer* was the fonne of on *Hugh Latymer* of *Thirkefon* in *Licefterfhire*, a husbandman of right good eftimation. When he came to 14. yeares old he was

Fox pag. 1570. The ftory of Hugh Latymer.

Fox pag. 1571.
,,
,,
,,

O 3   fent

,, fent to *Cambridge*, where for a tyme he was a
,, zealous Papiſt, and feruile obferuer of the Ro-
,, man decrees, perſuadinge himſelfe moreouer
,, that he ſhould neuer be damned yf he were

Latymer
once a Ca-
tholike.

,, once a profeſſed Fryar. He made a publike
oration againſt *Phillipp Melanchthon*, nor could
,, not abide *Maiſter Stafford* (a proteſtant reader in
, thoſe dayes) but moſt ſpitefully railed againſt
,, him, *&c.*

52.   Thus decribeth Iohn Fox the firſt beginninge of *Latymer* in Catholike Religion,
wherein yf he had perſeuered, he had byn a

Ibidem.

happy man. But he ſaith by hearinge of *Tho-*
,, *mas Bilney* his confeſsiõ one day in his ſtudy, he
,, was conuerted to be a Proteſtant. A ſtraunge
and ſtronge confeſsion by like, that could
make the confeſſor to chaunge his religion
vpon the ſuddayne: yet muſt we beleue many
ſuch ſtraũge ſucceſſes at Iohn Fox his hands,
without any other proofe at all, but only his
bare word. But yf yt were ſo, then the turninge againe of *Bilney* to Catholike Religion

* *Supra*
*March.*10.

and abiuringe his hereſie (as * before we haue
ſhewed) ought to haue moued *Latymer* alſo to
haue returned with him. But yt is eaſier to
inſtill poiſon, then to take yt out againe; and
this young Prieſt *Latymer* hauinge taſted once
the liberty of ghoſpellinge in thoſe dayes,
could not be retyred ſo ſoone againe, at leaſtwiſe with his harte and affection, though
with his mouth and tounge he often did recant, as after ſhall appeare.

53.   Well then *Latymer* being now affected
and

and infected with noueltyes, he began to
seeke occasions in his preachinges and other
actions to vtter the same, but yet couertly &
with difsimulation, left he might be difcouered; and he was a very fitt inftrument for
the beginninges of fuch a ghofpell, which in
those dayes confifted fpecially in fcoffinge, &
ieftinge at rites and ceremonyes of the Catholike Church, and carpinge at clergy mens
liues: for which enterprife *Latymer* naturally
had a fingular talent, being in deed borne (as
yt were) to be a *Buffone* or publike iefter.
Wherefore goinge vp into the pulpitt (faith
Fox) vpon the funday before Chriftmafle-
day in the Church of *S. Edwards* in *Cambridge*
anno Domini 1529. he made a fermon of playing
at Cards, and taught them how to play at
Triumph, how to deale the Cards, & what euery fort therof did fignifie, & that the *Hart* was
the *Triumph,* addinge moreouer (faith Fox)
fuch prayfes of that Card (the Hart, when yt
was Triumph) that though yt were neuer fo
fmall, yet would yt take vp the beft Cotecard
befides in the bunch, yea though yt were the
Kinge of the Clubbes himfelfe, &c. Which
handlinge of this matter was fo apt for the
tyme, and fo pleafantly applyed by him, that
yt not only declared a fingular towardnes of
witt, but alfo wrought in the hearers much
fruyt, to the ouerthrow of Popifh fuperftition,
and fettinge vp of perfect religion.

54. Thus wryteth Fox of the beginninge of
Latymers preachinge in *Cambridge,* and of his

*The fcof-
finge vaine
of Laty-
mer.*

Fox ibid.

playinge at cards in the pulpitt : a fitt *exordium*
for such a ghospell, as after he vvas to preach,
vvhich commonly vvas euery vvhere begon
vvith playes, comedyes, apes, poppets, iestung,
rayling, raysing of sedition , or other like practises (vvhich heere Fox calleth setting vp of
perfect Religion) and not as Christs ghospell be-

gan vvith *Agite pœnitentiam*, doe pennance, *&c.*
And yow must know that this Cardinge-sermon of *Latymer* in Cambridge, was one of the
most spiterull , and seditious , that euer vvas
heard before in England. For that vnder pretence of commendinge the *Hart*, vvhich vvas
Triumph in the Cards, & represented (forsooth)
his new Religion; he inueighed most bitterly
against most points of Catholike Religion, as
though they came not from the *Hart*: and consequently also compared the teachers therof
to Scribes and Pharisees , and the Bishops and
Prelats to the knaues of *Clubbes*, and other like
ribaldry, and seditious raylinge.

55.   Wherfore against this seditious Christmasse sermon of *Latymer* , there stepped vp in
to the pu'pitt diuers Catholike preachers, and
some as pleasant as he. And first (saith Fox)
came vp the prior of the dominicans vvhose
name vvas *Buckenam* , but called by the new
men of that tyme *Doctor Dusance,* or otherwise
Domine labia for that he had great lipps; and he

offered to *Maister Latymer* , that for so much as
yt vvas Christmasse tyme , and that the other
had begon at Cards in the pulpitt , he vvould
play at dice vvith him also , castinge at *cinque*
and

and *quater* before the whole audience, which he expounded thus: that he had brought fiue places of scripture, and foure of ancient Doctors to conuince *Latymer* with all. And after him came vp a gray friar called *Doctor Venetus,* an outlandishman, who raged soare against *Maister Latymer* (saith Fox) calling him *a madd & brainlesse man.* This happened in Cambridge in the yeare of Christ 1529.

A contention at Cambrige out of the pulpitt.

56. For this and other such matters, *Latymer* was at length called vp to London to *Cardinall VVolsey,* where he recanted & forsware soone after all that he had preached before, and so returned to Cambridge againe in good credit, and from thence after some tyme came backe to London, preached at the court, and gatt a benefice which Fox relateth in these words: *He was called vp to the Cardinall* (saith he) *for heresie, where he was content to subscribe and graunt vnto such articles, as then they propounded vnto him; after that he returned to the vniuersity againe,* &c. *Then went he to the court againe, where he remayned a certayne tyme in Doctor Butts chamber the Kings phisition, preachinge in London very often, and then at the sute of the L. Cromwell and Doctor Butts, the Kinge gaue him the benefice of VVest Kingston in VViltshire,* &c,

Latymer abiured protestats religion.

Fox pag. 1574.

D. Butt the Kings Phisition.

57. Lo heere *Hugh Latymer* reformed vpon the suddaine from his Cardinge-sermon, and now he preacheth often in London, that is to saye Catholike doctrine, in shew forsweareth the Protestant Religion, & enioyeth his benefice in the countrey: but yet (saith Fox) for that *S. Paul* telleth vs, that whosoeuer will

Ibidem.

liue

,, liue godly in Chrift muft fuffer perfecution:
,, this bleffed man vvas not longe after againe
,, accufed, and brought to *Quorum* for preaching
,, againft our Lady, the Saints, purgatory and
,, the like, and this not only by the countrey
,, Priefts, but by *Doctor Powell*, Doctor *VVilſon*, Do-
,, *ctor Sherwood* and others, and fo vvas brought
,, before *VVarham* B. of Canterbury, and fome
,, other Bifhopps in the yeare of Chrift 1531. So
vvryteth Fox, and that after diuers publike
meetinges, he abiured the Proteftants Religion againe, and fubfcribed to all points in

Latymer abiureth the ſecōd tyme.

controuerfie, vvhich points he fetteth downe
in a large Catalogue, and then being afhamed
to fee his bleffed man fubfcribe againe againft
him, and his Religion, he would gladly make
the matter doubtfull by foolifh fhufflinge to
& fro, as yow fhall heare by his owne words:

pag. 1577.

*To thefe articles (faith he) vvhether Maifter Latymer
did fubfcribe or no, it is vncertayne; yt appeareth by his
epiftle that he durft not confent; yet vvhether he vvas
compelled afterwards through the cruell handlings of
the Bifhops, yt is in doubt: by the vvords and title in Bifhopp Tonftall his regifter prefixed before the articles,*

Fox his fhufflinge to excufe Latymer.

*yt may ſeeme, that he fubfcribed, yf thofe words be true;
but vvhether he ſo did, or not, no great matter, nor
maruayle, the iniquity of the tyme being fuch, that eyther he muft needs ſo do, or els abide the Bifhops bleſſing,
that is, the cruell fentence of death,* &c.

58.   Behould, heere Fox playeth the Fox,
trafinge vpp and downe, and would call in
doubt the truth of the Bifhopps publike regifter, for excufinge his Saint, and yet ac-
comptech

compteth yt he neyther *matter nor maruayle,* though he had abiured his Religion now the second tyme againe; which is a straunge liberty that he alloweth to his people: his reason is, for that otherwise he must haue suffred much, but yf this reason had byn good, all old Martyrs might haue denied their Religion, but let vs passe on and come to the third tyme of Latymers denyinge his new Religion. Soone after this he behaued himselfe so earnest in preachinge againt the Protestants, as Kinge Henry gaue him the Bishopricke of Worcester; at vvhat tyme he tooke his oath also against the heresies of that tyme, as other Bishops were wont to do; which point though Fox doth sleightly passe ouer in silence, yet in effect he yeldeth thervnto, when he wryteth : *that albeit Maister Latymer durst not but preach and liue accordinge to the tyme, yet in* some thinges he procured reformation like a good Bishop; as for example he made 4. verses in Rithme, and caused them to be wrytten ouer the holy water stocke, for men to read vvhen they tooke holy water. The verses are these, as Fox cyteth them.

Latymer made B. of VVorce-, ster.

Fox *ibid.* 1578. ,, ,, ,, ,, ,, ,,

Remember your promise in baptisme,
Chrifts mercy, and bloudshedinge,
By vvhose most holy sprinkelinge,
Of all your sinnes yow haue free pardoninge.

59. And other like foure verses he compounded, and gaue to the Priests and Clarks of his Church to be said to the people, when they gaue them holy bread, to the end they might

The important points vvhich Latimer reformed vvhen he vvas a Bishopp.

might perceaue what they receaue. And then
as though Fox had recounted great and worthy
exploits done by this Prelate in his Bishoppricke;
he commeth in with this graue
Epiphonema: By this (faith he) *yt may be considered*
vvhat a diligent cure this Bishop had, in doinge the duty
of a faithfull Pastor, &c. And are not these great
exployts, to prayse his Bishopp for? to witt
that he made eight verses in Rithme, foure for
holy water, and foure for holy bread: is this
sufficient with Fox to recompence *Latymers*
triple abiuration of his Religion before? yow
see with how little the poore Reynard is contented,
so he may draw Saints any way into
his caue and Calendar. But let vs go forward.

60.   It was not longe after but *Latymer* vvas
accused agayne to K. *Henry* (saith Fox) for heresie
and sedition, vvhich story *Maister Latymer*
himselfe doth relate in a sermon of his before
K. *Edward*, and I thinke good to vse his ovvne
vvords vvhich are these: *In the Kings dayes that*
,, *dead is,* (saith *Latymer*) a great many of vs were
,, called togeather before him, to say our mynds
,, in certayne matters; and in the end one kneeled
,, downe and accused me of sedition, and
,, that I had preached seditious doctrine; a heauy
,, salutation and a hard point of such a mans
,, doinge, as yf I should name him ye would not
,, thinke yt. The King turned to me, and said,
,, what say yow to that Syr? then I kneeled
,, downe, and turned first to my accuser, and required
,, him: Syr, vvhat forme of preachinge
,, would yow appoint me, *&c.* Then I turned
     my

Ibidem.

Latymer
accused a-
gaine of
heresy and
sedition
to King
Henry.

Fox *pag.*
1578.

my felfe to the Kinge and fubmitted my feife
to his Grace &c. And I thanke almighty God
that my fayings vvere vvell accepted of the
Kinge; For like a gracious Lord, he turned into another communication &c. Thus efcaped
Latymer this third or fourth tyme as yow fee
by fubmitting himfelfe to the King, to preach
and teach what he fhould appoint, or thinke
beft. And albeit he do not name the Bifhopp
that accufed him, yet by his defcription, yt is
moft likely, that yt was eyther *Cranmer* or *Rid-*
ley that were of the new Religion, and moft
creditt in *K Edwards* dayes, in prefence of
which Kinge this was fpoken. And the fame
men kept *Latymer* backe in the faid Kings
tyme, that he could neuer recouer his Bifhopricke againe.

Latymers fourth denyinge nevv Religion.

61. But yet once more after this againe was
Latymer brought to *quorum* before *K. Henry* for
preachinge herefie, after the comminge forth
of the ftatute of fix articles *anno* 1540. and then
he was in danger in deed, for the King depriued him of his Bifhoppricke, fent him prifoner to the Towar, and yf he had not recanted
againe and humbled himfelfe in deed, euen
vnto the very ground, the faid Kinge would
haue burned both him, and *Doctor Shaxton* Bifhopp of *Salisbury*, whome he depriued togeather with *Latymer* for the fame caufe. And yt is
fingular impudency in Fox, to fay heere, that
both *Latymer* and *Shaxton* refigned vp their Bifhoppricks vvillingly, and that *Latymer* gaue a fkipp for ioy
in his chamber, vvhen his rochet was taken of; though
for

Latymer his fift and laft accufation and recantatiō.

D. Shaxtō. B. of Salisbury.

Fox *pag.* 1378.

for the skipp I will not stand, for that he was
held full light euer, both in head, tongue, and
feete, whilst he liued; and yt may be also that
he was glad to redeeme his life with the losse
of his Rochet & Bishopricke, but yet that they
gaue ouer freely their Bishoppricks (as Fox
here saith) is plaine impudency, for so much
as *Bishopp Shaxton*, (who was in the same cause
with *Latymer*) was made to recant publikely
at the fire-side for pennance , when *Anne Ascue*
with her fellowes were burned. For so wryteth *Stow* in these words.

Stow anno
Domini
1546.
62. *Vpon the 16. of Iuly 1546. vvere burned in*
Smithfield for the Sacrament, Anne Ascue, aliàs Kinne,
Iohn Lassells, Nicolas Otterdon priest, Iohn Adlam tay-
lor; and Doctor Shaxton sometymes Bishop of Salisbury
preached at the same fire, and there recanted, persua-
dinge them to do the like , but they vvould not. Now
yf K. Henry did force *Doctor Shaxton* after his
depriuation to recant so publikely, and with
so great shame , is yt like that he would haue
spared *Latymer* , except he had recanted, and
double recanted in the Towar, where he was
prisoner ? And I would aske Iohn Fox, why
did K. Henry keepe him in the Towar afterward all dayes of his life , as Fox here confes-
Ibidem.
seth, sayinge: *Till the tyme that blessed K. Edward*
entred , by vvhome the goulden mouth of this preacher
longe shutt vp before , vvas now opened againe, &c.
Why was this (I say) but for that the old King
knew well inough how seditious a fellow
this foule-mouthed *Latymer* was, though Fox
heere calleth him the goulden-mouth. But let

vs

vs see now, what this goulden-mouthed man did vnder *K. Edward,* whē he was set at liberty.

63.   *Doctor Saunders* that liued with *Latymer* in K. Edwards dayes, wryteth thus of him in his booke De *Schismate Anglicano: Eodem tempore ex publicis pulpitis, aperuit impurum os, Hugo quidam Latimerus, &c.* At the same tyme, a certayne man named *Hugh Latymer*, opened his impure mouth out of the pulpits, whome *K. Henry* before, had thrust out of the Bishoppricke of Worcester for suspition of heresie, & for that he had eaten flesh vpon good friday in the holy weeke; he was a man of the spiritt & speech of Lucian, by whose iests, scoffes, and wantonesse of tongue (wherin he excelled all other sectaryes lightly of his dayes) he did so delight and bewitch the common vulgar people, as they called him the Apostle of England, &c.

* lib. 2. pag. 160.

D. Saunders testimony of Latymer.

,,
,,
,,
,,
,,
,,
,,
,,

So wryteth *Doctor Saunders* of him : which thinge is testified also by diuers other graue men that knew him, and were present at his raylinge sermons in K. Edwards dayes; the subiect wherof was commonly the masse, or rather the *marrow-bones of the masse* (for that was his phrase) in so much as boyes, when he was goinge vp to the pulpit would cry: *Now Father Latymer, at the Marrow-bones of the masse.* And this foolish phrase was so ordinary with him, as Iohn Fox himselfe setteth it downe, in a conference he had with *Maister Ridley,* wrytinge vnto him thus : *The very marrow-bones of the masse are altogeather detestable, and therfore by no meanes to be borne withall,* &c.

Latymer his marrovvbones of the masse.

Fox pag. 1560. col. 2. num. 62.

64. But

64. But now what his *Lucianicall* spirit meant
by the marrow-bones of the masse is hard to
say, but that the word pleaseth him, and his
Satyricall veyne. For yf he meant substantiall
points of the order of masse, or prayers therin
conteyned, they are the epistle and ghospell
and words of Christ in consecration: (all taken out of the scripture) but yf he meane the
inward substance of the Sacrament yt selfe,
I will rather beleeue ould *S. Austen*, then a
thousand new scoffing *Latymers*, which Saint
calleth yt; *Sacrificium sanctum sanctorum, quod cor-*
pus Christi est. The holy sacrifice of Saints
which is the body of Christ, *quod omni die popu-*
lis immolatur in altari, that euery day is sacrinced
for Christian people vpon the Altar. What
would S. Augustine haue said yf he had heard
this scoffing Ribald preach or prate so scorne-
fully of the masses marrow-bones? which he
and all the rest of the ancient Fathers call, *tre-*
mendum Christianorum sacrificium, the dreadfull
sacrifice of Christians; and yet yow must note
that this vize *Hugh Latymer*, as yf he had byn
vpon a stage, was wont to play vpon certayne
other words and iests also to the same effect,
for bringinge the holy sacrifice in contempt,
as for example of *pascere* and *massere*, feedinge
and sayinge masse; cryinge out and complayninge greatly, that *massere* had driuen out *pas-*
cere, and that *pascere* could haue no place for
massere, for tha *massere* was gainfull and *pascere*
painfull: And then would he cry out and say:
O good pascere, who shall defend thee against massere,
                                                        and

Aug. lib. 2.
quaest. Enäg.
c. 3. & l 1.
cont. aduers.
leg. & pro-
phet. c. 19.
Aug. ep. 23.
ad Bonifac.

Latymers
scurrilous
veyne of
scoffinge.

and other ſuch like ſtuffe fitter for a ſtage, then a pulpitt; and yet this drew the people infinitely after him, as yt is wont to do. And thus much for his tongue, which as yt was gratefull to the vulgar, ſo was yt odious to all wiſe and diſcreet men, euen of his owne religion; wherby yt came to paſſe alſo, that in all K. *Edwards* raigne he could neuer be reſtored to his Biſhoppricke of *VVorceſter* againe, which K. Henry had taken from him for ſuſpition of that hereſie, which now he openly profeſſed: but *Cranmer* and *Kidley* and moſt of the counſell, knowinge his turbulent and dangerous ſpiritt, kept him downe, and would rather permitt that *Hooper* ſhould haue that Biſhoppricke togeather with *Gloceſter* (as before hath byn ſhewed) then that ſo vnquiett a fellow as *Latymer*, ſhould come to be Biſhopp againe.

65. But aboue all the reſt, he loſt his creditt moſt by his wicked dealing againſt *Syr Thomas Seymer* the Admirall, whome he was induced by the Ducheſſe of Somerſett, & her husband the Protector, to accuſe publikely in a ſermon : wherof the foreſaid *Doctor Saunders* that was preſent therat in Oxford, wryteth thus: *Facile tanquam à Iezabele crimen excogitatũ eſt, &c.* When the Protector had reſolued, at the inſtance of his wife to make away his brother, a cryme was eaſily diuiſed by her againſt the ſaid *Admirall*, as by another Iezabell. But how ſhall yt be publiſhed, and beaten into the peoples eares? They vvent to the Engliſh Apoſtle *Latymer* perſuadinge him to accuſe the

Sand. ibid. pag. 1596.

„
„
„
„
„
„
„
„

P   *Admyrall*

„ *Admyrall* in a sermon of treason: *Latymer* whose
„ Apostleshipp consisted in lyinge , refused not
„ the office, but came foorth into the pulpitt,

Latymer procureth the death of S. Thomas Seymer by lying and slandering him.

„ accused *Syr Thomas Seymer* to haue committed
treason against the Kinge, by seekinge his brother the protectors death, and therby to haue
deserued death himselfe : the people did not
applaud vnto him as they were wont , being
now ashamed of such a lyinge and malitious
„ Apostle, *&c.* So wryteth *Doctor Saunders.*

66.   And truly he that shall read the most
bitter and bloudy statute of condemnation
made against the foresaid *Syr Thomas Seymer,*
extant in print, shall find the most part therof
eyther to be of pickt matters, or odyous en-
forcements of the same, to witt, his great ambition and powre throughout the realme, and
that he desired to marry the young King at his

See the Statute of Attaynder of S. Thomas Seymer an. 1. and 3. Eduuard. 6. cap. 18.

pleasure , that he persuaded him to take the
gouernement into his owne hands, and that
he sought to make them of the priuy chamber
to be at his deuotion; that he desired to marry
the lady *Elizabeth* , and other like suspitions,
which points notwithstanding , this old sico-
phant *Latymer* vrged against him, for great &
hainous crymes at the Duke and Duches re-
quest , and so in the end , they gott him condemned in parlamēt, without euer comming
to his answere, (a strange kind of condemnation) & executed vpon the 20. of March 1549.

67.   And thus much of *Latymer* his acts, gests
& monuments vnder K. *Henry* and K. *Edward,*
but when Q. *Mary* came to the crowne, and
                                        Catho-

Catholike Religion was restored againe, yt was thought meete in consideratió of the great hurt he had done by his licentious tounge in *K. Edwards* dayes, and some seditious behauiour also reported of him against the said Queenes entrance, to call him to accoumpt amonge others, but namely with *Cranmer* and *Ridley* of whome he most depended: For as for his owne learninge yt was held for small, as both himselfe professed euer, and was seene in effect by his answeres, both in the disputations at Oxford with the vniuersity Doctors (which after we shall sett downe in a speciall treatise) as also by other conferences, and examinations had before *B. VVhite* of Lincolne, *B. Brookes* of Glocester, and other Commissioners sent downe from *Cardinall Poole* to that effect. Iohn Fox almost euery where, when he speaketh of this *Latymer*, endeauoreth to bring him in as a very venerable man, with a staffe in his hand, many night caps on his head, with a kercheife vnder, and a towne-capp vpon the same, with other implements of age and gratuity, as his spectacles hanginge on his brest, his new testament at his girdle, &c. *He had* (saith Fox) *a kerchife vpon his head* (when he appeared before the commissioners) *and vpon yt a night-capp or two, & a great capp such as townes-men vse with two broad flappes to butté vnder the chin; wearinge an old threadbare Bristow frize-gowne, girded to his body with a penny leather girdleat, the which haged, by a long string of leather, his testament & his spectacles without case depéding about his necke vpó his brest, &c.*

P 2   68. This

Latymer called to accoumpt for his doctrine.

See the review of 10 disputations in the end of this booke.

The description of Latymers habit by Fox. Fox pag. 1599.

68.   This is Fox his defcription of his Saint *Latymers* habit, whereby he would make him feeme fome old *S. Antony* or *Hilarion* in the defert, for the fimplicity & grauity of his attyre, but his mynd and tounge was as light and vaine, as yf he had worne feathers in his capp, or had come in with a rapier and dagger at his fide infteed of his teftament and fpectacles, for prefently he fell to fcoffinge before the commiffioners, pickinge a quarrell to a place in a booke of the Bifhop of *Glocefter*, newly fett foorth, wherein the Bifhop had made this inference or collection; that yf the Priefts of the old law had authority to decide controuerfies, as appeareth *Deutron.* 21. then much more ought that authority to be graunted to the new lawe; vpon which occafion *Latymer* began to play and fcoffe after his cuftome, about the word *regere*, as he had done before

Fox peg. 1660. vpon the words *pafcere* and *maffere*. S. Peter (faith he) was bid *regere*, but this *regere* muft
„ be hedged in, and digged in; Popes muft *regere*,
„ but *fecundum verbum Dei*, accordinge to the
„ word of God; they haue turned *regere fecun-*
„ *dum verbum Dei*, into *regere fecundum voluntatem*
Latymers fcoffings before the comiffioners. *fuam, &c.* What geldinge of fcripture is this? what clippinge of Gods coine, *&c.* With the which termes (faith Fox) the audience fmi-
„ led, *&c.* Then faid *Latymer*, now I truft (my
„ Lord) I doe not raile; *Lincolne.* No *Maifter La-*
„ *tymer*, your talke is more like taunts then rai-
„ linge, *&c.* With that the people laughed againe, *&c.* Thus Fox of *Latymers* fpeech: and
then

then a little after againe he doth iterate the ,,
same sayinge: *then the audience laughed againe, and* ,,
Maister Latymer spake vnto them , sayinge ; vvhy my
Masters, this is no laughinge matter, I doe answere vpon
life and death; then the *Bishop of Lincolne, commaun-*
ded silence and said, Maister Latymer yf yow had kept
your selfe vvithin your bounds, yf yow had not vsed such
scoffes and taunts this had not happened; vvhereunto ad-
ded the B. of Glocester: Maister Latymer, heerby euery
man may see vvhat learninge yow haue : Latymer; lo
yow looke for learninge at my hand, which haue gone so
longe to the schoole of oblinion, &c. So wryteth Fox
of that colloquy , whereby yow may see the
humor of the man in scoffinge ; and as for his
aunsweringe to arguments , yow shall heare
the same afterwards.

69. Now only will I recite yow a peece of
the said *D. Brookes* B. of *Glocester* his exhortatio,
to *Ridley* and *Latymer* a little before theire condemnation, as Fox himselfe setteth it downe:
thus he began : Yf yow would once empty
your stomakes, captiuate your senses, subdue
your reason , and together with vs consider ,,
what a feeble ground of your Religion yow ,,
haue; I doe not doubt but yow might easily ,,
be perduced, to acknowledge one Church ,,
with vs, to confesse one faith with vs , and to ,,
beleue one religion with vs, for what a weake ,,
& feeble stay in Religion is this, I pray yow? ,,
Latymer leaneth to *Cranmer, Cranmer* to *Ridley,*
and *Ridley* to the singularity of his owne witt,
so that yf yow ouerthrow the singularity of ,,
Ridleyes witt , then must needs the Religion of ,,

A speach
of the B.
of Gloce-
ster to Ri-
dley and
Latymer
before
theire co-
demnatio.

Fox pag.
1602.

P 2   *Cranmer*

,, *Cranmer* and *Latymer* fall alfo, yow remember
,, well *Maifter Ridley* that the Prophett fpeaketh
,, moft truly fayinge, *vvo, vvo, be to them, vvho are*
,, *fingular and vvife in their owne conceits:* but yow
,, will fay it is true that the Prophett faith, but
,, how know I that I am wife in my owne
,, conceyte? yes *Maifter Ridley* yow refufe the de-
,, termination of the Cath. Church, yow muft
,, needs be fingular and wife in your owne con-
,, ceyte, for yow bring fcriptures for the proba-
,, tions of your affertions, & we alfo bring Scri-
,, prures; yow vnder ftand them in one fenfe, &
,, we in another, how will yow know the truth
,, heerin? yf you ftand to your owne interpreta-
,, tion, then are yow fingular in your owne con-
,, ceipt, *&c.* Wherefore for Gods loue ftand not
,, fingular, be not vvife in your owne conceipt,
,, pleafe not your felfe ouer much: how were
,, the *Arrians, Manichies, Eutichians,* other heretiks
,, fuppreffed, and conuinced, by reafoninge or
,, difputations? no truly, the *Arrians* had more
,, places of fcripture for their herefie, then the
,, Catholiks for defence of the truth; how then
,, vvere they conuinced? only by determination
,, of the Church; and indeed except vve doe
,, conftitute the Church our iudge, we can haue
,, no end of controuerfies, no end of difputa-
,, tion, *&c.*

70.   This vvas the beginninge of the graue
and vveighty fpeech of the Bifhop of *Glocefter*
to thefe miferable men, which yf they would
haue harkened vnto (as there vvas great reafon they fhould) they might haue faued both
bodyes

bodyes & foules, & what could be more rea-
fonable then this, that they fhould not ftand
to theire owne conceits alone, and to theire
owne cytinge and interpretinge of fcriptures,
after their owne fancy, to their owne vnderftandinge, or collections therof, as all heretiks
had donne before them, but rather to the vniforme confent of Chrifts vifible Church from
age to age, and was not this reafon? was not
this piety? was not this duty? Fox addeth alfo that the Bifhopp of *Lincolne* made the like
exhortation to them. The Bifhopp of *Lincolne*
(faith he) *vrith many vvords, and gentle holdinge his
capp in his hand defired them to turne, &c.* But all
was in vaine, and fo they were both of them
burned together in the towne-dich of *Oxford*,
vpon the forefaid 19. of *October* each of them
takinge gunpowder to difpatch himfelfe
quickly as by Fox is feene, which yet is not Fox *pag.* 1605.
read to haue byn practifed by old Martyrs, &
yt feemeth that thefe men would haue the
fame of martyrdome without the paine, and
now they haue incurred the euerlaftinge
paine, yf by their end we may iudge. And fo
much of thefe men: lett vs paffe to the remnant of this moneth.

71. *Next after the death of the two former moft
vvorthy champions and ftanderd-bearers* (faith Fox) Fox *ibid.*
*Nicolas Ridley and Hugh Latymer at Oxford, there
followed three other ftout & bould fouldiours:* to witt, Iohn
Iohn VVebb, George Roper and Gregory Parke, bur- VVebbe.
ned at *Canterbury*; all fimple & vnlerned men. Roper.
Their articles (faith he) *vvere the ordinary articles:* Gregory
P 4   and

and so he setteth them not downe. Only he saith that *Iohn VVebbe* aunswered for them all, touchinge the Sacrament of Christs body. *That they vtterly denyed the true body of Christ to be there, but only a remembrance:* And for this they all three dyed at on fire. And more particularityes then these Fox telleth not, but only that *Roper* comminge to the fire, gaue a great leap for ioy. But whether this leap was towards hell or heauen, yf yt should be disputed betweene *Iohn Fox* and *Martyn Luther,* it would goe hard on Fox his side, seeing *Martyn* did expressely hould that *Zwinglius* was damned for inuentinge that opinion, for which these men willfully leaped into the fire, as yow ** Sup. Fob. 17.* haue heard * before, & shall againe afterward: which being so, their leap must needs be to hell, yf Luthers censure be any thinge worth: or yf himselfe be lept to heauen as Fox holdeth that he is, for that other wise he could not be a Saint of his Calendar.

72.   After these three vnder Q. Mary *anno Domini* 1556. Fox bringeth in extrauagantly *Adam VVallas a Scottish-man.* one *Adam VVallas* a Scottishman burned in *Edenborough* vpon the yeare of Christ 1449. K. Henry the sixt raigninge in England, and in Scotland K. Iames the second of that name: he was a poore simple fellow accordinge to Fox his narration, and being accused in sollemne iudgment for diuerse heresies, namely againist the Sacrament and sacrifice of the Al- *Fox pag. 1552.* tar: his aunswere was. *That he held nothinge but that he found in the Bible. And that hauinge reade the Bible*

Bible ouer three tymes, he found not the maſſe therein.
And from this aunſwere he vvould not goe, A fond anſvvere.
but vvould dy for yt in the fire as he did; neyther could any perſuaſiõ or reaſon to the contrary reuoke him from this madd obſtinacy;
vvhich yf he had lighted vpon any other article of our beleefe, he vvould belike haue
byn no leſſe inflexible then in this.

73.   And vvith this Scottiſhman, Fox ioyneth two other Engliſh, as holy martyres as
hee; the one a ſhippman called *Marke Burges* Marke Burges & his ſhipp boy. Fox *ibid.*
burned in *Lisbone* of *Portugall* the yeare 1560.
and the other a ſhipp boy ſtoned to death (yf
vve may beleue Fox) vpon the ſame yeare in
Syuill of Spaine, *by the youthes of that citty as Ste-*
phen vvas by them, of Hieruſalem. But thoſe that
haue liued in *Spaine* and eſpeciallly in *Syuill,* and
doe know the ſtraight iuſtice and ſeuere diſcipline vſed in that place againſt priuate tumults, and that a man cannot ſo much as offer
violence to another but only by the hand of
the magiſtrate, without greeuous puniſhmẽt;
doe laugh at this diuiſe of *Iohn Fox,* that would
haue vs beleue that a man ſhould be ſtoned to
death *by the youthes of that citty,* without help or
protection of the people or magiſtrate. But
lett vs leaue Fox to his fancyes and draw to Simpſon Prieſt, Friar
an end of this moneth.

74.   After this ſtoned Martyr, he bringeth in Beuerick, Keyler Blacke Friar, Dauy Stratton, Norman Gorley.
vpon the next three dayes following a whole
rablement of 9. or 10. other in theiſe vvords:
Simpſon Prieſt, Beuerich Friar, Keyler Blacke Friar,
Dauie Stratton gentleman, Norman Gorley Vicar of
Dolor,

Black Canon vvith 4.others.

Dolor, a Blacke Canon vvith foure other Martyrs, but vvhat martyres they vvere, how, or vvhy, he telleth vs not, nor can I find any particular thing related of them in all his Acts and Monuments, no not so much as once named in his Index or table, and therefore I am forced to be silent of them as a fiorish only of bare names, like to Apothicaryes Boxes that haue superscriptions without druggs.

75. Finally then to furnishe vp and finithe this moneth of October, he asigneth vpon the 29. day three Confessors that dyed in prison in Chichester-castle, but he knoweth not their names, and much lesse theire Acts and Gests. And for the last two dayes he asigneth *Mother Seaman* and *Mother Bennet* for confessors, two poore vveomen of *Norwich*, vvho though they died both in their owne houses, yet for that they had byn called before the commissioners for nevv opinions, Iohn Fox bestoweth vpon them a canonization of holy confessors, vvhich yf vve confer vvith the venerable Saints of the opposite rancke of our Catholike Calendar, vvill appeere most ridiculous, and this is so much as occurreth for this moneth.

Three Cōfessors vvithout names.

Mother Seaman. Mother Bennett.

The ende of October.

O F

OF THE MARTYRS
AND CONFESSORS
OF FOX HIS CHVRCH,

For the Moneth of Nouember,

Both vnder Kinge Henry the eyght, and Qu. Mary.

CHAP. XV.

THE first and last dayes of this **Moneth of Nouember**, are left by Fox to the **Saints** of our ancient Calendar; the first to the feast *of all Saints* (for which we are much beholding vnto him) & the last to *S. Andrew* the Apostle: and after these two, all the other dayes are replenished vvith new diuised Saints of his owne: as for example the second day of this moneth, that before conteyned in our Calendar the *Commemoration of all soules departed*, is quite put out, and in place therof, is put in the festiuall day of one *Richard Mekins* a poore boy of London, burned in Smithfield, vnder *King Henry* the eyght, the next yeare after the statute of six articles vvas published; and that (yf Fox say truely) for speakinge only against the Sacrament of the Altar. And then after him vpon the next two dayes: **to witt**, the third and

Richard Mekyns. Fox, pag. 1097.

and fourth, are fett downe for Martyrs, three
others as good as the former, vvho are *Richard*
Spencer an Apoftata prieft, become a ftage-
player for lacke of a better occupation, togeather vvith his fellow commediants *Ramfey*
and *Hewyt*, of vvhome Fox vvryteth only
thefe vvords.

Richard
Spencer.

2.　　*About the fame tyme alfo* (to witt *anno Domini*
1541.) *a certayne Prieft vvas burned at Salisbury vvho*
leauinge his papiftry, had marryed a vvife and became
a player in Enterludes vvith Ramfey and Hewyt,which
three vvere all condemned and burned; againft whome,
and efpecially Spencer, vvas laid matter concerning the
Sacrament of the Altar, &c. This is all that Fox
vvryteth for canonizinge thefe his comme-
diant-martyrs, and ftill note that the beginninge of proteftancy in Priefts, is the gettinge
of a woman; but now yf fome of his other
Saints, that ftand in this Calendar, fhould be
iudges in thefe mens caufes that were Sacramentaryes, as *Luther, Melancthon, Erafmus, Farrar,*
Taylor, Barnes and others that defended the
reall prefence, which thefe men denyed; they
would giue fentence that they died heretiks,
and not Martyrs, as * before we haue fhewed.
And of the laft named : to witt, *Doctor Friar*
Barnes, Fox takinge in this very place occafion
to fpeake, (for that the forfaid boy *Mekins* faid
at the fire fide, that he had learned his herefie
againft the Sacrament, of the faid *Friar Barnes*)
very grauely noteth in the margent thefe
vvords: *And how could he take that learninge of D.*
Barnes, when D, Barnes was neuer of that opinion?

Fox ibid.

Ramfey &
Hewyt
commen-
diants.

* *Sup. 07.*
num. 38.

Fox pag.
1097.

3. This

3. This is Fox his queſtion; and I would aske him againe another, to witt; how could *Mekins*, *Spencer* or *Hewyt*, be fellow-martyrs and placed in the ſame Calendar with *Doctor Barnes*, yf they died for that opinion, which *Doctor Barnes* did neuer allow of, but was earneſtly againſt yt? And I take yt, that my queſtion is harder to ſolue, then his: for that to his, yt is eaſily anſwered, that any heretike or ſectary may open the dore to further hereſies, then himſelfe doth like or hold for the preſent, as *Arrius* did to many ſects after him; and *Luther* to the Anabaptiſts and Sacramentaryes: and the reaſon is for that they once infringing the authority of the Church (which holdeth all in order,) and preferring their new diuiſes and ſingular opinions, they do ſhew the way for others to inuent alſo as they did, and euer to add ſomewhat of their owne heads. And ſo much of this.

Hovv one may teach the vvay to more hereſies, then himſelfe holdeth.

4. Vpon the next three dayes after this againe, to witt, the 5.6. and 7. Iohn Fox ſetteth downe three other Martyrs, vvhich are *Iohn Porter*, a young ſeruingman or apprentice that died in Newgate, and *Thomas Bernard* & *Iames Morton* artificers burned at Lincolne, the next yeare after 1542. Of *Porter* Fox wryteth no more but this: *This Porter vvas a freſh young man and bigg of ſtature, vvho by diligent readinge of the ſcripture, and by hearinge ſuch ſermons, as then vvere diligently preached by them, that vvere ſetters forth of Gods truth, became very expert, and becauſe he could read vvell and had an audible voyce, he read the Bible*

Iohn Porter. Thomas Bernard. Iames Morton.

Fox pag. 1101.

to great

to great multitudes of people that did resort to beare him in London. Thus Fox of his freſh younge man. And then he ſaith that *B. Bonner* takinge the matter very greuouſly, and accuſinge him that he did not only read the ſaid Engliſh Bible to all commers (which was permitted at that tyme by K. Henryes order) but made hereticall comentaryes alſo, expoſitions and interpretations vpon the ſame, ſent him to Newgate, where he died, and ſo became a Martyr. And more then this is not to be found of him in Fox: and conſequently I do not ſee with what equity he can make him a Martyr, ſeing he died in his bedd naturally, but he maketh and vnmaketh what he will in this kind.

Ibidem.

5. Of the later two, he wryteth only theſe words: *About the ſame tyme Iohn Longland, Biſhop of Lincolne burned two vpon one day, the one named Thomas Bernard, the other Iames Morton; the one for teachinge the Lords prayer in Engliſh, the other for keepinge the Epiſtle of S. Iames tranſlated into Engliſh, &c.* So he. And truly yf a man will beleeue Fox in his narration, he may: but to me it appeareth cleerly a moſt abſurd fiction, that men ſhould be burned for this only, but that they might perhaps be apprehended and examyned vpon like ſuſpition, by hauinge and vſinge prohibited books, and after found to be heretiks; and ſtandinge in the ſame, might come to be burned, but for bare hauinge ſuch books, is incredible; and as for *S. Iames epiſtle*, whome their maiſter Luther (for that it ouerthroweth euidently the foundation of his

new

new ghofpell of *only faith*) called *ſtramineam,* that is, *a ſtrawy or ſtubble epiſtle,* I ſe no probability in the world , that eyther the Proteſtants of thoſe dayes ſhould ſo much delight themſelues with yt, or that the Biſhopp ſhould take the reading therof ſo heinouſly, as to puniſh it by death; but rather he ſhould be glad to haue Proteſtants read that epiſtle , by which ſo cleerly their doctrine is confuted. But theſe are the improbable lyes and fictions of Iohn Fox, which he frameth with great facility euery where, for the feeding of his owne, and other mens fancyes.

About S. Iames Epiſtle in Engliſh.

6. Next after theſe vpon the eyght day of this moneth, is placed *Maiſter George VViſchart* Scottiſhman martyr, accuſed of ſedition and hereſy in Scotland in the yeare of Chriſt 1546. the laſt yeare of K. Henryes raigne of Englād. He was condemned and hanged on a gibbett, and burned vnder the ſame. His arraignment and condemnation was very ſollemne in the preſence of the Gouernor of *Scotland,* the Earle *Hamelton* afterward Duke of *Schatelroy,* & moſt of their nobility, as alſo of the *Cardinall Beton* Archbiſhop of *S. Andrewes* & primate of Scotland, togeather with all , or moſt of the Biſhops : Which great meetinge being made in the citty of *S. Andrewes,* the ſaid *George VViſchart* was brought forth publikely to anſwere to his accuſations, which you may ſee ſet downe in Fox at large, euery article of accuſation (being 18. in number) beginninge thus yf Fox ſay truely. *Thou falſe heretike , renagate , traytor,*

George VViſchart.

The arraignement of Maiſter George VViſchart Scottiſhman. Fox *pag.* 1156.

and

*and theese, deceyuer of the people thou despisest the holy
Kirke, & contemnest my L. Gouernours authority, &c.*
7.   This was the exordium to euery article. But the substance of all the accusations,
conteyneth (as I haue said before) partly sedition, and partly the common heresies of that
tyme, against the number of 7. Sacraments
held by the Church, as also in particular
against Confession, Confirmation, fastinge,
vowes and the like; but his seditious, and rebellious contempt, consisted in that he presumed to preach without licence, and being forbidden both in the Cardinalls and Gouernors
name, he perseuered therin. And further being
excommunicated by his ordinary the Bishop

The con-
téptuous
behauiour
of *George
i Vishearty.* of *Brothen* for his said contempt, he continued
therin notwithstandinge. And when he was
accused therof in this publike audience he answered no otherwise, but contumeliously ap-

Malach. 2. plyinge that of the Prophett *Malachias*, to his
Pastors and Superiors: *I shall curse your blessings
and blesse your cursings.* And to the other points
and articles about heresie, he answered, accordinge to the ordinary scoffinge and contemptuous manner of new ghospellers in
those dayes, though not very resolutely or distinctly, as not being yet thorowly settled in
all points of what sect to be, as may appeare
by his answers to sundry articles, and namely
to the sixt about the *reall presence*, which he
was accused to haue denyed, but he would
not yeeld thervnto: sayinge only, that he had
reported, *that a Iew in Germany had scoffed therat,*
but

but he denyed the fame to haue byn fpoken
by himfelfe ; fo as yt feemeth he was yet but
fome Nouice in Lutheranifme, by his trauayle
through Germany, & no perfect Zwinglian,
yf he were of any fetled fect at all, which is
more like that he was not at that day, though
accordinge to the veyne and feruour of herefie in thofe dayes, he was content to dye for
any one of his opinions rather then to recall
the fame.

8.   And thus much for his religion : but for
his perfon, Iohn Fox fetteth downe a certayne defcription of him when he ftudied in
Cambridge, fome three yeares before he was
burned in Scotland. And by this defcription
he may feeme to haue byn fome extrauagant
phantafticall fellow, fitt to begin or broach
any herefie or new fancy whatfoeuer. Yow
fhall heare Fox his relation, and therby iudge
of him, for that he cyteth the fame out of the
teftimony of one that liued with him. *About
the yeare* (faith he) of our Lord 1543.there was
in the vniuerfity of Cambridge one *Maifter*
George Vvifchart , commonly called *Maifter*
George of *Bennetts Colledge*, a man of tall ftature,
pold-headed, and on the fame a round french
capp of the beft , iudged of melancholy com-
plexion by his phyfiognomy, blacke hayre,
long-bearded, coomely of perfonage, well
fpoken after the countrey of Scotland , *&c.*
He had on him for his habitt of clothinge,ne-
uer but a mantle freefe-gowne to the fhowes,
a blacke *Millan* fuftian dubblett , and playne

Fox pag.
1155.
„
„
„
„
„
„
„
„
„
„
„
„
„

Q.   **blacke**

,, blacke hofen, courfe canauafe for his fhirts,
,, white fallinge bands, and cuffes at the hands,
,, all which apparell he gaue to the poore, fome
,, weekely, fome monethely, fome quarterly,
,, as he liked, fauinge his french capp, which he

A defcri- keeped the whole yeare, *&c.* He lay hard
ption of   vpon a powffe of ftraw, and courfe new cana-
George   uafe fheets, which when he changed he gaue
vvifchart, away: he had commonly by his bedd fide a
one of the tubbe of water, in which, his people being in
firft Prote-
ftants of   bedd, the candle put out, and all quiett, he
Scotland.

,, vfed to bath himfelfe, *&c.* He taught with
,, great modefty and grauity, fo that fome of his
,, people thought him feuere, and would haue
,, flayne him, but the Lord was his defence, *&c.*
,, 9. This is *VVifchart* his defcription by a Proteftant, that liued in houfe with him in *Cambridge*. And yf yow weigh the fame well, yow
will thinke, that he was as fitt to madneffe as
martyrdome; and his continuall hauinge a
tubbe of water by him, may fmell of fome
Iewifh or *Morifh* fuperftition. But yet finally
after much diligence vfed to recall him from
his opinions, ftandinge obftinately therin, he

The cruell was condemned and burned in Scotland,
tragedy of whervpon infued foone after a lamentable
murde-
ringe the   Tragedy to the Cardinall Beton, by whofe
Cardinall authority he was condemned. For that at the
of S. An- very fame tyme that this *VVifchart* was bur-
drewes.   ned, fome of the nobility and gentry of Scotland, being infected with herefie, and fearing

Lefleus in their owne fkynnes by *VVifcharts* example,
hift. Scot. (faith *B. Lefley*) and others enuyinge the faid
anno 1546.
                                    Cardi-

Cardinalls greatnes in Scotland conspired his ,,
murder,& performed the same in most barba- ,,
rous sort vpō the 29. of May next ensuing, nine ,,
persons were the cheefe doers therof, the prin- ,,
cipall of whome, was one *Normā Lesley*, togea- ,,
ther with an vncle of his, of the same name, *&c.* ,,

10. It is horror to read this story, how cruelly the murder was commytted, first by getting
into his Castle of S. Andrewes by treason, and
then breakinge into his chamber by violence,
and murderinge him in his bed, he crying out
(saith Fox) *alas, alas, slay me not, I am a Priest.* The   Fox *ibid.*
circumstances of their villanous behauiour
towards him, in hanginge him out at the
wyndow tyed by the pryuy parts, and other   Note Fox
such beastlynes as are not to be vttered : yet   his vvic-
doth the cruell and hypocriticall hart of this   ked and
our Fox seeme greatly to reioyce therin, ad-   bloudy
dinge further most blasphemously, *that yt vvas*   spiritt.
the spiritt of the Lord, that styrred them vp to do this
fact; wherin yow may see his desperate spiritt
in puritanisme. But yf yow will read the last   The booke
chapter of the fourth booke of *Dangerous Posi-*   of dange-
tions, sett forth in England by publike authori-   rous posi-
ty against the said Puritans, in the yeare of   printed at
Christ 1593. yow shall see this whole story sett   London
downe at large out of Scottish wryters, and   *anno* 1593.
censured by our Protestants of England, for
an vniust, barbarous, & villanous act, though
allowed at that tyme by *Caluyn*, *Knocks*, and
others; which *Knocks* being then in Scotland,
and priuy to the conspiracy as yt seemeth,
ranne presently to the said Castle of S. An-

drewes fupprifed by the murderers and there defended by the word, that which they had cruelly commytted before by the fword: fo as Fox and they were all of one fpiritt and religion, notwithftandinge his hypocriticall diffimulation of meekenes in other places. And thus much of *VVifchart,* and his burninge.

Io. Kirby. Roger Clarke.

11.   Vpon the next two dayes after this martyrdome of *George VVifchart* in Scotland, there follow in England *Iohn Kirby* and *Roger Clarke* martyrs in Fox his Calendar, the one burned at *Ipfwich,* the other at *Bury* vnder K. Henry the 8. vpon the fame yeare 1546. They were both poore labouring men wholy vnlearned, yet being peruerted once, with the perfuafions of certayne of Zwinglius fect, they offered to dy moft willfully *for denyall of the reall prefence in the Sacrament,* gloryinge & boaftinge

Fox *pag.* 1122.

therin fo much, that Iohn Fox wryteth, *Kirby* the former of the two to haue faid to a gentleman that vifited him in the prifon: *Ah Maifter*

An infolent and foolish bragg of Kirby.

VVinkefield be at my burninge, and yow fhall fay, there ftandeth a Chriftian fouldiar in the fire. He wryteth further of the faid *Kirby,* that when he came to the fire fide at *Ipfwich* to be burned, a learned man named *Doctor Rugham* being appointed to preach vpon that article of the *reall prefence* of Chrifts body in the Sacrament, *Kirby* though he were ignorant, and wholy vnlettered (as Fox himfelfe confeffeth) yet tooke he vpon him to cenfure that fermon from fentence to fentence. But let vs heare the words, of Fox his narration, themfelues.

12. *Then*

12. Then *Maiſter Doctor Rugham* (ſaith he) *entered into the ſixt Chapter of S. Iohn* (about the Sacrament) *who in handlinge that matter*; *ſo often, as he alleaged the ſcriptures, and applyed them rightly, Kirby told the people that he ſaid true, and badd the people beleeue him, but when he did otherwiſe; he told him agayne,* yow ſay not true ; *and to the people, beleeue him not good people, wherevpon they adiudged Doctor Rugham for a falſe Prophet, &c.* Lo, is not here a goodly matter, and the world turned vp ſide downe, that ſo poore and ignorant a fellow ſhall iudge the learned ? and that the people muſt hold the Doctor for a falſe Prophet, for that yt pleaſed the labourer to iudge him ſo in expoundinge S. Iohns ghoſpell, and to miſlike this or that in his ſpeech about ſo high a miſtery, as the labourer could not poſſibly vnderſtand the ſame? I would *Martyn Luther* had the handlinge of theſe ignorant preſumptuous men in this article, we ſhould haue quickely heard what iudgmēt he would haue giuen vpon them, as yow may perceaue by that yow haue read *before, and ſhall do more afterward, in the 17. Chapter of this treatiſe, where his words and cenſures are put downe more largely. And ſo we leaue theſe two willfull fellowes, there being nothinge wrytten ſingular of the ſecond (that is *Clarke*) for that he ſeemed only to follow the other and to applaude what he ſaid, and ſo for good fellowſhip burned with him alſo, ſo went the world in thoſe dayes of maddinge ſpirites.

13. From theſe fellowes Iohn Fox leapeth

backe

Fox ibid.

Strange folly and preſumption of the ignorant.

*Sup.menſ. Oct. nu. 38.

backe fome 15. yeares, and telleth vs a longe

Richard
Bayfield
Monke of
Bury.
ftory of the martyrdome of one *Richard Bayfield* who had byn a profeſſed monke and Prieſt of the Abbey of *Bury*, and being Chamberlayne (as he ſaith) of that Abbey, and therby his office requiringe him to prouide for gheſts and pilgrymes that came to the houſe, he fell acquaynted at length with two brickmakers of

Maxnell
and Stacy
brickema-
kers made
Bayfield an
heretike.
London, *Maxnell* and *Stacy*, that ſould briks to the monaſtery, and they being ſecretly infected with new opinions by reading the books of *Tyndall*, and other Engliſh Sectaryes of that tyme, they perſuaded the monke to read ſuch bookes alſo ; and for fittinge his turne, they preſented him two ſeuerall Treatiſes of *Tyndall*, the one called *The Wicked Mammon*, the other ; *The obedience of a Chriſtian man* ; *wherin*

Ibid. pag.
931.
(faith Fox) *this monke proſpered ſo mightely in two yeares ſpace, that he was caſt into the priſon of the houſe, and ſore whipped, &c.* And after this being brought before the Biſhop of *Wincheſter* and others, vpon the yeare of Chriſt 1528. he abiured all his forſaid new opinions, and did pennance for them, for ſo ſay the 6. and 7. articles here now obiected againſt him, to witt, *that*

Ibid. art 6.
& 7. pag.
931.
he iudicially abiured the ſaid articles, before the ſaid Biſhopps, and made a ſollemne oath vpon a booke, and the holy Euangeliſts to fulfill his pennance, &c. But after this he comminge acquaynted with a more learned Doctor and nearer to his vocation, which was *Friar Barnes*, that came ſometymes as a gheſt to the foraſtiery of the ſaid Monaſtery of Bury wherof *Bayfield* had the
care,

care, by his good counfell and inftructions he
refolued to go further then the brickemakers
had brought him before, that is to fay to be a
good Proteftant and renagate friar indeed,
and to caft of quite his monks weede, as he
did prefently, and ftole out of the monaftery,
ran ouer the Seas to Tyndall, tooke a woman
by his direction, nay as *Syr Thomas More* wryteth, he affured himfelfe to two weomen at
once, one in *Brabant* and another in *England,*
and after this made himfelfe a great marchant
of hereticall books, and came into England
with diuers packs of them, which were taken
with him, and are named in the Iudiciall fentence giuen againft him, & recorded by Fox,
to witt diuers volumes of *Martyn Luther*, and
others of *Oecolampadius,* fome alfo of *Zwinglius,*
others of *Pomeranus, Lambert, Melanchthon, Brentius, Bucer, Filinus, Capito, Tyndall* and others, and
then he being demaunded; *whether he beleued the
forenamed books to be good, and of the true faith ?* he
anfwered faith Fox, *that he iudged they were good,
and of the true faith.* And being asked further,
whether *Zwinglius, Oecolampadius,* and others,
whofe books he brought in, were of one faith
with *Luther ?* he anfwered *that he fuppofed they
held the fame doctrine that Luther did, but varyed in
fome points.* And being asked of what Sect
Zwinglius was, he faid, *he thought that he held
with Luther in fome points, &c.*

14. Thus Fox. Wherby yow fee the wife-
mans anfwere, fayinge; firft, that they varyed
in fome points, and then that they agreed in

*Bayfield
after per-
iury caft
of his
coole, and
affured
himfelfe
to tvvo
vveomen
at once.*

*Fox pag.
932.*

*Bayfields
confeffion
about Lu-
theran &
Zvvingliã
hooks.*

some points, and yet that all held the same doctrine, and were of one Religion and faith.
See Syr
Thomas
more in
his pre-
face to the
anſvvere
ofTindall.
Syr Thomas More ſaith, that this *Bayfield* being
taken now the ſecond tyme, offered to abiure
againe, & diſcloſed all his brethren, but when
he perceaued that for his relapſe he muſt be
burned notwithſtandinge; he choſe to dy an
heretike, then to recant, ſo ſaith *Syr Thomas
More* that liued in thoſe dayes, and knew the
man; neither hath Fox any thing to reply to
this graue teſtimony of *Syr Thomas More*, *but*

Fox ibid.
*only that he is not to be beleeued in his affirmation
againſt Bayfield, for that he vvas partially affected to
the Popes Religion.* But whether *Syr Thomas More*
or Iohn Fox be more credible in their aſſertions, the one affirminge yt vpon his owne
knowledge, as being preſent and liuing at the
very ſame tyme, the other denyinge yt vpon
heare-ſay or fancy of his owne 40. yeares after; I leaue to the iudgement of the diſcreete
reader, eſpecially yf he compare the conditions of the partyes togeather, the one being a
man of ſtrict truth, the other of looſe & large
conſcience in lyinge vpon euery occaſion, as
by infinite examples yow haue ſeene and ſhall
ſee in this Treatiſe againſt him.

15.   There enſue after this Apoſtata monke-
martyr, in the Calendar fiue Confeſſors that
I. Clarke.
I. Archer.
Dunſtan
Chitendē.
VVilliam
Foſter.
Alice Pot-
kins.
died in the Caſtle of *Canterbury*, where they
were impriſoned for their new religion; their
names are *Iohn Clarke* labouringe man, *Iohn Ar-
cher* weauer, *Dunſtan Chitenden* and *VVilliam Fo-
ſter* artificers, and *Alice Potkins* wife of *N. Potkins*.
All

All thefe (faith Fox) *did not only dy in the forfaid* Fox pag. 1773. *Caftle of Canterbury, but vvere alfo ftarued, and pined away , for lacke of meate, &c.* Which how probable a thinge yt is, there is no man of reafon, but will eafily difcerne. But howfoeuer they died, moft obftinate and peeuifh people they were, whileft they liued. *Alice Potkins* being asked of her age, anfwered, *that accordinge to her* The age *old age fhe had* 49. *yeares; but accordinge to her yonge* of Alice Potkins. *age, fince fhe learned Chrift , fhe vvas but of one yeare old, &c.*

16. *VVilliam Fofter* being asked why he could not abyde, that the Croffe fhould be borne in proceſsion, & why he refufed to cary a candle in his hand vpon Candlemaffe day, he said: *That for the Croſſe, yt was as needfull to carry the gal-* Fox ibid. *lowes about yf his Father vvere hanged, as the Croſſe: for that Chriſt died theron , and that a dung-forke in his hand , vvas as good as a candle on Candlemaſſe day.* Which was a fitt anfwere, (yow fee,) for a dung-former, one of his occupation. And as for their agreement of beleefe in matters of Religion, we may eafily imagine what it was, they being-ignorant and each of them fo obftinate, as what once they apprehended, they would defend euen vnto death: and partly alfo yow may gheffe by Fox himfelfe, who wryteth thus: *Although certayne of thefe vpon igno-* Fox pag. 1773. *rant fimplicity fvvarued a little in the number of Sacraments, fome grauntinge one Sacrament, that is the body of Chriſt hanginge on the Croſſe ; yet in the principall matter touching the doĉtrine of faluation for faith to ftay vpon, and in difagreeing from the dreaming de-*
                                                            termi-

*terminations of the Popish Church , they most agreed,
&c.* So wryteth Fox appointinge the vnity of
his people as yow fee , to confiſt in the diſagreeinge from vs , rather, then in agreeinge
amonge themſelues. And as for the Sacrament
of Chriſts body hanginge vpon the Croſſe,
which Iohn Fox faith heere that ſome of his
people, *did only graunt to be a Sacrament, and ſome
more* , I know not what he meaneth thereby,
nor how ſome could graunt this to be not
only a Sacrament, but the only Sacrament of
Ghriſtians. And yet Fox relateth yt heere as
yow fee , and feemeth not greatly to miſlike
yt , wherby yow may perceaue, that he and
his people were wiſe alike in many things.
And ſo much of them.

*Phantaſti-
call do-
ctrine al-
lovved by
Fox.*

17.   After theſe Confeſſors do follow other
foure Martyrs, *Iohn Hooke, Iohn Hallingdale, VVilliam Sparrow* , and *Richard Gibſon.* Of the firſt
Fox wryteth no more words but theſe: *I read
that in this preſent yeare* 1556. *vvas burned one called
Iohn Hooke, a true vvittneſſe of the Lords truth at Che-
ſter.* And this is all that he hath of that his *true
wittneſſe of the Lords truth,* not telling vs any further, eyther what that truth was , for which
he was burned , nor how truly he defended
the fame.

*Io. Hooke.
Iohn Hal-
lingdale.
VVilliam
Sparrovv.
Richard
Gibſon.
pag.* 1772.

18.   As for the other three, *Hallingdale, Sparrow*
and *Gibſon,* whome he calleth alſo *conſtant wittneſſes of Chriſt* ; they were all three burned in
Smithfield vpon the yeare 1557. after much labour in vaine taken with them , to inſtruct &
reduce them. *Hallingdale* being a ſimple ignorant

rant man , besides other particular herefies,
ftood refolutely vpon this point. *That generally*
(faith Fox) *thofe that of late had byn burned* (vnder Fox *pag.* 1838.
Q. Mary) *were no heretiks at all, but did preach truly*
the ghofpell, vpon whofe preaching he grounded his faith
and confcience, according to the fayinge of S. Iohn in
the 18. *Chapters of his Reuelations vvhere he faith, that* Halling-dales faith
the bloud of the Prophetts and of the Saints , and of all grounded vpon the
that were flayne vpon earth was found in the babyloni- preaching
call Church. By vvhich (faith Fox) *is vnderftood the* of here-tiks.
Church, vvherof the Pope is head, &c. Behould the
franticke prefumption of this ignorant artificer, who would needs proue out of the Apo-
calips, that all thofe that were burned in Q.
Maryes tyme were true Saints of God , and
that his faith and confcience was fufficiently
grounded vpon them , and their preachings,
without any further triall ; and this for that
they *vvere put to death by the Popes Church.* By
which argument he may found himfelfe alfo
vpon the faith and preachings of the Anabaptifts , and all other fectaryes burned by the
fame Church. But to go forward ; Fox faith
of his conftancy in this affertion, that he being
of B. Bonner further demaunded, whether he
would perfeuer , and ftand in thefe his opinions, he made anfwere ; *that he would continue*
and perfift in them to the death, &c.

19.   And the very like courfe tooke the other
two his companions *Sparrow* and *Gibfon,* who
had one circumftance more then *Hallingdale* to
aggrauate their fault , which was , that they
had fubmitted themfelues before , and were
fallen

vvilliam
Sparrovv a
ballad-fel-
ler.

fallen into relapse. *VVilliam Sparrow* was a fel-
ler and spreader of wicked and seditious ballads, and was conuinced of some in the open
court as Fox also Confesseth. *He granted* (saith

Bid. col. 2.

Fox) *to the sixt article, that he did sell the said ballads
then shewed and read before him, &c.* And then
being charged with his former submission
made in the yeare before to the Bishopp: he
answered: *I am sory that euer I made yt, for yt was
the worst deed that euer I did;* adding further vnto
them: *hold vp your abhomination so long as yow can,*

The obsti-
nacy of
VVilliam
Sparrovv.

&c. And then being demaunded what ground
of learninge he had, to cleaue to these his opinions, he made answere, and said ; *that all the
lawes now vsed* (meaninge the Ecclesiasticall
lawes) *are naught and abhominable, &c.* Thus
farre Fox. Wherby yow may perceaue what
manner of people they were , that answered
nothinge directly to any point demaunded,
but only raged and rayled . And yet when
B. Bonner asked this ballad-seller , whether he
would not be content to be persuaded to
change his mynd ? he made aunswere (saith

Bid. col. 2.

Fox) *that he would not go from his opinions;* and adding thervnto said: *That vvhich yow call heresie*
(speakinge to the Bishopp) *is good and godly: And
yf euery hayre of my head vvere a man, I vvould burne
them all,rather then to go from the truth,&c.* So hee.

20.   The same answers or very like , made
the third companion of his crew, *Gibson* , but
that in some things he was more arrogant and
obstinate then the other two. For he refused
to sweare before his ordinary *B. Bonner* , and
denyed

denyed him to be his ordinary. And when the Bishop spake vnto him to put him in remembrance of himselfe; he said, *he could not beare the Bishops bablinge, boldly protesting and affirming* (saith Fox) *that he was contrary and enemy to them all, in his mynd and opinion, although he had aforetyme kept yt secrett, for seare of the law, &c.* And being told of excommunication, he said to the Bishopp: *blessed am I, that am cursed at your hands.* And for that many articles were obiected by the Bishopp against him, about new heresies; he exhibited nine other articles or demaunds vnto the Bishopp most presumptuously, to be answered by him, conteyninge very fond and arrogant matters; *as, whether any man of what state or calling so euer may vse Lordshipp or power ouer any man, for faithes sake, or secresie of his conscience?*

Item, *by what euident tokens Antichrist may be knowne and his ministers?*

Item, *what the beast is, in the reuelation, that maketh warre with the Saints of God?*

Item, *what the gorgeous and glitteringe whore of Babylon is, &c.* And other the like demaunds appertayning all to contumely and contempt, as yow see; wherby yow may perceaue the spiritt of those men, full dronken with hereticall pride and obstinacy. Of whome yet Fox concludeth this story, with these patheticall words: *Thus this valiant souldiar fightinge for the gospell and sincere doctrine of Gods truth and Religion, against falshood and error, was committed with his fellowes vnto the secular power, &c.* And thus much of them.

21. There

(marginal notes:)
Fox *pag* 1839.

The pride and arrogancy of Richard Gibson. *Ibidem.*

Gibson poseth his Bishopp.

pag. 1839.

Ibid. col. 2.

21. There followeth the yeare of Chrift 1558. and laft of Q. Mary; in beginninge wherof vpon this moneth are placed two Foxian Martyrs burned at Ipfwich, *for the ghofpell of* *pag.* 1857. *Chrift* (faith Fox) *and his euerlaftinge teftament*, to witt, *Alexander Gouch*, and *Alice Dryuer*, or rather Alexander Gouch.
Alice Driuer. *Alice Dryuer* and *Alexander Gouch*, for that the woman was the doctor of the man, which yet yow muft note was not her husband, but a craftefman dwelling not farre from her, and by occupation (as Fox faith) a weauer of fhredded-couerletts, who vfing to her houfe at *Grosborrow* in Suffolke, was inftructed by her in the new ghofpell. And at length they two being taken togeather in a *Haygulfe* (as he faith) by a Iuftice of peace (no fitt place for fuch a coople to be conuerfant togeather) they were carryed to the Afsifes at *Bury*, and from thence afterward fent prifoners to *Ipfwich*. *Alexander Gouch* was about 36. yeares old, and *Alice Dryuer*, the wife of a certayne hufbandman, was of 30. There is no mention at all of her husband, but only of this fufpitious takinge of them togeather in the forfaid *Hay-* Alice Dri-
uer a fa-
mous do-
ctrix. *gulfe*, wherby a man may eafily gheffe, how light a ghofpellinge fifter fhe was: yet doth Fox make fuch accompt of her, and of her rare learninge in the fcriptures, as of no one fifter more in all his hiftory, fettinge downe two large difputations which fhe had with *Doctor Spencer* Chancelour to the Bifhop of *Norwifh*, & other Doctors that afsifted him; All which fhe brought to be dumme and mute, by her

wife

wise oppositions, answers, and alleaginge of
scriptures, yf yow will beleeue Fox, who
playeth also the notorious Reynard, and fraudulent companion in this, as in many other
things: and so I thinke yow will say also,
when yow haue heard the conferences, wherof heere I shall sett downe part in his owne
words, and therby yow may make a ghesse of
all the rest.

22. But yet before we enter to relate her
disputations; yow must note, that at the for-
said assise of *Bury, where* (saith Fox) *she did boldly* pag. 1857.
stand to confesse Christ crucified, defyinge the Pope with col. 2.
all his papisticall trash, she likened Q. Mary then
raiginge to *Iezabell, for vvhich her eares were cutt* Alice Dri-
of immediatly (saith he) *by commandement of Syr* uers ears
Clement Higham cheefe iudge, and she ioyfully yel- vndutifull
ded to the punishment, thinkinge her selfe happy, that vvords.
she vvas accompted vvorthy to suffer any thinge for the
name of Christ, &c. So as now hauinge lost her
eares for the liberty of her tongue, she came to
dispute with the said Doctors at Ipswich
without her eares in the forme followinge.

23. First (saith Fox) she comminge into the *Ibid. col. 2.*
place where she should be examined with a ,,
smylinge countenance, Doctor Spencer the ,,
Chancelor said: why woman dost thou laugh ,,
vs to scorne? ,,

Alice. Whether I do, or noe, I might well ,,
inough, to see what fooles ye bee. Thedispu-

Chancelor. Why are ye brought before me? tation of
and why are ye laid in prison? uer vvith

Alice. Yow know yt better then I. D. Spencer.

Chancelor.

,, *Chancelor.* No by my troth woman, I know
,, not why.

,, *Alice.* Then haue ye done me much
,, wronge, thus to imprifon me, and know no
,, caufe why.

,, *Chancelor.* Woman, woman, what faift
,, thou to the bleffed Sacrament of the Altar?

,, At thofe words (faith Fox) fhe held her
,, peace, and then a great Chuff-headed Prieft
,, ftandinge by asked her, why fhe anfwered not
,, the Chancelor?

,, *Alice.* Why Prieft (quoth fhe) I came not
,, to talke with thee, but with thy maifter. Yf
,, thou wilt that I talke with thee, command
,, thy Maifter to hold his peace. And with that
,, (faith Fox) the Prieft put his nofe in his capp
,, and faid no more.

,, *Chancelor.* Anfwere to that I demaund
,, of yow.

,, *Alice.* I neuer read nor hard of any fuch Sa-
,, crament in the fcripture.

,, *Chancelor.* Why? what fcriptures haue yow
,, read I pray yow?

,, *Alice.* I haue, I thanke God, read Gods
,, booke.

,, *Chancelor.* Why? what manner of booke is
,, that yow call Gods booke?

,, *Alice.* It is the old, and new Teftament.
,, What call yow yt?

,, *Chancelor.* That is Gods booke indeed.

The arro-
gancy of
Alice Dri-
uer.

,, *Alice.* And that fame booke haue I read
throughout, but yet neuer could find any fuch
,, Sacrament there, Notwithftandinge I will

grant

graunt yow a Sacramēt called the *Lords supper.* „
And seing I haue graunted yow a Sacrament, „
shew me what a Sacrament is? „

    Chancelor. It is a signe. And then one *Doctor* „
Gascoyne standinge by said : It was a signe of a „
holy thinge. „

    Alice. Yow haue said the truth Syr *:* It is a „
signe indeed, I must needs graunt yt : and ther- „
fore seing yt is a signe , yt cannot be the thing „
signified also. „

    Gascoyne. Then stood vp *Doctor Gascoyne* and „
made an oration with many faire words, little „
to the purpose, & in the end therof asked her, „
yf she did not beleeue the omnipotency of „
God, and that he was able to performe what „
he promised? „

    Alice. Yea truly. But I pray yow, did he „
euer promise that he would make the bread „
his body, in the Sacrament? „

    Gascoyne. What say yow to *take, eat, this is* „
my body? are they not his words? „

    Alice. Yes I cannot deny them. But I pray „
yow was yt not bread, that he gaue them ? „

    Gascoyne. No, yt was his body. „

    Alice. Then was yt his body , that they did
eat ouernight. Marke the
argument
of a spin-
cer against
a Doctor.

    Gascoyne. Yea, yt was his body. „

    Alice. What body was yt then , that was „
crucified the next day? „

    Gascoyne. It was Christs body also. „

    Alice. How could that be, when his disciples „
had eaten him vp ouer night , except he had „
two bodyes, as by your argument he had : one „

           R   they

„ they did eate ouer night, and the other was
„ crucified the next day. Be ye not aſhamed
„ to teache the people, that Chriſt had two
„ bodyes?

„ *Gaſcoyne.* With that Gaſcoyne held his
„ peace, and made her no anſwere (ſaith Fox)
„ for as it ſeemed he was aſhamed of his doings.
„ Then the Chancelor lift vp his head from the
„ cuſhion, and commanded the gaylor to carry
„ her away.

Alice Driuer triumpheth ouer the Doctors.

„ *Alice.* Now when ye be not able to reſiſt
the truth, ye commaund me to priſon: well
the Lord in the end ſhall iudge our cauſe, I
wis, I wis, this geere will not go for good pay-
„ ment then, &c.

24.   Thus farre Fox. And this was the end
of the firſt diſputation, wherin *Alice* the ſpin-
ſter ſett vp (as yow ſee) and blanked both *Doctor Spencer* the Chancelor, and *Doctor Gaſcoyne*
his aſſiſtant, as alſo the chufheaded Prieſt
with his noſe in his capp, by her learned anſwers framed out of Fox his owne braine. For
no man of wiſdome will imagine (I weene)
that *Alice Driuer*, though ſhe were neuer ſo pra-
chant & forward in hereſie, and bold through
the pride therof, could make ſuch a conference of her ſelfe, with ſuch learned men as
the aforenamed were, eſpecially yf yt be true,
that ſhe had loſt her eares firſt for her intem-
perate ſpeech; yet was her bragg of hauinge
read the Bible throughout, fitt for a woman
of her trade.

25.   The two obiections which ſhe is taught
to

to make before may feeme perchance to the
fimple and vnlearned, to haue fome little fhew
of difficulty: the firft that yf the Sacrament of
the Altar be a *figne, yt cannot be alfo the thing figni-*
fied: and that yf Chrifts difciples did eat his body really,
in the fupper, the fame could not be crucified the next
day vpon the Croffe, thefe are (I fay) two oppofi-
tions framed out of I. Fox his highe & deep
diuinity, and attributed to the woman, as
though fhe had vttered them of her felfe;
which yet euery meane fcholler amongft Catholiks can eafily anfwere. For firft wheras
S. *Auften* faith; that *a Sacrament is a vifible figne of*
an inuifible grace (which Fox would make as
though the Doctors of *Ipfwich* had not byn
able to bring forth) this definition, I fay, is
fully verified in the Sacrament of the Altar.
For that albeit there be not the fubftance of
bread and wyne, after the words of confecration; yet are there the externall accidents of
bread and wyne, as colour, quantity, taft, and
the reft, which are vifible fignes both of inuifible grace, receaued, (vvherin principally
confifteth the trew nature of a Sacrament)
and befides are fignes of Chrifts reall body
conteyned vnder them, and of his body in
heauen remayninge their after an other manner, and of his death vpon the Croffe, and of
the vnion of his myfticall body the Church,
& other fuch mifteryes fignified therby as ancient Fathers do expounde & declare, and yet
neuer any of them did heerby go about to exclude the trew reall prefence of Chrift vnder

R 2   thes

thes signes as Sacramentaryes do at this day,
wherof we haue said more in the third Chapter of our reuew of disputations, in the end of
this booke.

26.   And as for the second point, touched by
Alice Dryuer of Chriſts body receaued by
Chriſt himſelfe, & his Apoſtles the night before his paſſion, we ſay accordinge to the Catholike faith, that the ſame body of Chriſt our
Sauiour, that died on the Croſſe, was eaten by
his diſciples (yea by Chriſt himſelfe alſo)

Hier ep. ad
Hedibid.
queſt. 2 .
the night before in the ſupper; *ipſe comedens, &*
qui comeditur (ſaith S. *Hierome*) he that was eaten was one of the eaters alſo: and yt was the
ſelfe ſame body , though not in that ſenſible

Ioan. 6.
fleſhly ſhape, as the *Capharnaites* moſt groſſely
immagined, but exhibyted in another forme;
and the very ſame that now is eaten dayly by
infinite Chriſtians throughout the world, and
hath byn euer ſince his paſſion and reſurre-
ction, and ſhalbe to the worlds end ; and yet
this body is neyther multiplyed nor dimini-

Chriſ. hom.
24. in 1.ep.
ad Cor.
ſhed therby: to which effect S. *Chryſoſtome* ſaith,
vve eate now the ſelfe ſame body vvhich vvas crucified
on the Croſſe , vvhich vvas beaten and putt to death,
vvhich the Magi did adore in the maunger, &c. And

Ibid. hom. 2.
in ep. 2. ad
Tim.
againe in another place. *Eadem eſt oblatio, quam*
modò ſacerdotes cuiuſcunque meriti conficiunt, quamā̃
dedit Chriſtus ipſe diſcipulis ſuis. It is the very
ſelfe ſame oblation, that our Prieſts now,
though neuer ſo vnworthy do make, and
vvhich Chriſt himſelfe deliuered to his diſ-

Ibidem.
ciples. *Nihil habet iſta quam illa minus :* this oblation,

K 3

tion hath nothinge leſſe in yt , then that had,
vvhich vvas the true fleſh and bloud of
Chriſt .

27. Now then yf Iohn Fox and his ghoſpellinge ſiſter, haue not eyther ſo much faith as
to beleeue this, or vnderſtanding to conceaue
yt , no maruayle though ſhe inſulted ſo foo-
liſhely vpon the Doctors of *Ipſwich* , ſayinge,
that they muſt graunt Chriſt to haue two diſtinct bo-
dyes , for that the one vvas eaten the night before , the
other crucifyed the next day after. But the Catholike faith vvhich yeldeth ſo much to the omnipotency of Chriſt, as to confeſſe and beleeue
that he can make his body , to be in many
places at once , and to be receaued wholy of
infinite people at one tyme , remayninge ſtill,
one, and the ſelfe ſame body; this faith (I ſay)
hath no more difficulty in beleeuinge this article, then diuers others as repugnant to vulgar ſenſe, and appearance of humayne reaſon
then this. And ſo I leaue Fox and his woman
to their infidelity, and ſhall go forward to recyte another diſputation, which this his *Alice*
had with the ſaid Doctors of *Ipſwich* , wherin
he diſcouereth much more vanity, & humour
of lyinge then in the former.

28. For firſt he bringeth in his *Alice* vanting
and triumphing, that ſhe had ouercome them
the day before. Yeſterday (ſaith ſhee) I asked
yow vvhat a Sacrament vvas , and yow ſaid
yt vvas a ſigne, and I agreed thervnto, confir-
minge the ſame vvith the ſcriptures, and now
yow come, and aske me againe.

Chance-

„ *Chancelor.* Thou lyeſt, naughty woman, we
„ did not ſay that yt vvas a ſigne.

„ *Alice.* Why Maiſters, be ye not the ſame
„ men yow vvere yeſterday? vvill yow eat
„ your owne vvords? are ye not aſhamed to ly
„ before all this multitude?

„ *Gaſcoyne.* Then ſtood vp *Doctor Gaſcoyne*, and
„ began to talke of the Church, &c.

A good
doctrix
that knevv
not the
vvord
Church to
be in the
ſcripture.

Alice. I pray yow, vvhere fynd ye this
vvord *Church* vvrytten in the ſcriptures.

Gaſcoyne. It is vvrytten in the new Teſtament.

„ *Alice.* I pray yow ſhew me the place.

„ *Gaſcoyne.* I cannot tell the place, but there
„ yt is.

„ *Alice.* I thought ſo much indeed, that yow
„ vvere little acquainted vvith the new Teſta-
„ ment: ſurely yow be a good Doctor.

„ *Gaſcoyne.* I am as good a Doctor as yow.

„ *Alice.* Yow may vvell know I thanke God,
„ that I haue exerciſed the Bible, els could I not
„ haue anſwered yow (to Gods glory be it ſpo-
„ ken) as I haue done.

Ibid. col. 2.

Fox. Thus ſhe put them all to ſylence, that
„ one looked on another, and had not a vvord
„ to ſpeake.

Fox a more
foole then
all the reſt.

Alice. Haue ye no more to ſay? God be honoured, yow be not able to reſiſt the ſpiritt of
„ God in me a poore vvoman. I vvas an honeſt
„ poore mans daughter neuer brought vp in
„ vniuerſityes, as yow haue byn, but I haue
„ dryuen the plowgh before my Father many a
„ tyme I thanke God; yet notwithſtandinge in
defence

defence of Gods truth, and in the caufe of my
maifter Chrift, by his grace, *I vvill fett my foote*
againft the foote of any of yow all, in the maynte-
nance, and defence of the fame. And yf I had
a thoufand liues, they fhould go for payment
therof, *&c.*

29. Thus farre Fox. And I haue thought
good to put downe thefe two conferences
more at large, that therby yow might perceaue his veyne in vauntinge and lyinge, for
fettinge forth the veyne glory of his ghofpellers: and yet had he not witt fufficient to
fee vvhat is for him and vvhat is againft him.
For vvhat can be alleaged more ridiculous,
then for *Alice Driuer* to ftand vvith the Doctors
that the vvord *Church* vvas not to be found in
the new Teftament, which allmoft is found
in euery Chapter, or that none of them could
fhew any fuch place, or that they vvould deny
that vvhich they had faid the day before, that
the Sacrament *vvas a figne?* (except they meant
an only bare figne) or vvhat can be diuifed
more prefumptuous and intolerable, then this
laft glorious fpeach of this his foolifh ghofpelling fifter, affirming that fhe had *vanquifhed thofe*
Doctors by the fcriptures? and that *the fpiritt of God*
fpake in her, and that fhe would *fett her foote to any*
mans foote vvhatfoeuer, and other like fooleryes;
vvhich, yf Fox had had any one dramme of
vvitt or difcretion, he vvould neuer haue
brought forth in this place as to her prayfe;
of vvhome he addeth in the end, that laftly
fhe vvas burned at *Ipfwich,* togeather vvith

R 4   *Alexander*

Alexander Gouch the couerlett-weauer before mencioned, vvho vvas taken vvith her in the hay-mowe; of vvhome Fox speaketh very little, but, *that he vvas constant, denyinge the reall*

Fox *ibid.* col. 2. *presence in the Sacrament, accordinge to the doctrine deliuered by Alice Dryuer, vvith vvhome he vvas condemned, & burned at Ipswich the fourth of Nouember* 1558. And so much of them.

30. In this same yeare 1558. Iohn Fox appointeth vs out three other Martyrs burned at *Bury* in Suffolke vpon one day, though he allow them diuers dayes in his Calendar; but in relatinge their Acts and Gests he only telleth vs their names: to witt, *Phillipp Humfrey,*

Philipp Humfrey Io. Dauy. Henry Dauy.
Iohn Dauy, and *Henry Dauy* his brother, addinge these words; *that these three good men suffered martyrdome at Bury for the true testimony of Iesu Christ,*

Fox *pag.* 1859.
and that *Syr Clement Higham a fortenight before the Queene died, did sue out a vvryte for the burninge of these godly & blessed Martyrs.* And this is all which he vvryteth of them.

31. The last that vvere burned in this moneth and yeare, and in the vvhole raigne of Q. Mary (that died vpon the 17. day therof as is knowne) vvere fiue at *Canterbury,* three men and two vveomen not aboue six dayes

Io. Cornford. Christophor Brovvne. Io. Hurst. Alice Snoth. Katherine Knight.
(saith Fox) before the death of Queene Mary, vvhose names are *Iohn Cornford* of *VVortham, Chrystophor Browne* of *Maidstone, Iohn Hurst* of *Ashford* artificers & poore labouringe men, togeather vvith *Alice Snoth,* and *Katherine Knight* spinsters and labouringe vveomen: of all vvhose condemnations and articles Iohn Fox wryteth

teth

teth thus: *The matter vvhy they vvere iudged to the fire, vvas, for beleeuinge the body of Chrif̄t not to be in the Sacrament of the Altar, vnles yt be receaued: ſaying moreouer, that vve receaue another thinge alſo beſids Chrif̄ts body, vvhich vve ſee, and is a temporall thinge, accordinge to S. Paul. The things that be ſeene be temporall, &c.* This was their firſt article, vvhich of likelyhood, neyther they themſelues vnderſtood, being ſimple people, nor Iohn Fox that relateth the ſame; for partly this article ſauoureth of Lutheraniſme, acknowledginge the body of Chrif̄t to be in the Sacrament *in vſu,* when yt is vſed or receaued; and that with Chrif̄ts body we receaue alſo ſome temporall thing, to witt bread: wheruпto notwithſtandinge the place of *S. Paul* to the *Corinthians* is moſt abſurdly applyed.

Fox pag. 1862.

2. Cor. 2.

Moſt abſurd applyinge of ſcripture by ignorãt people.

32. For that *S. Paul* talking of the glory and benefitts of the life to come, and comparinge them with thoſe of this life, ſaid : *Quæ enim videntur, temporalia ſunt, quæ autem non videntur, æterna.* Thoſe things that are ſeene with our eyes in this world, are durable for a tyme only: but „ thoſe things that are not ſeene with the eyes „ of the fleſh, but hoped for in the next life, are „ euerlaſtinge. Now, vvhat application may „ theſe vvords haue (I pray yow) to the purpoſe heere alleaged by theſe fond heretiks? to witt, that for ſo much as the things of this life are viſible, and the things of the next life inuiſible, therefore muſt there bee as well the ſubſtance of bread in the Sacrament, as the body of Chrif̄t, accordinge to the Lutherans opinions,

2. Cor. 4.

nions, for that they see the accidentes: Do
yow not see how these people that talke nothinge but of scriptures, do abuse scriptures,
when they come to alleage them euery one to
their owne purpose?

33.   But let vs heare some other articles togeather with their reasons out of the scriptures: *Item* (saith he) *they vvere condemned for
confeßinge that an euill man doth not receaue Chrifts
body; becaufe no man hath the fonne, except yt be giuen
him of the Father.* How hangeth this togeather
trow yow? But heare further. *Item for fayinge*
(saith Fox) *that yt is idolatry to creep to the Croffe,
for that S. Iohn saith: Little Children beware of
images.* And by these few places of scripture so
fondly alleaged and applied by these ignorant
sectaryes, for reasons of their hereticall assertions, a man may see what people they were,
and how learnedly and fittly they alleaged
the scriptures, amonge whome the weomen
were euer lightely the most forward; And
Iohn Fox telleth vs heere a wonderfull tale
of *Katherine Knight* aliàs *Tynley,* one of this company, how shee became first to be a scriptu-
rian; *shee fell* (saith he) *vpon this place of scripture in
Ioel the prophett, vvhich she had seene, not by readinge
of the scriptures (for she had yet in manner no taft of
religion) but she had found yt by chance in a booke of
prayers: I will powre out my spiritt vpon all flesh , and
your fonnes and your daughters shall prophefy ; your old
men shall dreame dreames;and your young men shall see
vifions; and vpon the maydes , and vpon the feruants in
thofe dayes I vvill powre out my spiritt , &c.* VVhich
place

Ioan. 6.

*Fox pag.
1862.*

Ioel. 2.

place *of scripture after she had shewed to her sonne Ro-*
bert Tynley dwellinge in Maydstone, and he had ex-
pounded the same vnto her, she began to take hold of the
ghospell, growinge more and more in zeale, and loue
therof, and so continued vntill her martyrdome, &c.
Thus wryteth Fox of one of his prophetisses,
how she came to take hold of the ghospell, to
prophesie, dreame dreames, see visions, and to
assure her selfe that she had the same spiritt of
God in her.

Hovv Ka-
therine
Knightbe-
came first
a ghospel-
ler, and to
knovv that
she had
the spirite
in her.

34. Of the other vvoman also *Alice Snoth* he
telleth another tale, that she being at the fire
side, called for her God-fathers and God-mothers, asking them; *vvhat they had promised for*
her at her baptisme? and then immediatly (saith Fox)
she rehearsed her faith, and the Commandements of
God, and required of them yf there vvere any more that
they had promised in her behalfe? And they said no. And
then said shee: beare witnesse then, that I dy a good Chri-
stian vvoman, &c. This heroicall act recounteth
Fox of his maid *Alice Snoth*; and as though by
this he had giuen a great blow to B. *Bonner,* that
in his articles and interrogatoryes was wont
to aske, why they departed from the faith
wherin they were baptised, he maketh this
note in the margent: *Heerby B. Bonner may see*
that the Martyrs died in the same faith, vvherin they
vvere baptized, by their God-fathers and God-mothers.

Ibid. col. 2.

Fox his
tale of
Alice
Snoth.

Fox *ibid.*

35. But who doth not see the folly of this
marginall note? For B. *Bonner* meant the ancient Catholike faith, wherin they for the
most part and all their ancestors were baptised; and for their perseuerance in that faith
did

did their God-fathers & God-mothers make
their promises. And yf *Alice Snoth* had rehearsed or professed that faith to her God-fathers
and God-mothers at the fire side, she needed
not to haue byn burned; and so Fox (yow see)
playeth the foole in this place, both in text &
margent, as he doth also in tellinge vs finally;
that vvhen his forsaid fiue Martyrs vvere excommunicated, & separated from the Church
by sentence of *B. Bonner*, they excommunicated him and his part againe, beginninge their
sentence thus:

39.   *In the name of our Lord Iesu Christ sonne of the*
most mighty God, and by the power of his holy spirit, &c.
VVe do giue heere into the hands of Sathan to be de-
stroyed, &c. And vvith this they vvent to the
fire; vvhere vve leaue them togeather vvith
their curse, vvhich no doubt fell vpon themselues for their owne vvillfullnes. God blesse
vs from all such obstinacy in blyndnes: And
so an end of this moneth, remittinge the comparison, as in the former, vnto that vvhich
hath byn declared in the first two or three
monethes.

The ende of Nouember.

Fox his
Martyrs
do excom-
municat
their Bis-
hops.

Fox his

Fox *pag.*
1862.

O F

OF THE LAST MONETH,

VVHICH IS DECEMBER;

VVhat Martyrs and Confessors it compre-
hendeth of Fox his Church;

And that the number of Confessors therin is greater then of Martyrs, vvherof K. Edward the sixt is the last, and shutteth vp this moneth and vvhole Calendar.

Chap. XVI.

§. 1.

THIS moneth being the laſt of all the twelue, Iohn Fox his ſtore of Martyrs grew ſhort, either forrayne or domeſticall, and therfore leauinge fiue dayes free to the old Saints of our Calendar (the greateſt liberality that hitherto he hath vſed) which are, *S. Thomas* the Apoſtle, the *natiuity of Chriſt*, the feaſts of *S. Stephen*, and of *S. Iohn Euangeliſt*, and *Childermaſſe* (for ſo he calleth the feaſt of the Innocents ſlayne by *Herod*): he ſo ſhuffleth to-geather all theſe old Saints, as he obſerueth neyther the day, nor manner in his Calendar, which he found in ours: For that he placeth the feaſt of *S. Thomas* the Apoſtle (for example) vpon the 18. day which we celebrate vpon the 21.ͭ then thruſteth he togeather betweene
the

the 21. and 22. dayes (not allowinge them any more roome) foure feafts, to witt, the *natiuity of our Lord, S. Stephen Martyr, S. Iohn Euangelift,* and *Childermas:* vvhich feafts vve do ferue vpon 4. diftinct dayes, to witt the 25. 26. 27. and 28. and the next day after, vvhich is the 29. is the feaft of *S. Thomas of Canterbury* vvholy difplaced by Fox, vvherat I maruayle not, confideringe his affection towards him; but why after him againe he fhould difplace *S. Sylueſter* Pope of Rome, that baptized our *Conſtantine* the great, and vvas accompted ſo holy a Pope by all antiquity, I know not, except yt vvere to place *K. Edward* the fixt in his roome, a young head of a Church for an old.

2.   But vve muſt beare all this toſſinge and tormoylinge of Iohn Fox, and take vvhat he giueth vs: and ſo hauing allowed vs but three dayes in this moneth for fiue ſo great Saints, as yow haue heard, and theſe alſo ſo diforderly allotted; all the other dayes vvhich are 28. he deuydeth out to his Saints, but yet ſo, as he giueth the more places to Confeſſors or rather Profeſſors of his religion, vvhether they haue ſuffered any thinge for yt or no. Which courſe yf vve vvould follow in framinge out a Catholike Calendar of this our tyme only (that is to ſay of Engliſh alone that haue ſuffered for their faith vnder one only Prince, to vvitt, the late Queene), vvho gloryed notvvithſtandinge much in the ſtile of rare clemency;no man is there of diſcretion,that will not eaſily ſee and confider, that beſides great
numbers

numbers of excellent Martyrs, we might also
fett downe Confeſſors twenty for one, to the
number of thoſe which Fox picketh out, both
from at home, and from all forrayne nations,
to furniſh his Calendar in this kynd of Confeſſors.

3. And that which is moſt ridiculous of all,
he gathereth them not only from all partes of
the worlde, but alſo from all kynds of ſects &
profeſsions, though neuer ſo different and repugnant in opinions amonge themſelues,
wherof I may giue yow ſundry examples,
euen in this one moneth. For he hath ſome
vnder *K. Richard* the ſecond, which were *Lol-*
lards, as two gray friars, on the fifth day: ſome
vnder *H. Henry* the ſixth, as *Thomas Rhedonenſis*,
that was a Frenche Wickliffian vpon the 24.
day; diuers vnder *K. Henry* the eyght, of diuers
countreyes & ſundry religions, as *Melanchthon*,
a Lutheran, *Peter Martyr* a Zwinglian, *Martyn*
Bucer, frend to both, *Eraſmus Roterodamus*, frend
to neyther, *Picus Mirandola* a zealous Catholike
againſt them all: yea Fox fetcheth in a Iew alſo, put to death in *Conſtantinople*, for being conuerted to Catholike Religion, and ſtandinge
therin vntill death. So as Fox compoundinge
his Calendar for this one moneth, of ſo different ſorts and ſectes of men, and religions;
doth ſhew what he hath done in all the reſt
togeather. But now from this generality we
ſhall paſſe to examen the particulars, according as euery ones meritt requireth, deuyding
the ſame into two parts; the firſt ſhall conteyne

VVhat
manner of
Côfeſſors
Fox ga-
thereth
togeather
of his
Church in
this mo-
neth.

teyne the Martyrs and Confessors that haue
suffered any thinge in this moneth, for Fox
his Religion; the second shalbe of other certayne Confessors, or Professors that he put
in only for honouringe his Calendar, vpon
persuasion that they fauored somewhat his
religion though they suffred nothing for yt.

Of Foxian Martyrs and Confessors, that suffered in this moneth vnder K. Henry the 8. Qu. Mary, and other forraine Princes, for heresies. §. 2.

4. The first two dayes of this moneth are
assigned to *VVilliam Tracy Esquier Confessor*, and
to *Peter Sapience Martyr* : and they seeme in his
Calendar to be referred both to one yeare, to
witt, 1534. which was the 25. yeare of the
raigne of K. *Henry* the eyght, but seekinge afterward for the said *Peter Sapience* his story in
Fox his Acts and Monuments, I find nothing
at all of him; nor the man so much as named
eyther there, or in his Index of the whole
worke. For which cause, and for that his said
name soundeth not as though yt were English, we are driuen to thinke that he was some
out-landish poore companion, whose name
Fox did borrow to fill vp a place in his Calendar, puttinge out the noble virgin and
Martyr *S. Bibiana*, whome he found in our
Calendar vpon the second day of this moneth,

VVilliam
Tracy.
Peter Sa-
pience.

neth, to make this his Martyr roome.

5. But as for the other squire *Tracy*, Fox wryteth that he was of *Totingdon* in Glocestershire,
and cominge to dy he made a certayne extrauagant Testament, with diuers words soun-
dinge towards the new doctrine of Luther,
which was freshly spronge vp in those dayes;
and amonge other things he saith therein (as
Fox relateth): *Touchinge the buryinge of my body,
yt auayleth me not, vvhatsoeuer be done thervnto, &c.*
This draweth to *Diogenes* his religion, yf yow
remember, who would be cast to the dunghill
with a staffe by him. But what more? passeth
he no further? yes. For presently after he proceedeth to speake against the meritts of good
works, sayinge: *that a good man maketh good works,
but good works do not make a good man, &c.* And
other such things, tending to hereticall senses,
as was easy to see. Wherfore the said Testament being brought (accordinge to order) to
the Bishopp of Canterburyes court by *Tracyes*
sonne to be proued, after his Fathers death;
the Bishopp would not passe yt, but callinge a
conuocation of Bishopps and learned men,
adiudged the same to be hereticall, & so gaue
sentence that the body of the said *Tracy* (hauinge proued belike that he was an heretike
indeed) should be cast out of holy ground, and
burned, and so yt was executed as Fox saith,
vpon the yeare 1532. which is two yeares different from that he assigneth in his Calendar;
and for this cause yt pleased Fox to make him
a Confessor of his Church, as in like manner

Tracy his
hereticall
Testamēt
anno 1531.
Fox *pag.*
951.

Ibidem.

Tracyes
Testamēt
proued he-
reticall by
the Archb.
of Canter-
bury.

S   he

he made *VVickliffe* a Martyr before, for the very same cause; to witt, for being burned after he was dead, though yt be likely that the one felt as much payne as the other, in their burninge. But Fox hath authority to bestow the titles of Martyrs or Confessors as he pleaseth, and vpon whome he pleaseth, eyther with meritt or without. And so we will not stand with him in this point of *Tracyes* canonization, but passe to those that ensue.

6.   Vpon the third day of this moneth, he placeth the festiuall triumph of martyrdome, of one *George Bucker*, otherwise named *Adam Damlipp*, who was hanged, drawne, and quartered in *Cales* for treason against K. Henry the eyght, as his processes do shew, and Iohn Fox confesseth; but yet for that he had byn an Apostata Priest, and had byn heretofore called before B. *Cranmer*, and other Bishopps at *Lambeth* about the Sacrament of the Altar, and for denyinge the *reall presence (for that the learned, godly & blessed Martyr Cranmer* (saith Fox) *vvas then yet but a Lutheran,*) and for that at the same tyme, he deceaued the said Bishops, geuinge them the slipp, when he should haue appeared the second tyme before them (and this by warninge and collusion of *Cranmer* himselfe, betrayinge his fellow Bishopps, and the Kings commission also, yf Fox say truly:) for this cause (I say) though afterward this *Damlipp* being taken againe and sent ouer to *Cales*, he was hanged, drawne and quartered for treason as hath byn said, and not burned

at

Adam Damlipp an apostata priest, hanged dravvne and quartered in *Cales*, an. 1545.

Fox *pag.* 1115.

at all : yet will Fox needs haue him a Martyr,
For thus he wryteth of his death.

7. At his death (faith he) *Syr Rafe Ellerker* *pag.*1120.
knight-marfhall of *Cales*, would not fuffer the „
innocent and godly man to declare eyther his „
faith, or the caufe he died for , but faid to the „
executioner; *difpach the knaue, haue done*; and *Syr* „
VVilliam Mote a Prieft being appointed there to „
preach, declared to the people how *Damlipp* „
had byn a fower of feditious doctrine, and al- „
beit he had byn pardoned for that by the ge- „
nerall pardon, yet he was condemned for „
being a traytor againft the Kinge: to which „
when *Adam Damlipp* would haue replyed, the „
forefaid knight-marfhall would not fuffer „
him, &c. *And fo moft meekely, patiently and ioyfully* „
the bleffed and innocent Martyr tooke his death, &c. „
And thus you fee Iohn Fox canonizeth Mar- „
tyrs at his pleafure, yea maketh them Inno- Damlips
centes.   death for
                                                                        treafon.

8. There follow vpon the fourth and fifth
dayes in Fox his Calendar, firft, *an old man of*
Buckingamfhire Martyr , and then, *two gray friars*
Martyrs. But of the friars, I find no narration Tvvo gray
afterward in Fox his Acts and Monuments: friars faid
and accordinge to the yeare which he appoin- to be mar
teth to their martyrdome, yt feemeth impro- der K. Ri-
bable , that they fhould be martyred in Eng- chard the
land that yeare, being 1381. which was the 2. 1381.
fifth of the raigne of *K. Richard* the fecond,
when Wickliffes fauourers were in their ruffe
and borne out by *Iohn of Gaunt*, Duke of *Lanca-*
fter that ouerruled all, & Fox himfelfe confef-

seth that duringe this Kings raigne none suffered greatly for *VVickliffes* Religion ; so as I
know not where to find out these two friars
in those dayes', nor I thinke Iohn Fox himselfe. But as for the *old man of Buckinghamshire,*
(yf he be the same) Fox wryteth thus : *About*
vvhich yeare (to witt 1500.) *or in the next yeare*
followinge, the 12. day of Iuly, vvas an old man burned
in Smithfield, &c. And this is all that I can find
recorded in Fox his Acts and Monuments of
any such old man; yet for that he agreeth here,
neyther in day, moneth nor yeare, with that
which he assigneth in his Calendar, yt putteth
me in some doubt, whether he be the same or
noe; albeit it be a very ordinary matter in Fox
his Acts & Monuments, to differ in day, yeare,
and moneth from himselfe in his Calendar, as
often I haue noted before; and so no great argument can be grounded theron to or fro.

9.   Next after these three, ensue fiue other
each one occupyinge his day in the Calendar,
to witt 3. Confessors, *Iohn Hilton, Iohn Coignes*
and *Robert VVard,* for that belike they were called to accompt for new opinions; and then
two Martyrs, the first, *a scholler of Abbeuile* in
France (as yt seemeth) as the other a *Iew* martyred in *Constantinople.* And as for the first 4.
I canne find nothinge in all his Acts and Monuments of them, nether by way of his table
or Index, or of the yeares he assigneth of their
trouble, which are 1513. 1517. and 1522. But of
the *Iew* martyred in *Constantinople* vpon the
yeare 1528. he hath a short legend, ioyned with
                                    a pa-

The old
man of
Buckin-
gamshire.
Fox pag.
671.

I. Hilton.
Io. Coi-
gnes.
Robert
VVarde.
A scholler
of Abbe-
uile.
A Iew
martyr.

a pageant in print, wherin the Iew lyeth dead, and 2. or 3. Turks ſtaring wickedly vpon him. But Fox doth not tell vs how the Iew was put to death, but only wryteth this: *There was a certaine Iew dwelling in the Citty of Conſtantinople, and there receauinge the Sacrament of Baptiſme, vvas conuerted, and became a good Chriſtian; vvherof when the Turks vnderſtood, they were vehemently exaſperate againſt him, and fearinge leaſt his conuerſion ſhould be a detriment to their mahemeticall law, they ſought meanes how to put him to death, vvhich in ſhort tyme after they accompliſhed, &c.*

10. Behould heere the whole legend or narration of this martyred Iew. About whome I would aske of Fox, how he prooueth him rather to be his Martyr, then oures, if he were a Martyr at all? For that being conuerted in *Conſtantinople* in the tyme heere mencioned, yt is not like that he could be a Proteſtant; but rather of that religion, wherof Chriſtians are in *Conſtantinople*, where they haue maſſe publikely, proceſſion with the *bleſſed Sacrament,* images in their Churches, and other ſuch points, which in Fox his Religion is Idolatry and abhomination. And how then doth he ſay that *this Iew became a good Chriſtian, &c.* And ſo putteth him in for a Martyr of his Church? But this we muſt aſcribe vnto the pouerty & impurity of his ſaid Church, that taketh vp all ſcrapps whatſoeuer, and from whence ſoeuer to make vp a number. But now are we to paſſe from theſe petty Martyrs, to a famous Saint and Martyr indeed, that hath his feſti-

uall

uall day vpon the 10. of this moneth, named

Richard
Hunne
marchãt-
taylor ac-
cuſed of
hereſy &
ſedition
an. 1514.

Richard Hunne a marchant-taylor of London, who in the fifth yeare of the raigne of Kinge Henry the eyght (which was of Chriſt 1514, and three yeares before the beginning of Luther) was called before *Richard Fitz-Iames,* then Biſhop of London, and accuſed of certayne articles to the number of ſix, tendinge partly to ſedition and partly to open hereſie: as for example, the firſt was that he had read, taught, preached, publiſhed, and obſtinately defended; *that payinge of tithes, vvas neuer ordayned by God, but by couetuouſnes of Prieſts.* Which was a ſpeciall article of * *VVickliffe* to make Prieſts odious, as before hath bin ſhewed. The ſecond article was, *that Biſhopps and Prieſts be the ſcribes and pharaſees, that crucyfied Chriſt, &c.* The third, that one *Ioane Baker* abiured of many great hereſies a little before, *vvas wrongefully puniſhed by the Biſhop, for her opinions, vvhich he himſelfe* (to witt *Richard Hunne*) *offered to defend, &c.*

11. Vpon theſe articles & ſome other, partly denyed by *Hunne,* and partly confeſſed & ſubmiſſion offered for them, he was commytted priſoner to *Lollards Towar*; & there ſome dayes after found dead hanginge vpon a ſtaple of Iron, in his owne girdle of ſilke, and herevpon a roſe a great queſtion, whether *Hunne* had hanged himſelfe for feare of future iudgement and puniſhment (eſpecially hauinge a booke of his taken by the Biſhopp, which had both theſe and more odious hereſies in yt, as after ſhalbe ſhewed) or vvhether he vvas made
away

away by the procurement of him, that had the
cheefe commandement ouer that prifon,
which was an old aged man named *D. Horfey*
the B. of London his Chancelor. In which
controuerfie, *Iohn Fox* will needs haue yt
that he was murdered, and confequently alfo
martyred. And for proofe therof he dilateth
himfelfe exceedingely, and alleageth diuers
coniecturall reafons fett downe, as he faith,
by fome of the crowners queft in thofe dayes,
who went vp, and found the body hanginge,
as namely for that his countenance was faire,
his head combed, his cap ftanding right on his
head, his necke leaninge to one fide as broken,
his eyes clofed, the ftoole ftandinge by vpon a
bolfter, and fome other like probabilityes,
whervpon the faid crowners queft, being
fimple men (as yt feemeth) were induced to
thinke, that yt was not fo likely that *Hunne*
had hanged himfelfe altogeather by himfelfe,
but that he had fome other help. And this in
effect is faid on *Iohn Fox* his fide, with diuers
other allegations of examinations, letters, and
wrytings tendinge to that purpofe.

Allegatiōs of Fox for Hunnes murder.

12. But on the other fide, *Syr Thomas More*
firft, and then againe *Alanus Copus* handling the
matter; the former againft *Tyndall*, the fecond
againft *Iohn Fox* himfelfe, who in his firft edition of his *Acts and Monuments* had fet forth this
Hunne for a very principall Martyr of his
Church, for that he was one of the firft that
held new doctrines vnder K. Henry the 8.
Yea a double martyr (faith Fox) *for that he died both*

Syr Tho. More and Alanus Copus de-fend that Hun flevv himfelfe.

S 4   *for*

for religion and Iustice togeather: Syr *Thomas More,*
I say, who liued in those very dayes when the
fact fell out, sheweth great authority and arguments to the contrary, which after yow
shall heare. But *Alanus Copus* taketh vpon him
to shew two things: First that the death of
this *Hunne*, being very doubtfull for the causes
which after shall appeare, yt is much more
probable that he made himselfe away, for
auoydinge greater punishment; then that any
of the B. of Londons people should do yt,
especially *Doctor Horsey* his Chancelor, slaunde-
red therwith by Fox, and other heretiks. The
second point is, that albeit yt could be proued, that he had suffered some violence in prison by the hands of some priuate men (as
shalbe proued that he did not) yet could not
that iustly be called martyrdome, no more
then they are properly martyrs, that are slayne
by theeues on the high way, but chiefly for
that *Hunne* was giulty of many vile hereticall
doctrines also, which Fox himselfe will scarse
hold for tolerable, as after shall appeare. And
these are the two points which the said *Alanus
Copus* doth verify.

13.   And for proofe of the first point he beginneth with the argument of *Cassius, Cui bono?*
what commodity could the Bishops Chancelor or any other Catholike officer expect by
committinge so foule a murder vpon *Hunnes*
person? For as for his goods, they were all
cōfiscate to the K., so as they, nor any of them
could receaue any profit thereby; as on the
con-

Alan. Cop. dial. 6. pag. 114.

The first proofe of Alanus Copus.

contrary also no hurt or losse by his life. Neyther is yt so much as pretended by the aduersary, that he had any secretts to vtter against
any of the Cleargy, wherby they should seeke
to take away his life by so great iniustice. But
yow will say perhaps, that yt was hatred, and
reuenge that moued them, for that he had endeauoured to gett out *a premunire* against a
Priest, that had sued him in the Archbishops
Court for a mortuary, which *Hunne* pretended should haue byn donne in the K. Court.
This *Alanus* proueth to be vayne, for that the
temporall iudges hauing sitten vpon the case,
had determyned, that yt belonged to the same
Archbishops Court, which was thought no
small cause of *Hunnes* desperation also, & indu-
ctiõ to this wicked fact, for that he saw himselfe abandoned by that iudiciall sentence, of
all hope of reuenge which he had threatened.
14. And besides this, yf the Bishopp, and his
officers had had so great hatred & desire of reuenge against *Hunne*, they had the occasion in
their hands, which was to burne him for heresie, yf he had lyued; For that besides the former six articles which he had in substance acknowledged (though in some he had denyed
the manner of vtteringe them) *he had collected
13. more out of the prologue* (saith Fox) *of his English
Bible*, remayning in the Bishops hands: wherof the fifth is; *that poore men and idiotts haue the
truth of the scriptures, more then a thousand Prelats,
religions men, and Clarks of the schooles*. The eleuenth was; *that the very body of Christ is not in the*

Fox *pag.*
738.

Sacrament

Sacrament of the Altar. The 12. *that he damned the vniuersity of Oxford vvith all degrees and facultyes in yt, &c.* Vpon which articles & other proofes, the said *Richard Hunne* after his death was condemned publikely of heresy, by a iudiciall sentence of the Bishops of *London, Durham* & *Cales,* & thervpon accordinge to Ecclesiasticall cannons, his body was commaunded to be deliuered to the fire. For feare of which sentence in his life, and for greeife that he could not preuayle in his sute of *Premunire* against the parish Priest, that sued him for a buryingesheete or mortuary for his sonne, yt is presumed that he tooke that desperate course by help of the diuell to hang himselfe.

Nevv hereticall articles against Hunne.

15. And yet for that he was welthy, and had a daughter marryed to one *VValpole* a marchant in London, that was of some power in the citty, and the most of his kinred and acquaintance being thought to be somewhat infected by him also with Wickliffian heresies (as diuers also of the Crowners Quest were suspected to be) they made a great clamour about his death both in the citty & court, for which cause the King did diuers tymes (saith *Syr Thomas More*) commaund the same to be examined, himselfe sometymes being present; And finally after all examinations made both by law and otherwise, the K. Attorney generall, gaue sentence for the acquitting of *Doctor Horsey* and others, that had byn called into suspition for the same, which* Fox also confesseth, but saith yt was vpon fauour and sollicitation,

Hunnes frends suspected of heresy.

p.741.

tion. But none setteth downe the matter more substantially then *Syr Thomas More* himselfe, who was present, and then a Counselour, and therfore yt is reason we should heare him. Wherfore he being asked of his frend (as in his dialogue he wryteth) whether he knew *Hunnes* matter well, or noe, he answereth thus:

Syr Tho. Mores relation of Hunne, *lib.*3.*dial. cap.*15. *pag.*235.

,, Forsooth (quoth I) so well I know yt from
,, top to toe, that I suppose there be not very
,, many men that know yt much better, for I
,, haue not only byn diuers tymes present my
,, selfe at certaine examinations therof, but haue
,, also many tymes sunderly talked with almost
,, all such, except the dead man himselfe, as most
,, knew of the matter, which matter was many
,, tymes in sundry places examined, but special-
,, ly at *Baynards Castle* one day at great length,
,, euery man being sent for, that could tell any
,, thinge about the same. And this examination
,, was before diuers great Lords both spirituall
,, and temporall, and others of the Kings Coun-
,, sell, &c. I was present also at the iudgement
,, giuen in Paules, whervpon his books and bo-
,, dy were burned, &c.

16. Thus farre *Syr Thomas More*, addinge further, that hauinge vsed great diligence to
search out the same; could neuer find but that
Hunne made himselfe away, and that the partyes were guiltles, that were odiously slaun-
dered therwith. Which only testimony of *Syr
Thomas More*, made vpon his owne knowledge
he being the man he was both in learninge,
iudgement and tender conscience, and liuinge

The authority of Syr Tho. More.

in that tyme, place, and dignity, wherby he
might eafily informe himfelfe, is, and ought
to be of more credit with euery difcreet man,
then a hundred of Fox his tales, made vpon
coniecturall reafons only. But howfoeuer
this matter was, for the manner of his death,
certayne yt is, that he could not be a Martyr
of Fox his Church, as *Alanus Copus* well proueth; partly for that he côfeffeth in this place,

peg. 743.　that *in moft points, Hunne was a Papift, heard maffe,
and vfed his beads in the prifon*; partly alfo for that
diuers of thofe hereticall articles, wherin he
differed from vs, and was condemned by vs
(as before yow haue heard) do not agree with
the doctrine of Fox his Church at this day.
In which refpect he wryteth in the margent
of his text thus: *Hunne no full Proteftant.* So as
euery way, this our Fox fheweth himfelfe a
fimple fellow, in makinge fo great accompt of
this Martyr, whome yet he graunted not to
haue byn fully of his religion. Perhaps he may
be at the full moone. And fo much of him.

17. Next vnto *Richard Hunne*, commeth in

*Io. Tevv-
exbury
leather-
fellnr.*　*Iohn Tewexbury* martyr, a leather-feller of
London vnder King Henry the eyght, who
being infected with readinge certayne feditious books of *Tyndall*, efpecially that which
he intituled: *The wicked mammon* (vvhich
booke conteyned nothinge in effect, but an
odious inuective againft Bifhops and Prelates
of the Church) grew to be fo willfull and obftinate, in likinge and approuinge therof, as
being called before *Tonftall* B. of London, and
brought

brought into open confiftory about the fame,
he offered to defend all points of doctrine
therin held, as yf yt had byn the ghofpell.
Whervpon he was examined of diuers particular articles therin cōteyned, as for example:
That the diuell holdeth our harts fo hard, that it is im-
poßible to confent to Gods law. Whervnto he anfwered (faith Fox) *that he found no fault in yt.*
Another article was; *that* Peter, *and* Paul; *and*
other Saints, that be dead, are not our frends, but their
frends, whome they did help, when they were aliue. To
that he faid alfo, *that he found no yll in it*. Another was, *that euery one is Lord of what foeuer ano-*
ther man hath. To that he anfwered (faith Fox)
what law can be better then that? Another article
was, *that the Iewes of good intent and zeale, put*
Chriſt *to death*: To that he anfwered: *That yt is*
true, and the text is playne inough for yt, &c.
18.   Thefe and fuch like were his anfwers to
diuers propofitions, taken out of that mifche-
uous booke of *VVicked Mammon.* And he being
at fundry appearances gently and charitably
exhorted by the Bifhopp, that for fo much as
he was a fimple and vnlearned man, he fhould
not ftand fo ftiffely, in peculiar opinions; but
he would not harken thervnto, a long tyme,
which greatly contenteth Iohn Fox, who
wryteth thus vauntingly of this Martyr: *In all*
points of religion, he openly did difpute in the Bifhopps
Chappell and pallace, and rvas fo expert and prompt in
his anfivers, as Tonſtall, *and all his learned men vvere*
afhamed that a leather-feller fhould fo difpute vvith
them, vvith fuch power of the fcriptures and hea-
                                                uenly

Fox *pag:*
935.

Tyndalls
opinions
allovved
by the le-
ther-feller
as alfo by
Fox.

Fox *pag:*
934.

uenly vvifdome, that they vvere not able to refift him, &c.

19.　Thus wryteth Fox of the ftoutneffe of his Martyrs for 2. or 3. of the firft fefsions, approuinge (as yow fee) his hereticall doctrine, as well for the community of all things with the Anabaptifts, as other blafphemyes before noted, to haue proceeded from the heauenly wifdome of God. *But* (faith he) *in the next fefsion, he fubmitted himfeife, and abiured his opinions vpon the eyght of May* 1529. *and vvas inioyned pennance of bearinge faggots, &c. Notwithflandinge the fame Iohn Tewexbury after two yeares confirmed by the grace of God, and moued by the example of Bayfield aforefaid, that vvas burned in Smithfield, did returne, and being apprehended againe, vvas condemned and burned alfo in Smithfield, &c.*

Fox ibid.

20.　And this is the ftory of *Iohn Tewexbury* the leather-feller; to whome Fox adioyneth two Confeffors, *Iames Gore* that dyed in the prifon of *Colchefter, for the right and truth* (faith he) *of Gods word*; and *VVilliam VVifeman* clothmaker of London, that diceaffed, in *Lollards Tower,* and was buryed in the fields. And from thefe Fox paffeth to his rubricate Martyr *Iohn Philpott* preacher, of whome now we muft alfo fpeake in order, though with much breuity in refpect of the tedious prolixity vfed therin by him.

Iames Gore.
Fox pag.
1629. &
1630.
VVilliam
VVifemā.

21.　Firft then this *Iohn Philpott* was a gentleman borne of Worfhipfull houfe in *Hampfhire,* & afterwards brought vp in ftudy of the *Cyuill* law in new Colledge in *Oxford,* for the fpace of

The ftory
of Iohn
Philpott
burned for
herefie.

of 6. or 7. yeares, where Fox noteth that he
gaue himselfe to the study of tongues, especially to the Hebreue tongue, which he being a
lawyer doth well shew, that euen then he
was touched with some humor of new fancyes, the Hebreue tongue being litle needfull
to that profession. Afterward he trauayled
into *Italy*, and *Rome*, & returning home Priest,
got the aduouson of the Archdeacon-shipp of
Vvinchester through *B. Gardeners* fauour, by vertue wherof he gott also at length the present-
ment, when yt fell voyd vnder *Doctor Poynett*,
who in *K. Edwards* dayes was intruded in *Gardeners* place, that was depriued by *Cranmer* and
Ridley. In which depriuation, this *Philpott* also
was a wittnesse & agent against *Gardener*, and
reiected by him as more then halfe franticke
or madd, or (to vse his phrase) *altered in his wits*:
which humor was discouered in him diuers
wayes, not only during the tyme of *K. Edwards*
raigne, but also by his furious and phantasticall behauiour in the conuocation-house in
the beginninge of *Q. Maryes* raigne, wherof
yow shall heare more particulars afterward in
the *Re-vew* of the ten disputations: for that
matters of religion being referred by *Q. Mary* to the said conuocation-house to be discussed first amonge themselues and the Ecclesiasticall persons, being the same yet that had
byn in dignity vnder *K. Edward*, except some
two or three that had byn committed before
vpon speciall causes; they all subscribed vnto
the Catholike articles proposed, and namely
the

the *reall presence, Transubstantiation*, and the *sacrifice of the masse*, except fiue or six, to witt *Phillips* deane of *Rochester, Haddon* deane of *Exceter, Philpott* Archdeacon of *VVinchester, Cheyney* Archdeacon of *Herford, Elmer* Archdeacon of *Stow*, and one other (saith Fox) but what he was he declareth not.

Fox *pag.*
1282.

22.   These halfe dozen then had licence to propose their doubts & arguments, & so they did for fiue or six dayes togeather, some Catholike man being alwayes appointed *ex tempore* to answere them, as *Doctor VVatson, Doctor Morgan, Doctor Moreman* and others ; the prolocutor being *Doctor VVeston* : but when the Catholiks would haue had them to aunswere againe in their turnes, accordinge to promise, yt was * refused by them ; but as for *Iohn Philpott*, of whome the story is, he behaued himselfe so intemperatly, or rather impotently, in that assembly, as oftentymes by the prolocutor he was said to be fitter for bedlam, then for disputatiõ. Among other things he made this Protestation there publiquely, *that in the Sacrament of the Altar* Christ is not present in any wise : *and this his sayinge* (saith Fox) *he offered to proue before the vvhole house, yf they listed to call him therevnto, yea before the Queens grace and her Counsell: and before the face of six of the best learned men of the house of the contrary opinions and refused none; and yf I shall not be able* (quoth he) *to mayntaine by Gods vvord that I haue said, and confound those six vvhich shall take vpon them to vvithstand me in this point, lett me be burned vvith as many faggotts as be in London before*

Theoppositions of six Protestants in the connuocation house, being the 28. of Septembre 1553.

Fox * *pag.*
1288.

Fox *pag.*
1289.

before the court gates; *and this he vttered* (said Fox) *vvith great vehemency of spirite:* but yt was indeed with great vehemency of folly or rather fury, for he was not the best learned amonge them, though perhaps, the lightest witted; and his fond assertion ioyned vvith his ridiculous vaunt, doth make the thinge more manifest; for that none of his fellowes will hold commonly and in plaine words, that Christ is not any wayes present in the *Sacrament*: nay most of them to delude the people, and to auoyde the cleare testimonyes of the ancient Fathers will graunt in words, that his body and bloud are there *truly, substantially, naturally*, yea the very same body that he tooke of the virgin *Mary*, the very same blood that was shedd vpon the Crosse, as yow shall see oftentymes and ordinarily graunted by *Cranmer*, *Ridley* and *Latymer* in their disputatiōs, which we shall set foorth in the end of this booke especially in the fifth Chapter, of the ensuinge *re-viewe*, where they answere the Fathers, and else where: and for example doe yow heare one place only of *Ridley* in his last examination before the Bishop of *Lincolne*: *both yow & I* (saith he) *doe agree herein, that in the Sacrament is the very, true, and naturall body and blood of Christ, euen that which was borne of the virgin Mary, vvhich ascended into heauen, &c. Only vve differ in modo, in the vvay and manner of being, vve confesse all one thinge to be in the Sacrament, and dissent in the manner of being there, &c.*

23. Thus he, which is a farr different thinge from that which *Philpott* auerreth, that *Christ is*

Philpotts desperate protestation.

Fox *pag*. 1598. The disagreing of heretikes about Christs being in the Sacrament.

T

no wise present in the Sacrament. And Fox himselfe, that allwayes conformeth his assertion

See before
in the in-
troductiō.

with those hereticall opinions which for the
present he relateth, affirmed before, as yow
haue heard, that Christ is present in the Sacrament, neyther *spiritually nor corporally*; but heere
to conforme himselfe to *Ridley* saith the quite
contrary, makinge this note in the margin;
*Papists and Protestants in grauntinge the presence doe
agree; only in the manner of being they differ*: Which
yf yt be true then we ar agreed indeed, for all
our controuersie is about the thinge yt selfe,
to witt, whether the true body of Christ, the
same which is in heauen, be truly & substantially in the *Sacrament*; and as for the manner,
we graunt also that yt is a spirituall and Sacramentall manner of being there, farre different
from that of Christs being in heauen, but yet
the selfe same *true, reall & naturall* body; which
yf *Fox* and *Ridley* do graunt heere truly, as in
found of words they professe; then are we
agreed indeed; and then, what needed *Ridley*
to haue gone to the fyre for this article, as he
did; or what reason had *Philpott* to follow him
therin, yf after they agreed in one opinion? or
yf they were not (as by their words and con-

Philpotts
braggin
the Con-
uocation
house.

trary assertions may appeare, the one holding
Christ to be present truely, substantially and
naturally; the other in no wise at all) then
how madd a vaunt was this, that e would
confound by Gods word six of the learnedest
men of the Conuocation-house, that should
oppose themselues against his assertion?

                                                        amongst

amongſt which ſix , *Ridley* muſt be one as yow
ſee, and Fox an other ; and when they of the
conuocation-houſe laughed at this his folly,
he fell downe vpon his knees, cryed out, and
wept, which was after obiected vnto him in
his examinatiõs for a point of madnes, though
Fox indeuour to excuſe the matter ſayinge; *he* Fox pag.
fell into an exclamation, caſtinge vp his eyes towards 1285.
heauen, and ſaid: o Lord vvhat a vvorld is this, that the
truth of thy holy word may not be ſpoken , and abidden
by, & for very ſorrow & he auineſſe the teares trickled
out of his eyes. So Fox , but himſelfe excuſeth
the matter otherwiſe afterward in his ſaid
examinations, ſayinge *that he vvept vpon them, as* Fox pag.
Chriſt did vpon Hieruſalem, Scribes and Phariſees. 1658.
24. And no leſſe diſtractedly, or rather furi-
ouſly, did he behaue himſelfe in his conferences afterwards, & examinations with the
Biſhopps, eſpecially in that vpon *S. Andrewes*
day in the B. of Londons gallery, fiue Biſhops
being preſent, and 9. or 10. Doctors and learned men beſides, where conferringe with *Do-*
ctor Morgan , that ieſted ſomewhat at the aſſurance of his particular ſpirite, wherof he had
vaunted exceedingly , *Philpott* fell into plaine
fury, ſo as *Doctor Morgan* ſayinge: *yow rage now*; Fox pag.
Philpott replyed , *thy fooliſh blaſphemyes haue* 1653.
compelled the ſpirite of God; *vvhich is in me, to*
ſpeake that vvhich I haue ſaid vnto thee , thou enemy „
of all righteouſnes. Morgan. Why doe yow iudge „
me ſo? *Philpott*; by thine owne wicked words „
I iudge thee : thou blynd and blaſphemous „
Doctor, *&c.* and againe a litle after; *I tell thee* „

plaine, thou art not able to answere that spirite of truth
vvhich speaketh vvithin me, for defence of Christs true
religion: I am able by the might therof, to driue thee
round about this gallery before me. And yf yt will please
the Q. Maiestie to heare thee and me, I vvill make thee
for shame to shrink behind the dore. Thus he; and
by this yow may know the mans veyne.

25. Fox setteth downe 14. seuerall examinations or conferences had with him, partly before particular commissioners, partly with
the B. of London, and other learned men,
partly before the Lords of the Councell, partly before many Bishops togeather, and this
both in priuate and publike, besides many
other conferences, which Fox affirmeth not
to haue byn wrytten. All which paine and
trauell was taken (no doubt) with him, in respect of his worshippfull parentage, whereby
he was of kynne also to diuers of the Councell, as namely to the *Lord Riche*; who being
present at his sixth examination, tooke great
compassion of him to see so fond and willfull
a humor ouer-rule him; in so much as hauing
heard *Philpott* to make a large discourse of his
Church, different from the *Roman*; and perce-
auinge that after all was said and done, he and
his would rest vpon their owne particular
spiritts and iudgements, for triall of the true
Church; the said *Lord Riche* aunswered in
these words.

26. *Rich.* All heretiks doe boast of the spiritt of God, and euery man would haue a
,, Church by himselfe, as *Ioane of Kent* (burned of
late

late in *K. Edwards* dayes) whome I had my
felfe for a fennight in my houfe, after the
wryte was out, for her to be burned; where
my Lord of Canterbury (*Cranmer*) & *B. Ridley,*
reforted almoft dayly vnto her: But fhee was
fo high in the fpirit, as they could doe nothing
with her, for all their learninge, but fhe went
willfully to the fire, as yow do now.

Speaches
betvveene
the *Lord
Rich.* and
Philpott re-
lated by
Fox.

Philpott. As for *Ioane of Kent,* fhe was a vaine
woman, I knew her well, and fuch vaine fpiritts be foone knowne from the true fpiritt of
God; for that the fame abideth within the limitts of Gods word, nor ftubbernely main-
tayneth any thinge contrary to the word, as I
haue Gods word throughly on my fide, *&c.*

Rich. By whome will ye be iudged? yow
demaunded euen now ten learned men of the
realme to deale with yow: what yf meanes be
made to the Queene that yow may haue your
requeft: will yow promife to abide their
iudgement?

Philpott. I will make your honors iudges
that fhalbe hearers of vs.

Rich. Yea, but will yow promife to agree
to their iudgement.

Philpott. There be caufes wherfore I may
not fo doe, vnleffe I be fure they will iudge
according to the word of God.

Rich. Oh, I perceaue yow will haue no man
iudge but your felfe, *&c.*

27. Thus they went on, as Fox relateth.
And by this litle taft, yow may imagine, how
all or the moft part of the tyme was fpent in
thofe

T 3

those large & many examinations with those
kynd of men; which Acts notwithstandinge,
ar not sett forth accordinge to the Originall
in the Bishops Registers, as Fox heere confesseth. For he saith, *that they ar but slenderly handled*
therin , especially in behalfe of the answeres. So that
yow must thinke , that all these conferences,
are sett downe by Fox , accordinge as *Philpott*
did wryte them with his owne hand ; who
we may be assured, would not giue the worst
part to himselfe, nor the victory to his aduersaryes. And this is the creditt of most of these
large relations found in Fox , that they were
wrytten by the partyes, who had most interest
to lye, as before yow haue heard in diuerse
narrations, aswell of *Maundrell* the Cowheard,
Allerton the Taylor , *Fortune* the Black-smyth;
and others that wryte their owne triumphes.

28.   Well then, after all conferences, examinations, exhortations, instructions , persuasions, and the like in vaine vsed; *B. Bonner* was
forced to giue sentence against this man. And
therefore comminge forth in publike consistory at *S. Paules*, vpon the 13. day of December
anno 1557. hauing first obiected diuers articles
of heresie vnto *Philpott*, two were, that he had
blasphemously spoken against the sacrifice of
the masse, and *reall presence* of Christs body in
the same. Wherunto *Philpotts* aunswere (saith
Fox) in the register is this: *That as touchinge the*
sacrifice of the masse, and Sacrament of the Altar, I ne-
uer spake against the same. Vpon which words
Fox maketh this note in the margent. *Heere*
eyther

pag. 1658.

Philpotts
ansvvere
qualified
by Fox.
*pag.*1658.

*eyther the regifter belyeth Maifter Philpott, or els he
meant, as not offendinge the law, therby to be accufed, &c.*

29. Thus patcheth vp matters Iohn Fox, and after few words he concludeth thus: *Bon-* Fox ibid.
*ner then not able vvith all his learned Doctors to fatisfie
him* (M. Philpott) *fell to perfuadinge of him, &c.*
But *Philpott* anfwered: *yow, and all other of your
fort are hypocrytes, and I vvould all the vvorld did
know your hipocrifie, your Tyranny, ignorance, and
idolatry, &c.* Yow fee heere this vncharitable
anfwere, vnto the charitable perfuafion of the
Bifhopp. And yet further, a little after in his
laft examination, he faid aloud before the
people, anfwering to the Bifhopp and his af-
fiftants in iudgement feat: *God faue vs from fuch* Philpotts
hypocrits, that would haue things in a tongue that men rayling v-
do not vnderftand. pon the
Bifhopps.

Bifhop. VVhome do yow meane?

*Philp. Yow, and all others, that be of your genera-
tion and fect, &c.* And then turning him to the
people, he further faid: *Oh all ye gentlemen, beware of thefe men and all their doings, &c.*

Lond. and others Bifhopps. VVith vvhat can ye „
charge vs? „

Philp. Yow are enemyes to all truth, and all your „
doings be naught, and full of Idolatry, fauinge the ar- „
ticles of the Trinity, &c. Thus farre Fox. „

30. And after all this, and much more iniury
receaued from him in wordsʳ, the Bifhopps
made him a new large exhortation, which
Fox alfo fetteth downe; but yt auayled nothinge; for he being in a furious veyne of rai-

T 4   linge

linge and blaspheminge, rendered nothinge
but contumelious auntwers; as when the Bishopps, which were *London, Bath, VVorcester* and
Lichfield, asked him againe about the Sacramēt
of the Altar, he answered: *Yf ye call yt the Sacra-*
ment of the Altar in respect of the Altar stone (vpon
which yt is offered) *then I defy your Christ, for*
that it is a rotten Christ, &c. Behold this miserable blasphemous tongue, & what could the
Bishops doe with such a tongue, but burne yt?
And then (saith Fox) after other particular
matters brought forth against him, especially
after the comminge in of the *Lord Mayor, the*
Bishopps vvaxinge now vveary, &c. fell by fayre and
flatteringe speach to persuade with him, &c. Thus
much confesseth Fox, and yet complayneth of
cruelty against him, for that after all, they
condemned him to be burned. And thus much
of him.

31.   In the next place after *Philpott*, do follow
two other Foxian Martyrs, *Iohn Rough* and
Margarett Mering, burned togeather at one stake
in Smithfield. *Iohn Rough* was a Dominican
friar of Scotland, who runninge from thence
into England in the beginninge of K. *Edwards*
dayes, tooke a woman for his wife named *Ka-*
therine, (for this is alwayes their beginninge as
often I haue noted) and procured himselfe a
benefice neere vnto *Hull* in Yorkeshire: but after Q. Mary was entred, he fled out of England into *Frizeland*, & there with his woman
became a knytter of cappes, and when yarne
fayled them (saith Fox) and other necessaryes
    for

Fox ibid.

Io. Rough
a Scottish
minister.

Fox pag.
1640.

for their occupation, they returned both into
England againe, and learninge out that there
was a fecrett congregation of Proteftant brethren and fifters in London, he gatt to be minifter therof, as before we haue * fhewed in
the ftory of *Simpfon*, that was deacon of the
faid congregation. Where alfo we haue made
mention of a certaine vifion that *Rough* had by
night, of the faid *Simpfons* apprehenfion, whervpon he cryed out twife to his vvoman; *Kate,
Kate, my brother Simpfon is gone, ftrike fiar and gett
vp:* but himfelfe being foone afterward taken
at Ifflington, vvhere the congregation fhould
meete, he vvas brought before the Councell,
and by them remitted to the Bifhopp of London, to be proceeded againft accordinge to
forme of law in cafe of herefie. For which, after diuers examinations, he vvas condemned
and burned in Smithfield togeather with the
forfaid *Margaret Meringe*, a poore bufy pratling
vvoman of London, and fifter of the fame
congregation; of vvhome Iohn Fox vvryteth thus:

32.　*Maifter Rough* being cheefe paftor to the
congregation (of vvhich *Margaret Meringe* vvas
one) did not vvell like the faid *Margarett*, as
fomewhat to bufy, *&c.* Now vvhat they faw
or vnderftood further in her, we know not,
but this followed: *Maifter Rough*, the friday before he vvas taken, in the open face of the
congregation did excommunicate her, out of ,,
the fame company, and fo feemed vvith the ,,
reft, to exclude and cutt her of from their fel- ,,

lowfhipp

*19. *Matth
cap. 7.*

Margarett
Meringe
excõmu-
nicated
by Rough
the mini-
fter.
Fox *pag.*
1842.

,, lowſhipp and ſociety; vvherat ſhe being mo-
,, ued, did not vvell take yt, nor in good part,
,, but thought her ſelfe not indifferétly handled
,, amonge them. Whervpon, to one of her
,, frends in a heate ſhe threatened to remoue
,, them all, but the prouidence of God was
,, otherwiſe, &c. Lo heere the fallinge out betweene the paſtor, and the ſheepe, and how
B. Bonner made the attonemet betweene them
afterward, by burning them both at one ſtake.
For *Margaret* was as froward in matters of religion towards the ſaid Biſhopp, as ſhe had
byn in points of diſcipline towards her *Rough*
miniſter, that excommunicated her. For ſhe
auouched before *B. Bonner* (as Fox recordeth)
that the maſſe was abhominable before the ſight of God,
Ibid. col. 2. *and before the ſight of true Chriſtian people; that yt is*
the playne cupp of fornication, and the vvhore of Baby-
lon. And that as for the Sacrament of the Altar; *ſhe beleeued there was no ſuch Sacrament, in the*
The inſo- *Catholike Church, and that ſhe vtterly abhorred the*
lency and *authority of the Biſhopp of Rome, vvith all the Religion*
obſtinacy *obſerued in the ſame Antichriſts Church, &c.* And
of Marga- then being demaunded (ſaith Fox) yf ſhe
ret Me- would ſtand to theſe her aunſwers, ſhe ſaid:
ſing. *I vvill ſtand to them vnto the death: for the very Angells*
of heauen do laugh yow to ſcorne; to ſee the abhomina-
tion, that yow vſe in the Church, &c. And with this
ſhe went to the fyre. And what would yow
do to ſuch willfull people as theſe? or vpon
See Stovv what ground of knowledge could this madd
an. 4. & 5. obſtinacy be founded? but only vpon ſelfe-
Edvvardi will, as in the Anabaptiſts, *Ioane of Kent, George*
ſaxti. *Paris,*

Paris, and the like, burned by the Proteſtants
themſelues. Wherefore let theſe people go
into their place.

33.   Next vnto theſe Martyrs, Fox ſetteth vs
downe a ranke of halfe a dozen Confeſſors
togeather, that occupy ſix ſeuerall dayes in his
Calendar. The firſt three are *Thomas Tyler, Ma-*
thew VVithers, and *Iohn Dale,* all poore Crafteſmen, that were in trouble for the new ghoſpell vnder Q. Mary, vpon the yeare 1558. yet
about the firſt two, Fox wryteth no ſtory or
declaration in his Monuments that I can find,
but of the third, which is *Iohn Dale,* he ſheweth
how that for a ſpitefull raylinge ſpeech made
publikely againſt the parſon of *Hadley* his paſtor, named *Maiſter Newell,* in the Church, and
that openly, and in tyme of diuyne ſeruice, he
was put into the common cage of the towne
for three or foure dayes, and afterward ſent
by *Iuſtice Moyle* to the goale of *Bury,* where he
died, and therby was made a Confeſſor.

34.   The other three were *Iohn Glouer, VVilliam*
Playne and *Elizabeth Lawſon,* who, for their impriſonment only for new opinions, are preferred heere by Fox to the dignity of Calendar-
ſaints and Confeſſors. The firſt was impriſoned at *Lichfield* and *Couentry:* the ſecond in
London, the third at *Bedfield* in Suffolke. And
now how many Catholike Calendars vve
might fill vp with people, that haue byn
troubled and impriſoned for Catholike Religion only vnder the gouerment of the laſt
Queene, euery man may conſider, yf vve
                                          would

Thomas
Tyler
Matth.
VVithers
Io. Dale.

I. Glouer.
VVilliam
Playne.
Elizabeth
Lavvſon.

Fox *pag.*
1556.1927
1877.

vvould vvryte Acts and Monuments, as Fox hath done.

35.   Neyther are his Martyrs, vvhich presently to thefe he adioyneth, of much more confideration, to witt *Nicolas Burton* an Englifh marchant burned in *Syuill* of Spayne for Zwinglian opinions, vpon the yeare 1562. and *Thomas Rhedon* a french Carmelite friar (though Fox make him an Earle in his Calendar) burned at *Rome* for Wickliffian herefies, aboue a hundred & twenty yeares before that againe, to witt *anno Domini* 1436. duringe the raigne of *K. Henry* the fixt of England, though of each of thefe Martyrs, Fox fetteth forth a pittifull painted pagent of their burninge and hard handlinge. The marchant (he faith) was taken in *Cadiz* by a familiar of the Inquifition, caft into prifon, and after 14. dayes fent to *Syuill*: But *in the meane fpace, he fo inftructed* (faith Fox) *the poore Spanish prifoners in the word of God, that in fhort fpace he had vvell reclaymed fundry of them, &c.* For vvhich he vvas afterward condemned and burned in *Syuill*, as he had vvell deferued, yf he vvent about to infect vvith herefie, the inhabitants of that moft Catholike countrey and citty. Though Fox his tale of his *inftructinge the prifoners vvith the word of God*, hath no probability: For that fuch as are in prifon for fufpition of herefie in thofe countreyes, are not fuffered to conuerfe with other prifoners, as Fox imagineth, as it vvas permitted in Q. Maryes tyme in England, vvherof vve fhall haue occafion to fpeake more afterward

ward in the 17. Chapter of this Treatise. And
so much of *Burton.*

36. As for the Carmelite friar, *Rhedonensis,*
(whome Fox in his Calendar calleth Earle;
but it may be, it was of error, & that it should
haue byn left to the other followinge, which
is *Iohn Picus* Earle of *Mirandula*) he telleth vs,
that he goinge into Italy, and carryinge vvith
him diuers books of *Iohn VVickliffe, Iohn Husse,*
and the like, thinkinge to reforme the friars of
his order there, he was by them accused to
the Inquisition of *Rome,* and there after conuiction he was finally degraded and burned.
Neyther are there any particularityes vvhich
are vvorth the notinge in this behalfe. But
now hauinge considered further, I find that
Fox hath put this man twise into his Calender, both tymes vnder one yeare, to witt 1436.
and therfore in this place I meane to leaue
him out, especially for that the foolish madd
fellow hath made such an embrullery betweene his Saints and Catholike Saints in
this moneth, as that, except vve accommodate
the matter amonge them, they cannot stand
togeather, no, not the natiuity of Christ yt
selfe, nor *Saint Stephen, Saint Iohn Euangelist,* nor
Saint Thomas the Apostle can haue their due
places, as before vve haue shewed more largely in the beginninge of this Chapter.

Thomas
Rhedo-
nensis a
French
Carmelite
friar bur-
ned at
Rome
anno 1436.

The

The second part of this moneth, contey-
ninge seauen singular Confessors.

§. 2.

37. Wherfore to draw to an end of this moneth and of the whole yeare, Iohn Fox assigneth vs for the last seauen dayes, seauen sea-
uerall Confessors and Saints to furnish the
same, which yf we consider them well, we
shall scarce find any one of them all to agree
with his fellow, or with Fox himselfe in all
points of Religion. Their names are, *Picus*
Earle of *Mirandula* an Italian; *Erasmus Roteroda-*
mus a Flemminge; *Martyn Bucer, Paulus Phagius,*
and *Philipp Melanchthon* Germans: *Peter Martyr*
an Italian, and *K. Edward* the sixt of England.
Of vvhome breifly vve shall speake in order.

The story And as for *Iohn Picus* Earle of *Mirandula*, yt is
of I. Picus strange madnesse in Fox to bring him in for a
Earle of Saint of his Church, being a man in all points
Mirādula. so opposite vnto his Religion, as any man
lightly that liued in his tyme; nor can I imagine, why the madd fellow should draw him
vnto his Calenlar, except yt were for that he
was a great frend of Friar *Hieronymus Sauonarola*
* 3. May. of Florence, whome before * yow haue heard
cap. 9. treated of, and haue seene him taken out of
Fox his Calendar againe; and the like shall
yow now heere of this *Picus Mirandula*, of
whome (though Fox make him a Confessor
of

of his Church in the Calendar) yet comming
to his hiſtory of Acts and Monuments, I do
not find any ſufficient narratiō made by him,
of the Acts and Geſts of this *Picus*; but only Fox *pag.*
that he nameth him amongſt other learned 670.
men of his tyme, in the beginninge of the
raigne of K. *Henry* the 7. But on the other ſide,
there are againſt Fox, to proue him a foole in
this point, many arguments. Firſt the life of Syr Tho-
the ſaid *Picus* wrytten in Engliſh at large by mas More
Syr Thomas More, in the beginning of his works; of Picus
vvhich doth ſhew him in all things to haue Mirādula.
byn a Catholike,

28. There is another life alſo of the ſame
man, vvrytten in Latyn by *Franciſcus Picus*
nephew to the ſaid *Iohn Picus*, vvherein the
ſame thinge is moſt euidently proued, and
that amongeſt other points, he declareth,
that this Earle *Iohn Picus*, had a purpoſe
(yf he had liued) to haue wrytten a great
worke againſt all hereſies and heretiks, that
haue rebelled againſt the Roman Catholike *Franc. Picus*
Church, from the beginning of Chriſtian Re- *in vita Io-*
ligion vnto our dayes, but eſpecially againſt *Pici.*
ſuch heretiks, whoſe reliques remayned in his
tyme in diuers corners of the world, as *VVal-
denſians, VVickliffians, Lollards, Huſsits*, and the like.
Againe the ſame ſtory ſheweth, that euery friday in the yeare, this Earle *Picus* chaſtized his
body in remembrance of the bleſſed paſsion
of our Sauiour, with faſtinge, diſcipline, and
other mortification; & that at his death, after
receauing moſt humbly the bleſſed body and
bloud

bloud of Chrift, he would neuer let go out of his hand a certayne Crucifix, which he held, and therin for his fpeciall deuotion, which are no fignes of a good Proteftant. And finally that he had a firme intention to haue made himfelfe a Dominican friar, yf he had liued, which he would not haue done, yf he had byn but lightly touched with any motions of Fox his faith.

Tho. Mor.
in vita Io.
Pici cap. 4.

39.   And *Syr Thomas More* addeth further, that *Picus* had certaine reuelations from God about that vocation. And befides all this, are extant his owne wrytinges, that more clearly then any thinge els, fhew him a Catholike: which vvrytinges vvould not haue byn permitted among vs, yf they fauoured any thing at all of herefie, fo vigilant are the gouernours of our Church, and haue byn euer in all ages, to note and forbidd all books and wrytinges, that are but fufpected to conteyne different doctrine from the vniuerfall and Catholike, that is taught amonge vs, and that vvith very great reafon as vve haue fhewed at large in the

* VVarn-
vvord.En-
count. 1.
cap. 15.

* *VVarn-word* againft *Syr Francis Haftings* and *O. E.* And therfore to thinke that fo many of *Earle Picus* his vvorks fhould be permitted amongft vs, yf they did conteyne any herefie at all, is great fimplicity in Fox. For as the works of *Erafmus Roterodamus* are forbidden for fome errors, though he were no Proteftant: (as prefently fhalbe fhewed) fo vvould thefe other alfo yf they gaue the like caufe. Which is not fo, but rather are permitted read and highly

highly comended by Catholiks, namely thofe of *Picus Mirandula*, as yow may fee not only in the two forfaid wryters of his life, *Syr Thomas More*, and *Iohn Francifcus Picus*, but alfo by a later graue learned vvryter *Antonius Poffeuinus* of the Society of I E s v s, in his *Bibliotheca Selecta*, or *Choice-library*, vvhere he maketh profefsion to giue his cenfure of all authors that are allowable, and fpeakinge of this *Ioannes Picus*, he fheweth firft, that he had his excellent learning moft ftrangely by his only ftudy and particular infpiration of God. And then talkinge of his 12. learned and pious books wrytten by him *contra aftrologos iudiciarios*, againft thofe that fortell thinges to come by aftrology, he faith thus.

Ant. Pof-
feuum. l. 1.
Bibl.Selecta,
cap. 3º.

40. *Picus Mirandulanus Princeps, duodecim libros fublimitate eruditionis referfit, quibus iftam, vt diximus, aftrologiam expugnauit.* Picus Prince of *Mirandula*, made twelue bookes, replenifhed " with all height of learninge, wherby he ouer- " threw all this kind of Aftrology iudiciary, as " before we haue faid, *&c.* Neyther doth he " giue any worfe cenfure of him and his works then this, which he would not do, yf he had wrytten conforme to Iohn Fox his new learninge. Yet true yt is, that *Earle Picus* being extraordinarily forward in learninge, had certaine phylofophicall controuerfies with fome fchoolemen, proceeding from his great fharpneffe of witt, but nothinge tendinge to difference of faith or matters of religion; which I could wifh we myght fay truly of the fecond

Ant. Pof-
l. 15. c. 13,

V man

man named in this ranke, to witt *Erasmus Rote-rodamus* who vpon like, though leſſe ſharpenes of wytt, and farre meaner knowledge in ſchoole diuinity (but yet more raſh and confident in himſelfe) paſſed further in his youth to reprehend and ieſt at certayne defects or abuſes, as to him they ſeemed, then afterward in his old age, he receaued eyther comfort or creditt therby, or could ſo eaſily remedy, as he ſaw the inconueniences and hurts that had enſued therof.

41. And this his caſe is; as yf ſome one or other in England, diſguſted with ſome things that paſſe in gouernment, and offended with ſome particular magiſtrats or officers of the Prince; ſhould ſpeake or wryte ſo bitterly and contemptuoſly againſt the ſame, that albeit himſelfe had no meaninge to condemne the whole gouernment, or to ſet other men in rebellion; yet others lighter, or worſe affected then himſelfe, and lyinge in wayte for ſuch an occaſion, ſhould by his wrytings be animated to paſſe further, and to breake forth into open defection; and ſo after all the realme ſett on fire and infinite ſlaughters, thefts, rapynes, ſacriledges and other hurts commytted, the cauſe therof ſhould be layd vpon the other mans wrytinge, who meant not ſo farre perhapps, but yet guilty of high cryme (no doubt) and great fault, for giuinge ſuch occaſion.

42. And in very like ſort paſſed the matter with *Erasmus*, who ſeing himſelfe better learned

ned (as he thought) then many others of his tyme (efpecially in the tongues, and ftudy of humanity) and therby made high mynded, (which is euer commonly the next ftepp to a downefall) pricked on alfo with emulation againft certayne religious orders, whofe vocation he had more rafhely, then religioufly left; contemninge moreouer their manner of fchoole-ftudy, which in great part he vnderftood not, and offended with their rude fpeach; thought yt the beft way for remedy in the one, and fome reuenge in the other, and for oftentation alfo of fingularity in them both, to wryte bytterly, ieft, and carpe freely at whatfoeuer he lifted. Which liberty of fpeeche *Martyn Luther*, and his brood comming foone after, and findinge yt in his wrytings, they tooke occafion thereby to paffe further then yt feemeth *Erafmus* euer meant, whereof enfued the prouerbe before mentioned, *that Erafmus layed the egges, and Luther hatched the fcorpions*: and as fome others do note very fittly to the purpofe, to fhew the beginninge and progreffe of herefies. *Erafmus innuit, Lutherus irruit, Erafmus dubitat, Lutherus affeuerat.* Wherfoeuer ,, *Erafmus* did but point with his fingar, Luther ,, rufhed vpon yt, where *Erafmus* did but doubt, ,, Luther affirmed. So as vpon *Erafmus* dubitations, Luther framed affertions and affeuerations; And not only Luther and Lutherans, but all the peftilent fect of new Arrians in our dayes, began vpon certayne doubtfull queftions, and interpretations of *Erafmus*, whether

V 2   fuch,

such, or such places of scriptures vsed against them by the auncient Fathers, were well applyed, or no? Wherof yow may read at large in the forsaid *Posseuinus* in his *Bibliotheca*, and not only these Arrians and Lutherans, but all sects and sectaryes lightly that after rose vp, would needs persuade the world (as Fox doth heere of his sect of Caluinists also) that *Erasmus* was of their opinion, Church, and congregation, which though himselfe denyed most earnestly vpon euery occasion, yet would they haue yt not so beleeued.

Posseu. in bilioth. Select. lib. 1. cap. 20.

All heretiks drawv *Erasmus* perforce to their Church.

43.   And on the contrary side, Catholiks seeing his rash & temerarious wrytings, both in censuringe the Fathers works, and otherwayes (in which kynd one author only noteth aboue 600. errors of his censuring *S. Hieroms* epistles) as also that all sects, and heresies founded themselues vpon him, wrote no lesse sharpely against him, then against heretiks themselues, which himselfe seeing, was in a miserable plight, and could not tell what to say or do: yet tooke he this resolution to wryte against the head of all these sectaryes, to witt, *Luther* himselfe in the controuersie of free will, takinge vpon him to refute that brutish booke of his, intituled, *de seruo arbitrio,* of slauish will; where amonge other things *Erasmus* wryteth thus, as *Cochlaus* also relateth the same.

Marianus Victorius in Scol. in S. Hier.

44.   *Vide, quam sibi non constent hominum iudicia, &c.* Behould how different mens iudgements are, Martyn Luther cryeth out, that I do not

Eras. apud Cochlaum an Domini 1531. *pag.* 268.

so

so much as vnderstand those things, that he „
wryteth against Papists, and that I do scarse „
conceyue these grosse and ordinary points, „
and so do say nothinge indeed to the purpose; „
but on the other side, the other side obiecteth „
against me, that Luther hath taken these his „
subtilityes for the most part out of my books; „
but I say againe, the most that I wryte, I „
tooke out of the books of ancient Fathers: but „
as for Luthers books, yf yow take out of them „
exaggerations, reproches, iests, idle bablings, „
extrauagant speaches, exorbitant asseuera-
tions, and other such things, that agree with „
Iohn Husse and *VVickliffe* and some other secta- „
ryes; there would little remayne of his owne „
for him to glory of: so that I for my part, am *Erasmus*
content rather to delight my selfe with these iudgment
grosse things (as he calleth them), then with *of Luthers*
his subtilityes to trouble the peace of all Gods & spiritt.
Church, as he doth, and to sett one citty with „
another in tumult, the people with their „
Princes, and Bishops, and Princes with them- „
selues togeather by the eares: albeit I am not „
so dull neyther, as not to vnderstand those pa- „
radoxes of *Martyn Luther*, which coblers and „
spinsters can sing vnto vs without booke. And „
truly yf there were in his books nothing false „
and erroneous in doctrine, yet the vnbrideled „
liberty which he vseth of rayling, doth infect „
and poyson the mynd of his readers, especial- „
ly simple people, and doth breed nothinge els „
but schisme and diuision. „

45. This iudgement gaue *Erasmus* in those

dayes of Luthers spiritt & wrytinge: & when
Luther waxinge angry with him, obiected
atheisme, and that he beleeued nothinge indeed, but sought secretly to bring all religion
in contempt by wrytinge on both sides (behold the misery that falleth on them, who are
cold and indifferent in matters of Religion)
Erasmus being maruelously afflicted therwith,
aunswereth thus: That which Luther obie-
,, cteth against me, to be an Atheist, and to en-
,, deauour to weaken all Religion by my wry-
,, tings, and therby to bringe in paganisme; is so
,, foule a sinne, as yt belongeth rather to diuells,
,, then to men; And I nothinge doubt that so
,, impudent a slaunder will euer be beleeued
,, against me, by any that hath read my works, or
,, haue, by domesticall life, knowen my man-
,, ners; would God I had so well kept his diuine
,, commandements in life, as I am free & quiett
,, in conscience, for those things that appertaine
,, to faith, and beleefe. For touching my life and
manners, I do euery day with sighes and sorrow of my hart cry to God for mercy, whome
,, yet I do not desire euer to be mercifull vnto
,, me, yf euer any least cogitation of Atheisme,
,, or of this diabolicall purpose obiected to me
,, by Luther, did euer so much as mooue my
,, mynd, I do not say for weakening of all Chri-
,, stian faith, as he obiecteth, but yf I haue euer
,, had cogitation to slyde away my selfe from
,, the Catholike faith, *&c.*

Erasmus accused by Luther of Atheisme.

Coelaus ib. pag. 268.

Erasmus his prote-station of being a Catholik.

    46.   Lo *Erasmus* his protestation for his con-
stancy in the Catholike faith. But yet one
place

place more I cannot omytt, out of his said
worke wrytten for *free will* againſt Luther,
whereby yow may perceaue his opinion of
him and his : *Certè multi Lutheri diſcipuli, &c.* Eraſm. l. 3.
de libero ar-
Truly many ſchollers of *Luther* (ſaith he) are *bitrio.*
ſo vnapt to publike tranquillity , that the ,,
Turke himſelfe is ſaid to hate the Lutheran ,,
name, only for the hatred of ſedition, and to ,,
haue forbidden them to liue in his dominions, ,,
though he tolerate with Chriſtians, that are ,,
contrary to his doctrine. What ſhould I re- ,,
count heere the diſſention that is amongeſt ,,
theſe ghoſpellers? their bloudy hatred? their ,,
bytter contentions, nay their ſingular incon- ,,
ſtancy? Luther himſelfe hauinge changed his ,,
opinion ſo often,& yet new paradoxes ſprin- ,,
ginge vp from him dayly? Of which diſſen- ,,
tion and inconſtancy, what euery man ought ,,
to thinke, let vs learne, yf yow pleaſe, out of ,,
Luther himſelfe, to the end , that this here- ,,
tike with his owne ſword may cutt his owne ,,
throate. *Chriſt* (ſaith Luther in his commen- ,,
tary vpon the fifth pſalme) *doth not fight with he-* Luther
retiks any other way commonly ſo much, as by ſendinge held for
amonge them a certayne factious ſpiritt of diſſenſion. tike by
For that by this diſcord amonge themſelues, there fol- Eraſmus.
loweth euer their owne ruyne and perdition. Behould ,,
a notable propheſie of *Luther* concerning him- ,,
ſelfe and his followers, &c, ,,

47. Thus farre are the words of *Eraſmus* touchinge Luther, and Lutherans. By which
yow may ſee, that *Luther* and he can hardly
ſtand for Saints in one Calendar, as Fox heere

V 4 ap-

appointeth them, seeing *Erasmus* pronounced him for an heretike, as yow haue heard. But what of the *Zwinglians*? did *Erasmus* agree (thinke yow) any better with them? No truly. For in all his works he defended euer the *reall presence* in the blessed Sacrament, with great constancy; And liuinge in *Basill* amongst the Zwinglians, he euer said his masse very deuoutly to his last day; nor would he take any promotions or fauours offered by them, as both *Cochlæus*, *Surius* and others do testifie. And in particular *Surius* wryteth, that when certaine Zwinglians gaue out in diuers places, that he fauoured them, he purged himselfe by all meanes possible.

Erasmus euer defended the reall presence.

48. *Hoc tempore* (saith *Surius*) *Conradus Pellicanus, &c.* At this tyme *Conradus Pellicanus*, that of a Franciscan friar was become a Zwinglian, and had in tymes past, whilst he liued a friar, in *Basill* heard the Confessions of *Erasmus*, began to giue out amonge his secrett frends at *Zuricke*, that *Erasmus* did fauour Zwinglianisme: which slaunder *Erasmus* did presently seeke to shake of by diuers wayes. But soone after that againe, there was another Zwinglian named *Leo Iuda*, who settinge forth a German booke, did wryte therin, that *Erasmus* and *Luther*, did agree in tymes past with *Zwinglius*: which thinge *Erasmus* tooke in most euill part, and albeit by his inconsiderate wrytings, he had giuen no small occasion of such suspitions and speaches of him; yet certayne yt is, that the Zwinglians could neuer draw him

Sur. in hist. anno 1526.

Conradus Pellicanus.

Leo Iuda.

Erasmus purgeth himselfe from fauouringe Zwinglianisme.

him to their opinions, though he liued longe „
amonge them in *Basill*. And this very yeare, he „
wrote an epistle vnto the *Heluetians*, that were „
gathered togeather at *Badyn*, to purge himselfe „
from all suspition of fauouringe Zwinglia- „
nisme, *&c.* Thus farre *Surius.* „

49. But *Erasmus* himselfe doth best declare
himselfe, and his owne meaninge, especially
towards the end of his dayes, when he now
grew ould, and saw what suspitious opinions
men had of him, and namely in a certayne
booke called: *Spongia aduersus Huttenum:* that is
to say a sponge to wipe away the blotts of heresy, which *Huttenus* had laid vpon him, where
amonge other words he wryteth thus : *Ante*   *Erasmus in*
triennium, &c. It is now three yeares gone   *Spong. ad-*
since I protested publikely, in a certaine addi- *uers. Hutte-*
tion to familiar conferences had at *Louaine;*   *num.*
that I was most auersed, and euer should be, „
from the faction of these new ghospellers; „
neyther am I only auersed from them my „
selfe, but do exhort also and procure all my „
frends to be alienated from them, so much as „
I can, *&c.* And in a certayne epistle to a frend
of his, he wryteth thus : *Qui Luthero fauere vi-* *Eras. l.* 16.
dentur, &c. Those that will seeme to fauour *ep.* 11.
Luther, do endeauour by all meanes to draw „
me vnto their parts, and those that are against „
Luther, do seeke to dryue me into that faction „
by preachinge more odiously against me, then *Erasmus*
against Luther himselfe. But I cannot be dry- acknovv-
uen from my settled mynd by any such diuise of Rome
or battery: *Christum agnosco, Lutherum non agnos-* and not
co, &c. Luth.

" *co, &c.* I acknowledge Chrift, and I do not
" acknowledge Luther, I acknowledge the
" Roman Church, and her will I follow: what-
" foeuer is oppofite to the dignity of the Ro-
" man Church, beleeue moft certaynely that
" this commeth not from *Erafmus*, vnder what
" title foeuer yt be carryed abroad.

50. Thus and much more hath *Erafmus* in
many parts of his works, to declare his owne
difagreeing with the fectaryes of our tyme; as
alfo to teftifie, what a bad conceyte he had of
them both for their life and learninge. And as
for life, he wryteth his iudgement in diuers
places, as namely in his forfaid Sponge: *Cir-*
cumfpice mihi populum iftum Euangelicum, & obferua,
&c. Looke vpon this ghofpelling people, and
confider whether there be leffe lafciuioufnes,
pride, couetoufnes, and fuch like vices in

Erafm. in
fpong. ad-
uerf. Hut-
tenum.

" them, then amonge the papifts, whome they
" deteft,? bring me forth but one, whome this
" ghofpell hath made fober in dyett, of a ban-
" chetter; gentle and meeke, of a fearce man:
" liberall, of a rauenous or couetuous man:
" gentle fpoken, of a rayler: modeft, of vnfham-
" faft. But on the contrary I will fhew yow
" many, that by this ghofpell are made worfe
" then they were before. It may be that yt is an
" euill lucke to fall vpon the worfe fort of
" them, but truly yt neuer happened to me yet

Erafmus
iudgment
of the ef-
fects of
the new
ghofpell.

to know any one man, that became not worfe
by this ghofpellinge. And befids this, when I
go at any tyme into their Churches, I do fee
them come out from their fermons as poffef-

fed

fed with a wicked fpiritt, their countenance „
fhewing anger & fearcenes, as fouldiars com- „
ming from the warlike fpeach of a Captayne, „
exhortinge them to fightinge. Who did euer „
fee one man in their fermons hitherto, eyther „
to fhedd teares, or knocke his breft, or figh for „
his fynnes?

51. Thus wrote *Erafmus* vpon his owne experience, liuing dayly with thefe ghofpellers.
And in another place he telleth many particulars of his owne knowledgealfo, as for ex-
ample. *Noui monachum qui pro vna duxerit tres,&c.*   *Erafm. l.ad*
I haue knowne a monke who infteed of one   *fratres in-*
wife, marryed three, and I know a Prieft, that   *fer. Germa-*
after he had married a wife, found out that fhe   *nica.* „
was marryed to another before. And many „
other like examples are heere related of the „
marriages of monks, & nunnes, who do leaue „
one another after marriage by the fame law „
or right, wherby they married them. I will „
not name vnto yow a certayne Prieft, whipt „
heere in *Bafill* about the ftreets for his wic- „
kednes, being of the fame profeffion that „
thefe ghofpellers are; and when the execu- „
tioner had brought him without the gates of „
the citty after whippinge, and lett him go, he „
teftified publikely, that after he once addicted „
himfelfe to that fect, he ran into all kynd of „
wickedneffe. I will not fay what he tould of   *Vvhat E-*
the whole fect, &c. Hitherto are the words   *rafmus* re-
of *Erafmus*, wherby we may perceaue his good   *counteth*
opinion of the Proteftants in his dayes, and   *of the pri-*
yet that was their primitiue Church, which   *mitiue*
                                             ought   *Church of*
                                                         proteftats.

ought to be the beſt, and thoſe men wherof *Eraſmus* ſpeaketh had *primitias ſpiritus*, the very firſt fruits of that new ſpiritt, ſuch as yt was.

52.　And finally the longer *Eraſmus* liued, the more he was alienated from theſe ſorts of men, & entred more and more into himſelfe, ſeemed ſorrowfull for his former doings and vvrytings, vvherby he might any vvay ſeeme, to haue fauoured or furthered them; but eſpecially afcer the death and martyrdome of *Syr Thomas More* his deareſt, and greateſt frend, which happened in London vpon the yeare of Chriſt 1535. a little more then a yeare be-

The death of Syr Thomas More moued greatly Eraſmus to deteſt hereſie.

fore *Eraſmus* death in *Baſill*; to vvhome the ſaid good knight had often told in his life tyme, that his manner of vvryting ſo ſcoffingly and dangerouſly in matters of Religion, vvould one day make his vvorks odious, & contemptible, and forbidden by the Church of God, vvhich he ſaw in great part to fall out in his owne dayes, and vvas incredibily afflicted therwith; And after the death of the foreſaid *Syr Thomas More*, he neuer ſeemed to take ioy or comfort of this vvorld, but pyned away; And *Surius* wryteth, that he ſaw and read an epiſtle of *Eraſmus* vvrytten vvith his owne hand, to a certayne charter-houſe monke about this tyme, vvhen he ſaw the vvorld go vvorſe and vvorſe, vvhich declared vvell the affliction of his mynd, eſpecially hauinge vnderſtood that this monke his deare frend, was ſore tempted by the heretiks to leaue his monaſtery, and to follow them. We ſhall ſet downe heere ſome

vvords

vvords of the said epistle, as they stand in
Surius:

53.   *Vereor* (saith he) *ne imponant tibi quorundam*   Sur. in hist.
præstigia, &c. I am afrayd, least the deceyts &   an. Domini
inchantements of certayne men do deceyue   5536. pag.
yow, vvho vvith gorgeous vvords do sett   ,,
forth, and bragg of their Euangelicall liberty: ,,
Beleeue me, yf yow know how matters go   ,,
abroad, yow vvould be lesse vveary of the life   ,,
yow haue taken in hand there. I do see a cer-   ,,
tayne kind of men spronge vp, from vvhome   ,,
my heart and soule do vehemently abhorre.   ,,
I see no man made better, but all vvorse, for   ,,
so many at least as I haue knowne; in so much   ,,
as I am vvonderfully greeued now, that I did   ,,
in tymes past, preach & set forth in my books   ,,
the liberty of spiritt, *&c.* Diuers cittyes of   Erasmus
Germany are filled vvith Apostatates and re-   soule ab-
nagats of monasteryes, vvith marryed Priests,   retiks be-
the most of them hungry and naked, but yet   death.
followinge sensuality, dancinge, eatinge, drin-   ,,
kinge and svvillinge; neyther do they teach or   ,,
vvill learne; no sobriety of life, no sincerity is   ,,
among them; vvheresoeuer they be, there all   ,,
good discipline and piety is cast vnder foote.   ,,
I vvould vvryte vnto yow more about this   ,,
matter, but that yt is not safe to commyt such   ,,
things to letters, *&c.*   ,,

54.   By this vve may vnderstand, that the
poore man was not only in affliction of mind,
but also in feare of body, for that he lyued a-
mong heretiks at *Basill*, that began to rage, this
yeare more then before; yet goeth he forward
in

Ibidem.

" in the same epistle sayinge: what ghospell-li-
" berty is this, where yt is not lawfull for a man
" to say his prayers? nor to sacrifice? nor to fast,
" nor to abstayne from flesh? consider what can
" be more miserable then these men, euen in
" this life, *&c.* I would I were dead, but that yf
" this little body of myne had neuer so small
" strength to susteyne life there with yow, I
" had rather lead your life, then to be the chiefe

Erasmus vvisheth himselfe a carthusian tovvards the end of his dayes.

in Cæsars pallace. Wherfore my most-dearly
beloued in our Sauiour, I do pray, beseech &
obtest yow, by our old frendshipp, yea by our
euerlastinge frendshipp, and by Christ himselfe, that yow will vtterly cast out of your
" mynd that wearynes which yow haue con-
" ceyued,& do not yeld your eares to the perni-
" cious fables of these men, who after they haue
" drawne yow into the pitt of perdition, they
" will yeld yow no help at all, but only scoffe at
" yow. Thus *Erasmus.*

55.   And now lett Iohn Fox glory of him, in
his Calendar, as a Confessor of his Religion.
Yf *Erasmus* were aliue againe; and should heare
that a Zwinglian or Caluinian wryter had
putt him into a Calendar for one of the Saints
of his sect, how would he haue laughed at yt,
seing he could not absteyne from laughinge,
that the Zwinglias in his daies began to make
Catalogues of their Saints, comparinge them
to the old Saints, and Martyrs of the Catho-

Erasin l.ad fratres Inf. German.

like Church : *Vix temperabam à risu, &c.* (saith
he) *I could scarse hold my selfe from laughing, vvhen I*
" *heard them compare themselues to Christ Apostles*
                                                      and

and Martyrs, &c. And againe. *Scio multos, non sine* „
risu lectures, &c. I know that many will not „
read without laughter , that thefe men do „
compare their Martyrs with the ancient Mar- „
tyrs of the Church, *&c.* So faith *Erafmus.* But
what yf he had read this ftory of Iohn Fox, *Fox ep. ad*
who doth not only compare, but preferre his *doctum le-*
Martyrs alfo , *before the ancient Martyrs , euen the* *pag. 6.*
beft of them all, that be in the Roman Calendar? for fo
he faith in his Latyn epiftle to the Reader , as
* before we haue fhewed. ** Supra*
cap. 2c

56. Well this fhalbe fufficient to declare &
make euident, that whatfoeuer other worthy
Saints Fox may haue of his Church or Religion, yet that *Erafmus* by no reafon can be his;
of whome though the Catholike Church
haue giuen a grieuous cenfure, for his rafh and
erroneous wrytings : yet may we hope that
by his laft repentance, he hath obtayned remifsion at the mercifull hand of almighty
God. And *Syr Thomas More , Beda Natalis* , and
fome others of his frends, did exhort him
greatly to make a vew and retractation of his
works, after the example of S. Auguftine, and
by his owne cenfure of them , to preuent the
cenfure of the Church; and fome thinke, that
he meant fo to haue done , yf he had lyued
fome yeares longer , yet for that this is vncertayne , we muft leaue all to the iudgement of
God. And fo inough of him. Now lett vs
paffe to the other, that do follow him in the
Calendar.

57. There do follow for Saints vpon the 27.

and

Martyn
Bucer.
Paulus
Phagius.

and 28. dayes of this moneth, *Martyn Bucer* and *Paulus Phagius*, two german marryed Priefts, & the firft a friar, who were with their wyues banifhed from *Strasburge* a Protestant Citty in Germany, where they had preached diuers yeares. The caufe yow fhall afterward heare, which fell out about the beginninge of *K. Edward* the 6. his raigne, and fo they were glad to haue the occafion to come into England, the refuge at that day for all fuch Apoftataes; For that at the fame tyme. alfo, came in like manner two Italian friars, each man with his

The com-
ming into
Englād of
diuers A-
poftatates.

woman, *Peter Martyr* and *Bernardine Ochinus:* The former two were fent to Cambridge to infect that vniuerfity: the third to Oxford, & the fourth was left to preach in Italian at London, we fhall fpeake fomewhat of each one of them in order.

The ftory
of Martyn
Bucer.

58. Firft then as concerninge *Martyn Bucer* the chiefe Cambridge-Saint (for that of *Paulus Phagius* there is leffe to wryte, he being of leffe accoumpt, & dyinge quickely after he came to that vniuerfity) yt appeareth by diuers wryters as well Proteftants as Catholiks, that though *Bucer* were a man of great accoumpt among the new ghofpellers at the beginning; yet through his inconftancy in turninge from one fect to another he loft much reputation in the end. *Surius* in his chronicles, doth more exactly then others, obferue his proceedings accordinge to the yeares; which heere breefly we fhall runne ouer. Firft then he was by lin-

Bucer a]
Ievv by
lynnage.

nage a Iew, and then made a Dominican friar,

of

of quicke witt, and more then ordinary learninge, but inconstant and giuen to Sensuality; whervpon breakinge his vow of chastity,
he tooke three weomen, one after another,
for his wyues.

59. But his first manner of conuersion, *Surius*
wryteth in this order, by the testimony of
many graue wittnesses, as he saith: Soone after Luther had opened the way to new doctrines, *Bucer* went vnto him, to offer himselfe for a follower, and to leaue his habitt, &c.
But for that he seemed not as yet thorowly
persuaded, Luther asked him whether his
conscience were quiett or no, in the new way
he had taken in hand? Wheruto he answeringe no; the other said; *abi igitur & pugna con-*
tra hanc conscientiam, donec ea prorsus conticescat. go
and fight against this conscience of thine vntill yt be quiett, and repugne no more. And
so he did, & therby became a perfect follower
of Luther for a tyme, and was placed by him
in a benefice; But some years after, he began
to like better the sect of Zwinglius, and other
Sacramentaryes, vnto whome he adioyned
himselfe in such feruour of spiritt, as he inueighed eagerly both against Luther and his doctrine, vsinge very hard words against the
same, as appeareth by an epistle of his to the
cittizens of *Norenburge,* wherin he auoucheth,
that the doctrine of Zwinglius was sent from heauen,
and that the doctrine of Luther was new and quite op-
posite to scriptures; and in another epistle to those
of *Eislinga,* he calleth the Lutherans *fanaticos,*

suyr-

Surius in
Comment.
an. Domini
1526.
"
"
"
"
"
Sur. ibid.
pag. 152.
"
"
"
"
"

Bucer in ep.
ad Noren-
berg & El-
slingens.

fuyrmeros, furiofos, &c. fanaticall people, fwer-
merans; furious, and the like. Wherof yow
may read alfo *Genebrard*, in his cronograghy,
to the fame effect.

*Genebr. in
chron. an.
1526.pag.
446.
Stur. in cō-
ment. anno
1529.pag.
153.*

60.   And furthermore *Surius* teftifyeth, that
wheras vpon the yeare of Chrift 1524. a certayne Lutheran named *Ioannes Pomeranus*, had
,, wrytten certayne commentaryes vpon the
,, pfalmes, which worke *Luther* and *Melanchthon*
,, had highly commended by their feuerall pre-
,, faces, to the fame; *Bucer* feeing that the faid
,, worke was read with great applaufe, did
tranflate the faid commétary into the Dutch
tongue, and impudently corrupted the fame
in fauour of the Zwinglian herefie, namely in
the third pfalme, makinge *Pomeranus* to feeme
a Sacramentary, wherof the faid *Pomerane*
complayned publikely out of hand, by diuers
printed letters, both to *Brentius* and *Agricola*,
which letters are yet extant. And the very
,, fame fraud vfed *Bucer* foone after, in tranfla-
,, tinge Luthers owne commentaryes vpon the
epiftle of *S. Paul* to the Hebrues, peruertinge
the fame of purpofe, as Luther himfelfe did
complayne in his letters to his frends.

*The im-
poftures
of Martyn
Bucer at
the begin-
ning.
Vide epift.
Pomeran.
ad Brent.
& Ioannem
Agricolam
an.1526.*

*Vide epift.
Luther. ad
Typograph·
Wittberg.*

61.   And this was the art of *Bucer* at the beginninge to fett forward the Zwinglian fect,
for which being made odious to the Lutherans, he forfooke Saxony, & went to *Zuricke*,
and other townes of the Zwitzers, perfua-
ding them (therby to be the more gratefull to
them) that Luther did not differ indeed from
them in fubftance of doctrine, but only in
manner

manner and forme of speach, which neyther
they would beleeue, nor Luther yeld vnto,
but denounced them euery where for heretiks, as before yow haue heard in his story, and
shall againe after in the next chapter. Thus
passed on *Bucer* vntill the yeare of our Lord
1536. (in which yeare *Q. Anne Bolen* was beheaded in England) at what tyme Luther calling
a Synod at his owne house in *VVittenberge, Bucer* came thither with many other Zwinglians, and was by the authority and earnest persuasions of his old Maister Luther, & of other
Lutherans there present, recalled and drawne
backe from Zwinglianisme againe, and made
to renounce the same publikely, as do testifie
both *Funccius* a Lutheran, in his chronicle of
this yeare, and *Lauaterus* a Zwinglian in his
Sacramentary history. And the Acts publike
of the said Synod yet extant, do make it cleere:
Yea *Bucer* himselfe afterward in his commentaryes vpon the sixt Chapter of *S. Iohn,* and
vpon the 26. of *Mathew,* doth aske forgiuenes
publikely of God and his Church; *Quod multos
Zuinglij hæresi fascinauerat,* that he had be wiched
many with the heresie of Zwinglius, *&c.*

62. Of this notable defection also of *Bucer*
from the Zwinglians, maketh mention the
forsaid *Martinus Crusius* his appassionate scholler, vpon the yeare 1551. wherin he died, sayinge: *Defunctus est Bucerus, &c.* Bucer died at
Cambridge in England vpon the second of
February in this yeare 1551. he hauinge byn
first of the opinion of Zwinglius, about the

A Synod
in Luth.
house at
VVitten-
berg *anno*
1536.

Bucer re-
canteth
Zwinglia-
nisme.

*Martinus
Crusius p.
3. annal.
Sueu li. 11.
cap. 25.*
,,
,,
,,

,, Supper of Chriſt, did vpon the yeare 1536.
,, yeld to the ſentence of Luther, togeather with
,, the miniſters of *Sueuia*, and ſubſcribed with his
,, owne hand: he was my maiſter and ſingular
,, benefactor, &c. So he. But he doth not tell
of his other changes afterwards, eſpecially in
England, where he made ſhew to fauour
Zwinglian doctrine againe, according to the
humors of thoſe that their gouerned, but lett
vs ſee yet ſome more of his behauiour, whilſt
he remayned in Germany, before he entred
England.

Bucer
doubleth
betvvene
both ſects.

63.   After *Martyn Bucer* had made his peace
with Luther and Lutherans, and returned ſolemnely to their part againſt the Sacramentaryes, he was much troubled by the ſaid Sacramentary party their frends, as though he
had betrayed them, and committed Apoſtaſy
from their religion: whervpon he gat himſelfe to *Tigurine* aliàs *Zuricke*, the cheefe Zwinglian Citty of Zwitzerland, perſuading them
that he could diuiſe a way of compoſition betwene them and Luther, as before hath byn
ſaid: but they would not beleeue him, nor
like of any ſuch compoſition, but proceeded
on ſtill againſt Luther. And finally vpon the
* 13. Febr. yeare of Chriſt 1544. (as * before we haue noted in the hiſtory of *Luther*) they ſet forth their
publike confeſsion and profeſsion againſt him
and all his, holdinge them for heretiks. Whervpon *Bucer* being much greeued, retyred himſelfe from thence to *Straſburge*, and Luther on
his part excommunicated them againe, with

as grieuous a cenfure, as euer was giuen a-
gainft any heretiks in the world.

64.　But yet from this tyme forward, *Bucer*
bare himfelfe as indifferent betweene both
fects, or as a mediator, to compofe or vnite
them togeather, as yow may perceaue by *Cal-*
uyns letter of him to *Pharellus*, wherin he holdeth both *Bucer* and *Melancthon* in one predica-
ment, as concerninge this point. But two
yeares after this againe, he was forced once
more to declare himfelfe an open Lutheran,
at the conference of *Ratisbone* appointed by
Charles the Emperor, betwene Catholiks and
Proteftats of the confeffion of Augufta, vpon
the yeare 1546. which was the yeare that K.
Henry of England & Luther died, and *Charles*
the Emperor began his warre in Germany.
And in this Colloquy *Martyn Bucer* in the abfence of *Melancthon*, & fome other his fellowes,
being procurator for the Proteftants, there
was on the other fide one *Doctor Maluenda* a
learned Spanyard, fpeaker for the Catholiks,
who for more cleare proceedinge in the matter, caufed firft the Confeffion of Augufta to
be openly read, which the Proteftants had giuen vp vnto the Emperor, vpon the yeare
1530. for the grounded forme of their religion, wrytten by *Melanchthon* and allowed by
Luther, and all their followers. Which confeffion being publikely read, *Maluenda* demaunded of *Bucer* & the reft, that feeing there
had byn many editions of this confeffion,
whether they would ftand to that which was

The Col-
loquy at
Ratisbon.
anno 1546.

X 3　　　　　read,

read, and condemne all other wrytinges contrary to the same, as well their owne, as of other mens? Wherat *Bucer* at the firſt began to ſticke and ſtagger, but at length being vrged, he ſaid plainly, that he would ſo do for his part. Whervpon he confeſſed himſelfe once againe a perfect Lutheran, as yow ſee, & condemneth all Zwinglian and Caluinian wrytings, that refuſe the ſame; which yet is like he would not haue done, yf he had knowne that he ſhould haue byn forced ſo ſhortly after to go into England, & teach Zwinglian doctrine there againe. Or at leaſt to pretende to do yt, for that in his harte he is thought neuer to haue beleeued the ſame, eſpecially in their principall article againſt the reall preſence, for which cauſe he was left out of the publike diſputatiō, held at Cambridge by *B. Ridley* about that matter, as after ſhall appeare.

Bucer cōfeſſeth himſelfe a Lutherā the third tyme at the colloquy of Ratiſbone *anno* 1546.

See the reuevv of 10.diſput. after c.1.

65. I leaue to proſecute what paſſed in the ſaid Colloquy at *Ratiſbone*, remyttinge the reader to * *Surius,* and other wryters, that do ſett the ſame downe at more length, eſpecially the particular abſurdityes, whervnto the forſaid *Maluenda* brought *Bucer* in diſputation, though *Bucers* ſcholler the forſaid *Cruſius* be not aſhamed to write, that he did ſo contemne *Maluenda,* and his aſſiſtents; that while they framed their arguments, he wrote letters hither and thither to his frends abroad, and then anſwered them in a word or two, & turned to wryte againe, all the whole auditory lookinge vpon him. Which thinge how probable it is, euery

* *Sur. in comment. an.*1546.

Cruſius p. 3 annal. Sueuic. lib. 11.c.25.

man

man of iudgement will eafily fee, and therby difcerne the fhamelefſe pride of hereticall wrytings. And ſo much of that Colloquy.

66.   From this ſpeache of *Ratubone*, Bucer beingwholy out of credit now, as yt ſeemeth, with the Zwinglians and Caluiniſts, retyred himſelfe vnto *Argentina*, where the Lutheran fect bare rule at that day, and there the friar marryed one of his daughters vnto *Chriſtophorus Sellius*, a miniſter of the ſame tribe and towne, as appeareth by *Cruſius* in his ſtory *anno* 1551. when he talketh of this ſonne in law of *Bucer*, who with two other miniſters of *Straſburge Hedio* and *Lendglinus*, *equitarunt* (ſaith he) *ad VVittenbergenſes Theologos, de Concilio Tridentino deliberaturi*: they did ryde to *VVittenberge*, to conferre with the diuines of that Citty about the Councell of Trent, begon ſome 4. or 5. yeares before. And heere yow may conſider what a goodly conſultation this was, when 2. or 3. riding-miniſters, take vpon them to deliberate of ſo great and graue a generall Councell, at that of Trent was. *Cruſius ib.*

67.   But not long after *Bucers* returne to *Straſburge*, he and *Paulus Phagius* (who was another marryed Prieſt of the ſame Citty) were forbidden to preache any more, but rather to packe out of the towne, for their ſedition, which the forſaid *Cruſius* though greatly their freind, ſetteth downe in theſe words: *Argentinæ* 2. *Martÿ interdictū eſt Bucero & Fagio, ne amplius concionarentur*, *&c.* Vpon the ſecond day of March *anno* 1549. prohibition was made at *Cruſ.ibid. lib.* 11. *annal.c.* 23

,, *Strasburge* to *Bucer* and *Phagius,* that they should
,, preach no more, whervpon the next day they
,, made their last sermons, *Phagius* his speach
,, was very graue and patheticall, out of the 7.
,, of *Saint Mathew,* and after his sermon he added
,, these words: 1. I was called hither, and to
,, the citty of Constance by order to preach.

Paulus Pha-
gius his
graue and
pathetical
speache.
2. I haue taught & preached according to
the confessiō of Augusta these 30. yeares past.

3. Yow subiects must be quiett, and at-
,, tempt nothinge by force, for vpholdinge the
,, office of preachinge.

,,   4. The magistrates are not guilty in this
,, matter, they haue proued all they could for
,, vpholdinge all the ghospell.

,,   5. Read diligently at home Luthers Bible;
,, admonish one another; remayne constant in
,, the knowne doctrine; keepe your children
,, hard to the Catechisme.

,,   6. Young men, pray to God, for that he may
,, chance to heare yow sooner, then the elder
,, sort, that haue more synnes.

,,   7. Keep your preachers as long as they liue,
,, in honor; thinke not that they remayne with
,, yow for their bellyes sake, the diuell perse-
,, cuteth them chiefly, who can do him most
,, harme.

,,   8. No body hath conuinced vs, that we
,, haue a false doctrine, out of the scriptures; but
,, wheras men deale with force, we must com-
,, mend all to God.

,,   9. I am held for a seditious preacher, not-
,, withstāding I haue neuer set on any man, *&c.*

10. Pray

10. Pray God for me, that I remayne constant in all crosses, I am a man, Peter did also fall. „ „ „

11. Yow Superiors, punish the exterior grosse vices of those that be vnder yow. „ „ „

12. Read the 7. chapter of *Daniel*, the 15. of the first Epistle to the *Corinthians*, the 20. of the Acts, and the Epistle of *Iudas*, &c. „ „ „ „

68. This is the graue and patheticall speach, which *Crusius* sayth, that *Phagius* had at his expulsion out of *Argentina*, and that himselfe was present when he spake these words, wherin he professed himselfe to haue bin a Lutheran, accordinge to the confession of *Augusta* for 30. yeares togeather; and now both he and *Bucer* were banished from thence for seditious preachers, not by Catholiks, but by Protestants themselues, which is euident by *Crusius*: for that he wryteth, that two other Lutheran Doctors, *Gaspar Hedio*, and *Ioannes Marbachius*, (who afterward was superintendent of *Strasburge*, and set forth a terrible booke against all Sacramentaryes) were appointed to preach in their places. And albeit the day of their banishment was appointed the first of Aprill, yet went they not forth of *Argentina* (as *Crusius* saith) vntill the fourth of Aprill: *Interea namq; latuerunt domi Catherinæ Viduæ Zelsy*; for that in the meane space they lay hidden, at home in the house of *Catherine* the widdow of *Zelsius*, *teste hospita nostra Froschesserina, cuius sororem Agnetam Phagius in matrimonium habebat*; the wittnes wherof (saith he) is our hostesse *Fros-* „ „

choschesserina

See Sur. sio commentar. anno.1565.

Crus. ibid. l. 11. c.23.

cheʃʃerina whoʃe ʃiʃter *Agnes*, *Phagius* had marryed, *&c.*

69. Lo heere the ʃtory of theʃe two Apoʃtles,
or rather Apoʃtates expulʃion out of *Strasburge*,
related briefly by their owne ʃcholler. And
from thence they came into England leading
their ʃiʃters with them, and were ʃent to *Cambridge* to infect & peʃter that vniuerʃity, as before yow heard, teachinge for lucres ʃake, and
for pleaʃinge thoʃe that were in authority at
that tyme in our countrey, the Sacramentary
ʃect; againʃt which they had made proteʃtation as yow haue heard, at their very departure out of *Argentina*. Theʃe then are the two
famous *Cambridge-Saints*, vvhich Fox ʃetteth
downe for Confeʃʃors of his Church : Of
which two, *Phagius* died ʃoone after his comminge to Cambridge in the yeare 1549. but
Bucer liued ʃome 2. or 3. yeares after, to witt
vnto the yeare 1551. Of his death men report
diuerʃly. For that ʃome conʃidering his inconʃtancy in diuers ʃects, & that his linage was of
the Iewes, & that in diuers queʃtiõs aʃked him
about diuorcemẽts, vʃury, poligamy, & other
ʃuch points, he ʃeemed to inclyne to Iewiʃh
opinions, or vpon what other arguments, I
know not, they beleeued & gaue out that he
died a Iew, wherof both *Surius*, *Genebrard*, *Lindane*, & other forrayne wryters, do make mention, out of the report of Engliʃhmen that trauayled beyond the ʃeas. But howʃoeuer this
was, ʃure yt is, that both he and *Phagius* died
heretiks, and no man can tell of what ʃect.

70. But

Yt is
thought
that Bu-
cer died a
Ievv.

70.   But as for *Bucer*, the sentence of his condemnation sett downe by *Cardinall Pole*, for the burninge of his body in Q. Maryes dayes in Cambridge, hath, (besides other common & ordinary heresies) that of the Manichies, *Omnia fato, & absoluta necessitate fieri*, that he held all things to happen by destiny and absolute necessity. And more then this *Doctor Perne* maister afterward of *Peter House*, held for a principall learned man, euen amonge the Protestants of thos dayes, for whome he disputed vnder *B. Ridley* in the publike *Cambridge* disputation, as after yow shall heare, gaue in publike testimony against him, as one that had byn his scholler, and very familiar with him in K. *Edwards* dayes; that touchinge *diuorcements* and *vsury, he held them lawfull, as the Iewes did, and that God was the author of sinne absolutely and properly*: howbeit for offendinge diuers mens consciences, he said that he durst not teach the same openly. All which points and many other, yow may find in the depositions of *Cambridge-Doctors* at that tyme, which Fox also setteth downe, and chafeth wonderfully with D. *Perne* for testifying these things against him, which he seeketh to wipe of with this Rhetoricall defence. *Bucer* (saith he) *brought all men into such admiration of him, that neyther his frends could sufficiently praise him, neyther his enemyes in any one point, could find fault with his singular life and sincere doctrine; a most certayne token whereof may be his sumptuous buryall, solemnized with so great assistance and gladnes of all the degrees of the vniuersity, &c.*

71. So

Bucers bones burned in Cābrige.

A ridiculous argument of Fox pag. 1775.

71. So Fox. And yf this be not a defence worthy of so wise a man, I leaue to the reader to consider: For the same argument I may better vse against him; seeing that all the vniuersity afterward in Q. Maryes dayes, demanded to haue his bones taken vp againe, & burned for an heretike, as Fox himselfe doth confesse, relatinge at large, both their orations, speaches, sermons, conferences, sentences and iudgements about the same. So as heere I will make an end to speake any more of *Bucer* and *Phagius*; only I must add a word of the testimony of the right honourable the *L. Pagett* in Q.

lib. 2. de Schism. Angl. pag. 272.

Maryes dayes, cyted by *Doctor* * *Sanders* who heard him relate the same; And yt is, that the said *L. Pagett*, hauinge byn a Protestant in *K. Edwards* dayes, and imployed in forraine Embassages, was interpreter one day betwene the *L. Dudley* Duke of *Northumberland* and *Bucer*, & thervpon recounted, that the Duke asking *Bucer* in confidence, whether the body of Christ were truly & really in the Sacrament?

,, He answered: that yf all be true, which the
,, Euangelists do sett downe, yt must needs be
,, there, but whether we be bound to beleeue
,, absolutely euery thinge sett downe by them,
,, to be true or noe, he would not be iudge:

Which answere moued greatly both the *Duke* and the *Lord Pagett*, to beleeue the Catholike

* *Cap. 5.*

opinion in that affayre, * and afterward in the revewe of disputations yow shall see *Bucers* authority in this article, refused flatly by *Cranmer* and his fellowes. And so much
of

of thefe eompagnions *Bucer* and *Phagius*.

72. In the next place after thefe, cometh in
Philip Melanchon for a Confeffor alfo of Fox
his Church ; but yf the former two were
Sainéts for being Zuinglians, and for denyall
of the reall prefence in the Sacrament, then
can not *Melanchon* any way be a fainét with
them, who ftoutly affirmed and defended the
fame reall prefence cötrary to the Zuinglians,
as partly yow haue heard teftified before by
Tyndall hymfelfe in his letter to *Fryth*, where
he faith ; *Yf Philipp Melanchon be admitted into*
France (as the newes went, that he was) *then*
will he certainly plant the affirmatiue part in that
kingdome ; and thervpon he perfuaded *Frith* to
go foft and fayre in that controuerfy, vntill he
did fee the euent what would fall out. Now
yf *Philipp Melanchon* were fo refolute in the
affirmatiue of that doctrine, wherof Fox and
his fellowes do hold the negatiue, and for holding of which negatiue he hath canonized fo
many for Sainéts and Martyrs before; how
can he and they be Sainéts of one Church
or Calendar?

73. But to the end yow may perceyue, what
manner of Sainét Fox hath picked out heere
from the Lutherans, to beare a roome among
his Caluinian Sainéts, we fhall recount fomwhat more particularly what *Melanchon* was.
He was borne (faith *Crufius*) in a towne called *Bretta* in the countrey of Germany, named
Suetia or *Swoabenland*, vpon the yeare of Chrift
1497. So as when Luther began his breach,
he

Philip Me-
lanchon
his ftory.

Die 2. Iulij,

he was iuſt 20. yeares old: and the next yeare
after he began to read publikely in *VVittenberge*
where Luther liued, both *Homer*, and *S. Paules*
epiſtle to *Titus* (ſaith *Cruſius*) that is to ſay, both
Grammar and Diuinity, and ſoone after get-
ting him a wife, he ioyned himſelfe in ſuch
ſtrayte frendſhipp to Luther, as comonly they
were called by their followers, *Paul* and *Titus*.

Hovv Phi-
lipp Me-
lanchthō
toke his
name. And Luther was wont to ſay, when he would
ſpeake of great matters to be done by great
men, *Philippus meus & ego*, my Philipp and my
ſelfe. This *Melanchthons* name in Dutch was
Swartz erd, which ſignifyeth *blacke earth*; but
by counſell of Luther, who had changed his
owne name alſo from *Luder*, (as before yow
haue heard in his ſtory) he called himſelfe
Melanchthon, after the Greeke phraſe, which
ſignifyeth as much as blacke earth in Dutch.

74.   This man then being Luthers dearling,
and profeſsinge ſome extraordinary ſkill both
in the Latyn & Greeke tongue, Poetry, Rhe-
thorike, and ſuch other ſciences, drew many
other young mē after him of the like humour
at the beginninge of Luthers ghoſpell, profeſsinge themſelues Champions thereof by
their pennes and wrytings: and this endured
ſome 4. or 5. yeares, vntill the abſence of Luther from *VVittenberge* at his *Pathmos* (as he called yt) vpon the yeare 1522. at what tyme *Carolſtadius* Archdeacon of *VVittenberge* hauing taken a wife, and being as yt were a ſpirituall
Father to *Melanchthon*, in Luthers abſence,
had perſuaded him (as *Surius* relateth) to con-
temnē

temne and burne all bookes of Philofophy, Rhetoricke, and other fciences, and only to ftudy the fcripture; and therwithall to take vpon him fome Mechanicall art, as many other fchollers had done in *VVittenberge* by like perfuafions; wherypon *Melanchthon* refolued to be a baker. But Luther returninge home brake all thefe defignements, and foone after draue out *Carolftadius* from *VVittenberge*, with his new wife, & made him to be a labouring man in the countrey. *Melanchthon* then being newly confirmed by Luther, tooke hoatly his part againft all his contradictors, as namely the forfaid *Carolftadius*, *Oecolampadius*, and *Zwinglius*, that foone after began their Sacramentary fect againft him, whome *Melanchthon* by many wrytinges endeauoured to refute: but efpecially to preffe and confound them the more, he gathered togeather a whole booke of fentences, & authorityes out of the ancient Fathers for proofe of the *reall prefence*, againft the Noueltyes of the Zwinglians doctrine. In the preface of which worke, being fent to *Fredericus Myconius*, he wryteth thus:

75. *Mitto tibi, &c.* I fend vnto yow the places of ancient Fathers of the fupper of our Lord, as I promifed, wherby yow fhall fee, that the faid Fathers did thinke and beleeue, as we do; that is to fay, *that the body and bloud of our Sauiour is truly prefent in the faid fupper.* It is not fafe for ,, vs to go from the common fentence of the ,, ancient Church: we feeme dull vnto fome, for ,, that we do not fee a Metaphore in the words ,,

of

Sur. in hift. anno 1522.

Melanchthons temptation to be a baker.

Melanck. ep. ad Fred. Mycon. praf. veter. fentent. de Cana Domini editie. anno 1530.

,, of the ghofpell, *this is my body, &c.* But I do fol-
,, low the fentence of the auncient Church,
,, which doth affirme the true body of Chrift to
,, be in the fupper, & do iudge that this beleefe
,, hath with yt the teftimony of holy fcripture;
,, nor do I find any reafon, why we fhould in-
,, terprete the word *body* (affirmed to be pre-
,, fent) to be the figne only of an abfent body,
,, &c. I know that *Carolftadius* was the firft that
Carolftadius ftyrred vp this tumult about the matter, he
tended to being a rude barbarous fellow, without lear-
Iudaifme ninge or common fenfe, fo farre of was he
according from hauing in him any figne or fignification
to Me- of a holy fpirit;nay there were manifeft fignes
lanchthons of impiety in him, for that in all his doctrine
teftimo- he tended to Iudaifme, and began this con-
ny. trouerfie of the fupper,only for hatred of Lu-
,, ther, not vpon any perfuafion of piety. For
,, when Luther reproued his breakinge downe
,, of Images, he being inflamed with a beaftly
,, greedynes of reuenge, fought this plaufible &
,, vendible caufe (of denying the reall prefence)
,, wherby to reuenge himfelfe & hurt Luthers
,, creditt, &c.

76.   Thus vvrote *Melanchthon* of this vvhole
controuerfie and authors therof, againft Fox
and his fellowes. And in the fame place he
vfeth many other reafons to conuince the
Ibid. cap. 3. truth, as namely *cap. 2. Quid adferri poteft, præter*
humanæ rationis iudicium, &c. What can be
brought for the Sacramentaryes,but only the
iudgement of humaine reafon, that Chrifts
body cannot be but in one place, *&c. Sed omnes*
                                    veteres

veteres senserunt, iudicium rationis debere scripturæ cedere. But all ancient Fathers were of opinion that the iudgement of humaine reason should yeld in this point to scripture. And in another place : *Fieri potest, vt alia sententia blandiatur otioso animo, quia est magis consentanea humano iudicio.* Yt may be that the other opinion of the Sacramentaryes, may please an idle mynded man, for that yt is more conforme to humaine iudgement : but what tentation would these men feele in the end, when their owne consciences shall dispute against them, what cause they had to depart from the receaued sentence of the Church : *tunc ista verba; hoc est corpus meum, fulmina erunt:* then these vvords of Christ, *this is my body,* vvill be terrible thunderbolts vnto them, *&c.* Thus he.

Good reasons of Melanthon to be considered for reall presence. Ibid. cap. 4.

77. And yt were to long to alleage the many proofes and reasons, which he bringeth for this doctrine, in this and other parts of his works, and therfore I will end with these his words to *Martinus Gerolitius* a pastor and preacher : *Ego mori malim quam hoc affirmare, quod Zuingliani affirmant, Christi corpus non posse nisi in vno loco esse, &c.* I had rather dy, then to affirme as the Zwinglians do, that Chrifts body cannot be but in one place at once. Lo heere *Melanchthon* was ready to dy against the Zwinglians. And how then can he be a Saint or Confessor of their Church?

Melanthon ready to dy in defence against the Sacramentaryes. epa ad Mart. Gerolit.

78. And this were inough to shew Fox his folly, in settinge one downe in his Calendar for a Saint of his Church, that was his profes-

Y   fed

fed enemy in beieefe. But yf we will confider
further, not fo much what Catholike wryters
haue left recorded of this *Melanchthon*: (for
with this I know Proteftants will not greatly
be mooued) but what euen his owne men
alfo, both Lutherans & Sacramentaryes haue
left written of him; we fhall find that *Melanch-*
thon could fcarcely be a Confeffor of any fect
or religion, for that he was conftant and refolute in none, though at the beginning, as hath
byn faid, he was one of the chiefeft pillars of
the new ghofpell in generall, vvhen as all
ftood in wrytinge againft the Pope; vvhich
Melanchthon did by Luthers direction at fome
22. or 23. yeares of age; but afterward vvhen
many diftinct fects grew vp, and each one defired to eftablifh yt felfe, then was yt hard to
fay, of vvhich fide *Melanchthon* vvas efpecially
towards his end. For as he grew more mature
in iudgement; fo difcouered he more difficultyes on all fides, and thervpon became fo
doubtfull euery vvay, as no man could tell of
vvhat Religion he vvas indeed.

79.   For firft the Sacramentaryes, notwithftandinge all that yow haue heard him vvryte
againft them before, vvill needs haue him to
be of their opinion. *De Melanchthone* faith Caluyn in an epiftle to *Pharellus* in the yeare 1539.)
nihil dubites, quin peni'us nobifcum fentiat, &c. Of
,, Melanchthon do yow doubt nothinge, but that
,, he is altogeather of our opinion, *&c.* And in
,, his aunfwere to *VVeftphalus* a certayne Luthe-
,, ran, the fame *Caluyn* vvryteth thus about the

Calui ep. 12.
ad Pharell.

                                                    contro-

controuersie of the Sacrament. *Quod dixi, & quidem centies, si opus sit, confirmo, non magis à me Philippum, quam à proprys visceribus posse in hac causa divelli.* That vvhich I said of *Philipp Melanchthon,* I vvill say againe a hundred tymes, yf yt be needfull, that *Philipp Melanthon* can no more be separated from me in this cause of the Sacrament, then from his owne bowelis. Thus confidently vvrote Caluyn of *Philipp Melanchthon* to be of his side. And the like did bragg other Sacramentaryes, as namely *Thomas Neogeorgius: Philippus non ausus est, viuo Luthero, palam fateri, quid sentiret de Cœna Domini, &c.* Philipp Melanchthon, durst not vvhilst Luther vvas aliue to confesse openly, vvhat he thought of the supper of our Lord (behould how good a Confessor he was) for yf he had done, vvhat styrres and tumults thinke yow, vvould fierce Luther haue moued against him? *&c.*

80. I might alleage many testimonyes more, but these are sufficient to shew vvhat a confessor *Melanchthon* vvas, vvhich durst not vtter vvhat he thought in so great an article of faith as this is. *Caluyn* vvill needs attribute yt to a certayne *molliti es animi,* vveaknes or delicacy of mynd, much like vnto *Bucer,* that turned with euery vvynd, and vveather, vvhome in this point he compareth togeather. For vvrytinge to the forsaid *Pharellus* his Companion, vpon the forsaid yeare 1539. Caluyn telleth a notable fiction and ly for creditt of the cause of his new ghospell, vvhich vvas that K. Henry of England had demaunded a certayne embassage

　bassage

Calu. in admonit. vlt. ad VVostphal.

All sectaryes dravv Melanchthon vnto their side.

Tho. Neogeorgius.

,,
,,
,,
,,
,,
,,
,,
,,
,,

baſſage to be ſent vnto him from the Proteſtant Princes of Germany, and that *Melanch-*
thon in particular ſhould be one: *Angli petitio fuit*
(ſaith he) *vt legatio ad ſe noua mitteretur, cui adiun-*
geretur Philippus, &c. The petition of the King

" of England vvas to theſe German Princes,
" that a new embaſſage ſhould be ſent vnto
" him,and that *Philipp Melanchthon* ſhould be ioy-
" ned thervnto, to the end that the King might
" haue him by him,to vſe his counſell for orde-
" ringe of his Church. The Princes made no
" doubt to ſend the embaſſage, but did not like
" to ſend Melanchthon, *quod mollitiem animi eius*
" *ſuſpectam haberent*, for that they held for ſuſpect
" the ſoftnes or weakenes of his mynd.Neyther
" is *Philipp* himſelfe ignorant, or diſſembleth
" vvhat opinion men haue of him in this be-
" halfe, though vnto me he did ſwere moſt ſo-
" lemnely,that this feare which the Princes had
" of him, vvas vayne; and truly ſo farre forth as
" I may perſuade my ſelfe, to know his mynd,
" I vvould truſt him in ſuch a matter, as much
" as *Bucer*, eſpecially the buſynes being vvith
" ſuch men, as vvould haue ſomewhat yelded
" to them, *&c.*

    81.   Behould heere two points out of Cal-
uyns teſtimony: the firſt that K. Henry the 8.
did deſire Melanchthon to be ſent vnto him,
to put in order his Church of England by his counſell;
vvhich I hould to be a very ly, & only ſpread
abroad in Germany in thoſe dayes (as many
others were) for credit of their new ghoſpel,
and Proteſtant Religion. For that K. Henry
                      in

Calu.ep.13.
ad Pharell.
anno 1539.

in the very end of this yeare 1539. named by *Caluyn*, began the parlament, wherin the terrible Statute of 6. *articles* vvas decreed; against vvhich Melanchthon wrote a large and long discourse, yf we beleeue Iohn Fox ; as in the Latyn *Certamen* of our English Catholike Church we haue sett downe more at large: So as yt was not likely, that K. Henry being of that mynd in religion, which then he was, and resolued to make that Statute against all Protestants, vvould send for *Melanchthon* to take his iudgement in such a cause. The second point in Caluyns letter is, that both *Melanchthon* and *Bucer* were men of no fortitude nor Constancy in Religion; but as weaklings, were ready to yeld to Princes what they demaunded. Which *Beza* also doth signifie plainly of *Melanchthon*, when he wryteth, that he deferred to preach publikely Caluyns doctrine: *Quia nondum satis, ad hæc instillanda, Principum aures ei patebant.* For that Princes eares lay not yet open inough vnto *Melãchthon*, to instill these things (of Caluyns doctrine) vnto them. And thus much of the Censure of Caluyn and Caluinists and other Sacramentaryes touchinge *Melanchthon*.

82.   But as for Catholiks yt were ouer longe to see what they do note against this vnconstant and effeminate Confessor *Melanchthon*, especially concerninge his mutability in opinions, vttered in two principall works of his, to witt his *Common places* and *Confeßion of Augusta*, with the Apology therof, wherin he hath

Cert. Eccl. Angl. anno 1550.

Theod. Beza l. cont. Pap. pag. 143.

Y 3   byn

VVhat
Catholiks
opinion is
of Melanc-
thon.
* *ap. de*
signis.

byn as varyous as the rayn-bow, changinge in
euery edition diuers articles of Religion. As
for example, in his firſt edition of *Comon places,*
* he reiecteth the very name yt ſelfe of *Sacra-*
ment; but in the laſt edition he admitteth yt
plainly. Againe in the ſecond edition of his
comon places, he ſaith, that *there are two Sacra-*
ments only, baptiſme and the *Lords ſupper* : but in
his Catechiſmes ſet forth after that, he ſaith,

there are three, to witt, *baptiſme, abſolution,* and
the *ſupper of the Lord*; which he confirmeth alſo
in the Apology of his *Auguſtane Confeßion,*
where he calleth abſolution *Sacramentum pœ-*
nitentiæ : the Sacrament of pennance. But in
his laſt edition of *Comon places* hauinge better
thought of the matter, he holdeth foure Sacraments, for hauinge numbred the former
three he adioyneth theſe words: *Mihi maximè*

placet etiam addi Ordinationem, vt vocant, id eſt, vo-
cationem ad miniſterium Euangelij : It pleaſeth me
,, moſt of all, that the Sacrament of *Order,* which
,, men call *Ordination,* that is to ſay, the vocation
,, to the miniſtery of the ghoſpell, be added to

the former number of Sacraments. So as heere
yow ſee *Melanchthon* his pleaſure muſt ſtand for
a law of beleefe. For in his firſt edition of the

Cap de par-
tic:p. mēſ;
Domini.

ſame *Comon places* he wrote thus : *Quid in men-*
tem venit ijs, qui inter ſigna gratiæ, ordinem numerâ-
runt? What came in their mynd, I pray yow,
,, that did number takinge of *Orders* among the
,, ſignes of Grace? Whervnto a man might anſwere by asking of *Melanchthon*: And what came
in your mynd to add that now, which yow
ſhut

shut out before; & to change your opinion so often, not only in these points, but in so many more as are obserued by Catholiks? which were ouer longe to be recyted in this place.

83. But now yf we leaue as well Catholiks as Sacramentaryes, and consider what his owne men the Lutherans thought of him, & his inconstancy, we shall see how fittly he is brought in by Iohn Fox for a principall Confessor. For first *Melancthon* himselfe, seeing his owne men to murmure at his often changes, in hi- *Augustane Confession* and Apologv therof, he wrote thus of that matter to Luther. *In Apologia quotidiè multa mutamus, subindè enim mutanda sunt, & ad occasiones accommodanda.* We do change euery day many things in our Apo'ogy, for that they are to be changed, & accommodated vnto occasions as they fall out. And the whole Synod of Saxon diuines in their meetinge and Colloquy at *Altemberge*, in the yeare of Christ 1568. do sett downe in their printed Acts these words. That Martvn Luther did oftentimes chide with *Philipp Melancthon* for his frequent changes of the Confession of *Augusta,* sayinge: *Philippe, liber iste non tuus est, sed Ecclesiae confitentis, ideò, non est tibi integrum toties immutare.* Philippe, this booke, is not thine, but of the confessinge Church, and therfore yt is not lawfull for thee to change yt so often. So Luther. And by this yow may see the sure law of beleefe, which the Lutherans haue, who depend of this Confession of *Augusta,* as the ground of all their beleefe.

Melancht. ep. 1. ad Luth.

The iudgment of Lutherans touchinge Melancthon.

Theol. Saxon. in colloq. Altemberg. fol. 520. ,,

Y 4   84. But

The iudg-
ment of
Saxon di-
uines con-
cerning
Melanctho.
84.   But yt were to iong to shew now these
Lutheran Saxon diuines do disgrace, and dis-
creditt *Melancthon* in the Acts and Gests of this
Synod, for his inconstancy in matters of Religion. For speakinge of one controuersie they
wryte thus: *Affirmamus Philippum in hac controuer-
sia non sentire cum Luthero, neque cum verbo Dei.* We
*Bid. vt sup.
fol.* 377.
do affirme that Philipp in this controuersie
doth not agree eyther with Luther, or with
the word of God; And this is (forsooth) for
that these Saxon diuines were strict, & riged
Lutherans, defendinge all things absolutely
that Luther did defend. And *Melancthon* when
he came to be of more mature yeares, was a
soft, and temperate Lutheran, defendinge
Luthers opinions by discretion, takinge and
leauinge what he thought best, whervpon
*Bid. fol.
463. 464.
465.*
they call him a *good-fellow*, and his *locos Theolo-
gicos,* theologicall places, they call *iocos Theologi-
cos,* theologicall iests or playes. And albeit their
narration of him be somewhat longe, yet shall
I heere sett downe some part therof, therby to
know what *Melancthon* was, we shall say somewhat (say they) of Philipps Theologicall
,, places, but in few vvords and with mode-
,, sty, &c.

*In actis
colloq. Al-
tem. erg.
Fol.*402.
85.   First yt is knowne (say they) that he
changed his said places so oftentymes both in
words and sense, as yt is doubtfull what we
,, may beleeue, and what not. Secondly yt is
,, certayne that Luther did mislike this often
,, changinge of his. Thirdly his old *places* were
,, more pure then his later, as pious men do
iudge

iudge. Fourthly that Luther did not so much as looke ouer his later *places*. Fifthly that Luther being old, and especially after his death the same *places* were chãged. Sixtly, that many things are found in these later *places*, which do disagree with the wordof God, and with Luthers wrytings, *&c.* And so much for his *places*. And as for the *Confession* of *Augusta*, we say in like manner, yt hath often tymes byn changed by *Philipp*, which he had no authority to do, seing other men had now made the same to be theirs by their subscriptions, and he by so often changinge yt opened the way to the Sacramentaryes to creepe into yt also; And as for his other bookes they haue diuers things of great moment in them, which do neither agree with the Augustane Confession nor with the word of God, as about *freewill*, about the *ghospell* and *law*, about *Iustification*, about the *supper*, about *Magistrates*, about *Antichrist*, and the like; and how often Philipp was deceyued in many things, and suffered humaine infirmity, we had rather conceale in this place, yf by occasion of this Colloquy we were not forced to call the same to memory. In the very tyme when the *Confession* of *Augusta* was first wrytten, yt is knowne, and may be seene by epistles yet extant, how couragiously Luther did erect and confirme *Melancthon*, who seemed to stagger; and what ado *Luther* had with him to make him leaue of all respect to the primacy of the Pope (which is the synew of Antichrist) and how often Luther

,, ther did pull backe *Melan&hon* , when he was
,, runninge beyond his bands ; and laftly how
,, often Philipp did change and vary his owne
,, books, is ouer truly obie&ed vnto vs by the
,, papifts, *&c.*

86. Hitherto is the difcourfe of the faxon
diuines concerning the Inconftancy of *Philipp*
Melan&hon ; but fome other graue authors a-
monge them, do go further yet, and do touch
him of impiety, as namely *Conradus Schuffelbur-*
gius, in his worke, intituled *The Diuinity of Cal-*
uiniftes, wryteth this hiftory of *Melan&hon* : *Ma-*
gifter Ioannes Coliander, &c. Maifter *Iohn Colian-*
der , and a faithfull Do&or of the Church of
Brunfwicke , did recount vnto me, that he did
conferre at a certayne tyme with Maifter *Phi-*
,, *lipp Melan&hon* , that before tyme had byn his
,, Maifter, about this controuerfie, that we haue
,, now with Caluinifts, (touchinge the *Reall pre-*
,, *fence*) vfinge many reafons to perfuade him to
,, wryte, though yt were but one fide of paper,
,, to refolue men, that doubted whether he held
,, with Luther therin , or noe : wherat *Maifter*
,, *Philipp* was very angry, and faid he had wryt-
,, ten inough ; and yf he were forced to wryte
,, againe, he would wryte that which fhould
,, awaken the whole world ; & when the other
,, fought to pacifie him, and faid yt was only for
,, their fatisfa&ion , that doubted whether he
,, beleeued the bread of the fupper to be the
true naturall body of Chrift ; *Maifter Philipp* takinge vp a little peece of paper from the
,, ground , and caftinge yt away againe , with
great

great difdayne, faid : yf the true naturall body „
of Chrift, be in the bread confecrated, as you „
beleeue; why then may not the body of Chrift „
be in this paper alfo, which blafphemous „
word being heard out of the mouth of *Maifter* „
Philipp himfelfe, *Maifter Coliander* departed from „
him fadd and wonderinge. *&c.* Thus wryteth
he, fhewinge therby *Melancthon* to be falne to
the moft abfurd herefies of vbiquitaryes, that
hold Chrifts body to be in euery thinge, as
much as in the Sacrament.

87.   The fame author alfo alleageth another
example of one *Doctor Ioachinus Morlinus* of the The hard
Citty of *Brunfwicke,* who faid one day in a pu- fentence of
blike leffon, fpeakinge of *Philipp Melancthon* Ioachinus
Morlinus of
(himfelfe alfo being a Lutheran) that albeit Melancthon
he had deferued well of the Church, and of all
learned men, by diuers of his wrytings, and
had byn his Maifter, yet doubted he greatly of
his faluation, by reafon of his errors about the
articles of the *fupper, freewill, Iuftification* and the
like. And therfore he faid : *In his (Philippe) lau-* *Ioach. Mor-*
det te Diabolus, & non ego. In thefe points let the *lin. in publ.*
lect.
diuell praife thee (Phillipp) and not I : And
then turninge to his hearers to fhew his good
will towards him, but euill iudgement, he
faid : *Si poffem ego redimere falutem Philippi noftri* *Ibidem.*
praeceptoris, &c. Yf I could redeeme the falua- „
tion of our *Maifter Philipp,* with the perill of my „
body and life, I would do yt ; but he is taken „
out of this world, and carryed to the iudge- „
ment of the horrible Tribunall of the lyuinge „
fonne of God, to plead his caufe there, *&c.* „

And

And foe there muft vve leaue him .

88.   Thus vvryteth he'; and now hauinge

Melanchon iudged to be of no religion vvhen he vvas old.

brought *Philipp Melanchon* from Iohn Fox his Calendar to the Tribunall of Chrift, like inough to be damned by the iudgement of his owne fcholler, who knew him better then Fox; vve muft leaue him there alfo and Fox vvith him, befeechinge almighty God vve may find a morehappy acceffe thither, by keepinge one and the felfe-fame Catholike faith, and liuinge accordinge to the precepts therof; then they and other fectaryes haue found, or are like to fynd by their innouation, changes, and felfe-will choyces, wherof *Melanchon* had made fo many, as in his old age findinge nothing to reft in but his owne iudgmēt, he feemed to be of no religion at all, though he had framed a certayne fect of himfelfe called *Adiaphorifts*, or indifferent men, but properly *Melanchonifts*. And *Vigandus* one of the Centuriators of *Magdeburge*, recountinge the heretiks amonge the new ghofpellers, calleth this fect

Ioan. Vigand.

of *Melanchon Coturnifices, feu Concionatores Chrifti & Antichrifti*, vveauers of fhipmens hofes, that ,, preach partly Chrift, and partly Antichrift. So faith that hoate Lutheran. But *Melanchon* vvas none of them, but rather weary of them.

89.   And yt is to be thought, that yf he could with his honour and fafty haue returned againe to Catholike Religion, he might eafily haue byn intreated. And a thinge fell out not longe before his death, vvhich doth much confirme this opinion. For that he makinge a

certayne

certayne voiage in Germany, and comminge into an Inne, where a yonge gentleman was lodged before him, vvhen his name was knowne to be *Melancthon*, the said gentleman though there was scarse roome, yet was content, that the host should place him in part of the lodginge, which he had taken vp; soe they supped togeather, and had much curteous talke, and went to bedd. And in the morning being to depart (the said gentleman being a Catholike, and hauinge vsed his prayers both at his goinge to bed, and rysinge, which Catholikes are wont to do) *Melancthon* asked him of what Religion he was, who aunsweringe that he was a Catholike, the other with great inward feelinge as yt seemed, wished him to continew so, for that albeit (said he) some abuses be in their Religion; yet had they pious order and discipline amonge them, which sectaryes haue not. This history diuers graue men of that nation do recount for most certayne. And that *Melancthon* died vpon the yeare 1560. of no certayne Religion at all. And so will we leaue him, and passe to *Peter Martyr* the next Confessor that followeth after him in Fox his Calendar.

Melancthon seemed to vvish himselfe a Catholike in his old age.

90. This *Peter Martyr* then being an Italian by his country, and by profession a friar, had his ordinary vocation to the new ghospell by desire to haue a woman, as had also *Bernardinus Ochinus*, that had byn in like manner a friar of the order of *S. Francis*, both of them hauinge runne out of Italy to enioy the new Euangelicall

The story of Peter Martyr & Bernardinus Ochinus.

licall liberty in Germany; & afterward when
Charles the fifth had obtayned the victory
ouer the Proteſtants, vpon the yeare 1547. they
both made their refuge to England, each of
them leadinge with him a nunne for his companion. And though *Bernardinus* ſtayed not
long in England, he yet went ſo faſt forward
in that ſenſuall ghoſpellinge liberty of weomen , as he did not only praiſe poligamy, (as
Bucer alſo had done accordinge to the teſtimony of *Eraſmus Alberus, B Gardner* and others)
but wrote a booke moreouer therof, & printed the ſame allowinge openly the vſe of many wyues at once.

Bernardinus Ochinus his booke of poligamy.

91.   But as for *Peter Martyr*, after great variety
of new opiniôs, which he had paſſed through
in Germany, before his comminge into England, when he came thither , he was content
to offer himſelfe to the Archbiſhop Cranmer,
and to the L. Protecter (as *Bucer* and *Phagius*
alſo did) to hould and teach that Religion
which ſhould be appointed him by the Act of
Parlament, not as yet gathered togeather;
vvhervpon he was ſent to read at *Oxford*, as
Bucer was to *Cambridge*, and *Ochinus* was retayned to preache in *Italian* in *London*; but he
takinge the matter in dudgen , that the other
two were perferred before him, quickly retyred himſelfe backe againe out of England.
And after his departure, there inſued that ridiculous accident , which we haue recounted
before in the ſecond * part of this treatiſe, out
of the teſtimonyes of *Doctor Saunders D. Allen,*
our

*Sandrus l.
2 de Schiſm.
Anglic.*

** Cap. 12.
num. 34.*

our late Cardinall and others, who were then present in the vniuersity: to witt, that *Peter Martyr* beginninge to read the first Epistle to the Corinthians, & presuminge that the Parlament would be ended before he should come to the 11. Chapter, where the controuersie of the Sacrament is handled, and consequently that yt would be determyned by the said parlament, what part he should hould, eyther with *Luther*, *Zuinglius* or *Caluyn*, yt fell out contrary to his expectation, that he came to the said place of the Apostle, before the Parlament could agree of the matter; vvhervpon he deferred and delayed, and sent posts oftentymes to *B. Cranmer* to haue it dispached, which at last was done; And Peter went vp the next day to read and defend the same, as though there had neuer byn any doubt thereof.

Peter Martyr fore imbroyled by the delay of the parlamēt.

92. The same *Peter* confessed also to *Barklett Greene gentleman martyr* (as * before yow haue heard in his story) that at his first comminge into England, he was in diuers points a papist (though he had taught heresies in Germany many yeares before) & this affirmed *Greene* in publike consistory, but the good cheere of *Oxford*, togeather with the company of his woman, and other libertyes & dissolutions of that tyme, made him iump of the English states Religion; and yt is a markable point, which diuers did obserue, that this man with his fellowes, comming as new Apostles to reforme and conuert the whole kingedome to

* *Ian.* 13.

Peter Martyr not fully resolued in Religion vvhen he came into England.

their

their Religion, were neuer knowen to faſt one day (which yet was in frequent vſe with the Apoſtles of Chriſt, and with our Engliſh firſt Apoſtle *S. Auſten)* nor otherwiſe to chaſten their bodyes with *S. Paul*, but all was ſinginge of Pſalmes, all was banquettinge, and feaſtinge, merry tales and conuerſation, with theſe men, and their weomen, and frends, at the firſt entrance of their ghoſpell in England: ſo as yt was a ghoſpell of good newes indeed for them, that had run out of Italy, and Germany, or had byn baniſhed thence before.

93.   But to returne to *Peter Martyr* in particular, he was noted preſently by all men, that were not partially affe cted or blynded with the paſsion of hereſie, to be of a very light behauiour and ſpeach, and that he would talke willingly of his woman, & of their too great loue & affe ctions the one towards the other, more then modeſty might beare, euen in a ſecular man, and much leſſe in a friar. And at length when his ſaid nunne was dead, he did not only praiſe her publikely in a ſermon, but wrote a ſtrange complaint and wofull lamentation, of the great want he found of her preſence, to *Syr Iohn Cheke* the Kings ſchoole-maiſter (then a great Proteſtant but after a Catholike in Q. Maryes dayes ſayinge amonge other vnſeemely points, that by loſſe & lacke of her, he was but *dimidiatus homo*, that is only halfe a man. And when afterward he went out of England againe, he is ſaid to haue gotten another preſently, though he were then ould

The effeminate mynd of *Peter Martyr*.

ould. So as yf he came not to be *trigamus* with *Bucer*, yet was he *bigamus* at leaſt.

94. And now yt happened, that about the very tyme when *Peter Martyr* was ſent forth of England, *Conradus Pellicanus*, the Zwinglian preacher at *Strasburge*, who had byn a Franciſcan friar before, came to dye, and by that chance *Peter Martyr* had his place the yeare 1556. And ſome few yeares, after that againe he was appointed to go with *Beza* and other ten miniſters, to the conference of *Poiſye* in France in the yeare of Chriſt 1561. (the moſt part wherof were marryed friars and monks) there was he partaker alſo of the extraordinary delicacy prouided for him, & his fellowes, by certayne noble men, but eſpecially by weomen of France, that fauoured their ſects. Of which point I haue treated * largely before out of the Relation of *B. Claudius Sainctes*, that was preſent, and of *Genebrard* and other wryters of France yt ſelfe; as alſo of the irreconciliable diſagreement that was betweene *Theodore Beza* and *Peter Martyr* in points of doctrine at that conference, namely about the Sacraments of *Baptiſme*, and of the Lords ſupper; And this teſtifyed by their owne letters publiſhed by the Biſhop of *Metz* in a particular booke. And the originall letters were ſeene and teſtified by *B. Claudius Sainctes* in a booke wrytten to *Beza* himſelfe.

95. Biſhopp *Genebrard* alſo that was preſent at the ſaid Colloquy or diſputation of *Poyſie* wryteth, that *Peter Martyr* was ſo vehement

Sur. in hiſt. an. Domini 1556.

Peter Martyr went to the cōference of Poiſy.

* *VVarn. vvord ens. 2.6.4.n.12, 13. &c.*

B. Pegnillus l. de diſenſ. miniſtrorū in coll. Poiſſe Sainct. in reſponſ. ad Apol.Beza.

Z   agaínſt

againft the Caluinifts opinions about the prefence of Chrift in the Sacrament, that he
cryed out in the faid conference, *that for his part*
he vvould neuer agree to their monftrous opinion,
wherby they affirmed, *reipfa quidem abeffe corpus*
*Chrifti, reipfa tamen fumi,*that the body of Chrift
was really abfent from the bread,& yet really
receyued therwith. By which diffention,and
other his proceedings as well with *Caluinifts,*
Lutherans , and *Vbiquitaryes,* who do hold that
the body of Chrift is euery where according
to the former fpeech of *Melancthon,* when he
caft away the broken paper (which *Melancthon*
died the yeare before this Colloquy , to witt
anno 1560.) *Peter Martyr* (I fay) became fo vn-
gratefull to all kind of fects , as the very next
yeare after his goinge from *Poyfie,*to witt 1562.
of very greefe of mynd , as fome thinke, he
died , though others add fufpition of poyfon
alfo : for fo wryteth *Genebrard* in the place before cyted. *Peter Martyr* (faith he) *the* 12. *of No-*
uember 1562. *gaue vp the goft, not without fuppition of*
poyfon giuen by Caluinifts , from vvhome he had difa-
greed in the meetinge at Poyfie. And he died at the ve-
ry tyme , when he was preparinge to wryte againft
Brentius the Lutheran, who endeauored to bring in the
monftrous herefie of Vbiquity, &c. Thus he.

96.   And this was the end of *Peter Martyr*
vpon the yeare of Chrift 1562. neyther do I
fee , what great caufe Fox hath to bragge of
this Saint , or to putt him into his Calendar,
more then many other his companions , but
only perhaps,for that he was more inconftant
and

Geneb. l.4.
chron *anno*
1562. *pag.*
459.

Geneb. ibid.

About Pe-
ter Mar-
tyrsdeath.

and fingular then diuers others. Wherfore I
shall stand no longer vpon him, but passe to
the last Saint of this moneth, and whole Calendar, which is K. Edward the sixt, a worthy
Confessor, to shutt vp so large and worthy
a lift of Foxian Saints.

97. But first of all, why Fox determined to
make this yonge *K. Edward* the sixth a Confessor of his Church, I do not fee any speciall
reason, but only his owne will; and for that
perhapps he thought yt honourable to haue
one King at least in his whole Calendar; therby to be able to compare in part with our Catholike Calendar, that hath so many Kings
and Queenes, both Martyrs, and Confessors
of the English bloud, but Fox found none of
his Religion, but only this child to bestow
that title on. For albeit he calleth K. Henry
the eyght, now and then, a ghospeller, yet for
that he burned so many of Iohns Gospellinge
people, he durst not putt him in for a Saint in
this his Calendar. *Q. Anne Bolen* also he praiseth
exceedingly in his Acts and Monuments, as a
more forward ghospeller then the King himselfe, and holdeth her indeed for a very Saint
in his narration of her, and yet I knowe not
how or why she came not into this Calendar;
But *K. Edward* the sixth at his very entrance
to his gouernement, though he were then
but nyne yeares old; yet doth Fox place
him, as the head of the Church in a high
throne, deliueringe the Bible, and distribu-
tinge the ghospell to the whole Realme,

Z 2 and

VVhy Fox maketh King Edward the sixth a confessor.

K. Edward the 6. confessor.

Fox pag. 961.

and the like, as we haue shewed largely in

† *Part. 1.*
c. 12. part.
cap. 12.

the first and second * part of this Treatise.
98. But in deed yf yt be true which most
men do thinke, that the innocent child was
made away afterward, & holpen to his death
by those that raigned vnder him, and would
be loath that he should haue come to raigne

The Cala-
mity that
fell to K.
Edvvard
and the
realme by
the nevv
ghospell.

ouer them; but to serue to sett vp new Religion in his name: then may he better be called
a Martyr then a Confessor of Fox his ghospell;
seeing yt is most likely, that yf that ghospell
had not entred, nor the fatall mutation byn
made from that which his Father left; & that
the faithfull Counselors assigned by K. Henry had byn suffered to continue about the
child, who were remoued by pretense of their
not fauouringe this new ghospell; most likely
(I say) yt is, that the said yonge kynge might
haue lyued many fayre yeares afterward, yea
euen to this tyme, seing he would not haue
byn so old by diuers years, as the late Queene
was at her death. And might haue left behind
him much faire yssew, for so much as the principall cause, which the nobility and people of
Scotland alleaged in the yeare 1547. before
the field of *Mustleborrow*, why they would not
consent vnto the marriage agreed betweene
the said K., and their yonge Q. his Maiesties
mother; was the difference of Religion, and
the late innouation made therof in England.
99. Now how heynous a cryme this was in
those English Counselours, to imbue the innocent age of that young Prince with a contrary

trary Religion to his Father, and all his anceſtors, from the firſt Conuerſion of England
to his dayes; & contrary to the expreſſe will,
order, and commaundement of their Lord
K. Henry, and their oath and promiſes for the
ſame; God himſelfe did ſhew ſoone after by
the euent that enſued; For that none of them
all eſcaped vnpuniſhed, one cuttinge of the
other, as was conuenient, for the puniſhment
of ſo barbarous and heynous a ſinne.

The hay-
nous crime
of peruer-
tinge King
Edvvard
in his Re-
ligion a-
gainſt his
Fathers
vvill.

100. In the Catholike doctrine founded
both in reaſon, law of nature, and word of
God, yt is held for a firme principle, that the
power of the parents is ſo great ouer their
children, vntill they come to full vſe of reaſon,
that the children of very infidelis may not be
baptized, nor made of another Religion, then
their parents are, without the free conſent of
their ſaid parents; for that as their parents
themſelues may not be forced to Chriſtian
Religion by violence, except themſelues will:
ſo may not their children in preiudice of their
paternall authority. And yf this be true in
drawing children to Chriſtian Religion from
infidelity; and that the ſame were a moſt wicked Act in Catholike doctrine to attempt;
how much more wicked was yt in theſe men
to inſtill to the yonge Prince, a plaine contrary and oppoſite Religion, to the King his Father; he being yet vnder yeares of diſcretion
to iudge therof, and his ſaid Father hauing vtterly forbidden the ſame vpon his death-bedd
and Teſtament.

D. Thom.
p. 3. q. 68.
art. 10. &
ſecunda ſe-
cunda q. 10.
art. 11. &
omnes ſcha-
laſt. ibid.

Z 3　　101. And

101. And albeit his said Lord and Father was now dead; yet did *patris potestas*, his power both of Father and King ouer him, continue all the tyme of his minority, and consequently his will and commaundemement being knowen, togeather with his speciall detestation of the Sacramentary sect, vttered at his death, did cry out against this so notorious an iniury offered to his sonne, and realme. But much more was this seene some yeares after, in the neerest yong Prince of bloud, countrey, and kyn, vnto K. Edward in the world, who in the life, and sight of his owne dearest mother and Queene, (that both by words, protestations, and teares reclaymed against the same) was by much more forcible violence taken from her, in the very first monethes of his age, and made to be her enemy, whome yet he knew not, and was imbued with an opposite Religion vnto her, without her will, consent, or likinge, an Act against all rule of reason, iustice, piety and Religion.

The violence vsed to the K. and Q. of Scotland anne 1566.

102. And truly, yt Princes may iustly, when they come to years of discretion and gouernement, take accoumpt of temporall iniuryes & abuses commytted against them, in their minority, by such, as in their names did tyrannize both ouer their person and state; how much more may, and ought they do yt in spirituall matters, that concerne their soule, and eternall saluation? But alas; the infirmity and corruption of mans nature is such, as we feele more worldly and temporall losses, then spirituall

rituall and euerlaftinge : and the diuell hath a
more crafty and couert meanes to worke the
fame euen by our owne will, and approbation, eyther before or after the fact, offeringe
the firft iniury to our faid will and vnderftandinge yt felfe, and drawinge the fame to like
of the iniury ; euen as yf fome company of A dange-
theeues, had fuch an art of ftrange enchaunt- rous en-
ment, as after they had robbed and fpoyled a mēt ofhe-
man of the greateft treafure in the world,they reticall
could with fome potion or charme make him education.
like of yt,yea glory in yt,and thanke them for
the fame. And were not this a pittifull cafe
thinke yow ? yes truly. And this is the very
cafe of Infants and Chriftian children fpoyled
of their parents Religion, and brought vp in
herefy againft their wills,with fuch inchaunt-
ments of flattery, & inftillations of liking the
robbery yt felfe commytted vpon them,as by
fraud they are brought to allow the fame,and
to loue & remunerate the robbers themfelues.
103. And for example of this, I would aske
any Englifh noble-man at this day, whether
yf his fonne fhould be ftollen from him by
Turkes or Mores,and made of their Religion,
againft the will of his parents, were this robbery,or violence,or no ? and were this iniury
to the child himfelfe, or not ? Truly I thinke
no man of common reafon will deny, but
that yt were the higheft iniury that could be
diuifed, both againft Father and fonne. And
yet notwithftandinge, yf a man fhould aske
diuers of them that haue fuffered this iniury;

(as for example *Ochelli Baſſa* and *Cicala Baſſa* in our dayes, borne of moſt Chriſtian parents, the one in *Calabria*, the other in *Sicilia*, but taken in their infancy, robbed of their Religion and countrey and made Turks) they will deny to haue receaued iniury, but rather great benefitt therby; & yet all true Chriſtians will iudge otherwiſe. And this is the caſe of all other hereſies in like manner.

104.   But to returne to our K. Edward, of whome we began this ſpeache, albeit he had run this daunger alſo yf he had liued, to like of the iniuryes done vnto him by heretiks, and vpon that hope and preſuppoſition, no doubt they were donne by ſuch as were the authors therof; yet ſome are of opinion, that if he had had longer life indeed, yt would haue fallen out otherwayes, & that the feare therof ſhortened his dayes and haſtened his diſpatch. Truly I haue heard a very wiſe, and honourable man affirme, from the mouth of Q. Mary her ſelfe (of whoſe Councell he had byn) that ſhe with teares would often lament the memory of her deare brother K. *Edward*, ſaying that yf he had lyued, ſhe hoped verily to haue ſeene him a good Catholike, and to haue puniſhed exemplarly all thoſe wicked men, that ſo egregiouſly abuſed his youth & realme in his name. For that in diuers ſpeaches which ſhe had with him, wherein ſhe recounted to him what deadly hatred their Father K. Henry did beare againſt heretiks in his dayes, but eſpecially againſt the Sacramentaryes, whome now

now they had brought into England vnder
his authority, and that he was the firft Kinge
of all Englifh bloud, that euer allowed or im-
braced the fame , or admitted yt into that
realme, and that all this would remayne vpon
his foule afterward : thefe things (I fay) and
other the like, when fhe tould the yong King,
with thofe effectuall words , which fhe well
could , the innocent child would fall a weepinge with her , and fay that he was priuy to
none of thefe doyngs ; but yf euer God gaue
him life, he would take accoumpt of them all
one day ; And further promifed his faid fyfter
to remember his Father & grand-father, and
to keep fecrett what fhe had told him , without vtteringe any of thefe conferences to his
vncle the Protector , or others; as indeed he
did not (which fhewed his difcretion and fidelity to his fifter) albeit thofe of the chamber
feeing him fadd after fuch talke, began to fu-
fpect fome fuch thing, and thervpon in his later yeares would not permitt her to haue acceffe vnto him but very feldome , and with
great iealofy. And this was all the Confefsion
of Fox his faith which K. *Edward* euer made,
to our knowledge , and therby lett the reader
iudge , how worthily he is made heere a Calendar Confeffor of his Church & Religion.
And fo with this we fhall leaue both the one
and the other, and end this our examen of Fox
his whole Calendar, other matters fhalbe
handled afterwards in their dew place, & particularly in the obferuations followinge.

E Y G H T

EYGHT SEVERALL OB-

SERVATIONS AND CONSIDERA-

TIONS ABOVT THE PREMISSES:

*VVherin is considered vvhat persons are left out, and
vvhat are put into Fox his Calendar; how they are
canonized; vvhat spiritt and agreement of
Religion they had among themselues; whether they were lawfully punished, or
no, and such like pointes.*

C H A P.   XVII.

ALBEYT I cannot doubt, but that the difcreet and iudicious reader, in pervsinge
ouer the former Story of Foxian Martyrs and
Confessors, hath made diuers notes and obseruations vnto himselfe, for his better memory and iudgement therin : yet some few also I
thought good to lay togeather in this place,
which are these that ensue. First, that as sundry people are put into this Calendar, for holy
Martyrs and Confessors, very impertinently,
and without any iust reason at all, as in pervsinge yow haue seene : so sundry are left out
also, that seeme should haue had their place
therin, with as great reason or greater then
other of the best sort that are preferred.

First con-
sideration
vvhy some   2.   As for example, amonge the Lutheran
Protestants, seeing Fox is content to admitt
some

fome of them for Saints, yt feemeth that *Flaccus Illyricus*, *Vigandus*, *Faber* and their fellowes the *Magdeburgians* moſt highly deferuinge of the Proteſtant Religion, by wrytinge their laborious and lying centuryes, fhould haue byn admitted among the reſt. And the like may be faid of *Ioachinus VVeſtphalus* head fuperintendent of Saxony, *Ioannes Brentius*, *Heſhuſius* and other fuch chiefe German pillars of that fide, who as well might haue byn Calendred, as *Melancthon*, *Phagius*, *Bucer*, and fuch other, that haue their roomes in that ranke, except yt be perhaps, for that thefe men wrote more earneſtly againſt *Caluyn* and Caluiniſts; but fo did alſo fometymes *Melancthon* and *Bucer*, as before hath byn fhewed.

3.   But yet a farre greater queſtion yt is, why the very firſt Fathers and founders of Sacramentary Religion yt felfe are left out of this Calendar, to witt *Carolſtadius*, *OEcolampadius*, *Zuinglius*, and *Caluyn*, though for the firſt three, that were immediate fchollers of *Luther*, and firſt brake from him to begin the Sacramentary fect, his feuere fentence and condemnation of them, which we haue fett downe before in the * ſtory of his life at large, togeather with his deteſtation of their fpiritt (he being a Saint himfelfe alfo of this Calendar) might perhaps deteyne Iohn Fox, from canonizinge them in this place. But of *Iohn Caluyn* fome other reafon muſt needs be, which I cannot imagine to be other, but the notorious infamy of his life, as alſo the little likinge which

Febr. 18.

the

the ſtate of England had of him,& his actions, as well for denyinge the ſupremacy Eccleſia-ſticall, to temporall Princes (which is the cheefe wall of their Religion) as alſo for ſet-tinge vp the dangerous plott of Puritaniſme, and ſpreadinge yt from *Geneua* into *England, Scotland, France,* and other places, as yow may ſee in the bookes of *Dangerous Poſitions; Suruey of diſciplinary doctrine,* and other ſuch Treatiſes written by our Engliſh Proteſtants againſt the Puritans, wherin they are ſo farre from ma-kinge *Caluyn* and *Beza* Saints, as albeit for ci-uilityes ſake, they giue them the titles of *Mai-ſter Caluyn,* and *Maiſter Beza:* yet yf yow reſpect the ſubſtance of that they write againſt them, they do make them the moſt notableſt decey-uers & cogginge companions,that euer were, and very knaues indeed, & firebrands of hell, vnder the titles of maiſters.

Of *Caluyn* and *Beza.*

4.   And in this point do our Engliſh Prote-ſtants ioyne with the moſt learnedſt Prote-ſtants of all Germany, concerninge the noto-rious wickednes of *Iohn Caluyn.* For firſt the foreſaid Superintendent of Saxony *Ioachinus Weſtphalus* doth lay open the ſame egregiouſ-ly in an Epiſtle to Caluyn himſelfe, wrytten *anno Domini* 1557. prouing him therin to be a moſt lyinge,and deceytfull heretike; And then in another booke written the next yeare after, intituled : *A Confutation of Caluyns lyes,* he per-formeth the ſame more largly ; as doth alſo a famous Lutheran preacher,named *Samuell Au-ſterinus* in his booke intituled; *A demonſtration of*
the

the fallacyes of Iohn Caluyn *, &c.* Imprinted at *Lauginga anno Domini* 1591. And two yeares af-ter him againe *Doctor Aegidiu Hunnæus* in his booke intituled *Caluinus Iudaizans, Caluyn play-inge the Iew in corruptinge, falſiſyinge, &c.* printed at *VVittenberge* 1793. And fiue yeares after that againe *Doctor Albertus Grauerus* Reader of Diui-nity, declaymeth the ſame more largely in his booke intituled : *Bellum Ioannis Caluini &* I E S V *Chriſti, &c.* The warre betweene Iohn Cal-uyn and I E S V S Chriſt, *&c.*

5. And laſtly, (for I will paſſe no further in this place) the booke of *Doctor Zacharias Riuan-drus ,* intituled *Lupus Caluinianus excoriatus ,* the Caluinian wolfe ſkynned or yncaſed, doth giue vs aboundant teſtimony of this matter, to wit, to yeld vs ſome cauſe, why Iohn Fox, like a Fox indeed, did leaue out his *Maiſter Caluyn* from the Calendar of Saints, notwith-ſtandinge the great furniture therof is of his ſchollers and diſciples, ſo as in this particular, the ſayinge of our Sauiour holdeth not: *Non eſt diſcipulus ſuper magiſtrum.* The ſcholler is not aboue his maiſter.

6. And now as this firſt conſideration hath byn of them, that haue byn left out : ſo may the next be of thoſe that are putt in, which is a point of more length then the former, yf we would proſecute the ſame: but I will only as yt were with the fingar point towards yt, and therwith leaue yt to the Readers for their contemplation. It is then to be noted, that in the Calendar and ſtory therof, are compriſed

The ſecōd conſidera-tiō, vvhat people be put into the Calen-dar of Fox.

all

all the heades of factions,and sects, that haue
byn different from the knowne Catholike
Religion,and opposite among themselues for
these three or foure last hundred yeares, as
VValdo of *Lyons*, and his *VValdensians*, the Earle
of *Tholosa*, and his *Albigensians*, *Iohn VVickliffe* of
England and his *VVickliffians*, *Iohn Husse* of *Be-
meland*,and his *Hussits*, *Iohn Zisca* of the same nation, and his *Thaborits*, *VValter Lolhard* in Germany, and his *Lollardians*: and in our dayes
Martyn Luther and his *Lutherans*, both sectes
Molles and *Rigidi*, *Vldericus Zuinglius*, and his
Zuinglians, *Iohn Caluin* and his *Caluinists* both
mingled and Puritans; and other the like: All
which are allowed and commended by Fox
eyther in his Calendar or history,though they
did not a little disagree, as well among themselues, as with the Catholike Church,both in
words,actions,manner of life,preachings and
wrytings, as before hath byn shewed.

7.   And wheras we that follow Catholike
doctrine, are so exact for holding vnion therin, as we reiect and hould for wicked (accordinge to the Creed of *S. Athanasius*, and first
Councell of Nice) whosoeuer doth not beleeue inuiolably the said Catholike faith
wholy and entirely in euery point, and do
sometymes condemne euen to death, and
burne some for dissentinge in one only point
of faith, (as Iohn Fox himselfe hath diuers
tymes complayned) how can yt be, that he &
his Church can gather vp and ty togeather in
one vnion of faith and communion of Saints,
all

See before
in *Taylor*
burned
1. *Martij*.

all theſe different and oppoſite heads, togeather with their members & followers? Truly,
no other way, but only as Sampſon tyed his
Foxes togeather by the tayles, though their
heads and faces were oppoſite, and contrary
one to another, which ſerued him not to
plowgh or ſow, plant or tyll, but only to ſett
a fire, waſt & deſtroy the corne vvhich others
had ſowed before, which is the only office &
peculiar vvorke, that theſe wranglinge oppoſite hereticall heads do bringe forth in the
Church of God, to witt, pull downe, digg vp,
deſtroy, diſcreditt & diſgrace that which was
ſowen, planted and eſtabliſhed before them,
& therby to bring all to miſdoubt, vnbeleefe
and atheiſme. And ſo I leaue them to Iohn
Fox to be diſpoſed of.

8. The third conſideration may be, of the
different manner of proceedinge in the Catholike Church for declaringe mens holynes,
from that which is vſed by heretiks and ſectaryes: For as we, out of the common ſenſe and
reaſon of all men, do ſay and affirme, that all
are not of one holynes or meritt of life in this
vvorld: ſo to publiſh or make declaration
therof, after their death, appertayneth rather
to ſome publike authority, vvhich may or-
dayne more certayne & exact enquiry therof,
then to any particular man, vvho may be carryed away eyther vvith paſsion, or deceyued
by ignorance, or otherwiſe abuſed by falſe information, more eaſily then a publike magiſtrate. Whervpon yt is ſeene, that vvhen
among

The third
conſidera-
tiõ of dif-
ferẽt man-
ner of Ca-
nonizatiõ

among Catholiks any one is to be canonized, that is to say, to be declared for a holy man or woman, great and long search is made about the matter first, and many hundred persons examined; many records also are sought out, of the life and actions of the person, of his vertues and miracles, and such other points appertayninge to sanctity.

9. And for so much as the publike & highest Ecclesiasticall magistrate, in whose name and authority the examen is made, cannot be presumed to haue interest or passion therin, yt is euident that the matter must needs passe with farre more indifferency, grauity, sincerity, and truth, then yf yt passed vpon the word, credit, or assertion of any one particular man, as amongst heretiks & sectaryes yt doth, where euery man canonizeth or condemneth according to his owne fancy: For that they hauing no one generall, or supreme head acknowledged by all, do fall at diuisiō or strife among themselues, one part sanctifyinge and canonizing such for holy men and weomen, as the other commonly do reiect and condemne, as yow haue heard before in the storyes of *Luther, Zuinglius, Caluyn,* and other like: yea some one man of a particular sect, will presume to canonize sometyme some for Saints of his sect, whome other of the very selfe same sect will hould for wicked, as heere in Fox his Calendar are many examples; as that of *Cowbridge,* vvhoe denyed Christ; that of *Colins,* who held vp the dogg to be adored, and Fox himselfe con-

confeſſeth that he was madde: That of *Flower*
the Apoſtata monke, that wounded the Prieſt
at *VVeſtminſter*, & ſaid yt was the ſpirit of God
that had moued him thervnto: That of *Roger
Oneley*, hanged for coniuringe, and *Eleanor Cob-*
ham condemned of wichcraft: That of *Old-*
caſtle, Acton, and other rebells, hanged in *Saint*
Gyles fields, for conſpiringe the death of King
Henry the fifth and his brethren: That of the
famous ruffian and murderer *Ziſca*: That of
the three theeues *Kinge, Debnam,* and *Marſhe,*
hanged in chaines by commandement of *King*
Henry the eyght, for robbinge the Church of
Douer-court in Kent. All theſe I ſay, and other
like vnholy Saints, hallowed heere and canonized by Iohn Fox for Martyrs and Confeſſors of his Church, I nothing doubt, but will
not be allowed for ſuch, by many of the diſ-
creeter ſort of Proteſtants in England, but rather reiected, and thought fitter to be flunge
to the dunghill, then to be placed in an Eccleſiaſticall Calendar. And this is the good agreement, that ſectaryes can haue amonge themſelues in theſe points.

10. The fourth conſideration may be, what
perſons Iohn Fox hath put out of his Calendar, that were in ours before, and what recompence he hath made for them, by putting
in others, in their places. For albeit he hath
byn ſo courteous, as to lett ſtand all the
Apoſtles, and ſome other old Saints alſo; as
S. *Mary Magdalen,* S. *Marke,* S. *Luke,* and ſome
few others: yet doth he put out both S. *Barnaby*

The 4. cõ-
ſideration
vvhat
Saints
Fox put-
teth out
and into
the Ca-
lendar.

A a   their

their equall, & all the Doctors of the ancient
Church, Greeke, and Latyn, with about 200.
Martyrs and Virgins, as yow may fee in our
Calendar; and in place therof, hath putt in
fuch a multitude of artificers, labourers, fher-
men, weauers, cowherds, coblers, taylors,
fmithes, and fpinfters, as yow may fee in his
Calendar: who as they could not be true Martyrs for the reafons before alleaged, to witt,
for dyinge for their owne difagreeinge fancyes: fo neyther Confeffors, partly for the
fame caufe, & partly for that their lyues were
nothinge eminent in vertue aboue the common fort of men and weomen, by Fox his
owne Confefsion. For what fingular thinge
doth he commonly recyte of any of thefe his
Confeffors, that exceeded the vulgar fort of
Chriftians, vvhat extraordinary faftinge,
prayer, almes-deeds, mortification of the flefh,
doth he alleage in any of them? Nay it is to
be noted, that fcarfe any one of them all, man
or woman, is recorded to haue obferued virginity or continent life? And yet will not
Fox deny, but that thefe thinges are great
graces and gyfts of God, which did fhine both
in our Sauiour, and his bleffed mother, and in
moft of all Chriftian Saints after them; and
yet that none of Fox his Saints fhould haue
this gift to conteyne, but that all all of them
yelded to the pafsion of the flefh, is a very bafe
matter, yf yt be well confidered, as yt is well
worth the confideration.

**None of
Foxes
Saints
hath the
gift of cō-
tinency.**

11.   But yf we paffe further yet and confider
the

the reſt alſo of their actions,& compare them
with the liues and actions,wrytten,and deliuered vnto vs, by antiquity of ancient Saints;
we ſhall ſee the compariſon ſo baſe and ridiculous , as any modeſt Proteſtant himſelfe
would bluſh to abide the triall. As for example, he that ſhould read the rare vertues of
S. Francis , (whoſe feaſt is vpon the fourth of
October) his prayers, his mortifications , his
wonderfull miracles, recorded by *S. Bonauen-
ture*, a Saint alſo himſelfe; and then ſhall come
to Fox his Calendar, and find him ſtriken out,
and one *Catelle* a ſchoole-maiſtres in France,
put in his place , who will not laugh or byte
his lippe theratt ? And the like yow ſhall find
in hundreds beſides of no leſſe indignity , yf
yow will go ouer the former Calendar: as for
example the forſaid Apoſtle *S. Barnaby*, being
ſtroken out vpon the 11. of Iune (for what
cauſe God knoweth) , *Halliwell* and *Bowier*
are put in his place, the firſt a Smith, the other
a weauer; and what a change (thinke yow) is
this ? *S. Antony* the Abbott, of whome *S. Atha-
naſius* and *S. Auguſtine* , and ſo many other ancient Fathers do vvryte moſt admirable
things, is put out vpon the 17. of Ianuary, and
Iſabell Foſter a Cutlers wife, is put in his roome.
S. Tymothy Biſhopp and Martyr , ſcholler to
S.Paul, is put out vpon the 24. of the ſame moneth, & *VVilliam Hay* artificer of Kent, entreth
in his place. The like yow may ſee in the feaſts
of *S. Polycarp* ſcholler to *S. Iohn Euangeliſt* , and
of *S. Chryſoſteme*, and *S. Cyrill*, both of them fa-

A a 2   mous

mous Doctors, (all which feasts follow in
this moneth one the other) who are thruſt out
by Fox, and three kentiſh artificers, *Lowicke,*
Prowtinge, and *Finall* put in their places; And ſo
may yow goe ouer all the whole Calendar, &
find ſufficient matter of muſinge to furniſh
this fourth conſideration withall.

11. Wherfore the fifth conſideration may
be, that Iohn Fox hath made the farre greater
part of all his Martyrs and Saints in this Calendar, and throughout his whole volume (to
witt to the number of 268. as before hath byn
noted) for denyinge the *reall preſence* of Chriſts
true body, and bloud in the Sacrament after
the words of conſecration, and for that they
deryded, ſcoffed at, and blaſphemed the ſame,
alleaginge always certayne reaſons of ſenſe
or humaine iudgement againſt that moſt high
miſtery of beleeue. In which, ſuch vayne
weomen, and thoſe that were moſt ignorant
and vnlearned of all others, beare away the
bell, in that kynd of contempt and raylinge, as
before yow haue heard in the examen of all
the 12. moneths. But now theſe Saints of
Iohn Fox, whome he confidently placeth in
heauen, & aſſureth vs that they are partakers
of Gods euerlaſtinge bliſſe, *exalted and inthro-*
ned (to vſe his phraſe) *in his eternall ſeat of glory:*
theſe people (I ſay) dyinge for that cauſe, cannot be ſaued, except all the reſt, that held and
defended the contrary, be reiected and damned, who are firſt all the holy Fathers, accordinge as yow heard confirmed before by *Do-*
ctor

ctor *Philipp Melancthon*, a Saint of this *Calendar, who gathered out their fayings and fentences about this article into a particular volume, and affirmeth not only, that all the faid
ancient Fathers beleeued, and taught the reall
prefence of the very body of Chrift in the Sacrament, but that himfelfe would be content
to dy in defence of that beleefe againft the Sacramentaryes.

12. And not only thefe ancient holy Fathers
of the primitiue Church, and all others that
haue followed them, and their beleefe vntill
our dayes, muft be damned, yf Fox his Sacra-
mentary-Saints be faued (which were a pittifull cafe) but euen *Doctor Martyn Luther* himfelfe, and all his followers, as yow may partly
fee by that, which in the firft confideration of
this Chapter we haue touched about the opinions of *Iohn Caluyn:* but heere in this place, we
fhall briefly heare the fame about all forts of
Sacramentaryes both Zwinglians and Caluinifts, whome the moft learnedeft Proteftants
of our tyme do hould for damned heretiks.

13. And firft for *Doctor Martyn Luther* himfelfe
a cheefe Saint of this * Calendar, who had
primitias fpiritus amongft the Proteftants, yt is
fufficient to remytt the Reader, to that which
we haue noted before vpon his feftiuall day,
where amonge other thinges he holdeth, as
yow may remember, not only that *Carolftadius, Oecolampadius,* & *Zuinglius* the firft authors
of the Sacramentary doctrine, are damned rather then faued, but giueth alfo this refolute

sentence of them all, as well authors and maisters; as schollers and followers, that they are
all heretiks: *Hæreticos ſeriò cenſemus* (ſaith he)
&c. We do ſeriouſly iudge for heretiks, and
cutt of from the Church of God, both the
Zwinglians, and all other Sacramentaryes,
that do deny the body and bloud of Chriſt to
be receyued in the venerable Sacrament, by
our bodily mouth, &c. Lo heere, yf all Sacramentaryes be heretiks, and cutt of from the
Church of God by Luther, how can they be
Saints by Fox? I will not ſtand heere to alleage the ſentence of all other Lutheran Doctors and diuines, the learnedſt that haue
wrytten in this behalfe, who with one voyce
do condemne all Sacramentaryes, and namely
Zwinglians, and *Caluiniſtes* for damnable heretiks. And to repeat nothinge of that which
we cyted before about *Caluyn*, in the firſt conſideration, yow may ſee *Tilmannus Heſhuſius* a
great Lutheran Doctor, who calleth *Zwin-*
glians and *Caluiniſts: Sacrilegas ſectas contra teſta-*
mentum filij Dei. Sacrilegious ſects againſt the
teſtament of the ſoonne of God. *Ioannes Schutz*
another famous Doctor and wryter ſaith: *Sa-*
cramentariorum ſecta, ſentina quadam eſt, in quam
multæ hæreſes confluunt; vltima ſatanæ ira, quam is
furijs exagitatus, contra Chriſtum, eiuſq̃ Eccleſiam
exercet. The doctrine of Sacramentaryes is a
certayne ſinke, wherinto many hereſies do
runne: yt is the laſt wrath of Sathan, which
he being vexed with fury, doth exerciſe a-
gainſt Chriſt and his Church. And the ſame
author

Luth. contr.
Art. Loua-
nienſ. theſ.
27.

Luther
holdeth
all Sacra-
menta-
ryes for
hereticks.

Heſhus in
defenſ. cont.
Caluinum.
The iudg-
ment of
Lutheran
Doctors.
Ioan. Scutz
in 50. cauſ.
Præfat. a. 6

author afterward wryteth thus: He that followeth the ſect of Sacramentaryes, is a manifeſt and ſworne enemy to God, and hath forſaken his faith which he promiſed to Chriſt in
his baptiſme.

14. And now let any man iudge what Saints
Zwinglians and Caluiniſts be, accordinge to
theſe learned Proteſtants iudgements. But for
that yt were ouerlong, to recyte heere the ſe-
uerail ſentences of all theſe Lutheran Doctors againſt Sacramentaryes; I ſhall only
touch the titles of certayne books & volumes
ſett forth by Lutheran Proteſtants againſt
them, vvherby the reader may gheſſe vvhat
ſtuffe is conteyned in the works themſelues:
Firſt then read the worke of the foreſaid Superintendent *VVeſtphalus* intituled; *Farrago con-*
fuſianarum, &c. A heape of confuſed opinions
of Sacramentaryes, contrary the one to the
other. *&c.* Where you ſhall ſee a ſtraunge confuſion among theſe men. Read alſo the worke
of *Tilmannus Heſhuſius,* another Superintendent,
intituled; *A refutation of the Pelagianiſme and Ana-*
baptiſme of Caluiniſtes, about the articles of Baptiſme
and Originall ſinne; printed at Erphord. The worke
alſo of *Doctor Iocobus Andreas* of the vniuerſity
of *Tubinga,* intituled *Breuis admonitio de crimine*
ſtellionatus Caluinianorum. A briefe admonition
or detection of the crime of Treaſon or fraudulent impoſture of Caluinians. And another
worke of the ſame Doctor intituled; *Of the In-*
carnation of the ſonne of God, againſt the impious and
blaſphemous errors of Zwinglians and Caluiniſts;

Books a-
gainſt the
Zuingliãs
and Cal-
uiniſts.
Anno Do-
mini 1583.
Anno Do-
mini 1582.

A a 4 printed

printed at *Tubinga in* 4. wherin he sheweth that Zwinglians & Caluinists do hould many blasphemous errors about, the Incarnation of Christ our Sauiour.

15. See also the worke of *Philippus Nicolaus* a principall pastor of the Church of *Herdican* whose title is : *A discouery of the foundations of the Caluinian sect, agreeinge in all things vvith the old Arrians and Nestorians*: and that yt is impossible for any Christian to follow Caluinists, but that he must be guilty also of Arrianisme, and Nestorianisme ; printed at *Tubinga in* 4. There followeth also the worke of *Ioannes Modestius* printed in 4. in the same vniuersity of *Tubinga,* intituled : *A demonstration out of the holy scriptures, that those of the Sacramentary sect are not indeed Christians, but rather baptized Iewes and Machometans.* The worke of *Ieremias Victor,* printed at *Frankeford* in 4. whose title is : *A trew and cleare demonstration that Zwinglians and Caluinists are no Protestants, nor conteyned vnder the Confession of Augusta, exhibited to Charles the Emperor, an.* 1530. The worke also of *Doctor Conradus Schuffelburgius* contayned in three large books, printed at *Frankeford* in 4. whose title is : *Three books of Caluinian diuinity, vvherin, as in a cleere table, is shewed to the eye, out of* 223. *Sacramentary wrytinges vnder the names of their proper authors ; eos, de nullo ferè Christianæ fidei articulo rectè sentire, &c.*

16. I omit many other works extant, as that of *Ioannes Mathew, de cauendo Caluinistarum fer-* *mento,* of auoydinge the leuen of Caluinists. The great worke of *Theologorum VVittenbergen-*
sium,

fium, of all the diuynes of *VVittenberge*, printed in *fol.* at *Tubinga*, and intituled: *A confutation of the Zwinglian and Caluinian patchinge togeather of fcriptures and Fathers of the ould Church, called by them Confenfus Orthodoxus Chriftianus*. Titelmans booke alfo, printed in 4. at *Magdeburge* intituled: *Ten greeuous and Pernicious errors of Zwinglians about the doctrine of finne, and baptifme, taken out of their owne bookes,&c.* All this (I fay) being feene and confidered, and that thefe moft learned Proteftants of this our age, do hould the Sacramentary fect of Zwinglians and Caluinifts for fuch pernicious and damnable heretiks, as yow haue heard; yea not for Chriftians indeed, but rather for enemyes of the fonne of God, corrupters of his word, peruerters of his will, deprauers of his teftament, and traytors of his Religion: I would aske with what affurance or probability can Iohn Fox make fo many of them Saints in this his Calendar? For yf thefe be Saints; then muft the other be diuels,that wryte thus againft them. And this fhalbe fufficient for this fift confideration.

Anno Domini 1584.

Anno Domini 1592.

17. The fixt confideration may be,how that all this notwithftandinge euery one of Iohn Fox his Saints (but efpecially thofe of the Zwinglian fect) did bragge exceedingely of their peculiar fpiritt, of their election, predeftination, and affurance they had therof by the inward teftimony of the faid fpiritt; yea many of them did infult and vaunt ouer their Bifhopps and Paftors, and other ordinary Iudges, for that they durft not affure themfelues

felues as thefe men did, that they had the true
fpiritt of God in them : as yow haue feene by
many examples before, efpecially of *V Voodman*
the Ironmaker, *Allerton* the Taylor; *Iohn Fortune*
the fmith, *Iohn Maundrell* the Cowheard , and
many other both men and weomen,but efpecially weomen, who, the leffe knowledge
they had, the more obftinately did they reft
themfelues vpon this perfuafion of their inward fpiritt, which is the laft refuge of any

See a no-
table ex-
ample of
Alice Dry
uer,*Now.*
22. and
others.

heretike whatfoeuer. For when once he contemneth the externall authority of the vifible
Church, and retyreth himfelfe to only fcriptures (for this is the firft leap , which commonly he maketh) and then being preffed
about the meaninge or interpretation of fcriptures; he muft prefently, yf he be vnlearned,
and not able to ftand in that combatt , retyre

The fancy
of a pecu-
liar fpiritt
is inexpu-
gnable.

himfelfe to the laft hold of his owne peculiar
fpiritt: & yf he be learned,though he wrangle
for a tyme , yet this muft needs be his laft refuge and refolution; for that herefie being nouelty and fingularity, cannot finally defend yt
felfe, but by this only fhift, and deceyt of the
diuell, which for the moft part is fo fortifyed
by him , as yt is inexpugnable. For whatfoeuer yow alleage againft them , eyther reafon,
authority, fcriptures, fathers, or other perfuafion , yt is all reiected by this only perfuafion
of theirs, that they being elect, their fpiritt
and iudgement cannot erre : vvherin I haue
feene my felfe ftrange examples of obftinacy, but yet ftranger cannot be, then in the
                                                former

former examples yow haue feene and read.
18.   Only I will add one example out of a
printed booke, dedicated to the Lords of the
late Q. Counfell intituled ; *The feduction of*
Henry Arthington by Hackett , in the yeare of Chrift
1592. In which this *Henry Arthington*, being an
earneft Proteftant or rather Puritan, doth difcourfe of 2. fpiritts of his, the firft from the
tyme of his being a Proteftant vnto the death
of *Hacket*, the fecond from that tyme forward:
His firft fpiritt duringe *Hacketts* life, he affured
himfelfe to be of the holy ghoft, for that yt
was founded in the hatred of Papifts and Papiftry, whome he held for traytors; yt moued
him to follow Puritan fermons, as alfo their
faftes and exercife vpon the Lords day, and
befides this, *he felt himfelfe poffeffed* (to vfe his
owne words) *vvith a burninge heat within him,*
and his loue and affection greatly placed towards the
preachinge miniftery, to ftand vvith them in their iuft
defence, &c.

19.   Thus defcribeth he his former fpiritt,
which induced him by little & little to ioyne
with the forfaid *Hackett* and *Coppinger*, and to
beleeue that the faid *Hackett* was Chrift, and
Coppinger and himfelfe two Prophetts, who
iointly at laft proclaymed him for fuch, in
Cheapfide of London vpon the 16. of Iuly
1591. and were condemned all three for the
fame. *Hackett* was hanged, *Coppinger* died in
Brodwell, and this *Arthington* was repriued, who
afterward vpon hope of life, (as yt feemeth)
was content to condemne his former fpiritt

for

The ftrāge ftory of H. Arthia gton.

Seduct. pa, 2.& 56.

Stovv in his chron. anno 1591.

for wicked and diuelilh, which hitherto he
had held to be of the holy ghoſt, and to take
another ſpiritt, though it differed in nothing
els, but only that he held not *Hackett* now for
Chriſt, but in all other points it was the ſame,
to witt in hatred of Catholiks, in zeale towards the preaching miniſters, and their opinions, in heat of feruour towards faſts and
exerciſes vpon the Lords day, in the inward
teſtimony of his ſaid ſpirit that cryed *Abba Fa-*
ther and the like. Yow ſhall heare him ſpeake
himſelfe breefly of both ſpiritts, and therby
iudge what reaſon he had to be aſſured more
of the one, then of the other.

20. *VVee all returned* (ſaith he) *after ſermon vnto*
Hackets chamber, where we finiſhed our exerciſes in
prayer by courſe, &c. And before we departed I felt
my ſelfe very hoate within, which I verily thought had
byn an extraordinary motiue of the holy ghoſt (*as Chriſts*
diſciples had goinge to Emaw) *vvhich the Lord had ſent*
downe for a bleſſinge of his loue vpon our exerciſes; ſo I
departed a very glad man; and the next morninge fol-
lowinge as I lay in my bed, I found my ſelfe moued to
penne a curſe againſt the Citty of London, which I pro-
ſecuted vvith vvatry plants, &c. This is the deſcription of his former ſpirit, which according to
the definition of a Proteſtants ſpiritt, I do not
know why yt ſhould be reiected. For as for
his familiarity in ſcriptures (which is wont to
be a clauſe in the definition of a new ghoſpellinge ſpiritt) yow may ſee yt plainly in this
man, for that at euery turne of his ſaid booke,
he alleageth the ſame aboundantly. So as
layinge

Seduct. pag.
14.

Luc. 24.
verſ. 32.

Arthingtō
his firſt
ſpiritt.

layinge afide the condition of a Catholike
fpiritt, (which is to be gouerned by others, &
not by yt felfe : I fee not how this firft fpiritt
of *Arthington* may iuftly be condemned by the
rule of Proteftants, for that fpirit affureth him
certainely that he was elected, and chofen to
eternall bliffe, & gouerned by the holy ghoft,
which is the cheefeft priuiledge & commendation of Proteftants fpiritt. But let vs now
heare the defcription of his fecond fpiritt,
which he called the true fpiritt of the holy
ghoft indeed, and the former to haue byn of
Sathan.

21. Firft of all he cyteth and heapeth togeather many fcriptures, out of which a man may
certainely gather, accordinge to this his new
fpiritt, whether one be predeftinate or noe &
fo did he of himfelfe in thefe words : *VVherby*
(faith he) *I certainely know my felfe to be referued for*
faluation in Chrift &c. Yea I did expoftulate vvith
Gods mercifull Maieftie (after my fall vvith Hackett)
vvhether I vvas a reprobate or noe, and prefently the
holy ghoft did affure my hart, that I was no reprobate,
but that my cafe in effect, was much like S. Paules,&c.
Lo, this is the affurance of *Arthington* his new
frefh fpiritt, wherof afterwards he alleageth
alfo many arguments and proofes, to affure
himfelfe that yt was a true fpiritt : *I was affured*
(faith he) *of my fpiritt by thefe tokens followinge:*
Firft by experience of Gods prouidence in ftill prefer-
uinge me, &c. (to witt from hanginge when
Hackett was hanged) *Secondly for that God hath*
fent his fpiritt into my hart to cry Abba Father, &c.
Thirdly

Seduct pag.
24.

Ib. pag. 24.

The argu-
ments of
Arthing-
tons ipi-
ritt.

*Thirdly for that God doth still encrease my faith, &c.
Fourthly in that I know my faith to be founded in the
fruits of Gods spiritt, proceedinge from the same, &c.
VVherbyI do certainely know my selfe to be surely reserued for saluation in Christ, &c.*

22. These be his arguments and this his affurance: And this 'spiritt' he faith that he
knoweth to be of almighty God, the other of
Sathan, which before he thought to be as
much of God, as this, and would haue gone
to the fire for asseueration thereof, yf he had
byn pressed therevnto. And in truth, the one
hath as much assurance as the other, but only
the madd persuasion of his owne hereticall
brayne. And the like is to be held of the particular spiritts of all Fox his sectaryes before
rehearsed, who were possessed in deed, with
that Whirl-wynded lyinge spiritt, whereof

3.*Reg.* 22.
Esa. 19.

both *Elias* and *Esayas* the Prophetts do speake,
as sent of purpose to deceaue such vvillfull
heady people. And so much of this confideration about hereticall spiritts.

The 7. cõ-
fideratio n
about pu-
nishing of
heretiks &
sectaryes.

23. There followeth the seauenth confideration vpon the premisses, to witt, that sup-
posinge the former peruersity of hereticall
people in England, and that they would nether be instructed nor reduced themselues,
nor ceafe from peruertinge of others; what
fhould or could the Paftors of England, and
such as had charge of confcience ouer their
flocke, do in fuch a cafe? Fox doth euery-
where exclayme and make fierce inuectiues
againft the Bifhops & Cleargie, for punifhing
                                                      thefe

thefe people, condemninge yt, (as yow haue heard) for barbarous cruelty, iniuftice, murder, and the like. For anfweringe whereof yt feemeth to me, that three points may be confidered: Firft whether the punifhinge of fuch as be condemned for heretiks, by the externall and vifible Chriftian Church of euery age, be lawfull or noe? and Secondly whether in Q. Maryes time and in the raignes of former Catholike Englifh Princes, yt were expedient to punifh fuch people, as they did, fuppofinge yt were lawfull. And thirdly whether the fame vvere executed vvith cruelty, or rather vvith compafsion vpon necefsity.

24. To the firft, yf we talke of matter of fact, there can be little controuerfy betweene Englifh Proteftants and vs at this day, for that they do burne alfo Anabaptiftes, Arrians, and other fuch like heretiks, as is euident by *Ioane* of *Kent*, and of *George Paris*, burned in King Edwards dayes, and diuers others condemned to death by our Proteftant Bifhopps for Anabaptifme, and burned for the fame vnder Q. Elizabeth. And *Michel Seruetus* was burned by the procurement of *Caluin* in *Geneua:* And *Valentinus Gentilis* was burned in like manner by the Proteftant Magiftrates of *Berna*, vvhich facts were not only allowed, but alfo highly commended both by *Caluyn & †Beza, as conforme to the word of God, which appeareth by their feuerall bookes wrytten of that matter. And the fame fact of burninge the forfaid *Seruetus* in *Geneua*, is much commended in like

manner

Three que ftions to be hädled.

Steuu anno 1549. 22. *April. & anno* 1550. 20. *Maij & anno* 1551. 24. *April. & 2. Iunij.*

* *Calu. l. de fupplicio Serueti.*
† *Beza l. de haeret. à ciuili magiftratu puniendis.*

Melancthon in loc. com. Manly cap. de Ecclef.

manner by *Philipp Melancthon* a fpeciall Saint of Fox his Calendar. So as heereby he hath no-thinge iuftly to make aduantage of.

25.	But now yf we paffe from the fact vnto the iuftice and lawfulnes in generall, as little doubt can be made therof, as of the fact yt felfe and much leffe; For that from the tyme of Conftantine and the firft Councell of Nice downeward, which conteyneth the fpace of thirtene hundred yeares, yt is cleere and eui-dent, that all vertuous and Catholike Empe-

Emperors Edicts a-gainft he-retiks.

rors for many ages togeather, haue promulga-ted fharp lawes for the punifhinge of all forts of heretiks; the firft of whome was Conftan-tine himfelfe, who at the motion of the faid Councell of Nice, publifhed diuers fharp de-clarations & edicts againft *Arrius*, and his fol-lowers, and befides them alfo againft the *No-*

Eufeb. l. 3. de vit. Conftant. c 62. Niceph. l 8. hift. c 25. Zozom. l. 1. cap. 20.

uatians, Valentinians, Marcioniftes, Paulinians, Mon-tanistes and *Cataphrigians* by name, *& quicunque alienam ab Ecclefia opinionem & doctrinam fequuntur,* and whofoeuer did follow a different opinion or doctrine from the knowne Catholike Church of his tyme; which Edicts his three

Lib. 1 Cod. c. de hær. & Manich. & c. de Apoft. leg. Arrian. & l. Cæter. & in Noss. valent. tit. de Manich. Theod ep ad Ifiod. Praf. Valent. ep. ad Pallad. Prafectum.

fonnes after him renewed and amplified, and fo did after them againe the moft Catholike Emperors *Gratian, Valentinian, Theodofius, Arca-dius, Honorius,* and others. as appeareth by their decrees extant in the *Codex,* and all the holy Fathers that liued with them, both Greekes and Latyns, did highly commend their zeale and iuftice in that behalfe. In place of all the reft yow may read S. *Auften* approuinge and
defen-

defending moſt largely this matter againſt the
Donatiſts in many places as *lib. 2. cont. epiſt.
Parmen. cap.7. & lib.2. contr. litteras Petiliani c.*10,
& lib. 2. cont. epiſt. Gaudent. cap. 17. *&* 26. and in
many other places. And in his ſecond booke
of * *Retractations* and other where, he doth re-   * *Cap.5.ep.*
call & retract his former opinion which once   4 8. & 50.
he had held, that heretiks were not to be puniſhed with violence. And vnto the Donatiſts that complayned of the puniſhment of
death appointed againſt them, he anſwereth
thus: *Occidunt animas, affliguntur in corpore: ſempi-* *Aug.tract.*
ternas mortes faciunt, & temporales ſe perpeti con- 11. *in Ioan.*
queruntur. Hereriks do murder ſoules, and are
themſelues but puniſhed in body: they inferre
eternall deathes vpon others,and yet do complayne that they do ſuffer temporall death: as
though he would ſay they had no reaſon.

26. And this vvas the diſcipline of the
Church for puniſhinge heretikes after the
Councell of Nice, when ſhe began to haue
externall power and tribunall: For that before while ſhe was in perſecution,ſhe vſed only the ſpirituall diſcipline or ſword of excommunication, and deliueringe hereriks ouer to
Sathan, which yet yf we beleeue *S. Auguſtine*   The ter-
was a more terrible puniſhment, then any   ror of ex-
temporall,that could be layd vpon them: *Her-* munica-
ribilius eſt (ſaith he) *tradi Sathanæ per excommuni-* tion.
cationem, quàm gladio feriri, flammis abſumi, feriſúe *Aug.lib.1.*
ſubijci ad deuorandum. It is more horrible to be *cont.aduerſ.*
deliuered ouer to Sathan by excommunica-   *leg. &*
tion, then to be ſlaine by ſword, or conſumed   *proph c 17.*

by fire, or to be caft out to wild beafts to be
deuoured. So faith *S. Auguftine.* And of the
fame opinion and iudgement alfo, were the
moft anciét Fathers of the primitiue Church,
and nearest vnto Chrift himfelfe, who did fo
exactly and carefully fly, and deteft the very
fight and conuerfation of heretiks, after they
vvere once detected and denounced by the
Church for fuch, as yf they had byn damned
foules already feparated to the fire of hell. For

Iren. lib.3. aduerf.har. cap.3.

fo we read teftified by *S. Irenæus* in the very
firft age after that of the Apoftles, that *S. Iohn
Euangelift* would not fo much as abide in the
bath or hoat-houfe, where **Cerinthus** an heretike was. The fame Father relateth alfo a like
example of *S. Polycarpe,* fcholler to the faid *S.
Iohn Euangelift,* that he meeting in Rome a certaine Arch-heretike named *Marcion,* (author
of the *Marcionifts,* as the other was of the *Ce-
rinthians)* he would not fo much as falute him,
wherat the other being moued, asked him

Iren. ibid.

(faith *Irenæus*) *Non cognofcis nos?* Do yow not
know vs? wherunto the holy man aunfwe-
red, *cognofco te primogenitum Sathanæ.* Yes, I know
yow for the principall or firft begotten fonne
of Sathan: both which facts are conforme to
the doctrine of the faid Euangelift in his fecond epiftle, where talkinge of heretiks he

2 Ioan.

faith: *Do not fo much as receaue them into your houfe,
nor giue them a falutation, &c.*

27.   And after that bleffed *Irenæus* hath recyted thefe two examples of feuerity, in flyinge
communication with heretiks, he geueth this
generall

generall and notable admonition in that behalfe : *ſo great a feare* (ſaith he) *had the Apoſtles &*
Diſciples of Chriſt, to communicate or haue conuerſa-
tion in any one word with heretiks, accordinge to the
precept of S. Paul : Fly *an hereticall man after one or*
two admonitions, knowinge moſt certaynely that ſuch a
one is ſubuerted, and of himſelfe damned, &c. Behold
what a leſſon this is of old *S. Irenæus,* out of the
words and examples of the Apoſtles, for them
that liue among heretiks, and haue no ſcruple
at all to participate with them. And all this
no doubt was founded vpon thoſe words of
our Sauiour *Math.* 18. *Si Eccleſiam non audierit, ſit*
tibi tanquam Ethnicus & Publicanus. Yf he heare
not the Church (which is proper to heretiks)
let him be vnto thee as a Heathen or Publicã;
with whome the Iewes had neyther conuerſation nor dealinge. Wheruppon inſue thoſe
ſpeaches of *S. Iohn,* and *S. Paul* before recyted
of flyinge hereticall men. And *S. Irenæus* (as yow
haue heard) calleth yt a precept, and ſaith that
the Apoſtles and firſt diſciples of Chriſt, *did*
feare to do the contrary; which appeareth not only in the example of *S. Polycarp,* before rehear-
ſed ; but of *S. Clemens Romanus,* and *S. Ignatius,*
both ſchollers of the ſaid Apoſtles, the former
wrytinge thus: *Do yow ſeclude from you, wicked*
heretiks; let faithfull people declyne them by all meanes
poſsible, in ſuch ſort as there be no communication with
them eyther in ſpeach or prayers, &c. For that theſe
men are more impious then Iewes, and more hatefull
to God then the gentils, &c. Conſider this ſeuere
ſentence of *S. Clement.*

Bb 2   28. The

Iren. ibid.

Marke
this infe-
rence of
S. Ire-
næus.

Tit. 3.

Matt. 18.

The ſeue-
rity of an-
cient Fa-
thers in
flying he-
retiks.

Clem. Rom.
Conſtit. A-
poſt. cap. 18.

28.   The fecond, to witt *S. Ignatius*, is no
leffe earneft and precife in this behalfe ; for
hauinge defcribed the wickedneffe of an heretike, he addeth thefe words : *Do not come in*
Ignat. ep. ad *company of fuch a one, leaft yow perußh vvith him,*
Philadelph. *though he be your Father, though he be your brother,*
Deut. 53. *though he be your houßhould frend : Non parcat oculus*
vefter fuper eum. Lett not your eye haue pitty
vpon him, &c. By which laft words taken out
of Deuteronomy for putting to death of falfe
Prophetts, yt is euident, that yf the Church of
God had had externall iurifdiction, & power
to putt heretiks to death in thofe dayes, *S. Ig-*
natius would haue allowed therof. And albeit
Chrift our Sauiour out of that manfuetude
wherin he walked vpon earth, did not appoint any fuch rigorous bodily punifhment to
be laid vpon them (as neither he did vpon
malefactors, which notwithftandinge now
are lawfully put to death) : yet is yt cleere by
the fimilitudes vfed againft heretiks by him,
Math. 7. to witt of *vvolues, theeues, robbers, murderers,* and
Act. 20. the like (all which may iuftly be refifted and
Ioan. 10. punifhed by death , yf otherwife they cannot
be repelled) yt is lawfull to putt heretiks alfo
to death, when the defenfe of Chrift flocke
requireth the fame·
29.   Well then in all this I do not fee, how I.
Fox can ftand with vs, but that heretiks may
be punifhed, not only fpiritually by Ecclefiafticall cenfures, but corporally alfo with the
fword, when need requireth ; only perhapps
he will wrangle with vs when we come to
th e

the particulars, who are heretiks, and how
they may be knowne, though this indeed
haue as little doubt in yt, as any of the reſt:
for that the very words of the Decrees and
Edicts, ſett forth by Councells and Emperors
againſt them, do ſhew plainly who be heretiks, & who be Catholiks, as is declared largely in the * *VVarn-word* againſt *O. E.* or masked-
miniſter *Sutcliffe* lately ſett forth. As for example when Conſtantine the great wryteth
thus in his decree againſt heretiks, as before
hath byn ſhewed; *that they are heretiks who follow*
a different opinion or doctrine from the Church, &c.
Is it not euident whome he meaneth? to witt
ſuch as held different opinions from the
knowne Catholike Church of his tyme.

30.   And againe when he ſaith thus : *O yow*
Nouatians, Valentinians, Marcioniſts, Paulinians, Ca-
taphrigians, know yow this law, &c, Is it not alſo
manifeſt what manner of men he meaneth?
to witt, ſuch as had their names from particular authors, and not from the Catholike
Church. And when *Gratianus, Valentinianus* and
Theodoſius moſt Chriſtian Emperors made their
firſt decree, that is extant in their *Codex,* beginninge *Cunctos populos,* and ſaid that they would
haue all their people to liue in that Religion
which *S. Peter* had deliuered to the Romans,
and had endured vntill that day, vnto the
tyme of *Damaſus* B. of Rome, and Peter B. of
Alexandria, and was called Catholike, & therof
do commaund their ſubiects to take the name
of *Chriſtianorum Catholicorum:* of Chriſtian Catholiks:

* *Fol.* 15.
& 16.

Conſtant.
apud Euſeb.
l 3. *c.* 64.
de vita
eius.

Ilid. c. 62.

Lib. 1. *cod.*
de ſumma
Trinitat.

tholiks: And that all others followinge other
doctrine, they would haue them called and
accoumpted heretiks. This defcription (I fay)
of Catholiks and heretiks made by thefe auncient Emperors, is it not cleere to whome yt
agreeth? And yf we would bringe yt downe
from that tyme to this, and confider in euery
age who did follow the common knowne
Catholike Religion, vnder the Succeffors of
*Damafus,*and who followed different opinions
rayfed by particular authors,is not the matter
cleere? not only to Catholiks but euen to heretiks themfelues? And do not the teftimonyes of the very Lutheran wryters before alleaged, declare that the names of Lutherans
and Caluinifts (wherof Iohn Fox profeffeth
himfelfe to be one, and againft whome we
ftriue principally in this place) are in deed not
inuentions of ours, but as properly agreeinge
to them in refpect of the particular authors of
their opinions and fects, as the names of Arrians, Nouatians,and the like,are afcribed before by the Emperors to the old heretiks?

31. Wherfore to ftand no longer vpon this
point (which yet is of great importance) we
fhall fay a word breefly to the fecod & third,
which fhall conteyne the laft confideration of
this place; the fecond point being, whether
it were expedient in Q. Maryes dayes(though
yt were lawfull)to burne fo many heretiks,as
heere Fox fetteth downe, and feeketh by the
number to make the matter odious, wherin
truly I will firft confeffe of my felfe, that in
reading

The 8. &
laft confi-
deration
vvhether
it vvere
expedient
to burne
fo many
heretiks
in Q. Ma-
ries tyme.

readinge them ouer, I was greatly moued to
compaſsion,not only towards themſelues, in
reſpect of their euerlaſtinge miſery, and obſtinate madneſſe, but alſo towards their Biſhopps, Paſtors, and other Catholike Magiſtrates, that were forced to puniſh ſo great a
number of ſuch a baſe quality for ſuch opinions, as neyther themſelues could well vnderſtand, nor haue any ſurer ground therof
then their owne fooliſh apprehenſions. And
albeit I be not ignorant that diuers learned,
godly & wiſe men do much doubt, whether
the courſe held in thoſe dayes of burning ſuch
people were expedient or noe : yet is there
much to be conſidered alſo on the other ſide.

32.   The cheefe reaſon of theſe men that put
the matter in doubt, is founded on the euill
ſucceſſe , and that albeit the thinge was lawfull in yt ſelfe, as now hath byn ſhewed ; yet
the raigne of K. Edward the ſixt hauing gone
imediatly before, & corrupted infinite mynds
with that nouelty of doctrine, which vnder
him was ſpread contrary both to that of his
Father,and to the Catholike doctrine, yt ſeemeth to theſe men, that yt had perchance byn
better in Q.Maryes dayes, to haue giuen place
to thoſe words of the parable of our Sauiour,
when he was demaunded about weeding out
the darnell from the good corne, to witt, *that
both ſhould be permitted to grow togeather vntill the
harueſt , leaſt in goinge about to weed out the darnell,
the good corne alſo might chance be pulled vp therwith.*
Which parable *S. Auſten* againſt *Parmenian* the

Donatiſt

Mett. 18.
The para-
ble of the
Cockle
expoun-
ded.
*Aug.lib 3.
cont.epiſt.
Parm. c.11*

Donatiſt that alleaged the ſame (as diuers do
in our dayes) to proue that no heretiks ought
to be puniſhed,doth ſhew at large to haue this
only meaninge, thar prudence and circum-
ſpection is to be vſed in rootinge out as well
heretiks, as other malefactors, and not to aduenture vpon yt raſhely, or violently, when
they are ſo many, or ſo ſtronge, or ſo euill diſpoſed , as great perturbation and perill of the
common welth might be expected therby,
and ſo the good wheat pulled vp with the
darnell, *&c.*

33.   And this to be the true meaninge of this
place,and not that hereſies generally are to be
permitted,the ſaid Doctor proueth euidently,
for that otherwiſe all other malefactors in
like manner muſt be permitted , for that they
are comprehended alſo vnder the names of
euill ſeed,cockle, & darnell. And in this ſenſe
muſt be vnderſtood in like manner both *Saint*
Cyprian, in his epiſtle to *Maximus* & *Vrbanus,* &
S. Chryſoſtome vpon *S. Mathew,* who otherwiſe
may ſeeme to fauour the permittinge of hereſies ; but their meaninge is, that ſome tolera-
tion may be vſed with them when they cannot be rooted out,without danger of the good
corne , which ſome men thinke to haue byn
the ſtate of tyme vnder Q. Mary.

*Cyp. lib. 3.
ep. 3. Chry-
ſoſt. coment.
in cap. 13.
Math.*

The rea-
ſons and
argumē̄ts
for pro-
ceeding a-
gainſt he-
retiks in
Q. Maryes
dayes.
Art. 10.

34.   But on the contrary ſide is to be conſidered the charge of conſcience, that lay vpon
the Biſhopps and Paſtors in thoſe dayes for
lookinge to their flocke , whome euery houre
they perceaued to be infected more and more
by

by thefe hereticall Foxes and wolues. And yf
Chrift our Sauiour did côdemne for hirelings
in the ghofpell thofe Paftors, which did fly for
feare of the wolfe, to witt, when they faw
the wolfe ftronge, and potent, & armed with
authority, againft whome they fhould haue
fpent their bloud, for preferuinge their flocke;
what would he fay of Paftors that had authority on their fide, and power alfo to refift and
punifh the wolfe? yf thefe men (I fay) not of
feare (which is fome excufe) but of negli-
gence, or of fome compafsion towards the
wolues and Foxes themfelues, fhould haue
permitted fuch noyfome willfull beafts, to
haue liued freely among their flocke, doing all
hurts they could without reftraint or punifhment; what would our Sauiour haue faid of
fuch men? Truly it is like, he would not only
haue blamed them as hirelinges: but rather
haue condemned them, as priuy betrayers of
his flocke. And this was their cafe in Q. Maryes dayes, for that none of thefe willfull ignorant people then burned, could be brought
eyther to reuoke their herefies, or to keep
them to themfelues, or not to infect others,
or any way to enclyne themfelues to quiett-
neffe.

35.   Now then as to the laft point, whether
cruelty were vfed towards them or no, as euery where Iohn Fox doth exclayme, the matter is eafy to be iudged by indifferent men.
Firft, for that true iuftice lawfully adminiftred
cannot be called cruelty, and fecondly much

Whether
cruelty
vvere vfed
tovvards
heretiks in
Q. Maryes
dayes.

leffe,

lefle , where necefsity ftandeth on the part of
the Magiftrate , and felfe will on the behalfe
of the delinquent. Thirdly yf we confider the
manner and circumftances of this execution,
vfed then againft thefe heretiks and fectaryes,
Fox himfelfe is forced to fett downe fo many
particularityes euery vvhere , of fauour and
compafsion vfed towards them by the Bifhopps, and other Ecclefiafticall Iudges, as do
confound his owne vayne accufations of
cruelty , fhewinge fomewhere that the faid
iudges did weepe , when they gaue fentence
againft them , confideringe their madd obftinacy , other where that they intreated them,
fpake them fayre , repriued them after their
condemnation, delayed the execution , offered them pardon and remifsion , euen at the
very laft caft, and the like.

36.   And fome thinges alfo the faid Bifhopps
permitted of ouer much indulgence,which in
moft mens opinions ought not to haue byn
permitted , for that they were noyfome and
pernicious both to the fectaryes themfelues
and others, as for example, their meeting togeather and conference in their prifons ; their
continuall intelligence abroad by letters and
meffengers; their wrytinge out and penninge
their owne examinations & difputations , by
their owne hands after their owne fafhion;
the flockinge of frends vnto them in the prifons, efpecially after fentence of condemnation paffed againft them , when their words
did more pearce and penetrate then before,as
being

being now deſigned Martyrs amonge their
owne people; their goinge accompanyed to
the fire; their takinge leaue ſeuerally of all
priſoners vvhen they departed; their meetinge of their frends and kinred on the vvay;
and amonge them, diuers thruſt in of purpoſe to animate them in their folly by glorious vvords; their drinkinge and pledginge
at the fire ſide, vvith geuinge their apparrell
heere and there, and ſendinge tokens to diuers that vvere abſent for memoryes ſake:
Theſe thinges (I ſay) togeather vvith liberall ſpeache at their burninge, being permitted to fond men and vveomen, puffed vpp
vvith pride and vanity, as they could not
chuſe but be greatly hurtfull both to the partyes themſelues and to others, that heard and
ſaw them: ſo yet did they ſhew a great confidence, and extraordinary gentlenes in the
Biſhopps that permitted them, and thereby
do quite ouerthrowe Fox his clamour of
their cruelty. Though when God almighty
ſhall againe put the menaginge of thoſe matters into Catholike mens hands, cleere yt is,
that a farre different courſe vvere now to be
taken, namely as well by publike diſputations as priuate conferences, and all other fitt
meanes to attend in all charity, manſuetude
and longanimity, to the inſtruction and reduction of thoſe, vvhich haue byn miſled
vvith the ſo longe ſway of hereſie, rather then
by any kind of ſeuerity; vvhereof hauinge
aboundantlye and of purpoſe treated els
                                    *where,

* *Lib 1. de*
reform:
Eccl. Angl.
per aliquot
capita.

* vvhere, I vvill not enlarge my selfe any further heere. And this is so much as in this
place I haue to treat about these considerations.

A BRIEF CENSVRE

OF IOHN FOX AND HIS

VVRYTINGES,

*Against vvhich other two larger bookes are also said to
be hand, the one in Latyn, the other in English: and
by occasion heerof the author giueth his iudgement, why the history of England so much
desired both by Catholiks and Protestants, cannot vvell be vvrytten
by eyther of them in these
our dayes.*

CHAP. XVIII.

NOtwithstandinge that throughout the
whole course of this our Treatise against
Iohn Fox, and his Acts and Monuments, we
haue often had occasion to giue our opinion
aswell of the man, as of his wrytings; yet now
drawinge towards the end of that we designed to wryte in this behalfe; yt shall not be
amisse perhapps, to repeate heere briefly that,
which els where dispersedly hath byn vttered about this point, to the end that the discreet Reader may see more cleerly in what
accoumpt

accoumpt both the wryter and his wrytinges are iuftly to be held.

2. And firft then to fay nothing of the mans perfon, he being now dead, nor of the notorious infirmityes commonly related of him, as that he imagined himfelfe fometymes to be an vrinall of glaffe; fometymes a crowinge cocke, & other like fancyes which might fall vnto him eyther by weaknes of brayne, or by other difturbance of his fenfes through ouermuch ftudy, phrenfy of herefy, or other like caufes; Thefe perfonall thinges (I fay) that might happen vnto him without his default, and confequently are rather to be pittyed in him, then any way exprobrated vnto him; I fhall wholy lay afide, and treate in this place only of fome points that muft needs be prefumed to haue proceeded from his free-will and iudgement, and thereby the more reprehenfible, they being eyther falfe or wicked, and not iuftifiable in themfelues. Albeit in this kind againe, I muft needs help to excufe him alfo in diuers things, which I afcribe rather to his lacke of vnderftandinge and iudgment, then to meere malice, as are thofe vvhich make more againft him then for him, or are fo impertinent, as no man of learninge & iudgement would haue alleaged, or noted in that fafhion which he doth.

Many of Foxes errors are afcribed rather to lacke of iudgment then othervvife,

3. To which head or branch I do reduce all thofe large difcourfes, vvhich he maketh of our Church in many ages againft himfelfe; his relations alfo and prolix narrations of the

Walden-

Waldenfians , Albigenfians , Wickliffians, Hufsits and the Lutherans affayres , vvhich conteyne a great part of his volume, and haue infinite things in them againft Fox his fect of Sacramentaryes: In like manner his coopling togeather of fo different and repugnant fecta-ryes , as Saints of one Calendar and Church, can be excufed by no other meanes then by this , that the good man vnderftood not or confidered not, how farre his narrations made for his caufe or againft yt, fo they might feeme to found fomwhat againft the Romã Church or Religion. And for that the greateft part of his whole volume may be comprehended vn-der this branch , I will not ftand heere in dif-cufsing the particulars, but referre the Reader to the firft and fecond parts of this Treatife, that do runne ouer the whole worke,& make the matter cleere to the faid Readers eye , in euery age from the Apoftles.

4. Now then thofe things remoued, we fhall only call into confideration for the prefent, fuch other points, as concerne his falfhood & lacke of confcience, or rather (to mitigate the matter alfo in this point fomewhat) his error of confcience, wherby it feemeth that he came to perfuade himfelfe in confcience , that fup-pofinge (as he did) that the Proteftant or Pu-ritan profefsion of England was the only true Religion, he might fay or wryte any thinge in furderance thereof, without fcruple of con-fcience, whether it were in deed true or falfe. And that this was his perfuafion I am induced

ced to beleeue rather (as I haue faid) for his
excufe then commendation : For that otherwife , yf he had not had that opinion , I can
hardly thinke fo euill of any man Chriftened,
as that he vvould recoumpt fo many falfe
thinges, as Fox doth againft his owne confcience. For truly to fpeake as I thinke , after
I had read ouer the whole worke with fome
attention , and to fpeake without all exaggeration or pafsion,as one that doth hartily pitty the mans cafe, and muft follow him out of
this world ere yt be longe (though I hope to
another place) I do not thinke there be many
ftoryes in this whole volume(though fo huge
& vaft as yow fee)but that one way or other,
yf they belonge to matters of controuerfie, he
corrupteth or falfifyeth fome part therof, eyther in the beginninge , endinge , entrance,
goinge forth, matter, manner of handlinge,or
fome other kind of adulteration; and yet doth
he vfe euery where fuch holy proteftations of
piety, as neuer perhapps other author before
or after him, addinge alwayes wherfoeuer he
promifeth any thinge, or fpeaketh of the tyme
to come , thefe deuout phrafes ; *the Lords holy*
fpiritt afsiftinge me therin; The Lords diuine grace ge-
uinge me leaue: yf IESVS *fhall lend me his helpinge*
hand : by the Lords good leaue and pleafure; and
other like moft fainctlike phrafes, repeated &
iterated aboue a thoufand tymes throughout
this worke; And for that comonly foone
after thefe godly proteftations, yow fhall find
him in diuers falfhoods, falfifications, deceyts
and

It fee-
meth that
Fox did
thinke it
lavvfull to
ly for fet-
ting for-
vvard his
caufe.

and fhifts, I am rather induced to thinke that he efteemeth this manner of dealinge lawfull in fo good a caufe , as he prefumed his owne to be , then that he did yt expreffely againft his confcience and iudgement.

5.   The particular proofes, examples and de-monftrations of this kind of dealinge in him, were ouer longe and tedious to profecute in this place , and yow haue had ftore of them before , both in this third part , as alfo in the former two, and in the Warn-word,where it fhalbe fufficient to referre the Reader to the word (*Fox*) in the table of each booke; and the next enfuinge Chapter fhall giue a fuller taft, of his manner of proceedinge in this behalfe, though it be not the hundreth part of the falfe and deceytfull dealinge, which is to be noted out of thefe his lyinge Acts and Monuments; a booke compofed wholy to deceyue , and by iudgemét of many men , hath done more hurt alone to fimple foules in our countrey , by in-fectinge and poyfoninge them vnwares , vn-der the bayte of pleafant hiftoryes , fayre pi-ctures and painted pageants,then many other the moft peftilent bookes togeather.

The fpeci-
all caufes
of infe-
ction by
Iohn Fox
his Acts
& Monu-
ments.

6.   For firft as I haue faid , the variety of the hiftory it felfe,draweth many to read yt: then the forefaid fpectacle and reprefentation of martyrdomes (as they are called) delighteth many to gaze on, who cannot read; thirdly the hypocrify of the wryter , makinge thofe proteftations which before haue byn mentio-ned,and otherwife,gayninge opinion of piety
with

with the common people, by a certayne affected ſimplicity of life: Fourthly certayne tender ſpeaches attributed by him to ſectaryes at
their deathes, with his owne ſanctifying & canonizinge them for Saints: theſe things I ſay,
& other circuſtances togeather, with the very
greatnes of the booke yt ſelfe, obtruded to be
read in very many pariſh Churches, and other
publike places, haue byn cauſes of infinite ſpirituall hurt, to many thouſand ſoules of our
countrey, for which this miſerable man, and
his abetters haue, no doubt, to yeld a ſtraite
and heauy accoumpt to their redeemer, at the
moſt dreadfull accoumpting-day.

7. And to the end yow may the better perceaue the deadly hurt, which this moſt poyſe-
ned Fox-den hath brought forth, & wought
not in ſimple ſoules only, but in many of
iudgement and ſome learning alſo, yow muſt
conſider, that from the beginninge to the end
of this whole volume, he commonly ſetteth
downe nothinge affirmatiue or poſitiue of his
owne in matters of Religion, nor any certaine
rule what to beleeue, but only carpeth, or ſcof-
feth at that which was in vſe before: ſo as the
Reader is brought only into vnbeleefe, diſtruſt and contempt of that, which was accoumpted piety and Religion by his forefathers, and nothinge certayne taught him in
place therof, but only negatiue or ſcornefull
taunts, the proper meanes to make Atheiſts &
infidells. For proofe wherof yow may pleaſe
to conſider, that yf yow begin (for examples
C c   ſake)

fake) with the firft planting of Chriftian faith
in the Englifh nation by *S. Gregory* & *S. Auften,*

The fcof-
finge at
our firft
founders
of religion
in Englād.
* Cap. 8.

and other Englifh Apoftles, Iohn Fox and his
fellowes do ieft euery where at them, and at
the Religion brought in by them, as we haue
fhewed at large in the firft part * of this Treatife : fo as thefe our firft Fathers in Religion,
as alfo our predeceffors & anceftors in bloud,
that vvere conuerted from paganifme to
Chriftian Religion by them, being proued
now by thefe later Doctors, to haue byn no
true Chriftians in deed but only in name, as
thefe men hold, what good doth the Reader
receaue by this doctrine, but only remaine in
miftruft of all, and to thinke that the whole
hiftory of the Englifh Church for a thoufand
yeares togeather, is a meere fable?

8.   Againe, when Fox his hiftory commeth
downe for 600. yeares togeather after this
our firft conuerfion, to witt, beneath the conqueft, iefting ftill and fcoffing at moft things
that paffed in that Church and time, and after
that beginneth to recoumpt the Acts & Gefts
of diuers new-fangled people, condemned
for herefie, as the Acts of Saints & holy men,
fent efpecially from God, & illuminated par-

Coinqui-
na ion by
hereticall
opinions.

ticularly by his holy fpiritt, as the *VValden-*
fians, Albigenfians, Lollards, VVickliffians, Huffitts,
*Thaboritts. Lutherans,*and in all thefe or the moft
of them he is forced to acknowledge many
hereticall opinions, which himfelfe and his
Church (yf he haue any at all) condemneth,
and yet, as I faid, fetteth them forth for great
                                                    Saints

Saints and men of perfection, without repro-
uinge their falſe opinions; how is yt poſsible
but that the Readers mynd muſt remayne
heere poyſoned, and coinquinated with theſe
dregges ſett before him by Iohn Fox, ſeing
that no cleere rule is put downe for diſcerninge the ſame, but only referringe ouer each
man and woman to the examination of ſcriptures, which both theſe heretiks, & all other
alleage moſt aboundantly for themſelues, and
the interpretation ſtandeth in each ones particular iudgement to allow or follow?

9. Thus then the mynds of Engliſh Chriſtians ſtandinge firme and fixed in one Religion, before the readinge of Iohn Fox his
booke, for more then a thouſand yeares togeather, and attendinge only to the exerciſes of
piety and godly life preſcribed by that Religion; now by readinge this booke, they are all
put out of ioint; and being brought into doubt
& contempt of their ſaid old Religion, which
had endured from their firſt conuerſion; they
are now to chuſe new opinions what each
man liketh beſt, eyther of the *VValdenſian, Al-
bigenſian, VVickliffian, Lutheran, Caluinian*, and
other ſuch opinions or ſects, and vpon theſe
they are to reſt their ſoules, & to receaue the
authors of theſe opinions into their Eccleſiaſticall Calendar, in ſteed of the old Saints, that
were there before, and for that, where ſuch
choyce of Religion is giuen, yt is hard for
ſimple men and weomen, as alſo for the learned to determyne vvhat they like beſt, or

wheron

Men
brought to
be of no
Religion;

wheron they will lay hand in so great a matter, as concerneth their eternall saluation or
condemnation; we must imagine that infinite people remayne in suspence, & doubtfull
in our countrey at this day, and haue not
yet determined, what certayne sect to be of;
but only to doubt or contradict the Catholike, and for the rest to hould of this or that
sect what euery one liketh best, when they
shall resolue to determine of any; which is the
most miserable estate that can be imagined;
for that it is indeed to haue no Religion at all.
And this is the very principall effect of Fox
his booke or history.

10. For better confirmation wherof, do yow
read with attention but any one of the historyes before mentioned, as for example of *Iohn
Husse*, or *Iohn VVickliffe*, and albeit I know yow
will be weary before you come to the end, yet
do marke with diligence, what yow can gather, or what Fox doth gather out of all that
history for your profitt, but only their contradiction against the Catholike Church (which
he might gather also out of all ould heretiks:)
but for the rest yow shall see, that sometymes
he will tell yow matters indifferent of them,
sometymes others that seeme to sound towards his Religion, sometymes other that
make flatt against him, & not seldome others
that are opposite to vs both, to witt, Catholiks
and Caluinists: and yet are the men auouched
by him to be good and holy, but no particular
conclusion is made about their whole Religion;

gion; whether yt were good or badd. And
what then can the Reader gather out of thefe
difcourfes, but only doubtfullnes and breakinge of his owne braine, for that moft tymes
Fox concludeth thus, after he hath rehearfed
both good and badd of thefe new Saints, that
he leaueth all to the Reader, both men and
matters, to iudge thereof as he fhall thinke
beft, and therby to take and leaue what he lifteth or liketh beft: fo as in very truth he hath
no certainty at all, nor fure direction how to
find yt. Wherby a man may pronounce of
this Fox-den booke more fitly, then one did
of another in old tyme: *Hic liber ex ftultis infanos*
facit, this booke is fitt to make madd men of
fooles, to witt heretiks of ignorant people.
And this is another principall effect of Fox
his booke.

Mad men
made of
fooles,
that is het
retiks of
ignorant
people.

11.   Wherfore not to proceede any further
vpon this fubiect, my counfell fhould be vnto
my Countrymen, not to leefe any more time
in readinge ouer fo vaft and vayne a heape of
vntruthes laid togeather, as this worke of
Fox conteyneth, wherin there is neyther certainty of truth in the narration, nor good order in the method, nor any exact diftinction
of tymes obferued, as in the firft * part of this
Treatife we haue declared, albeit the fame is
like to be difcuffed more exactly and particularly in two other books, that I heare are in
hand againft the fame, the one in Latyn the
other in Englifh, wherynto I meane to remit
my felfe in this place, being content to fett

*Cap.9.10.
11.

Tvvo nevv
bookes in
hand a-
gainſt Fox
his Acts
and Mo-
numents.
downe only the arguments of the ſaid two
books, with this intent, that yf a man haue
matter of importance apperteyninge to the
ſaid arguments, or eyther of them, eſpecially
of the firſt booke in Latyn, which will conteyne diuers *Tomes* or *Volumes,* he vouchſafe to
impart the ſame with the author for better
furniſhinge the worke.

12.   The title of this booke is *Ecclesia Anglicana*
pro fide Catholica certamen, aduersus hæreses, &c.
„   The conflict of the Engliſh Church in de-
„   fence of Catholike Religion againſt hereſies,
„   euer ſince her firſt beginninge vnto theſe our
„   dayes, but eſpecially vnder foure Princes *King*
Henry the eyght and his three Children, *Ed-*
ward, Mary, and *Elizabeth, &c.* The argument
and occaſion of this worke, is taken out of the
Epiſtle of *S. Iude* the Apoſtle, who forwarning
Chriſtians to beware of certayne libertine &
licentious heretiks, he deſcribeth them ſo, as
he may ſeeme particularly to haue painted out
ours of this age: *Homines impij* (ſaith he) *Dei no-*
ſtri gratiam transferentes in luxuriam: Impious
men that do abuſe the grace of Chriſt to licen-
tiouſnes; againſt whome he maketh this exhortation: *De communi veſtra ſalute neceſſe habui*
ſcribere vobis, deprecans ſupercertari ſemel tradita ſan-
ctis fidei. I was forced to wryte vnto yow of
your comon ſaluation, and to beſeech yow to
ſtriue and fight for defence of that faith,
which was once deliuered vnto the Saints of
God, *&c.*

13.   In which few words the holy Apoſtle
doth

doth fhew very effectually the care he had,
that Catholike Chriftians fhould ftand and
ftriue for the faith once deliuered them, and
that this highly commended their common
faluation. Which holy exhortation of the
Apoftle this worke intituled : *The conflict of the
English Church*, doth pretend to fhew and declare at large by way of hiftoricall deduction,
that the Englifh & Brittifh Church hath obferued no leffe carefully and exactly, then any
other Church lightly of the Chriftian world
fince her firft plantinge vnto thefe our dayes,
for that the Brittifh Church from the Apoftles
tyme to *S. Gregory*, for more then 500. yeares,
and the Englifh Church from *S. Cregory* and
K.Ethelbert vnto *Pope Clement* the feauenth, and
K.Henry the eyght, for the fpace of more then a
thoufand yeares, haue fought and ftriuen a-
gainft all herefies and heretiks, in defence of
their firft faith and Church erected amonge
them. And that albeit, they had two famous,
or rather infamous heretiks of their owne nation, to witt the Brittans *Pelagius*, and the
Englifhmen *VVickliffe*, which infected many
with their herefies both at home and abroad:
yet could not they preuayle or haue the vpper
hand in eyther nation, but were refifted, and
fuppreffed, & finally alfo extinguifhed by the
faid faith of the Catholike Church, togeather
with all other herefies for the fpace of 1500.
yeares, vntill *K. Henrres* tyme.

14. And when in his tyme *Luther*, *Zwinglius*
and *Caluyn*, and other heretiks began afrefh to

The aun-
cient con-
flict of the
English
Church a-
gainft he-
retiks.

come

come in with their new diuifes, K. Henry
withall his realme oppofed themfelues manfully & moft religioufly, & began to conflict
againft them alfo, as appeareth by diuers famous books wrytten in thofe dayes, afwell by
the learned B. of *Rochefter*, S. *Thomas More*, and
other Englifhmen, as alfo by *K. Henry* himfelfe,
whofe notable learned booke, conteyninge a
defence of the feauen Sacraments, and other
Catholike articles of Religion againft *Martyn
Luther*, printed in London vpon the yeare of
Chrift 1521. and dedicated to Pope *Leo* 10. and
exhibited to him in publike confiftory, by *Iohn
Clarke* B. of *Bathe* & *VVelles*, his Maiefties Em-
baffadour & Refident in Rome: This worthy
booke (I fay) and Monuments of that Kings
moft pious ftriuinge againft heretiks, is yet
extant, and diuers copyes therof figned and
fubfcribed both in the beginning, and ending
with the Kings owne hand, are to be feene in
the libraryes both of the Pope and Englifh
Colledge in Rome, as alfo of fundry Cardinalls, to whome they were in the fame King
name prefented.

15. And when afterward the fame King moft
vnfortunately came to breake from the vnion
of that fea, and in fome things to hold with
heretiks (which in effect was but only the
article of fupremacy) and thervpon began to
perfecute Catholiks for the fame (whome
before he had defended), then did they fu-
fteyne the conflict alfo againft him, and ftood
in the maintenance of the firft ancient deli-
ueredꞋ

(margin note:) K. Henryes combat a-gainft he-retiks.

uered faith euen vnto death, and sheddinge of
their bloud. And the same did they vnder, and
against his two children *Edward* and *Elizabeth*,
and against other heretiks vnder Q. Mary his
Catholike daughter; so as this *Certamen* or
conflict, so earnestly commended and persuaded by *S. Iude*, hath byn notably performed by
the English nation from age to age, as this
worke in particular doth declare; albeit for
default of diuers records and testimonyes,
which are necessary, and which through the
difficultyes of these tymes, and by the persecution of Catholike Religion in our countrey, cannot so easily be had from thence: and
for that the worke will grow to more length
then at the beginning was expected, (to witt,
to diuers Tomes or volumes:) for these and
some other difficultyes, lets and hinderances,
yt cannot so soone be expected, though yt be
in some reasonable good forwardnes; And
being particularly directed against the narration of *Iohn Fox* (which promiseth a deduction
of his Church, and performeth nothing therof) I thought good to mencion the same in
this place.

The diffi-
culty for
the set-
ting forth
the history
of Englãd.

16.   The other booke in English, is designed
to be of much lesse volume, but yet depending
of this, and for the most part taken out therof,
whose title is; *The hunt of an English Fox*, *&c.*
Which was begon vpon this occasion, for that
in search of the yeares and ages for the fur-
nishing of the forsaid *Certamen* or *Conflict*, Iohn
Fox being found to shift vp and downe from
hole

The secõd
booke in
English a-
gainst
Fox.

hole to hole, and to make leapes hither & thither without ftanding to any thing conftantly, yt feemed good to the author to putt forth this hunt a part in our vulgar language, therby to lay open the egregious falfe dealing and hereticall fhifts of this our Englifh Fox, which is like alfo to grow to a worke of fome bulke before yt be ended, wherof the reader may take a taft by that, which hath byn difcouered of him in thefe three parts of this prefent Treatife. And this fhall fuffice for this breife cenfure in this place.

17.   Only I muft note by the way, that by readinge ouer this hiftoricall volume of Fox, and by the progreffe of the other intituled *Certamen*, I find yt to be true, which oftentymes I haue thought with my felfe, that the hiftory of England, efpecially the Ecclefiafticall, cannot pofsibly be well wrytten in thefe our dayes eyther by Catholiks or Proteftants, which yet feemeth much to be defired not only by vs, but by them alfo, as appeareth by their fettinge forth in print of old hiftoryes, *Henry Sauel* and prefaces made theron, wherin they ex- *in præfat. in* preffe this their earneft defire, that fome man *Gul. Mal-* of our dayes, would take in hand the abfolute *mesiunr. &* wrytinge of our Englifh hiftoryes; but my *Gul. Camb-* opinion is that yt cannot be done, tymes ftan- *den præfat.* dinge in England as now they do. The reafon *in Affer* heerof is, for that Catholike wryters cannot *Menewenf.* haue a fufficient inftruction or authenticall *The rea-* records, eyther for the tyme paft or prefent, *fon why* they being in the hands of their aduerfaryes. *English* And *hiftoryes*

And as for Proteſtant wryters, yf they ſhould take the matter in hand, they muſt eyther feigne of their owne, or wryte wholy againſt themſelues, or trifle out the matter with impertinent ſtuffe, as *Iohn Fox* hath done throughout the moſt part of his Acts & Monuments.

18. The Magdeburgians as in other * places we haue noted, takinge vpon them to wryte the vniuerſall ſtory of the whole world, had much variety to ſtuffe their books with ſuch things, as are indifferent both to vs and them, and wherin the ancient Fathers may be alleaged at large; but yet when they came to matters of controuerſie, they muſt eyther leaue them out, or miſconſter or diſcreditt them as they do in euery age, wherof yow may ſee ſtore of examples in the firſt part of this * Treatiſe. But yf we will treat of the matters of England only, I do not ſee what ſubſtance a Proteſtant wryter can haue to his aduantage, to make vp a booke of any few leaues in good ſenſe and conſequence, before the entrance of *Martyn Luther*, except he will imitate the folly of Iohn Fox in promiſinge much and performinge nothinge, and in triflinge out the tyme in deſcribinge a few burned heretiks, agreeinge neyther with him, vs, or them ſelues. And therfore this worke of wryting the Engliſh hiſtory muſt be reſerued to other tymes and men, when God ſhall reſtore peace to his Engliſh Church, and giue meanes to go forward with that hiſtory by Catholike wryters, which by men of that

Religion

Religion hath byn begone and continued vnto our age. And so much for this point : now
shall we passe to giue you the tast, before promised, of Iohn Fox his threescore lyes within
the compasse of two leaues , and therby yow
may make a coniecture of the mans integrity.

A NOTE OF MORE

THEN A HVNDRED AND TVVENTY

LYES VTTERED BY IOHN FOX,

In lesse then three leaues of his Acts and Monuments;
and this , in one kind only of perfidious dealinge,
in falsifyinge the opinions of Catholikes,
touchinge diuers chiefe pointes
of their Religion.

Chap. XIX.

ALBEYT there be many sorts of lyinge and
false dealinge to be noted in Iohn Fox,
as before we haue said , yet are two most notorious in generall, each of them conteyninge
sundry members and branches vnder them.
The first may be called historicall , when in
his narrations he purposely vttereth falshood;
For when he doth yt by error , or false information concerninge any fact, as when for example in his former edition, he putteth downe
Iohn Marbecke singingman of *VVindesor,* & some
others for Martyrs, and describeth the particularityes

Tvvo
sorts of
lyes histo-
ricall and
dogmati-
ca..

cularityes of their burnings, and yet were neuer burned ; this I accoumpt for error and no
ly, to be made accoumpt of, becaufe his intention (perhapps) was not to ly . But when he
cannot chufe but know, that the thing which
he wryteth was falfe, this I call a willinge or
willfull ly; of which kind yow haue heard
ftore of examples before.

2.   The fecond kind of lyinge may be called
dogmaticall , when not only in matter of fact
and actions, but of doctrine alfo he falfifyeth
and lyeth of purpofe , which is fo much the
more greeuous then the former , by how
much leffe he cannot pretend ignorance, or
mifinformation of others, but with his owne
greater reproach, whoe will reprehend that
which he knoweth not . And of this kind
principally we are to giue exaples heere, partly for the Readers inftruction , and partly for
difcharge of a promife made, in a certayne relation of a conference betweene the Catholike Bifhopp of *Eureux* in France, now Cardinall, and *Monfieur Pleßis Mornay* Proteftant , in
prefence of the King himfelfe, vpon the yeare
of Chrift 1600. In which conference diuers
manifeft falfhoods, & vntruthes were proued
euidently againft the faid *Pleßis* , by the fentence of his moft Chriftian Maieftie there
prefent , wrytten to the Duke of *Efpernone* on
the fifth of May in the fame yeare , and 500.
lyes more were offered to be fhewed out of
the faid *Pleßis* owne books by the faid Bifhop,
yf he would haue ftood to yt, and haue continued

See the
relation of
the triall
made be-
fore the K.
of France
&c. 1600.
in the 3.
part of
this
vvorke.

tinued the conference , but his hart fayled
him, and his health alfo , vpon fore greife of
mynd , as is prefumed , and many great Proteftants in France haue byn conuerted thervpon fince that tyme.

3.	And for fo much as that wifh was made
by this occafion , in the faid relation, that the
late Q. of England , by this noble example of
the moft Chriftian Kinge, would permitt the
like tryall to be made of her cheefe Proteftant
wryters in England , namely *Iewell* , *Fox* and
fome others , with affurance that as great, or
farre greater number of lyes and falfifications,
fhould be conuinced out of their wrytings, yt
was faid for examples fake , that a certayne
Catholike ftudent , had gathered aboue 30.
manifeft lyes out of little more then two

See of Fox
his lyes in
the prin-
ted relatiõ
before
mẽtioned.

leaues, lyinge togeather in Fox his Acts and
Monuments, and that in the relators opinion,
there might be obferued double that number,
wherin Fox , concerninge diuers important
articles of Religion , belyeth falfely the Catholiks , and fetteth downe the ftate of the
queftion or controuerfie, betweene them, and
him , farre different from that in truth yt is.
And for that this is a common fhift of the heretiks of our tyme, alwayes to fett downe the
ftate of the queftion guilefully , and neuer to
fuffer the reader fincerely to fee how the cafe
ftandeth betweene them and vs; I haue the
more willingely byn induced to lay forth this
handfull of examples in this place , which I
fhall runne ouer with the greateft breuity that
I may;

I may, without any large refutation, but only ſhewing ſome Authenticall author or place
of ours, where we hold the contrary to that
which he affirmeth. And commonly the author ſhalbe eyther the Councell of Trent,
whervnto all Catholiks do ſubiect themſelues, or *S. Thomas* of *Aquin*, which is an vniuerſall Doctor that wrote 300. yeares gone,
and is generally receaued by all, which point
amonge Proteſtants is not to be found. And
by the way alſo I muſt aduertiſe the reader,
that hauinge pervſed the ſaid two leaues in
Fox with ſome attention, to note out the forſaid threeſcore lyes, the whole number is
growne to aboue an hundred, as yow will
now perceaue in the accoumpt.

4. Firſt then wheras *pag.* 22. of his worke   Foure lyes
num. 26. he relateth our opinion about faith &   about iu-
iuſtification, he makes foure lyes togeather, in   ſtificatiō,
ſetting downe foure neceſſary meanes of Sal-
uation, as held by vs, to witt, the Sacrifice of
the maſſe, meritts of Saints, holy orders and
the Popes pardons; after which aſſertion he
inferreth this relation: *So as* (ſaith he) *Chriſts ſacrifice, ſtripes, and ſufferinge, by this teachinge (of the
Papiſts) doth not heale vs, nor is not beneficiall to vs,
though vve beleeue neuer ſo well, vnleſſe we adde alſo
theſe works and meritts aboue recyted.* Thus he.
And the works and meritts before by him recyted, are theſe foure amonge diuers other
thinges; vpon which for breuityes ſake, we
will not ſtand at this preſent. But the foure
are foure manifeſt vntruthes; for that we do
                                        not

not hould them for so absolutely necessary to
euery mans saluation, as no man can be saued
without them; and much lesse that Chrifts sacrifice is not beneficiall, without addition of
these, wittnesse the Councell of *Trent sess. 6.
cap. 6. 7. & 14.* where the necessary meanes of
our saluation being recoumpted, (to witt, the
grace of God that preuenteth vs, and our cooperation by faith, hope and charity, pennance
and receauinge the Sacrament of baptisme)
none of these foure are mencioned, and consequently are not absolutely necessary to each
mans saluation ; so as they are foure seuerall
lyes. And as for two of them, to witt, *holy orders*, and *the Popes pardons*, they be double lyes;
for that holy orders are receaued but of few
men, and therby can be no necessary meanes
of saluation to all: pardons are so farre of from
iustifying vs, as we hould that they can remitt
no sinne at all, but only temporall paynes, remayninge after sinnes already remytted; and
therby we see as well the fraud, as folly of
Iohn Fox.

A ly about
the condi-
tion of
saluation,
vvhich
might
make ten.
5.   In the same *pag. 22. num. 50.* is a fiftth ly,
and so much the greater and more heynous,
in that it is directly against God himselfe, and
conteyneth many lyes in it. For he saith, *that
almighty God assigneth none other condition (for our
saluation) eyther of law, or any works, but only of faith.*
Wheras expressely to the contrary Christ, in
the 19. of Mathew, being asked by one what
he should do to haue life euerlastinge, he aun-
Math. 19. swered: *Si vis ad vitam ingredi, serua mandata.* Yf
yow

yow will go into life euerlaftinge , keepe the
commandements. And when the other replyed againe, *vvhat commandements?* our Sauiour
anfwered: *thou fhalt not kill, thou fhalt not committ
adultery, &c.* Which are works of the law. And
the very fame repeateth S. Marke againe in
the fixt Chapter, but that he reporteth Chrifts
anfwere more refolutely, *nofti mandata: yf thou   Marc. 10.
vvilt be faued,* faith he, *thou knoweft the commandements that thou muft keep.* And the fame recordeth alfo S. Luke in the 18. Chapter in the   Luc. 18.
very fame words : So as indeed this ly conteyneth fo many lyes vnder yt , as there be
commandements afsigned by God to be kept
of vs. But I will fpare Iohn Fox, and fcore vp
but one lye , for I fhall haue ftore inough afterward .

6. In the forfaid *pag. num.* 70. Fox faith, *that   A ly aboue
by our impious doƐrine vve leaue men in a doubtfull di-   diftruft of
ftruft of Gods fauour, and of their faluation, &c.* But   faluatiō.
this is conuinced to be a great ly by the words
of the Councell of *Trent, feß. 6. cap. 13.* where
talking of the truft and confidence, that euery
man ought to haue in the afsiftance of almighty God for his faluation , their words
are; *In Dei auxilio firmißimam fpem collocare & re-
ponere omnes debent, &c.* All men ought to place „
a moft firme hope in the help of almighty „
God, (for their faluation) for that God, except „
they be wantinge to his grace , will end the „
good worke he hath begone in them , wor- „
kinge in them both will and performance. „
Behould, yf we teach a moft firme hope , in
D d   Gods

Gods fauour, then we teache not a doubtfull distrust therin as Fox affirmeth.

Tvvo lyes about hope and charity.

7.   In the next page after *num.* 22. he saith, *that the vvord of God doth precisely exclude from the conditions of our iustification, both hope and charity.* These are two manifest lyes against the two excellent vertues of hope and charity, or rather against the word of God yt selfe, which is so farre of from excludinge precisely these two theologicall and diuine vertues, as of the first of them to witt *hope,* the holy ghost saith:

Psalm. 36. vers. 40.

Saluabit eos quia sperauerunt in eo : God shall saue them (speaking of the good) for that they haue hoped in him. Behould saluation attributed by hope, *ergo,* yt is not expressely excluded as Fox saith. And of charity *S. Paul* wryteth to the Corinthians: *Yf I should haue all faith, and yet not haue charity, I am nothinge*; *ergo* faith without charity doth not iustifie, and consequently charity is not excluded, but rather included in the worke of our saluatiō. Moreouer when *S. Paul* talketh of a iustifyinge faith indeed, he

1. Cor.13. vers. 2.

Galat. 5.

saith, it is that, *quae per charitatem operatur,* which worketh by charity, *ergo* charity is necessary to be ioyned with faith, to the end a man may be saued.

Tvvo lyes about Gods lavv and the Popes lavv, and many more omytted,

8.   Againe in the same *pag. nu.* 66. Fox wryteth thus: *VVhose error about goods works* (to witt of Papists) *standeth in this, that they do call good works, not such as are properly commaunded by the law of God, but such as are agreeable to the Popes law, &c.* Out of which words though I might gather many lyes, as presently yow shall see, yet will

I score

I fcore vp only two in this place. The firft, where he faith , that we do not call good works, *fuch as are properly commaunded by the law of God, &c.* Which lye conteyneth as many other lyes in yt,as are good works commaunded by God, & acknowledged by vs for fuch; as are loue of our neighboures, fafting,prayer, giuinge of almes , defendinge the oppreffed, afsiftinge the widdow or orphane , giuinge good counfell , preaching the truth, vifiting the ficke, and imprifoned, and finally all *opera mifericordia,* works of mercy, both fpirituall & corporall, commended and commaunded by God. The fecond lye in this matter is not much inferiour to this, to witt , *that we do only call thofe works good , which are agreeable to the Popes law, &c.* Which is euidently refuted , by that all our fchoole diuines allow generally the common definition of fyn, taken out of *S.Au guftine,* to witt, *Peccatum, eft dictum , factum, vel concupitum contra legem æternam:* fyn is a word, fact,or defire againft the eternall law of God, *ergo* , we do meafure good works by Gods law , and not only by the Popes law , yf we define finne by the breach of Gods law.

9. After this in the fame *pag. num.* 76. Iohn Fox takinge vpon him to explane vnto vs, what works we do call good by the Popes law, which are not commaunded or allowed by Gods law (whervnto notwithftanding he faith, *that the Pope giueth more pardons, then to any other good works commaunded by Gods law*) he re- coumpteth vp a great beadrole, *as buildinge of*

D d 2 *Abbies,*

A heape of lyes par- doned to Fox.

D. Thom, 1.2. q. 71. art.6 & q. 76. art. 2. *Aug. l.22. cont. Fauft. cap.* 27.

Ten lyes about good vvorks by the Popes lavv , and pardons giuen to them.

Abbies , geuinge to the high Altar , foundinge of chan-
tries, hearinge of maſſe, goinge on pilgrimage, fightinge
for the holy croſſe, guildinge of images,entringe into or-
ders, creepinge to the croſſe,and prayinge to Saints,&c.
All which works (ſaith he) *are not only reputed for*
good works (by papiſts doctrine) *but are ſo prefer-*
red alſo before all other vvorks , that to theſe is giuen
pardon from the Pope, double and triple fold more, then
to any other good works of charity, commaunded in the
law of almighty God. Out of which words there
are as many lyes to be noted , as he nameth
heere good works of the Popes law,preferred
by vs, before the works of Gods law, to witt,
ten in number yf yow coumpt, which number yet might.be much more encreaſed , yf I
would deale ſtrictly with I. Fox. For that of
moſt of them he vttereth a triple ly. Firſt,that
theſe works heere named , are good works
only by the Popes law,and not by Gods law,
which is euidētly falſe in all theſe that belong
to piety,liberality & almes-geuing,recōmen-
ded vnto vs in Gods law. The ſecond is, that
he affirmeth vs to preferre theſe works *before*
other works commaunded by God; which is a meere
calumniatiō:For that we preferre the neceſsity of the leaſt worke cōmaunded by God, before the higheſt worke,that is but coūſeled; &
cōforme to this doctrine do teach,that he that
doth not obſerue the precepts of God,cānot be
ſaued by obſeruing counſeils or workes of per-
fection.The third triple ly is;*that the Pope giueth*
double and triple fold more pardons vnto theſe works,
then to any other works commaunded by God; Which

is

is euidently falfe: For that all indulgences are
commonly giuen for fafting, praying, almes-
giuinge, *&c.* Which works are commended, &
commaunded vnto Chriftians by Gods law.

10. In the fame page *col.*1.*num.*80. Fox wryteth thus: *Albeit all Papifts confeſſe in their books,
that gratia Dei gratis data, is the cheefe and principall
cauſe of good works, and worketh in vs Iuſtitiam primam (as they call yt): yet their good works after regeneration they referre to other ſubordinate cauſes* vnder
God, as to freewill to *habitum virtutis,* or *integra
naturalia,* and nothinge at all to faith, *&c.* In
thefe words of Fox, as there is conteyned
much ignorance, fo are there diuers manifeſt
& malitious lyes alfo, & I might make vp my
whole number of 60. in this place yf I would
difcuffe matters narrowly. For firſt where as
he faith, that all Catholike wryters do hould
in their books that *gratia gratis data,* is the
cheife and principall caufe of good works, I
might fcore vp fo many lyes, as there be Catholike authors that do not wryte fo, which
would make vp more then my whole number promiſed. For that Catholike Schoole-
men do diftinguifh betwene *gratia gratis data,*
and *gratia gratum faciens,* affirming that the former of the two, to witt *gratia gratis data,* a grace
freely giuen, may be in an euill man, and is
principally giuen to help other men to their
faluation, as the gyft of preachinge, of tongues
and other talents: and confequently is neither
any neceffary caufe of good works in him, to
whome yt is geuen, and much leffe worketh

A ly 'that
cōteyneth
many cō-
cerninge
*gratia gra-
tis data.*

The di-
ftinction
betvveene
*gratia gra-
tis data,* &
*gratia gra-
tum faciens.*

D d 3   *Iuſtitiam*

Iustitiam primam, as Fox wryteth not well vnderstandinge what he faith.

11.   But the fecond grace which is *gratia gra-*
tum faciens, that is the grace which maketh a
man gratefull to God, fanctifyeth the receyuer himfelfe, and it is geuen vnto him for his
owne faluation, yf he vfe yt well. And this distinction Fox may fee fett forth at large, both
in *S. Thomas* 1. 2. q. 111. *art.* 1. and other * wryters, wherby the reader may fee how well
Iohn Fox hath studied our wryters, and how
wife a fellow he is to affirme, that all of them,
without exception, do fpeake as he doth of
gratia gratis data. And this is the first lye, concerninge all our authors.

12.   Next to this there follow in the fame
words by Fox alleaged, three other apparent
lyes. Firft where he faith, *that we do referre good*
works, after regeneration, to free will. For that we
do referre good works after regeneration no
otherwife to freewill, then we do before regeneration, to witt, that our free-will preuented & afsifted by Gods grace, is enabled therby to concurre with her confent to do good
works. The fecod ly is, that we attribute good
vvorks *ad habitum virtutis*, to the habitt of
vertue, which habitt we teach only to ferue
for the more eafy workinge in any vertue, but
not attributinge thervnto the meritt of good
works. And as for *Integra naturalia*, which Fox
afsigneth for a third caufe of good works, yt
may be doubted that he had *lafa naturalia*,
when he wrote yt: For that we do not hould,

that

@ *Barth. de*
Medina co-
ment. in
eundem lo-
cum. *Du-*
rand. in 5.
dist. 15. *q.*
1. *n.* 6.

Three lyes
about fre-
vvill and
good-
vvorks.

that there are *integra naturalia* in any man after
the fall of Adam our firſt Father, and much
leſſe can they be the origin of any good works
that are meritorious, as yow may ſee expreſſely defined in the Councell of Trent *ſeſ. 6. c. 16.
Can. 1. & 2.* and in S. Thomas 1. 2. q. 109. art. 9.
& q. 114. art. 2.

13.   But the moſt ſhameleſſe of all this rablement of lyes, is that, which he vttereth in the
very laſt words of the former ſentéce, to witt, A foule ly
about
faith.
that in good works, we attribute nothing at all to faith,
wheras expreſſely to the contrary, the ſaid
Councell of Trent, ſpeakinge of the ſelfeſame
matter *Seſ. 6. cap. 8.* hath theſe words: *Fides eſt
humana ſalutis initium, fundamentum, & radix omnis
iuſtificationis.* Faith is the beginning of mãs ſaluation, & the foundation & roote of all iuſtifi-
catiõ, &c. And how then can I. Fox ſay, *that we
do attribute nothing at all to faith in mans iuſtification?*
14.   In the ſame page *col. 2. num. 26.* he hath
theſe words concerninge the old law of
Moyſes: *They take and apply no other end to the law,
but to make vs perfect, to keepe vs from wrath, and to
make vs iuſt before God.* In which words are con- Foure lyes
about the
lavv of
Moyſes.
teyned three members as yow ſee affirmatiue,
and in them three notorious vntruthes; and
beſides this one negatiue, that conteyneth
another more groſſe then all the reſt, and ſuch
a one indeed, as comprehendeth diuers other
lyes vnder yt. The three affirmatiue lyes are,
that we do apply the end of Moyſes law, *to
make vs perfect, to keep vs from wrath, and to make vs
iuſt before God.* For confutation wherof it were

Dd 4   inough

inough to cyte the firſt Chapter of the forſaid
ſixt Seſsion of the Councell of *Trent* , whoſe
title is; *of the infirmity of the law to iuſtifie men, &c.*
For yſ vve hold the law of Moyſes to be
vnable to iuſtifie any man, then can yt not be
true, that we attribute, *both perfection and defence
from Gods wrath, and iuſtification vnto the law.* But
lett this fond fellow read our Catholike authors and wryters about the nature & force of
the old law, and he ſhall ſee his owne madnes,
yſ he be capable therof. Or yf yt be much for
him to read all, lett him inſteed therof at this
tyme, read *S. Thomas* 1. 2. *q.* 91. *art.* 5. *& q.* 117.
art. 10. Where he diuideth Gods law into the
new law of the ghoſpel, & old law of Moyſes,
tanquam in perfectum & imperfectum, as into a perfect and imperfect law, *ergo,* we do not hould
that the old law maketh vs perfect, which is
imperfect in it ſelfe.

15.   And againe the ſame Doctor wryteth

Gal. 3.   1. 2. *q.* 98. *art.* 5. *theſe words: The new law* (by the
Apoſtle) *is likened to a man, as a perfect law, but the
old law to a child, for that it is vnperfect, &c.* Behould
heere our doctrine. How then can we be ſaid
to hould, that this law maketh vs perfect, yf it
be infirme and imperfect in yt ſelfe ? But yet
furrher the ſaid Doctor in the ſame worke
q. 98. *art.* 1. and in many other places, teacheth,
*that the law of Moyſes could giue no grace, for that this
priuiledge was reſerued to the comming of Chriſt.* And
how then do we apply yt, as Fox lyeth, to
keep vs from wrath ? ſeing that cannot be
done but only by grace, which this law giueth
     not.

not. And finally *S. Thomas* hath a speciall article 1.2. *q.* 100. *art.* 12. vvith this title; *vvhether the precepts of the old law, can iuftifie or no?* and he holdeth that they cannot; vvherby yow fee Iohn Fox his three lyes affirmatiue. The negatiue ly is,that vve apply the law to no other end, but to thefe three named; which is falfe, and conteyneth fo many vntruthes, as there be thinges whervnto we apply the fame, befides thefe fictions diuifed by Fox. As for example, to be an introduction or pedagoge to the new law, as *S. Paul* faith *Gal.* 3. Item to fignifie & prefigurate Chrift, & his law,and to teach vs what is to be done or auoyded in our actions, though yt giue not grace for the performance therof *&c.* See S.Thomas 1.2.*q.*107. *art.*2. *& in commentar. ad Rom.*10. *lect.* 1.

16.   Further-more in the fame place *num.* 30. he vvryteth thus of our doctrine concerninge good works: *They do teach, as though the end of good works were to meritt remiffion of finnes,and to deferue grace, &c.* In vvhich two members to omitt other points, are conteyned two egregious lyes,refuted by the words of the Councell of Trent it felfe *feff. 6. cap. 8. Nihil eorum quæ Iuftificationem præcedunt, fiue fides, fiue opera, ipfam iuftificationis gratiam promeretur.* None of thofe things that go before our iuftification, eyther faith or works, can meritt the grace of our iuftification. *ergo* we do not teach,that our good works, can eyther meritt remifsion of finnes, included in iuftification, or deferue grace, which is our formall iuftification,as yow may

fee

Tvvo lyes about meritinge remiffion of finnes and deferuing grace by vvorks.

see in the same Councell & session *cap.4. & 7.*
and more at large in S. Thomas *1.2.q.* 114.*art.5.*
and later schoole diuines vpon that place, as
also in the comentaryes vpon the second
booke of sentences *dinstinct. 27. &c.*

Tvvo lyes about originall and actuall sinnes.

17.   In the same page *num.* 35. he vvryteth
thus: *They teach most wickedly and horribly, sayinge,
that Christ suffered for originall sinne , or sinnes goinge
before baptisme, but the actuall sinnes which follow after baptisme, must be done away by mans meritts, &c.*
Heere are two wicked and horrible lyes, in
steed of this wicked and horrible doctrine of
ours. For first we say not that Christ suffered
only for originall sinne, but for all sinnes, both
originall, and actuall, precedent, and subse-
quent after our baptisme. *S. Thomas* his words
are cleere, *part. 3. q.1.art. 4. Certum est, &c. It is
certayne* (saith he) *that Christ came into the world to
blot out, not only originall sinne, but all sinnes, &c.* The
second point also, that actuall sinnes after baptisme, can not be done away by mans merit,
as Fox feigneth vs to teach, but by the merits
of Christ & by the grace and vertue of his said
passion, is no lesse euidét in all our wrytings,
as yow may see in S. Thomas *1. 2. q.* 114. *art.7.*
and the Councell of Trent, *Seß. 6. cap. 14.
& 16. &c.*

A ly about outvvard & invvard obedience to the lavv.

18.   Againe in the same page *nu.* 66. he wryteth thus: *They affirme that the law doth requyre
but only outward obedience of man , and therwith is
contented, &c.* This is a wicked lye also, for that
we teach that the law of God doth require
not only externall obedience, but also internall

nall of the will and iudgement, which yow may fee handled at large by *S. Thomas* in diuers places, & namely 1. 2. *q.*100.*art.*9. where he doth diſtinguiſh and put a difference betwene humayne lawes, and Gods lawes in this point. *Man (ſaith he) when he maketh a law, can iudge but of externall acts, but God iudgeth of the internall motion of our will, according to that of the Pſalme,* God ſearcheath the hart and reynes, *&c. So* Pſal. 7. *humayne law doth not punish him that hath a ſecret will to murder, yf he do not committ the fact, but Gods law doth as Chriſt teacheth vs Matth.* 5. Behold heere not only externall obedience of the fact, but internal alſo of the will, is taught by vs, and conſequently Fox is an egregious lyar to calumniate vs for the contrary.

19. In the ſame page *num.* 70. Fox hath theſe words: *Alſo there be ſay they, among other, certayne works of the law, which perteyne not to all men, but are conſilia, counſells, left for perfect men, as matter for them to meritt by, and theſe they call Opera perfectionis, or Opera indebita, adding alſo vnto theſe new deuiſes to ſerue God after their owne traditions, beſides the word of God, as monaſticall vowes, willful pouerty, differences of meats and garments, pilgrimage to reliques, worshipping of the dead, roſaryes,* &c. *And theſe they call works of perfection, which they preferre before the other commaunded in the law of God. In ſo much that in compariſon of theſe, the other neceſſarye dutyes commaunded, and commended by the word of God, as to beare office in the common welth, to lyue in the godly ſtate of matrimony, to ſuſtayne the office of a ſeruant in a houſe, is contemned and accoumpted as prophane,*

phane, &c. So Fox. And heere are fuch a heap
ofignorant and malitious lyes, as well may
become fuch a Doctor. For firft we do not
hould, *that confilia are works of the law,* as he faith,
for then they were not coufells, but precepts.
Secondly we do not call the laft foure works
heere mentioned, to witt, difference of meats,
pilgrimage to reliques, worfhipping of the
dead, and Rofaryes, *&c.* properly Euangelicall counfells or works of perfection, but only thofe three recomended by Chrift in the
ghofpell, namely voluntary pouerty, chaftity,
and obedience, as yow may fee in *Saint Thomas*
1. 2. q. 108. art. 4. *&c.*

20.   Thirdly yt is a follemne lye, that we do
preferre the works of Counfell, before the
works commaunded in the law of God, touching necefsity of faluation. For we hould the
quite contrary, to witt, that the workes commaunded by almighty God, are abfolutely neceffary to be obferued by euery man, that
will be faued, but not the workes of coufell or

perfection. *This is the difference* (faith S. Thomas)
*betwene a counfell and a precept, that a precept impor-
teth necefßity, but a counfell is left in the choyfe of him,
to whome yt is geuen, & therfore in the new law, which
is a lavv of freedome, Confells vvere conueniently geuen*

befides precepts, &c. And the fame Doctor in diuers other places fheweth, that the obferuation of Counfells, is ordeyned to keep therby
the better, the obferuation of precepts; and
that wherfoeuer any precept and counfell
cannot be obferued togeather, there we muft
leaue

leaue che counfell, and obferue the precept,
wherby appeareth the falfhood of Fox his affertion, that we preferre counfells before precepts, or things commaunded.

21.   And as for the three laft things affirmed
by Fox to be neceffary and commaunded by
God, to witt, *to beare office in the comon vvelth, to*
marry, and to be a feruant in a houfe, thefe do make
three other moft foule lyes alfo (yf he meane
ofparticular men, as needs he muft, feeing he
reprehendeth thofe that would liue chaft, or
do leaue the world, and rather ferue God,
then particular maifters, for that God hath
not commaunded thefe to particular men, but
only hath left the fame as indifferent to take
them or leaue them) and the fourth may be
that we do contemne, and accoumpt them
prophane. For we accoumpt Matrimony (for
example) holy, and to be a Sacrament & giue
grace, which Fox, and his fellowes do not.
We accoumpt alfo the other two named by
him for lawfull, and commendable, though
of leffe perfection, then the Euangelicall
Councells, commended by Chrift, and his
Apoftles. So as this is a notorious ly alfo in
this matter.

22.   *Page* 24. *col.* 1. *num.* 3. he faith, that we
do hould externall actions againft our will
to be fynne. T*hey fuppofe fynne (faith he) to be*
nothing els, but the invvard actions, vvith confent of
vvill, or the outvvard actions fuch as are againft vvill;
and then he noteth in the margent ; *Erroneous*
doctrine of the later Church of Rome, cocerninge fynne.

But

Foure lyes
about
vvorks of
precept.

A ly, that
outvvard
actions a-
gainft our
vvill are
finnes.

But this is erroneous foolery in Iohn Fox, that vnderstandeth not what he saith, nor we. For we are so farre of from holding eyther inward, or outward actions to be sinne, without consent of the will, as both S. *Thomas*, and all other schoole diuines do hould with *Saint Augustine*, affirming, that yt is so necessary, that synne be voluntary, as yf yt be not voluntary, yt cannot be sinne. See S. Thomas 1.2. *q. 71. art. 5. & q. 76. art. 3. & q. 80. art. 1. &c.*

Aug. l. de vera relig. cap. 14.

23.   Againe in the same page *num. 22.* he saith that we do hould about originall sinne ; *that concupiscence in vs, is no deprauation of the higher, but only of the lower parts of man.* Wheras our doctrine is quyte contrary, as yow may see in S. Thomas, 1. 2. *q. 83. art. 3.* whose words are. *Infectio peccati originalis per prius respicit atque inficit voluntatem, quam alias potentias.* The infection of originall sinne, doth respect and infect our will, before the rest of our powers . *Ergo*, yt is first a deprauation of the higher powers , accordinge to our doctrine , quite contrary to Fox his assertion.

A ly about concupi- sence.

24.   *Page* 24. *num. 30.* he saith, *that the later Lateran Church of Rome hath made of late a Sacrament of pennance.* This is an euident ly; For that long before the Councell of Lateran , which was *anno* 1215. Schoole diuines, to omitt all others, did ordinarily wryte of pennance, as of a Sacrament, as yow may see in the *Maister of Sentences l. 4. dist. 14.* and all others that followed him many yeares before the Lateran Councell. Besides that we hold generally, that the whole

A ly about the Sacrament of pennace.

whole Church hath not authority to make
any Sacraments at all, nor yet to change the
matter and forme therof, as yow may fee in
S. Thomas *part. 3. q. 6. art. 5. & q. 64. art. 20.*
and therby note the fhamelefle dealing of our
aduerfaryes.

25. In the fame page *num. 33.* he wryteth of
vs thus: *Contrition (as they teach) may be had by
ftrength of free will, vvithout the law & the holy Ghoft,
per actus elicitos, through mans ovvne action and indeauour ; vvhich contrition firft muft be fufficient, and
fo yt meriteth remiffion of finnes, &c.* Heere are diuers lyes, but two moft fingular. The firft, *that
vve hould contrition may be had by ftrength of mans
freevvill vvithout the help of the holy Ghoft by actus elicitos.* The fecond, that the fame contrition fo
had, *doth meritt remiffion of finnes.* Both which
propofitions are in exprefle tearmes condemned, and anathematized by the Councell of
Trent, *Sef. 6. & can. 3.* in thefe words: *Si quis
dixerit, fine prauĕniente Spiritus fancti infpiratione, atque eius adiutorio, hominem pœnitere poffe, ficut oportet, vt ei iuftificationis gratia conferatur, Anathema
fit.* Yf any do fay that a man may repent as he
ought to do, without the infpiration and cooperation of the holy Ghoft, in fuch fort as
therby he may obtayne his iuftification, lett
him be accurfed.

26. Thus determineth the Councell of both
thefe points; which doctrine is fo certayne a-
monge vs; that not only of contrition, but of
faith alfo, and all other works whatfoeuer
goinge before iuftification, the faid Councell
pro-

*Tvvo lyes
about cō-
trition.*

pronounceth, as before hath byn shewed; *Nihil*
eorum , quæ iustificationem præcedunt , siue fides , siue
opera , ipsius iustificationis gratiam promeretur. No-
,, thinge that goeth before our iustification,
,, being it faith or works, can merit the grace of
,, our iustification , and consequently neyther
,, contrition which goeth before iustification,
,, can meritt remission of our sinnes. And where
Fox , to seeme that he knoweth somewhat,
putteth in *per actus elicitos,* and doth Inglish yt,
through mans owne action and indeauour, excluding
therby as yt were the cooperation of Gods
grace from *actus eliciti ,* he sheweth himselfe a
silly fellow, that vnderstandeth not the ordinary tearmes of Schoole ; For that *actus eliciti,*
are also those actions, which our freewill bringeth forth by the assistance of grace. And the
opposition is betweene *actus eliciti* and *actus im-*
perati, and not in respect of grace or not grace.
See S. Thomas 1. 2. *q.* 6. *art.* 6. *& 2.* 2. *q.* 3. *art.*
1. *ad* 1.

27. In the same page *num.* 42. Fox hath these
words of satisfaction: *Satisfaction* (say they) *ta-*
keth away, and changeth eternall punishment into tem-
porall paynes, which paynes also, yt doth mitigate. This
is a manifest ly: For we teach plainely the
contrary, that our satisfaction, neyther taketh
away or changeth eternall punishment , nor
satisfieth for yt , but only for temporall punishment due for sinnes, already remitted by
vertue of the Sacrament of absolution, which
only can remit eternall punishment. Heare
the Councell of Trent, and tell me (good reader)

Di.f. 6. c. 8. [left margin]

A ly about
Satisfa-
ction. [left margin]

Di.f. 6. c. 14. [left margin]

der) whether Fox be an honeſt man or no. ,,
Satiſfaction (ſaith the Councell) by faſting, ,,
almes, prayer, and other pious exerciſes of a ,,
ſpirituall life doth ſatiſſie , *Non quidem pro pœna*
æterna (quæ vel Sacramento vel Sacramenti voto, vnà
cum culpa remittitur)ſed pro pœna temporali. Not for
eternall puniſhment (which is remitted to- ,,
geather with the guilt, by vertue of the Sacra- ,,
ment of pennance, or deſire therof) but only ,,
for temporall paynes. And yet will Fox needs
haue vs teach the contrary , that yt taketh
away and changeth eternall puniſhment.

28. In the ſame page *num.* 66. he ſaith: *They*
teach the people , that vvhatſoeuer the law ſaith , the
ghoſpell confirmeth , and that vvhatſoeuer the ghoſpell
ſaith, the ſame is agreeable to the law, & ſo they make
no difference betweene Moyſes & Chriſt, ſaue only that
Moyſes(they ſay)vvas the giuer of the old law,& Chriſt
is the giuer of the new , and a more perfect law . And
thus imagine they the ghoſpell to be nothinge els , but a Fiue lyes
new law geuen by Chriſt,byndinge to the promiſe ther- about the
of, the condition of our doings and deſeruings, no other- of Chriſt
wiſe then to the old law. Thus wryteth Fox, and & Moyſes
then triumpheth in the margent with theſe lavves.
notes. *The blynd ignorance of the Popes Church.*
*A Babylonicall confuſion in the Popes doctrine,*and the
like. But heere are nothinge but heapes of
lyes proceedinge of ignorance and malice, as
preſently yow ſhall ſee.

29. For firſt yt is an euident lye , that we
teach the people,*that vvhatſoeuer the law ſaith,the*
ghoſpell confirmeth. For who doth not ſee , that
vve neyther vſe any ceremoniall part of
E e Moyſes

Moyſes law, nor yet do teach the people that the ghoſpell alloweth or cōfirmeth the ſame. And *S. Thomas* 1. 2. *q.* 103. *art.* 3. *& 4.* doth euidently teach the ſame, his principall queſtion in the fourth article being this: *Vtrum poſt paſſionem Chriſti, legalia poßint ſeruari ſine peccato mortali?* Whether thoſe things that do perteyne to the law (of Moyſes) may be obſerued after the paſsion of Chriſt, without mortall ſyn? And he holdeth no. And how then ſaith Fox that we teach the people, *that vvhatſoeuer the law of Moyſes ſaith, the ghoſpell confirmeth?* And lett this be the firſt lye of this ſpeach.

30. The ſecond is out of the next words: *that vvhatſoeuer the ghoſpell ſaith, the ſame is agreeable to the law.* This is ſo euident a lye, as euery child may refute the ſame. For the ghoſpell, for examples ſake, commaundeth vnder mortall ſinne not to circumciſe *Gal.* 5. (and we hold the ſame, as appeareth in the place imediatly before cyted, out of *S. Thomas:* and the law of Moyſes commaundeth vnder mortall ſinne to be circumciſed *Gen.* 17. And how then do we teach, *that whatſoeuer the ghoſpell ſaith, the ſame is agreeable to the lavv?*

1.2.q.103. art. 4.

31. The third lye is, *that vve make no difference betvvene Moyſes and Chriſt, ſaue only, that Moyſes vvas the giuer of the old lavv, and Chriſt of the nevv, &c.* This is moſt impudent. For let any man read *S. Thomas* 1. 2. *q.* 106. and diuers other whole queſtions and articles, that follow, and he ſhall ſee him aſsigne many other differences betwene Moyſes, and Chriſt, and their two lawes.

lawes. The cheefe and principall wherof is,
that Moyses gaue the law, but not force of
grace to fullfill yt; but Chrift gaue his law, togeather with grace of the holy Ghoft to performe the fame, accordinge to thofe words of
S. Iohn: *Lex per Moyfen data eft*; *gratia & veritas* Ioan. 1.
per Iefum Chriftum facta eft. The law was giuen
by Moyfes, but grace and verity was brought
by Iefus Chrift. To which effect alfo, fee the
Councell of Trent *Seß. 6. cap. 1. & Can. 1. & 2.*
and tell me what a fellow Iohn Fox is.

32. There follow the laft words of this fentence of his, to witt, *that vve imagine the ghofpell
to be nothing els, but a new law, byndinge to the pro-
mifes therof, the condition of our doings and deferuings,
no otherwife then to the old law.* In which words
are two other feuerall lyes. The firft, *that vve
imagine the ghofpell to be nothing els, but a new law,
conteyninge new precepts, &c.* Which is refuted
before, and S. Thomas his words are cleere.
*Id quod eft potißimum in lege noui teftamenti, & in quo
eius virtus confiftit, eft gratia Spiritus fancti, quæ da-
tur per fidem Chrifti.* That which is the principall in the law of the new teftament, is the ”
grace of the holy Ghoft, giuen by the faith of ”
Chrift, wherby we are made able to performe ”
the precepts. And the fame Doctour in the ”
fame and fequent article, concludeth, that the
precepts *pertinent ad legem Euangelij fecundariò*, do
appertaine to the new law fecondarily; wherby alfo yow fee the other ly next followinge,
where he affirmeth vs to hould, *that the new
law of the ghofpell doth bynd to the condition of doings,*

no otherwise, then did the old law, vvhich is false: For
that the new law byndeth and geueth grace
to performe, and the old byndeth with out
help of grace, which is farre otherwise, as often hath byn shewed.

33.   In the same page *num. 76.* he wryteth

thus : *And as for the ghospell , they say yt is receaued
for no other cause to the vvorld , but to shew more perfect precepts and Counsells , then vvere in the old law,*
&c. *bringinge the people therby into a false opinion of
Chrift, as though he vvere not a remedy againft the law.*
In these words there are two apparant lyes.
For firft , befides the caufe feygned heere by
Fox, we do afsigne diuers other of reueylinge
the ghofpell. Firft to performe that indeed by
Chrift, vvhich vvas promifed and prefigured
by Moyfes law. Secondly to giue grace and
force, to be able to performe the precept of
this new law, as imediatly before we haue declared. The fecond ly is, *that vve hould Chrift not
to be a remedy againft the obligation of the old law*;
vvhich is refuted by that we haue faid before,
in that he both tooke away the faid obligation, of the ceremoniall & iudiciall part therof, and gaue force of grace to fullfill the morall part that remayneth, to witt the ten commandements; which may content Iohn Fox,
except he will haue licence by his new ghofpell to abrogate this part alfo, and therby obtayne leaue to lye, fteale, kill, commytt adultery and the like, prohibyted in the faid deca-
logue by the very law of nature yt felfe , and
confequently retayned alfo and confirmed by
the

the law of the ghofpell, wherof yow may fee
S. Augustine at large *lib.*10. *cont. Fauft.cap.*2.*& lib.
de spiritu & lit. cap.*14. *& tract.*3. *in Ioan.* and infinite other places.

34.   In the fame *pag.* 24. *col.*2. *num.*2. he wryteth yet further about the fame law in thefe
vvords: *They, contrary to the vvord of God, make the
lavv to haue no end nor reafigne , but giue vnto yt immortall life and kingdome equall vvith Chrift : fo that
Chrift and the lavv togeather do raigne ouer the foule
& confcience of man,&c.* In which words among
other abfurdityes, two lyes are euident; *Firft,
that vve put no end to the law of Moyfes.* And the
other, *that we affirme the fame law to raigne vvith
Chrift ouer Chriftian mens confciences.* For yf he
fpeake of the ceremoniall part of the law, yt is
too too impudent, for we haue fhewed before
out of *S. Thomas* 1.2.*q.*103.*art.*4. & other places,
that we hould the law of Moyfes concerning
this part , to haue ceafed with the pafsion of
Chrift, & fo neyther liueth nor raigneth. But
if Iohn fpeake of the morall part of the law, to
witt the ten cōmaundements before touched,
which were geuen to be obferued not for a
tyme, but for euer, as hath byn fhewed, then is
yt true that they do liue & laft , but falfe that
they do raigne. For that Chrift hath geuen vs
grace to raigne ouer them, that is to fay to performe them, which *S. Paul* meaneth, when he
faith; *vve are no more vnder the law.* Wherof alfo
fee *S. Auguftine lib. de continent. cap.* 3. *& in Pfal.*1.

35.   Further *pag.*25. *num* 80. he wryteth thus:
See now how farre this later Church of Rome hath de-
                                          generated,

E e 3

Tvvo lyes about the kingdome of Chrift & Moyfes lavv.

Rom. 10.

generated, vvhich holdeth & affirmeth that men vvithout grace may performe obedience of the law, and prepare themselues to grace by vvorking; so as these vvorks
may be meritorious, and of congruity obtayninge grace.
But as for the infirmity vvhich still remayneth in nature, that they nothinge regard, nor once speake of,&c.

Foure lyes about performinge the lavv & our infirmity. Heere there are foure most shameleste lyes, to
omytt the rest. For first we do not hould, *that
men vvithout grace, can performe the obedience of the
law,* but rather the quite contrary, as yow may
see in S. *Thomas* 1. 2. q. 109. *art.* 9. vvhere he
sheweth, that euen a iust man, though he haue
receaued his grace of iustification, yet needeth
he another speciall help from God to worke
accordinge to the law, and much lesse can he
that is not iustified, performe the law vvithout grace. Secondly we say not, that a man by
works may prepare himselfe to grace, but the
plaine opposite is defined by the Councell of
Trent *Seß.6.c.5.* & *S. Thomas* in the forsaid *art.9.*
whose title is : *VVhether a man may prepare himselfe to grace by his owne vvorks, or no?* And he determineth no. And in the very same place he
refuteth the third lye of Fox, to witt, *that vve
hould vvorks vvithout grace to be meritorious, and to obtayne grace of congruity*; as also in the ninth article he refuteth the fourth lye; *that vve regard
not, nor once speake of the infirmity that remayneth in
nature after baptisme.* For in that place S. Thomas asigneth two infirmityes remayninge
euen in the iust man, after his iustification;
Albeit (saith he) *man by grace be healed touchinge his
mynd, yet remayneth there a certayne corruption and
infection*

infection touchinge his flesh, vvherby he serueth to the law of sinne, as S. Paul saith to the Romans: There re- Rom. 7. *mayneth also a certayne obscurity of ignorance in the vnderstandinge, vvherby vve know not how to pray as* Rom. 8. *vve should, as the same Apostle saith in the same epistle.* Thus he. And yow may see further the Councell of Trent *Seß. 5. num. 5.* And where then is Fox his shame, that sayeth we neuer so much as speake of this infirmity?

36.   In the same page *col.2. num.6. They affirme* (saith Fox) *that Christ vvas a mediator only in the* A ly about the media- *tyme of his passion, vvhich is contrary to S. Paul Rom.8.* tion of Christ. *Christ, vvho is on the right hand of God, vvho also maketh intercession for vs, &c.* But this is malitious foolery. For schoolemen distinguish two offices of a mediator in Christ, the one to pay our debt for vs, which he did only vpon the Crosse; the other to be our intercessour, which he performeth now also and for euer in heauen, as *S. Paul* affirmeth. This doth *S. Thomas* and other wryters declare in their comentaryes vpon the said place of *S. Paul* to the Romans; wherby yow may see how falsely Fox affirmeth vs to deny, that Christ is a mediator of intercession.

37.   Againe *num. 26. They prophane also* (saith he) *the Lords supper, in settinge yt to sale for money, and falsely persuading both themselues and others, that the Priest doth meritt both to himselfe, that saith the masse, and to him that heareth ex opere operato, siue bo-* Three lyes about the *no motu vtentis, &c. that is only by the meere doing of* vse and *the vvorke, though the party that vseth the same, hath* meritt of *no good motion in him.* Heere is another heap of Sacraments. lyes.

lyes. For firſt yt is moſt falſe , *that vve ſett to ſale
the Lords ſupper for money.* For that we holding
yt to be the very body of Chriſt, yt vvere Sy-

* See Canſ.
1.q.3.cap.
Altare.

mony in the higheſt degree,vvhich ſinne* our
Religion condemneth for moſt greuous by
Eccleſiaſticall canons. And yf he meane that

* Se Suarez
to.3.in p.3.
diſput. 86.
Sect.1.

ſome Prieſts * take almes for ſayinge maſſe, yt
is foolery ; for ſo doth the miniſter alſo for a
communion. And S. Paul ſaith. *He that ſerueth
the Altar , may liue of the Altar,* vvhich yet can
hardly agree to a communion table , as yow
vvill eaſily conſider. And this is the firſt lye.

38. After this are conteyned diuers other lyes
in the ſame vvords, as for example , *that vve do
hould and teach , that the Prieſt doth meritt by ſayinge
Maſſe both to himſelfe, and to him, that heareth yt, by
the meere doinge of the vvorke , vvithout any good invvard motion, &c.* For firſt touchinge the Prieſt
himſelfe that ſaith maſſe , yt is a ly , that vve
hould him to meritt to himſelfe , yf he do yt
vvithout any inward good motion. For that
meritt, accordinge to all ſchoole-diuines, requyreth a good inward motion, vvherof. See
S. Thomas 1.2.q.71.art.3.& q.110.art.4. Secondly
yt is no leſſe , but rather a farr greater ly, that
a Prieſt ſayinge maſſe vvithout any good invvard motion , doth meritt to him that heareth the maſſe. For albeit the hearer may meritt to himſelfe by his owne deuotion, vvhen
the Prieſt meriteth not ; yet is yt falſe that the
Prieſt vvhich meriteth nothinge for himſelfe,
can meritt for his hearer.See *S. Thomas* at large
1.2.q.114.art.4. And as for the phraſe *ex opere
operato,*

operato, vvhich Fox heere vseth and vrgeth a-
gainst vs, he vnderstandeth not, what it meaneth ; For that this phrase is vsed only to expresse the manner of working of Sacraments,
vvhich are said to vvorke their effects of geuinge grace, not *ex opere operantis,* that is accordinge to the dignity or meritt of the person,
that doth administer them, but *ex opere operato,*
that is by the very application of the Sacrament, accordinge to Chrifts inftitution, from
vvhich inftitution yt hath this force. For that
Chrift vvould not haue the effect of his Sacraments depend of the goodnes or badnes of
the minifters therof, yf the person that receaueth them do putt no lett by his vnworthi-
nefle. As for example the effect of baptifme,
vvhich is the vvafhinge away of our fynnes,
doth not any vvay depend of the goodnes or
badnes of the prieft, or minifter that baptizeth,
but only of Chrifts inftitution, and therfore
taketh away finnes from euery one that is baptized, *ex opere operato,* yf the party baptized put
no lett. But this inferreth not the malitious
conclufion of Iohn Fox, that a naughty Prieft
baptizinge, may meritt both to himfelfe and
others, without any good motion in himfelfe;
for that meritinge and workinge of the Sacraments are two diftinct things. See *Bellarm.* of
this matter largely *tom. 2. controu. lib.2. cap.1.*
39. Next after this in the fame page *num.* 44.
he vvryteth thus: *VVhere the vvord hath ordayned*
thofe Sacraments (to vvitt *Baptifme and Eucharift*) *to*
excite our faith, and to giue vs admonitions of fpirituall
things,

things, they contrary vvife do teach, that the Sacraments do not only ſtyrre vp faith, but alſo that they auayle and are effectuall vvith out faith ex opere operato, ſine bono motu vtentis, &c. as is to be found in Thomas Aquinas, Scotus, Catharinus and others more, &c. In vvhich vvords, to omitt all other obſeruations, fiue manifeſt lyes are to be conuinced at leaſt, to witt, in that he auoucheth of the 3. ſeuerall authors heere named, and of others more, vvhich muſt be two at leaſt, vntill he bring them forth, vvhich he can neuer doe, the contrary doctrine being vvith vs a matter of faith, to witt, that in baptiſme, to obtayne the effect therof (vvhich is the remiſsion of our ſinnes) faith is abſolutly neceſſary, as the Councell of Trent decreeth *Seſſ. 6. cap.* 8. and proueth the ſame out of *S. Paul Heb.* 11. *without faith yt is vnpoſſible to pleaſe God.* And as for the Sacrament of the Euchariſt, our authors do require a farre greater diſpoſition in the receauer, then for baptiſme. As for example, not only to beleeue, but alſo to be contrite, confeſſed and the like, vvherof yow may ſee the Councell of Trent *Seſſ.13. cap.3.* And as for the three authors heere by Fox named, but no place cited or quoted out of them for the ſame; they hold the quite contrary, as may be ſeene in *S. Thomas pag. 3. q. 68. art. 8.* as alſo in *Scotus in 4. Sentent. diſt.4.q.4.* And albeit I haue not *Catharinus* lyinge by me, yet is yt certayne that he agreeth with the reſt in this point.

23. lyes, about the applicatiō

40.   Next after this *num.* 52. he faith, that *we apply our Sacraments both to the quicke and the dead,*

and

and to them alſo that be abſent, to remiſſion of ſinnes & releaſinge of paynes, &c. *And vvheras the vſe of the old Church of* Rome (ſaith he) *vvas only to baptiſe men, vve baptize alſo belles, & apply the vvords of baptiſme, to vvater , fire , candells , ſtocks and ſtones , &c.* In vvhich vvords are another heape of lyes intollerable. For firſt there are ſo many lyes as there are Sacraments, vvhich vve apply not to the dead, vvhich are ſeauen, for albeit vve apply the holy ſacrifice of Chriſts body , to the releeſe of thoſe that are in purgatory; yet not as yt is a Sacrament, which is adminiſtred vnto them only that be aliue and preſent; and as for the other ſix Sacraments I thinke he will not ſtand vvith vs in earneſt, for that vve neither baptize the dead, neyther confirme the dead , nor giue holy orders to the dead , nor heare the deads confeſsion , nor marry the dead , nor giue them extreeme vnction. Secondly vvheras he ſaith, *that vve do baptize bells, vvater, fire, candles, ſtocks and ſtones,* as the old Roman Church did baptize men , and do apply the vvords of baptiſme vnto them , there are as many lyes, as there be things named, to wit ſix more. For that the baptiſme , vvhich the old Church of Rome, and the new alſo at this day (yf Fox vvill haue it new) vvas a Sacrament & required faith , and other diſpoſition in the receauer , as before hath byn ſhewed, vvhich cannot be in *bells , candles , fire , vvater, ſtocks and ſtones.* And ſecondly the vvords of baptiſme, as yt is a Sacrament are: *I do baptiſe thee in the name of the Father, the Sonne and the holy Ghoſt,* vvhich

which were neuer vfed to bells, or candles,&
other fuch thinges heere named, as appeareth
in the pŏtificiall & ceremoniall booke, where
the formes of hallowing bells, water,candles,
& fuch other creatures, appropriate to diuine
feruice are fett downe, where though the bell
(for exáple) be appointed to be wafhed with
holy-water, yet can ꝙt no more properly be
called the Sacrament ofbaptifme,then when
Iohn Fox(for example)fprinkled holy-water
vpŏ his fonnes face, that was foule,or that the
geuinge a peece of browne bread to a poore
man,may be called the Proteftáts communiŏ.
41.   And now I begin to be vveary (good
reader) to profecute this mans folly any further,fo as I vvill make haft to difpach the reft.
Num. 80. after many opprobrious blafphe-
Two lyes myes, vtteredagainft the blefled body of our
about the fauiour in the Sacrament, he faith ; *that vve do*
putrifying
and bur- *ordeyne, that yf he corrupt and putrifie in the pix* (to
ninge of witt Chrift,) *then that he be burned to poulder and*
Chrifts
body. *afhes, &c.* Wherin are two blafphemous lyes:
for neyther we hould,that the body of Chrift
can corrupt or putrifie, nor yet do we or-
dayne, that yt be burned. Thefe are Fox his
hereticall fictions, and not our doctrines. For
we hould, that Chrifts body is immortall and
incorruptible, vnder the corruptible formes
of bread, and wyne, which formes and accidents, yf they do at any tyme putrifie or corrupt, then ceafeth to be vnder them the body
& blond of Chrift,wherof fee *S. Thomas par.* 3.
*q.*77.*art.*4. So as thefe are two impious lyes.
42. *Pag.*26.

42. *Pag.*26.*n.*8. he belyeth *S.Paul* apparantly,
sayinge that in his epiftle to Timothy, *he vehe-*
*mētly reproueth them that reſtraine marriage.*Which
is nothinge fo. For in that place he fortelleth
only of certayne heretiks to come, that fhould
forbid marriage,*prohibentes nubere,&c.*as a thing
vncleane & vnlawfull in it felfe,& fuch were
the Manichees,as *S.Auſten* declareth. But as for
reſtrayninge of marriage , for a more perfect life,
S. Paul himfelfe hath a whole Chapter to the
Corinthians,affirminge that yt was better to
abftaine,then to marry, which alfo *S. Auguſtine*
cyteth,& proueth that *S. Paul* was of the fame
opinion,that we are: *Ille prohibet*(faith *S.Auſten*)
qui hoc malum eſſe dicit, non qui huic bono,aliud melius »
anteponit. He doth prohibite marriage (accor- »
ding to *S.Paules* words)who faith it is euill (as »
yow Manichies do),& not he who preferreth »
before this good thing, another that is better, »
(to witt virginity) as the Apoftle doth.

43. Againe *num.* 14. he wryteth thus. The
new *Catholiks of the Popes Church do repute and call*
marriage a ſtate of imperfection , and preferre ſingle
life, be yt neuer ſo impure,before the ſame. And then
in the margent of his booke , he maketh this
note for the reader:*ſingle life,be yt neuer ſo impure*
preferred before matrimony. Which are two fha-
melesfe lyes, the one in the text, the other in
the margent. For that we hould the ftate of
an impure fingle life for damnable , but the
ftate of matrimony for holy,and indued with
grace by vertue of the Sacrament , as appeareth in the Councell of Trent *Seſſ.*24. *cap.* 1.

though

A lye a-
gainſt S.
Paul.
1. *Tim.* 3.

Aug. l.30.
cont. Fauſt.
cap. 6.
1. *Cor.* 7.

A.

Two lyes
about the
ſtate of
matrimo-
ny.

though yet leſſe perfect in yt ſelfe, then the
ſtate of virginity, as immediatly before hath
byn ſhewed out of *S. Paul* and *S. Auguſtine*. So
as this lying ſpirit of Iohn Fox is euery where
apparant; as namely alſo in this place, where
he ſaith, *that we teach the earth only to be repleniſhed by the ſtate of matrimony; but heauen to be filled by
impure ſingle life;* vvheras contrary wiſe we ſay,
that heauen is repleniſhed with thoſe marryed folkes that liue well, and only hell is
furniſhed with thoſe that liue impurely in
ſingle life.

44. Againe in the ſame page *num.* 18. *Further-*
Tvvo lyes   *more* (ſaith Fox) *as good as the third part of Chri-*
about co-   *ſtendome, yf yt be not more, both men ad vveomen they*
acted   *keep through coacted vowes from marriage.* Heere
vovves.   are two manifeſt lyes more. For who but Fox
will ſay, that they are the third part of Chriſtendome that liue vnmarryed *by obligation of*
vowes? At leaſt in our Iland, and ſome other
parts of Chriſtendome he will not ſay, they
are the 13. part, through the good doctrine of
Fox, and his fellowes agreeing to their owne
ſenſualityes. Secondly who but Fox will ſay,
that vowes are coacted, vvhich are freely offered
by the vowers, vvithout any coaction at all,
and not accepted, but vpon long and mature
deliberation, and at leaſt one whole yeares
probation, yf not more, after the vower hath
purpoſed to make them? VVherof ſee the
A ly about   Councell of Trent *Seſſ.* 15. *cap.* 26.
dayes ex-   45. Againe *num.* 26. *As good* (ſaith he) *as the*
empt frō   *third part of the yeare, they exempt and ſuſpend from*
marriage.   *liberty*

liberty of marriage. Behould heere our pro&er
of marriage, he would haue men to be marryinge euery day, and as though two parts of
three in the yeare (yf Iohns accoumpt had
byn true) were not fufficient to ioyne people
togeather in marriage, and as though fome
dayes for more reuerence or deuotion, prayer
and pennance, might not be exempted, from
this exercife, and yet is Iohn Fox much deceaued in his accoumpts, and therby fheweth,
that he was yet neuer good parifh Prieft, for
they haue the exa& number of dayes, vvhich
are exempted, to witt the aduent and lent,
which make not the fourth part of the whole
yeare; fo as this lye is both flaunderous and
foolifh.

46. Furthermore *pag. 26. num. 51.* he faith:
the Pope withall his cleargy exempt themfelues from all
obedience Cyuill, &c. And this alfo to be a mani-
feftly, appeareth plainly by all our wryters,
and namely, by *Cardinall Bellarmine* in his difputation *de exemptione Clericorum cap. 1.* where
he teacheth expreffely, that cleargy men are
not exempted from the obferuation of Cyuill
lawes in the countreyes where they dwell,
except they be repugnant to the holy canons
of the Church or to the office of clergy men.

A ly about
exemptiõ
of clergy-
men.

47. Further in the fame page *num. 33.* he
wryteth thus: *Lett vs examine the vvhole Religion*
of this later Church of Rome, and we fhall find yt wholy
from topp to toe, to confift in nothinge els, but altogea-
ther in outward, and ceremoniall exercifes, &c.
Note heere the exaggerations of Iohn Fox,

that

that our Religion consisteth vvholy from topp to toe, in nothinge els, but altogeather, &c. Which foure or fiue fond exaggerations, are so many notorious lyes, whervnto I might adioyne so many others, as there are inward vertues belonginge to our Religion. For yow must note, that quite contrary to this shamelesse assertion of Fox, we teach that all the good of our Religion consisteth and commeth from the inward, to witt, faith, hope, charity, zeale, piety, and other like inward vertues, in so much that we hold no externall act for good or meritorious, except it proceed from internall goodnes of the mynd first, and S. Thomas 1.2.q.20. *art.* 4. holdeth this proposition; *that the goodnes of any externall act, proceedeth from the goodnesse of the internall, from which yt cometh, and addeth nothing thervnto.* And how then doth this miserable fellow say, that all our whole Religion, *doth vvholy from topp to toe, consist in nothinge els, but altogeather in externall exercises?* there are as many lyes as words, wherby yow see his veyne of lyinge.

48.   Moreouer in the same place, he wryteth, *that the doctrine of Christ, is altogeather spirituall, consistinge vvholy in spiritt, and verity, and requyreth no outward thinge, to make a true Christian man, but only baptisme, which is the outward profession of faith, and receauinge the Lords supper, &c.* In which words are conteyned as many lyes, as there are outward works commaunded by God to Christian men. As first of all the seauen works of mercy, named corporall, as to

feed

feed the hungry, giue drinke to the thirfty,
apparell the naked, redeeme the captiue, vifitt
the ficke & imprifoned, harbour the pilgrime,
and bury the dead; wherof Chrift expreffely
faith in *S. Mathewes* ghofpell, that he will aske
vs an accoumpt at the laft day, and fend them
to heauen that haue done them, and damne
others that haue omitted them: *ergo*, there are
fome outward things neceffary to a Chriftian
befides baptifme and the fupper. And I might
adde diuers of the other fort of fpirituall
workes of mercy, at leaftwife fiue of the fea-
nen, that are outward workes alfo, as to correct finners, to giue good counfell to them
that be doubtfull, to teach the ignorant, to
comfort the fadd, and to pray for our neighbour, commended alfo by the * fcriptures,
wherby are made vp a dozen of lyes togeather, to omitt other that might be recoumpted, as preachinge, marryinge and fuch other
externall actions.

Efa. 58.
Rom. 12.
Tobi. 4.
2. *Cor.* 9.

Math. 25.

Math. 18.
1. *Tim.* 5.
Eph. 4.
& 5.

49. Befides this Iohn Fox drawing towards
the end of his enumeration of our doctrines,
after much raylinge and calumniation, inferreth this conclufion : *So that by this Romish Reli-*
gion (faith he)*to make a true Chriftian and good Ca-*
tholike, there is no vvorkinge of the holy Ghoft almoft
required, &c. It is well that Iohn Fox did put
in almoft, for otherwife his owne people,
would haue cried fhame vpon him, (efpecially hauinge heard now fo often repeated, that
no one action is accoumpted good and meritorious with vs, except yt proceed from the

A ly about
the con-
currance
of the ho-
ly Ghoft,
to our
good
vvorks.

F f   inward

inward motion of the holy Ghoſt, and is expreſſely defined in the Councell of *Trent)as
they may do alſo now, for that this dimini-
tiue (*almoſt*) is put in only for a ſhift by Fox,as
appeareth by his note in the margent which
ſpeaketh abſolutely, ſaying: *All doctrine of the
Popes ſtandeth only in outward things.* Marke *all* and
only, and conſider the impudence of the vayne
fellow, as though our diuinity had no Trea-
tiſſe of any inward vertues at all. But infinite
books of oures do cry the contrary, and ſhew
therby that Fox is a famous lyar. And albeit
I do note this but for one lye in this place,yet
yf yow conſider yt well,yt conteyneth ſo many leaſings,as therby goods works & actions,
wherynto we require the neceſſary concurrance of the holy Ghoſt, which make a greater number, then that I promiſed of Fox his
lyes in this place,and conſequently the whole
might be comprehended in this.

50.   Laſt of all in the ſame page *num.* 25. Fox
hath a certayne definition of a true Chriſtian
Catholike man, according to the Popes Religion, wherin are as many lyes as lynes,yf not
more, as yow ſhall ſee examined more particularly in the next Chapter. Out of which
heap of lyes, I will only now take a dozen to
adde to the former number,though in examination they will arriue at leaſt to thrice as many. And ſo by the example of this one Chapter, yow may conſider, in what deceatfull
dreames the more ſimple ſort of Proteſtants
are held, about our opinions in matters of

con-

controuersies, not knowinge for the moft part
the true ftate of the queftion in any one thing
treated beweene vs,, but are fedd with fuch
fancyes & diuifes, as pleafeth beft their guides
to diuife, and deliuer vnto them, for our opinions. Aud yf they pleafe to do this in their
printed books, that are extant to the vew of
all the world, what will they feare to doe in
pulpitts and priuate fpeaches, vvhich paffe
more free from examination and controle-
ment, & the moft ignorant are wont to fhew
moft audacity in flaunderinge vs, and our doctrine, which ordinarily they lay forth fo fau-
fed, and poudered, as yt may feeme the moft
abfurdeft doctrine in the world, & themfelues
iolly fellowes in refutinge the fame. But this
fraud being detected euery where by our
vvrytings, may iuftly vvarne thofe, that are
difcreet and ftudious of truth, and their owne
faluation, to take heed vvhat they beleeue
vpon fuch mens creditts. And this fhall fuffice
for a fhort admonition out of this Chapter,
the number of lyes proued againft Iohn Fox,
arryfing to the number of more then fix fcore,
which is more then double to the number by
me laftly promifed, and more then quadruple
to the firft promiffe of thirty, befides many by
me pardoned to him, which the reader will
eafily haue obferued in readinge yt ouer.

Ff 2   B Y

BY OCCASION OF A

FALSE AND RIDICVLOVS

DEFINITION,

Sett downe by Fox, of a Christian man, according to the Popes Religion; there is examined, the true distinction and description of a Catholike and Protestant of our dayes.

Chap. XX.

I Promised (gentle reader) in the table of the former Tome of this Treatise, that yf tyme did giue place, and that desire of breuity did not make me to leaue yt out, I would add for the finall end of this last part, the examination of a certayne ridiculous definition of a Catholike man, diuised & sett downe by Fox in the end of his former lyinge recytall of our opinions. And further that by this occasion I would say somewhat, of the true description or distinction of a Protestant and Catholike man, as in our dayes they are to be found, togeather vvith their differences, as vvell in matter of faith and doctrine, as in life and actions. This was my promise, which albeit I might iustly pretermitt in this place, for that this booke hath growne to a bigger bulke, then in the beginninge was pretended, yet for that being come thus farre forward, and that

the

the difference of few pages more or leſſe can make no great matter, I will breifely touch the ſame, layinge firſt before yow the forſaid definition of Iohn Fox, which muſt be the ground of all, that is to be ſaid in this behalfe.

2.   Firſt then Iohn Fox, hauinge laid togeather all the foreſaid abſurdityes of our doctrine, treated in the precedēt chapter (which yet yow haue ſeene to be rather his fictions & calumniations then our opinions) he layeth downe this firme & generall concluſiō, which before yow haue heard, of all our Religion, to witt, *that to make a true Chriſtian and good Catholike by Popiſh Religion, there is no workinge of the holy Ghoſt required.* Whervnto we haue aunſwered in the laſt Chapter. But he goeth forward to verifie the ſame in theſe words; *As by example* (ſaith he) *to make this matter more demonſtrable, let vs heere define a Chriſtian man after the Popes makinge, wherby we may ſee the better, what is to be iudged of the ſcope of his doctrine.* Thus Fox. And preſently hee ſetteth downe a new title in theſe words: *A Chriſtian man after the Popes makinge defined:* And in the margent: *A Chriſtian man defined after the Popes doctrine.* By all which promiſes and preambles, yt ſeemeth, that he byndeth himſelfe to deliuer vs an exact definition of the nature, and eſſentiall points, that make a Roman Catholike, accordinge to the Popes Religion, eſpecially ſeeing in the end, after he had recited the ſaid definition, he maketh this ſeuere illation thervpon: *Now* (ſaith he) *looke vpon this definition, and tell me good reader*

Iohn Fox his fond propoſitiō about our Religion.

Fox *pag.* 26. *col.* 2. *num.* 46.

F f 3   *what*

*vvhat faith or spiritt , or vvhat vvorkinge of the holy
Ghost in all this doctrine is to be required.* Well then,
now lett vs heare his worthy definition after
all these promises, and by this one act of his,
lett the reader make conceyte of the man, and
his conscience in all the rest he wryteth.

Fox *ibid.*

Fox his
definition
of a Ro-
man Ca-
tholike.

3.   *After the Popes Catholike Religion* (saith he) *a
true Christian man is thus defined. First to be baptized
in the Latyn tongue, vvhere the Godfathers professe they
cannot tell vvhat : then confirmed by the Bishopp; the
mother of the child to be purified: After he is growne in
yeares, then to come to the Church; to keep his fastinge
dayes; to fast the lent; to come vnder* Benedicite: *that
is to be confessed of the Priest; to do his pennance; at easter to take his rites ; to heare masse, and dinine seruice;
to sett vp candles before images;to creepe to the crosse;to
take holy bread and holy-water ; to go on procession; to
carry his palmes, and candle, and to take ashes ; to fast
Ember dayes, Rogation dayes and Vigills, to keep the holy-dayes ; to pay his tithes and offeringe dayes; to go on
pilgrimage; to buy pardons; to vvorshipp his maker ouer
the Priests head ; to receaue the Pope for his supreame
head; & to obay his lawes; to receaue S. Nicolas Clarks;
to haue his beads; and to giue to the high Altar; to take
orders yf he vvill be Priest ; to say his mattyns , and to
singe his masse; to lyft vp fayre; to keep his vow and not
to marry ; vvhen he is sicke to be anneyled, and take the
rites of the holy Church ; to be buryed in the Church-
yard; to be rung for ; to be song for ; to be buryed in a
friars coole; to find a soule Priest, &c. All which points
being obserued, vvho can deny, but this is a deuout man,
and a perfect Christian Catholike, and sure to be saued
as a true faithfull child of the holy mother Church?*

4. This

4. This is Iohn Fox his definition,& his demaund made theron: Whervnto I aunswere, that euery man that hath witt, and knoweth our doctrine, will deny both these points of Fox his demaund. For first he will deny that these externall thinges, when they be performed, do make a perfect Christian Catholike, or are any way meritorious of themselues, as before we haue shewed, except they do proceed from internall vertues of faith,hope,charity, obedience, deuotion, piety, and the like. And secondly yt will much more be denyed, that whosoeuer performeth these exteriour things, though flowinge also from the forsaid internall vertues, is sure to be saued. For that in the Catholike doctrine, no man is sure of his perseuerance, as teacheth the Councell of Trent *Seß. 6. cap.* 13. vvherfore these two are most absurd and palpable lyes of Iohn Fox his inference.

5. But now to the whole definition, which is no definition at all, but rather a beggarly coaceruation and fardell of scurrility laid togeather, wholy impertinent to the purpose: For that a definition should conteyne nothing els but essentiall and substantiall points,necessarily agreeing to the thing defined, and to all that which is comprehended vnder yt; as the definition of a man in generall agreeth to euery man also in particular. But heere in this wise definition of a Catholike man in generall, most of the points which he setteth downe are not necessary to euery man, that is

F f 4 a Ca-

An examination of Fox his definitiō.

a Catholike in particular: as for example, a man may be a Catholike, though he were baptized in English & not in the Latyn tongue, as many be in England at this day, & though he go not in procession, nor carry his palmes, nor go in gilgrimage, nor buy pardons, nor receaue S. Nicolas clarks, nor haue his beads, nor giue any thinge to the high Altar, and the like. And againe on the other side, a man may do all, or most of these things heere named in this definition, and yet not be a true Catholike; For he may lacke faith, hope and charity, which are the first three foundations, of the definition of a true and good Catholike man, accordinge to our true Cath. doctrine, as we may see declared by the Councell of Trent *Seß.6. cap.7.8.9.11.13.14. &c.*

The infinite number of lyes in Fox his definition of a Cath. man.

6.   So that the number of Fox his lyes in this definition is exceedinge great, yf we consider all points: For first there are as many lyes in this definition, as there are points sett downe of externall things, actions and ceremonyes, which are not essentiall or necessary to the true nature of a Catholike man, which are thtee parts of foure at least, of all that is heere sett downe: Secondly there are so many lyes more, as there are internall vertues omitted, necessary to make a perfecte Christian Cath. and denout man, & sure to be saued, as he describeth him, which internall vertues are many also; and heerby yow may gheße at the number of lyes in this definition, wherof I haue only taken a dozē in the former chapter.

7. Now

7. Now then to contemplate the wyſdome of Iohn Fox in this his plauſible diuiſe, to make vs odious and contemptible , yow may conſider yf yow pleaſe two points. Firſt how many triflinge thinges he hath ſett downe in this definition as eſſentiall to a Cathol. man, which in no wayes are ſuch. Secondly for ſo-much as he holdeth all theſe points to be pro-per, and peculiar to Catholiks , wherby they differ, and are diſtinguiſhed from Proteſtants; yf a man ſhould frame the definition of a true Proteſtant , by the negatiue of theſe points heere ſett downe, yow would eaſily ſee how naked a thinge yt were, & might agree to any ſort of forelorne people , heretiks, atheiſts, or what elſe ſoeuer. As for example lett vs take a man, that is baptized only in Engliſh, not con-firmed by the Biſhop, nor his mother was euer purified, nor himſelfe after he was growne to yeares euer came to any Church, nor kept any faſtinge dayes in his life, nor euer came vnder *Benedicite* , nor euer heard maſſe or diuine ſer-uice , nor euer ſett vp candles before images, but rather pulled them downe and made mo-ney of them, nor knoweth what aſhes or em-ber-dayes meane, nor keepeth any holy-dayes one more then another, nor payeth any tithes to any man, nor goeth on pilgrimage, but ra-ther in purchaſe and pyracye; that receaueth not the Pope for his ſoueraigne head , nor obayeth his lawes, that hath no beads, nor yet books, that ſaith neyther mattyns nor euen-ſonge, that giueth nothing to the high Altar, but

Proteſtāts according to Fox his negatiue definitiō.

but taketh rather away and fpoileth Altars; that breaketh his vowes when or whatfoeuer he maketh, that when he is ficke contemneth all rites of holy Church, and will be buryed as foone in the dunghill, as the Church-yard, & will neyther be rung for, or fong for, &c.

8. This good fellow (I fay) that beareth only the name of a Chriftian, for that he was baptized in Englifh, and hath all thefe negatiue parts oppofite to a Roman Catholike, that was baptized in Latyn, is he not a holy man thinke yow, by this negatiue defcription? or may not this defcription agree to any fort of wicked men whatfoeuer? and yet is this a good and true defcription accordinge to Fox, whofe affertion is, as a little before yow haue heard, *that no one outward thing is required in Chrifts doctrine, to make a Chriftian man, but only baptifme, and the Lords fupper.* Vnto which generall negatiue propofition of his, yf yow add alfo the particular negation of thofe externall things, which he nameth in his forfaid definition, &, amonge others; *of goinge to Church, hearinge of diuine feruice, obferuinge of faftinge dayes, payinge of tithes, keepinge of vowes, buryinge in Curch-yard, &c.* And then fuch other alfo, as a few lynes before that againe he excludeth, *as buildinge of Churches, fett prayers, keepinge of holy dayes, outward vvorks of the law, outward geftures, difference of tymes & places, externe fucceffion of Bifhops, and of S. Peters Sea, externe forme and notes of the Church,* &c. All thefe (I fay) thus expreffed in his owne words, being excluded, yow may imagine, what

Fox pag. 26. nu.40.

what kind of men such Proteſtant people
would make, as are comprehended in this negatiue definition, & what a common-wealth
or Church they would be, yf they were much
multiplyed in the world.

9· For do yow conceaue with your ſelfe a
multitude of men bearinge the name of Chriſtians, that haue no externall worke of Religion at all amonge them after their baptiſme,
but only to meet now and then at the *Lords
ſupper,* which is nothinge in effect, but eatinge
of bread, and drinking of wyne. But for other
externall actions, they haue no vſe or exerciſe
of any particular outward works of the law,
at all; to witt they haue no works of mercy
corporall or ſpirituall, before mentioned, no
outward Church or diuine ſeruice, no outward feaſts or ſett prayers, no outward ge-
ſtures, as for example ſalutinge, diſcoueringe
the head, no bowinge, kneelinge or other like;
no outward payinge of Tythes or keeping of
vowes, no outward obſeruing of holy-dayes,
nor differéce of tymes or places; ſo as all that is
lawfull in one time or place, is lawfull to them
in any other, no outward ſucceſsió of Biſhops
in their Church, nor any outward marke to
know the ſame by. Do yow lay before your
eyes (I ſay) ſuch a multitude of Chriſtians,
as Fox doth heere deſcribe in his new *Idæa,* &
conſider what a comon welth they would
make, but eſpecially yf yow compare them
with the comon welth of Catholiks, whoſe
oppoſits Fox would haue them in all points.

10. And

10.   And albeit this only hitherto fpoken, were fufficient to lett yow fee the difference betweene them, yet to make the matter more cleere ; I fhall not fticke to runne ouer fome other points alfo in this place, with the greateft breuity I can, to lay before yow, a true vew of their natures, proprietyes, ftates, and conditions. Firft then the Roman Catholike, whome Fox calleth *Papift*, touchinge matters of faith & beleefe, compofeth himfelfe to that humility, as whether he be learned or vnlearned, or what arguments foeuer he hath on the one or the other fide; yet prefumeth he to determine nothing of himfelfe, but remytteth that determination (yf any thing be doubtfull or vndetermyned) vnto the iudgement and decree of the vniuerfall Church, and gouernours thereof. And hence proceedeth the agrements and vnity of faith, which they haue held and conferued in fo large a body, for fo many ages, as haue paffed fince Chrift and his Apoftles. Wheras Proteftants in this behalfe followinge another fpiritt of felfe will, and felfe iudgement, and loofinge the raynes of liberty to the pregnancy of each mans witt, do hold and determine what their owne iudgements for the time do thinke to be true, or moft probable, and are fubiect to no authority in this behalfe, but to their owne fpiritt; which is variable, accordinge to the variety of arguments and probabilityes that do occurre. And heerof do enfue the great variety of fects and opinions amonge them, euen in this one

age,

age, since they began, as yow may see by that
we haue sett downe before, especially in the
third and seuententh Chapters of this booke.
11. Next to this, for so much as appertayneth
to life and actions; the Catholike man holdeth that we can do nothinge at all of our
selues, no not so much as to thinke a good
thought, but we must be preuented and assi-
sted by Gods holy grace, as before we haue
shewed out of the Councell of Trent, which
teacheth with *S.Paul*, that our sufficiency is of
Christ; yet is the force of this grace so tempe-
red notwithstanding, as yt vseth no violence,
nor excludeth the free concurrance of mans
will, also preuented (as hath byn said) and
stirred vp by the forsaid grace of our Sauiour
and motion of the holy Ghost: So as freely by
this help, we yeld to the said good motions,
and do beleeue in God, and his promises: and
this act of faith (as yow haue heard out of the
said Councell) is the first foundation & roote
of all our iustification: but yet not sufficient
neyther of yt selfe, except charity and hope
(two other theologicall vertues) do accompany the same; so as we do both loue & hope
in him, in whome we beleeue. And out of
these, & by direction of these, do flow againe
other Christian vertues, called morall; for that
they appertayne to the direction of life and
manners, which vertues do consist principally in the inward habitts and acts of the mind,
and from thence do proceed to the externall
actions; and operations, wherby we exercise
our

our felues in keeping Gods commandements, and works of piety with our neighbour, as

Externall actions flovvinge of internall vertues.

clothinge the naked, feedinge the hungry, vifitinge the ficke and the like. In works of deuotion in like manner, as finging, and praying to God, kneelinge, knockinge our breafts, mortifying our bodyes, by fafting, watching, & other fuch like. All which exteriour actions are fo farre forth commendable and meritorious, as they proceed from the inward vertues and motion of Gods fpiritt.

12.   And albeit (as before we haue fhewed

* In the former Chapter.

out of S. * Thomas,) thefe extetior acts do add nothing in fubftantiall goodnes to the inward acts, but haue their meritt from thence; yet for that man confifteth both of fpiritt and flefh, yt was reafon that he fhould be bound to honour God with both, that is to fay both with inward acts of vertue, proceeding from Gods grace and motion, and with outward vertuous acts teftifyinge the inward, wherby we fee, what an excellent Chriftian comonwealth the Catholike Religion doth appoint, yf it were executed according to her doctrine, to witt, that all mens mynds fhould be replenifhed with all fort of vertues, towards both God, and our neighbour, & that their actions fhould be full of all righteoufnes, piety, and charity in exterior behauiour; fo as neyther in thought, word, nor deed, they fhould offend eyther of them both. And thus much for the Catholike man concerninge his actions, life and manners.

13. But

13. But this Catholike Religion doth not stay heere, nor teach only in generall what actions a Christian man should haue, & from what internall principles of grace and vertue they should flow, but doth offer vs diuers particular meanes also how to procure, conserue and increase this grace, which is the fountaine of all goodnesse. For first yt exhibiteth vnto vs, besides all other meanes of prayer, and particular endeauors of our part, seauen generall meanes & instruments left vs to that purpose, by the institution of Christ himselfe, vvhich are seauen Sacraments, that being receaued with due disposition of the receauer, do alwayes bringe grace by the vertue and force of Christs meritt and institution, without dependance of the merit, or demerit of the minister that administreth them. By vse of which Sacraments, infinite grace is deryued dayly by Christ our Sauiour vnto his Church, and particular members therof, in euery state and degree of men.

The Cath. doctrine of 7. Sacraments and their vse.

14. Moreouer, Catholike Religion not contented with these generalityes, doth come yet more in particular to frame, direct, and help a Christian man in the way of his saluation, euen from the first houre of his byrth in Christ, vntill his soule, departinge from this world, be rendered vp againe into his creators hands. For first, he hauinge all his sinnes forgiuen cleerly & freely by the grace of Christ, receaued in *Baptisme*, he is strengthened to the fight and course of a true Christian life, by the

The particular direction of a Christian man from his baptisme, vntill his death, by help of diuers Sacraments.

Sacra-

Sacrament of *Confirmation* and imposition of hands : his soule also is fedd, & nourished spiritually by the sacreed food of our Sauiours body in the *Eucharist* : two seuerall states of Christian life are peculiarly afsisted with grace of two particular Sacraments, Priests & Cleargy-men by the Sacrament of *holy-orders*, and marryed people by the Sacrament of *Matrimony*. And for that in this large race and course of life, as *S. Paul* calleth yt, we often fall, and offend God by reason of our infirmity, there is a most soueraigne Sacrament of *Pennance* for remedy heerof appointed by our prouident Sauiour, founded in the meritts of his sacred passion, called *Secunda tabula post naufragium* by holy Fathers, that is, the second table or planke, wheron we may lay hands & escape drowninge, after the shipwracke of our pardon, grace & iustification receaued in our baptisme, which was the first table : by which second table of *pennance* all sorts may rise againe how often soeuer they fall; which Sacrament consisteth of three parts, sorrow for our sinnes, and confessinge the same, for the remission of the guilt, and some kind of satisfaction on our behalfe for remouing the temporall punishment remayninge : the true vse wherof bringeth such exceedinge help and comfort, to a Christian soule, as is vnspeakable. For that by the first two parts a man is oftentymes brought sweetly to sigh for his sinnes, to thinke vpon them, detest them, aske pardon of God for them, to make new pur-

poses

Margin notes:

Baptisme.
Confirmation.
Eucharist.

Holy-order.
Marriage.

Pennance.

Hier. in c. 3.
Esa. & ep. 8.
ad Demetr.
Pacian. ep.
1. ad Sympron.

Contrition.
Confessiō.
Satisfaction.

poſes of better life for the tyme to come, to
examine his conſcience more particularly, &
other ſuch heauenly effects, as no man can
tell the comfort thereof, but he that receaueth them.

15. By the third part alſo, which is ſatisfaction, though a man performe neuer ſo little
therof in this life, yet doth yt greatly auayle
him, not only in reſpect of the gratefull ac-
ceptation therof at Gods hands, for that yt
cometh freely of his owne good will, but alſo *The force*
for that yt humbleth euen the proudeſt mynd *of Satisfa-*
in the ſight of almighty God, yt refreyneth *ction.*
alſo greatly our wicked appetites from ſynne
for the tyne to come, when we know we
muſt giue a particular accoumpt and ſatisfie
alſo for our ſenſualityes ſomewhat euen in
this world. And finally yt is the very cheefe
ſynnow of Chriſtian conuerſation and behauiour one towards another. For when the
rich man knoweth (for examples ſake) that
he muſt ſatisfie one way or other,& be bound
by his ghoſtly Father to make reſtitution ſo
farre, as he is able, of whatſoeuer he hath
wrongefully taken from the poore; when the
poore alſo are taught, that they muſt do the
ſame towards the rich, the ſonne towards his
Father, the ſeruant towards his maiſter, yf he
haue deceaued him; when the murmurer in
like maner knoweth that he muſt make actuall reſtitution of fame (yf he haue defamed
any:) this Catholike doctrine, I ſay, and practiſe therof, muſt needs be a ſtronge hedge
G g to

to all vertuous, & pious conuersation among
men, that beleeue and follow the same.

16. And finally not to passe to more particularityes, wheras Catholike doctrine teacheth
vs, that all or most disorders of this life in a
sensuall man (to omitt the infirmityes of our
higher powers in like manner) do proceed
originally from the fountayne of concupiscence, and law of the flesh remayninge in vs
after our baptisme, and *ad certamen*, as holy Fathers do tearme yt, that is to say, for our conflict and combatt, to the end our life may be
a true warfare, as the scripture calleth yt: This
concupiscence, I say, or sensuall motion, being
the ground of our temptations, though yt be
not sinne of yt selfe, except we consent vnto
yt, yet is she busy in styrringe vs dayly to
wickednes, as a Christian mans principall exercise, and diligence, ought to be in resistinge
her, which he may do by the help, and asi-
stance of Chrifts grace, merited by his sacred
passion, wherin he extinguished the guilt of
this originall corruption, though he left still
the sting and prouocation for our greater meritt, and continuall victory by his holy grace,
in them that will striue & fight, as they may,
and ought to do.

17. But yet for that this fight is comber-
some, and fastidious in it selfe, and deadly also
to many; that suffer themselues to be ouercome, the Cath. Religion doth teach a man
how he shall fight in this conflict, what armes,
& defence he may vse in particular to defend
him-

The warre
of concu-
piscence
and help
of Gods
grace for
the same.

himfelfe, and to gaine the victory. And to this
head or braunch are reduced all our fpirituall
books and volumes about mortification, as
well of our will, iudgement, and affections
of mynd, as all other parts alfo of our inferiour fenfuality, to witt, how yow may refyft
this and that temptation; what preuention
yow may make, what bulwarke yow may
raife, what defence yow may reft vpon, wherin do enter all particular directions, of fafting,
prayer, watchinge, hearcloth, lyinge on the
ground, and other bodily afflictions fo much
vfed by old Saints, and may be vfed alfo now
by all (yf they will) for gayninge of this important victory. There entreth alfo amonge
other defences, that great and foueraigne remedy of flyinge the world wholy, and rety-
ringe to the port of a religious life, for fuch as
otherwaife fee themfelues either weake, or in
danger to be wholy ouercome by this veny-
mous beaft of concupifcence, or els do defire
to meritt more aboundantly at Gods hands,
by offeringe themfelues wholy and entyrely
to his feruice, and to the more neere imitation
of their Lord, & fauiour. By all which helpes,
afsiftances, and directions, deliuered in this
behalfe by Catholike doctrine to euery mans
ftate and degree of life, a Cath. Chriftian paffeth on more fecurely, duringe his life, and at
his laft goinge out of this world, receaueth finally the grace and comfort of the laft Sacrament of *Extreme vnction*, inftituted by Chrift,   Extreme
and recommended ynto vs by *Saint Iames* his   vnction.
   Iac. 5.

Apoftle; and from thence paffeth to receaue that eternall ioy & kingdome at his Sauiours hands, which he hath prepared for them, that beleeue in him, and ftriue and fight for him in this life againft fynne and iniquity.

18.   And thus haue we defcribed breifely but ferioufly and truly, the ftate and condition of a Roman Catholike man, to oppofe the fame againft the ridiculous vayne definition, or rather fiction of Iohn Fox before mentioned. But now if we would paragon the fame with the Proteftants doctrine and practife, in all thefe points before métioned, we fhall quickly fee the differences. And as for the firft point of all concerninge faith and beleefe, we haue fett downe fome kynd of paralel or comparifon before, now fhall we profecute the fame very breifely.

The com-
parifon of
the forfaid
Cath. do-
ctrine,
with that
of the
Proteftäts. 19.   In the firft point then about the inward principles of our outward actions, truth yt is, that they agree with vs in fomewhat, to witt, that all good commeth originally from Gods holy grace, and motion, but prefently they difagree againe, for that they hold our grace of iuftification to be no inherent quality, but only an externall imputation, and that Gods motion to our mynd is fuch, as yt excludeth wholy all concourfe and cooperation of our freewill, wherby they cutt of at one blow, all endeauors of our part to do any goodneffe at all, and leaue vs as a ftone or blocke to be moued by God only, wherof alfo enfueth, that he muft needs be author of our finnes & other
blafphe-

blasphemyes, & infinite inconuenyences, not
only in matter of faith, but in life and actions
also; For that this principle being once receaued, that our freewill, though yt be preuented, moued, and ftrengthened by Gods grace,
can do nothinge at all, nor cooperate to any
good worke, or refift any euill, who will haue
care afterward to endeauour, labour, ftriue, or
weary himfelfe about any thinge that is difficult, or difpleafant vnto him?

20. Next to this concerninge the vertues
theologicall, of faith, hope and charity, Proteftants are content with faith only to our iuftification, as yow fee by Iohn Fox, who * faith
that the fcriptures do expreffely exclude both
hope and charity. And albeit fome other of his   * *Cap. præ-*
fect will feeme to couer the matter, by faying,   *ced.*
that hope & charity do follow faith as fruites
thereof, yf yt be true faith; yet in practife is
there no man of them in deed, that will permitt his faith to this triall: but whether he
haue thefe fruits or noe, will he defend his
faith to be good, and that himfelfe is iuftifyed
thereby: So as from hence yow fee another
gapp opened to all prefumption and libertye
of life. For howfoeuer a Proteftant liueth,
yet will he not yeld thereby, that his faith
is naught (and indeed the argument inforceth yt not), and then followeth yt that his
faith being good, he is iuftified, and confequently howfoeuer he liue, yet is he a
iuft man, and vvho vvill trouble himfelfe
vvith the labour of a good life, yf beleeuinge
only

only be fufficient. And this for internall vertues.

21. But as for externall actions, euen thofe of the law and ten commaundements commaunded by Chrift himfelfe, Fox derideth them in our people, as before yow haue heard in his definition, and requireth only two exterior actions in his people, to witt, *baptizinge* and fuppinge, or celebratinge *the Lords fupper:* For all other matters, he faith, no one thinge is neceffary for the exercife of his new ghofpell, or to make a perfect Chriftian after his definition. So as yf yow lay before yow two forts of people, the one labouringe and wholy occupyinge themfelues in all godly life,

Coloſſ. 1.
verſ. 10.

fructificantes in omni bono opere, fructifyinge in all good works (as the Apoftles words are, who alfo in the fame place calleth this worke, the true wifdome and right vnderftandinge of Gods heauenly will, and worthy walking before him:) yow may behold, I fay the one fort of thefe people, which Fox calleth Papifts, not only endued with inward good defyres,

The continuall exercifes of Catholiks in good works.

but externally alfo bufyed altogeather in good deedes, fhewinge the fame by the fruits of their inward vertues, to witt, in buildinge of Churches, Hofpitalles, Monafteryes, Colledges, giuinge almes, maintayning orphanes, wyddowes, and pupills, receauing pilgrymes and other fuch Chriftian exercifes, as alfo meeting at Churches, praying on their knees, fighinge and fobbinge and weepinge for their finnes, and confefsinge the fame vnto Gods

fubfti-

fubftitute, to witt, their ghoftly Father, af-
kinge pardon alfo of their neighbours, and
makinge reftitution, yf any thinge with euill
confcience they haue taken or withholden,
&c. Whiles in the meane fpace the other fort,
accoumpted Saints of the new makinge by
Fox, do walke vp and downe, talking of their
beleefe, but lay their hands vpon no good externall worke at all by obligation, yf we beleeue Fox, except only the Lords fupper, nor
is it incident to their vocation. And heerby alfo may we confider, how great a difference
there is, betweene thefe two forts of people
in a common-welth, where they liue togeather, and what an infinite gate is laid open by
this loofe new doctrine, to idlenes and lafy
behauiour in Chriftian conuerfation, quite
oppofite not only to the doctrine and practife
of auncient Fathers, & the primitiue Church,
but to the whole courfe of fcriptures, in like
manner, which euery where do inculcate
with all follicitude, the cōtinuall performance
of externall good works, and that therby indeed true Chriftians are knowne, in exerci-
finge themfelues in Chrifts cōmaundements.

22. And as for Sacraments, which according to our doctrine, are heauenly conduicts,
and moft excellent inftruments appointed by
God for deriuing of grace vnto vs in euery
ftate and condition of Chriftian men; thefe
fellowes do firft cutt of fiue of the feauen, and
the other two they do fo weaken and debafe,
as they are fcarce worthy the receauinge: for

The diffe-
rence a-
bout Sa-
craments
and effects
therof.

they do not hould, that eyther their *Baptisme*
or the *Lords supper* doth giue any grace at all, to
him that receaueth them, though he prepare
himselfe neuer so well therynto, but only
that they are certayne signes of their election
and iustification, which signes notwithstanding, hauing no more certainty in them, then
themselues list to apprehend by their speciall
faith, concerning their owne iustification, and
the matter standinge in their owne hands to
shew themselues iustified, when they will; by
these signes yt cometh in deed to be a very
iest or comedy, but yet breaketh downe a
mayne banke of Christian discipline, care and
sollicitude, that is to be seene in our men,
when they receaue any Sacrament, for that
beleeuing (as Catholike faith teacheth them)
that all Sacraments bringe grace to them, that
receaue them with due preparation, and of
their owne part, put no lett by their indisposi-
tion; do labour and endeauour to prepare
themselues worthily, to the said due receauinge therof, by pennance, fastinge, prayer,
almes-deeds, and other like holy endeauors,
assuring themselues also on the contrary side,
that negligent receauing of Sacraments doth
not only not bring grace, but increaseth rather their offence: So as this preparation of
Catholike people to the receauinge of Sacraments, is a continuall kynd of spurre to good
purposes, vertue & renouation of life: wheras
this other sort of good fellowes, persuadinge
themselues, that their Sacraments are only
bare

*The diffe-
rent pre-
paration
to receaue
Sacra-
ments.*

bare signes of things already past; and as it were a continuall reprefentation of iuftification already receaued, there needeth not any fuch laboursome endeauor for due preparation, nor yet care or follicitude for life or manners, For that already they haue the thinge, which they defire, and that thofe are but fignes, tokens and teftimonyes that they haue receaued yt indeed, which yet as I faid hath no more affurançe, then euery mans owne perfuafion and apprehenfion.

23. Laftly concerning the forfaid fountaine of temptations in our flefh and fenfuality, called *Concupifcence*, they differ from vs in two effentiall points: Firft that they hold this concupifcence, not for a temptor only, but rather for a conqueror, for fo much as they teach that euery motion of her to fenfuality in vs, is a fynne, whether yt be yelded vnto by our will or noe. The fecond point following necefſarily of this firft is, that all refianſtçe of our part to the motions of this concupifcence, is either needleſſe or booteleſſe: For that the motion it felfe being fynne without our confent, yt followeth confequently, that the matter is not remediable by our endeauors; and heere now breaketh in a whole fea of diforders to Chriftian life, for that fuppofinge firft, that which is moft true, that euery Chriftian man hath this affault of concupifcence within him; and fecondly by this new doctrine, that no man can auoid to fynne therby vpon euery motion that is offered, what needeth or what auayleth

The differences about mortifying & refifting of our concupifcéce.

leti any resistance of ours, or any conflict to the contrary? Sinne yt is though we resist neuer so much, and but sinne yt is, yf we yeld. And seing that by another principle of this new doctrine, all synnes are equally mortall, what is gayned by striuinge, or what is lost by yeldinge? and to what end are all those large Treatises of auncient Fathers about fightinge against this concupiscence and mortification of her appetites & motions? What do auayle all their exhortations to this purpose, as also those of the scriptures, to continency, chastity, virginity, abstinence, sobriety, and other like vertues; for so much as euery first motion of our concupiscence to the contrary (which first motions we cannot auoyd) is syn in it selfe; to what purpose (I say) are we persuaded and animated, to fight and striue against this enemy, seing there is no hope of victory, but that at euery blow, she conquereth and ouerthroweth vs, as the Protestants teach?

24.   Wherfore to proceed no further in this comparison, yow may easily by this, that is said, consider the differences betweene these two people, and in particular yow may with greefe and teares contemplate amonge other points, fiue generall inundations of loosenes and wicked liberty, brought into Christian conuersation, by the forsaid fiue seuerall principles of these mens doctrine, to witt, first in takinge away wholy all concurrance, and good endeauour of mans will to any vertuous action whatsoeuer, though neuer so much

Fiue principall inundations of licentiousnes broughtin by Protestants doctrine.

preuented

preuented or afsisted by the help of Gods grace: fecondly in afcribinge all iuftification to only faith, and therby remouinge the concurrance of hope, charity, piety, deuotion, and other vertues: thirdly in difgracinge and denyinge the necefsity of the exercife of externall good works, proceedinge from thofe internall vertues, and commended vnto vs to walke therin: Fourthly in debacing the force, dignity and number of Sacraments, appointed for inftruments and conduicts of Gods holy grace vnto all forts of men. And laftly in attributinge a kingdome of finne irrefyftable, to our cocupifcence in fauour of temptations & fenfuall motions, and difcomfortinge therby all people from fightinge againft the fame.

25. VVhich fiue principles being vvell weighed and confidered, togeather with the practife and fucceffe that haue enfued vpon them, throughout Chriftendome, where this new doctrine hath preuayled; no indifferent man can be fo fimple, but that he will eafily difcouer the true differences betweene thefe two people, and their religions; as alfo betweene Fox his lyinge fond definition, fett downe in the beginninge of this Chapter, concerninge Catholiks alone, and this our defcription of both forts of people, conteyninge the moft fubftantiall points of faith and life, both of the one and the other. And thus much for this matter.

A N

AN INDEX

OR TABLE

aſwell of the names of men, and weomen ; as of particular matters, conteyned in this examen of the ſecond ſix Monethes.

In this Table (good Reader) I haue thought good for thy better direction, to remitt thee for all particular names both of Catholike and Foxian Saints, vnto the day of the moneth vvherin they are named and ſett downe in the Calendar : for that turninge to the place, thou ſhallt alwayes find further direction vvhere to read more of them. And againe touchinge Syr-names and Chriſtian-names, I haue thought beſt for breuities ſake, to put the Syr-names firſt, vvith a note of their Chriſtian-names after, except yt be in certayne perſons of more moment then others, vvhome you ſhall find ſett downe twiſe vnder the Alphabet of both their names.

A   *Catholike Saints.*

SS. **A**ARON & Iulius m. m. Iul. 1.

SS. Abdon & Sennon. m. m. Iul. 30.

SS. Adauctus & Fælix m. m. Aug. 30.

S. Aedigius Abbas conf. ſept. 1

SS. Africanæ virgines m. m. Decemb 16.

S. Agricola mart.   Nouemb. 4

S. Aidanus ep. conf.   Aug. 31

S. Alexis confeſſ.   Iul. 17

S. Ambroſius ep. conf.   Dec. 7

S. Andreas Apoſtolus. Nou. 30

S. Antoninus ep. m.   ſept. 12

S. Anatolia v. mart.   Iul. 9

S. Anacletus pp. & m.   Iul. 13

S. Anna mat B V. M.   Iul. 6

S. Apolinaris ep. m.   Iul. 23

S. Arcadius & Soc. m.   Nou. 13

S. Artenius mart.   Oct. 20

Aſſumptio B. V. M.   Aug. 15

S. Auguſtinus ep. conf. Aug. 28

S. Andochius mart.   ſept. 24

A   *Foxian Saints.*

Abbes Iames m.   Aug. 2

Abbonile ſcholler m.   Dec. 8

Abraham Father m.   Sept. 1

Aleſworth Iohn conf.   Iul. 6

Allen Roſe mart.   Aug. 28

Allen VVilliam mart.   Sept. 4

Allerton Raph mart.   Sept. 19

Andrew

Andrew VVilliam conf. Sept.6
Atch:r Iohn conf.   Nou.16
Afhdon Iohn mart.   Sept.27
Athoth Thom. m.   Sept.26
Atkyns N. mart.   Iul.18
Auftow Iames and Margery m.
    Sept. 20.

Bafilicæ Saluatoris dedicatio,
    Nou. 9.
Bafilica Petri & Pauli Apoft,
    Nou. 18.
S. Babiana v. & mart.   Dec.2
S. Bonauentura ep. conf. Iul.14
S. Bruno confeffor.   Octob.6

A   *Particular things.*

Age of Alice Potkins martyr,
    *cap.*15. *num* 15
Alice Driuer the Doctrix, *cap.*16.
    num. 21. 22. Her difputation
    vvith the Doctors, *ibid. &*
    num. 28.29.
Alanus Copus his proofe againft
    Hunne that he hanged him-
    felfe, *cap.*16. *num.* 13.
Antiquity & vnity of the VVic-
    kliffians, *cap.*13. *num.* 4.
Allerton the Taylor his ftory,
    *cap.*13 *num.* 27. his difputation
    vvith *B. Bonner, ibid.*
Apoftataes flocking into Englad
    in K. Edwards dayes, *cap.*16
    num 57.
Arthington and *Hackett* their
    ftrange attempts, and ftory,
    cap 17. *num.* 18.
Atheifts & *Atheifme*, how they
    are brought thervnto, *cap.* 18,
    num 9.
S. Auguftine vvrefted by *Bradford.*
    a Foxian martyr, *cap.*11. *n.* 34.

B   *Catholike Saints.*

S. Bartholomæus Apoftolus.
    Aug 24.
S. Bernardus Abbas   Aug.20

B   *Foxian Saints.*

Barnes Robert mart.   Octob.13
Bayfield Richard m.   Nou.11
Bembricke Thom. m,   Iul.31
Bennold Thom. m,   Aug.21
Bennet Mother conf. Octob.31
Beuerich friar mart.   Oct.25
Bernard Thomas. mart. Nou.6
Bland Iohn m.   Iulij 10
Black-friar Keyler m.   Oct.26
Bongeot VVilliam m.   Aug.19
Bongeor Agnes m.   Sept.22
Bradford Iohn m.   Iul. 6.
Bradbridge Georg. m.   Sept.11
Browne Chriftophor mart.
    Nou. 26.
Burward Anton. m.   Sept.10
Bungay Cornelius m,   Sept.14
Burges Marke m.   Oct.24
Bucker Georg m.   Dec.3
Buckingam-fhire old man m.
    Dec. 4.
Burton Nicolas m.   Dec.19
Bucer Martyn conf.   Dec 23
Burge de Iohn m.   Oct. 2.

B   *Particular things.*

Bale his ridiculous praifes of
    Iohn Frith. *cap.*11. *num.* 12.
Bayfield the Apoftata monke his
    Story, *cap.*15. *num.* 13.

His

His confession about hereticall books *ibid.*

Bishopps excōmunicated by Fox his martyrs, *cap.* 5. *num.* 35.

Blynd woman of *Darby* her story, *cap.* 12. *num.* 21.

Her pennyworth of Scripture, *ibidem.*

Black-smithes conference vvith the Bishops and Doctors, *cap.* 13 *num.* 37. 38.

Bradford his story condemnation and burninge, *cap.* 11. *n.* 22. 23. 24. 25. *& deinceps.* His barly-bread, *ibid. num.* 22. His seditious behauiour at Paules-Crosse in Q. Maryes dayes, *ibid. num.* 25. His liberty in prison, *ibid. num.* 26. His iudgement about the reall presence, *ibid num.* 31.

Brainford-martyrs vnder Q. Mary, their opinions, condemnations and deaths, *cap.* 11. *n.* 60.

Doctor Brooks Bishop of Glocester his speach to Ridley and Latymer, *cap.* 14. *num.* 69.

Bucher his disputation with Doctor Dunnings, *cap.* 13. *n.* 16.

Bucer his story, *cap.* 16. *num.* 58. His coming into Eng'and. *ibid.* A Iew by byrth, *ibid.* His impostures at the beginning, *ibid. num.* 60. His recantation of Zwinglianisme, *ibid. num.* 61. His bones burned in Cambridge vnder Q. Mary, *ibid. num.* 70.

C.

S. Calixtus pp. m.   Octob. 14
S. Carpus Episc. conf.   Oct. 13

SS. Cassianus & Hippol. mart. Aug. 13.

S. Catulinus diac. m.   Iul. 15

S. Catherina v. m.   Nou. 25

S. Cæcilia v. m.   Nou. 22

S. Christina v. m.   Iul. 24

S. Charitina v. m.   Oct. 5

SS. Chrisanthus & Darius m. Octob. 25.

S. Chrisogonus mart. Nou. 24

S. Chæremon mart. ep. Dec. 22

S. Clemens PP. m.   Nou. 23

S. Clara v. conf.   Aug. 12

SS. Cosmas & Damian. mart. Sept 27.

S. Cordula v m.   Oct. 22

Comemor. omnium fidel. def. Nouemb. 2.

SS. Coronati quatuor mart. Nouemb. 8.

S. Columbanus Abbas Nou. 21

Conceptio B. Virg.   Dec. 8

S. Cyriacus & Soc. m.   Aug. 8

S. Cyriaca vidua.   Aug. 21

SS. Cyprianus & Iustina mart. Sept. 26.

C.

Carelesse Iohn conf.   Iul. 17
Caruer Diricke m.   Iul. 11
Cauches Catherine m.   Iul. 19
Catmer George m.   Sept. 8
Carelle school-maistresse mart. Octob. 5.
Cannon blacke m.   Oct. 17
Chittiden Dunstan confes. Nouemb. 12.
Chichester 3. Confessors Oct. 29
Clarke Iohn conf.   Nou. 12
Clarke Roger m.   Nou. 16
Cooper Elizab. m.   Iul. 24
Cotten Stephen m.   Iul. 28
                         Cokes

Coker VVilliam m.   Aug, 6
Colliar Richard m.   Aug. 9
Cob Thomas m.   fept. 5
Coo Roger m.   fept. 5
Colias & Coubridg. m   Oct. 10
Cornforth Iohn m.   Nou. 25
Coignes Iohn conf.   Dec. 6.

C.

Calamity that fell to England by the new ghofpell, *cap.* 16 *n.* 98.

Capper of Couentry his ftory, *cap.* 3 *n* 19 His difputation & opinion of the Sacrament, *ibid.*

Cardinall of Saint Andrewes in Scotland murdered by Proteftants, *cap.* 15 *num* 15.

Card playinge Sermons of Latymer in Cambridge, *cap.* 4. *n.* 54

Carmelite friar burned at Rome for herefie *anno Domini* 1436. *cap.* 16. *num* 36.

Catholike man defcribed by Iohn Fox. *cap.* 20. *perto um.*

Charity and hope belyed by Fox, *cap.* 19. *num.* 7.

Chrifts law and Moyfes belyed by Fox, *ibid. num.* 34.

Chrifts mediation belyed, *ibid. num.* 36.

Church notes affigned by a Foxian artificer martyr, *cap.* 13 *n.* 23.

Coinquination by hereticall opinions, *cap.* 18 *num.* 8.

Colloquy at *Ratifbone* anno 1546. *cap* 16. *num.* 64.

A *Cooke* difputed vvith the B. of London, *cap.* 12. *num.* 12.

His communion vvith a pint of malmefy vvhen he vvas to be burned. *ibid. num* 14.

Commedian martyrs in Fox his Calendar, *cap.* 15. *num.* 2.

Confiderations of moment, *cap.* 17. *pertotum.*

Concupifcence, and a lye therof, *cap.* 19. *num* 23.

Concupifcence and vvarre thervvith, *cap.* 20 *num.* 16.

Contrition belyed by Fox, *cap.* 19. *num* 25.

Comparifon of a Catholike and Proteftant in matter of doctrine, *cap* 20 *num.* 10.

Coubridge his ftory, *cap* 14. *n.* 36. His blafphemous opinions confuted by *Alanus Copus, ibid. num* 37.

Confeffors of all fects in Fox his Calendar, *cap.* 16. *num* 3.

D.

SS. Damianus & Cofmas. m. fept. 27.

S. Damafus Papa conf. Dec. 11

SS. Darius & Chrifanthus m. Octob. 25.

Dedicatio S. Mariæ ad niues. Aug. 5.

Dedicatio S. Michaelis fept. 29

Dedicatio Bafil. Saluatoris. Nouemb. 9.

Dedicat. Bafil. SS. Petri & Paul. Nouemb. 18.

Decollatio S. Ioan. Baprift. Aug. 29.

SS. Dionyfius & Eleuther. m. Octob. 9.

Dormientes feptem. m.   Iul. 10

S. Dominicus conf   Aug. 4

S. Donatus Epifc. m.   Aug. 7.

D.

Dale Iohn conf.   Dec. 17
Damlipp George. m.   Dec. 3
                Dauy

Dauy Iohn and Henry mart.
Nou. 24.

Denley Iohn mart.   Aug. 3
Dighill VVilliam mart.   Iul.13
Dynes Robert mart.   Iul.30
Dogg and Collyns m.   Oct.10
Driuer Alice mart.   Nou.22
Dungate Thom. m.   Iul.20

D.

Dangerous Positions printed in
London and vvrytten againſt
the Puritans, *cap.* 17. *num.* 3.
Definition of a Catholike and 12.
lyes therabout made by Fox,
cap. 19. *n.* 50. *& cap.* 20. *per totum.*
The ſame examined, *cap.* 20. *n.* 5.
Definition of a proteſtant. *ib. n.* 7.
Denley his opinion about the
rea'l preſence, *cap.* 2. *num.* 6.
Deſperate Act of VVilliam Garde-
ner in Lisbone of Portugall,
cap. 13. *num.* 9. *&* 10.
Deſcriptiõ of Fortune the blacke-
ſmith, *ibid. num* 37.
Deſcription of Latvmers habitt
by Fox, *cap.* 14. *num.* 67.
Dialogue betweene the Biſhopp
of London a cooke & a pain-
ter, *cap.* 12. *num.* 12.
Dialogue betwene the ſame B.
and a ſherman, *cap.* 13. *num.* 15.
Difficulty in ſettinge forth the
Engliſh Eccleſiaſticall hiſtory
in theſe dayes, and vvhy *cap.* 28.
num. 15. *&* 17.
Diſtruſt of Saluation, *cap.* 19 *n.* 6.
Diſtinction of Fox his profeſſed
and not profeſſed Saints, *cap.*
14. *num.* 35.
Doctrine moſt vvicked about
Baptiſme *cap.* 11. *num.* 42.
Dreames of Samuell the mar-

ryed Prieſt martyr, *cap.* 12. *n.* 18.
His kiſſing in the ſtreets when
he vvent to be burned, *ibid.
num.* 19. *&* 20.
D Dunnings conference vvith a
butcher, *cap.* 13. *num.* 16.

E.

S. Edilburga v. conf.   Iul.7
S. Editha v conf.   ſept 16
S. Edmundus ep. conf.   Nou.16
S. Edmundus Rex m.   Nou.20
S. Egidius Abbas conf.   ſept.1
SS. Eleutherius & Dionyſ. m.
    Octob. 9.
SS. Elizabeth & Zachar. Nou.5
S. Euſebius Confeſs.   Aug.14
S. Eutichius Confeſs.   Aug.23
S. Euſtachius & ſoc. m.   ſept.20
SS. Eualdi fratres m.   Oct.26
S. Euariſtus PP. m.   Oct.3
S. Eutropia v. & m.   Oct.30
Exaltatio S. Crucis.   ſept.14

E.

Eagles George m.   Aug.30
Eagles Siſter m.   Aug.31
Eraſmus Roterodamus   Dec.22
Edvvard the ſixt K. conf. Dec 31
Eske Iohn mart.   Iul. 1
Euringe Ellen m.   Aug.23

E.

Edicts of Catholike Emperours
againſt heretiks, *cap.* 17. *n* 25.
Epiſtle of S Iames in Engliſh,
cap. 15. *num.* 5.
Eraſmus Roterodamus his ſtory,
cap 16. *num.* 40. 41. 42.
His iudgement of Luther, *ibid.
num.* 44.

Eraſ-

Erasmus a Catholike, *ibid. n.45.*
His sorrow for *Syr Thom.* More
his death in England, *ibid.*
num. 52.

Excommunication, and the terror
therof, *cap.17. num.26.*

Extreme vnction a Sacrament &
force therof, *cap.20. num.17.*

F.

S. Faustus mart.   Iul. 16
S. Ferreolus mart.   sept.18
Festum omnium sanctorum.
    Nouemb.1.
S. Firminus episc. m.   sept.25
Fidelium omnium defunctor.
    Nouemb.2.
SS. Fælix & Nabor m. Iul.12
SS. Felix & Adauctus m Aug.30
S. Franciscus conf.   Oct.4
S. Fredesuida virgo.   Oct.19

F.

Filmer Henry m.   Iul.5.
Foreman Thomas m.   Iul.21
Folkes Elizabeth m.   Aug.25
Fortune Iohn m.   sept.30
Forge de la Stephen m.   Oct.6
Foster William conf.   Nou.14
Frankish Iohn m.   Iul.11
Frith Iohn m   Iul.2
Friar & his vvoman m.   Aug.31
Friars gray two m.   Dec.5
Fust Thomas m.   Aug.16

F.

Faith belyed by Fox, *cap.19.n.13.*
Fox his bragg of his martyr
Frith cap.11. num.4.
Fox his martyrs excommunicate
their lavvfull Bishoppes, *cap.*
18. num.35.

Fox his endeauour to find out
Saints for furnishinge of his
Calendar, *cap.14. num 2* His
lyinge tale of 1 amberts burninge, *cap.14. num.30.*

Fox his vvrytings censured, *cap.*
18.per totum. His errors ascribed rather to lacke of iudgement then otherwise, *cap.18.*
num.2.

Fox his lyinge seemes to him
lawfull, *ibid. num.4.*

Fox his 120. lyes in lesse then
three leaues of his booke, *cap.*
19 per totum.

Fortune the blackesmith his description & story, *cap.13. n.37.*
His disputation vvith the Bishopps, *ibid. num.38.* His ridiculous aunsvvers and behauiour, *ibid.*

Freewill and good vvorks belyed by Fox, *cap 19. num.12.*

French seditious Saints, *cap.14.*
num.3.

French Carmelite friar burned in
Rome for heresie, *cap.16.n.36.*

Friar Barnes his story, *cap 14.n.18.*
His recantation and flyinge
beyond the seas, *ibid.*

Frith his story, condemnation,
and burninge, *cap.11.n.2.3.4.5.*
6. & deinceps. His doctrine
about the blessed Sacrament,
ibid num.4. & 5.

Frith his vvife content that her
husband should be burned, ib.

G.

S. Germanus episc. conf. Iul.31
S. Gorgonius mart.   sept.9
S. Gratianus ep. conf. Dec.18.

G.

German Peter m.	Oct.11
German Giles m.	Oct.12
Gerrard Thomas m.	Oct.14
Gardener VVilliam m	sept.4
Gilbert Gillemyne m.	Iul.19
Gibson Richard m.	Nou.20
Glouer Robert m.	sept.15
Glouer Iohn conf.	Dec.18
Gor vay Iohn m.	sept.12
Gorley Norman m.	Oct.26
Gouch Alexander m.	Nou.21
Gore Iames conf.	Dec.12
Gray friars two m.	Dec.5
Grouer Christofer m.	sept.25
Guyn Iohn m.	Iul.18.

G.

Gardener his story, cap.13 n.8.9.
10. His desperate Act in Lisbone of Portugal, ibid.

Gernesey martyrs their story condemnation and death, cap.11. num.45.46 & deinceps.

Gods law belyed by Fox, cap.19. num.8.

Good works by the Popes law belyed ibid.nu.9 Item good vvorks and freewill belyed ib. num.12.

Gratia gratis data belyed by Fox, ibid.num 10.

H.

S. Heddus Episc. conf.	Iul.7
S. Heliodorus ep. conf.	Iul.3
S. Helena Imperatrix	Aug.18
S. Hero Episc. mart.	Octob.17
S. Heualdi fratres m.	Oct.3
S. Hieronymus presbyt. conf. septemb.30.	
S. Hilarion Abbas.	Oct.21
SS. Hippolitus & Cassianus m. Aug 13.	
S. Hugo Episc. conf.	Nou.17
SS. Hyacinthus & Protus m. septemb. 11.	

H.

Hall Nicolas m.	Iul.16
Hallingdaie Iohn m.	Nou.8
Hart Iohn m.	sept.6
Harwood Stephen m.	Aug.15
Hayle VVilliam m.	Aug.17
Hayward Thomas m.	sept.12
Hewitt Andrew m.	Iul 3
Hewitt Andrew alter m.	Nou.4
Hierome VVilliam m.	Oct.15
Hilton Iohn m.	Dec.6
Hooke Richard m.	Iul.9
Hopper VVilham m.	Aug.7
Horne Iohn mart.	sept 17
Hooker VVilliam m.	Oct.24
Hooke Iohn mart.	Nou.17
Humfrey Phillipp m.	Nou.23
Hunne Richard m.	Dec.10
Hurst Iohn mart.	Nou.17

H.

Hackett and Arthington their strange attempt & story in Q. Elizabethes dayes, cap.17.n.18.

Hereticall Testament of Tracy Esquier, cap 16. num.5.

Heretiks shunned by ancient Fathers, cap.17. num.26. 27.

Heretiks by vvhat meanes to be knovven, ibid. num 29.

Heretiks punished in Q. Maryes dayes, vvhether yt vvere lawfull & expedient or no? ib.n 35.

Heape

Heape of lyes pardoned to Fox at once. *cap.* 19. *num* 8.

Henry the sixt his letters for apprehension of Norfolke heretiks, *cap.* 13 *num.* 2.

History of England hard to be sett forth in these dayes, and vvhy? *cap.* 18. *num.* 15. & 17.

Hope and charity and a ly therabout by Fox, *cap* 19 *num.* 7.

Hunt of an English Fox in wryinge, *cap.* 18. *num.* 16.

Hunne his story. *cap.* 16. *num.* 10. 11. & 12. He hanged himselfe in the towar. *ibid.* His defence by Fox about the same matter, *ibid.*

I.

S. Iacobus Apostolus.   Iul.25
S. Iacobus intercisus m. Nou. 27
S. Ianuarius & soc. m.   sept.19
Inuentio S. Stephani p. or. Aug.3
S. Innocentius PP. & conf Iul.28
SS. Innocentes m. m.   Dec.28
Iesu Christi natiuitas.   Dec.25
S. Ioanes Apostol. & Euangel Decem. 7.
S. Ioan Bapt. Decollat. Aug.29
S. Ioannes mart.   sept 7
SS Iulius & Aaron.   Iul.1
S. Iulius Senator. m.   Aug.19
SS. Iudas & Symō Apost. Oct.28
S. Iustus ep conf   sept.2
S. Iustinus presbiter. m. sept. 7
S. Iustina v. & m.   sept.26

I.

Iew a martyr   Dec.9
Iohnson Iohn m.   Aug 19
Iucson Thomas m.   Iul.15

I.

Iew martyred at Constantinople *cap.* 16. *num* 9.

Inundations of Licentiousnesse brought in by Protestants, *cap.* 20. *num.* 14.

Iustification and many lyes therabout by Fox, *cap.* 19. *num.* 4.

K.

Keyser Leonard m.   Aug.1
Keyser black-friar m.   Oct. 26
Kerby Iohn m   Nou 9
King Edvvard conf.   Dec 31
Knight Catherine m.   Nou.29
Kurd Iohn mart.   sept.18

K.

King Henry the sixt his letters for apprehension of heretikes in Norfolke. *cap.* 13 *num.* 2.

King Henry the 8. his condemnation of *Tyndalls* translation of the Bible, by Act of Parlament, *cap.* 14. *num.* 12.

King Henry the 8. his combatt vvith *Lambert*, *ibid.* *num.* 15. & *cap.* 18. *num.* 14.

King Edvvard the sixt a Confessor of Fox his Calendar and vvhy, *cap.* 16 *num.* 97 The calamity that fell to England in his dayes by the new ghospell, *ibid. num.* 98.

King and Q. of Scotland violently vsed in K. Edvvard the sixt his dayes, by the nevv ghospellers in England, *cap.* 16. *num.* 101.

L.

L.

SS. Largus & Smaragdus m.
  Aug. 8.
S. Laurentius mart.   Aug. 10
S. Laurentius ep. conf. Nou 14
S. Lazarus ep. conf.   Dec. 17
S. Leonardus conf.   Nou. 6
S. Leocadia v. & m.   Dec. 9
S. Linus PP. & m.   sept. 23
S. Ludouicus Rex conf. Aug. 25
S Lullus episc. conf. Oct. 16
S. Lucas Euangelista. Oct 18
S Lucius Rex m.   Dec. 3
S. Lucia v. & m.   Dec. 13

L.

Lambert Iohn m.   Oct. 9
Lancelott N. m.   Oct 12
Latymer Hugh m.   Oct 20
Launder iohn m.   Iul. 14
Laurence Henry m. Aug. 8
Lawson Elizab. conf. Dec 18
Layton VVilliam mart. Oct 8
Leafe Iohn mart.   Iul. 7
Lenes Ioyce m   sept. 19
Leyes Thom. conf. sept. 7

L.

Lambert his ftory. arraignment,
and condemnation, *cap*. 14 *n*.
20. 21. 22. 23. 24. &c. His combate vvith *K*. Henry the eyghr,
ibid. num. 25.

Latymer his ftory, *cap*. 14. *num*. 51.
His card playing fermon at
Cambridge, *ibid num*. 54. His
abiuration of herefie, *ib. num*.
56. 57. 58. & 60. He vvas
made B. of Glocefter, *ib. num.*
58. The reformation of his

Bishopricke, *ibid*. His accufation of Treafon to *K*. Henry
the 8. *ibid. num* 60. His marrow-bones of the maffe, *ibid.*
num. 36. His habitt and apparell defcribed by Fox, *num*. 67.
His burning at Oxford, *ib n*. 70.
Libell of *Daungerous pofitions*
vvrytten againft the puritans,
cap. 15. *num*. 10. & *cap* 17. *num*. 3.
Licentioufnes of hereticks defcribed, *cap*. 18. *num*. 11.
A *Logitian* made of a pewterer,
cap. 12. *num*. 7.
Lollards abiuration vnder *King*
Henry the 6. *cap*. 15. *num*.
Luthers condemnation of all
Zuinglian fectaryes, *cap*. 4.
num 21. & *cap*. 17. *num*. 13.
Lyes of Fox infinite, *cap*. 19. *per*
totum. & *cap*. 20. *num*. 6. 7. & 8.

M.

S. Machutus epifc. conf. Nou. 15
S. Maglorius ep. conf. Oct. 24
S. Mammians mart. Aug. 17
S. Margarita v. m, Iul. 20
S. Macrina Virgo   Iul 19
S. Maria Magdal.   Iul. 22
S. Martha Virgo.   Iul. 29
S. Maria ad Niues. Aug. 5
S. Marcellus mart. fept. 4
S. Mariæ v. natiuitas. fept. 8
S. Marcus PP. & conf. Oct 7
S. Martinus ep, conf. Nou. 11
S. Martinus PP. & m. Nou 12
S. Mariæ v. concepio. Dec. 8
S. Mathæus Apoftolus fept 21
S. Mauritius & foc. m, fept 22
S. Melchiades PP. & m. Dec. 10
S. Michaël Archangelus fept. 29

M.

Martyr Peter conf.	Dec.30
Massy Perotine m.	Iul.19
Mekings Richard m.	Nou.2
Melancthon Philipp	Dec.29
Mering Margarett m.	Dec.15
Middleton Humfrey m.	Iul.11
Miller Symon m.	Iul 23
Milles Robert m.	Iul 30
Millan Bartolett m.	Oct.1
Ming VVilliam m.	Iul.8
Mirandula Picus	Dec.20
Morton Iames m.	Nou.7
Munt VVilliam m.	Aug.26
Munt Alice m.	Aug.27

M.

Mad men made of fooles, *cap*.18. *num*.10.

Magdeburgians and their Centuryes, *ibid. num*.18.

Marbecke the Organ-player of VVindesore his story, *cap*.11. *num*.10.

Martyrs of VVindesore, tippling at the fire side when they were to be burned, *ibid. num*.19.

Marrow-stones of the masse. *cap*. 14. *num*.63.

Martyr Peter his story, and comminge into England, *cap*.16. *num*.90. His presence at the conference of *Poysy* in France anno 1556. *ibid.n*.94. His death, *num*.95.

Matrimony and state therof belved by Fox *cap*.19. *num* 43.

Melancthon his story, *cap*.16 *n* 77. Howv he tooke his name, *ibid*. His temptation to be a baker,

ibid. num.74. He vvas an enemy to the Sacramentaryes, *ibid.* His inconstancy, *num*.82. Hovv he became an vbiquitary, *ibid. num*.86. The sentence & iudgement of the Germans concerninge *Melancthon, ibid. num*. 83. 84. *& deinceps.*

Mirandula Picus his story, *cap*.16 *num*.37. His life vvrytten by Syr Thomas More, *ibid.*

Moyses law belyed by Fox, *cap*.19. *num*.14.

N.

SS. Nabor & Fœlix m.	Iul.12
S. Narcissus Episc. conf	Oct.29
Natiuitas B. M. V.	sept.8
Natiuitas Domini.	Dec.25
S. Nemesius mart.	Dec.19
S. Nicolaus conf.	sept.10
S. Nicolaus Epise. conf.	Dec.6
S. Nicomedes mart.	sept.15
S. Nimpha v. & m.	Nou.10

N.

Naunts Receauer m.	Oct.3
Newman Iohn m.	Aug.4
Norman Gorley m.	Oct.26

N.

Norfolke heretiks apprehended by K. Henry the sixt, *cap*.13.*n*.2.

Notes of the Church assigned by a Foxian martyr, *cap*.13. *num*.23.

O.

S. Olimpias mart.	Dec.1
Omnium Sanctorum fest.	Nou.1
	Omnium

Omnium fideliũ defunct. Nou.2
S. Onesiphoꝛus m.   sept 6
S. Osmundus episc.conf, Dec.4

O.

Old man of Buckingham mꝰ
  Decemb.4.
Ormes Cecily m.   sept.8

O.

Obedience of the law, and a ly
  therabout by Fox, cap.19. n 18.
Ochinus Bernardinus his cominge
  into England, cap.16. num.90.
  His booke of Poligamy, ibid.
Opinion of the Capper of Coꝰ
  uentry about the Sacrament of
  the Altar, cap.13. num.19.
Organ-player of VVyndesoꝛ
  made a Martyr by Fox, & yet
  aliue, cap.11. num.20.

P.

S. Pantaleon m.   Iul.27
S. Paulinus ep. conf.   Oct.10
S. Petr. ad Vincula.   Aug.1
SS. Petr. & Paul. Basil. dedicat.
  Nouemb.18.
S. Petrus episcop. Alexandr. m.
  Nouemb.26.
S. Philippus m.   sept.13
S. Philogonius ep. conf. Dec.20
S. Pius P.P. & m.   Iul.11
S. Praxedes virgo.   Iuꝉ.21
S. Priuatus mart.   sept.28
SS. Proꝰus & Hiacinthus mart.
  sepꝉenb.11.
S. Pontianus m.   Nou.19

P.

Palmer Iulius m.   Iul.18
Patingham Patricke m.   Aug.5
Parke Gregory m,   Oct.22

Paynter Iohn m,   Oct.12
Person Antony m.   Iul.3
Peter a German m.   Oct.11
Peter Martyr conf.   Dec.30
Philpott Iohn m.   Dec.13
Phagius Paulus conf.   Dec.24
Philipp Melancthon   Dec.29
Picus Mirandula   Dec.20
Pigott Robert m,   Oct.17
Pikes VVilliam m.   Iul.27
Poyle Henry m,   Oct.4
Porter Iohn m.   Nou.5
Potkins Alice m,   Nou.15
Pulley Margery m.   Iul.8
Purcas Robert m.   Aug.20
Playne VVilliam conf.   Dec.18
Puttedew N. mart.   Oct.9

P

Painters disputation vvith the
  B. of London, cap.12 num.12.
S. Paul belyed, cap.19. num.42.
Pennance; and a lye about the
  same, ibid. num.24.
Pewterer become a Logitian,
  cap.12. num.7.
Phagius his expulsion out of
  Germany and comming into
  England, cap.16. num.67.
Philpott Archdeacon of VVin-
  chester his story, cap.16. num 1.
  His conference vvith the Lord
  Rich. ibid. num.26. VVith the
  Bishopps. num.29.
Picus Earle of Mirandula his stoꝛ
  ry cap.16 & 17. His life vvryt-
  ten by Syr Thom. More in Eng-
  lish, ibid.
Popes law, and a ly therabout,
  cap.19. num 8.
Preparation to receaue Sacra-
  ments, and difference therof,
  cap.20. num 22.
                           Hh 4   Proꞇe-

Proteſtant defined, *cap.20.num.7.* & 8.

Q.

SS. Quadraginta virg. m. Dec.24
SS. Quatuor Coronati mart. Nouemb. 8.
S. Quinctinus mart. Oct.31
Quinquaginta Milites m. Iul.8

Q.

Queene Mary her title to the crowne preached againſt by Ridley B. of London, *cap.14. num.44.* Her conference with the ſaid Ridley at her houſe of *Hunſdon, ibid num.* 49.

Queene Maryes report of K. Edward her brothers diſpoſition, *cap.* 6. *num* 104. Her puniſhinge of hereticks, and whether yt were lawfull and expedient or no? *cap.17.n* 35.

R.

S. Remigius ep. conf Oct 1
S. Reſpicius & Triphon mart, Nouemb. 10.
S. Romulus ep. m. Iul.6
S. Romanus mart. Aug.9
S. Rufus ep. conf. Aug. 27
S. Rufus mart. Nou.28
S. Ruſticus mart. Oct.9

R.

Rauenſdale Iohn m. ſept.16
Receauer of Naunts m. Oct. 3
Rhedonenſis Thom. m. Dec.19
Ridley Nicolas m. Oct.19
Roth Richard m. ſept.19

Roper George m. Oct 31
Rough Iohn m. Dec.14
Roterodamus Eraſmus Dec.22

R.

Ratiſpone colloquy of hereticks *anno Domini 1546. cap.16.n.64.*
Rebell martyrs in S. Giles field, *cap* 12. *num.2.*
Ridley his ſtory, *cap.14. num.43. 44.45 & deinceps.* His ioyning with Cranmer in wickednes and treaſon, *ibid* His ſermon at *Paules Croſſe* againſt the Princeſſe Mary her ſucceſſion to the Crowne of England, *ibid.n.44.* His conference with the ſaid Princeſſe at her houſe of *Hunſdon, ibid. num.49.*

S.

S. Sabinus ep. m. Dec.30
S. Sabba Abbas Dec.5
SS. omnium feſtiu. Nou.1
SS. quatuor Coronati m. Nou.8
S. Saluatoris Baſil. dedicat. Nouemb. 9.
S Saturninus mart. Nou.29
S. Sarmas mart, Oct.11
SS. Septem dormiētes m. Iul.10
SS. Sennon & Abdon.m. Iul 30
S. Serapia v. & m. ſept.3
S. Silueſt. PP. conf Dec.31
S. Simphroſa cum 7.fil.m Iul.18
S. Simplicianus ep.conf Aug.16
S. Simphorianus mart. Aug 22
S. Spiridion ep conf. Dec 14
S. Smaragdus m. Aug.8
S. Stephanus PP. &. m. Aug.2
S Stephanus protom. Dec.26
S. Symeon conf, Oct.8

SS

SS. Symon & Iudas Apostol.
Octob. 28.
S. Susanna v. & m. Aug. 11
S. Synesius mart. Dec. 12

S.

Samuel Robert m. Aug. 18
Sapience Peter m. Dec. 2
Sheterden Nicolas m. Iul. 12
Sheater VVilliam m. sept. 9
Sharpe Edward m. sept. 15
Scholler of Abbonilem. Dec. 8
Siluerside Agnes m. Aug. 22
Simpson Priest m. Oct 25
Slade Iohn m. Iul. 29
Seaman Mother Oct. 30
Smith Robert m. Aug. 14
Spurdance Thom. m. sept. 28
Spenser Rich. m. Nou. 3
Sparow VVilliam m. Nou. 19
Snoth Alice m. Nou. 28
Steere VVilliam m. Aug. 10
Stephen de la forge m. Oct. 6
Stratton Dauy m. Oct. 25

S.

Sacraments; and therteene lyes
about the application of them,
cap. 19. num. 40.
Sacraments 7. and the vse therof
in the Cath. Church impugned
by Fox, cap. 20 n. 13. & 14.
Satisfaction, and force thereof,
cap. 20. n. 15. The false dealing
of Fox therabout cap. 19. n. 27.
Saints exchanged by Fox, cap. 13.
num. 1.
Scripture applyed fondly by ig=
norant artificers, cap. 15. n. 31.
Scripture read by the penny=
vvorth, cap. 12. num. 21.

Scottishman in Syuill of Spaine
his willtull obstinacy an. 1595.
cap 14. num. 9.
Seruing maid martyr her obstinacy in heresie, cap. 12. num. 7.
Shermans disputation vvith the
B. of London, cap. 13. num. 15.
D. Shaxton B. of Salisbury his
story and depriuation, cap. 14.
num. 40 & 60.
Story of Iohn Frith & Bradford,
cap. 11. num. 2. 3. 4. & num. 22.
23. 24. &c.
Synod held in Luthers house at
VVittenberge, cap. 16. num. 61.
Synnes originall and actuall. cap.
19. num. 17. Fox his false dea=
linge therabout to deceaue his
reader, ibid.

T.

S. Thecla v. & m. sept 23
S. Thecla Abbatissa. Oct 15
S. Theodorus ep. m. Iul. 4
S. Thomas Hereford. ep. Oct. 2
S. Theodorus presbyter. mart.
Octob. 23.
S. Theodorus mart. Nou. 9
S. Thomas Apost. Dec 21
S. Thomas Cantuar. ep Dec. 29
SS. Tiburtius & Susanna mart.
Aug. 11.
Transfiguratio Domini Aug. 6
SS. Triphon & Soc. Nou. 20

T.

Tankerfield George martyr.
Aug. 12.
Testwood Robert m. Iul. 4
Tewkesbury Iohn m. Dec. 11
Thrustan Margarett m. sept. 23
Tiler

Tiler Thom. conf.　Dec.16
Tracy VVilliam conf.　Dec.1
Tutty Iames m.　Sept.11
Tyndall VVilliam m,　Oct.7

S. Vincentius mart,　Oct.27
S. Vrsula v. & m.　Oct.21
S. Vitalis mart.　Nou.4
S. VVillebrordus ep.cont,Nou.7
SS.Virgines Africanę m. Dec 16
SS.Virgines 40. mart.　Dec.24

T.

Taylors disputation vvith the B. of London, cap. 13. num. 27.

Testament of VVilliam Tracy esquier, cap 16. nu. 5. The same proued to be hereticall, ibid.

Syr Thomas Seymers death procured by Latymer,cap.14.n.65. His attaynder by parlament, ibid. nu.66. his beheading, ibid.

Syr Thomas More his proofes against Hunne that he hanged himselfe in the Towar, cap. 16. num. 13. 14. & 15.

Trudgeouer-the-vvorld his story, cap.12.num.33,34.& 35.

Tyndall maister to Iohn Frith in heresie, cap.11.num.2. His letters to him out of Flanders, ibid, n.10. & 11. His stoiy and progresse in heresie, cap. 14. num.5 6. & 7. His opinion of the Sacrament of the Altar, ibid.num 8. His translation of the Bible condemned by act of parlament, ibid. num.12.

V. and VV.

9. Valerianus ep. m.　Dec.15
S VVenefrida v. & m.　Nou.3
S. VVillebaldus ep. conf.　Iul.7
S. Victor PP. & m.　Iul. 28
S. Victorinus ep. m.　Sept.5
S Victoria v. & m.　Dec.23
Visitatio B. M. V.　Iul. 2
S VVlfridus ep. conf.　Oct.12

V. and VV.

VVarne Elizab. m.　Aug.11
VVast Ioane m.　Aug.19
VVaddon Iohn m.　Sept.3
VVade Iohn conf.　Sept.6
VVarner Iohn m.　Sept.24
VVallace Adam m.　Oct.23
VVard Robert conf.　Dec.7
VVhite VVilliam m.　Sept.2
VVichart George m.　Nou.8
VVisman VVilliam conf, Dec.12
VVithers Mathew cont. Dec.16
VVebb Iohn m.　Oct.21
Vos Henry m.　Iul.1
VVolsey VVilliam m.　Oct.16
VVright Stephen m.　Iul.29
VVright Rich. mart.　Aug.11
VVoman vvith her child mart, septemb.17.

V. and VV.

VVicked doctrine about Baptisme, and force therof,cap 11. num. 42.

VVickliffians their antiquity and vnity, cap.13. num 4.

VVinde-sore-martyrs tipplinge at the fire-side, vvhen they vvere to be burned, cap.11.num.19.

Violence vsed to the K. & Q of Scotland in K. Edwards dayes by new ghospellers, cap. 16. num. 101.

Virginity not professed amongst any

any of Fox his Saints, *cap.* 17. *num.* 10.

VVifchart the Scottish-martyr his ftory, arraignement, and condemnation for herefie, *cap.* 15. *num.* 6. 7. His defcription by Fox, *ibid num.* 8.

Vowes coactiue, and 4. lyes about the fame by Fox, *cap.* 19. *n.* 44.

Y.

Yeoman Richard. m,   Jul. 26

Z.

S. Zacharias & Eliz.   Nou.5
S. Zephetinus PP. m.   Aug. 27
S. Zoa mart.   Jul.5

Z.

Zuinglian Sacramentaryes condemned by Luther, *cap.* 14. *num.* 41.

FINIS.

A REVIEVV

OF TEN PVBLIKE

DISPVTATIONS

Or Conferences held vvithin the compasse of foure yeares, vnder *K. Edward*
& *Qu. Mary,* concerning some principall points in Religion, especially of
the Sacrament & sacrifice of the Altar.

VVHERBY,

*May appeare vpon how vveake groundes both Catholike Religion
vvas changed in England; as also the fore-recounted Foxian
Martyrs did build their new opinions, and offer themselues to
the fire for the same, vvhich vvas chiefly vpon the creditt of the
said Disputations.*

By N. D.

Aug. lib. 2. against *Petilian* the *Donatist .*
VVe are constrayned to heare, discusse, and refute
these trifles of yours: least the simpler and weaker
sort should fall into your snares.

Imprinted vvith licence
Anno M. DC. IIII.

The contentes of this Reuievv.

THe *Preface shewing what vtility disputation may bring, for discussion of matters in controuersy; and how farre: togeather with the causes, why the reuiew of these ten disputations is now published.*

1. Of ten *publike disputations, recounted by Iohn Fox to haue byn held in England, about controuersies in Religion, especially concerninge the blessed Sacrament of the Altar, vvithin the space of foure yeares, at two seuerall changes of Religion vnder K. Edward and Q. Mary; besides many other more particular, held in Bishops consistoryes and other places about the same matters.* CHAP. I.

2. The *state of the cheife question handled in the forsaid disputations, concerninge the* Reall *presence,* Transubstantiation, *and the* Sacrifice of the Masse; *with the cheese grounds that be on eyther side.* CHAP. II.

3. *Certayne obseruations to be noted, for better answeringe of hereticall cauillations against the forsaid articles.* CHAP. III.

4. The *examination of such arguments, as in the former disputations were alleaged by the* Zwinglians *and* Caluinists, *against the Reall presence of Christs body in the Sacrament.* CHAP. IV.

5. *VVhat Catholike arguments were alleaged in these disputations for the reall presence: & how they were answered or shifted of by the Protestants.* CHAP. V.

6. *Of two other articles about Transubstantiation, and the Sacrament of the Altar, what passed in this disputation.* CHPP. VI.

THE

THE PREFACE,

Shewinge what vtility disputation may bringe, for discussion of matters in controuersie, & how farre: togeather vvith the causes, vvhy the reuievv of these ten disputations is now published.

THAT disputation is a good meanes and profitable instrument, to examine and try out truth, euen in matters of faith, yf yt be rightly vsed, & vvith due circumstances, no man can deny; for that experience in Gods Church doth teach yt, to vvitt, that great vtility hath often-tymes byn receaued by such disputations: and vve read amonge other examples, that in the tyme of *Antoninus* the Emperour sonne of *Seuerus*, that died in *Yorke*, a little more then a hundred yeares after Christ, the

Mon-

Montanifts herefy, vvho vvere called alfo *Cataphrigians*, grovving ftrong, and dravvinge to it diuers pricipall men, and namely *Tertullian*, vvith the admiratiõ of the vvhole vvorld; one *Caius* a Cath. man moft excellently learned, and of rare and vertuous life , tooke vpon him to difpute publikely in *Rome* in the prefence of the vvhole Church , vvith licéce of *Zepherinus* the Pope, againft a chiefe principall man of that feĉt called *Proclus*, and fo confounded him therin, as frõ that day forvvard the feĉt began greatly to decline; of vvhich difputatiõ do make mentiõ both *Eufebius* & *S. Hierome*, & yt did much profitt that Catholike caufe.

2.   And about 2. hundred yeares after this againe , vve read of another profitable difputation held in our countrey, by *S. Germanus* & his fellovves, French Bifhopps, vvith the

Anno Dominis 215.

Eufeb. l. 6. hift. c. 14. Hier. de vir. Ill uft. in Caio.

Brittifh

Brittiſh *Pelagians* vpon the yeare of
Chriſt 429. vvherby they vvere ſo
confuted,as alſo vvith the miracles
vvrought by *S.German,* by certaine
reliques brought from *Rome,*as their
hereſie neuer proſpered there aftervvard,but vvas ſoone extinguiſhed.
VVe read in like manner of diuers
publike côflicts & diſputatiôs, held
by *S.Auſten* vvith diuers learned heretiks of ſundry ſects , as namely
vvith *Fortunatus* a *Manichean* prieſt,
in the citty of *Hippo* in *Africa,* vpon
the yeare 392.al the clergy & people
being preſent, & publike notaryes
appointed to ſet dovvne both their
argumêts: & the iſſue of this diſputatiôs vvas,that vvhê the *Manichean*
heretike could not anſvvere,he ſaid
(ſaith *Poſſidonius)ſe cum ſuis maioribus*
collaturum, that he vvould conferre
thoſe difficultyes vvith his betters,
& then if they could not ſatisfy him

Bed. l. 1.
hiſt. c.14.
& Conſt.
presbyt.
in vita
s. Lupi
epiſc.

A 3 *ſe*

See the acts of this disputatiō *in Possid. l. de vita Aug. c. 3.*

se animæ suæ consulturum, that he vvould haue care of his ovvne soule. But this care vvas (saith the same *Possidonius*) that he ranne a-vvay from the citty, and neuer appeared there againe. VVhich point

Aug. epist. 244.

S. Augustine himselfe obiecteth, in a certayne epistle, to another *Manichee* Priest, that came to succeed in *Fortunatus* his place in that citty, prouokinge him also to like disputation, but the heretike refused the combatt.

3   And after this againe, the said Father being novv made Bishopp, vpon the yeare of Christ 405. he disputed publikely for tvvo dayes togeather, vvith another principall *Manichean* heretike named *Fœlix*, in presence of the vvhole people,

S. Austens disputa-tion with *Fœlix Ma-nicheus*

notaryes being appointed on both sides to take their arguments. In vvhich disputation, *S. Austen* did so

eui-

euidently conuince his aduersarie,
as he in the end yelded (a strange
example in an heretike) and renounced his heresie, and became
a Catholike, vvhereby the *Maui-
chean* heresie vvas so shaken and
discredited throughout all *Africa*,
as no man euer openly aftervvard
durst defend the same in disputation, but it vanished avvay by little
and little, as a smoke vvhen the fire
is putt out. This vvhole disputation is to be seene at large in *S. Austen*, laid forth in tvvo books of his
de actis cum Fælice Manichæo. And
this for the *Manicheans*.

4. But vvith the Donatists and
Arrians, he had many other like
conflicts : as for example,vpon the
yeare of Christ 411. there vvas a sollemne disputation held at *Carthage*
in *Africa*,for diuers daies togeather,
betvvene the Catholike and Do-
A 4 natist

natift Bifhopps, the Cath. Bifhopps
being in number 286. vvherof the
Breuic.
collat.
primi
diei.
principall difputer vvas *S. Auften*
himfelfe;& of the Donatift Bifhops
279. vvhich fhevveth the multitude
of heretiks in thofe parts to haue
byn great, notvvithftandinge they
had bin much diminifhed by Cath.
Bifhops labours and vvrytings: for
that 17. yeares before, there mett togeather againft the Catholiks 400.
Donatift Bifhopps, exceptinge fix:
this difputation vvas before the
Conte Marcellinus gouernour of that
countrey , and publike notaryes
vvere prefent to take the argumēts
on both fides; and all being ended
the Iudge pronounced this fen-
Aug. in
Breuic.
tence: *Omnium documentorum mani-*
feftatione , à Catholicis Donatiftas con-
futatos. That the Donatifts vvere
conuinced by the Catholiks, by the
manifeft truth of all kind of arguments.

ments. *S. Auguſtine* himſelfe ſetteth
forth a breefe relation of all that
meeting & diſputation, intituling
yt *Breuiculum*. And in a certayne
epiſtle of his teſtifieth moreouer
of the euent, that albeit thoſe miſerable Biſhops vvere not conuerted
therby, but rather made more obſtinate & obdurate: yet that many
of their people vvere, & eſpecially
of the furious *Circumcellians*, that
vvere ready to murder men vpon
zeale of their hereſie.

Epiſt. ad Gaudent.

5. I lett paſſe another diſputation
vvhich the ſaid Father had, ſome 10.
or 11. yeares after that, by the order
of *Pope Zozimus* of Rome, in the
Citty of *Cæſarea* in *Mauritania*, vvith
one *Emeritus* a Donatiſt B. of that
Citty; all the vvhole people of the
Citty, togeather vvith diuers Biſhopps, being preſent; but little
good could be done vvith him, his
obſti-

Acta apud Aug. ep. 157. & l. 2. Retract. c. 51. & Possidon. in vita Aug. c. 14.

obstinacy vvas so great and peruerse. The acts of that disputation are extant in *S. Austen*, & often mention therof is made by himselfe, & by *Possidonius* in his life. And this for the Donatists.

6.   But vvith the Arrians I find the same Father to haue had sundry disputations also, as namely once vpon the yeare of Christ 422. the

Possid. ib. ap. 17.

Gouernour *Bonifacius*, hauinge many Gothes in his campe vvho vvere of the Arrian sect : they had also an Arrian Bishopp that gouerned them, named *Maximinus*, vvho in their opinion vvas very learned, and therfore they made instance, that he might dispute vvith *S. Augustine*, vvhich the good Father accepted, for he refused none, and so

S. Augustines disputatiõs vvith the Atrians.

they had their meetinge and disputation, and the acts thereof are extant in his vvorks, togeather vvith
a cer-

a certaine booke of his ovvne added thervnto, for explication of diuers points, vvherof thefe heretiks
vvere vvont to vaunt aftervvard, as
though they had gott the victory;
vvhich happened to the fame Father in another combatt, held the
very fame yeare, vvith one *Conte
Pafcentius* of the fame Arrian fect,
vvho vvas cheefe fifchall or trea-
fourer of the Emperor, and moft
arrogantlie chalenged to difpute
vvith *S. Auften*, but yet in priuate
& vvithout notaryes, in refpect of
the Emperiall lavves, that did forbidd publike difputations in fauour of fects and herefies. VVhich
difputation *S. Augustine* accepted;
and the fame vvas held priuatly, in
the prefence of many noble and
learned men, but the heretikes
vvould not yeld, but rather publifhed foone after (as their fafhion is)
that

Aug.epist.
73.74.75.
76.77.

that they had the victory, vvhich *S.*
Austen vvas forced to refute by many feuerall epistles, and by settinge
forth the disputation it selfe, as yt is
to be seene in his vvorks.

7.   And this may suffice for a tast
of some disputations, held at diuers
tymes and in diuers countreyes,
vvith heretiks of sundry sects in the
ancient Church: And I might recite many more, as that of *Maximus*
a learned Catholike monke in *Afri-*
ca , vvho vpon the yeare of Christ
645. held a very famous disputation
against one *Pyrrhus,* Archbishop of
Constantinople, a great pillar of those
heretiks called *Monothelits,* that held
one only vvill, and not tvvo to be
in Christ our Sauiour , vvhich disputation being made in the presence of many Bishopps, and of the
gouernour of that *Country* , named
Gregorius Patricius , the hereticall
Arch-

Photius in
Bibliothe-
ca.
Anasta-
sius hoc
anno.

Archbifhopp vvas fo confounded, as he left his herefie , vvent to *Rome*, and gaue vp a booke of his pennance to *Pope Theodorus*, and vvas receaued by him into the Catholike communion againe : and that vvas the euent of that difputation.

8. And not full 20. yeares after this againe, to vvitt vpon the yeare 664. vvas that great difputation alfo in England, betvvene the Englifh and fcottifh Bifhops, about the obferuation of *Eafter* , in the prefence of tvvo Kings *Ofwyn* and *Egfrid* his fonne , *Kinges* of *Northumberland* and of the *Mercians:* the cheefe difputers, on the Scottifh Bifhopps parte, vvere *Colman* and *Cedda*; and of the Englifh, *Agilbertus* Bifhopp of the *VVeſtſaxons* and *VVilfrid* : and the iffue of this difputation vvas, that Kings *Ofvvyn*

Beda l. 3. hiſt. cap. 25.

vvas

vvas conuerted to the vnion of the Roman Church, and caufed the vfe thereof to be practized in his countrey.

9. And fo vve fee by thefe examples, and many more that might be alleaged, that difputations in points of Religion are fometymes neceffary, & do much good, vvhen they are taken in hand vvith equall and due conditions, and conuenient lavves for indifferency in tryinge out the truth, for that othervvayes they may be pernicious, & haue byn refufed by anciēt Fathers, as vve read of one reiected by *Saint Ambrofe* in *Milayne,* vpon the yeare of Chrift 286. vvhen *Auxentius* the Arrian-Bifhopp, being puffed vp vvith pride & arrogancy, by the fauour of the Empreffe *Iuftina,* infected vvith the fame herefy, had not only prouoked *S. Ambrofe* to publike

Publike difputation refufed by *S.Ambrof.* vpon iuft caufes.

blike difputation, but had further
procured that *Valentinian* the yong
Emperour, being yet a child, & not
baptized but only *Cathecumenus*,
did make a publike edict, to commaund the faid difputations to be
held vpō fuch a day, in his publike
court or confiftorie, before himfelfe & the faid Empreffe, certaine
learned Pagans and Ievves being
appointed for iudges in that matter. But *S. Ambrofe*, by the counfell
of diuers Bifhopps gathered togeather vvith him, refufed to come to
thofe difputatiōs, vvryting a booke   *Ambrof.*
to the Emperour *Valentinian* for his   *epift.* 31.
                                          vvhere is
excufe, fhevvinge the iniuftice and   extant
                                          alfo *the*
vnequality of the order, and of   booke
thofe tymes, and perfuadinge him   fent by
                                          Ambrofe
to recall the faid lavv. And yf he   to *Valen-*
                                          tinian.
vvould haue that controuerfie in
religion, betvveene them and the
Arrians, treated againe, he fhould
                              follovv

follovv therin the excellent example of his predeceſſor *Conſtantine* the great, vvho ſuffered Prieſts
and Biſhopps only to handle that
matter in the Councell of *Nice*, and
ſo vvas this diſputation broken of:
& preſently there happened a thing

*Paul. in
vita Am-
broſij.* of great admiratiō (ſaith *Paulinus* in
the life of *S. Ambroſe*) vvhich vvas,
that a certaine principall learned
Arrian, *acerrimus diſputator*; *&
inconuertibilis ad fidem Catholicam*,
being a moſt eager diſputer, and
eſteemed not poſſible to be con-
uerred to the Catholike faith;being
deceaued, at it ſeemeth, of his hope
and expectation to diſpute in this
conflict, vvent to the Church, to
heare at leaſt vvhat *Ambroſe* could
ſay out of the pulpit in his ſermons:
vvhere ſeing an Angell to ſpeake as
it vvere in his eare, he vvas by that
miracle not only conuerted to be a
Ca-

Catholike, but became alſo a moſt vehement defendor of that faith a-gainſt the heretiks.

10. To returne then to our purpoſe of diſputation, yt is of great mo-ment, hovv, and in vvhat tyme and place, and vvith vvhat lavves and conditions they are made, vvherof yovv vvill ſee the proofe and expe-rience alſo in theſe ten, that heere vve are to preſent; vvherof ſix being held vnder the gouernemēt of Pro-teſtants, and 4. vnder Catholike magiſtrates, yovv ſhall ſee com-plaints on both ſides of inequality vſed: but he that ſhall read and con-ſider them indifferently, and vvith-out paſſion, euen as they are ſett dovvne by Fox himſelfe (for vve could gett no other records therof for the preſent) he ſhall eaſily ſee no ſmall differences to appeare. For that the diſputatiōs both at *Oxford*

B   and

The com-pariſon bet ene Cath & hereticall diſputa-tions.

and *Cambridge* in K. Henryes dayes, vvere only certaine oftentations of light fkyrmifhes a farre of, fo vainly and fondly performed, as they haue no fubftance in them at all. And fo he vvill fee that fhall read thefe examinations. The other vnder *Queene Mary*, though the firft of them in the conuocation-houfe, vvherin Proteftants only vvere opponents, vvas not much vnlike the former for fubftace, or rather lacke of fubftance: yet the other three held in *Oxford* againft *Cranmer*, *Ridley* and *Latymer* by Catholike difputers, are of a farre different kynd, as hauinge both iudges, notaryes, and arbitrators to the likinge of both parts appointed. And albeit in the manner of vrginge arguments, there vvant not complaints of the Proteftant party, as after yovv fhall heare: for that diuers

uers somtymes are said to haue spoken togeather, & one man to haue
putt himselfe into the profecution
of another mans argument, somevvhat diforderly as to them yt feemed: yet touchinge the thinges
themfelues, to vvitt the arguments
& proofes there laid forth & profecuted, there vvere fo many cleere,
fubftantiall & vveighty, as the reader vvill côfeffe there vvas no tyme
loft in thofe 3. dayes difputation of
the Cath. party. And fo to the examination therof I remitt me.

11.   One thing of no fmall importance there is to be côfidered in this
preface about the nature of difputation;to vvitt,that as it is a fit meanes
to ftyrre vp mans vnderftandinge
to attêd the truth, by layinge forth
the difficultyes on both fides; fo
is yt not alvvayes fufficient to refolue his iudgement, for that yt

Difputa-
tiô fitter
in fome
to moue
doubts&
examine
thetruth,
then to
refolue
the fame,

moueth more doubts then he can
aunfvvere or diſſolue. And this
happeneth not only in vnlearned
people, vvhich by no meanes can
deſcerne vvhich party hath the better, vvhen both parts are learned &
alleage arguments for themſelues,
in matters aboue their capacity, but
euen the moſt learned alſo, yf they
haue no other meanes of reſolution then arguing to and fro by diſputation, are brought many-times
to be more doubtfull therby then
before, & this euen in matters both
naturall and morall of this life. The
reaſon vvherof is, that mans vnderſtandinge being limited, and the
light of knovvledge imparted vnto
him from God, being but a little
particle or ſparkle of his infinite diuine knovvledge: yt cometh to
paſſe, that the more this ſparkle is
exerciſed, & inkendled in ſearching
out

out Gods vvorks and secrets in this life, the more yt seeth her ovvne vveaknes, and beginneth to doubt more, & to be more ambiguous in herselfe, vvhether that vvhich shee apprehendeth be truly apprehended or no, or vvhether by further search shee shall not find it othervvise, and see herselfe deceaued in this apprehensio, as she hath found in many other apprehensions that vvent before, vvhen she had lesse knovvledge.

12. And vpon this ground no doubt came those philosophers, called the *Academicks*, to found their sect & profession, that they vvould beleeue or affirme nothing, but dispute of all things to and fro vvithout assent. And heere hence came also the sayinge of that other philosopher: *Hoc vnum scio, me nihil scire.* I knovv only this, that I knovv no-

B 3   thing

thinge. And *S. Austen* himselfe before his conuersion, being yet a *Manichee*, & vvearyed out vvith this search by vvay of arguments to and fro, vvhich should be the true Religiō (for this vvas one of their principall groūds, as himselfe testified, to beleeue nothinge, but that vvhich vvas euidēt by reason) fell at length to forsake the *Manichees*, & to ioyne himselfe to the Academiks: but after long search finding no certainty also therin, and hearing their sect euery day impugned by *S. Ambrose* Bishopp of *Millayne* (vvhere then *Augustine* remayned) he returned in the end by the motion of almightie God, to consider vvhat more grounds the Catholike Religion had, to stay a mans iudgement or cōscience, then the vncertainty of disputations, and findinge the same, resolued himselfe to renoūce all

Aug. l. de moribus Ecclesiæ contra Manicheos.

Aug. confess. lib. 5. cap. 13. & lib. 6. c. 1. 2, 11.

all sects and to be a Catholike, as in his ovvne confessions at large he declareth.

13. By this then vve do see, that albeit disputation rightly vsed, be a good meanes to discouer truth by mouinge doubts to and fro, yet is yt not alvvayes sufficient to resolue and quiett a mans iudgement, euen in naturall thinges: and yf not in these, hovv much lesse in supernaturall and diuine, vvherin humaine disputation hath farre lesse force? For that humaine sciences, deducinge their disputation from principles that are euidently knovvne vnto vs by light of nature, may farre better resolue a man by force of those disputations, and enforce him to yeld his assent, then in matters of diuinity, vvhere the first grounds and principles, are not knovvne to vs by light of nature,

VVhat force disputatiõ hath in resoluing matters of faith.

B 4   as

as in humaine sciences, but are receaued only by light of faith, & reueyled from God : vvherfore these
disputations may serue to examine
and discusse matters, for stirring vp
our vnderstanding, but the resolution & determination, must come
frõ a more certaine meanes vvhich
is infallible, and this vve see practi-
sed in the very first cõtrouersy, that
euer vvas handled in the priuitiue
Church, as is recorded by *S. Luke* in
the Acts of the Apostles, vvhere the
question being, vvhether Christiãs
conuerted of gentills, should be
bound to the obseruation of the
mosayicall lavv or no? there vvas
(saith the text) first *magna conquisitio*,
a great search or disputation about
the matter; and then secondly the
Apostles declared their sentences
in order; and finally the determination vvas in all their names, repre-
senting

Act. 15.

The manner of procee-ding vn-der the Apostles.

senting the vvhole Church, *visum est spiritui sancto & nobis*, yt seemed good to the holy-ghost and vs, and so vvas the matter determined, and the like forme hath byn obserued euer since that tyme in the Cath. Church, determining all côtrouer-sies that haue fallen out, to vvit, that first there should be great search & discussion of the matter, by lavvfull and free disputation, to vvhich end the most learned men of all na-tions are sent cômonly to generall Councells, to performe this point. And secondly all argumêts on both sides being heard & examined, the Bishops presêt do giue their voices, and accordinge to the greater part, vvith concourse & generall appro-bation of the generall head, do they determine *visum est spiritui sancto & nobis.* So as heere disputatiô serueth not to determine but to examine.

14. And

14. And for that the sectaryes of our dayes haue not this found meane to determyne matters, but do depend only vpon probability, and perfuafibility of fpeach, or vvryting one againft the other, *by which* (as *Tully* faith) *nothinge is fo incredible, that may not be made probable* : therfore are their queftions and controuerfies endleffe and indeterminable ; and though they haue had aboue a hundred meetings, conferences, difputations, Councells and fynods from their firft difputation held at *Lypfia*, vpon the yeare 1519. vnto their fynodde in *Vilna*, vpon the yeare 1590. vvhereof yovv may fee more largely in *Staniflaus Refcius* his obferuations : yet could they neuer agree, nor vvill hereafter, lackinge the forfaid meanes of refolution and determination vpon their difputations.

15. And

The wāt which sectaryes haue to determyne matters by *Cicero in Paradox.*

15. And yf this do fall out euen in the learnedst of our sectaryes, that they cannot by disputations alone resolue soundly eyther themselues, or others in matters of cōtrouerfy, for that still there remaine doubts and difficultyes, vvhether matters vvere vvell profecuted or no; and nevv arguments do offer themselues dayly to and fro: vvhat shall vve thinke of the vnlearned and ignorant people, that cannot vnderstand that is argued, and much lesse iudge therof? and yet vpon the creditt of such disputations do aduenture their foules, as yovv haue feene by many lamentable examples before in both mē & vveomen, that vpon the fame & creditt of thefe English disputations heere fett dovvne by Fox, partlie vnder *K. Edward,* & partlie vnder *Queene Mary,* and vpon the probabilitie of fome

The will-
fulnes of
Foxian
vnlear-
ned sectaryes in
disputation

some fond and broken arguments vsed therin for the Proteftants fide, as fomevvhat apparant & plaufible to their fenfes & capacity, haue not only ftood therin moft arrogantly againft their Bifhopps, and learned Paftors by open difputatiõs in their Courts and Confiftoryes, but haue runne alfo to the fire for the fame, vvherof *Allerton*, *Tankerfield*, *Crash-field*, *Fortune*, and others * before mentioned being but *Cooks*, *Carpenters*, and *Coblars* by occupation: yea vveomen alfo as *Anne Alebright*, *Alice Potkins*, *Ioan Lashford*, *Alice Dryuer*, and others may be ridiculous but lamentable examples.

*Menfibus
Ian Mart.
Sept. &
Nouemb.*

16. Neither is this a nevv or ftrange thinge, that hereticall vveomen fhould grovv to fuch infolency, as to ftand in difputation vvith the learnedft Bifhops of the Catholike fide, for that vve read it recorded in

Eccle-

Eccleſiaſticall hiſtoryes aboue 12. hundred yeares gone, to vvitt vpon the yeare of Chriſt 403. that a certayne vvillfull vvoman of the citty of *Antioch* named *Iulia*, infected vvith the abhominable hereſie of the *Manichees* and feruent therein, came vnto the citty of *Gaza*, vvherof *S. Porphyrius* a holy learned man vvas Biſhop, & beginning there to peruert diuers Chriſtians, & being for the ſame reprehended by the Biſhopp, ſhe contemned him, yea chalenged him to open diſputatiō, vvhich the good man admittinge, ſhe behaued herſelfe ſo inſolently therein as vvas intolerable : So as vvhen he had ſuffered her a great vvhile to alleage her blaſphemous arguments, & could by no meanes reduce her or make her harken to the truth, he fell from diſputation to vſe another meane, turning himſelfe

The ſtory of a *Manichean* woman that diſputed vvith a Biſhopp.

felfe to God, fayinge: *O Eternall God which haft created all thinges, and art only eternall, hauinge no beginninge or endinge, who art glorified in the bleffed Trinitie, ftrike this womans tongue, and ftopp her mouth that fhe fpeake no more blafphemyes againft thee.* VVhich vvords being vttered, *Iulia* began to ftammer, and to change countenance, fallinge into an *extafis,* and fo leefing her voyce, remained dumme vntill fhe died, vvhich vvas foone after, vvherat tvvo men and tvvo vveomen that came vvith her fell dovvne at the Bifhopps feete askinge pardon, and vvere conuerted, as vvere diuers gentills alfo by the fame miracle.

17.   And this vvas the conclufion of that difputation; and though it pleafed not almightie God to vfe the like miracles externallie in *Qu. Maryes* dayes, for the repreffinge of thofe

thofe infolēt vveomen that difputed fo malepartlie, and vttered fo
manie blafphemous fpeaches a-
gainft the foueraigne mifterie of
Chrifts reall prefence in the Sacrament; yet can there be no great
doubt, but that invvardlie he vfed
the fame, or no leffe iuftice vnto
them, efpeciallie feing he fuffered
them to go to the fire all vvithout
repentance, and fo to perifh both
bodilie and ghoftlie, temporallie
add eternallie. And for that in re-
cytinge their ftoryes before fett
dovvne, intendinge all breuitie
poffible, I could not conuenientlie
lay forth their feuerall arguments
in difputation, as neyther of thofe
that vvere their maifters and in-
ducers to this maddnes; I haue
thought good heere to examine
all togeather in this *Re-vievv*,
vvhereby yovv fhall fee vvhat
grounds

The caufe of the Edis ion of thefe difputa= ions.

grounds they had of so great an en-
terprise, and of so obstinate a prosecution therof. And this shall suffice
by vvay of *Preface :* Novv vvill vve
passe to the recytall of the said disputations .

O F

OF TEN PVBLIKE

DISPVTATIONS,

*Recounted by Iohn Fox, to haue
byn held in England,*

About Controuersies in Religion, especially
concerning rhe blessed Sacrament of the
Altar, within the space of 4. yeares,
at two seuerall changes of Religion, vnder K *Edward,*
and *Queene Mary;*

*Besides many other more particular, held in Bishops
Consistoryes, and other places, about
the same matters.*

C H A P.   I.

N o v v then to come more neere to the
matter yt selfe, we are breefly to recount the forsaid ten disputations, or
publike meetinges and conferences, that after
the change of the outward face of Catholike
Religion in England, were held in our countrey within the space only of 4. or 5. yeares,
and the effects that ensued thereof, which in
great part were not vnlike to the successe of
all those disputations, meetings, conferences,
colloquies and other attempts of triall before
mentioned, to haue ben with little profitt of
C   agree-

agreement, made in Germany, Polony, France
and other places amongst the Proteſtants of
this age, ſince the beginning of their new ghoſpell, the cauſes and reaſons wherof, haue in
part ben touched by vs in our precedent preface, and ſhall better appeare afterward by the
examination of theſe ten publike diſputatiõs,
from which, as from generall ſtorehouſes, or
head ſchooles, were borrowed the armour &
arguments, for theſe other leſſer bickerings of
particular Foxian Martyrs, which they had
with their Biſhops, Prelates & Paſtors at their
examinations & arraignemẽts, vpon the confidence & pride wherof, they were induced to
offer themſelues moſt obſtinately & pittifully
vnto the fire, as in th'examẽ of *Iohn Fox* his Calendar, you haue ſeene aboundantly declared.

First Diſputation. §. 1.

First di-
ſputation
of *Peter
Martyr* at
Oxford.
I,49.

2. Wherfore to recount the particulars as
breifely as we may, the firſt publike diſputation of theſe ten, wherof we now are to treat,
was held at Oxford againſt the *reall preſence* of
the bleſſed body & bloud of our Sauiour in the
Sacrament of the Altar, by *Peter Martyr* an Italian Apoſtata friar, vpon the yeare of Chriſt
(as Fox ſetteth it downe) 1549. which was the
third of *K. Edward* the ſixt his raigne, about the
moneth of *Iune* for he expreſſeth not the very
day, and the cheife moderator or iudge in this
diſputation, was *D. Cox* Chancelour at that
tyme

tyme of the vniuersity; but after vnder *Q. Eli-*
zabeth was B. of *Ely*, and his assistents were
Henry B. of *Lincolne*, *D. Haynes* deane of *Exceter*;
M. Richard Marison Esquier, and *Christophor Ne-*
uison Doctor of *Cyuill* law; all comissionars (saith
Fox) of the Kings Maiestie, sent downe for
this effect to authorize the disputations.

Fox pag. 1249.

3.   For better vnderstandinge wherof yow
must note, that albeit *K. Edward* had raigned
now more then full two yeares, and that the
protector *Seymer* and some others of his humour, would haue had change of doctrine
established euen at the beginninge, about the
point of the blessed Sacrament; yet could they
not obtayne it in Parlamēt, partly, for that the
farre greater part of the realme was yet against
it, but especially for that it was not yet resolued by the Archbishopp *Cranmer* himselfe, of
whome if you remember, *Iohn Fox* doth com-
plaine in one place vnder *K. Henry*; *that good*
Cranmer had not yet a full feelinge of that doctrine.
Whervpon we see, that in the first parlament
of *K. Edwards* tyme, begon vpon the 4. of *No-*
uember & ended vpon the 14. of *December* 1547.
there was an act made with this title. *An act*
against such persons, as shall vnreuerently speake against
the Sacrament of the body and bloud of Christ, &c.
Wherin magnificent words are spoken of this
Sacrament, and all those greatly reprehended,
that in their sermons, preachings, readings, talks, rymes,
songes, playes, or gestures, did name and call yt,
by such vile and vnseemely words(saith the Statute)
as Christian eares did abhorre to heare yt rehearsed;

Fox pag. 1115 & 1205.

See Statute booke an. 1. Edvv. 6. cap. 1.

C 2   and

and this was the the firſt ſpiritt of that Calui‑
nian humor in England, miſliked by *Cranmer*
and the reſt at that tyme, but ſoone after al‑
Fox *pag.* lowed well by *Iohn Fox* in ſuch of his Martyrs,
1548. as call yt *wormes-meate, idoll,* and the like.

4. And finally this party ſo much preuayled
with them that gouerned, as not longe after,
that is to ſay, in the ſecond parlament begone
Zuingli‑ the 4. of Nouember 1548. and ended the 14.
aniſme ad‑ of March 1549. they gott their new commu‑
mitted. nion booke to be admitted, wherin their new
1546. doctrine alſo againſt the *reall preſence* was con‑
teyned, and then *Peter Martyr,* who, as in his
* *Sup. De-* ſtory we haue * ſhewed, was ſent to Oxford
cemb. 26. before with indifferecy, to teach what ſhould
be ordeyned him from higher powers in that
See *Doctor* parlament, hauing expected all the lent long,
Saunders l. whilſt the parlament endured, what would
2. *de ſchiſm.* be decreed about this point; and finding him‑
Angl. ſelfe in ſtraytes, for that he was come to the
place of *S. Paul* to the Corinthians, where he
1. *Cor.* 11. muſt needs declare himſelfe, receauinge now
aduertiſment of the new decree, did not only
accomodate himſelfe to teach and preach the
The diſ‑ ſame doctrine preſently: (which yet the other
ſemblinge friar, his companion *Martyn Bucer* would not
of *Peter* doe in Cambridge) but alſo was content vpon
Martyr & requeſt & order from the Councell, to defend
Bucer. the ſame in publike diſputations, for better
authorizinge yt through the whole body of
the realme. This then was the occaſion of this
firſt publike diſputation, to giue ſome counte‑
nance and creditt to the new receaued opi‑
nion

nion and paradox of *Zuinglius*, *Oecolampadius*, and *Carolstadius*, three schollers of Luther himselfe, againft the *reall prefence*, which as often yow haue heard before, *Luther* did condemne for damnable herefie, and them for heretiks that mayntayned yt.

Luth. lib. cont Sacrament. & alibi fæpe.

5. The queftions chofen by *Peter Martyr* were three: Firft about Tranfubftantiation, *whether after the words of confecration, the bread and wyne be turned into the body and bloud of Chrift.* The fecond about the reall prefence ; *whether the body and bloud of Chrift be carnally and corporally* (for fo are his words) *in the bread and wyne, or otherwife vnder the kinds of bread and wyne.* The third was: *whether the body and bloud of Chrift be vnited to bread Sacramentally?* But of this laft queftion Fox relateth nothing, that yt was eyther handled or touched in this difputation. About the former two, this manifeft fraud was vfed, that wheras the firft about *Tranfubftantiation*, dependeth of the fecond of the *reall prefence*, it fhould haue byn handled in the fecond place, and not in the firft, as heere yt is; for cleerer conceauing wherof, the Reader muft note, that the mayne controuerfie betweene the Sacramentaryes & vs, is about the reall prefence, to witt whether the true body of Chrift be really and fubftantially in the Sacrament after the words of confecration, which we do hould affirmatiuely, and fo doth Luther alfo, & then fuppofing that it is fo, there followeth a fecond queftion *de modo effendi*, of the manner of Chrifts being there, to witt, whether yt be there to-

Three queftions to be difputed at *Oxford* 1549.

geather

geather with bread, or without bread, or whether the bread be anihilated by the ptesence
of Chrifts body, or whether yt be turned into
the very fubftance of Chrifts body, as we haue

See the
defence of
the relatiō
of *Pleßis*
his difpu-
tation
vvith B.
Peron of
Eureux
tom 2 part.
3. or our
three con-
uerſions,
fhewed out of *Scotus* and *Durand* before, in the
difcufsion of *Pleßis Mornay* his Triall; and euery one of thefe opinions, about the manner of
Chrifts being there, do prefuppofe the *reall prefence,* denyed by the Sacramentaryes: So as to
difpute firft about this particular manner of
Chrift his being there by *Tranfubftantiation,*
before yt be difcuffed whether he be really
there or noe, ys to fett the cart before the
horfe, and the foote before the head.

6.   And yet for that they do perfuade themfelues, that they haue fome more fhifts or
fhewes of probability againft *Tranfubftantiation,*
then againft the *reall prefence,* or can delude better our arguments in the fimple peoples eyes,
they alwayes runne to this, & leaue the other:
And it is, as if the queftion being, firft whether
gold were in a purfe, & then whether yt were
there alone or els togeather with ledd, tynne,
or fome fuch bafer mettall; fome wrangeler
would firft difpute the fecond queftion before
the firft; or as if two demaūds being propounded, firft whether in fuch a veffell (where wat-
ter was knowne to be before) there be wine
put in, and fecondly whether this wine haue
turned that water into it felfe or noe? or that
water & wine do remaine togeather, and that
one would pretermit the firft queftiō, to witt,
whether wine be really & truly there or no? and cauil
only

only about the second, *vvhether the vvater be tur-*
ned into wine, or remaine togeather with the wine? In
which cafes yow fee firft, that this manner of
dealinge were prepofterous and impertinent
wrangling, but efpecially, yf thewrangler did
deny expreffely that there was any gold at all
in the purfe, or wine in the veffell, for then yt
were too too much folly for him to difpute
the fecondary queftions whether the faid gold
were there alone, or with other mettalles; or
whether the wine had côuerted the water into it felfe or no; for yf neither gold nor wine
be really there prefét, then is there no place for
the fecôd difpute at all. And fo fareth it in our
côtrouerfy of the *reall prefence* of Chrifts body.
For if the faid body be not really & fubftâtially
in the Sacramét at all, as the *Zuinglians* & *Cal-*
uinifts do hould; then is it impertinét for them
to difpute the fecond queftion, whether it be
there without bread or with bread, or whether
bread be turned into it or no by *Trâfubftâtiation*,
for fo much as they fuppofe it not to be there
at all; only *Luther* & *Lutherans* may haue côtrouerfy with Catholiks, about the máner how it
is there, feing they beleeue it to be there in
deed; but *Zuingliãs* & *Caluinifts* cánot, but only
about the firft queftion, whether it be there or
noe; which queftion notwithftanding, for fo
much as they fly and runne alwayes to the fecond, as we haue fhewed; notorious it is that
they runne frô the purpofe, & fhew thefelues
not only wráglers but alfo deceauers, feeking
to dazell the eyes of the fimple in this behalfe,

as

Tvvo fi-
militudes
to expreffe
the vayne
vvrâgling
of Sacra-
métaryes
about
Tranfub-
ftantiatiô.

as in this firſt diſputation at *Oxford*, *Peter Mar-tyr* begon with Tranſubſtantiation, and was much longer therein, then in the controuerſie of the reall preſence.

7. And in the ſecond diſputation of *B. Ridley* in *Cambridge*, two only queſtions being propoſed; the firſt was by prepoſterous order of *Tranſubſtantiation*, and the ſecond of the *Sacrifice*; but the *reall preſence* was wholy omytted, and the like in the fourth diſputation vnder *Maiſter Pearne* for the Proteſtants, as after yow ſhall ſee. And when laſtly *Maiſter Ridley* came to reſolue vpon all three diſputations, held vnder him in *Cambridge*, and the queſtions handled therin, he quite paſſeth ouer the controuerſie of *reall preſence*. And ſo yow ſhall obſerue the like tricke in moſt of the other diſputations, and yet (as I ſay) yf there be no reall preſence, the queſtion of Tranſubſtantiation hath no place at all, no nor the ſacrifice neyther, as *Ridley* confeſſeth in his ſaid reſolution, and this for the firſt ſhift of *Peter Martyr* & his fellowes in this diſputation.

Fox *pag.* 1249.

8. The ſecond ſhifte is, that he putteth downe fraudulently the ſecond queſtion about the *reall preſence*, whether the body of Chriſt be there *carnally or corporally*, for albeit we do hold that both *Caro & Corpus*, which is the fleſh and body of Chriſt our Sauiour, be there truly and really, yet not after a fleſhely and corporall manner, as theſe words ſeeme to import, but rather Sacramentally, that is to ſay though *truly*, and *really*, yet *after a Sacramen-tall*

Fraudulēt dealing of Proteſtāts, in diſputation.

2. fraud.

tall and spirituall manner, euen as our soule is in
our body, and an Angell in a corporall place.
And albeit some authors and Fathers do vse
sometymes the word *Corporaliter*, speakinge of
the reall presence, yet do *Fox* and *Martyr* mali-
tiously euery where call *yt a carnall and corporall* See after-
presence, therby to deceaue the simple reader, vvard *c.* 3.
as though yt were there with locall dimen-
sions, after the manner of other bodyes, and
not after a spirituall manner of being.

9.   The third fraude in settinge downe this
first disputation is, that wheras Fox doth tell Fox *pag.*
vs in this place, that the principall disputers *ibid.*
against *Peter Martyr* were *Doctor Tressam, Doctor*
Chadsey, and *Maister Morgan*, yet doth he not tell 3. fraud.
vs one word what they said against him, nor
doth he relate any one of their arguments or
answers, but only the arguments of *Peter Mar-*
tyr against them with triumph, as who would
say, he had gotten the victory without resistance: but yow shall see in the ensuing Chapters, what manner of arguments *Peter Martyrs*
were, and how easy to be answered, as no
doubt but they were by them, yf Fox had
thought good to haue related both parts (as
he ought to haue done) or haue left both parts
out. But this is his ordinary custome of dealing. Wherfore that you may vnderstād partly how the matter went in deed, by the relation of one that was present, to witt *D. Saun-*
ders, I will set downe breefely his words of the
action in generall, as yt passed. Thus then he
wryteth about this first *Oxford* disputation.

10. *Pe-*

Sand.l:b.2.
de schism.
Angl.

10. *Petrus Martyr* (faith he) *&c.* Peter Martyr, of
whome many of the Sectaryes promised to
„ themselues great matters, for that he was pu-
„ blike reader in *Oxford*, being challenged in
„ those dayes by many of that vniuersity,to de-
„ fend his doctrine by disputation, and namely
„ by D. *Rich. Smyth* who had byn his predecessor
„ in the same chaire,neuer durst to yeld thervn-
„ to, vntill he had obtayned that D. *Cox* a secta-
„ ry of his owne side, and a man of very loose
„ life should be sent from the court,to be mode-
„ rator and iudge in the same disputation: And
„ that D. *Smith* was called from the vniuersity,
„ *&c.* But when the said disputation had endu-

D. *Saunders*
relation of
this di-
sputation
at *Oxford*.

red for three dayes,and that *Cox* had seene his
Peter Martyr much more pressed then he looked for, and almost hissed out of the schooles
by all the schollers and hearers, he was forced
„ to say that he was sent for away in all hast to
„ London,& consequently could no longer at-
„ tend to these disputes.Wherfore hauing giuen
„ great praises publikely to *Peter Martyr*, and ad-
„ monished the schollers to keep peace,he brake
„ vp those disputations,& so departed with in-
„ famy in the sight of all men : yet *Peter Martyr*
„ afterward set forth these disputations fraudu-
„ lently, as heretiks are accustomed, and would
„ needs seeme to haue had the victory, but by
„ the iudgment of that vniuersity he was twise
„ vanquished,first in that he durst not encounter
„ D. *Smith*, & secondly for that he could not an-
„ swere the arguments of the other Cath. Doctors. Thus he. Wherby we may perceaue.the
reason

reaſon whereſore Fox would not ſet downe at length the particulars of this firſt diſputation at *Oxford,* as he did of ſome of the others after.

Second Diſputation. §. 2.

11. The ſecond diſputation was held at *Cambridge* about the ſame tyme (ſaith Fox) to witt vpon the 20. of Iune *anno* 1549. the defendant for the Proteſtant ſide was *D. Madew*; the opponents *D. Glyn, M. Langdale, M. Sedgewike,* and *M. Yonge,* the moderator was *D. Ridley* B. of *Rocheſter* at that time, but ſoone after of *London* by depriuation of *D. Bonner.* The commiſſionars ſent from the King to aſſiſt as iudges, beſides the ſaid *Nicolas Ridley,* were *Thomas* B. of *Ely, Syr Iohn Cheke* ſchooimaiſter to the King, a forward Proteſtant in thoſe daies, though vnder *Q. Mary* he left them, *D. May* a Ciuilian, and *D. VVenday* the Kings phiſition. The queſtiōs diſputed were two, as before hath byn ſaid. The firſt, *whether there were any Tranſubſtātiation* & the ſecond, *whether there be any externall & propitiatory ſacrifice in the maſſe.* The queſtion of the *reall preſence,* wherof both theſe do depend, was not handled at all, for the cauſes yow muſt thinke before mentioned, and he that ſhall read ouer this whole diſputatiō, ſhall find it a very cold & trifling thing, much of the time being ſpent in ceremoniall words of courteſy, much in impertinét excurſions frō the purpoſe, out of all ſcholaſticall forme of diſputing or ſtrayning the defendant, & when any thing drew neere

to

The ſecōd diſputation held by *D. Ridley* in *Cambridge.*

Triflinge diſputations of our firſt Proteſtants.

to vrge or preſſe, eyther the moderator would
diuert the ſame by intrudinge himſelfe, or the
proctors by their authority would interrupt
yt. *Heere* (ſaith Fox) *the proctors commaunded the*
opponent to diuerte, &c. And againe, *heere the pro-*
ctors commaunded Langdale to giue place to another.
And further; *heere he was cōmaunded to reply in the*
ſecond matter. And yet further, *heere M. Sedgewike*
was commaunded to ceaſſe to Maiſter Yonge. Which
Yonge, hauinge ſcarce made three inſtances in
proofe of the Sacrifice againſt *Ridley,* ended all
the diſputations with theſe words: *VVell I am*
contented, and do moſt humbly beſeech your good Lor-
ſhipp, to pardon me of my great rudeneſſe & imbecillity
vvhich I haue heere ſhewed, &c. Which indeed
ſheweth great imbecillity, yf he ſaid ſo in
deed, and that Fox hath not made him to
ſpeake as beſt pleaſeth himſelfe.

12.   I could alleage diuers other ſimplicityes
out of this diſputation, yf I would ſtand vpon
them, yea on the part of *Fox* and *Ridley* themſelues; for in one place Fox maketh this note
vpon a certayne anſwere of *Ridley: Heere is to be*
noted (ſaith he) *that Peter Martyr in his anſwere at*
Oxford, did graunt a change in the ſubſtances of bread
and vvyne, vvhich in Cambridge by the Biſhopp Doctor
Ridley vvas denyed. Behould heere the goodly
agreement, that was betweene the firſt founders of Sacramentaryes doctrine in England,
and how worthy to be noted by themſelues.
Friar *Martyr* in *Oxford* graunted a change in the
ſubſtances themſelues of bread and wyne, by
the words of conſecration; but *Biſhop Ridley* in

Fox pag.
1254.

Fox pag.
1255.

Fox no-
teth the
diſagree-
ment of
his ovvne
men.

Cam-

Cambridge denieth the same, so great difference is there betweene *Oxford* and *Cambridge* , the *Friar* and the *Bishopp*: and is not he well holpen vp that hangeth his soule on these mens opinions? this then is one simplicity of Fox, but lett vs heare another of *Ridley* related by Fox his owne pen, in his answere to *Maister Sedgewicke*, who began thus.

13. *Right VVorshippfull Maister Doctor I do aske of yow first of all, whether the Greeke article* (this) *being of the neuter gender, be referred to the vvord* (bread) *or to the word* (body) ? *to the first yt cannot be, for that it is of the masculine gender, ergo to the second.* This was the obiection or demaund, lett vs heare the Bishopps solution. *Forsooth* (saith he) *that article is referred to neyther of both, but may signifie vnto vs any other kind of things.* Thus the Bishopp. So as by this exposition, Christ might as well signifie a staffe, or a stoole, or any garment or thing that lay on the table, or whatsoeuer els any man will diuise, as well as bread, or his body, when he said of bread, *this is my body.* And is not this a Bishopplike aunswere? But of the arguments and aunswers of this second disputation, we shall haue occasion to speake afterwards, when the controuersies themselues shalbe discussed in particular, and so we shall passe forward to recoumpte the other disputations that ensue.

Ridleyes fond aunsvveringe.

Fox pag. 1256.

Third

Third Disputation.   §. 3.

14.   The third disputation was held at *Cambridge* vpon the 23. of Iune in the same yeare 1549. as Fox recounteth, wherin two propositions were held affirmatiuely for the Catholiks, by the aforesaid *D. Glyn* defendant, to witt for the reall presence & sacrifice of the masse. The opponents for the Protestants were *M. Perne*, *M. Gryndall* B. afterwards of *London*, and *Canterbury*, *M. Ghest* and *M. Pilkinton*, which last vnder *Q. Elizabeth* gott the Bishopricke of *Durham*. The moderator and iudges were the same as in the former disputation, to witt *Ridley* and his fellowes, and the manner and forme not much vnlike, though somewhat more disorderly, each one puttinge in his verdict to and fro at his pleasure. But yet whosoeuer shall peruse the same vvith equality, will easily perceaue an eminent difference for learninge, discretion and clere aunsweringe betweene the said *Doctor Glyn* and his opponents, which principally is to be attributed to the difference of his cause from theirs; they neuer prosecuting commonly one *medium* for aboue one or two instances, but leaping presently to another: so graue and substantiall a disputation was this for poore people that heard yt, or heard of yt, and followed the resolution therin sett downe, to hange their soules vpon the certaynty therof.

Maister

15. *Maister Perne* beginneth with a complaint, against *D. Glyn*, that he had left *Transubstantiation* & taken vpon him to defend the reall presence in the Sacrament, *vvheras we deny nethinge lesse* (saith he) *then his corporall presence or absence of his substance in the bread.* Wherby yt is euidently seene, that *Maister Perne* was not of *Ridleyes* opinion, but held the reall presence, though with *Luther* perhaps he did not beleeue *Transubstantiation*: and this is euident by his arguments which after he vsed, nothinge in deed against the *reall presence*, but only to proue that Christ his body was togeather with bread. The like manner of impertinent dealinge vsed *Ridley* himselfe in diuers of his arguments; as for example: *this is that bread* (saith he) *vvhich came downe from heauen, ergo, yt is not Christs body, for that his body came not from heauen*: which proueth also that yt was not bread, for that *Ridley* will not say (I thinke) that the materiall bread which Christ had in his hand, came downe from heauen. The like argument vseth *Pilkinton* thus: *vvheresoeuer* (saith he) *Christ is, there be his ministers also, for so he promised: but Christ as you hould is in the Sacrament, ergo his ministers are there also.* Which were a foule incouenience as you see, if all our English ministers should be in the Sacrament for the poore people to byte at. And yet this argument seemeth so graue vnto Iohn Fox, as he maketh this marginall note theron. *VVhere Christ is, there are his ministers.* And the poore fellow hath not so much witt, as to see that those words of Christ were meant

of

D. Perne confesseth the corporall presence of Christ in the Sacrament.

Fox pag. 1257.

Fond arguments of Sacramentaryes.

of his glory in the life to come, and not of the Sacrament which is ministred vpon earth.

16.   But to the end yow may the better perceaue, how disorderly this and the former disputation at *Cambridge*, was made by the new Protestants to ouerbeare the Catholike cause, I shall sett downe some lynes of a narration of *D. Langdale*, Archdeacon of *Chichester*, a *Cambridge* man who was present at the said disputation, and confuted afterward in print the said *Ridleyes* determination vpon these disputations. Thus then he wryteth: *Vix dum finita Collegiorum visitatione, &c.* The Colledges of Cambridge were no sooner visited by the Kinges Commissionars, but there appeared

Albanus Langlandus in confut. Determ. Nicol. Ridley.

„ vpon all the gates two conclusions sett vp, the
„ first against *Transubstantiation*, the other against
„ *the sacrifice of the masse*, and presently the bedells
„ of the vniuersity went about to giue warning,
„ that yf any man had any thinge to say against
„ these conclusions, he should come forth the
„ third day after, (which was *Corpus Christi* day,)
„ to dispute, or otherwise all to be bound to
„ perpetuall silence for euer after. The con-
„ course of noble men, & all other degrees was
„ great, and scaffolds made for the place of di-
„ sputation that the multitude might the better
„ heare : but all that were indifferent, did see
„ matters to be handled with great inequality;
„ for that whosoeuer spake for the Catholike
„ side presently his speach was eyther interrup-
„ ted, or for breuity shifted of to another tyme,
„ and *Ridley* that was the Captayne of all step-

pinge

pinge in at euery turne to afsist his defendant, „
did eyther with threates or fayre words, or by „
scoffes and bytter taunts seeke to diuert the „
Catholike disputers. „

17. And when the first dayes disputation „
was in this manner ended, yt was denounced „
to the auditory, before the dismission of the „
schooles, that yf any man would come forth **The par-**
and defend within a day or two, the Catho- **tiall dea-**
like parte of those questions, he might, but af- **linge of**
terwards it should not be lawfull for any man **in their**
to speake therof : which vnexpected denun- **disputa-**
tiation being heard, one man looked vpon **tions.**
another, and all for a tyme were silent, vntill „
at length a most learned and graue man, pious „
and skillfull, as well in knowledge of the „
tongues, as also in diuinity, wherof he had „
byn there publike reader before (to witt *Do-* „
ctor Glyn) stept forth and offered himselfe to „
the combatt, and performed yt the third day „
after, takinge the place of defendant without „
help of any moderator, but all rather against „
him, beginning his declaration, (which *Cam-* „
bridge men call his *position*) with the words of „
the Prophett : *Credidi propter quod locutus sum.* **Psalm. 115.**
And the Protestants were so vrged in these „
disputations about the *reall presence*, that not- „
withstandinge they auoyded and dissembled „
that question so much as they could, yet were „
they driuen to such shifts, to putt of the cleere „
places & authorityes of ancient Fathers about „
the same, as was ridiculous to heare ; for that „
sometymes they said Christs body was present „

in the

,, in the Sacrament by signification, then by re-
,, prefentation, then by meditation, then by ap-
,, pellation, fometymes by propriety, other
,, tymes by nature, then by power, then againe
,, by grace, then by memory or remembrance,
,, then by vertue & energy, and by many other
,, diuifes of deluding or fhifting of the matter.
,, All which being done, and another third day
,, of difputation paffed ouer in like manner,
,, *Ridley* tooke vpon him to giue the determina-
,, tion of all, as though he had gotten the victo-
,, ry. Thus farre out of *Doctor Langelands* booke;
,, wherby may be gathered how the matter
,, paffed in thefe difputations.

Fourth Difputation.   §. 4.

18.   The fourth difputation was held alfo in
Cambridge foone after the former, wherin, ac-
cording to Fox his relation, the forfaid *Maifter
Perne* was defendant for the Proteftants, and
the opponents for the Catholike part, were
Maifter Parker, *Maifter Pollard*, *Maifter Vaucfour*,

and *Maifter Yonge*: the moderator and iudges
was *Maifter Ridley* of *Rochefter* togeather with
his fellowes aforementioned: the two queftions were about *Tranfubftantiation*, and the
Sacrifice; the other of the *reall prefence* was pre-
termitted (according to the former declared
fleight) though yt were the principall and the
ground, wheron thefe other two do depend,
& concerneth the very fubftance of the *Zuim-*
                                           glian

glian and *Caluinian* sect, now newly set vp and authorized by these disputations, and consequently should first and principally haue byn discussed, yf eyther good method or shew of true dealinge had byn obserued. But *D. Perne* the defendant beleeued the *reall presence*, as in the former disputation yow haue heard him protest, though in this disputation he sought to expound himselfe in these words: *I graunt that Christ is in the Sacrament truly, wholy and verily after a certayne property and manner. I deny not his presence, but his reall, and corporall presence.* But this is a difference without a diuersity (by *M. Pernes* licence) for yf Christs body be there *truly, wholy and verily*, he must also be there *really*, as to euery mans common sense and reason is euident; and so *Maister Perne* by this distinction sheweth, that he beleeued nothing at all really, truly, or verily at that tyme, yf his heart were accordinge to his words.

D. *Pernc* speaketh doubtfully & doubly about the Sacramēt.

19. And albeit, as I haue said, *Maister Perne* propoundeth the questions of *Transubstantiation* & *sacrifice of the masse*, yet when they came to ioyne issue, their speach was most of all about the *reall presence*, and I call yt a speach rather then disputation, for that yt had neyther order, method, nor substance in yt, but was a most ridiculous colloquy of one to another, without vrginge or answeringe any one argument substantially, but as little beagles lyinge togeather, one starteth vp and giueth a barke or two, and lyeth downe againe; so these disputers, aunswerers, and moderator

The fond manner of this disputation.

D 2 handled

handled the matter; as for example, M. *Parker*
being to argue first, began to alleage three
vayne reasons (as Fox calleth them in the
margent) for the *reall presence*, to witt, that yt
was *prophesyed promised*, and *performed* as he proued by diuers places of scripture, which being
done Iohn Fox, without tellinge vs any aunswere at all giuen by *Maister Perne*, hath these
words. *Heere they were forced to breake of through
the want of tyme*, yet Maister Parker *replyed thus*

Fox pag.
1260.

with a prayer against Maister Perne ; *vve giue thee
thankes most holy Father, that thou hast hidden these
things from the wise and prudent, and hast reueyled
them to babes, for pride is the roote of all heresies whatsoeuer, &c.*

20.   Now heere I vvould aske Iohn Fox
what he meaneth by this note ; *that they were*

Contradi-
&ction in
Fox his
vvords.

forced to breake of for lacke of tyme? and yet that
Parker replyed, and began his reply with a
prayer? For yf they brake of, how did he reply, especially his reply being somewhat long?
And yf he replyed in so large a manner as Fox
setteth it downe, how did they breake of?
& how ridiculous a thing is it, that a sollemne
disputation being begon in presence of the
whole vniuersity, and of so great an audience,
and *Maister Parker* being the first opponent, the
matter should be broken of without hearing
any one answere of the defendant? But these
are Fox his fooleryes, and these were the first
and most firme foundations of our new Caluinian sect in England. Many other particulars might be sett downe, especially of *Ridleyes*
mode-

moderatinge, who at euery turne made himſelfe defendant & anſwered farre worſe then
Perne himſelfe, but we ſhall haue better occaſion to touch the ſame afterward, when we
ſhall examine more particularly what paſſed
about euery controuerſie, in each of theſe diſputations; only *Vaueſour* of all the opponents
ſeemeth to haue ſpoken beſt to the purpoſe
(as Fox relateth him) for that he alleaged an
authority of *S. Auguſtine in Pſalm.*98. which *Rid-*
ley, not able to anſwere, ridiculouſly ſhifteth
of as yow ſhall ſee afterwards, when yt commeth in ranke to be examined, and in his preface he cited two ſayings of *Zuinglius* and *Oeco-*
lampadius, of their owne doubtfullneſſe at the
beginninge, in the doctrine with they firſt
broached againſt the *reall preſence.* Zuinglius
his words are : *Albeit this thinge that I meane to*
treat of, doth like me very well; yet notwithſtandinge
I dare define nothinge, but only ſhew my poore iudge-
ment abroad to others,&c. Oecolampadius his words
are wrytinge to his brother. *Peace be with thee.*
As farre as I can coniecture out of the ancient Fathers,
theſe words of Chriſt (this is my body) *is a figura-*
tiue locution, &c. Thus they at the beginninge
very doubtfully, as yow ſee, but afterward,as
thoſe that tell lyes ſo often, as at length they
beginne to beleeue them to be true themſelues, ſo did theſe men; and yet others were
ſo fooliſh as to follow them in their doubtfull
fancyes, a pittifull caſe in the cauſe of our
ſoule. Well, *Iohn Fox* concludeth this whole
diſputation with theſe words : *Heere endeth*

D 3　　　　　(ſaith

M. *Vaua-*
ſour com-
mended.

Zuinglius
and *Oeco-*
lampadius
doubtfull
of their
doctrine
at the be-
ginninge.

Fox pag.
1261.

54   *A review of ten publike*
(saith he) *the third and last disputation holden at*
Cambridge 1549.

Fifth Disputation. §. 5.

The 5. di-
sputation
or deter-
mination
at *Cam-
bridge* by
M. Ridley.

21. The fifth disputation was the publike determination made by *B. Ridley*, as iudge and moderator vpon the questions, before handled in the three disputations of *Cambridge*, vvhich determinatiō I do reckon among the number of the other disputations publike, and colloquyes, both for that yt was made vpon a seuerall day most sollemnely, and with no lesse concourse of people then the former, as also for that yt setteth downe all the heads of his principall arguments, as the first disputation doth those of *Peter Martyr*, though without the answers or replyes of his aduersaryes. And indeed this being a collection of all the substantiall points, of whatsoeuer had byn alleaged by the Protestants in all three disputations, as also whatsoeuer himselfe could adde thervnto; and being done with so great study & deliberation, as to be deliuered in the greatest concourse and expectation of people (for the nouelty therof) that euer perhaps were seene togeather in *Cambridge* before; yt being the first publike determination against the truth of Christs sacred body in the Sacramēt, that euer that vniuersity, from her first foundation had heard of: For all these reasons and respects (I say) this determination may perhaps

haps be numbred amongſt one of the moſt
follemne conferences, or diſputations held
by the Sacramentarye Proteſtants in our
countrey.

22. *Ridley* then began the aſſembly with theſe
words: *There hath byn an ancient cuſtome amonge*   Fox pag.
you, that after diſputatiōs had in your common ſchooles,   1261.
*there ſhould be ſome determination made of the matter
diſputed and debated, eſpecially touching Chriſtian Religion, becauſe therfore it is ſeene good to theſe worſhip-
full aſſiſtants, ioyned with me in commiſſion from the
Kings Maieſtie, that I ſhould performe the ſame at this
tyme, I will by your fauourable patience declare, both*   Ridley his
vvhat I do thinke and beleeue my ſelfe, and what all   entrance
other ought to thinke of the ſame, vvhich I vvould that   to his de-
afterward ye did with diligence weigh and ponder, eue-   termina-
ry man at home ſeuerally by himſelfe, &c. This is his   tion.
preface, wherin yow may note firſt, what a
different aſſurance it is for a man, to repoſe the
ſaluation of his ſoule vpon this new beleefe
and thinkinge of *Maiſter Ridley,* which was not
yet as yt ſeemeth full three or foure yeares old
with him (for vntill *K. Henryes* death he was
euer held of another opinion) or vpon the generall determination, learninge, iudgement,
piety, & conſent of the worthieſt in the Chriſtian world, aſſembled togeather in councells,
wherof ten, (as in our preface we haue tou-   Diuers cō-
ched, and ſhall againe afterward) had deter-   ſideratiōs
mined for the *reall preſence* in the ſpace of the   about the
laſt 500. yeares, before this contrary determi-   vncertain-
nation of *Ridley,* to witt after the queſtion was   ty of Pro-
once moued by *Berengarius,* vntill yt was mo-   teſtants
                       D 4   ued   beliefe.

ued againe by *Zuinglius* and *Oecolampadius*; lett
euery difcreet man, I fay, confider what a dif-
ferēce this is, for a man to aduenture his foule
and euerlaftinge inheritance theron. For yf a
man had demaunded of *Ridley* himfelfe 4.or 5.
yeares before this day, what a man *was bound to
thinke and beleeue* in this point for fauinge his
foule , he would haue faid the quite contrary
to that he determineth now.

23.   Secondly yow may confider another
difference in this priuate determination , of
Ridley & his affociates from that of Catholike
Councells , for that Councells after enquiry
and difputations made for the truth, do determyne by generall confent of the Bifhopps
affembled, with affured afſiſtance of the holy
ghoft ; wheras *Maifter Ridley* remytteth all to
the priuate iudgement *of euery one at home, feue-
rally by himfelfe*; which is as much to fay , notwithftanding all the difputation , and his determination, yet muft euery man and woman
follow their owne fancy *at home*, and be iudge
of all that hath byn difputed, or determyned:
& this is the certainty that Proteftants haue
for common people to rely vpon.

24.   Thirdly yt is to be noted, that notwithftanding Fox calleth this decifion, *the determination of Doctor Nicolas Ridley B. of Rochefter, vpon
the conclufions aboue prefixed*, yet handleth he only
two queftions in this his determination videlicet; *Tranfubftantiation*, and the *Sacrifice of the Altar*, but the firft much more amply and aboundantly, pretermitting the very cheefe & principall

cipall queſtion in deed, wherof all the reſt dependeth, which is of the *reall preſence*, which
maketh the very eſſence of *Caluinian* and *Zuinglian* ſect, wherby they do differ from both
Lutherans and vs : of which abſurd impoſture
we haue ſpoken ſufficiently before, and ſeing
ſo much had byn ſaid in the former diſputations about that point, though greatly againſt
the Proteſtants inclination, me thinketh he
ought not to haue left out wholy that queſtion in this his determination. But as I haue
often ſaid, their principall ſhift in thoſe dayes
was to ſtepp from the mayne point, whether
Chriſt were really in the Sacrament or no; &
to leape vnto a quiddity of the manner of his
being there, to witt by Tranſubſtantiation. Fiue pre-
About which notwithſtandinge. *B. Ridley* be- tended
heades of
ginneth his reſolution with great oſtentation Ridleyes
of words ſayinge; that he had fiue principall determi-
nation.
grounds or head ſprings for the ſame: *Firſt* (to 1.
vſe his words) *the authority. Maieſtie, and verity of
the ſcriptures: ſecondly the moſt certayne teſtimonyes of* 2.
ancient Catholike Fathers: thirdly the definition of a 3.
Sacrament: fourthly the abhominable hereſie of Eu- 4.
tiches, that may enſue of Tranſubſtantiation: fifthly, 5.
the moſt ſure beleefe of the article of our faith; he aſcended into heauen, *&c.*

25. Theſe be *Maiſter Ridleyes* fiue bulwarks or
caſtles of defence builded in the ayre, which
he handleth ſo fondly and childiſhely, as after
yow ſhall ſee in the particular examinations
of his arguments. Only heere I will ſay in
generall, that the reader ſhall find his *authority,*
Maieſtie,

maieſtie, and *verity* of ſcriptures againſt Tranſubſtantiation, to be a meere vaunt and vanity, for he hath no one cleere or ſubſtantiall
place at all. And as for his certayne teſtimonyes of the ancient Fathers, they will proue
ſo vncertaine for his purpoſe, as yow ſhall ſee
them moſt certaynely againſt him. His third
caſtle of the definition of a Sacrament, vvill
proue a cottage of no ſtrength at all, for that
the true nature of a Sacrament ſtandeth well
vvith Tranſubſtantiation. His fourth head
ſpringe about the hereſie of *Eutiches*, will proue
a puddle, and himſelfe puzzeled therin, for
that the hereſie of *Eutiches* confoundinge two
diſtinct natures in Chriſt, hath no more coherence vvith *Tranſubſtantiation*, then *Rocheſter*
with *Rome*. And finally his laſt ground about
the article of Chriſts aſcendinge into heauen,
hath no ground to reſt on, but is a meere imagination in the ayre, to witt, that for ſo much
as Chriſt aſcended into heauen, *ergo* there is
no Tranſubſtantiation.

26.   Wherfore to leaue this firſt queſtion of
Tranſubſtantiation, and paſſe to the ſecond of
ſacrifice, yow muſt vnderſtand, that when
Maiſter Ridley had ſpent moſt of the time about
Tranſubſtantiation, he had little left concerning
the ſacrifice of the maſſe, but concluded his ſaid
determination in very few words thus: *Now
for the better concluſion* (ſaith he) *concerning the ſacrifice, becauſe yt dependeth vpon the firſt, I will in few
vvords declare what I thinke. Two things do perſuade
me, that this concluſion* (againſt the ſacrifice of the
maſſe)

*Ridleyes
reſolution
about the
ſacrifice of
the maſſe.*

*Fox pag.
1262.*

masse) *is true, that is certayne places of scripture, and
certayne testimonyes of the Fathers.* Lo heere the
graue and weighty motiues that *Ridley* had, to
aduenture vpon so great a change in beleefe
as this was, after so many yeares, being a
Priest and Catholike Bishopp, and offeringe
sacrifice after the manner of the Catholike
Church, from the first day of our contreyes
conuersion, vnto th'end of K. Henryes raigne.
His motiues were, as yow heare, *certayne places
of the scripture,* which were only taken out of
the Epistle to the Hebrues, talkinge of Christs   *Hebr. 9. &*
bloudy sacrifice on the crosse, which was but   *10.*
one, & certayne places of the Fathers, to witt,
two or three misvnderstood out of *S. Augustine,*   The mise-
and one out of *Fulgentius,* all which notwith-   rable pro-
standinge proue nothinge for his purpose, as   ceeding of
after yow shall see declared in their place, and   *Ridley.*
turne. And the selfe same Fathers haue so ma-
ny other cleere places to the contrary, as we
will desire no better iudges for proofe of our
Catholike cause, then yf *Ridley* would remitt
himselfe to these two Fathers iudgements, by
him cyted against vs; for that both of them do
professe themselues to be Priests, and to offer
externall sacrifice, vpon the Altar as our
Priests do now.

27.   Consider then how wise and constant a
man *Ridley* was, to leaue his ancient faith so
generally receaued throughout all Christendome in his dayes, and so many yeares practi-
sed by himselfe, vpon two such motiues, as
are *certayne places of scripture misvnderstood by himselfe,*

felfe, and certayne teſtimonyes of *Fathers*, that ſeemed to him to haue ſome difficulty. Which
leuity vvas ſo diſpleaſaunt vnto almighty
God, as by the effects we ſee, that wheras at
the beginning he ſeemed to doubt vpon theſe
two motiues, leauinge other men to iudge
therof, he became by little and little to be ſo
obſtinately blinded at length therin, as albeit
ſome foure or fiue yeares after, he were openly conuicted in diſputations at *Oxford*, as by
his anſwers yow ſhall afterwards ſee, yet was
he content to burne for the ſame, which was
the higheſt degree of calamity that could fall
vpon him, in body and ſoule. And thus much
of him and his determination for the preſent.

Sixt Diſputation.   §. 6.

The ſixt
diſputatiõ
at *Cam-
bridge* by
Bucer 1549.

28. In all the former diſputations both at
Oxford and *Cambridge*, yow ſhall find nothinge
of friar *Martyn Bucer*, no not ſo much as that he
is once named in all theſe conflicts, about the
bleſſed Sacrament. And yet yow muſt remember, that he was principall reader of diuinity
in *Cambridge* at this tyme, as *Peter Martyr* was
in *Oxford:* and therfore as the firſt place was
giuen to the ſaid *Peter* in *Oxford*; ſo yt is likely,
that the ſame would haue byn to *Martyn* in
Cambridge, yf they had found him ſo pliable to
their hands in his opinions about the Sacrament, as the other was ; but in no caſe would
he be induced as yet, to accommodate himſelfe

felfe therin , and therfore had he not any part
allowed him in this comedy, eyther of defendant, opponent, difputer, counfelour, moderator, afsiftant, or other office or imployment:
nay yt is thought that he incurred fo great
difgrace about this matter , as he could willingly haue departed the realme againe , (as
Bernardinus Ochinus vpon fuch like difcontent-
ment did from London) had not the necefsity of his woman , and other impediments of
pouerty letted him, not knowinge well whither to goe, as being expulfed from *Argentina* at
his comming to England, as * before we haue
fhewed in the ftory of his life.

Martyn Bucer in great di-ftreffe.

'Menfe Decemb. cap. 16.

29.   Wherfore refoluinge himfelfe at length
to paffe ouer this mortification , and to giue
our Englifh Proteftants fome fatisfaction,
though not in the points which they defired,
he thought it good after *Ridleyes* departure, to
defend certayne other paradoxes, which Fox
recordeth in thefe words: *Ouer and befides thefe
difputations aboue mentioned , other difputations vvere
holden in Cambridge fhortly after by* Martyn Bucer, *vpon thefe conclusions followinge:* Firft, *that the
canonicall bookes of fcripture alone, do fufficiently teach
the regenerate all things neceffary belonginge to faluation.*
Secondly, *there is no Church on earth that erreth not, as well in faith, as in manners.* Thirdly *we
are fo iuftified freely of God , that before our iuftification , yt is finne and prouoketh Gods wrath againft vs,
whatfoeuer good worke we feeme to do. Then being iuftified, we do good works.*

Fox pag. 1262. & 1263.

1.

2.

3.
The que-ftions of Bucers di-fputatiõ.

30.   Thefe were *Bucers* conclufions, which
          well

well I may call paradoxes, for that euen in the common sense & iudgement of euery meane capacity, the falsity and absurdity therof is apparant. For as touching the first, though we graunt, that the diuine books of scripture, yf they were fewer then they are (respectinge Gods holy prouidence) are sufficient to teach both regenerate and not regenerate (that beleeue the verity therof) the true way of saluation, and that the said diuine prouidence hath, doth, and will so prouide, that albeit some parts of these we now haue should be lost (as diuers others before haue byn) yet should the remnant still be sufficient to that purpose, with such other supplyes of Gods assistance as he would send; yet to say, as this

Howv scriptures are sufficient to saluation.

man doth, *that the canonicall bookes of scripture alone, do sufficiently teach all things belonginge to saluation*; yt by *alone* he will exclude all other helpes of tradition, antiquity, testimony of the Church, interpretation of the Fathers, direction of generall Councells, and other like aydes, yt is a most absurd paradox; for neyther can we know which bookes are to be held canonicall, nor what they teach truly & sincerely, nor what may be deduced out of them; yf we remoue the former helpes; And the case is, as yf one of the Kings of our countrey goinge abroad, as some did to *Hierusalem*, or other forrayne warres, and intending to be longe absent, should leaue with his Councellors for their better gouernement certayne lawes wrytten with his owne hand, & other

dire-

A case re-
presen-
tinge the
heretiks of
our dayes
about cry-
inge for
scriptures
alone.

directions by word of mouth how to proceed, interprett, and vse them, commaunding
all men to obay them, and that some trouble-
some people after many yeares continuance
in their gouernement, should appeale from
them, to the Kings wrytten lawes only, praysinge the sufficiency therof (for better colou-
ringe their pretence) and suinge that yt were
a blott vnto the said lawes, and to the Kings
wisdome that made them, to acknowledge
any insufficiency at all in them for perfe&t direction of the common welth, which lawes
yet, themselues would expound, as pleased
them best for their owne purposes.

31. In this case, who seeth not whervnto this
practise tendeth, and for what causes so great
prayses are giuen to the sufficiency of these
lawes, vsed to make the praisers iudges of all,
and to exempt them from all controlment of
others? And the very same is seene in the
other case of the scriptures, which being written by the spiritt and fingar of God himselfe,
and deliuered vnto vs by the Church, whose
commission also and authority in the same
scriptures is sett downe, byndinge vs vnder
damnation to heare her from age to age, as the
pillar *and firmament of truth*, there stepp vp togeather diuers sorts of sectaryes in all ages, &
of this of ours, *Lutherans, Zuinglians, Caluinists,
Anabaptists, Trinitarians,* and the like chalenged
by the said Church of disobedience, and do all
appeale ioyntly and seuerally from her, to only scriptures, praysinge highly the sufficiency,
and

Matt. 18.
1 Tim 3.
Marc. vlt.
Matt. 16.

and excellency therof, and refuiinge all other meanes, eyther of tradition or ancient exposition, for vnderftandinge of the fenfe and true meaninge. And when we alleadge the Catholike Doctors and Paftors of euery age, as fpirituall Gouernours and Confelors vnder God in the Church, for explaninge his diuine will and meaninge in this behalfe; they refufe all, and only will be interpreters and expofitors themfelues, and this not only againft the Catho. Church, which they ought to obay, but one fect alfo againft another for their particular opinions, and diuerfityes, which by this meanes are made irreconciliable, and indeterminable, as experience teacheth vs. For when, I pray yow, will Luther & Zuinglius or their followers, come to any accord eyther with vs, or amongft themfelues by only canonicall fcriptures, expounded after each partyes particular fpiritt, iudgement and affection? The like I may aske of Anabaptifts & Arrians, Englifh Proteftants and Puritans, or of any other Sectaryes that yow can name vnto me, which neuer agreed by this way, nor euer will. And this is the firft paradox of *Martyn Bucer*, that only fcriptures are fufficient to teach euery man.

22.   The fecond is yet worfe (yf worfe may be) to witt; *that there is no Church on earth, which erreth not as well in faith as manners.* Which yf yt be fo, then erreth alfo in faith the true Church of Chrift, and is a lvinge Church, and may lead vs into error and herefie. And of this yt followeth

The fecōd paradox of *Martyn Bucer.*

followeth againe, that we can haue no certainty of any thinge in this life, and that almighty God doth damne vs very vniuftly for
herefie, wherinto we may be brought by his
true Church, and fpoufe, which on the other
fide, he hath commaunded *vs to heare, and obay* *Matth.18.*
vnder payne of damnation; yt followeth alfo that
S. *Paul* did falfely call the Church, *the pillar and* *1.Tim.* 3.
firmament of truth; for as much as yt may both
deceaue and be deceaued. Chrifts promife al-
fo was falfe, when he affured his Church, *that* *Marc. vlt,*
he weuld be with her by his fpiritt of truth vnto the
worlds end; and that, *the gates of hell fhould not pre-* *Matth.16.*
uaile againf her. All thefe abfurdityes, impofsibilityes and impietyes, do follow of this fecond paradox, befides infinite others, which
any meane capacity may deduce of himfelfe.
33.   The third paradox alfo is no leffe monftrous to common fenfe and reafon, then the The third
two former, to witt, *that vvhatfoeuer good worke* paradox of
any man doth, or may feeme to doe before iuftification, Martyn
is finne, and prouoketh Gods wrath. But I would Bucer.
aske this new opiniatour or paradox-defen-
der, how he would anfwere to that of *Exodus,*
where yt is faid of the Egyptian mid-wyues
(infidells no doubt) *quia timuerunt obftetrices* *Exod.* 1.
Deum, ædificauit illis domos. God gaue them a-
boundant children, for that vpon feare of offendinge almighty God, they difobayed their
King *Pharao* in fauinge the Hebrues children.
doth God vfe to reward finne? or to prayfe
that which prouoketh his wrath? Againe, the
Prophett *Ezechiell* fheweth vs how God did

E   tem-

Ezech. 20. temporally reward *Nabuchodonozor* and his army with the spoyle of Egypt, for that they had serued him faithfully in chastizinge of

*Hier. in
Comment.
in cap.* 20.
Ezech. *Tyrus.* And *S. Hierome* vpon that place hath these words: *By that Nabuchodonosor receaued this reward for his good worke, we learne that gentills also yf they do any good thinge, shall not leese their reward at Gods hands*; and how can God be said to reward that which offendeth him? The Prophet *Daniell* also to the same *Nabuchodonosor* an

Dan. 4. infidell, gaue this counsell, *peccata tua eleemosynis redime*: redeeme thy synnes with almes, which he would neuer haue done, yf yt had byn a synne, & prouoked Gods wrath to giue almes, or to performe any such other morall vertue before iustification, especially being styrred & holpen thervnto by Gods especiall help, which may be before iustification, as *Martyn Bucer* in this paradox supposeth. And lastly not to stand any longer in this which is of it selfe so euident; I would aske friar *Martyn*, whether *Cornelius* the centurion being yet a gentile, did sinne and prouoke Gods wrath in prayinge, and giuinge almes before his conuersion? Yf he say yea (as needs he must accordinge to his doctrine) the text of scripture is against him, for the Angell said vnto him:

Act. 10. *Thy prayers and almes deeds, haue ascended vp, and haue byn called into remembrance in the sight of God.*

*Aug. l. de
prædestinat.
sanct cap* 7.
& lib. 1. *de
Baptis c.* 3.
& l.4.c.23. Vpon which words *S. Augustine* in diuers of his works, doth call the said almes-deeds of *Cornelius*, before he beleeued in Christ, *Iustice, and the gifts of God*, which he would neuer haue

done,

done,yf they had byn ſynnes,and *prouoked Gods wrath* , as this new-fangled friar hath taken vpon him to defend.

34. And this ſhalbe ſufficient for this ſixt diſputation of *Martyn Bucer,* which is fiue tymes as much,as Fox ſetteth downe of the ſame,for that he relateth only the time and place of the ſaid diſpute , togeather with the concluſions afore mentioned, & that *Sedgewicke,Yonge,* and *Perne* were opponents to *Bucer* therin ; but all the reſt he remitteth to a larger diſcourſe at another tyme , ſupplyinge the breuity of this Bucerian diſputation , with another diſpute betweene cuſtome and verity, which he calleth: *A fruitfull dialogue , gathered out* (ſaith Fox) *of the Tractations of Peter Martyr , and other authors, by a certayne reuerend perſon of this realme, teachinge all men not to meaſure Religion by cuſtome , but to try cuſtome by truth, &c.*

Fox *pag.* 1263.

35. And this was another diuiſe of thoſe dayes of Innouations and noueltyes,to dazell ſimple mens eyes, as though *Cuſtome* and *Verity,* the handmayd and maiſtreſſe, were ſo fallen out,that one impugned the other,& could not agree or ſtand togeather any longer , and conſequently *cuſtome* and *antiquity,* muſt needs giue place to *nouelty* ; the fraud and folly of which diuiſe may in very few words be diſcouered, and their true frendſhipp and agreement eaſily be declared; yea their inſeparable coherence to be ſuch,as in our caſe of the controuerſie about the *reall preſence* (for in this point they are made to braule and full out)

An altercation betvveene cuſtome & verity.

E 2　they

they cannot pofsibly be feparated For yf verity in this matter haue not antiquity and cuftome with yt, yt is nouelty, and by confe-
quence not verity at all. And on the otherfide,
cuftome in points of Chriftian faith and beleefe, yf yt be generall, and of long tyme (for
otherwife yt cannot properly be called cuftome, in the fubiect we handle)may not pof-
fibly be found in our Chriftian Church without verity, for that otherwife the whole
Church fhould vniuerfally admitt a falfity, &
continue yt by cuftome, which to imagine
were folly and madneffe, yea moft infolent
madnes, yf vve beleeue *S. Auguftine*, whofe
words are: *Difputare contra id, quod tota per orbem
frequentat Ecclefia, infolentißima infania eft* . It is a
„ moft infolent madnes to difpute againft that,
„ which the whole Church throughout the
„ world doth practice. And he addeth in the
fame place,*though it be not coteined in the fcriptures.*
   36.   Wherfore for *Iohn Fox*, and his reuerend
maifter *Nicolas Ridley, Peter Martyr* and others,
to come out now with a dialogue or brauling
altercation, betweene *cuftome* and *verity* about
the matter of the Sacrament, and to feeke to
fett them by the eares, or make a diuorfe betweene them,for that cuftome had continued
from the beginning of our conuerfion to that
day without verity, was a very fimple and ridiculous diuife, & worthy Iohn Fox his witt
and grauity,for by this he confeffeth in effect,
that cuftome and antiquity was againft him,
wherof we in this matter do rightly alfo inferre,

Aug. epift.
118. ad Ia-
nuar.

Cuftome
and verity
cannot be
at odds in
the Chri-
ftian
Church.

ferre, verity I ſay in this matter concerninge
Chriſtian faith and beleefe, receaued in the
Church by cuſtome and tradition of former
ages, which our Sauiour Chriſt did promiſe
to aſsiſt with his ſpiritt of truth, whatſoeuer
Fox or his fellowes may obiect, or we admitt,
againſt Idolatry or other reprehenſible cuſtomes of former tymes amongſt the Iewes,
gentills, nations, contreyes, and common-
welthes different from the Chriſtian Church;
all which had no ſuch aſſurance of truth, for
beginninge and continuinge their cuſtomes,
as our Chriſtian Church hath. And ſo much
of this feigned fight, betweene cuſtome and
verity in Chriſtian Religion; whatſoeuer arguments of moment are alleaged in the combatt betweene them about the *reall preſence*,
ſhalbe afterward handled in their due places.
So as of this diſputation and *Martyn Bucers* we
ſhall make but one, to witt, the ſixt.

Seauenth Diſputation. §. 7.

37. Hitherto are the publike diſputations,
recorded by Fox to haue byn held by Proteſtants, for eſtabliſhinge and authorizinge their
new religion vnder *K. Edward*, and all within
the compaſſe of one yeare, to witt, 1549. there
enſue now foure other, appointed ſome foure
yeares after in the firſt of *Q. Maryes* raigne 1553.
vvhich albeit they were vnder a Catholike
gouernement, yet were they for giuinge ſa-

The 7. di-
sputation
in the cō-
uocation
house *anno*
1553.

Fox *pag.*
1284.

tisfaction only to Proteſtants of thoſe dayes,
when Catholike Religion was to be reſtored
to th'end that the other might ſee their owne
leuity in changinge the ſame. And the firſt of
theſe diſputations (being the ſeauenth in order) was held in the conuocation houſe, at
S. *Paules* Church in *London*, begon (as Fox
ſaith) vpon the 18. of October in the foreſaid
yeare, and during for ſix dayes togeather. The
queſtions vvere the accuſtomed about the
reall preſence and Tranſubſtantiation. The
manner of diſputinge was not in forme or after any faſhion of ſchoole, but rather of pro-
poſinge doubts, and anſweringe the ſame for
ſatisfaction of them that were not reſolued,
and ſo much leſſe then in the former was any
thinge purſued to any point of triall. *Doctor*

M. Doctor
VVeſton
prolocu-
tor.

Fox *ibid.*

VVeſton deane of *VVeſtminſter* was choſen prolocutor, who proteſted in his preface (as Fox
ſaith) *that this conference vvas not held to call any
points of Catholike Religion into doubt, but to ſolue ſuch
ſcruples or doubts, as any man might pretend to haue.*

38.   This conuocation conſiſted for the greateſt part, of all thoſe clergy-men that had
borne rule in K. *Edwards* dayes, exceptinge
Cranmer, Ridley, Latymer and *Rogers*, and I know
not yf any other that were commytted before. And the firſt point that was handled
therin, was about a certayne Caluinian Ca-
techiſme, ſett forth a little before vnder the
name of that conuocation, wherynto the prolocutor required ſubſcriptions, to teſtifie that
yt was not ſett forth by their conſents, meaninge,

ninge, as yt feemed, therby to conuince *Ridley*
or *Crammer*, or both of falfe dealinge therin.
The fecond point was of fubfcribing to the
reall prefence, wherynto all the whole houfe
agreed (faith Fox) fauinge fiue or fix, to witt,
Maifter Philips Deane of *Rochefter*, *Maifter Haddon*
Deane of *Exceter*, *Maifter Philpott* Archdeacon
of *VVinchefter*, *Maifter Cheyney* Archdeacon of
Hereford, & *Maifter Elmour* Archdeacon of *Stow*,
and one other whome he nameth not, and by
thefe ~~were~~ propounded all the doubts, that
were there difcuffed : and as for the firft two
dayes, there was nothinge done at all, but a
certaine communication. The third day came
the *Lord great-mafter*, with the Earle of De-
uonfhire and diuers other noble men, and
Cheiney afterward Bifhopp of Glocefter, who
confeffed the *reall prefence*, but not *Tranfubftantiation*, propofed fome doubts about the fecond point, which we fhall afterwards examine in their place. The prolocutor appointed *Doctor Moreman* to aunfwere him and the
reft *extempore*, wherby we may gheffe how
fubftantiall a difputation yt was, for that the
defendant came nothinge at all prepared. *Philipps* alfo propofed fomewhat about the reall
prefence ; *Elmour* and *Haddon* fpake little vpon
that day, though the next day *Elmour*, then
Chaplaine to the Duke of *Suffolke*, and after
Bifhopp of *London*, read certayne authorityes
out of a note-booke, which he had gathered
againft the reall prefence.

39. But of all other, the moft bufy was *Phil-*

Six only of all the côuocation houfe re-fufed to fubfcribe.

M. Cheiney.

D. More-man.

M. Elmour.

M. Philpot.

pott, both that day, and the other followinge, vauntinge and chalenginge the whole company to diſpute. *Then quoth Philpott* (ſaith Fox) *I vvill ſpeake playne Engliſh, the Sacrament of the Altar, which yee reckon to be all one with the maſſe ; is no Sacrament at all, neyther is Chriſt any wiſe preſent in yt , and this his ſayinge he offered to proue before the vvhole houſe, yf they liſted to call him thervnto, and before the Queens grace, and her counſell, and before the*

Fox pag. 1185.

face of ſix of the beſt learned men of the houſe of the contrary opinion, and refuſed none. And yf I ſhall not be able (quoth he) to maintayne by Gods word that I haue ſaid, and confound thoſe ſix which ſhall take vpon them to withſtand me , in this point, let me be burned with as many fag gotts as be in London , before the court-gates, &c. This was *Philpotts* vaunt, and yet yf yee conſider the poore arguments he brought forth in this conference, which afterwards ſhalbe diſcuſſed , togeather with his fond anſwers that he gaue in his 15. or 16. ſeuerall examinations , before the Biſhopps of *V.Vincheſter, London, Chicheſter, Bangor* and others (for ſo much payne was taken to ſaue him)

John Phil-potts vaūt in the cō-uocation houſe.

yow will ſay that his *B. Gardiner* had reaſon, when he held him for more then halfe madd, as in his ſtory we haue related. Conſider alſo, that his denying Chriſt to be preſent any wiſe in the Sacrament, is much different from that yow heard *Maiſter Perne* affirme before , by approbation of *Maiſter Ridley* the moderator, that Chriſts body was truly, wholy, and verily in the Sacrament after a certayne propriety; but theſe men muſt not be taken at their words.

40. And

40.   And finally, the conclusion of all this conference with *Philpott* was, that the prolocutor in the end, feing him out of all reafon to trouble the houfe, layed two comaundements vpon him; the firft that he fhould not come thither any more, vnleffe he came in gowne and typpett, as the others came : the fecond, that he fhould not fpeake but in order, and with licence as the reft did; whofe aunfwere *Fox* relateth in thefe words: *then quoth Philpott* Fox *ibid. I had rather be abfent altogeather*, fo infufferable was all order, or temperate manner of proceedinge to this diforderly man; and fo *Q. Mary* fent a wryte the next day to diffolue the conuocation : *And fuch as had difputed* (faith Fox) *on the contrary part, were driuen, fome to fly, fome to deny, and fome to dye, though to moft mens iudgements, that heard the difputation, they had the vpper hand, &c.* Thefe are hereticall bragges, as yow will better fee afterwards when we come to examining of arguments. And as for dyinge, none of the forfaid difputers died, to our knowledge, but only *Philpott* in his madd moode; *Cheyney, Elmour,* and *Haddon* gott Bifhopricks, & other dignityes vnder *Q. Elizabeth.* And fo much of this difputation in the conuocation houfe.

Eight, ninth, and tenth Difputation. §. 8.

41.   Thefe laft three difputations I do ioyne togeather, for that they were held fucceffiuely

in

in *Oxford* vpon three seuerall dayes in the moneth of Aprill, *anno* 1554. with *Cranmer, Ridley,*
and *Latymer* vpon the forsaid three questions
of the *reall presence, Transubstantiation,* and *the sacrifice of the masse.* The names (saith Fox) of the
vniuersity Doctors and graduates, appointed
to dispute against them vpon the said questions, were these of *Oxford,* Doctor VVeston prolocutor, *Doctor Tressam, Doctor Cole, Doctor Oglethorpe, Doctor Pye, Maister Harpesfield, Maister Fecknam.* Of *Cambridge ,* *Doctor Yonge* Vice Chaun-
celour, *Doctor Glynn, Doctor Seton,* Doctor VVatson,
Doctor Sedgewicke, and Doctor Atkinson, to witt six of
each vniuersity, all meeting at Oxford togeather to this
effect.* Thus farre Fox; who describeth also
the manner and forme of this disputation,
much more reasonable, orderly & indifferent,
then all the former disputations vnder the
Protestants, yf we beleeue Fox himselfe, who
saith; that in the middle of the Doctors, there
were appointed foure to be *exceptores argumentorum ,* wryters of the arguments (to vse his
words) *and a table sett in the middest, and foure notaryes sittinge with them ;* So as by his relation
there were eight indifferent men chosen to
register whatsoeuer passed : yet yf he relate
truly, the manner of arguinge, was not so orderly and schoolelike as might haue byn,
wherby yt came to passe, that scarce any argument was prosecuted to the end ; and the
answeringe was such, as comonly was wholy
from the purpose, as by diuers examples, yow
shall see afterwards declared; as also we shall
examine

Three di-
sputatiõs
in *Oxford*
against
Cranmer,
Ridley and
Latymer.

Fox pag.
1199.

Fox ibid.

The indif-
ferēt dea-
linge of
Cath. in
their di-
sputation

examine what arguments *Cranmer* could alleage againſt the *reall preſence*, vpon the fourth
day of diſputation, to witt the next day after
Latymer had ended. For that *Doctor Harpesfield*
anſweringe for his degree, defended the queſtion of the reall preſence, and *Maiſter Cranmer*
was courteouſly inuited to the ſaid diſputation, and ſuffered to ſay what he would or
could againſt that verity, & was fully anſwered; notwithſtandinge Fox will needs beare
vs in hand to the contrary, as his faſhion is.

42.   And wheras the ſaid *Doctor Harpesfield* in
his preface, did much commend the diligent
readinge of ſcripture with prayer, and confer-
ring one place with another, but yet ſaid that
this was no ſecure way or meane, for euery
particular man to reſolue himſelfe of the ſenſe
therof, but muſt rather beleeue the body of
the Catholike Church therin, then his owne
iudgement. Fox ſaith that *Maiſter Cranmer* in
his reply reprehended that direction, ſayinge:
*vvheras yow referre the true ſenſe & iudgement of the
ſcriptures to the Catholike Church, as iudge therof, yow
are much deceaued, &c.* And Fox himſelfe addeth
this marginall note: *Yf Maiſter Harpesfield (when
he ſaith we muſt not follow our owne heads and ſenſes,
but giue ouer our iudgement to the holy Catholike
Church) had willed vs to ſubmitt our ſelues to the holy
Ghoſt he had ſaid much better.* So Iohn. But I
would aske him, who ſhalbe iudge what the
holy Ghoſt teacheth vs? For that is the queſtion. For yf a particular man readinge the
ſcripture with prayer, and conferringe place
with

The foo-
liſh repre-
hentiõ v-
ſed by
Cranmer &
Fox.

Fox pag.
1326.

with place only, may be prefumed to attayne therby the true meaninge of the holy Ghoſt (which notwithſtanding cannot be certayne, for that an heretike may vſe the ſame meanes) how much more may the vniuerſall body of the Church, vſing the ſelfe-ſame meanes alſo, as many of her learned members no doubt do; how much more, I ſay, may ſhee be thought and preſumed to attayne to the true ſenſe of the holy Ghoſt, ſeing that ſhe hath a ſpeciall promiſe of his infallible aſiſtance to that eſ-fect, which particular men haue not, though heretiks are wont proudly to preſume therof? And ſo yow ſhall ſee yt appeare alſo in theſe diſputations, when we come to diſcuſſe the particulars.

43.   And heere it is to be noted, that preſently vpon the end of this *Oxford-diſputation*, vnder *Q Mary*, it was reported, that others ſhould be held at *Cambridge* betweene the Doctors of that vniuerſity, and the reſidue of the Proteſtant preachers that were in priſon; wherof they being aduertiſed by the warninge of *Doctor Ridley*, as yt ſeemeth by *Fox*, and caſtinge their heads togeather vpon the matter, determined to refuſe all diſputation except it were before the Queene and priuy Councell, or before the houſes of parlament, to which effect they ſett forth a publike wrytinge and proteſtation, with certayne reaſons of excuſes mouinge them thervnto, ſubſcribed by *Hooper*, *Farrar*, *Taylor*, *Philpott*, *Bradford*, *Rogers*, *Saunders*, and ſome others. And their cheefe excuſe was,

Fox *pag.* 1336.

The Proteſtāt Miniſters excuſe themſelues frō diſputation.

for

for that matters had byn determined by parlament before they were disputed of, not consideringe that in K. *Edwards* dayes, the same
course with farre lesse reason was held and
determined by Parlament, before the Protestants disputations in Cambridge.

Of diuers other Disputations held be-fides these ten. §. 9.

44.   These ten disputations I thought good
to sett downe, for that they were held vpon
the first chaunges of Religion in England,
within the space of 4. or 5. yeares, as before
hath byn said: diuers others I do passe ouer,
though some of them were as sollemne as
these; as that of K. *Henry* the 8. against *Lambert*,
vvherin *Doctor Cranmer* disputed for the *reall
presence*, and the *Lord Cromwell* gaue sentence
against him, as we haue shewed * before in
Lamberts story. That also which was held or
pretended in the beginninge of the raigne of
Q. *Elizabeth* at Westminster, betweene nyne
persons of the Catholike parte, and as many
of the Protestant preachers newly come from
beyond the seas. Those of the Catholike side
were fiue Bishopps, to witt *Doctor Iohn VVhite*
Bishopp of *VVinchester, Doctor Baynes* of *Lichfield,
Doctor Scott* of *Chester , Doctor Oglethorpe* of *Car-
liele, Doctor VVatson* of *Lincolne*, with foure other
Doctors adioyned vnto them , *Doctor Cole*

*The di-
sputation
of K. Hen-
ry vvith
Lambert.*

* *Sup. cap.
14 die 4.
Octob.*

Deane

Deane of London , *Doctor Langedale* Archdeacon of *Lewis* , *Doctor Harpesfield* Archdeacon of
Canterbury , and *Doctor Chadsey* Archdeacon of
Middlesex. And for the Proteſtant parte , were
Doctor Scory an Apoſtata friar , & *Doctor Cox* before mentioned , that fledd the realme vnder
Q. Mary , with whome ioyned M. *VVhitehead*,
M. *Grindall*, M. *Horne*, M. *Sandes*, M. *Gheſt*, M. *Elmour*, and M. *Iewell* , all freſhly come from beyond the ſeas , who all , except ſome one or
two, were ſoone after for their good deme-
ritts, made Biſhopps, and accommodated by
thruſtinge out the other, in reward of this diſputation, wherin notwithſtanding there was
not one argument made , nor ſolution giuen,
but only an oſtentation ſought to effectuate
that with ſome colour, which otherwiſe was
determined before, and lacked but a pretence,
for that the Queene and thoſe that were nea-
reſt about her , hauinge determined to make
a change of Religion, thought they ſhould do
yt beſt , and moſt iuſtifiable, yf they promiſed
ſome name of diſputation , wherin the Catholiks had byn ſatisfied or vanquiſhed ; to
which end, there were ſo many ſhifts, partia-
lityes, and diuiſes vſed, and ſo many iniuryes
offered to the Biſhops of the Catholike party,
as they thought good vpon the ſecond dayes
meetinge, to paſſe on no further, except more
reaſon or indifferency vvere vſed towards
them .

45. For firſt, in this diſputation ſummoned
& denounced throughout the whole realme,
by

A preten-
ded diſpu-
tation in
the begin-
ninge of
*Q. Eliʒabe-
thes* raigne
anno 1559.

by order of the Queene and Councell, *Syr Nicolas Bacon* lately made *Lord Keeper*, tooke vpon him to be president, and cheefe moderator, whome all men knew to be one of the greatest aduersaryes to Catholike Religion, that was in England, violent in condition, and vtterly ignorant in matters of diuinity. Secondly the questions appointed to be disputed on, were not chosen nor assigned by the said Bishopps, but by the same *Syr Nicolas* and his adherents in the name of the Councell, at the instance or pleasure of the Protestant new pretenders, wherof when the Bishopps complayned, the *Lord Keeper* answered: *the questions are neyther of their (to witt the Protestants) propoundinge, nor of your diuise, but offered indifferently to yow both.*

The great inequality & iniuryes offered in this preteded disputation.

Fox page 1924.

46. The questions were three, first *whether yt were against Gods word, and the custome of the primitiue Church, to vse a tongue vnknowne to the people in common prayer, and administration of Sacraments.* The second, *whether euery Church had authority to appoint, take away, and change ceremonyes and Ecclesiasticall rites, so the same be to edification.* Thirdly *whether yt can be proued by the word of God, that there is offered vp in the masse a sacrifice propitiatory for the quicke, and the dead: VVhich questions were to be handled* (saith Fox) *in the presence of the Queenes Councell, Nobility, and other of the parlament house, for the better satisfaction and enablinge of their iudgements, to treat and conclude of such lawes as might depend heerevpon.* By which words you may easily conceaue what the drift of this pretended di-

Three questions to small purpose.

Fox pag. 1919.

sputa-

sputation was, and how guilefully these questions were chosen, and sett downe, yf yow
marke their words and sense, especially the
former two, which only or principally were
to be handled, and how impertinent these
questions were to the great moment of the
whole matter and sequele, that was to ensue
therof, which was no lesse then the vniuersall
change of the whole body of Catholike Religion, throughout the realme.

47.   This then was the first hereticall fraud
in appointinge this disputation, and the questions to be disputed, but they were many
more and greater in the prosecution therof;
for first the Catholike cleargy lackinge their
cheife head, which was the Archbishopp of
Canterbury lately dead, the other Archbishopp
of Yorke, to witt, *Doctor Heath* was entertay-
ned with feyre words for a time, to effectuate
with his brethren, what the Protestant party
of the Conncell should thinke expedient:
wheruppon he being Chancelour yet in name,
though the effect of his office was giuen to
Syr Nicolas Bacon, vnder the little of *Lord Keeper*,
he was brought into the place of disputation,
and sate in his roome amongst other Coun-
cellours, togeather with the Duke of Norfolke, & other of the nobility as one of them,
and rather against the Bishops, then for them,
(though no doubt the good man meant yt not
so) then was yt appointed to the said Catholike Bishopps by the Archbishopp, in name of
the Councell, only two dayes before their
meeting

Diuers frauds.

1.

2.

meetinge at the conference (for so complay- Fox *pag.* 1923. *col.* 1. *num.* 1.
neth the Bishop of *Lincolne* in the second dayes
meetinge) that both they, to witt the Bishops,
should begin to say what they could for
themselues, & the Protestant preachers should
answere them. And secondly that the conference should be in English and not in Latyn;
and thirdly, that yt should not be by way of
arguinge or disputinge, but only of speach or 3.
readinge yt out of some booke or paper : All Three indignityes
which three points seeminge indignityes to offered
vnto the
Bishops.
the Bishopps, they complayned greeuously
therof at their first publike meetinge, which
was in *VVestminster* Church vpon the last of
March 1559. being friday; and *Bishop VVhite* of
VVinchester being the first to speake for his side,
said that they were ready to dispute & argue,
but had not their wrytinge ready to be read
there, but would do it at their next meeting:
yet for giuinge some satisfaction, *Doctor Cole* *D. Cole.*
extempore alleaged some breife reasons concerninge the former questions or propositions,
reseruinge the rest vnto their fuller booke or
wrytinge.

48.   But heerevpon presently the Protestant
preachers came out with their booke, or inuectiue against Latyn seruice, fraught with a
vayne shew of many allegations, Scriptures,
Fathers, Councells, and Constitutions of Emperors, sounding as it might seeme somewhat
to their party, though nothing at all in truth, An ostentation of
the Prote-
stant side.
yf yow examine them, as they ly in Fox himselfe; but with this ostentation they sought to

F   gett

get the applause of the people, & heerby well
declared that they had more then two dayes
warninge to prepare themselues; and albeit
when this was done, the Bishops offered to
refute all the same cleerely at the next me-
tinge, yet could they not be heard or permitted, as presently we shall shew, but that this
must needs stand for the whole resolution in
the first questio. And Fox like one of his kind,
seeketh to preuent the matter in these words:

Fox pag. 1922. *The same being reade (to witt the wryting of the
Protestant party) vvith some likelyhood as it seemed
that the same was much allowable to the audience, certayne of the Bishopps began to say, contrary to their former aunswere, that they had now much more to say
in this matter, vvherin although they might vvell haue
byn reprehended; yet for auoydinge of any more mista-
kinge, and that they should vtter all they had to say, yt
was ordered that vpon munday followinge, the Bishopps
should bringe their mynd and reasons in vvryting to the
second assertion, and to the last also yf they could, and
first read the same, and that done the other part should
bring likewise theirs, &c.*

49. Lo heere the indifferency that was vsed;
the Bishopps are accused of cauillation, that
they offered to aunswere in wrytinge to the
Protestants libell, which is not only denyed
Open inequali-ty. them, but yt is ordayned also, that after other
two dayes, they should bringe in whatsoeuer
they haue to say to the second and third questions, and readinge yt first, giue their aduersaryes leaue to triumphe in the second place, as
they had done vpon the first question the day
before.

before. But vpon munday, when all the affembly was fett, the Bifhopps ftood firmely
vpon this, that they would firft read publikely
their owne vyrytinge, vvhich there they
brought with them vpon the firft queftion of
Latyn feruice, in anfwere to that of the Proteftants at the laft meeting, but in no cafe would
yt be graunted them. Fox relateth the Altercation thus.

50. VVinchefter. *I am determyned for my part,
that there fhalbe now read that, vvhich vve haue to fay
for the firft queftion.*

Altercatiō
of the Bif-
hops vvith
*Syr Nico-
las Bacon.*

L. Keeper. *VVill yow not then proceed in the order appointed yow?*

Winchefter. *VVe fhould fuffer preiudice, yf yow
permitt vs not to treat of the firft queftion firft, and fo
vve vvould come to the fecond, and I iudge all my brethren are fo mynded.*

Bifhopps. *VVe are all fo determyned.*

L. Keeper. *Yow ought to looke vvhat order is appointed yow to keepe,* &c.

Winchefter. *Syth our aduerfaryes part haue fo
confirmed their affertion, we fuffer preiudice yf yow
permitt vs not the like.*

Lincolne. *VVe are not vfed indifferently, fithen
yow allow vs not, to open in prefent vvrytinge that, vve
haue to fay for declaration of the firft queftion,* &c. *for
that vvhich* Maifter Cole *fpake in this late affembly,
was not prepared to ftrengthen our caufe, but he made
his oration of himfelfe* extempore, &c. *VVe are alfo euill ordered as touching the tyme, our aduerfaryes
part hauing warning longe before and we were warned only two dayes before the laft affembly in this place,*

The refo-
lute fpe-
ach of *D.
VVatfon* B.
of *Lincolne.*

F 2   *and*

and vvith this busines and other trouble, we haue byn dryuen to be occupied the whole last night, for we may in no case betray the cause of God nor will not do, but susteyne it to the vttermost of our power, but heervnto vve vvant presently indifferent vsinge, &c.

L. Keeper. *I am vvillinge and ready to heare yow, after the order taken for yow to reason therin, and further or contrary to that, I cannot deale vvith yow.*

Lichfield. *Let vs suffer no disorder heerin, but be heard vvith indifferency.*

51.   Thus went on that contention, wherof I omitt much for breuityes sake ; but by this little, so partially declared by Fox, as may be immagined, and appeareth also by diuers circumstances, yow may ghesse how the matter passed, and which part had more reason. At the length, the Archbishop of *Yorke*, knowing belike that this standinge of the Bishopps would not preuaile against designements, already made by the Queene and Councell in disgrace of the Catholike cause, willed the Bishopps ro giue ouer in this matter, and to passe to the second question. But then began a new strife, which party should first begin to speake in this question also, the Bishops affirminge both in respect they had begonne the other day, and that the Protestant party was plaintife or accusant, they should begin, and the Bishopps would answere, but this in no case would be graunted, but that the Bishops must begin againe, and the other haue the last word as before : which indignity the Bishop of *Lichfield* being not well able to beare, recue-

ſted

sted humbly the Lords there pretent, that they might dispute, and try first which party was Catholike and of the Catholike Church, for that therby would appeare who had right to the first or second place of speach, and being somewhat earnest therin, spake to M. *Horne* in these words as Fox relateth.

52. Lichfield. *Maister Horne, Maister Horne, there are many Churches in Germany, I pray yow vvhich of these Churches are ye of?* Another altercatiõ vvith the L. Keeper.

Horne. *I am of Chrifts Catholike Church.*

L. Keeper. *Yow ought not thus to runne into wandringe talke of your owne inuentinge, &c.*

Lichfield. *Nay vve muft firft go thus to vvorke vvith them. yf vve vvill fearch a truth: thefe men come in and pretend to be doubtfull, therfore they fhould firft bringe vvhat they haue to impugne,* &c.

Winchefter. *Lett them begin, fo vvill vve go onward.*

Chefter. *They fpeakinge laft vvould depart* cum applaufu popu'i, &c. *furely vve thinke yt meete that they fhould for their parts giue vs place.*

Lichfield. *Yea that they fhould and ought to do, vvhere any indifferency is vfed.*

Elmour. *VVe giue yow place, do vve not? I pray yow begin.*

L. Keeper. *Yf yow make this affembly gathered in vayne, and vvill not go to the matter, lett vs rife vp and depart.*

Winchefter. *Contented, lett vs be gone: for vve vvill not in this point giue ouer.* And fo finally after fome other like altercation, *Bacon* diffolued the affembly with this threat.

F 3

L. Keeper. My Lords, for that yow vvill not, that vve ſhall heare yow, you may chaunce ſhortly to heare of vs. So he. And this hearinge was; *that ſoone after* (ſaith Stow) *the Biſhopps of* Lincolne *and* Wincheſter *vvere ſent to the Towar, and the reſt bound to make dayly, and perſonall appearance before the Councell, and not to depart the Citty of* London *and* VVeſtminſter, *vntill further order vvere taken vvith them for their diſobedience and contempt.*

Stovv anno Domini 1559.

53.   And this was the iſſue of the firſt diſputation vnder *Q. Elizabeth,* vvherof preſently there was a booke printed and publiſhed, accordinge to the faſhion of the new Doctors, giuinge the victory to the Proteſtants, and ouerthrow to the Cath. Biſhopps, who yet, as yow ſee, were neuer permitted to propoſe any one argument, or reaſon in due place and tyme.

The iſſue of this diſputation vvith the Biſhops.

54.   And with this ſhall we end our narration of publike diſputations, omitting many more priuate and particular, as the conference of *Ridley,* and *Secretary Burne, Doctor Fecknam,* and others in the towar, in the beginninge of *Q. Maryes* raigne: The colloquy of the foreſaid *Fecknam,* with the *Lady Iane* in the ſame place; the particular conferences and examinations of *Hooper, Farrar, Tavlour, Rogers, Philpott, Smyth, Bradford, Tyms, Saunders, Blandford,* and others of the learneder ſort of Proteſtants, but many more of crafteſmen, artificers, weomen, and ſuch like of the ignorant ſort, in the Biſhopps conſiſtoryes and other places: Out of which alſo we ſhall reduce the ſumme of the princi-

Fox pag. 1297.

pall

pall arguments or anſwers, yf yt be different from the reſt, when we come afterward to their due places.

55. And now all this being ſeene and conſidered, the reader will eaſily diſcerne, what ground of certainty may be drawne from all theſe diſputations, altercations, and conferences, to found theron the ſecurity of his ſoule in beleeuing, as the Proteſtants doe: yea and yeldinge themſelues to the fire for yt, as many did in *Q. Maryes* dayes, vpon the ſame and creditt of the torſaid diſputations, which yet many of them vnderſtood not, nor euer heard or read, but moſt of all were not able to reſolue themſelues by them, yf they had heard, read, or vnderſtood them, but only in generall they reſted themſelues vpon this point, that the Proteſtants were learned men, and had gotten the victory in diſputations againſt the Catholiks, for that ſo yt was told them. And this they thought ſufficient for their aſſurance.

The inference vpõ theſe diſputatiõs.

56. But now on the contrary ſide, yf a man would oppoſe to theſe ten publike diſputations before recyted, ten learned Councells of the Catholike Church, that diſputed, examined, and condemned this hereſie of theirs againſt the *reall preſence*, vvithin the ſpace of theſe laſt 600. yeares, ſince *Berengarius* firſt began yt, as namely thoſe foure named by *Lanckfranke*, to witt, that of *Rome* vnder *Leo* the 9. and another of *Verſells* vnder the ſame Pope; the third at *Towars* in France vnder *Pope Victor*

Ten councells examined & confirmed the doctrine of the *reall preſence.*

F 4   ſucceſſor

successor to *Leo*, the fourth at *Rome* againe vnder *Pope Nicolas* the second; In all which *Berengarius* himselfe was present, and in the last, not only abiured, but burnt his owne booke. And after this, six other Councells to the same effect, the first at *Rome* vnder *Gregory* the 7. where *Berengarius* againe abiured, as * *VValdensis* testifieth : The second of *Lateran* in *Rome* also vnder *Innocentius* the third: the generall Councell of *Vienna*; the fourth at *Rome* againe vnder *Pope Iohn* the 22. the fifth at *Constance* , and the sixt at *Trent*. All these Councells (I say) yf a man consider with indifferency of what variety of learned men they consisted , of what singular piety and sanctity of life, of how many nations, of what dignity in Gods Church, how great diligence they vsed to discusse this matter, what prayer, what conferringe of scriptures , and other meanes they vsed , and with how great consent of both Greeke and Latyn Church conforme to all antiquity, they determined and resolued against the opinion of Protestants in our dayes; he will easily discouer, how much more reason, and probability of security there is, of aduenturinge his soule of the one side then of the other , which yet he will better do, by contemplation of the vanity of new Protestants arguments and obiections, against so ancient founded and continued a truth. Which obiections we shall examine in the Chapters followinge. And so much for this.

Laufranc. contra Berengarius.

* *VVald tom. 1. de Sacram. cap. 43.*

THE

THE STATE OF THE
CHIEFE QVESTIONS
handled in the forsaid disputations,

Concerninge the reall presence, Transubstantiation, *and the* Sacrifice of the Masse,
*vvith the chiefe groundes that
be on eyther side.*

CHAP. II.

THE questions that were most treated, and
vrged on both sides, at the two changes of
Religion vnder *K. Edward* and *Q. Mary,* were
principally three, all concerninge the Sacrament of the Altar, as before hath byn shewed:
The first about the *reall presence* of Christ in the
said Sacrament: the second concerninge the
manner of his being there by *Transubstantiation:*
and the third about the same as it is a *Sacrifice.*
Which three points of Catholike doctrine
being left by *K. Henry* the 8. standinge in vigour, as he had found them deliuered, and preserued by all his ancestours Kings of England,
from the beginninge of our conuersion vnto
Christian Religion, they were all changed
within two yeares after the said Kings death,
by authority of his sonne, being then somewhat lesse then a dozen yeares ould, and by
force

force of a certayne act of parlament, confirmed by his name intituled: *An act for the vnifor-
mity of seruice and administration of Sacraments, &c.*
Which act though in shew yt conteyned nothinge els, but the admission and approbation
of a certayne new booke of *Common-prayer and
administration of Sacraments* (for so are the words
of the Statute) gathered togeather by *Cranmer,
Ridley,* and some others of the same humor, yet
for that in this new communion booke, togeather with many other articles of auncient
beleefe, these three also of the *reall presence,
Transubstantiation,* and *Sacrifice* were altogeather
altered, and a new manner of faith therin
taught, yt was giuen forth that all was established and setled by Parlament: and for that
this collection of new articles of beleefe, passed, as yow haue heard, in a bundell or fardell
shuffled vp togeather in hast, vnder the name
of a reformed booke of *Common-prayer,* without any great examination or dispute about
the particulars, but in generall only takinge
voyces in the parlament house, as well of lay-
men as other learned and vnlearned, whether
the booke should passe, or noe; wherin the
L. Seymour Protector and his crew, hauing the
Kings authority in their hands, and gettinge
Cranmer and *Ridley* on their sides for loue of
weomen, and other preferment, easily preuayled, as by the statute yt selfe may appeare:
yt was thought expedient, as before hath byn
noted, that presently after the statute published, two meanes should be vsed for authorizinge

See the
booke of
statutes
*an. 2. & 3.
Edou. 6.*

Hovv dif-
orderly
Catholike
Religion
vvas ouer-
throvvne
in *K. Ed-
vvards*
dayes.

zinge and better creditinge the same. The one
by persuasion of diuers meetings, conferences,
and disputations of the learneder sort, which
before yow haue heard related; and the other
by imprisonment & depriuing such Bishops,
and other cheefe Ecclesiasticall persons, as
should shew themselues most forward or able
to resist this course, which they began with
VVinchester, Durham, and *London:* And thus passed they on for those 4. or 5. yeares that remained of *K. Edwards* raigne after this change,
wherein notwithstandinge, almighty God
shewed wonderfully his hand of iudgement
and punishment soone after, vpon the principall authors of this innouation both spirituall
& temporall; as of the later, both the *Seamours,*
Northumberland, Suffolke, and diuers of their followers; of the former *Cranmer, Ridley, Hooper,*
Latymer, & the like, as to the world is euident.

2.   For vpon this followed the raigne of
Q. Mary for other 4. or 5. yeares, who seeing so
pittifull a breach made in the realme by this
vnlucky alteration, she as a zealous Catholike Princesse, endeauored to restore the old
faith and Religion againe, to the former vnity
of the vniuersall Church, and close vp the
wound that had byn made, vsinge to this effect the selfe same meanes of instruction and
correction, by arguments and punishments,
but in different manner, and with farre vnlike
iustice of proceeding. For that the arguments
were the very same, which euer had byn vsed
by ancient Fathers, against old heretiks in the
like

The en-
trance of
Q. Mary.

like controuersies: and the punishments were no other then such, as auncient Ecclesiasticall Cannons did prescribe, and were vsed only towards them, that eyther had byn cheefe authors of the innouations, or stood so obstinately in defence therof, as by no meanes they could be recalled.

3.   Now then yt is to be considered, which of these two sorts of people had more ground or reason, either those, that withstood the first change in K. *Edwards* dayes, which was from the old accustomed Religion to a new: or those that resisted the second change or exchange vnder Q. *Mary*, which was nothinge els indeed but a returne from the new to the ould againe. And heerby will appeare the state of the controuersie vvhich now vve are to handle. For as for the first sort, to witt Catholiks, the historicall state of their controuersie is manifest, concerninge these three questions about the Sacrament; for that no man can deny, but that the doctrine of the first, and third, which is the *reall presence*, and *Sacrifice*, had byn receaued and held for true throughout England, (wherein concurred also the vvhole Christian vvorld abroad) from the tyme before by me prefixed of our first conuersion, and more, euen from the Apostles dayes: neyther could any tyme be appointed, or memory brought forth, when, how, or by whome, the said doctrines had their beginnings in England, or els where, which accordinge to *S. Augustines* rule, and diuers particular demon-

The state of the cōtrouersie in three questions.

demonstrations layd downe by vs before, in the first part of the *Treatise of three Conuersions*, doth euidently couuince, that they came from Christ, and his Apostles themselues ; vvhich ought to be sufficient , though no other prooues of Scriptures, Fathers, Doctors, and Councells could be shewed in particular for the same , as may be almost infinite , and some yow shall heare a little after in this Chapter.

Aug. l. 1. de baptif. c. 7. l. 4. c. 6. & 24. & l. 5 c. 23.

4. And as for the second question of *Transubstantiation* , though yt be but a certayne appendix of the first, about the manner how Christ is really in the Sacrament, as * before hath byn shewed, & was not so particularly declared , and defined by the Church in this very tearme of *Transubstantiation*, vntill some 400. yeares gone in the generall Councell of *Lateran*, (as neyther the doctrine of *homusion* or *consubstantiality* was, vntill 300. yeares after Christ in the Councell of *Nice* , neyther the dignity of *theotocos*, wherby the blessed Virgin is called the Mother of God, vntill the Councell of *Ephesus* aboue 400. yeares after Christ:) yet was the same doctrine euer true before from the beginninge, and vttered by the Fathers in other equiualent words & speaches, *of changes, and Transmutations of natures*, *conuersions of substances*, and the like ; and when there had not byn such other euident proofes extant for the truth therof; yet the consent and agreement of so great and vniuersall a Councell of Christendome, as the said *Lateran* was, wherin

* Sup. cap. præced.

anno 1215.

The names of cosubstantiality , of Mother of God, and Transubstantiatio, determined after one manner.

both

both the Greeke and Latyn Church agreed;
and after great and longe searche by readinge,
disputinge, prayinge, conferringe of Scriptures and Fathers, and other such meanes,
concluded this doctrine to be truth : Yf there
had byn (I say) nothinge els for Englifh Catholiks to rest vpon in this point , but the generall consent, and agreement of so learned,
holy, and venerable an assembly ; yt might
iustly seeme sufficient in the sight of an indifferent or reasonable man to weygh, and ouer-
weygh, against the particular iudgements of
all the innouators of any age to the contrary;
and so no maruayle, though they stood so earnest against that innouation , this being the
state of the controuersie on their part.

5.   But now for the Protestants , the state of
their question was farre different. For first,
The state
of the
question
for the
Prote-
stants. wheras *Martyn Luther* about the 9. or 10. yeare
of *K. Henryes* raigne, had begon some noueltyes
about the second and third question of *Tran-*
substantiation and *Sacrifice* , holding still the first
of the *reall presence* for firme , and that three of
his first schollers *Oecolampadius, Carolstadius,* and
Zuinglius full sore against his will , takinge occasion of his innouations, had added others of
their owne, about the said first question , denyinge the *reall presnce* , though in different
forts : and that after them againe *Iohn Caluyn* a
French-man , had diuised a third manner of
beleefe therin, not a little different from them
all about the said doctrine, both affirminge &
denyinge the *reall presence* in different manner
and

and ſound of words: yt ſeemed good to our
Engliſh Proteſtants at that tyme, or the more
part therof, to chooſe the laſt and neweſt opinion of all, and to eſtabliſh yt by parlament,
baniſhinge thervpon the ould faith, that euer
vntill that day had byn held and beleeued in
our countrey, as well by themſelues as others.
6.   And thus came in the firſt new Religion
into England, by ſome ſhew of publike authority, which being ſett forth with ſo great ap-
plauſe, and oſtentation both of publike diſputations, colloquyes, conferences, lectures,
preachings, expoſition of ſcriptures, and conſent of Parlament, as yow haue heard, did
partly by this outward ſhew and oſtentation
of authority, partly by the pleaſinge face of
nouelty yt ſelfe, and ſweet freedome that yt
brought from all former Eccleſiaſticall diſcipline, ſo infect, and enchaunt the harts, iudgements, & affections of diuers of the common
people, and ſome alſo of the learned, (but the
lighter, and more licentious ſort) as afterward
when *Q. Mary* came to take accoumpt, and
vvould recall them againe to the ſtation
which they had forſaken; they choſe rather of
pride and obſtinacy, to ſuffer any thinge, yea
to dye, and go to the fire, then to renounce
theſe new fancyes once faſtened vpon them:
vnto which pertinacity the fame of the forſaid
Proteſtants diſputations, did not a little animate them; for that yt was giuen out generally (and ſo doth Fox ſtand ſtiffely in the ſame)
that the Sacramentaryes had the vpper hand

in

Motiues
that drevv
in nevv
Religion.

in all, as well againſt the Lutherans in the
firſt queſtion of *reall preſence*, as againſt the Catholiks in that and all the reſt: vvhich bragg
how vayne yt was, will appeare after when
we come to examine their arguments in particular.

7.   But yet before we come to that, two
other points ſeeme expedient to be performed, for better direction of the readers vnderſtandinge in theſe high miſteryes of our
faith: the firſt to ſee what ſure grounds the
Catholiks had, and haue at this day to ſtand
firme, and immoueable in their old beleefe
about theſe articles, notwithſtandinge any
plauſible or deceytfull arguments of ſenſe and
reaſon, that may be brought againſt them; &
ſecondly certayne obſeruations, wherby the
force or rather fraud of hereticall obiections
may be diſcouered, which ſo beguyled many
ſimple people in *Q. Maryes* dayes, and made
them runne headlonge to their perdition;
the firſt of theſe points I ſhall handle in this
Chapter: the ſecond in the next that followeth.

---

*Catholike groundes of theſe three ar-
ticles, and firſt of the reall preſence.*

§. 1.

8. The firſt ground that Catholike men haue
of theſe, and all other miſteryes of Chriſtian
faith

faith that are aboue the reach of common sense and reason, is the authority of the Catholike Church, by which they were taught the same: as points of faith reuealed from God. And this is such a ground, as we see by experience, that the most part of people of what Religion soeuer, being yonge or vnlearned, can yeld no other reason in effect, why they beleeue this or that article of theire faith, but for that they receaued the same from their Church and teachers therof, being not able themselues to searche out any other grounde therof: yea the most learned of all from their infancy, tooke all vpon this assurance only of their Church, which Church yf they held to be of infallible authority, so as she can neither be deceaued nor deceaue (as we do of the Catholike) then should they rest firme & sure in their opinion vpon this ground; but yf they hould that all Churches may erre, and bringe into error both in doctrine, and manners, as yow haue heard *Martyn Bucer* hold before in *Sup. cap. 1.* his *Cambridge* conclusions, and most sectaryes of our tyme do follow him in that assertion, then can they haue no ground or certainty this way, but each man and woman must seeke other grounds and proofes, and stand vpon their owne iudgements for triall of the same, which how well the most part of people can do, being eyther yonge, simple, vnlearned, or otherwayes so busyed in other matters, as they cannot attend thervnto, euery man of meane discretion will consider, and

G   conse-

consequently they must needs be said both to
liue and dye, vvithout any ground of their
faith at all, but proper opinion, and so perish
euerlastingely.

9.   The famous Doctor *S. Augustine* handleth
this matter in a speciall booke to his frend *Honoratus* deceaued by the Manichies, as himselfe
also sometymes had byn, and he intituleth his
booke *De vtilitate credendi* : of the profitt that
commeth to a man by beleeuing the Church,
and points of faith therin taught, without de-
maundinge reason or proofe therof, which
the Manichies derided, and said that they required nothinge to be beleeued of their followers, but that which first should be proued
to them by good proofe and reason, and not
depend only of mens creditt: but the holy Father scorneth this hereticall bragg and ostentation of theirs, and commendeth highly the
contrary custome of simple beleeuinge vpon
the creditt of the Catholike Church, for that
otherwise infinite people should haue no faith
at all, and exhorteth his frend *Honoratus* to take
the same course; first to beleeue, and after to
seeke the reason. His discourse is this : *Fac nos
nunc primum quærere, cuinam Religioni, animas no-
stras, &c.* Suppose that we now first of all did
„ seeke, vnto what Religion we should commit
„ our soules to be purged and rectified; without
„ all doubt we must begin with the Catholike
„ Church, for that she is the most eminent now
„ in the world, there being more Christians in
„ her, at this day, then in any other Church of
                                            Iewes,

*Aug. tom.
6.*

*Aug. lib. de
vtil. cred.
tom. 6.
cap. 7.*

Iewes,and Gentills put togeather: And albeit „
amongſt theſe Chriſtians, there may be ſects „
and hereſies, and all of them would ſeeme to „
be Catholiks,and do call others beſides them- „
ſelues heretiks: yet all graunt,that yf we con- „
ſider the whole body of the world, there is „
one Church amongſt the reſt more eminent „
then all other, & more plentifull in number, „
& (as they which know her do affirme) more „
ſincere alſo in truth;but as concerninge truth, „
we ſhall diſpute more afterward; now yt is „
ſufficient for them that deſire to learne, that „
there is a Catholike Church, which is one in „
yt ſelfe, whervnto diuers heretiks do feigne, „
and diuiſe diuers names, wheras they, (and „
their ſects) are called by peculiar names, „
which themſelues cannot deny, wherby all „
men that are indifferent, & not letted by paſ- „
ſion, may vnderſtand vnto what Church, the „
name Catholike,which all parts deſire & pre- „
tend, is to be giuen.

10. Thus *S. Auguſtine*: teachinge his frend
how he might both know and beleeue the
Catholike Church, and all that ſhee taught
ſimply, and without asking reaſon or proofe.
And as for knowing and diſcerning her from
all other Churches, that may pretend to be
Catholike, we heare his marks, that ſhe is
more eminent, vniuerſall, greater in number,
and in poſſeſsion of the name Catholike. The
ſecond that ſhe may be beleeued ſecurely, and
cannot deceaue nor be deceaued in matters of
faith, he proueth elſwhere, concluding finally

G 2   in

in this place: *Si iam satis tibi iactatus videris, &c.*
,, Yf thou dost seeme to thy selfe now to haue
,, byn sufficiently tossed vp and downe amonge
,, sectaryes, and wouldst putt an end to these
,, labours and tormoyles, follow the way of
,, Cath. discipline, which hath flowen downe
,, vnto vs from Christ by his Apostles, and is to
,, flow from vs to our posterity.

11. This then is the iudgement and direction

of *S. Augustine*, that a man should for his first
ground, in matters of faith, looke vnto the beleefe of the greatest & most eminent Church
of Christendome, that hath endured longest,
embraceth most people, & hath come downe
from our fore-fathers with the name of Catholike, not only among her owne professors,
but euen among her enemyes Iewes, infidells,

and heretiks, and so is termed & held by them
in their common speach, as the said Father in
diuers others places declareth at large. Which
rule of direction, yf we will follow about
these three articles of faith now proposed, the
reall presence, Transubstantiation, and *Sacrifice of the
masse,* yt is easily seene what ground we haue
for their beleefe, in this kind of proofe, so
highly esteemed by *S. Augustine,* which is the
authority of the vniuersall Cath. Church.
For that when *Luther* and his followers began
to oppose themselues in our dayes, no man
can deny, but that our beleefe in these articles
was generally receaued ouer all Christendome, as well *Asia* and *Africa,* where soeuer
Christians be, as *Europe,* and so vpward tyme
out

out of mynd; neither can any beginning be affigned to thefe doctrines in the Cath. Church,
but only a certayne definition and determination of fome Councells, about the name of
Tranfubftantiation, as after fhalbe declared.

12. Now then, hauinge found out this firft
ground which *S. Auguftine* and other Fathers
do make fo great accoumpt of, which is the
authority and beleefe of that Church, that generally is called Catholike: Yf we paffe further, and fee what grounds this Church had
or hath to admytt the fame, (which yet is not
needfull, or poffible to all fortes of men, for
that only can be done by the learneder fort)
we fhall find that fhe hath fuch grounds, as
may conuince any man that is not obftinate,
and indurate to the contrary. And firft to begin with the article of the *reall prefence*, what
ground, proofe, or Theologicall demonftra-
tion can there bee, which the Cath. Church
hath not for her beleefe in that high miftery?
which as it was to be one of the cheefeft, moft
facred, and admirable of Chriftian Religion,
fo was yt meet that yt fhould be confirmed, by
all the principall wayes that any article of
faith could or can be confirmed, that is to fay
both by fcriptures of the ould and new Teftament, and the true expofition therof by auncient Fathers, that liued before this controuerfie began with Sacramentaryes; by authority and tradition of the Apoftles and their
fucceffors; by teftimony of auncient Fathers
from age to age; by confent and agreement,

C 3   practife

Groundes
about the
reall pre-
fence.

practife and vfe of the vniuerfail Church; by
the concourfe and approbation of almighty
God, with euident and infinite miracles, by
confeffion of the aduerfaryes, and other fuch
generall heads of arguments, which Catholike diuines do produce for this truth, for iu-
ftifyinge the Churches faith therin.

Demon-
ftrations
out of the
fcripture.

13.   And out of the fcriptures their demon-
ftration is not fingle or of one fort only, but
in diuers manners, as to the height and dignity of fo diuine and venerable a myftery was
conuenient. For that out of the ould Teftament, they fhew how yt was prefigured and
prophefied, and in the new both promifed
againe, exhibited, and confirmed, and this not
by expofition of their owne heads only, as
fectaryes do, but by intendement, and interpretation, of the graueft and moft ancient Fathers, that haue liued in the Church of God
from age to age, who vnderftood fo the faid
figures and forefhewinges of the old Teftament. As for example, the bread and wine mi-
fterioufly offered to almighty God by *Melchi-*
fedeck King and Prieft, who bare the type of
our Sauiour *Gen.* 14. *Pfalm.* 109. *Heb.* 7. The
fhew-bread amonge the Iewes, that only could
be eaten by them that were fanctified *Exod.*

Three fi-
gures of
Chrifts
flesh in
bread.

40. *& 1. Reg.* 21. The bread fent miraculoufly
by an Angell to *Elias*, whereby he was fo
ftrengthened, as he trauayled 40. dayes without eating, by vertue only of that bread. Thefe
three forts of bread to haue byn expreffe figures of this Sacrament, and of the trew flefh

of

of Chriſt therein conteined, do teſtiſie by one
conſent all the ancient Fathers, as *S. Cyprian
lib.* 2. *epiſt.* 3. *Clem. Alexand. lib.* 4. *Strom. Ambroſ.
lib.* 4. *de Sacram. cap.* 3. *Hier. in cap.* 1. *ad Titum.
Chryſoſt. hom.* 35. *in Gen. Auguſt. lib.* 2. *cont. litteras
Petil. cap.* 37. *Cyrill. Catecheſi* 4. *Myſtag. Arnobius,
Euſebius, Gregorius,* and many others.

14.   Three other ſigures there are not expreſ-
ſed in the forme of bread, but in other things
more excellét then bread, as the paſchall lambe
Exod. 12. *Leuit.* 23. The bloud of the Teſtament   Three other ſignes of Chriſts fleſh.
deſcribed *Exod.* 24. *Heb.* 9. And fulfilled by
Chriſt *Luc.* 22. when he ſaid: *This cupp is the new
Teſtament in my bloud,* and againe: *This is my bloud
of the new Teſtament Matth.* 26. The *manna* alſo ſent by God from heauen was an expreſſe
figure of this Sacrament, as appeareth by the
words of our Sauiour. *Ioan.* 6. and of the
Apoſtle 1. *Cor.* 10. Out of all which figures, is
inferred, that for ſo much as there muſt be
great difference betweene the figure, and the
thing prefigured, no leſſe yf we beleeue *S. Paul,*   *Colioſ.* 2. *Heb.* 10.
then betweene a ſhaddow, & the body whoſe
ſhaddow yt is; yt cannot be imagined by any
probability, that this Sacrament exhibited by
Chriſt in performance of thoſe figures, ſhould
be only creatures of bread and wine, as Sacra-   An infe-rence vpõ the for-mer fi-gures.
mentaryes do imagine, for then ſhould the fi-
gures be eyther equall, or more excellent then
the thing prefigured yt ſelfe, for who will not
confeſſe but that bread for bread, *Elias* his
bread made by the Angell, that gaue him
ſtrength to walke 40. dayes vpon the vertue
G 4   therof,

therof was equall to our English-ministers
Communion-bread, and that the *manna* was
much better.

15.   And yf they will say for an euasion, as
they do, that their bread is not common
bread, but such bread as being eaten and receaued by faith, worketh the effect of Christs
body in them, and bringeth them his grace;
we answeare that so did these figures and Sacraments also of the ould Testament, being
receaued by faith in Christ to come, as the
ancient Father and Preachers receaued them:
And for so much as Protestants do further
hould, that there is no difference betweene
the vertue & efficacy of those old Sacraméts,
and ours, (which we deny) yt must needs follow, that both we & they agreeinge, that the
Fathers of the old Testament beleeued in the
same Christ to come that we do now, being
come, their figures and shaddowes must be as
good as our truth in the Sacrament, that was
presigured, if it remaine bread still after Christs
institution, and consecration. But Catholike
Fathers did vnderstand the matter farre
otherwise, and to alleage one for all, for that
he spake in the sense of all in those dayes, *Saint
Hierome* talking of one of those forsaid figures,
to witt, of the *shew-bread,* and comparinge yt
with the thinge figured, and by Christ exhibited, saith thus: *Tantum interest, &c.* There is so
much difference betweene the *shew-bread,* and
the body of Christ figured therby, as there is
„ difference betweene the shaddow and the
body,

Hier. in
comment.
in prmism
cap. ad Ti-
tum.

body, whose shaddow yt is, and betweene an „
Image and the truth, which the Image repre- „
senteth, & betweene certaine shapes of things „
to come, and the things themselues presigured „
by those shapes. And thus much of figures, & „
presignifications of the old Testament. „

16.   In the new Testament, as hath byn said, Proofes out of the new Testament.
are conteyned both the promise of our Saui-
our, to fullfill these figures with the truth of
his flesh, which he would giue to be eaten in
the Sacrament, as also the exhibition and performance therof afterward, the very night
before his passion, with a miraculous confirmation of the same by *S. Paul*, vpon conference
had therin with Christ himselfe after his blessed assension. The promise is conteyned in the
sixt Chapter of *S. Iohns* ghospell, where our *Io. 6.*
Sauiour foretelleth expressely, that he would
giue his flesh to vs to be eaten : *for that except
vve did eat the same, vve could not be saued : that his
flesh vvas truly meat, and his blond truly drinke*; and
that his flesh that he would giue vs to eat, *vvas
the same that vvas to be giuen for the life of the world:*
All which speaches of our Sauiour expoun-
ded vnto vs in this sense, for the *reall presence* of
his flesh in the Sacrament by the vniuersall
agreeinge consent of auncient Fathers, must
needs make great impression in the hart of a
faithfull Christian man, especially the performance of this promise ensuing soone after,
vvhen Christ being to depart out of this
world, and to make his last will and Testament, exhibited that which heere he promi-
                                                    sed,

sed, takinge bread , brake and diftributed the
same, sayinge : *this is my body that fhalbe deliuered*
for yow, which words are recorded by three seuerall Euangelifts, and that with fuch fignificant, and venerable circumftances on our Sauiours behalfe , of feruent prayer, wafhinge
his Apoftles feet, proteftation of his excefsiue
loue , and other deuout , and moft heauenly
fpeaches in that nearneffe to his pafsion , as
well declared the exceeding greatneffe of the
miftery which he was to inftitute: whervnto
if we add that excellent cleare côfirmation of
S. Paul, who for refoluing doubts as it feemed
had conference with Chrift himfelfe after his
afcenfion (for before he could not, he being no
Chriftian when Chrift afcended) the matter
will be more euident . His words are thefe to
the *Corinth. Ego enim accepi à Domino, quod & tradi-*
di vobis, &c. For I haue receaued from our Lord
himfelfe , that which I haue deliuered vnto
yow about the Sacrament ; and do yow note
the word (*for*) importinge a reafon why he
ought fpecially to be beleeued in this affayre,
for fo much as he had receaued the refolution
of the doubt frô Chrift himfelfe. And then he
fetteth downe the very fame words againe of
the Inftitution of this Sacrament , that were
vfed by Chrift before his pafsion, without alteration, or new expofition , which is morally moft certayne that he would haue added
for clearinge all doubts, yf there had byn any
other fenfe to haue byn gathered of them,
then the plaine words themfelues do beare.

Matth. 26.
Marc. 14.
Luc. 22.

1. Cor. 11.

S. Paules
confirma-
tion of
the *reall*
prefence.

Nay

Nay himfelfe doth add a new confirmation, when he faith, that he which doth eate and drinke vnworthily this Sacrament, *reus erit corporis & fanguinis Domini*, fhalbe guilty of the body and bloud of our Lord. And againe: *Iudicium fibi manducat & bibit, non dijudicans corpus Domini*, he doth eat & drinke his owne iudgement, not difcerninge the body of our Lord: Which inferreth the *reall prefence* of Chriftes body, which thofe, whome the Apoftle reprehendeth, by the fact of their vnworthy receauing doe fo behaue themfelues, as yf they did not difcerne it to be prefent. All which laid togeather, & the vniforme confent of expofitors throughout the whole Chriftian world, concurringe in the felfe-fame fenfe and meaninge of all thefe fcriptures, about the *reall prefence* of Chrifts true body in the Sacrament, yow may imagine what a motiue yt is, and ought to be to a Catholike man, who defireth to beleeue, and not to ftriue and contend. And thus much for fcriptures.

17. There followeth the confideration of Fathers, Doctors and Councells, wherein as the Sacramentaryes of our tyme, that pleafed firft to deny the *reall prefence*, had not one authority, nor can produce any one at this day, that expreffely faith, that Chrifts reall body is not in the Sacrament, or that yt is only a figure, figne, or token therof (though diuers impertinent peeces of fome Fathers fpeaches they will now and then pretend to alleage) fo on the cotrary fide, the Catholiks do behould

The fecōd ground about authorityes of Fathers.

for

for their comfort, the whole ranks of ancient
Fathers through euery age, standinge with
them in this vndoubted truth: Yea not only
affirming the same *reall presence* in most cleere,
and perspicuous words (wherof yow may see
whole books in Catholike wryters repleni-
shed with Fathers authorityes, laid togeather
out of euery age from Christ downewards)
but that which is much more, yeldinge reasons, & endeauoring to proue the same by manifest arguments, & theologicall demonstrations, vsing therin such manner of speach and
words, as cannot possibly agree vnto the Protestants communion of bare bread and wyne,
with their symbolicall signification or representation only. As for example, where the Fathers do shew how Christs true flesh commeth to be in this Sacramēt, *videlicet: by the true*
conuersion of bread into his body, and by, *that this body*
is made of bread, and by, *that the substances of bread*
and vryne be changed, and other like speaches, as
may be seene in *S. Ambrose 4. de Sacram. cap. 5. &*
lib. 6. cap. 1. lib. de myst. init. cap. 9. Cypr. Serm. de
Cœna. Chrysost. hom. 83. in Matth. & de proditione
Iuda. Cyrill. Catec. 4, Mystag. Nissenus orat. Catech.
37. and others.

18.   Secondly, yt is an ordinary speach of the
Fathers, to cry out & admyre the miracle that
happeneth, by the conuersion in this Sacrament, ascribinge the same to the supreme omnipotency of almighty God, as yow may see
in *S. Chrysostome l. 3. de sacerdotio: O miraculum, &c.*
S. Ambrose lib. 4. de Sacram. cap. 4. Iustinus Martyr
Apolog.

See *Claud.*
de Xanctes
reuet. &
Bellarm. l.
de Euchar.
tom. 2. and
9 thers.

The first
reason of
the Fa-
thers.

The secōd
reason of
Fathers.

Apolog. 2. sayinge : *that by the same omnipotency of God, vvherby the vvord vvas made flesh, the flesh of the vvord vvas made to be in the Eucharist*, which a-greeth not to a Caluinian communion.

19.　Thirdly, some of them do extoll and ma-gnifie the exceeding loue & charity of Christ towards vs, aboue all other humane loue, in that he feedeth vs with his owne flesh, which no shephards did euer their sheepe, or mothers their children, which is the frequent speach of *S. Chrysostome hom.* 83. *in Matth. &* 45. *in Ioan. & hom.* 24. *in ep.* 1. *ad Cor.* 2. *& homil.* 60. *&* 61. *ad Pop. Antioch.* And to the same effect *S. Augu-stine ep.*120. *cap.*27. *& in Psal.*33. which speaches can no wayes agree to the Protestants supper. The third reason.

20.　Fourthly, diuers of the said Fathers do expressely teach, that we do receaue Christ in the Sacrament not only by faith, but truly, really, and corporally; *semetipsum nobis commiscet* (saith *S. Chrysostome*) *non fide tantum, sed & reipsa*: Christ doth ioyne himselfe with vs (in the Sacrament) not only by faith, but really. And in another *place, he putteth this antithesis or opposition betwixt vs, and the *Magi*, that saw and beleeued in Christ lying in the manger, that they could not carry him with them, as we do now by receauinge him in the Sacra-ment, and yet no doubt they beleeued in him, and carryed him in faith as we do now; to which effect *S. Cyrill Alexand.* saith: *Corporaliter nobis filius vnitur vt homo, spiritualiter, vt Deus*: Christ as a man is vnited vnto vs corporally, (by the Sacrament) and spiritually, as he is God. The 4. reason.

Chrysost. hom. 60. ad Popul. An-tioch.

*De Sancto Phylogonio.

4. in Ioan. cap. 13. & 14. & l. 11. cap. 27.

Wher-

Whervnto yow may add *S. Hilary lib. 8. de Tri-nitate*, and *Theodoru* in the Councell of *Ephesus tom. 6. Appendic. 5. cap. 2.* and others.

The fifth reason.

21.   Firtly the Fathers do many tymes, and in diuers places, and vpon sundry occasions go about to proue the truth of other mysteryes, and articles of our faith, by this miracle of the being of Chrifts flesh and body in the Sacrament, as *S. Irenaus* for example, doth proue Chrifts Father to be the God of the old Teftament, for that in his creatures he hath left vs his body & bloud, and in the same place he vseth the same argument, for eftablifhinge the article of the refurrection of our bodyes, to witt, that he that vouchfafeth to nowrifh vs with his owne body and bloud, will not lett our bodyes remayne for euer in death & corruption. *S.Chryfoftome* in like manner, by the truth of his *reall prefence* in the Sacrament, doth confute them that denyed Chrift to haue taken true flefh of the Virgin Mary, which hardly would be proued by the Sacramentary fupper of bread and wyne, as euery man by himfelfe will confider.

Lib. 4. cont. haref. c. 34.

Ibidem.

Hom. 3. in Matth.

The sixth reason.

22.   Sixtly to pretermitt all other points handled to this effect, by the said Fathers, as that diuers of them do exclude expreffely the name of figure, or fimilitude from this Sacrament, as *S. Ambrofe lib. 4. de Sacram. cap. 1. Damafc. lib. 4. cap. 4. & 14. Theophilact. in Matth. 26.* Others yeld reafons why Chrift in the Sacrament, would be really vnder the formes or accidents of bread and wyne, to witt, that our faith

faith might be proued and exercised therby, & the horror of eating flesh & bloud, in their owne forme & shape, taken away, and so the same *S. Ambrose Ibid. l.4. de Sacram. c.4. Cyrill. in cap. 22. Luc. apud D. Thom. in catena.* Others do persuade vs not to beleeue our senses that see only bread and wyne, wherof we shall speake more in the obseruations following: so *S. Augustine, serm. de verbis Apost. & l.3. de Trinit. cap.* 10. Others do proue this reall presence by the sacrifice, affirminge the selfe same Christ to be offered now in our dayly sacrifice vpon the Altars of Christians, after an vnbloudy manner, which was offered once bloudely vpon the Altar of the Crosse, as more largely shalbe shewed: so *S. Chrysostome hom. 17. ad Habr. & 2. in 2. ad Tim. Greg. lib.4. dial. c. 58. Nissenus orat.1. in pascha, &c.* All these considerations I say, and many others that may be taken out of the Fathers wrytinges, I do for breuityes sake lett passe in this place, though most euidently they do declare the said Fathers plaine meaninge, and beleefe in this article, and cannot any way be applyed to the new Communion of Protestants, but by manifest impropriety and detortion.

Diuers euident reasons togeather.

23. And therfore I will end only with one consideration more, very ordinary with the said Fathers, which is, the diuine reuerence, honour, and adoration, that in all ages the said Fathers haue giuen vnto the blessed Sacramēt, whose authorityes were ouerlong heere to recyte in particular. The sayinge of *S. Austen*

The seauenth reason.

is

is knowne. *Nemo manducat nifi prius adorauerit,* no man eateth the Sacrament but firft adoreth the fame, and *S. Chryfoftome, Adora & manduca.* adore yt and receaue yt; And *Theodoret* to the fame effect, *Et creduntur & adorantur, quòd ea fint quæ creduntur.* They are beleeued and adored (*the flesh and bloud of Chrift*) for that they are in deed the things they are beleeued to be. And to fpeake nothinge of many other Fathers fayings to this effect, *S. Chryfoftome* his large dif-

courfes about this matter may ferue for all, who wryteth, *that at the tyme of confecration and facrifice, the very Angells come downe, and with tremblinge do adore Chrift their Lord. therin prefent;* which he would neuer haue wrytten, yf bread, and wyne were only there prefent.

24.   By all thefe wayes & meanes then, may

eafily be feene what the auncient Fathers in their ages did thinke, fpeake, and beleeue, of this high & admirable miftery of Chrifts reall prefence in the Sacrament. And albeit there were no Councells about this matter, for the fpace of a thoufand yeares after Chrift, the caufe therof was, that in all that fpace no one man euer openly contradicted the fame, at leaft after the tyme of *S. Ignatius* vntill *Berenga-rius,* (for yf any man had done yt, we may fee by the forefaid Fathers fpeaches, who muft haue byn the chiefe in thefe Councells, what their determination would haue byn againft

them) and when the faid *Berengarius* had once broached this Sacramentary herefy, the whole Christian world rofe vp prefently againft the

fame,

fame, as againft a blafphemous nouelty, and
ten feuerall Councells condemned the fame,
as in the former Chapter hath byn declared.

25. Wherfore the Catholikes hauinge with
them all thefe warrants of truth by fcriptures,
fathers, councells, tradition of antiquity, vniforme confent of all Chriftian nations , both
Greeke, Latyn, Afian, African, & other countreyes embracing the name & faith of Chrift,
and that no beginninge or entrance can be
fhewed of this doctrine in the faid Church,
nor any contradiction againft yt when yt firft
entred: as on the cōtrary fide the firft offpring
of the other, togeather with the place, author,
tyme, manner, occafion, refiftance, condemnation, and other like circumftances are and
may be authentically fhewed, prooued and
conuinced, yea that the very face of Chriftendome from tyme out of mynd, by their
churches, altars, offerings, adoration, and
manner of diuine feruice admitrted euery
where, without contradiction, doubt, or queftion, do teftifie the fame: the truth moreouer
therof being confirmed by fo infinite concourfe of manifeft miracles, recorded by fuch
authors, as no man with piety can doubt of
their creditt; the Catholiks I fay hauinge all
this *mayne cloud of wittneffes* (to vfe the Apoftles
words) for the teftimony of this truth, and
being practized and accuftomed in the beleefe
therof for fo many ages togeather without
interruption, and feing moreouer that *Luther*
himfelfe, and all the learned of his fide that

*The 4.
ground of
the Chur-
thes con-
fent.*

*Miracles.
Hebr. 12.*

H   were

were open professed enemyes in other things to the Catholike beleefe, yet in this protested the truth to be so euident, as they durst not impugne it, nay held the first impugners therof for damnable heretiks, addinge also heere-vnto that *Zuinglius* the first chiefe author, confesseth himselfe to haue byn moued thervnto by a certayne extrauagant spiritt, which he saith he knew not, *whether yt was blacke or white.*

Zuing. l. de re Sacramentaria.

All these things, I say, laid togeather, and the liues and manners considered of them, that haue held the one & the other faith; that is to say the infinite Saints of the one side, whome the Protestants themselues do not deny to haue byn Saints; and the qualityes and conditions of the others, that first began, or since haue defended the new Sacramentary opinions: lett the discreet reader iudge, whether the Catholiks of England had reason to stand fast in their old beleefe, against the innouations of our new Sacramentary Protestants in K. *Edwards* dayes. And the like shall yow see in the other articles that ensue of *Transubstantiation* and *Sacrifice,* dependinge of this first of the *reall presence,* as before yow haue heard. But much more will yow be confirmed in all this, when yow shall haue read ouer the disputations followinge, and seene the triflinge arguments of the Sacramentaryes in these so weighty & important articles of our beleefe, and the ridiculous euasions where- with they seeke to auoyd, or delude the graue tistimonyes of scriptures, and Fathers before mentioned.

VVeighty considerations.

tioned. For therby wilbe feene, that they feeke not truth in deed with a good and fincere confcience, & feare of Gods iudgements; but only to efcape and entertayne talke for continuaunce of their faction, which ought to be marked by the reader, yf he loue his foule. And thus much for the grounds of the reall-prefence.

Groundes of *Tranfubftantiation.*
§. 2.

26. Touchinge the fecond queftion about Tranfubftantiation, though yt be leffe principall then the former of the *reall-prefence*, for that yt conteyneth but the particular manner how Chrift is really in the Sacrament,& confequently not fo neceffary to be difputed of with Sacramentaryes, that deny Chrift to be there really at all, as before hath byn noted: yet fhall we briefely difcouer the principall grounds wheron Catholiks do ftand, in this receaued doctrine of the Church againft Lutherans efpecially, who grauntinge the faid *reall prefence,* do hold that bread is there togeather with our Sauiours body : which Catholiks for many reafons do hould to be abfurd. And albeit the word *Tranfubftantiation* & particular declaration therof,was not fo expreffely fett downe in the Church vntill fome 400. yeares gone in the generall Councell of Late-

ran vnder Pope Innocentius the third, as the word *Trinity, Homousion,* or *Consubstantiality* and cleere exposition therof, was not vntill the Councell of Nice 300. yeares after Christ; yet was the truth of this doctrine held euer before in effect and substance, though in different words: to witt *mutation, transmutation, conuersion of bread into the body of Christ, transelementation,* and the like, which is proued by the perpetuall consent of doctrine, vttered by the ancient Fathers in this point from the beginninge, which are recorded by Catholike wryters of our dayes from age to age: and one only alleageth thirty and two, that wrote heereof

Fathers authorityes reduced to tvvo heads.

before the Councell of *Lateran,* and are ouerlong to be recited in this place; only they may be reduced for more perspicuitie to two heads: the one of such as deny the substance of bread to remayne after the words of consecration; the other of such as do expressely auouch a conuersion of bread into Christs body.

Firsthead.

27.   Of the first sort, that deny bread to remaine, is *S. Cyrill* Bishop of Hierusalem, whose

Catech. 4. mystag.

words are: *hoc sciens, ac pro certissimo habens, panem hunc, qui videtur à nobis, non esse panem, etiamsi gustus panem esse sentiat, &c.* Thou knowing and being

,, certayne of this; that the bread which we see

,, is not bread, notwithstanding it tast as bread;

,, and the wyne which we see not to be wyne,

,, but the bloud of Christ, though to the tast yt

Lib.de San-
&. Baptis-
mo non lõge
ab initio.

still seeme to be wyne. And *S. Gregory Nissen: Panis iste panis est in initio communis, &c.* This
bread

bread at the beginninge is comon bread, but
when yt is consecrated, yt is called, and is indeed the body of Christ. Againe *Eusebius: Ante-*
quam consecrentur, *&c.* Before consecration
there is the substance of bread and wyne, but
after the words of Christ, yt is his body and
bloud: All which do exclude, as yow see,
bread after consecration. And to the same effect *S. Ambrose* : *Panis hic, panis est, ante verba Sa-*
cramentorum, sed vbi accesserit consecratio, de pane sit
caro Christi. This bread before the words of the
Sacraments, is bread , but after the consecration, of bread is made the fiesh of Christ. And
S. Chrysostome treating of this mistery, asketh
this question, and aunswereth the same. *Num*
vides panem? num vinum? absit, ne sic cogites! Dost
thou see bread? dost thou see wyne heere?
God forbidd, thinke no such matter. And to
this same effect many others might be cyted,
but yt would grow to ouergreat prolixity.

28. The second sort of testimonyes that do
affirme conuersion and change of bread into
the body of Christ, are many more, yf we
would stand vpon their allegation, and in
place of all might stand *S. Ambrose*, whose faith
was the generall faith of Christendome in his
dayes; & he doth not only oftentymes repeat,
that by the words of Christ vttered by the
Priest vpon the bread, the nature & substance
therof is changed into the body and bloud of
Christ, but proueth the same by examples of
all the miraculous mutations & conuersions,
recorded in the old and new Testament. *Pro-*

Hom. 1. *de*
Fast.
,,
,,
,,

De Sacram.
cap. 4.
,,
,,

Hom de
Eucha: en
Encæn.
,,

2. head.

bemus (faith he) *non hoc esse quod natura formauit,*
sed quod benedictio consecrauit, maiorémque vim esse
benedictionis quam natura, quia benedictione etiam ip-
sa natura mutatur. Lett vs proue then (by all
,, these other miracles) that this which is in the
,, Sacrament, is not that which nature did frame
,, (vsed bread and wyne) but that which the
,, blessinge hath consecrated, and that the force
,, of blessinge is greater then the force of nature;
,, for that nature herselfe is changed by bles-
,, singe; And againe: *Si tantum valuit sermo Elia, vt*

ignem de cœlo deponeret; non valebit sermo Christi, vt
species mutet elementorum? Yf the speach of Elyas
,, was of such force, as yt could bring downe
,, fire from heauen, shall not the words of Christ
,, (in the Sacrament) be able to change the na-
,, tures of the elemēts? *videlicet* (as I said before)
,, of bread and wyne. And yet further: *Yow haue*
read, that in the creation of the world, God said, and
thinges were made, he commaunded, and they were
created; that speach then of Christ, vvhich of nothinge
created that which was not before; shall yt not be able
to exchaunge those thinges that are, into other thinges,
vvhich they vvere not before? for yt is no lesse to giue
new natures to things, then to chaunge natures, but ra-
ther more, &c.

29. Thus reasoneth that graue and holy
Doctor, to whome we might adioyne many
more both before and after him, as namely
S. *Cyprian* in his sermon of the supper of our
Lord: *Panis iste quem, &c.* This bread which
,, Christ gaue vnto his disciples being changed
,, not in shape, but in nature, is by the omnipo-
                                                    tency

tency of the word made flesh. *S. Cyrill* Bishop
of Hierusalem proueth the same by example
of the miraculous turning of water into wine,
at the marriage of *Cane* in Galeley: *aquam mu-*
tauit in vinum (saith he *&c.*) Christ turned water into wyne, by his only will, and is he not
worthy to be beleeued *quòd vinum in sanguinem*
transmutauit, that he did chaunge wyne into
his bloud? For yf at bodily marriages he did
worke so wonderfull a miracle, why shall not
we confesse that he gaue his body and bloud
(in the Sacrament) to the children of the
spouse? wherfore with all certainty, let vs receaue the body and bloud of Christ, for vnder
the forme of bread is giuen vnto vs his body,
and vnder the forme of wyne his bloud. Thus
hee of this miraculous chaunge, wherof *Saint*
Chrysostome treatinge also vpon *S. Mathew* wryteth thus: *Nos ministrorum locum tenemus, qui verò*
sanctificat & immutat, ipse est. We that are Priests,
hould but the place of his ministers: (in this
great chaunge) for he who doth sanctifie all,
and maketh the chaunge, is Christ himselfe.
To like effect wryteth *Eusebius Emißenus; quando*
benedicenda, &c. When the creatures of bread
and wyne are layd vpon the Altar to be blessed, before they are consecrated by the inuo-
cation of the holy Ghost, there is present the
substance of bread and wyne; but after the
words of Christ, there is Christs body and
bloud. And what maruayle yf he that could
create all by his word, *poßet creata conuertere,*
could conuert, and chaunge those thinges

*Cyrill. Ca-
tech. my-
stag. 4.*

*Hom. 83.
in Matth.*

*Serm. de
corp. Do-
mini.*

H 4   that

that he had created, into other natures?

30.   I might alleage many other Fathers to this effect, but my purpose in this place doth not permitt yt: this shalbe sufficient for a tast, that the doctrine of conuersion or chaunge of bread and wyne, into the body and bloud of Christ, which is the doctrine of Transubstantiation, was not new at the tyme of the Councell of *Lateran*, but was vnderstood and held euer before, by the cheefe Fathers of the Catholike Church, yea and determined also by two Councells at Rome : and the first therof generall, wherin was present our *Lanfrancus* vpon the yeare of Christ 1060. vnder Pope *Nicolas* the second ; and the other 19. yeares after vnder Pope *Gregory* the seauenth, & both of them aboue an hundred yeares before the Councell of *Lateran,* wherin notwithstanding is declared expressely this doctrine, of the chaunge of bread & wyne into the body and bloud of our Sauiour, albeit not vnder the name of *Transubstantiation*; and yt is proued expressely out of the words of Christs institution, *This is my body*, which can haue no other probable exposition, but that the bread is chaunged into his body. And so yt is expounded by all the forsaid Fathers, and others that, before this controuersie fell out, interpreted the same words of our Sauiour.

31.   These grounds then had the English Catholiks in *K. Edwards* dayes to stand in the defence of this doctrine, that is to say, the cleere words of scripture so vnderstood by all antiquity,

Lanfranc. l. de corp. Domini Guit. l. 3. de corp. Domini & Ansel. ep. de corp. Domini.

The consent of the vniuersall Church.

quity, togeather with the affertions and affeuerations of all the Fathers, the determination of Councells prefently vpon the controuerfie firft moued, and namely of that great
famous *Lateran* Councell, wherin concurred Canon. 1.
both the Greeke and Latyn Church, there & 2.
being prefent, the Greeke patriarks of *Conftan-*
tinople and *Hierufalem*, 70. metropolitan Archbifhops, and aboue a thoufand and two hundred other Fathers of diuers ftates, & degrees,
(compare this with a meeting of fome twenty or thirty minifters impugninge the fame.)
All which hauinge difputed the matter, and The great-
confidered as well by fcripture, and by ancient neffe of
tradition of the Fathers and vniuerfall Cath. the Late-
Church, what had byn held before, did with ran Coun-
full agreement determine & declare this mat- cell.
ter, accurfinge whofoeuer fhould from that
tyme foreward, deny that doctrine of *Tranfub-*
ftantiation. Which decree of that *Councell* being
receaued generally, vvithout contradiction
throughout the Chriftian world, hath byn
confirmed by feauen other Councells fince
that tyme, as before we haue fhewed. And let
the difcreet reader vveigh vvith himfelfe,
vvhich party hath more fecurity for yt felfe,
eyther the Catholike that followed all this
authority & confent of antiquity, or our new
Proteftants, that vpon frefh imaginations of
their owne heads, diuifed a new doctrine contrary to all this antiquity. And thus much of
this article, for a taft of that which may be alleaged for yt.

Groundes

Groundes for the sacrifice of the masse.
§. 2.

32. The third question proposed to be handled in the foresaid disputations, was about the
sacrifice of the masse, to witt, whether the selfe-
same body of our Lord, whose reall presence
is proued in the first question, be not only a
Sacrament in the Christian Church, as yt is
receaued vnder a signe of bread and wyne by
the Priest and communicants, but a sacrifice
also, as yt is offered to God the Father by the
Priest vpon the Altar; and whether this externall and visible sacrifice be appointed by
Christ, to be iterated and dayly frequented in
the Church vnto the worlds end, and this
both for an externall worshipp peculiar to
Christians, whereby they are distinguished
from all other people, as also for propitiation
of sinnes, by applyinge the meritt and vertue
of the other bloudy sacrifice of our Sauiour
on the Crosse once offered for all, and euer
auayleable (as *S. Paul* at large declareth in his
epistle to the Hebrewes) for sanctifyinge the
redeemed: this then being the question, and
this being a doctrine so generally receaued
throughout the Christian world, both in the
Greeke, Latin, Aethiopian, Armenian, and other
Christian Churches, as there was no doubt or
question therof, when *Luther* and his offspring
began;

The state of the question.

began; yt fell out in England, that vnder the
child *King Edward* his raigne, name & authority, that the *L. Seymour* proteƈtour and his
followers, with some few Priests that were
weary of massinge, and desirous of marriage,
but cheefly *Cranmer* and *Ridley, Hooper, Latymer,*
and others, bad heads of the cleargy in those
dayes, tooke vpon them to pull downe this
publike vse of sacrifice, and afterward to examine, and call in question the doƈtrine therof.
At which chaunge and suddayne innouation,
neuer seene in England before, from the first
day that Christian Religion entred vnder the
Apostles, as all the realmes and contreyes
round about remayned astonished: so diuers
notwithstanding of the lighter sort, enclyned
to noueltyes, applauded to them, & followed
their diuise; others more prudent and respe-
ƈtiue to their owne saluation, consideringe
that there went more in this matter then the
pleasure and fancyes of a few particular men,
stood constant in that, which before they had
receaued, and that which generally they saw,
and knew to be in vse throughout all Christendome without cōtradiƈtion, which could
not be by *S. Austens* rule, but that yt must needs
come downe from the Apostles themselues,
for so much as all opposite doƈtrine to that,
which was first planted by them & receaued
from them, could neuer be so generally admitted without contradiƈtion.

*Aug. l. 2. de
baptis. c. 7.
lib. 4. cop. 6.
& 24. &
l. 5, c. 23.*

33. Wherfore entringe into due consideration of this matter, whilst all the ruffe ran the
other

other way for 5. or 6. yeares space, vnder that King Child, and those other little tyrants that bare sway, and one destroyed the other by Gods iust iudgement vnder him. These good men (the Catholikes I meane) fell to search what grounds they had, or might find out for this so receaued a doctrine & practise, as this of the masse and sacrifice was. And first they found, that wheras the first insult of heretiks was against the very name of the masse, as a new diuised thinge without reason or signification ; they found (I say) that it was a very ancient and vsuall word, for the externall sacrifice of Christians vpon the Altar, in the Latyn Church, for twelue hundred yeares past and downeward; in place wherof the *Grecians* haue vsed the word *Liturgie*, *Synaxis*, and the like, and this vse is not only to be shewed by the testimonyes of particular Fathers, as Saint [a] *Ambrose*, S.[b] *Augustine*, S.[c] *Leo*, S.[d] *Gregory*, [e] *Victor Vticensis*, [f] *Cassianus*, and other ; but by whole Councells also, as by that of [g] *Rome*, vnder *Pope Siluester* the first of 275. Bishops, held almost 1300. yeares gone; the second & fourth of [h] *Carthage* held the next age after, and the Councell of [i] *Agatha* in *France* the same age; the Councell of [k] *Ilerdum* and [l] *Valentia* in *Spaine*, and of [m] *Orleance* in *France*, all aboue 1000. yeares gone, which was sufficient matter against the vanyty of heretiks, that condemned the name & the words: for example of S. *Ambrose* sayinge *Missam facere cœpi*, *orare in oblatione Deum*. I began to say masse, and to

pray

The search of Catholiks vnder *K. Edw.* for the groūds of the masse.

About the name of masse.

a *l.5. ep.33.*
b *Serm.91. & 151. de sep & serm. 237. in domin.19. post Penterost.*
c *Ep.81. ad Dioscor & 28. ad episc. Germ.*
d *l 1. ep 12. & l.4.c.10.*
e *Lib. 2 hist. Vandal.*
f *Lib. 3. de sant. pf. ord.*
g *Can 1.*
h *In 2. Conc. can. 3. & 4. Ca. 84.*
i *Can. 47.*
k *Can. 4.*
l *Can. 1.*
m *Can. 28.*

Ambros. ibid.

pray to God in the oblation of the sacrifice,
and those of S. *Austen: In lectione qua nobis ad mis-* *Aug. ibid*
sas legenda est, audituri sumus. We shall heare of „
this matter more in the lesson which is to be „
read vnto vs at masse. These speaches I say, &
this practise of so ould learned & holy Priests,
as these and their fellowes were, did preuayle
more with the grauer sort of English people,
then the lightnesse & inconstancy of *Cranmer*
Ridley, and such other licentious Priests, as for
liberty fell to Apostasie.

34. And this for the name of the *masse.* But
for the nature and substance therof, which
conteyneth the externall true and proper sacrifice of the Christian Church, they found
such store of euident proofes, and most graue
authorityes, as might stay, confirme and satisfie any mans mynd, that were not willfully
bent to the contrary. And wheras I do vse the
words of *externall, true and proper* sacrifise, yow
must remember therby the fraud of these new
heretiks, who, as before about the reall presence, did go about to delude all the sayings of
holy Fathers, and other testimonyes of Antiquity, that spake of Christs reall being in the
Sacrament, by running to the words *spiritual-*
ly, sacramentaly, by faith, and the like: so heere
fyndinge the whole torrent and streame of
Christian antiquity to stand for this Christian
sacrifice, & to mention, reuerence, & auouch
the same; these fellowes for auoydinge their
authorityes do runne from the proper externall sacrifice, wherof we treate, vnto the internall,

ternall, and inuisible sacrifice of the mynd,
wherof K. *Dauid* saith, that a contrite spiritt is
a sacrifice to God. And when this cannot
serue, they run also to improper and metaphoricall externe sacrifices, (such as are, *mortification
of the body Rom.* 12. *sacrifice of thankesgeuinge.
Psalm.* 49. *Sacrifice of almes deedes. Hebr.* 13. and
other such good works, which by a certayne
analogy or proportion with the nature of
proper sacrifices, are called also *sacrifice* in scriptures & by the Fathers, but improperly. To
these then do our Protestants runne, when
they are pressed with the authorityes of auncient Fathers, that name the vse of Christian
sacrifice in the Church, and will needs make
vs beleeue, that the Fathers ment not properly of any true visible or externall sacrifice, but
eyther of inward or inuisible sacrifice of the
hart, mynd, and good desire; or els of outward
metaphoricall sacrifice of pious and vertuous
workes.

35. But all these are fraudulent shifts to ouerthrow one truth by another. For as we do
not deny, but that there is an inward and inuisible sacrifice of our mynd, in dedicatinge of
our selues to God, and to the subiection of his
Maiestie, without which the externall sacrifice is little worth to him that offereth the
same: And as we graunt that all good works
be sacrifices in a certayne sort, by some similitude they haue with true & proper sacrifices,
for that they are offered vp to God in his hu-
nour; yet do we say, that this is from our purpose

pofe in this place, who talke of a true proper externall facrifice offered vp to God, after a peculiar facred rite, or ceremonyes, by peculiar men deputed to this office in acknowledgement of Gods diuine power, maieftie, and dominion ouer vs, & proteftation of our due fubiection vnto him, fuch as were the externall facrifices in the law of nature, offered vp by patriarks and heads of familyes, and by Priefts of Aarons order vnder the law of Moyfes, and by Chrift and his Priefts accordinge to the order of *Melchifedech* in the new law; and for fo much as both the internall, & metaphoricall facrifices before mentioned of good affection, defires, and holy works, are not peculiar to any law, but were lawfull and needfull vnder all lawes, and in all tymes, and require no particular kind of men or minifters to offer them, but may be offered vp by any man or woman whatfoeuer: therfore do we exclude all thefe from the name of the facrifice, which heere is meant by our defcription, and comprehendeth as yow fee an externall vifible oblation, made by him or them, who are peculiarly deputed by God to this office, which are Priefts: So as whenfoeuer our aduerfaryes do flipp from this proper fignification of a facrifice to the other, eyther internall or metaphoricall, which may be offered by all forts of people, and therevpon do fay that all men are Priefts, they runne, as yow fee. quite from the purpofe, as they do alfo for examples fake, when to auoyd the necefsity of externall

The defcription of a true externall and vifible facrifice.

faftinge,

An exãple of an hereticall fraude about faſtinge.

faſtinge, they runne to the internall faſtinge of the mynd, ſayinge that true faſtinge, is to faſt from ſinne, which as we deny not in that ſenſe of ſpirituall faſtinge; ſo is it notwith-ſtandinge a plaine ſhift, and runninge from the purpoſe, and cannot ſtand with many places of the ſcripture, which muſt needs be vnderſtood of the externall faſt; as when Chriſt is ſaid by the Euangeliſts to haue faſted 40. dayes togeather; and *S. Paul* affirmeth that he and his fellow Apoſtles faſted frequently; It cannot be vnderſtood (I ſay) of faſtinge on-ly thoſe tymes from ſinne; for that Chriſt fa-ſted alwayes from ſinne without exception; and ſo do all good men both faſt and ſacrifice alſo, by offeringe vp good deſires and pious actions to almighty God, dayly and hourely without diſtinction of men or tymes.

36. But this is not the proper, viſible, & exter-nall ſacrifice which heere we meane, which was inſtituted by God, as peculiar to Chri-ſtian peopie vnder the law of the ghoſpell, for an externall worſhipp vnto him (beſides the internall) and teſtification of their inward ſubiection, loue, and piety towards him; which ſacrifice comming in place of all others that went before, both in the law of nature and of Moyſes that prefigured and foreſigni-

The excel-lency of the Chri-ſtian and externall ſacrifice.

fied the ſame; and being but one and ſingular inſteed of them all, and their great variety, is to be eſteemed ſo much more excellent then they all, as the law of the ghoſpell is more excellent then thoſe lawes, and truth aboue

ſhad-

shaddowes, & the sacred body of Christ God and man himselfe, to be preferred before the bodyes of beasts, byrds and other such creatures, vvhich vvere but signes and figures of this.

37. And in this sense do both scriptures, fathers, councells, and all holy Christian antiquity speake and treat of this most diuine, venerable and dreadfull sacrifice, wherof, as of the highest and most principall mystery and treasure, left by our Sauiour in his Church, there are so many testimonyes, as before hath byn signifyed, that yt shall not be possible for me in this place, and with the breuity which is necessary, to alleage the least part therof; yet some few generall heads shall I touch, which the learned reader may see more dilated, by diuers Catholike wryters of our dayes, and he that hath not commodity or tyme to do that, may geue a ghesse by that which heere I shall sett downe.

38. First then, for that this holy sacrifice of the Christian Church was so principally intended by almighty God for the new law, as hath byn said, many things were sett downe by the holy Ghost in the old Testament, both prefiguringe and prophecyinge the same, as first the sacrifice of the King and Priest *Melchisedech* in bread and wyne, *Gen.* 14. which all the auncient Fathers, by generall consent, do apply to the sacrifice vsed now in the Christian Church, and yt were ouerlong to alleage their particular authorityes, lett. *S. Augustine*

I   speake

Aug. l.16.
de ciuit.
cap. 22.
speake for all: *Primum apparuit* (saith he) *sacrificium* (Melchisedech) *quod à Christianis nunc offertur Deo toto orbe terrarum.* The first sacrifice ap-
„   peared in Melchisedech, which now is offe-
„   red to God by Christians throughout all the
Lib. 1. cont.
aduers. leg.
& Prophet.
cap. 20.
world. And in another place : *Vident nunc tale sacrificium offerri Deo toto orbe terrarum:* Christians do see the like sacrifice (to that of Melchisedech) to be offered to God, ouer all the world.
„   And all the other sacrifices, signes and oblations mentioned before, as presiguringe the reall presence of Chrifts sacred body, and true flesh in the Sacrament, are applied by the selfe same Fathers, whome before we haue named, to the presiguration also of this diuine sacrifice, conteyninge the selfe same thinge, which the Sacrament doth, but in a different sort, in respect of diuers ends, the one as yt is receaued by the communicants; the other as yt is offered vnto God the Father.

39.   After these presigurations there follow the predictions of Prophetts as that of *Esay* 19. and 66. where is foreteold the reiection of the Aaronicall priesthood and sacrifice, and a new promised vnder the Christians. The prophesy of *Daniell* also, where it is foretould, that in the last age of the law of grace, by the comminge
Dan. 8. &
12.
of Antichrist, *iuge sacrificium,* that is the dayly sacrifice shall cease. Of this (I say) is inferred by the ancient Fathers, that vntill Antichrists comminge there shalbe a perpetuall and dayly sacrifice amonge Christians; which is most of
Malach. 1.
all confirmed by the prophesie of *Malachias* in
these

these words: *Ad vos ò sacerdotes, &c.* To yow ò ,,
priests, that despise my name, and do offer ,,
vpon my Altar polluted bread, and do sacri- ,,
fice the beasts that are blind, lame and weake, ,,
I haue no more likinge of yow, saith the lord ,,
of hosts, and I will not receaue at your hands ,,
any gifts, for that from the east to the west my ,,
name is great amonge the gentills, and they ,,
do sacrifice vnto me in euery place, and do of- ,,
fer vnto my name a pure oblation, for that my ,,
name is great amonge the gentills, saith the ,,
lord of hostes. Out of which place the Fathers
do shew first, that heere the priesthood and
sacrifice of Aaron was to be reiected, & a new
priesthood and sacrifice, accordinge to the order of *Melchisedech*, erected amongst the gentills, wherby ordinarily are vnderstood the
Christian people conuerted chiefly (from gen-
tility) who were to succeed in their place, and
that with such certainty, as the present tense
is put for the future, accordinge to the manner
of prophesies; and the Antithesis or opposition
betweene the two sacrifices, the one reiected,
the other promised, doth make the matter
more plaine; for that as the Iewes sacrifice
could not be offered but in one place, to witt,
in the Temple of Hierusalem: so shall the
Christian sacrifice be offered vp *in omni loco,*
that is euery where without respect of places
from the east to the west. The Iewish sacrifices were many and of diuers sorts, but the
Christian sacrifice that should succeed in place
therof was to be but one. The Iewish sacri-

The op-
position
of the pro-
phesie of
Malachie.

fices

fices were polluted, not so much in respect of
great quantity of beasts bloud powred out
therin, and for that they offered defectuous
beasts, as for the wickednesse of them that offered the same; but the Christian sacrifice was
to be cleane & vnspotted, not only in respect
of the vnbloudy manner, wherin yt was to be
offered vnder the formes of bread and wyne,
but especially for the excellency of the thinge
yt selfe offered, being the most pretious body
of Christ himselfe, and for that the demeritt
of the offerer cannot take away the worth of
the offeringe.

40.   These circumstances then considered,
and that the heretikes heere cannot runne to
their shift of inward, and inuisible sacrifices,
(for that these could not be vnderstood by the
Prophett as new sacrifices, that should suc-
ceede to the ould, for that these were alwayes
in vse with good men, duringe the tyme of the

Circum-
stances
that proue
the sacri-
fice of the
masse to
haue byn
fore pro-
phesied.

old sacrifice also, and were lawfull, yea commaunded in all tymes, to witt, to haue inward
piety and deuotion, giue almes, and the like)
these things I say considered, togeather with
the expositions of holy Fathers, as well vpon
these as vpon other piaces of the old Testament, there can be no probable doubt, but
that this externall sacrifice of the Christians
was prophesyed by the holy Ghost longe before the comminge of Christ.

41.   Secondly, the same is proued out of diuers places of the new Testament: And first
out of S. Iohns ghospell, where as our Sauiour

pro-

promiſed in myſterious words the inſtitution
of this bleſſed ſacrifice, as before hath byn
ſeene; ſo alſo did he ſigniſie that this ſacrifice
ſhould ſucceed in ſteed of all ſacrifices that
went before. For wheras the *Samaritan* woman at the well, ſpeakinge of the ſchiſme betweene the Iewes & *Samaritans* about adoring
in the Temple of Ieruſalem, and in the hill
Garizim of *Samaria* (which word of adoringe
muſt needs in that place ſigniſie ſacrifycinge,
as yt doth alſo in other places of ſcripture, as
Gen. 22. *Act.* 8. and els where, for that the controuerſie betweene the Iewes and *Samaritans*
was about the vſe of ſacrificing, as the higheſt
externall act of adoration) our Sauiour aunſwereth to her queſtion, that the houre was
now come, when neyther in that hill of *Samaria*, nor in *Ieruſalem* they ſhould adore; that is
to ſay, vſe any more ſacrifice, but that a new
adoration in ſpiritt and truth ſhould ſucceed
the former; which adoration being vnderſtood of ſacrifice, as the circumſtance both of
the place and matter do enforce, yt followeth
that Chriſt did heere promiſe a new ſacrifice,
that ſhould be ſpirituall and true: ſpirituall,
both in compariſon of the bloudy ſacrifice
that went before, & for that the conſecration
of Chriſts holy body in this ſacrifice, is made
by ſpeciall worke and operation of the holy
Ghoſt; true alſo and in truth it may iuſtly be
ſaid to bee, for that yt is the fulfillinge of all
precedent ſacrifices, and the truth of all former figures.

Ioan. 4. &
6. *Ioſeph.
lib.* 10. *de
Antiquitat.
Iudaic.* 6. 8.

The expli-
cation of
the place
of *S. Iohn*
*ca.*4.about
Sacrifice.

I 3   42. There

42.   There ensue the places of *Saint Mathew,*
S. Marke, S. Luke, and *S. Paul* about the institution and first celebration, of this vnbloudy sacrifice of Christ in his last supper, where yf we
admitt that, which all the circumstances of
the places themselues do plainly insinuate or
rather inforce; the continuall exposition and
tradition of the auncient Church doth teach
vs, to witt, that Christ our Sauiour hauinge
consecrated his sacred body, did offer the same
vnto his Father as a most gratefull sacrifice
in his last supper; then must yt follow, that
the words *hoc facite in meam commemorationem,*
do this in remembrance of me, implyed a precept not only of receauinge and communica-
tinge the body of Christ, but to offer vp the
selfe same also to God in sacrifice, after the example of Christ himselfe; which is that we
call the sacrifice of the masse, & to proue that

Proofe of
the sacri-
fice by
Chrifts
Inftitu-
tion.
th'Apostles vnderstood these words (I meane,
do this in remembrance of me) so; and in this sense,
not only the most ancient Fathers, as hath byn
said, do testifie the same, but the ancient liturgies or rituails also of the Apostles and their
schollers, as namely of *S. Iames, S. Clement,* and
S. Dionysius Areopagita, do make the matter manifest, concerning the Apostles practise in this
behalfe, to witt, that they did offer vp this
Christian externall sacrifice in all places of the
world, where they liued, and that from them
the Church tooke the same precept and vse,
accordinge to the testimony of old *Irenæus* Bishopp & Martyr, that liued aboue 1300. yeares
                                          gone,

gone, whose words are: *Eum qui ex creatura pa-*
nu est, accepit, & gratias egit, dicens; Hoc est corpus meum; *& calicem similiter qui est ex ea creatu-*
ra quæ est secundum nos suum sanguinem confessus est,
& noui testamenti nouam docuit oblationem, quam Ec-
clesia ab Apostolis accipiens, in vniuerso mundo offert
Deo. Christ tooke that bread which was a ,,
creature and gaue thanks sayinge : *This is my* ,,
body; and that cupp or wyne in like manner, ,,
which accordinge to vs , is of a creature , he ,,
confesseth to be his bloud, and heerby taught ,,
a new oblation of the new Testament, which ,,
the Church receauinge from the Apostles, ,,
doth offer the same to God , throughout the ,,
whole world. ,,

Tren. lib. 4.
adu. hæreſ.
cap. 32.

43.　Heere now are touched all the points
that might be doubted of by sectaryes, to wit,
that this bread and wine being first creatures,
are confessed by Christ, after consecration, to
be his body and bloud: secondly that this was
not only an institution of the Sacrament, and
communion, but of a new oblation & sacrifice
for the tyme of the new Testament : thirdly
that yt was not only to be offered once and in
one place , as Christs bloudy sacrifice was
vpon the Crosse , but throughout the whole
world by the whole Church. And fourthly
that this manner of oblation was taught the
Apostles by Christ himselfe, and by them deliuered to the said Church. What can be spoken more cleerly or distinctly by so ancient a
wittnesse ? neyther can heretiks heere haue
any refuge to internall or inuisible sacrifices of

A most
cleere
place of
S. Irenæus
for the
dayly sa-
crifice.

　the

the mynd, or to vnproper externall sacrifices
of thankefgeuinge, almefdeeds, and the like,
for that they are many, and were before alfo
lawfull vnder the law of *Moyfes*, as often hath
byn noted, & heere is faid to be taught a new
particular and fingular oblation of the new
Teftament, in fteed of all the facrifices of the
ould Teftament, vvhich *Irenæus* confirmeth
prefently in the next words after, by the pro-
phecye of *Malachye* before mentioned fayinge:

Iren. ibid.   *Malachias fic præfignificauit, &c.* Malachy the Pro-
,, phet did fo foretell vs, (that this new facrifice
,, and oblation of the new Teftament, fhould
,, thus be inftituted by Chrift, and frequented
,, by the Church) when he faid to the Iewifh
,, Priefts, I haue no will or likinge in yow, *&c.*
*Manifeftiſſimè ſignificans, quoniam prior quidem popu-
lus ceſſauit offerre Deo; omni autem loco ſacrificium offertur Deo, & hoc purum in gentibus;* moſt mani-
feſtly ſignifyinge, that the former Iewiſh
people (being reiected) haue ceaſed to offer
facrifice vnto God; but that amonge the gentills (to witt, Chriftians conuerted of them)
a pure facrifice is offered in euery place of the
world, that is to fay, without refpect of any
certayne place, as the Iewiſh facrifices were.

44. With *S. Irenæus* Biſhop and Martyr, concurreth in the fame age, and fomewhat before
him, *S. Iuſtinus* philofopher and Martyr, who
fpeakinge of the felfe fame thinge, and of the
Iewes reprobatiõ, and of the facrifice of the
new Teftament ordayned by Chrift in place
therof, writeth thus in his dialogue, intituled,
Triphon

Triphon againſt the ſaid Iewes: *A nemine Deus* *Iuſtin. in dial. Triph.*
hoſtias accipit, niſi à ſacerdotibus ſuis, &c. God doth
accept hoſts and ſacrifice of none, but of his ,,
Prieſts; wherfore he preuenting all thoſe that ,,
do offer ſuch ſacrifice vnto him in Chriſts ,,
name, as Ieſus Chriſt hath deliuered to be ,,
made in the Euchariſt of bread and wyne, & ,,
are made by Chriſtians in euery place, doth ,,
teſtify that they are gratefull vnto him: but ,,
your ſacrifices (o Iewes) he doth reiect. Thus
he. And theſe two teſtimonyes, of two ſo famous Martyrs and Doctors, are ſufficient for
wittneſſes of the firſt and next age after the
Apoſtles, to declare what the ſaid Apoſtles
both taught and practiſed in this point of publike ſacrifice, and what the Church of that
time vnderſtood Chriſt himſelfe to haue done
in that behalfe, though I might adioyne other a *l.5. Conſt.*
foure teſtimonyes more auncient yet then *Apoſt. c.18. & l.8. c.5. & 36.*
theſe; which are S. a *Clement*, ſcholler to S. Pe-
ter S. b *Dionyſius Areopagita*, ſcholler to S. Paul; b *l. de Eccl. Hier. cap.3.*
S. c *Martiall* Biſhop of *Burdeaux*, and S. d *Alexan-* c *epiſt. ad Burdegal.*
der Biſhop and Martyr of Rome; All which do *cap 3.*
no leſſe cleerly then theſe two, declare vnto d *ep.1. De- cret. ad Or-*
vs the doctrine and practice of their tymes *thodox.*
vnder the Apoſtles.

45. But for auoydinge prolixity I muſt paſſe
them ouer, aduertiſinge only by the way, that
where in the Acts of the Apoſtles yt is wryt-
ten by S. *Luke*, cōcerning the miſſion of S. *Paul*, *Act. 13.*
and *Barnaby* to preach, *Miniſtrantibus illis Domino,* That the
& ieiunantibus, dixit Spiritus Sanctus, ſegregate mihi Apoſtles
Saulum & Barnabam, &c. They miniſtring vnto did ſacri- fice.
God,

„ God, and faftinge (to witt, *Barnabas, Symon,*
„ *Lucius, Manahen* and *Saul*, that were Prophetts
„ and Doctors faith *S. Luke*) the holy Ghoft faid
„ to them, take out for me *Saul*, and *Barnabas*, to
„ the worke that I haue chofen them for. Now
as concerning the myniftery which thefe men
were performing, when the holy Ghoft fpake

Litour- vnto them, the Greeke word vfed by *S. Luke,*
gounton. importeth rather facrificing, and fo doth *Erafmus* tranflate yt, who was no euill Grecian,
nor of fmall credite with our aduerfaryes:and
of that word proceed the names before mencyoned of *Liturgy*, conteyninge the order of
this facrifice in the Chriftian Church.

46. But howfoeuer this bee, yow haue
heard the iudgement of the firft age, after the
Apoftles, by two wittneffes of fingular credit,
S. Iuftinus, and *S. Irenaus*: for the fecond may
fpeake *S. Cyprian* to the fame effect: *Iefus Chri-*

Cypr. lib 2. *ftus Dominus & Deus nofter, ipfe eft fummus facerdos*
ep.ft. 8. *Dei Patris, & facrificium Deo Patri ipfe primus obtu-*
lit, & hoc fieri in fui commemoratione pracepit. Iefus
„ Chrift our Lord and our God, he is the high
„ Prieft of God the Father, and he offered vp
„ firft of all to God his Father a facrifice, and
„ commaunded this to be done in his comme-
„ moration. Lo he commaundeth vs to facrifice
as he did facrifice. And for the third age after
the Apoftles *S. Ambrofe* may only fpeake: *Ponti-*

Ambrof. *fex nofter ille eft*, (faith he) *qui obtulit hoftiam nos*
comment. *mundantem; ipfam offerimus nunc, qua tunc oblata*
in cap. 10.
ad Hebr. *quidem, confumi non poteft.* He is our high Prieft
„ that offered the hoft which made vs cleane,
the

the selfe same do we offer now, which then was offerred, and cannot be consumed. Behould that we offer the selfe same host that Christ offered, and cannot be consumed. And for the fourth age *S. Austen* may stand for all, who answering *Faustus* the *Manichee*, that obiected, that he and other Catholiks did offer sacrifice vnto Martyrs; the holy Father denyeth yt saying: *Sacrificare martyribus dixi, &c.* I said that we did not sacrifice vnto Martyrs, but I said not, but that we sacrifised to God in the memoryes of Martyrs, which we most frequently vse to do, after that only rite, which God in the manifestation of the new Testament hath comaunded vs to sacrifice vnto him.

Aug. l. 20. contr. Faust. Manich. cap. 21.
,,
,,
,,
,,
,,

47. By all which testimonyes is euident, that the Church of God, in the first foure ages after the Apostles, did both offer an externall sacrifice, which was the same that Christ had offered before, and this after a peculiar rite insinuated by Christ to the Apostles, and deliuered by them to their posterity (which peculiar rite is more expressed in the liturgies before mentioned) and that all this is done by the authority and example of Christ himselfe in his last supper, and by tradition of the Apostles, which is inough to settle any pious mans conscience. Now then thirdly, wheras I should by order passe to the consideration of ancient Fathers sayings & testimonyes about this matter, they are so many and copious, as I should be prolix and weary to the reader in produ-

producing so many as may be alleaged, no one
article or mystery of our faith, being so often
handled or inculcated by them, as this of the
Church sacrifice. For better comprehendinge

Diuers heads of Fathers authori-tyes.
1.

wherof, I shall, as for the mystery of the *reall*
presence before, heere note only vnto thee certayne generall heads, whervnto the said Fathers testimonyes may be reduced; as first, that
euery where in their wrytings, speakinge of
this oblation made in the masse, they vse the
words *sacrificium, hostia, victima, offerre, immolare,*
sacrificare, all which are words that peculiarly
and properly do signify sacrifice; which is certayne that the said Fathers would neuer so
comonly haue vsed, no more then the Protestants do vse them now of their supper, if they
had meant no otherwise then the Protestants
do for other Sacraments; as *Baptisme* for example they do not call eyther sacrifice, host, or
victime, nor that the act of *Baptizinge*, is offer-
ringe, immolation or sacrifice, as they do the
act of celebratinge masse, wherof yow may
read all the Fathers generally, as *S. Hyppolitus*
Martyr, Orat. de Antichrist. S. Ambrose in psalm.38.
Nissen. orat. de resurrect. Chrysost. hom.24. in 1.Cor.
& hom. 17. in epist. ad Hebræos. Cyrill. lib. de adorat.
Aug. l.2. quæst. Euang. q.8. & l.4. de Trinit. cap.14.

2.

48.   The second head is of those authorityes,
that do compare this Christian sacrifice with
the sacrifices of the Iewes, affirminge the one
to be of the flesh of beasts & spotted, the other
of the pure, and immaculate flesh of Christ,
which they would neuer haue done in like
manner,

manner, yf they had not meant properly of true externall facrifices, offered by Chriftians in the new law, wherof yow may fee at large *Tertullian lib. contr. Iudæos cap. 1. Iuftin. in Triph. Chryfoft. in pfalm. 95. Cyprian. lib. de vnitat. Ecclefiæ Ambrof. in cap. 1. Lucæ. Nazianz. orat. 2. de pafchat. Aug. lib. 17. de Ciuitat. Dei cap. 20. S. Leo. ferm. de pafsion.* and many others.

49. The third head is of thofe authorityes, that compare this dayly facrifice of the Chriftian Church, offered in euery place throughout the world, with the only facrifice of Chrift, offered once for all vpon the Croffe, wherin for differéce fake they vfe the words, *cruentum & incruentum facrificium*, that is bloudy and vnbloudy facrifice, for diftinguifhinge the máner of the oblatió, the one vpon the Croffe, the other vpon many Altars in the Church at once, till the worlds end, otherwife holding the thing it felfe offered to be the very fame in th'one & other facrifice. See *S. Chryfoft. hom. 24. in 1. Cor. & hom. 2. ad 2. Tim. Cyprian. lib. 2. ep. 3. Ambrof. in pfalm. 38. Niffen. orat. 1. de refurrect. Aug. lib. 3. cont. Donatift. cap. 19. & lib. 20. contr. Fauft. cap. 21. Ifichius in Leuit. cap. 8.* and others.

50. The fourth head is of thofe, that affirme this our dayly facrifice to be propitiatory both for the liue and dead, as well thofe that are abfent as prefent, and that for both thefe forts of people yt ought, and was accuftomed to be offered in their dayes, which doth euidently proue yt a true facrifice, for that a Sacrament only doth profitt only thofe that do communicate

nicate and receaue the same, and no Protestant will say that their communion is offered vp for those that are absent, quicke or
dead, as the ancient Fathers do euery where
say, that our host & Eucharist was offered vp
in their dayes, and consequently they held yt
not only for a Sacrament, but also for a sacrifice; wherof yow may see *S. Chrysostome hom. 79.
ad Pop. Antiochen*; where he saith yt was offered
for Bishopps and Gouernours of the Church;
& *hom. 72. in Matth.* for sicke men, & *lib. 6. de Sacerdotio* for the dead. For which effect see *S. Augustine lib. 22. de ciuit. cap. 8. & in Enchirid. cap. 110.
& lib. 9. Confeß. cap. 12.* where he professeth to
haue offered sacrifice of the masse for his mother S. *Monica.*

5.   51.   The fifth head is of those places wherin
the Fathers do vse the words *Altar, Priests and
Priesthood,* as proper, peculiar, and appropriated
to true sacrifices; For as the Protestants of our
tymes do not vse these words, for that they
hould not their supper to be a sacrifice, but rather do fly them, though neuer so much vsed
by the said Fathers, and in place therof do vse
the words, *table, minister, mynistry,* and other
such like of their new Religion; so neyther
would the Fathers haue vsed the same words,
yf they had had the same meaning that Protestants haue; For that well knew the said Fathers how to expresse their meaninge in proper words, and therfore when they say that
x Optat. l. 6. Altars amonge Christians, are, *sedes ª corporis
cont. Parm.* Christi* the seats of the body of Christ, and that

                                               in

in their d yes Christians did ^b *adgeniculare aris* ^{b Tertull. l.}
Dei, knele downe at the Altars of God, *& quod* ^{de Penitent.}
^c *obsculabantur altaria,* that they kissed the Al- ^{c Ambros.}
tars, and that the office of Christian Priests is ^{l. 5. ep. 33.}
to sacrifice vpon the said Altars, yt is euident
what they meant, to him that will vnderstand
them, wherof more may be read in *S. Cyprian*
lib. 1. *ep.* 9. *Euseb. lib.* 1. *demonstr. Euang. cap.* 6. *Athan. in*
vita Anton. Nazianz. orat. in Gorgon. Nissen. lib. de
baptismo. Chrysost. hom. 53. *ad Pop. Antioch. & hom.*
20. *in* 2. *Cor. Hieron. lib. cont. Vigilant. & dial. cont.*
Lucifer. Aug. lib. 8. *cap. vit.* and others.

52. The sixt consideration out of the Fathers, 6.
may be their lyturgyes or forme of diuine seruice or masse, for offeringe of this sacrifice in
those dayes, of which sort of liturgyes there
are extant vnto this day diuers, as that of
S. Iames the Apostle, *S. Clement* scholler and
successor of *S. Peter,* of *S. Basill, S. Chrysostome,*
S. Ambrose, which albeit in all particular forme
of prayer, do not agree with our forme and
canon of masse at this day, yet in the substance
of the sacrifice they do, as also in many other
particular circumstances, vsinge the words of
oblation, sacrifice, victime, signes, singings, blessings,
eleuations, and other such rites which Protestants cannot abide. And for the cannon, and
forme of our masse, which is vsed at this day
in the Latyn Church, most parts therof are to
be seene in *S. Ambrose* his books *de Sacramentis,*
and the whole order as now yt is hath endured without alteration from *S. Gregory* the first
downeward, wherof yow may see *Alcuinus,*

Amala-

Amalarius, VValfridus, and other ancient authors in their books *de diuinis officijs.*

Luther reiecteth all Fathers about the masse.

53.   By all which generall heads, yow may easily see the multitude of testimonyes, that may be alleaged out of the Fathers, yf we should prosecute euery one of these in particular; & how great reason *Martyn Luther* had to except against them all, or rather to defy them all, when first he begā to write against this sacrifice, *Hic non moramur* (saith he) *si clamitant Papistæ, Ecclesia, Ecclesia, Patres, Patres;* heere we care not, though Papists cry, Church, Church, Fathers, Fathers; And againe: *Heere I do professe against them that vvill cry out, that I do teach against the rite of the Church and ordinances of Fathers, that I vvill heare none of these obiections.* And in another place against our K. Henry of England, much more immodestly and wickedly, when the King alleaged the authorityes of ancient Fathers for the masse, this shamelesse fellow answered: *Thomisticos asinos, &c. I say that these Thomisticall asses haue nothinge to bringe forth, but only a multitude of men, and vse of antiquity.* And a little after he saith expressely; *that he careth not though a thousand Augustines, and a thousand Cyprians be brought against him.* So as this first Father and chiefe Captayne of our Protestants, did easily graunt, as yow see, that the whole consent of ancient Fathers was against him.

Lib. de Missa & l. de abrogand. miss. & lib. contr. Angliæ Regem.

Ponderations

Ponderations vpon the Premises.

§. 4.

54. All which being considered, there remayneth only to weigh, what a discreet man
may thinke or do in this important case: For
first heere is all the antiquity of the Christian
Church on the one side, that testifyeth vnto
vs not only what was beleeued and exercised
in their dayes, but vpon what grounds also,
both of scriptures of the old and new Testament, and by Christs owne institution, fact
and ordination, and by the practise and tradition of the Apostles themselues. Then is there
the continuance of all ages since, throughout
all countreyes and nations of Christendome,
as hath byn said. There is the agreement of all
generall Councells: The consent of all Ecclesiasticall historyes, wherin as there is continuall mention of both publike and priuate
exercise of this externall Sacrifice: So is there
no memory at all, of any tyme synce the
Apostles wherin yt began, or that euer any
contradiction, doubt, or question was about
the same, for 1200. yeares togeather after
Christs assension, which must needs haue happened, yf the vse therof had not byn prescri-
bed and left by Christ and his Apostles themselues. For what men or people would haue
attempted to begin, or bring in so great a mat-

Importāt considera-tions.

1.

2.

3.

4.

5.

K ter

ter as this? or who would haue receaued ye without oppofition, yf yt had not byn eftablifhed euen from the beginninge? I adde alfo

6.

another cófideration of no little importance, which is, that yf Chrift had left his Church & people without a particular externall facrifice, wherby they fhould be diftinguifhed from all other people; the Chriftian Church vnder the law of grace, fhould be inferiour to the Church of the patriarks vnder the law of nature, and vnto the Prophetts vnder the law of Moyfes: for that both of thofe Churches and people had an externall dayly facrifice, wherby to honour God, befides the internall facrifice of their mynd: neyther can yt be faid, that Chrifts owne facrifice on the Croffe, once offered for all, is this dayly facrifice apprehended by vs in faith, for that they alfo beleeued in him, and their facrifices were acceptable only by faith in him to come. And therfore as Chrifts one facrifice then to come, was no impediment, why their dayly facrifices, which tooke their valour from this one of Chrift, fhould not be dayly offered amonge them: fo the fame facrifice of Chrift vpon the Croffe, being now paft, fhould not take away our dayly facrifices offered in remembrance therof, and for the applying of the infinite valour of that one facrifice vnto vs, from which this other dayly facrifice taketh his fufficiency.

7.

55. Furthermore the very outward forme of all Chriftian Churches, there buildinge with Croffes, Altar, Iles, and the like, the
foun-

foundinge of monasteryes, Chappells, orato-
ryes, the ceremonyes in foundinge them, their
statutes for sayinge of masses for the dead,
which were in Britany both before our nation was conuerted, and much more after;
the whole Canon of our Latyn masse-booke
which is graunted by our aduersaryes, and
euidently proued to haue byn, as yt is now,
for aboue a thousand yeares togeather, and
brought in by *S. Augustine* our first Apostle: All
these things I say, do shew whether this were
a matter to be called in question by a few li-
bertyne Priests, and auaritious noble men, &
to be banished the realme vpon a soddayne,
vnder the name of a child Kinge, that knew
not what yt meant, as yt was in K. *Edwards*
dayes in our miserable countrey.

56. Moreouer yf yow ponder with your
selfe, what manner of Priests they were for
life, learninge, and vertue that acknowledged
themselues to haue offered sacrifices vpon Altars in their dayes, as *S. Irenæus, S. Cyprian, S.
Ambrose, S. Chrysostome, S. Augustine, S. Gregory.*
and others of the first ages, yea and for these
later ages, since *Berengarius* mooued first the
question about the *reall presence*, as *S. Anselme,
S. Bernard, S. Thomas* of *Aquin, S. Dominicke,* and
almost infinite other Saints, and holy men, of
whome all historyes do report wonderfull
extraordinary tokens, of almighty God his
speciall fauours towards them; and do compare them with the first marryed Priests and
Apostata friars, that were the first impugners

8.

The com-
parison of
Priests
that offe-
red or im-
pugned
the sacri-
fice of the
masse.

of

of this sacrifice in England or round about
vs, we shall find a great difference. And then
yf we consider, by what good spiritt or motiue *Luther* began the firlt contradiction in
Germany, which was by the diuells owne per-
suafion and personall appearance vnto him,
and disputinge againft yt (for yt seemed that
he esteemed so much both of the man and the
matter, that he would not send an Embassa-
dour vnto him, as he did soone after to *Zuinglius*, for impugninge the *reall presence*, but go
himselfe in proper person) and that all this
is confessed by themselues , and testifyed by
their owne wrytings: All this,I say,being laid
togeather , may strengthen him that hath any
faith at all, to stand constant in the beleefe of
the Catholike Church concerninge these articles: For yf there be any certainty or ground
in Christian Religion at all , yt muft needs be
in these, wherin authority,learninge,antiqui-
ty, consent, continuance, vniuersality, miracles, and all other sorts of theologicall arguments, both diuine & humane, do concurre,
and nothinge at all with the impugners , but
only selfe-will , passion, and malicious obstinacy, as yow will better see afterward, when
yow come to examine their obiections.

57.   Furthermore yt is to be pondered ,
what miserable men they were that firft in
our dayes , againft the whole army of Gods
Church did presume to impugne this blessed
sacrifice,vpon such simple and fond reasons as
before yow haue heard,to witt *Luther* in Ger-
                                                many,

many, vpon the motiue laid downe vnto him
by the diuell, in his diſputation with him, recorded by himſelfe in his wrytings, and *Nico-
làs Ridley* in England, vpon *certayne places of the
ſcripture, and certayne teſtimonyes of Fathers* (to vſe
his owne words) which made nothinge at all
for his purpoſe, as after moſt cleerly ſhall be
ſhewed in due place, and we may eaſily gheſſe
by that, which hath byn alleaged before out
of ſcriptures and Fathers : for that ſcriptures
cannot be contrary to ſcriptures ; nor are Fathers preſumed to impugne Fathers, in ſo
great a point of faith as this is.

58.   Wherfore miſerable & twiſe miſerable
were theſe men, that firſt vpon ſo ſmall
grounds aduentured to make ſo fatall a breach in Gods Church ; and thriſe miſerable
were other, who vpon theſe mens creditts,
ranne to aduenture both body and ſoule euer-
laſtingly, in purſuite of this breach and contradiction begunne, as were the moſt of *Fox*
his phantaſticall Martyrs of the ruder and vnlearned ſort, who in all their examinations &
anſwers, were moſt blaſphemous in defiance
and deteſtation of this *bleſſed-Sacrament*, as yow
haue ſeene in their hiſtoryes ; and therby did
well ſhew that they were gouerned by his
ſpiritt, that aboue all honours doth enuy this
that is done to almighty God, as the higheſt,
and moſt pleaſing to his diuine Maieſtie of all
others. And ſo much for this point.

CERTAYNE OB-

SERVATIONS

To be noted, for better aunſweringe of hereticall Cauillations, againſt theſe articles of the bleſ- ſed Sacrament.

CHAP. III.

HAVING exhibited a taſt in the former Chapter, of the many great and ſubſtan- tiall grounds, which Catholike men haue to ſtand vpon, in theſe high and diuine miſteryes of Chriſts ſacred body in the Sacrament and ſacrifice, and ſhewed in like manner that the faithleſſe and inſidious Sacramentary, that wrangeleth againſt the ſame, hath no one plaine place indeed, eyther of ſcriptures or Fathers for his purpoſe, but only certayne ob- iections, founded for the moſt part vpon ſenſe and humayne reaſon againſt faith, and aun- ſwered ordinarily by our ſchoolemen them- ſelues that firſt obiected the ſame, and out of whoſe books the heretiks ſtole them; I haue thought yt beſt for more perſpicuityes ſake, & for helpinge their vnderſtanding, that are not exerciſed in matters aboue ſenſe, to ſet downe a few obſeruations in this very beginninge,

wherby

wherby great light will grow to the reader, for difcouering whatfoeuer fhall after be treated about this matter. But yet before I enter into the obferuations themfelues, I would haue the reader confider two things; firft the inequality betweene our aduerfaryes and vs in this cafe, for that their arguments againft thefe myfteryes, being founded almoft all in the appearance of comon fenfe (as hath byn faid) the vnlearned reader is capable of the obie&ion, but not of the folution, which muft be taken from matters aboue fenfe, as prefently yow fhall fee.

Tvvo things diligently to be noted.

2. The fecond point is, that yf any of the old heretiks, or heathen philofophers fhould rife againe at this day, and bringe forth their arguments of fenfe & humaine reafon againft fuch articles of our faith, as in ould tyme they did impugne, for both improbable and impoffible in nature; as namely the creation of the world out of nothinge; three diftin& perfons of the bleffed Trinity in one, & the felfe fame fubftance; two diftin& natures in one perfon conioyned by the incarnation of Chrift; the refurre&ion of our putrifyed bodyes, the felfe fame fubftance, qualityes, quantityes, & other accidents, & fuch like points: Againft which, I fay, yf ould philofophers, & heretiks fhould come forth againe in our dayes, and propofe fuch arguments as in their dayes they did, which feeme inuincible and vnanfwerable to common fenfe and humaine reafon; do yow not thinke that they fhould haue infinite

people both men and weomen to follow them, especially yf they were countenanced out with the authority of a potent Prince and Kingdome, and suffered to speake their will, as our men were, that first impugned the *reall presence*, and sacrifice in England; and yet as the aunciene Fathers in their tymes, did not abandone these articles of faith for those difficultyes, or appearance of impossibilityes; no nor the common Catholike people themselues, that could not reach to the vnderstandinge therof; so must not we do now; though we could not aunswere in reason the aduersaryes arguments, which yet by the ensuinge obseruations, yow will easily be able to do. And this for an entrance; now to the obseruations themselues.

First Obseruation.

That vve are not in this myftery to follow eur fenfe, or Imagination. §. 1.

3. The first obseruation is taken out of the ancient Fathers wrytings, who treatinge of this myftery of Chrifts being in the Sacrament, do expreffely warne vs to beware, that we iudge not of the matter according to fenfe or humayne imagination: So faith *S. Cyrill* B. of *Hierufalem*, whofe words are: *Quamuis fenfu hoc tibi fuggerat, &c.* Albeit externall fenfe do ,, fuggeft vnto thee, that this Sacrament is bread ,, and wyne; yet lett faith confirme thee to the contrary,

[margin: Cyrill. Cathech.4. my stag. prope snissinus.]

Disputations, about Religion. Chap. 3. 153

; neyther do thou iudge by the taſt,
knowinge moſt certainely, that this bread,
which ſeemeth ſo vnto vs, is not bread in
deed, notwithſtandinge the taſt doth iudge it
to be bread; but is the body of Chriſt; and that
the wyne, which ſo appeareth to our ſight, &
by the ſenſe of our taſt, is iudged to be wyne,
yet is it not wyne, but the bloud of Chriſt.
Thus hee, neere thirteene hundred yeares
gone. And the like aduertiſment giueth in
the ſame matter *S. Ambroſe*, ſomewhat after
him, who hauing determined moſt cleerly the
truth of the *reall preſence*, ſayinge: *Panis iſte, panis*
eſt ante verba Sacramentorum, vbi acceſſerit conſecra-
tio, de pane fit corpus Chriſti: This bread is bread,
before the words of the Sacrament be vttered
(by the Prieſt) but when the conſecration is added thervnto, the bread is made the body of
Chriſt: He frameth an obiection of the ſenſes
in theſe words: *Fortè dicas, aliud video, &c.* Perhaps thou wilt ſay, I ſee another thinge *(to witt*
bread, and not the body of Chriſt) and how then
doſt thou ſay that I receaue his body? To
which queſtion *S. Ambroſe* aunſwereth at large
alleaginge many other myracles, wherein our
ſenſes are deceaued.

Ambr. l. 4. de Sacram. cap. 1.

Ambr. l. de myſter imitiand. c. 9.

4. The like obſeruation hath *S. Chryſoſtome*
in ſundry places, talkinge of this myſtery: *Cre-*
damus (ſaith he) *vbique Deo, nec repugnemus ei, etſi*
ſenſui & cogitationi noſtræ abſurdum eſſe videatur, &c.
Let vs alwayes giue creditt to God, nor let vs
reſiſt him, albeit the thing ſeeme abſurd to our
ſenſe and cogitation; for our ſenſe may eaſily

Chryſoſt. hom 83. in Matth.

be

,, be deceaued; and therfore for fo much as he
,, hath faid; *This is my body*, lett vs not doubt
,, therof at all, but beleeue him. *Saint Epiphanius*
ftandeth alfo vpon the fame aduertifment, reprehendinge them greuoufly, yea condemninge them that difpute and frame their arguments, from the teftimony of their fenfes a-
gainft the *reall prefence*, whofe words he brin-

Epiph. in Ancorat. circa medium.

geth in thus: *Et videmus* (fay they) *quod non æquale
eft, &c.* We do fee with our eyes, that this
which we do receaue in this Sacramē (to witt,
,, *the hoft*) is neyther equall nor like the image of
,, Chrift in flefh, nor to his inuifible deity, nor
,, to the formes or lineaments of his body, for yt
,, is of a round forme, &c. So they; but *S. Epi-*

Epiph. ibid.

phanius his conclufion is againft them thus: *qui
non credit effe ipfum verum, excidit à gratia & falute*;
,, he that doth not beleeue Chrift himfelfe to be
,, truly there (*vnder the round forme of bread that is
,, giuen*) is fallen both from Gods grace, and his
,, owne faluation.

5. And finally not to enlarge my felfe further in this behalfe, *Eufebius Emiffenus*, or who
els was the author of that excellent fermon *de
corpore Domini*, concurreth alfo in this note a-
gainft the iudgement of our fenfes fayinge;

Eufebius Emiff. ferm. 5. de Pafchat.

*Verè vnica & perfecta hoftia fide æftimanda, non fpecie,
non exteriori cenfenda vifu*; This only and perfect
hoft is truly to be efteemed by faith, and not
,, to be iudged by the externall fhape or veiw of
,, our eyes. Thus hee; wherof *S. Chryfoftome* gi-
,, ueth an example when he wryteth of this my-
,, ftery: *O quot modò dicunt, vellem formam, & fpeciem*

cius,

eius, vellem vestimenta ipsa, vellem calceamenta videre. *Chrysost. hom.,* 1. *& 83. in Matth.*
O how many are there *(videlicet* of the simpler
sort, and not so grounded in faith) that say, ,,
I would I could see Christ, his forme & shape ,,
in the Sacrament, I would see his apparell, ,,
I would see his very shooes. Thus said some
in those dayes, vpon simplicity perhappes; but
so say many more in our dayes, vpon heresie
and infidelity. And truly yf we consider most
of the arguments of all Fox his artificers, or
weomen Martyrs, they were such as these
heere mentioned, & deryded by *S. Chrysostome,*
and vpon these arguments went they to the
stake: *Let your God in the Sacrament* (said *Alice
Driuer* and her fellowes) *shedd some bloud, and vve
vvill beleeue.* The like cryed out many other
simple & rude people; *vve see bread, we see wyne,
vve see a round cake, we will neuer beleeue yt to be
God, except we see him worke some miracle.* What
would *S. Chrysostome* (thinke yow) and other
Fathers before mentioned haue said to these
people, yf they had heard them sound out
such blasphemous cryes of infidelity, and vnbeleefe in their dayes? And so much for this
first obseruation, which is vsually to be found
in all auncient Fathers wrytinges.

The

The second Obseruation.

*That not only sense and common Imagination, but ney-
ther philosophicall reason is necessary to be
followed in these mysteryes.* §. 2.

6.   The second obseruation is much like to
the firſt, but paſſeth ſome degrees further, and
is taken out of the auncient Fathers aduertiſ-
ments in like manner, to witt, that not only
ſenſe, and ſenſuall imagination is not to be
followed in theſe diuine myſteryes, of our Sauiours body; but neyther naturall, or philoſo-
phicall reaſon it ſelfe, is allwayes to be followed, notwithſtandinge yt reacheth farre
higher then ſenſe can attayne to: which is
proued firſt by the generall definition of faith,
vſed by *S. Paul* in his epiſtle to the Hebrues,
where yt is ſaid to be *argumentum rerum non ap-
parentium,* an argument or aſſent of things, that
do not appeare by reaſon, which yet is more
explicated by *Saint Gregory,* when he ſaith: *fides*
non habet meritum, vbi humana ratio præbet experi-
mentum; faith hath no meritt, where humane
,, reaſon doth yeld a proofe: *Saint Auguſtine.* alſo
ſaith: *This is the praiſe of faith, yf that which is belee-*
ued be not ſeene, for what great matter is it, yf that be
beleeued, vvhich is euident? And this is vniuerſally
in all points of our faith, the beleefe wherof
muſt not depend of the euidency of reaſon,
for then yt ſhould be ſcience (as philoſophers
tearme yt) and not faith, which faith dependeth

Gregor.
hom. 26. in
euang.

Aug. tract.
79. in Ioan.

deth on the authority, truſt and creditt we
giue to the reuealer, which is God himſelfe.

7. But eſpecially is this to be done in this
high myſtery of the bleſſed Sacrament of the
Altar, which is not only a myſtery, but a miracle alſo, and ſuch a miracle, as requireth no
leſſe power then the omnipotency of God to
performe the ſame: *Neceſſarium eſt* (ſaid *S. Chry-* *Chryſoſt. in*
ſoſtome to his people of Antioch) *myſteriorum* *ſerm. ad*
diſcere miraculum, &c. It is neceſſary for vs to *tioch.*
learne this myracle of myſteryes, what it is, „
why it was giuen vs, what vtility cometh „
therwith vnto vs & the like: And againe the
ſame Father in his bookes of Prieſthood, deſ-
cending to treat more in particular one point
of this myſtery, which is, how Chriſts body is
at one tyme in many places, he cryeth out: *Chryſoſt.*
O miraculum! o Dei benignitatem! O myracle! *l. 3. de Sa-*
o goodneſſe of God! and why? *qui cum patre* *cerdor.*
ſurſum ſedet, in illo ipſo temporis articulo omnium ma-
nibus petractatur, he that ſitteth aboue with his „
Father, in that very inſtant of tyme is handled „
by all Prieſts hands: And *S. Cyprian* to the ſame „
effect: *Panis quem Dominus diſcipulis porrigebat, non* *Cypr. ſerm.*
effigie ſed natura mutatus, omnipotentia verbi factus eſt *de cæna*
caro: The bread which our Lord gaue to his *Domini.*
diſciples (at the laſt ſupper) being changed not „
in outward ſhew (for yt appeareth bread ſtill) „
but in nature, by the omnipotency of Gods „
word is made fleſh.

8. Thus thought and ſpake the ancient Fathers of this high myſtery, and myracle in the
Sacrament. And conforme to this, they called

vs alwayes from reason to faith, from contention to humble beleefe, when they treated
therof, for so wryteth among other auncient
Fathers *S. Hilary* speakinge of this matter : *non* *Hilar.lib.8.*
est humano aut saculi sensu in Dei rebus loquendum. *de Trinit.*
„ We must not talke of works of God accor-
„ dinge to humayne and wordly reason, *&c.*
„ touchinge the naturall verity of Christ in vs
„ (by this Sacrament) that which we affirme
„ except we haue learned yt of himselfe, we'do
„ affirme the same folishly, and impiously, but
he hath said : *my flesh is truly meate, &c.* Vnto *Ioan. 6.*
whome *S. Ambrose* agreeinge, saith of the same
mystery: *Quid hic quaris natura ordinem, &c.* Why *Ambr. l 4.*
seekest thou heere the order of nature (tou- *de Sacram.*
„ chinge the body of Christ in the Sacrament) *cap. 4.*
„ forsomuch as our Lord Iesus was borne of
„ the Virgin beside the course of nature. Heere
yow see he compareth this mystery, and myracle of Christs being in the Sacrament, with
the myracle of his incarnation & myraculous
byrth, of the blessed Virgin. The very same
iudgement held *S. Ephrem* equall in antiquity *Ephrem.lib.*
to *S. Ambrose*. *Quid scrutaris inscrutabilia, &c.* *de natura*
Dei mini-
What dost thou search after thinges vnsear- *mè scrutan*
cheable ? Yf thou examine these thinges cu- *da cap. 5.*
„ riously, thou wilt seeme not to be faithfull
„ but curious: be faithfull and simple, and so
„ participate the immaculate body of thy Lord,
„ beleeuinge most certaynely, that thou dost
„ eat the very whole lambe yt selfe, *&c.* So he.
„ 9.   *Saint Augustine* also in many places doth
beat earnestly, against this standing vpon reason

son in matters of faith, but especially in his
epistle to *Volutianus,* sayinge : *Quæ sibi quisque fa-*
cilia, &c. The thinges which each man esteemeth easy for him to conceaue, though he
cannot make them, he is content to beleeue
them, but all that is aboue his capacity he holdeth for false and feigned. And againe: *Si ratio*
quæritur non erit mirabile, yf yow seeke reason
for euery thinge, yt will not be maruelous,
Demus, Deum aliquid posse quod nos fateamur inuesti-
gare non posse : Lett vs graunt that God can do
somewhat, whereof we cannot seekeout the
reason ; *in talibus rebus tota ratio facti est potentia*
facientis; in such matters all the reason, that can
be alleaged for the fact, or for that which is
done, is the power of the doer. And in another
place the same Father hauing spoken of the
blessed Sacrament and how Christ our Sauiour is therein *sub aliena specie,* vnder another
forme of bread and wyne, as the Angells also
appeare vnto vs vnder assumpted bodyes, he
concludeth thus: *Mihi autem omnino vtile est, &c.* *Ibidem.*
It is very profitable for me to remember my
owne feeble forces, & to warne my brethren
that they also be myndfull of theirs, to the
end that our humayne infirmity do not passe
further (in search of these mysteryes) then is
safe for vs to do. So blessed *S. Augustine.*

10.   And finally *S. Cyrill* Bishop of *Alexandria*
handlinge those words of the faithlesse Capharnaites, *Ioan. 6. How can he giue his flesh to be*
eaten. &c. reprehendeth greatly such curious
inquisition sayinge : *Numquam in tam sublimibus*
rebus

August. ep.
ad Volutian.
,,
,,
,,
,,
,,
,,
,,
Aug. ibid.
,,
,,

,,
,,
,,
,,
,,
,,
,,

rebus illud (quomodo) aut cogitemus aut proferamus. In
so high matters (as theſe of the Sacrament) let
vs neuer thinke or alleage this word *(quomodo)*
that is , *how yt can be* ? And in this manner did
the ancient Fathers proceed about this myſtery, by way of faith and humble ſubmiſſion of
their iudgements and vnderſtandings, and not
by feeding their imagination with probability of humayne reaſon againſt faith , as the ſectaryes of our tyme do , yea and placinge ſo
much confidence therin , as they were content to dy for the ſame (as after yow will ſee
by experience, when we come to handle their
arguments in particular , wherof the greater
part (yea almoſt all) relyed eyther vpon common ſenſe , or ſome little ſhew of humayne
reaſon . And thus much for the ſecond obſeruation .

Third Obſeruation .

That reaſon is not contrary to faith, but inferior vnto it. §. 3.

11.   The third obſeruation may be , that
though yt is iuſtly accoumpted a fault of folly,
pride, hereſie, or infidelity by the foreſaid Fathers, to ſtand too much vpon ſenſe & reaſon
in theſe myſteryes, which do ſurpaſſe them
both; yet are they not contrary to reaſon , for
that one truth cannot be contrary to another,
and God is the author of both lightes , the
one as a lower, the other as a more high and
                      eminent

eminent light, so as, though this lower cannot
reach to discouer that, which the higher doth
disclose & comprehend; yet is not this extinguished or violated by the other, but rather
perfected and strengthened. Reason reacheth
only to thinges that are probable in nature,
faith ascendeth to all that is possible, and not
only possible to man, but euen to God himselfe, which so farre exceedeth both the power
and vnderstanding of man, as *S. Paul* speaking
but of one point only of our faith, which is
the ioyes of heauen, saith that the hart of man
could not comprize the same.

12.   And yet yf we would enter into the
search of what is possible to Gods power and
omnipotency, the scripture in few words setteth yt downe : *Non est impossibile apud Deum* *Luc. 1.*
omne verbum : there is nothinge impossible to
God, which is as much to say, that all thinges
are possible. And againe our Sauiour speaking
to his Father said : *Omnia tibi possibilia sunt:* All *Marc. 14.*
things are to thee possible. And yf we would
require examples, the creation of the heauens, and of all things both in & vnder them,
will minister thousands, whervnto humayne
reason cannot reach. And *S. Iohn Baptist* gaue *Luc. 3.*
an example to the Iewes, that God of stones
is able to raise vp children to *Abraham*; but this
also is nothing in respect of Gods infinite and
incomprehensible omnipotency, which is
aboue the reach of our vnderstandinge.

13.   No limitation then at all is to be layd to
Gods almighty power, but that he may do

what-

whatfoeuer he pleafe, except only one, according to diuines, which is, that the thinge do not imply contradiction in yt felfe, as that

D. Tho. 1. part. q. 24. art. 3.

yt fhould be and *not be at once*, which is impoffible, or that yt fhould import any imperfection or impotency in God, as to fynne, or dye, which are effects rather of want of power, then of omnipotency. And in this do the more learned Proteftants alfo agree in word with vs, fayinge, that yf yt were cleere that God would haue yt fo, or had faid yt, that of bread fhould be made his flefh, and that one fubftance fhould be turned into the other, they would graunt that he could do yt by his omnipotency. Thus they fay in words, to auoid the odious note of infidelity, or limiting Gods power; but when they come to the point indeed, they found all their greateft arguments vpon the impoffibility thereof, as though God could not do yt. And fo fhall yow fee afterwards, when we come to difcuffe their ftrongeft arguments. And their great Grand-father *Iohn VVikliffe*, or rather *VVicked-beleefe*, as *VValfingham* calleth him, did

VValdenf. tom. 2. cap. 72. & 73.

abfolutely deny that God was able to do yt, as *Thomas VValden* teftifieth out of his owne wrytings. Aud *Iohn Caluyn* his fcholler in this point calleth vs madd-men, for that we beleeue that God was able to make bread his flefh in the Sacrament, and yet not to haue the externall forme, nature and propriety of

Calu. lib. 4. Inftitut. cap. 17. §. 24.

flefh: *Infane* (faith he) *quid à Dei potentia poftulas, vt carnem faciat fimul effe, & non effe carnem?* Thou
madd-

madd-man how doft thou demaund of the „
power of God, that he fhould make flefh to „
be flefh, and not flefh at one tyme? But how
doth *Caluyn* proue (thinke yow) that our beleefe of the Sacrament implyeth this contradiction of flefh and no flefh? Forfooth (to vfe
his words) for that we graunt, *that God can* *Calu. ibid.*
make, that the felfe-fame flesh of Chriſt can occupy di-
uers places at once, and that yt be conteyned in no cer-
tayne place, and that yt lacketh both the outward fhape
of flesh and proper manner of being, &c. And for beleeuinge of this he counteth vs madd-men, as
yow haue heard, and fo muft he account alfo
of necefsity all thofe holy Fathers before
mentioned, who beleeued the fame myftery,
as we do, notwithftandinge the outward appearances of impofsibility, for comprehendinge wherof they fledd from fenfe and reafon to faith and beleefe.

14. And yet further then this the reader muft
vnderftand, that for fo much as the faid reafon
and faith, are not contradictory the one to the
other, but more eminent the one aboue the
other, as before hath byn fhewed, Catholiks
do take vpon them to proue, that no one of
thefe difficultyes obiected by faithleffe Proteftants, is impofsible, or implieth contradiction
in reafon it felfe, as by the enfuing confideia-
tions fhall more particularly be declared; notinge only to the reader by the way, that yf
the particular intrinfecall natures and effences
of euery thing were cleerly knowen vnto vs,
as they are for example vnto Angells, and
　　　　　　　L 2　　　　other

other Saints, that be in glory, we fhould eafily fee what doth imply contradiction to the faid natures, and what doth not, but for that God, for our humility and greater meritt, would haue vs not alwayes to fee this; therfore are we forced to gheffe at the fame by way of difcourfe and reafon, and by one example to another, as yow fhall fee in the enfuinge obferuations.

Fourth Obferuation.

How a body may be vvithout an ordinary naturall place. §. 4.

15. One of the greateft difficultyes therfore obiected by the aduerfary, is, that a true and naturall organicall body, fuch as Chrifts is confeffed to be in the Sacrament, cannot be without the ordinary dimenfions of a peculiar place, which we deny in fuch fenfe, as heere we fhall declare. For better vnderftandinge wherof is to be noted, that three wayes a thinge may be in a place, firft naturally and ordinarily by extenfion and commenfuration vnto the faid place, foe as euery part and parcell of the thinge placed, do aunfwere to each part of the place yt felfe, which manner of being in place, philofophers do call *circumfcriptiuely*, for that all places of the body fo placed, are fo limited and circumfcribed by the parts of the place, as neyther that body can be in any other place, nor that place admitt another

Three vvayes or manners of being in place.

1.

ther

ther body, without penetratinge the one of the other, which by ordinary courſe of nature is held for impoſsible.

16. Another manner of being in place is   **2.** more ſpirituall, and hard to conceaue, to witt, when a thing is ſo in a place, as the parts therof are not extended to the parts of the place, as in the former example, but yet that the whole thing is ſo defined and limited within the compaſſe of that whole place aſsigned thervnto, as naturally yt cannot be in any other, whileſt yt is there, as for example, the ſoule of a man in the body thervnto aſsigned, is ſo conteyned therin, as yt is not elſwhere, and yet is it not ſo extended by commenſuration, as in the former example, that one part of the ſoule aunſwereth one part of the body, and another, another part, but the whole ſoule which is indiuiſible, and hath no parts at all, is wholy in the whole body, and wholy in euery part and parcell therof, which is a miraculous ſtrange being, yf yt be well conſidered, & notwithſtanding naturall as all philoſophers do graunt, for that the whole ſoule of man is as wholy (for example) in the fingar and foote, as in the breaſt and head, and yet is but one ſoule in all, and nether many ſoules nor one ſoule diuided into parts. And after the ſame manner, is an Angell alſo in a place definitiuely, and not circumſcriptiuely, that is to ſay wholy in the whole place, which he occupieth, & wholy in euery part therof, without multiplication or diuiſion in himſelfe, or ex-

tenſion

tenfion vnto the parts of the place wherin yt
is. But for that the example of the foule, is
more familiar and euident to our fenfe and
reafon, it doth better expreffe the matter. And
yt is to be noted, that yt doth fomewhat imitate the being of God himfelfe wholy, and
without diuifion in all parts of the world, and
in all creatures therof without limitation,
change, or multiplication, but only yt differeth in this, that the foule, or an Angell, being
both creatures, cannot be euery where, as the
creatour naturally is, and he cannot be otherwife; but yet by his diuine power, the faid
creatures may be in diuers places at once, as
after fhalbe fhewed.

17. Thefe two wayes then of being in a
place, as I haue faid, are naturall; the firft circumfcriptiuely, the fecond definitiuely. But
befides thefe two, there is a third fupernatu-
rall, and pofsible to Gods diuine omnipotency, and not repugnant to reafon yt felfe, as after fhalbe fhewed; which is, that one and the
felfe-fame thing, may by Gods diuine power,
be placed in two different places at once, that
is to fay, that the felfe-fame foule, as yt is naturally, wholy, and entyrely in the head, for
example, and in the foote; fo yt repugneth
not to the fame nature or effence of the foule,
to be putt in two different bodyes at once.
The like of an Angell in diuers places, and the
fame alfo may be held of a naturall body, yf
God will haue yt fo, as in the next obferuation fhalbe proued. And this way or manner
of

of being in place, for that the Cath. Church
doth hould yt to be in the body of our Sauiour in the Sacrament, is called by diuines a
sacramentall being in place, nor for that the
true body is not really there, as some hearinge
the word *Sacramentally*, vsed sometymes by the
Fathers and Doctors, do fondly apprehend,
but for that it is there after this speciall manner, as we haue declared, that is to say, so as yt
is also in other places at the same tyme.

18. Now then, these three wayes or manners
of being in place declared, yt remayneth, that
we shew how yt is possible to Gods power,
and not repugnant to naturall reason, that a
true body, which of his owne nature is in
place, only after the first manner of circumscription and commensuration, or extension,
may, by Gods power, be in place also after the
second and third way, that is definitiuely and
Sacramentally, without the first way of commensuration and extension to a place. And
first heere we shall shew the said possibility in
the second way, and then of the third in the
ensuinge obseruation.

How a body may be definitiuely in place.

19. The only cheefe ground, or reason obiected by the hereriks, why it may seeme to repugne or imply contradiction, that a true organicall body togeather with his quantity,
such as Chrifts is in the Sacrament, should be
definitiuely without extension in place, is, for
that yt appeareth contrary to the nature of
quantity to be without such extension: but
this ground Cath. Philosophers and diuines

L 4   do

do eafily ouerthrow , fhewinge that three things do agree to quantity or magnitude, wherof the firft is to be extended in yt felfe, and to haue diftinct partes one from the other among themfelues, though not euer vifible, or perceptible by our fenfe; and this firft point is fo effentiall to quantity and magnitude, as yt cannot be imagined feparable, fo as it remaine quantity. And therfore this is graunted to be in the body of our Sauiour in the Sacrament, though our fenfe doth not comprehend yt. The fecond property of quantity or magnitude, proceedinge from this firft, is ; not only to haue partes diftinct in themfelues, but to haue them extended alfo in place, accordinge to the commenfuration therof, as in the firft way of being in place we haue declared.

20.   And for that this fecond condition, or propriety, is later then the former, & enfueth therof, yt is not fo intrinfecall to the nature & effence of quantity, but that by Gods diuine power yt may be feparated, without deftroyinge the faid nature , which our diuines do fhew by examples of other thinges , where God hath feparated fuch fecondary proprie-tyes, without diffoluinge the natures, as hea-tinge, for example, from fyre in the fornace of Babylon , which heatinge notwithftandinge is as naturall to fyre, as yt is to quantity to oc-

Cap. 19.   cupy place. Chrift alfo in *S. Mathewes* ghofpell,
,, hauinge faid to his difciples, that yt was eafier
,, for a Camell to paffe through the eye of a
,, needle, then for a rich-man to enter into the
King-

Kingedome of heauen , and the Apostles wondringe therat, and sayinge: *vvho then can be faued?* our Sauiour anſwered, that, *that vvhich vvas impoſſible to men, vvas poſſible to God,* which yet could not be poſsible, but by ſeparatinge from the camell all his naturall extenſion, and commenſuration of place. Wherfore all the auncient Fathers vpon this place attributing this to myracle , do affirme , that by Gods diuine power yt may be done, to witt, that a camell remayninge in the nature of a camell , may paſſe through a needles eye: *quid prohibet* (ſaith S. Gregory Nazianzen) *quo minus hoc fiat, ſi voluntas ita tulerit?* What letteth but that this (of the camell) may be done , yf Gods will be to haue yt ſo? Some Proteſtant will ſtepp forth, and ſay that yt cannot be done, for that the Camell ſhould not in that caſe haue quantity and be organicall (for ſo they ſay of our Sauiours body in the Sacrament) , but *Nazianzen* was of another opinion: And ſo may yow read *Origen, S. Hierome , S. Auguſtine , S. Hilary, S. Chryſoſtome,* and other Fathers in their commentaryes, and expoſitions vpon this place of *S. Mathewes* ghoſpell.

Nazianz. orat. 36. quæ eſt quarta de Theolog.

Matth. 19. Luc. 18. Marc. 10.

21. The third naturall condition or propriety of quantity (proceedinge of this ſecond) is, that for ſo much as by the forſaid ſecond propriety, the thinge placed doth fill vp the place which yt occupyeth, euery part therof anſweringe to euery part of the ſaid place only , and one place conteyne one body ; ſo as naturally yt is no leſſe impoſsible for two bodyes to be

The third condition or propriety of quantity.

in

in one place, then for one body to be in many. Yet notwithstanding supernaturally, and by Gods omnipotent power, both the one & the other may be without implication, or contradiction of the essence, or nature of a true body. The reason wherof is this: for that this third propriety in quantity or magnitude, flowinge of the second, as hath byn said, may much more easily be separated from the essence of the said quantity and body, then the second, and consequently the former being separable, this is much more, wherof our diuines do giue diuers most euident instances, out of scripture yt selfe. As for example out of S. Iohns Ghospell, where twise yt is said, that he came in to his disciples, when the gates were shutt. And in *S. Mathew*, and *S. Marke*, where yt is shewed, how Christ after his resurrection came forth of the sepulcher, the stone also being shutt; and in his natiuity he came forth of his mothers wombe, without violation of her virginity, and in his assension he passed through all the heauens with his naturall body. In all which myraculouse examples (for so do the ancient Fathers hould and affirme them to be) there must needs be penetration of bodyes, or two bodyes in one place, which is no lesse repugnant to the ordinary nature of quantity (as hath byn said) then for a body to be without certaine dimension of any place.

22. Besides this our diuines do alleage the examples of the damned spirits, miraculously

Ioan. 20.

Math. 28.
Marc. 16.

Ephes. 4.

Se S. Aug.
ep. 3. ad Vo-
lus. & l. 22.
de Ciuit. Dei
cap. 8. &
Chrysost.
Euthim. Cy-
rill. &c. In
commenta-
rijs.

tyed

tyed to certayne locall places in hell; and that which is more maruelous, that the damned foules being fpiritts, fhould fuffer, and be tormented by corporall fire, wherof *S. Auguftine* treateth at large *lib. 21. de Ciuit. Dei cap. 1. 2. & deinceps,* which is no leffe againft the ordinary nature and propriety of fpiritts, to fuffer corporally,then yt is againft the nature of a body, to be after a certayne fpirituall manner without his locall dimenfion;by all which we may perceaue, that although yt be aboue naturall reafon, that organicall bodyes fhould want thefe externall locall pofitions; yet is yt not contrary,or contradictory thervnto, but fubiect to Gods omnipotent power, when, and where yt pleafeth him to make yt fo,and confequently yt may be fo alfo in the bleffed Sacrament, without deftroyinge the nature of a true body, as fondly Proteftants do pretend.

23. And heerby now falleth to the ground, a whole mayne multitude of vayne arguments, brought by Fox his Martyrs,as after yow fhall fee,againft the reall prefence,all of them founded vpon this ground, that a true organicall body cannot,by Gods power,be either without locall dimenfions, or in moe places then one at once. The firft of which two affertions hath now ben improued, and the fecond fhalbe in the next enfuinge obferuation.

The fifth Obseruation.

How a body may be in diuers places at once. §. 5.

24.   As the weake faith and learninge of the Sacramentaryes of our tyme, cannot reach to conceaue, that a body can be without an externall place; so much lesse, can they comprehend, that yt may be by Gods omnipotency placed in diuers places at once, for that yt seemeth to their sense, and humayne reason to be impossible; but the ancient holy Fathers, more wise and learned then our said Sectaryes, tooke another course in this point, which was to ascribe yt to miracle, and to Gods infinite power, which they could not by reason arriue vnto: I might cyte diuers Fathers, but one or two shall serue for all; *O miracle! (*saith *S. Chrysostome) o goodnes of God! that the same Christ who sitteth in heauen vvith his Father, is conuersant at the selfe-same tyme, in the hands of all that receaue him on earth!* And the same Father, wrytinge of the same sacred body of our Sauiour, as yt is a sacrifice, saith: *Vnum est hoc sacrificium, &c. This sacrifice is but one, for that otherwise, because yt is offered in many places, there should be many Christs, vvhich is not so, but one, and the selfe-same Christ is in euery place,* (when yt is offered) *here yt is whole Christ, and there it is whole Christ, and yet but one body: for as euery-where one body, and not many bodyes are offered, so is there also but one sacrifice, &c.*

Chrysost.
lib. 3. de
Sacerdotio.

Chrysost.
hom. 17.
in ep. ad
Hebr.

In

In which places you see *S. Chryfostome* to hould
& to affirme, that Chrifts true body, without
diuifion or multiplication, is offered vp in many places at once, yea innumerable places, yf
we beleeue *S. Gregory Niffen* whofe words are:
As Chrifts diuinity doth replenifh the world, and yet is   *Niffen. orat.*
but one; fo is his body confecrated in innumerable places,   *de Pafchate.*
and yet is but one body. So he. And do yow ob-
ferue, that the Father faith not, that Chrifts
body is euery where, as his diuinity is, as the
Lutherane Vbiquitaryes of Germany, do abfurdly affirme ; but that yt is in innumerable
places by confecration.

25. Well then thefe Fathers denyed not the
reall prefence, as our Sacramentaryes do, for that
they conceaued not the reafon, how one body
might be in diuers places at once, but moun-
ted by faith aboue reafon, afcribing the fame
to miracle and Gods omnipotency, as yow
haue heard : and fo do Catholiks at this day.
Heare the pious fpeach of a great learned man
aboue 400. yeares gone . *Yow vvill fay to me*   *Hugo de S.*
(quoth he), *how can one and the felfefame body , be*   *Victor. l. 2.*
at one tyme in diuers places, &c. *Do not maruayle, he*   *de Sacram.*
that made the place, made the body , and the place for   *p. 8. cap. 11.*
the body, and the body in the place; and vvhen he orday-
ned that one body fhould be in one place, yt was as plea-
fed him, and yf he would, he could haue made yt other-
vvife, &c. *Thou haft feene only that vvhich he hath*
made, and not that vvhich he can make, and heerevpon
doft maruayle when thou feeft any other thinge , then
that which thou art accuftomed to fee ; but do thou
thinke vpon the matter, and yt will ceafe to be maruay-
lous,

low, or at leastwayes, yt will not seeme to be incredible.
Thus he.

26.   But our diuines do go yet further, shewinge that this is not impossible, euen in nature yt selfe, for God to performe, as yow may
perceaue by that we haue declared in the former obseruation: For yf yt were repugnant
and contradictory to the nature of a true body, to be in diuers places at once, this must be
eyther in respect of the vnity therof, for that
yt should therby be diuided from yt selfe, or
multiplyed in yt selfe, and so not be one but
many bodyes; or els secondly yt should be impossible to be in diuers places, in respect of
the quantity, which a true body hath, wherby
yt should be limyted to some certayne space or
place; but neyther of these two difficultyes do
impossibilitate the matter, as now we shall
declare.

27.   Not the first about vnity, for that God
being a substance indiuisible, is euery where
wholy, and in euery one of his creatures, and
yet remayneth one still, nor can be diuided or
multiplyed: which is so wonderfull a consideration, as S. *Augustine* saith therof: *Miratur hoc
mens humana, & quia non capit, fortasse non credit.*
Mans mynd doth wonder at this, and for that
yt conceaueth yt not, perhaps yt doth not beleeue yt. Some likenesse also of this admirable
being is in an Angell, which though it cannot
be euery where at once, as God is, yet hath yt
a wonderfull being in place; notwithstanding,
as before hath byn touched, being placed
within

Twwo dif-
ficultyes
solued.

The first
difficulty
about
vnity.

*Aug. ep. 3.
ad Volus.*

within any compaſſe or circuite, as for example in a houſe or Church, yt is wholy in all that ſpace, and wholy in euery part therof, & yet remayneth one and ſimple without diuiſion in himſelfe: which example is more euident alſo in our ſoule, as before we haue declared, for that the ſelfe-ſame ſoule in a body, when yt is an infant, and when yt is at his full grouth, is wholy in the whole body, & wholy in euery part therof, and yet is yt not multiplyed therby, nor diuided. Whereby is made manifeſt, that yt repugneth not to the eſſence or vnity of any one ſubſtance, to be in diuers places at once, and this naturally, but much more ſupernaturallye, by the omnipotent power of God.

28. There remayneth then the ſecond difficulty about quantity, or a body indued with quantity, how yt is not letted therby to be in two places at once, wherof we haue treated in the former obſeruation, ſhewinge how actuall locality by circumſcription, being but a ſecondary propriety, following and flowing from the nature of quantity, may, by Gods power, be ſeparated from the ſame, ſo as the ſaid quantity may remayne with her true eſſence, of hauinge diſtinct parts in yt ſelfe, and yet no extenſiue location, or commenſuration of place, in which caſe yt repugneth no more for the ſelfe-ſame quantity to be in many places at once, then yt doth vnto a ſpirituall ſubſtance without quantity, ſuch as is an Angell, or the ſoule of man, and conſequently

the

The ſecōd difficulty about quantity.

the substance of Christs body, togeather with the quantity in this manner, may by Gods power be put in many places at once, as we see by course of nature it selfe, that the substance of mans soule without quantity, is put in many particular places of a mans body, without diuision or multiplication, remayninge still but one only soule, as hath byn declared. And this shall suffice for explication of this possibility, how yt doth not imply contradiction, and therfore is not impossible to God.

Diuers articles beleeued by Protestãts are more hard then this.

29.   Neyther do our diuines shew only, that this is not impossible in our Sauiours body, but further also, that we do beleeue diuers other mysteryes of our faith as hard or harder then this, yea much more impossible to sense and reason, yf we consider well the difficultyes therof, as the creation of the world of nothinge, the mystery of the blessed Trinity, the beleefe of Christs incarnation, our resurrection, and the like, for yt is much harder by humayne reason and naturall philosophy, to conceaue how the world could be created of nothinge, and how one and the selfe-same nature can be wholy in three reall distinct persons, without diuision or multiplication in yt selfe, and how one person can be in two diuers distinct natures, as yt is in our Sauiour, and how one, and the selfe-same thing being perished and corrupted, may be raised againe with the selfe-same accidents that perished before. These points I say, and diuers others

which

which both we and Proteltants do confeſſe to
be true, are more harde, and impoſſible in
naturall reaſon, then yt is to be beleeue that
one body is in diuers places at once.

30. Furthermore there be certayne familiar
examples in nature yt ſelfe, that do reſemble
ſomewhat the matter, and may induce a man
that is not obſtinate, and hath any meane capacity to conceaue ſomewhat of the poſsibi-
lity therof, as when a great lookinge-glaſſe
that repreſented but one face vnto yow when
yt was whole, being broken into many parts
euery part will repreſent wholy the ſelfe-
ſame face. The voyce alſo of him, that ſpeaketh to a great multitude, though yt be but
one in yt ſelfe, yet cometh yt wholy to euery
mans eares, which *S. Auguſtine* alleaged for a
wonderfull thinge towards the prouing of
Gods being wholy euery-where: *Omne quod
ſonat* (ſaith he) *& omnibus totum eſt, & ſingulis totum eſt.* All that ſoundeth is heard wholy of
all, and wholy of euery particular man. And
though theſe examples be not like in euery
reſpect, yet may they ſerue for a certayne induction to make vs comprehend the other,
wherof we now ſpeake.

31. Laſt of all, Catholike diuines do not only
ſhew the poſſibility of this point, that our Sauiours body may be in diuers places at once,
as alſo that ſundry other myſteryes of our faith
are beleeued, of more difficulty then this, yf
we regard common ſenſe and reaſon, but do
ſhew alſo out of the ſcriptures themſelues, that

Chriſt

(margin note beside §30:) Naturall examples inducing vs to this manner of being of Chriſtes body in diuers places.

(margin note:) Aug. ep. 13 ad Volus.

(margin note beside §31:) Examples of the being of Chriſts body in diuers places at once.

Christ after his assension hath byn in more then one place at once, as is manifest by that

Act. 9. & 22.

famous apparition of his to *S. Paul*, recorded in the acts of the Apostles, when he appeared vnto him in the way neere to *Damasco*, inuironed with a great light, and talked with him in such sort, as both the light and words were seene and heard by his companions, and many

Egesipp.l.3. de excidio Hierosol. Ambr. orat: cont. Auxentium Athan. in vita Anton. Greg. lib. 4. dial. c. 16. Paul. ep. ad Macarium. Ioan. Diac. li. 2. de vita Greg. c. 22.

other apparitions to *S. Peter* himselfe, testified by *Egesippus*, and *S. Ambrose*; to *S. Anthony* also testified by *S. Gregory*, & besides diuers others recorded by *S. Paulinus*, *Ioannes Diaconus*, and other authenticall wryters, from whome, except we will derogate all creditt and authority, we may not doubt, but that Christ remayninge still in heauen (for so hould both we and Protestants togeather, that he departed not from thence) appeared also in diuers

Marc. 16.

places of the earth to his Saints, and consequently his body could be in diuers places at once, wherby is broken and dissolued another

Hovv Christ is in heauen and in the Sacramēt after a different manner.

squadron of arguments, framed by the Sacramentaryes of our dayes to the simple people, as though Christs reall body could not be in the Sacrament, for that yt is in heauen; wheras we affirme, that both may be and stand togeather, though in different manner, for that in heauen he is *circumscriptiuely*, and in the Sacrament *sacramentally*, which tearmes we haue before declared.

The

The sixth Obseruation.

How Chriſtes body in the Sacrament, may be now vnder a greater forme, now vnder a leſſe, and the leaſt, that may be diſcerned.   §. 6.

32.   By this alſo which is ſaid may be conceaued, how the ſacred body of our Sauiour, in the Sacramēt vnder the accidents of bread, is ſometymes in a greater viſible quantity, and ſometymes in a leſſe, accordinge to the externall formes and accidents vnder which yt is, yea and in the leaſt part & parcell of the conſecrated hoſt, that is perceptible to our ſenſe, for that the ſaid body being remoued by Gods omnipotent power from all locall extenſion, it may be vnder a greater or ſmaller externall quantity, without alteration of the body yt ſelfe, as we ſee in the ſoule of man, which is the ſelfe-ſame in the leaſt part of the body wherin it is, as in the greateſt, or in the whole body, yea when the ſaid body is changed, or groweth from a leſſer to a greater quantity, as in an infant, who after commeth to be a great man, the ſelfe-ſame ſoule repleniſheth the one and the other without grouth or diminution in yt ſelfe, and ſo the body of Chriſt in a great hoſt or a little, or in any leaſt part therof, when yt is broken, is wholy, and the ſelfe-ſame body, with the ſelfe-ſame internall organicall quantity, which yt had vnder a great hoſt. And this point that the quantity of a

ſub-

Note this
example.

substance may be increased or diminished externally, in respect of place, without alteratiō of the inward quantity, or substāce, is euident by many examples, which we see dayly of rarefaction and condensation. As for example when a gallon of water is put in a great vessell ouer the fire, yt cometh by boylinge to fill the whole vessell, that is capable of many gallons, and yet as the inward substance is not increased, so neyther the quantity in yt selfe; and contrary wise, when the said water is againe cooled, it returneth to occupy as small a place, as yt did at the beginninge, and yet retayneth allwayes the selfe same both quantity and substance.

33. By which example, & many other that may be alleaged, some kind of notice may be gathered vnto our common sense and reason, how the substance of Chrifts body in the Sacrament, togeather with his internall quantity, may by his omnipotent power, be sometymes vnder a great externall quantity, or extension in place, & sometymes vnder a lesser; yea the least, that by our senses may be perceaued : and yet is Chrifts body wholy and entirely there, accordinge (in some proportion) to the lookinge-glasse before mentioned, which being broken into diuers small peeces, each one representeth the whole visage seuerally, which before was exhibited by the whole: And so, when any consecrated host is broken into many parts, that which was cōteyned before in the whole host, is now cōteyned who-

ly

ly vnder euery particular parcell therof, as yt
was also before. And to this effect, are those
words of *S. Epiphanius* before alleaged, against
them that said: *Videmus quod est æquale, &c.* We   *Vti supra.*
see that the host receaued in the Sacrament, is   ,,
not equall or like to the figure of Chrifts bo-   ,,
dy, but is round, *&c.* Wherfore all the arguments of Fox his Martyrs, that were founded
on this improportion of the host to Chrifts
naturall, and externall quantity, haue no
ground at all, but a little fraudulent shew and
appearance of sensible improbability, and yet
were many of their cheefest arguments builded on this only foundation, as yow haue
seene readinge ouer their historyes before recyted, and shall do more afterward, when we
come to examine their arguments seuerally;
and in the meance space this shall suffice for
an aduertisment about this obseruation.

The seauenth Obseruation.

How accidents may be without a subiect, and of their operations in that case. §. 7.

34. The seauenth obseruation may be, about
the accidents or formes of bread and wyne,
that do remayne by Gods omnipotent power
without a subiect, after the words of confecration, as they did before in the substance of
bread, wherypon the more simple sort of Sacramentaryes following sense, will needs argue, that the substance also of bread & wyne,

do remayne after the said consecration ; and
those that be more learned, do go about to
proue the same by philosophicall reason , for
that the nature of an accident is to be in another, as the nature of a substance is to be in yt
selfe , wherof ensueth, that for so much as no
accident can be in God , as in a subiect, (neyther are they in Christs body , as we also doe
confesse) they must needs be heere in their
proper subiect and substances of bread and
wyne: but all this is founded vpon a false
ground , for albeit naturally an accident cannot be but in a subiect, yet supernaturally, and
by the power of God susteyninge yt, and supplyinge the place of a naturall subiect, yt may
be , as we do confesse on the contrary side by
Christian faith , that the humayne nature of
Christ in the mystery of the incarnation, hath
not her proper subsistence in yt selfe (which
yet is as naturall to a substance to subsist in yt
selfe, as yt is to an accident to be susteyned by
another) but is susteyned by the diuine person
of Christ.

Aristot. 5.
Met:*ph.*
text. 35.

35.   And the reason of this , concerninge accidents, is, that albeit the intrinsecall nature of
an accident is to be vnperfect, and to depend
of another , and therby to haue an aptitude to
be in another, yet the act therof may be separated by Gods power , from the said nature,
as a thinge posterior, and followinge from the
said nature , as we haue shewed before in the
naturall propriety of quantity , to haue commensuration of place; and this to be, true that

this

that this actuall inherence of accidents, may be seuered from the essentiall aptitude thervnto, without destroing the nature of the said accident, many philosophers both Christian and heathen do affirme, whose sentences you may see gathered by diuers learned men, as well of ancient as of our tymes. Sundry Fathers also are of opinion, that this case happened *de facto* in the creation of the world, when the light being made vpon the first day, as the booke of *Genesis* recounteth, which being but a quality and accident, remayned without a subiect vnto the fourth day, when the sonne and moone weare created. And of this opinion expressely was *S. Basill,* in his explication of the works of God in those six dayes. And the same holdeth *S. Iohn Damascene, Procopius* in his commentary vpon the first Chapter of *Genesis,* and *Saint Iustine* in the explication of our faith.

See Auerr. in epitom. Metaphys. tract. 1. Auicebron. l. font. vitæ tract. 1. VValdensis tom. 2. cap. 76.

Basil. ho. 1. & 6. de oper. sex dierum Damascen. l. 1. cap. 7.

36. This then being so, that these accidents of bread & wyne may remaine, by the power of God, in the Sacrament, without their proper subiects, yt followeth to consider, what actions they can haue: And first yt is to be noted, that whatsoeuer actions, or operations are proper to them, as accidents, when they were in their proper subiects of bread and wyne, before consecration, the same they may haue afterwards, when they conteyne the body and bloud of Christ, without inherence therein, for that God supplyeth all by his power, which their said subiects or substances

Of the actiuity of accidents being seperated from their substance.

M 4   did

did performe, when they were present. So as
the effects, for example, that the accidents of
wine & bread did worke in our senses before,
by mouinge our sight by their colours to see,
our tast by their sauour, and other like effects:
the same do they performe also afterwards: So
as, for example sake, by drinkinge much consecrated wyne, though there be no substance
of wyne therin, but only the proper accidents
of wyne, as heat, smell, and other qualityes
and proprietyes of wyne; may a man be in-
censed, or distempered, as much as yf the substance of wyne were there in deed, for these
are the proper actions and operations of the
said accidents themselues; but where the con-
currace of substance is necessary to any action,
as in nutrition, generation, or corruption of
one substance into another, there doth God
supply the matter, that is necessary to that
action, when the body of Christ doth cease to
be there, which is, when those accidents of
bread and wyne are corrupted and not otherwise: As for example, in the resurrection of
our bodyes, where euery body is to receaue
his owne proper flesh againe, which yt had in
this life, yf some one body hauinge eaten another body, or parcell therof in this world, and
conuerted the same into his proper substance;
in this case (I say) almighty God must needs
supply otherwise, by his omnipotent power,
that part and matter of substance, that wan-
teth in one of these two bodyes, for that els
one of them should be vnperfect, and want

                                            part

part of his substance in the resurrection. And after the like manner we say, that when a consecrated hoast is eaten, and afterward is turned into the naturall norishment of the eater, which norishment requireth a materiall substance, God doth supply that substance in that instant, when the formes of bread and wyne perishinge, the body of Christ ceaseth to be there.

37. And this appertayneth to the prouidence of almighty God, for supplying the defects of particular naturall causes, when any thinge fayleth, that is necessary for their naturall operations. The very same also is to be obserued in generation, and corruption, as for example, when the accidents of the consecrated host perishinge, and some other substance should happen to be engendred thereof, as wormes, or the like, there the body of Christ ceaseth to be, when the said accidents do perish, and for the new generation insuinge thereof, God supplyeth fitt matter, as in the example before alleaged of the resurrection of our bodyes, wherof the one had eaten part of the other. By which obseruation yt wilbe easy afterward to dissolue many cauillations, proceedinge eyther of ignorance, heresie, or both, and obiected by Sacramentaryes against this mystery.

The

The eight Obseruation.

About the wordes Sacrament, signe, figure, type, commemoration, memory, &c. §. 8.

38.   For so much as the Sacramentaryes of our tyme, did forsee that they should be forced to oppose themselues, for defending their hereticall noueltye, sagainst the whole streame of scriptures, expositors, fathers, councells, reasons, practise, antiquity, and vniforme consent of the vuhole Christian vvorld, they thought best to diuise certayne tearmes and distinctions, which should serue them for euasions or gappes to runne out at, when-soeuer they should be pressed by our arguments: and these their shifts do consist principally, in the fraudulent vse of these tearmes of *Sacrament, signe, figure, type, commemoration, memory, sacramentally, spiritually* and the like. Wherfore we thinke yt needfull to explane and declare in this place, the natures, vses and abuses of these words.

39.   First then a Sacrament, according to the common definition ascribed to *S. Augustine, is a visible signe of an inuisible grace,* as in baptisme, the externall washinge by water, is the signe of the internall washing of the soule by grace: So heere also in this Sacrament of the Eucharist, the externall & visible signe are the consecrated formes of bread and wyne, as they conteyne the body of Christ; the internall or inui-

The vvord Sacramēt explicated.

inuisible grace signified, is the inward nou-
rishinge and feedinge of our soule: And this is
the first and cheefe manner how this Sacrament is *a signe*, that is to say *a signe of grace*, and
not of Chrifts body absent, as Proteftants are
wont moft fondly and fraudulently to inferre.
40. Secondly thefe externall formes and accidents of bread and wyne, are alfo a signe of
Chrifts body conteyned vnder them. And in
this sense is the Euchariſt called fometymes
by the Fathers, the signe of Chrifts body, but
of Chrifts body prefent, as hath byn faid, and
not abfent. Thirdly this Sacrament is a signe
of Chriſt his death and pafsion, and of the
vnion of his myfticall body the Church with
him: For that as bread and wyne reprefented
by thefe formes, are made of many grains and
many grapes; fo is Chrifts myfticall body, confiftinge of many members vnited to him; fo as
by all thefe wayes may this Sacrament be called *a signe*, to witt, a signe of the inward grace,
and norifhment of the foule obtayned therby,
a signe of Chrifts true body prefent, a signe of
Chriſt his death, and myfticall body, and yet
do none of all thefe figures exclude the true
reall being of his body in the Sacrament, but
do rather fuppofe the fame.

41. And the like may be faid to the other
words, or tearmes of *figure, type, commemoration,*
or *memory,* all which, when they occurre, are to
be vnderftood in fome of thefe fenfes, without
preiudice of the reality, or truth of our Sauiours being in this Sacrament, as for example,
this

The other
vvords of
tipe figure
&c. expli-
cated.

this Sacrament is *a forme, type, commemoration* & memory of Chrifts death on the Croffe, and yet this excludeth not his *reall-prefence* from hence. As for example, if a Prince hauing gayned in proper perfon a great & fingular victory, fhould inftitute a follemne triumph, to be made euery yeare in memory therof, & fome times fhould go in that triumph himfelfe alfo,

Note this
example. yt might be truly faid, that this triumph is a figure, type, commemoration, and memory of the other victory, & of the Prince, yet is the Prince truly alfo in yt himfelfe, and fo may be faid in like manner of this matter of the Sacrament, wherin Chrift in differēt manner, is a figure or type of himfelfe. And the like may be faid of the dayly facrifice alfo, which facrifice is a commemoration or memory of the other bloudy facrifice, once offered on the croffe, and yet conteyneth the fame reall body of our Sauiour, which the other did, after another manner. And by this will the reader eafily difcouer diuers poore fhifts & fallacyes of our moderne heretiks, efpecially of *Ridley* before named, who as yow haue heard him profeffe, was moued to leaue his ancient faith of the maffe, & his practice therin, for that in fome certaine places (for footh) of the Fathers, he found *that this facrifice* (of the maffe) *is called a commemoration of Chrifts paffion*; a ftronge argument, no doubt, to moue him to fo great a refolution. And fo much of this.

42. Now then are to be examined the other words, *facramentally, really*, and *fpiritually*: and as for

for the first, the common sense, and meaninge of schoole diuines is, that diuised this word, to signifie therby a peculiar manner of Christs supernaturall being in the Sacrament, different from his naturall and circumscriptiue being in heauen, and from the naturall being of an Angell definitiuely in a place, wherof we haue spoken before. So as, when they say that Christ is sacramentally vnder the formes of bread and wyne, they do not deny his true and reall being there in flesh, the very selfe-same that is in heauen; but he is there in another manner. And this is the chiefe proper signification of the word *sacramentally* amongest schoole-men, for which the word was inuented.

43. But in the common vse, and sense of our speach, *sacramentally* signifieth, that Christs body is there vnder a Sacrament or signe, which are the formes of bread and wyne, and not in his owne proper shape, euen as an Angell, when he appeareth in a body, he may be said to appeare bodyly, for that the body is the figure or forme, vnder which he appeareth; and conforme to this sense, we are said to receyue Christ *sacramentally*, when we receaue him truly and really, but yet not in his proper forme, but vnder another forme, that is to say of bread and wyne, wherby the fraudulent dealing of our moderne Sacramentaryes may appeare, who deceauing the people with this word *sacramentally*, do oppose yt to *really* and *truly*, as though when any author saith, that

we

Twoo signification of the word *sacramentally* and both against the Sacramentaryes.

1.

2.

we receaue Chrift facramentally in the Eucharift, yt were to be vnderftood, that we did
not receaue Chrifts body in deed and really,
but only a figne therof, and by this they endeauour to delude all the places, though neuer fo euident, of holy Fathers affirminge,
that Chrifts true flefh and body, the very fame
that was borne of the virgin Mary and crucified for vs, is receaued in the Sacrament, thefe
good fellowes aunfwere that yt is true, *facramentally*, which we alfo graunt, yf *facramentally*,
do not exclude really, accordinge to the true
fignification of the word: But yf by facramentally, they meane as they do, that only a figne
is receaued of Chrifts body in the Sacrament,
then is their deceyt manifeft as yow fee; for
that facramentally, hath no fuch fignification
at all amonge diuines, but only is diuifed a-
monge them for a fhift.

44.   The like fraud they vfe about the word
fpiritually, which in the fenfe of holy Fathers,
being oppofite to carnally and corporally, in
their ordinary materiall fignification, is by fectaryes alfo wrefted, as though yt were contrary to the word *really*, fo as whenfoeuer they
are forced to graunt Chrifts body to be fpiritually in the Sacrament (by which phrafe the
faid ancient Fathers do meane only, that he is
not there after a carnall, or common manner,
as he liued vpon earth) they will haue yt vnderftood, that he is there only by faith, and not
in deed really and fubftantially. They abufe
alfo the fignification of the forefaid wordes
carnally

(margin) VVhat the vvord fpi-ritually fi-gnifieth in this my-ftery.

carnally & corporally, which hauing a double
sense, the one that Christs body is naturally
and really in the Sacrament, the other that he
is there after the externall being of other bodyes, they deceytfully do take them now in
one sense, and now in another, and alwayes
oppose them to the word *spiritually*, which in
the former sense are not incompatible, but
may stand togeather, though not in the later.
And for auoydinge of this equiuocation, diuines do wish those two words, carnally and
corporally, though true in the foresaid sense,
yet to be more sparingly vsed, then the other
words really and substantially, that are equiualent in sense, and lesse subiect to equiuocation and mistaking.

45. Wherfore to conclude this obseruation,
all these words are to be noted, and their true
vse and signification remembred by him, that
will not be deluded by hereticall sleights and
impostures in this high mystery, but especially are to be obserued these three, wherby our
Sacramentaryes do most of all deceyue the
vulgar people, in their assertions and answers
to our arguments, to witt, *sacramentally*, *spiri-*
tually and *by faith*, as though they did exclude
the reall presence of Chrifts body in the Sacrament; which is most false, for that in the
true sense we admitt them al!. For example,
we graunt that Christ is sacramentally in this
Sacrament, both as sacramentally signifieth a
distinct manner of Chrifts being there, from
that in heauen, and as yt signifieth his being
there

there vnder a Sacrament or figne, but yet
really, we graunt alfo that he is there fpiritually, that is to fay, after a fpirituall, and
not corporall circumfcriptiue manner, yet
truly and really. We graunt further, that he
is in the Sacrament by faith, for that we do
not fee him, but apprehend him prefent by
faith, but yet truly and really, and not in faith
and beleefe only. And by this yow may perceaue our Sacramentaryes manner of difputinge; iuft like the Arrians of old tyme, and of
our dayes, who feeke to enacuate all places alleaged for the vnity and equality of Chrift
with his Father, by one only diftinction of
will and nature: So as when Chrift faid for
example *Ioan. 6. my Father and I are one,* yt is true
faid they, they are one in will & loue, but not
in nature; & thus they deluded all that could
be brought for naturall vnity, except only the
authority, and contrary beleefe of the vniuerfall Church, wherby at laft they were ouer-
borne.

Our here-
tiks cauill
like to
that of the
Arrians.

46.   And the very fame courfe held the Sacramentaryes of our dayes; for whatfoeuer
plaine and perfpicuous places you bring them
out of antiquity, affirminge the true naturall
fubftantiall body of our Sauiour, to be in the
Sacrament, they will fhift of all prefently, by
one of thefe three words; yt is true, *facramentally,* yt is true *fpiritually,* and yt is true *by faith
only,* as though thefe could not ftand with
really or *truly;* and heereof fhall yow haue ftore
of examples afterward in the aunfweringes of
Doct̃r

Doctor *Perne*, *Cranmer*, *Ridley* and *Latymer* for the
Sacramentary party to our arguments, taken
out of the ancient Fathers. For when the said
Fathers do auouch, that Christ our Sauiours
true naturall body is in the Sacrament, they
answere, *yt is true sacramentally*, and thinke they
haue defended themselues manfully therby,
and when in other places the same Fathers do
professe, that the very same flesh that was
borne of the virgin Mary and crucified for vs,
is there, they aunswere, *yt is true spiritually* and
by faith, but not really. And thus they do
euacuate and delude all that can be alleaged:
But yf they cannot shew (as they cannot) any
one Father that tooke or vsed the words *sacramentally, spiritually*, or *by faith*, in this sense, as
opposite to *really* and *truly* in this mystery, then
is it euident, this to be but a shift of their owne
inuention, to escape therby. And so much of
this obseruation.

The nynth Obseruation.

How Christ is receaued of euill men in the Sacrament,
and of good men both in, and out of the same. §. 9.

47. It followeth vpon the former declaration of the words, *sacrament, signe*, and the rest,
that we explane in this place, a certayne distinction insinuated by the ancient Fathers,
and touched in the Councell of *Trent*, of three ᴍᵃʳᵍⁱⁿ: *Concil. Tri-*
sorts of receauinge and eatinge Christ by this *dent. sess.*
13. Can. 8.

N   Sacra-

D.Tham.3. part.q. 80. art. I.
Sacrament: Firſt ſacramentally alone, the ſecond ſpiritually only, the third both ſacramentally and ſpiritually togeather. An example of the firſt is, when euill men do receaue the Sacrament vnworthily, for that theſe men, though they receaue the very Sacrament, to witt the true body of Chriſt vnder the formes of bread and wyne, yet do they not receaue the true ſpirituall effect therof, which is grace and nouriſhment of their ſoule, and of theſe doth S. *Paul* ſpeake expreſſely to the *Corinthians*, when he ſaith: *He that eateth and drinketh*

1. Cor. 11.
vnworthily (videlicet the Sacrament) *doth eat and drinke iudgement to himſelfe, not diſcerninge the body of our Lord.* And in this ſenſe do the auncient Fathers vpon this place, expound the Apoſtle, as yow may ſee in the commentaryes of *Saint*

Aug. l. 5. do bapt. cap. 8.
Chryſoſtome, S. *Ambroſe,* S. *Anſelme,* and other expoſitors both Greeke and Latyn; and S. *Auſten* in many places of his works doth expreſſely ſhew the ſame, alleaginge this text of the

Aug. epiſt. 162. & in pſalm. 10.
Apoſtle for proofe therof, *Corpus Domini* (ſaith he) *& ſanguis Domini nihilominus erat illis, quibus dicebat Apoſtolus, &c.* It was notwithſtanding the body & bloud of our Lord, which they tooke, to whome the Apoſtle ſaid; he that eateth and drinketh vnworthily, eateth and drinketh his owne damnation. And to the ſame effect he ſaith in diuers other places, that *Iudas* receaued the very ſelfe-ſame body of Chriſt, that the other Apoſtles did; and the ſame affirmeth S. *Chryſoſtome* in his homily intituled, of the *Treaſon of Iudas*; & generally it is the vniforme
opinion

opinion of all the auncient Fathers, whensoeuer any occasion is giuen to speake or treat therof.

48. The second manner of receauing Christ by this Sacrament, is tearmed *spiritually* only; for that without sacramentall receauinge of Chrifts body and bloud, a man may in some case receaue the spirituall fruite or effect therof, as yf he had receaued the same really, and this eyther with relation to the Sacrament, *videlicet*, when a man hath a desire to receaue yt actually, but cannot; or without reference thervnto, when by faith and grace good men do communicate with Christ, and participate the fruite of his passion. In which sense of spirituall communion, or eating Christ, *S. Austen* wryteth vpon *S. Iohns* ghospell, *Crede & manducasti*, beleeue, and thou hast eaten. And to the same effect do our Fathers often speake, when they treat of this spirituall & metaphoricall eating only without relation to the Sacrament which manner of speaches the Sacramentaryes of our dayes do seeke to abuse, as though there were no other eatinge of Christ in the Sacrament, but by faith alone, which is furthest of from the said Fathers meaninge, though sometymes they had occasion to speake in that manner.

Aug. tract. 25. in Ioan.

49. The third member of our former diuision is, to eat Christ both sacramentally and spiritually, as all good Christians do, when with due preparation & disposition, they receaue both the outward Sacrament and in-

ward grace and fruite therof: by obferuation
of which threefold manner of receauing, many obiections and hereticall cauillations will
eafily afterward be difcerned. And fo much
for this.

The tenth Obferuation.

*Touchinge indignityes and inconueniences obiected
by Sacramentaryes againft vs, in holdinge
the Reall prefence.* §. 10.

50.   As by the former obiections of naturall
impofsibilityes, yow haue heard this foueraigne myftery impugned, both by the learneder fort of old and new heretiks; fo do the
more fimple & ignorant infift & infult moft,
vpon certayne inconueniences, indignityes,
and abfurdityes, as to them do appeare. As for
example, that Chrift in the Sacrament, fhould
be eaten with mens teeth, go into the belly,
not only of men & weomen, but alfo of beafts
yf they fhould deuoure yt, that yt may putrifie, be burned, caft and fall into bafe and vnworthy places, be troden vnder mens feet,
with the like, which is a kind of argument
plaufible at the firft fight vnto vulgar appre-
henfions, and fuch as feemed to moue principally the moft part of Iohn Fox his artificers,
and fpinfter-martyrs, as may appeare by their
rude clamours, and groffe obiections, expro-
brations, irrifions, iefts and fcoffes at their
aunfweringe before their ordinaryes.

51. And

51. And heerin also they shewed their spirite of derydinge and blaspheminge that, which they vnderstood not, to concurre with that of the pagans and Iewes against the whole body of Christian Religion, and of auncient heretiks against the principall articles therof. Of the pagans S. *Augustine* wryteth thus: *In ipsum Christum non crederemus, si fides Christiana cachinnum metueret paganorum:* We should not beleeue in Christ himselfe, yf Christian faith did feare the scoffinge of pagans. S. *Paul* also wryteth both of Gentills and Iewes, that the Crosse of Christ (that is to say, that God should be apprehended, beaten, wounded and crucified) was to these a scandall, and folly to the others, though vnto the elect, yt was the very wisdome, power & vertue of God himselfe. We read also in the ghospell, that the *Saduces* amongst the Iewes, scoffed at the resurrection of bodyes, by asking Christ a question of a woman that had seauen husbands, whose wife she should be in the resurrection, purposinge therby to haue inferred an absurdity against the said article, to witt, that eyther seauen men should haue striued for one woman, or one woman haue byn wife of seauen men. And the *Marcionists* infamous heretiks, that tooke the same heresie from the Sadduces, as also the *Originists* concurringe therin against the said beleefe of our resurrection, went about to disgrace the same, as both *Tertullian,* and S. *Hierome* do testifie, by certaine absurd indignityes, which they imagined would ensue therof,

Aug. ep. 49. q. 6.

1. Cor. 1.

Math. 22.

Tertul. l. de resur. carn. Hier. in ep. ad Pamachium.

N 3   therof,

therof, as for example that difference of sexes
procreation, mydwyues, nurſes, priuyes, and
the like, muſt needs be in heauen, but the auncient Fathers anſwered them with the words
of our Sauiour to the ſaid *Sadduces, Erratis , ne-*

Matth. 11.   *ſcientes ſcripturam, & virtutem Dei.* Yow do erre,
not knowinge the ſcriptures , nor the power
of God .

52.   And the ſame aunſwere was giuen by
Catholiks to the firſt Sacramentaryes, that
euer publikely appeared , to witt the *Berenga-*
rians aboue 500. yeares paſt, who obiected the
very ſame abſurdityes, that our hereriks do at

Guitmun-   this day , as teſtifieth *Guitmundus* and *Algerus,*
dus lib. 2.&   that liued in that age and wrote againſt them;
Algerus
leb. 2. cont.   they were aunſwered (I ſay) that their error
Berenga-   proceeded of not vnderſtandinge the true
rium.   meaning of ſcriptures, nor the power of God,
which in the Sacrament conſerueth his body
without all leaſion, hurt, indignity, or inconuenience , whatſoeuer happeneth vnto the
formes, vnder which his body is, and that it is
nothing ſo baſe and vnworthy a matter, euen
in our ſenſe & comon reaſon, that Chriſt our
Sauiour being impaſsible in the Sacrament,
ſhould vnder another forme be ſaid to fall on
the ground , to be burned , to be eaten , &c.
then in his owne proper forme , when he was
paſsible , and ſenſible to ly in his mothers
wombe, or to cry and weepe in the cradle, or
to ſuffer hunger , thirſt , and other humayne
necefsityes, and to be whipped, wounded and
put to death, all which indignityes, ſuppoſing
that

that he was the selfe-same God that created
the world, might seeme more absurd, and improbable in common sense and reason, then
this of the Sacrament, and so they did seeme
to old heretiks, who obiected and derided the
same, as the torsaid *Marcionists*, that God should
be in a womans belly, and in a maunger; and
Nestorius the heretike, that God should be two
monethes old for example, and two cubitts
bigg, and other such iests and scoffes, as yow
may read of them in *Tertullian*, *Theodoret*, *Eua-
grius* and other wryters.

*Tert. lib. de
carn. Christi
& Theod.
l. 4. haret.
fabul. &
Euagr. l. 1.
hist. c. 2.*

53. Wherfore to conclude this obseruation,
two points are to be noted in this whole matter: First that many things that seeme to happen to Christ in these cases, do not touch him
indeed, but only the externall formes of bread
and wyne, as when they are burned for example, do putrifie, or the like, Christs body is
not burned, or putrified, but ceaseth to be vnder them, when the said formes or accidents
are corrupted, for that the substance of Christs
body, supplyinge the substance of bread, is no
longer there then the substance of bread
would haue byn there, yf yt had not ben conuerted into Christs body, but yf bread had remayned, yt would haue ceased by any kind of
corruption, as burninge, putrifyinge, or the
like, and so doth Christs body, though in a
different sort, so that the substance of bread
m ght, by the said corruption, be chaunged into some other substance, which Christs body
cannot be, but only ceasseth to be there, God

sup-

supplyinge some other matter for production of that, which is bronght forth or new, as in the former obseruation hath byn declared.

54.   The other point, that those other conditions which by reason of the formes are ascribed vnto Christ his body in the Sacrament, as to moue from place to place, when the formes are moued, to be seene, touched, eaten with our teeth and the like, which are frequent phrases among the Fathers, haue no inconuenience amonge them at all, no more for example, then when our soule is said to be moued with the motion of the body, which soule notwithstandinge of his owne nature is not moueable: so as an Angell being a spiritt, may be handled, seene, or stroken in the body which he taketh to appeare in, as is euident by the whole story of *Tobias* and other places of scripture, which Angell of himselfe notwithstandinge, is not capable of such thinges; and finally Gods eternall diuinity and maiesty is present in all places & things, the most basest and horrible that can be diuised, and yet suffereth no inconuenience therby: For though he be for example in the dunghill, yet he cannot be said to haue any euill smell therby, neyther to be burned in the fire, though the formes of bread and wyne be burned therin, nor to putrifie, though he be actually present in those things that rott and putrifie. And by this may yow see the vayne calumniations of fond heretiks, against the power of almighty God, out of their senses and foolish imaginations.

The

The eleuenth Obseruation.

About the nature of a sacrifice, as it is ordayned to diffe-
rent effectes, and how that of the Crosse standeth
vvith that of the masse.   §. 11.

55. The eleuenth and last obseruation shalbe
peculiarly about the last of the three questions
proposed, which is sacrifice of the masse, notinge therin two ends, offices, or effects to be
considered : First that yt is ordayned *ad cultum*
externum, to an externall worshipp of God peculiar to himselfe, in the highest degree of honour, called by the Gretians *Latria :* secondly
ad propitiationem pro peccatis, for pacifyinge of
Gods wrath for sinnes, and albeit both these
effects may be in one and the selfe-same sacrifice (and so we hould them to be in the sacrifice of the masse, for that yt was ordayned by
Christ, as well for a perpetuall outward honour & worshipp to be exhibited vnto God
in the Christian Church vnto the worlds end,
as also for remission of sinnes by application
of the meritt of Christs bloudy sacrifice on the
Crosse) yet may they be separated of their
owne natures, so as a sacrifice may be ordayned only *ad cultum,* that is to say, for an externall worshipp only, without power to remitt
sinnes: And so in a manner were the sacrifices
of the ould law, which little or nothing auayled for sinnes. And againe, sacrifice may be or-
deined only or principally to satisfy for sinnes,
                                                without

without relation therof *ad cultum*, to perseuere in any state of men, to be often offered by them, and such was Chrifts on the Crosse, which is not reiterated againe in the same bloudy and passible manner, as then yt was, but in another farre different fort in the masse, which is capable of both these effects, as hath byn said.

56,   Now then in the first sense, as a sacrifice is ordayned *ad cultum*, to an externall worship of God, yt conteyneth an outward protestation of our knowledge of Gods supreme Maiestie, power, and absolute dominion ouer vs, and in our subiection therunto, which is the highest honour that can be giuen by a creature vnto the creator, and is so particular to God alone, as hath byn said, as yt cannot be imparted to any creature, without the horrible sinne of Idolatry, and is so conioyned with the nature of Religion yt selfe, as no true Religion hath euer byn without this degree of externall honour, exhibited vnto God by his people; and so we see that all good men in the law of nature, by Gods instinct, did sacrifice vnto him, as *Adam, Abell, Noe, Melchisedecke,* and others, as afterwards also in the law of Moyses, the same was expressely ordayned by Gods owne commandement; & the Gentills did the same, though not to one true God, but to many idolls, by suggestion of the diuell, that therin emulated Gods honour exhibited vnto him by sacrifice. And this for the first effect or office of sacrifice.

57. The

57. The second is *propitiation*, or pacifynge of Gods wrath for sinnes, as hath byn said. Wherin for more perspicuityes sake, three degrees may be obserued. First of such sacrifices as were so weake & imperfect in themselues, touching this point of propitiation and satisfyinge for sinnes; as they profited little or nothinge, except only as they were morall good works; and accordinge to the piety of the offerer, they might help somewhat; but they had neyther sufficient force in themselues to remitt sinnes, neyther to apply the vertue and satisfaction of any other sacrifice, already exhibited, to the remission therof, but were only figures, and shaddowes of things to come: and such were the sacrifices of the old law of Moyses.

58. The second degree is quite opposite to this for excellency of perfection, power and meritt, being in yt selfe of so infinite valour, as yt is sufficient not only fully to satisfie for the sinnes of all the world; but also to giue vigour to all other sacrifices, both internall, and externall; And this was the sacrifice of Christ our Sauiour on the Crosse; & betweene these two sacrifices, to witt the weaknesse and imperfection, multitude and variety of the one vnder the old law, and the singularity, excellency, force and infinite power of the other, is the large *antithesis* & opposition, vsed by *S. Paul* in his 9. and 10. Chapters of his Epistle to the *Hebrewes*, shewing, that as the Iewes sacrifices were many in number, and of diuers sorts and infirme

infirme of themselues, & therfore offered vp
in great multitudes and often ; so the sacrifice
of Christ for the excellency therof, and infinite force and valour, was single, & but one,
and once offered for all , and not iterable for
acquiringe the price of mans redemption, and
perfect sufficiency for the sanctifyinge of all,
though yet he affirmeth not, that yt may not
be iterated in another manner, & to another
effect, to witt for applyinge the sufficiency &
meritt of this one sacrifice offered for all, to
the vtility of particular people : For albeit
Christ hath satisfied for all *quoad sufficientiam*
(to vse the termes of schoole) yet not *quoad effi-*
caciam, which is as much to say, as albeit Christ
hath redeemed all and paid the price for all,
yet all are not saued therby, nor do receaue the
efficacy or benefitt therof, for that they apply
not to their owne vtility that which is gayned for all.

59. Now then for applyinge this treasure
vnto people in particular, our aduersaryes do
confesse, that some things are necessary of our
parts, as faith & baptisme, but we do ad more
meanes, as ordayned by Christ himselfe, and
amonge other the sacrifice of the masse, not
for acquiringe any new price or sufficiency of
our saluation, but for applyinge the effect or
efficacy of that, which already is gotten by
Christ our Sauiour, through his passion on
the Crosse, & heerof resulteth a third degree
of propitiatory sacrifice, that is neyther so infirme as the sacrifices of the ould law were,
                                              that

that remytted not sinnes, nor yet in a manner of so potent effect, as to acquire the price of our saluation, for that yt is not offered vp to that end, but only to apply the vertue of the other sacrifice already gotten, and so may be iterated, not for any defect in it selfe, but for that sinnes dayly growinge haue need of day-ly application of the said sacrifice, as hath byn said.

60. And in this sense do all the ancient Fa-thers, in the places before alleaged, call this sa-crifice of the masse *iuge sacrificium*, a dayly sacri-fice, and iterable, notwithstandinge that the other on the Crosse could be offered but once, as *S. Paul* proueth. And now these obserua-tions being premised, we shall passe to exa-mine and aunswere the arguments of our aduersaryes, in all the former disputations brought forth.

THE

THE EXAMINATION

OF SVCH ARGVMENTES

*As in the former disputations were al-
leaged by the* Zuinglians *&* Caluinists, *against the* reall-presence
of Christes body in the
Sacrament.

C H A P.   I V.

Two
thinges to
be consi-
dered.

N o v v then to ioyne more neerly with
our Sacramentaryes, and to come to the
vew of particular arguments, brought forth
against the article of the *reall-presence*, yt is to
be held in memory, that which before we
haue noted: first, that these new Doctors hauinge no one direct place eyther of scriptures,
or Fathers for their purpose, that expressely
denyeth the said *reall-presence* (as we haue for
the affirmatiue) they are forced to runne to
certayne inferences, as *for that Christ is in heauen,
he cannot be in the Sacrament,* & such other like of
no validity, as presently yow shall see. And secondly it is to be remembred, that these arguments (the most wherof are founded on sense
and humayne reason against faith) are ordinarily to be found both alleaged, vrged and aunswered

fwered in all our fchoolmens books at large,
before our Sacramentaryes were borne, and
confequently thefe men bring no new things,
as worthy of a new labour. But yet for better
fatisfaction of them, that haue not read the
faid fchoolmen, nor are of fufficient learning
to fee the folution of themfelues, we fhall
breefely runne ouer in this place, whatfoeuer
was obiected by the faid Sacramentaryes, of
any moment in all the former difputations, or
other conferences, colloquyes, or examinations, reducinge all for more perfpicuityes
fake vnto certaine heads or groundes in manner followinge.

The firft head or ground of Sacramen-
tary obiections; for that yt feemeth
impoſsible to them, that Chriftes body
can be in many places at once. §. 1.

2. This is the firft principall ground of all
the Sacramentaryes vnbeleefe, and out of
which they draw the greateft fquadron of all
their arguments and obiections, as prefently
yow fhall fee, for that yt is a point very plaufible to comon-fenfe and humayne reafon,
that a naturall body naturally cannot be but
in one place at once: but he that fhall read our
obferuations in the precedet Chapter, where
we haue fhewed, that not only fupernatural-
ly and by Gods omnipotent power yt may be
done;

done; but that it comprehendeth not so much as any contradiction in nature it selfe; and further shall consider, that albeit Christs true and naturall body be in the Sacrament at many places at once, yet not after a naturall manner, but supernaturall and miraculous, as euery where the ancient Fathers do admonish vs (and we haue alleaged many of their admonitions before) he I say that shall consider this, will easily contemne and laughe at the vanity of so many Sacramentary arguments, founded vpon this weake ground and principle only, *that a naturall body cannot be in more places then one at once,* which is true naturally, that is to say by the ordinary course of nature, but by the power of God, that is aboue nature, yt may be, and this without an essentiall contradiction, as I haue said, in nature yt selfe.

3.   Well then, now will I sett downe the whole squadron of arguments, which out of this false principle, or rather true principle misvnderstood, Iohn Fox layeth foorth with great ostentation out of *Peter Martyr* his Oxford disputations, which arguments are 8. in number, and did seeme so insoluble vnto Fox his diuinity, and philosophy, as he putteth no answere at all giuen by the Catholike defendants to the same. I shall deliuer them also in dialecticall forme, as they ly in Fox this once, togeather with his foolery of cytinge the moods and figures of sophistry in the margent to euery argument, a thinge knowen to euery child that beginneth logique, & consequently

is ri-

is ridiculous to men of learninge, though
strange to the ignorant people, that may imagine great secrets to ly hidden in those words
of *Disamis*, *Darij*, *Baroco*, *Festino*, *Bocardo*, and
thinke that Iohn Fox doth go about to con-
iure vs his readers, by settinge them downe:
but now to the arguments themselues.

1. *Argument*.

Di- 4. ª The true naturall body of Christ is   ª It is
placed in heauen. *Matth.24. & 26. Ioan.*   graunted.
12. & 16. Act. 3. Colloss. 3.

sa- ᵇ The true naturall body of man can be   ᵇ It is true
but in one place at once, where he is.   naturally.
August. ad Dardanum, propter veri corporis
modum, saith he, that is for the manner
of a true body.

mis. ᶜ Ergo the true naturall body of Christ   ᶜ But yt
can be in noe place at once, but in hea-   may be su-
uen where he is.   pernatu-
rally.

2. *Argument*.

Da- ᵈ Euery true naturall body requireth one   ᵈ That is
certayne place.   by course
of nature.

ri- ᵉ Christs body is a true naturall body.   ᵉ True.

i. ᶠ Ergo. Christs body requireth one cer-   ᶠ True na-
tayne place.   turally.

3. *Argument*.

ᵍ Augustine giueth not to the soule of   ᵍ It is true
Christ   according

O

Chriſt to be in more places at once then one. *Aug. ad Dardan.*

[b] Ergo. Much leſſe yt is to be giuen to the body of Chriſt, to be in more places at once then one.

4. *Argument.*

[i] The nature of Angells is not to be in diuers places, but they are limited to occupy one certayne place at once. *Baſil. de ſpiritu ſanĉto. cap.* 22.

[k] Ergo. The body of Chriſt being the true naturall body of man, cannot fill diuers places at once.

5. *Argument.*

Ba-   [l] Whatſoeuer is in many & diuers places at once, is God.

ro-   The body of Chriſt is not God, but a creature.

co.   [m] Ergo. The body of Chriſt cannot be in more places togeather.

6. *Argument.*

Fe-   We muſt not ſo defend the diuinity of Chriſt, as we deſtroy his humanity.

ſti-   [n] Yf we aſsigne more places to the body of Chriſt, we deſtroy his humanity.

no.   Ergo. We muſt not aſsigne to the body of Chriſt plurality of places.

7. Ar-

7 . *Argument .*

Fe- • Whatsoeuer thinge is circumscribed,
that is to say, conteyned in the limitts
of any peculiar place, cannot be di-
spersed into more places at once.

sti- ? The body of Christ is a thinge circumscribed.

no. ¶ Ergo the body of Christ is not disper-
sed into more places at one tyme.

‣ This
graunted.

p It is true
de facto in
heauē, but
not in the
Sacramēt.
q True as
it is circū-
scribed.

8 . *Argument .*

Da- • Euery quantity, that is euery body hauing magnitude, length, and other dimensions, is circumscribed in one peculiar place. *Cyrill. de trinit. lib.* 2.

ri- ⸰ The body of Christ hath his dimensions,
and is a quantity.

j. • Ergo the body of Christ is circumscribed .

r True na-
turally but
not supper-
naturally.

s True,
though a
body is
not a quā-
tiry, but a
substance ‡
that hath
quantity.
‡ *Non se-
quitur.*

Aunswere.

℥. These are the doughty arguments, which
Fox affirmeth their great Patriarke *Peter Martyr* to haue alleaged against the *reall-presence,*
out of this first philosophicall ground, *that one
body cannot be in many places at once* ; Whervnto
I might aunswere in the words of *S. Augustine,*
to such kind of men, as measure Gods power
by their owne imagination: *Ecce qualibus argu-
mentis, omnipotentiæ Dei, humana contradicit infirmi-*

*Aug. l. 2 2.
de Ciuit. Dei
cap. 1 1.*

O 2   *tas,*

tas, quam poßidet vanitas: behould with what
kind of arguments, the infirmity of man, possessed by vanity, doth contradict Gods omnipotency. Yf yow read the fourth and fifth obseruations sett downe in the former Chapter,
yow will easily see both the infirmity, and vanity of all these arguments, & how this great
variety vpon one ground, are but minced-
meats guised in diuers sorts and fashions, by
the art of *Fox* and *Peter Martyrs* cookery, and yet
are they held for great demonstrations, and
stronge fortresses of the Sacramentary faith,
or rather infidelity, and vrged euery where
by their followers.

6.   *Iohn Rogers* vsed the same argument in his
defence before the Bishops, as yow may see in
Fox *pag.* 1351. *Chrift is corporally* (saith he) *in heauen only, ergò not in the Sacrament*, where he vseth
an equiuocation also in the word corporally,
for that we do not say, that Chrift is corporally in the Sacrament, yf by corporally he meane
not only really and substantially, but also after
a corporall manner, accordinge to externall
dimensions. *Thomas Tompkins* the weauer of
Shordich, vseth the same argument against his
Ordinary in like manner, to witt, *that Chrifts
body cannot be in the Sacrament, for that yt is in heauen.* Fox *pag.* 1395. *Maifter Gueft* in his Cambridge disputations against *Doctor Glyn*, leaned
principally to this argument, and *B. Ridley*, his
moderator, or president of these disputations,
vrged a place of *S. Augustine* ad *Dardanum* to the
same effect. *Tolle spatia corporibus, & nusquam erunt.*
                                        Take

Take away the spaces from bodyes (saith *S. Austen*) and they shalbe no where. But *D. Glyn* defendant answered him well, that *S. Augustine* spake expressely of the naturall being of bodyes, accordinge to their ordinary externall dimensions, and not how they might be by Gods supernaturall power and omnipotency.

7. But aboue all others, *Philpott* did keep reuell in the conuocation house about this argument, against *Maister Morgan*, & *Maister Harpesfield*, alleaginge diuers places of scripture for the same, but little to the purpose God wooteth, as that of *S. Paul*: *Christ is like vnto vs in all points, except sinne.* And therfore said he, as one of our bodyes cannot be at *Paules*, and at *VVestminster* togeather; so cannot Christ be in heauen, and in the Sacrament. But yt was told him, that these words of *S. Paul*, were true in *S. Paules* sense, but yet that Christs body was vnlike also vnto vs besides sinne, in diuers other points, as for example, in that he was begotten without the seed of man, and that his body was inuisible, when he would haue it soe, and that he rose out of the sepulcher the same being shutt, and diuers other like points, which our ordinary naturall bodyes haue not, though God of his omnipotency might giue the same to our bodyes also. Then he alleaged the sayinge of *S. Peter* in the Acts: *VVhome heauen must receaue vntill the consumation of the world.* Wherof he would inferre a necessity of Christs remayning in heauen, vntill the day

Philpot his styrre in the conuocation house about this argument.

Fox pag. 1288.

of iudgement. Then *Morgan* laughed at this (faith Fox) *Harpesfield* ftood vp, and asked him how he vnderftood that place, *Oportet Episcopum effe vnius vxoris virum*, A Bifhop muft be the husband of one wife. And whether this be of fuch necefsity, as he may not be without a wife, one at leaft? With which demaund *Philpott* was fo entangled, as he could not well go forward, as there yow may fee, and refufed to aunfwere *Maifter Morgan*, as the prolocutor would haue had him.

1. Tim.

8.   Well then, this is the firft and principall ground and bulwarke of all Sacramentary vnbeleefe in this article, that Chrifts body cannot be by Gods omnipotent power in two places at once, to witt both in heauen, and in the Sacrament, which we haue fhewed before in our fourth, fifth and fixt obferuations, to be a fond and temerarious pofition, wherevnto we referre the reader to fee the grounds more at large, and heere only we fhall fay a word or two to the former eight arguments, as they lye in order. Yet firft it fhalbe good for the reader to remember that, which we haue noted before in the ftory of *Melancthon*, who faith, *I had rather offer my felfe to death, then to affirme, as the Zuinglians do, that Chriftes body cannot be but in one place at once.* But yet *Peter Martyr*, *Philpott*, *Cranmer*, and their fellowes would dye, and fome of them alfo did dye for the contrary, fo as Saints of one Calendar, do heere dye for contrary opinions one to the other. But let vs anfwere the arguments.

Melancth.
Epiftola ad
Martinum
Garolituin

8. To

8. To the first we say, concerning the minor proposition, that a true naturall body, naturally, and by ordinary course of nature, cannot be at one tyme, but in one place, and that meaneth *S. Augustine ad Dardanum*, but supernaturally, and by Gods omnipotent power, that exceedeth nature, yt repugneth not to be in diuers places at once, yf God will haue yt so : as in our fifth obseruation is proued. To the second argument we say, that euery true naturall body requireth one certaine place by ordinary course of nature, and not otherwise. To the third, that soules and spiritts by their naturall course haue but one totall place, wherin they may be said to be, as one soule in one body, and one Angell in the place, that it pleaseth to occupye, or to haue operation therin : albeit yf we respect partiall places of the same body, as head, foote, fingar and the like, the selfe-same soule is wholy in diuers places at once, which is no lesse wonderfull and incredible to our sense, then for a bodily substance, to be in two distinct places at once. And the like is in the Angell, who may occupy, for example, a whole house or towne for his totall place, and yet be in euery particular and partiall place therof wholy and entyrely, which is graunted both by all philosophers and diuynes, though vulgar sense cannot apprehend yt.

9. To the fourth may be answered the very same, as to the former, that the being of Angells in place definitiuely, is like in all respects

O 4

to that of the soule. Read our fourth obseruation in the precedent Chapter. To the fifth argument the aunswere is easy, for we deny that whatsoeuer is in diuers places at once, is God, for that by his omnipotent power a creature may be: yt is Gods priuiledge that he is euery where wholy and entyrely, *ex vi natura diuina*, by force of his diuine nature, that is to say, he is so euery-where, as he cannot be but euery where, which is not true eyther in a spiritt, or in Chrifts body, or in any other creature whatsoeuer; for that all creatures, as they haue limited natures, so are they limited also in place, and reftrayned from vbiquity, or being euery where, which is proper and peculiar to almighty God alone : & so to speake of the body of Chrift in particular, yt is not euery-where; and we detest both the *Eutichian* vbiquitaryes, that held Chrifts body to be euery-where, as confounded with his diuinity ; and no lesse the Lutheran vbiquitaryes of our dayes, that hold Chrifts body to be euery where, by reason of the coniunction with Chrifts diuinity; the Catholike faith affirming only, that Chrifts body, though naturally it be but in one place, yet by Gods omnipotency it may be in more.

10. To the sixt argument we deny the *Minor*, to witt, that we destroy Chrifts humanity by grauntinge, that yt may be in diuers places at once; for that yt repugneth not to a humayne creature, to be in more places then one by Gods omnipotency ; this we haue shewed
more

more largely in our fifth obseruation. To the seauenth we deny also the *Minor* ; that Christs body in the Sacrament is to be circumscribed, or circumscriptiuely there , as yt is in heauen. The differences betweene three manners of being, to witt, circumscriptiuely, definitiuely, and sacramentally, yow may see more at large declared in our fourth and fifth obseruations. To the eight and last, we say that the maior is to be vnderstood naturally, and not supernaturally by diuine power: to the *Minor*, we aunswere , that Christs body hath not externall dimensions in the Sacrament, though yt haue in heauen: and in the Sacrament yt hath only internall and inuisible quantity, without extension to place; wherof yow may read more in the fourth and fifth obseruations. And this shalbe sufficient for this first ground of philosophicall arguments. Now will we passe to the second.

The second head or ground of Sacramentary argumentes, drawen from contrary qualityes or quantityes, &c. §. 2.

11. This second ground is not much different from the former, for both of them are founded on sense, and humayne reason , and heere I will not conioyne all the arguments

togea-

togeather, as before I did, but set them downe
seuerally, as Fox recordeth them out of *Peter
Martyrs* disputation.

1.   *Argument*.

Ba-   Yf Christ had giuen his body substantially and carnaily in the supper, then
was that body eyther passible or impassible.

ro-   But neyther can yow say that body to be
passible or impassible, which he gaue
at supper: not passible for that *S. Austen* denyeth yt *Psalm.* 98. not impassible, for that Christ saith: *This is my
body, vvhich shalbe giuen for yow.*

co.   Ergo he did not giue his body substantially at supper.

Annswere.

12.   And this same argument vsed others after *Peter Martyr*, as *Pilkilton* against *Doctor Glym*,
& alleageth the same place of *S. Austen*, as yow
may see in Fox *pag.* 1259. But the matter is easily answered, for that the minor or second
proposition is cleerly false, for that Christs
body giuen in the supper, though yt were the
same in substance, that was giuen on the
Crosse, the next day after, yet was yt deliuered at the supper in another manner, to witt
in manner impassible, & vnder the formes of
bread and wyne, so as according to the being,

                                    which

which yt hath in the Sacrament, no naturall
cause could exercise any action vpon yt,
though being the selfe same which was to
dye vpon the Crosse, yt is also passible, euen
as now in heauen it is visible, & in the Sacrament inuisible, though one & the selfe same
body,& now in both places glorious and immortall,& this meaneth expressely *S. Austen* in
the place alleaged, whose words cited by Fox
are : *Yow are not to eate this body that yow see, nor to
drinke the bloud that they are to shedd who shall crucifie
me.* Which words being spoken to them, that
were scandalized at his speach about the eatinge of his body, do shew that we are in deed
to eate his true flesh in the Sacrament, but not
after that carnall manner, which they imagined: *carnaliter cogitauerunt* (saith *S. Austen* in the
same place) *& putauerunt, quod præcisurus esset Dominus particulas quasdam de corpore suo, & daturus
illis.* They imagined carnally, and thought
that Christ vvould haue cutt of certayne
peeces of his body, and giuen vnto them;
which grosse imagination our Sauiour refuteth by tellinge them, that they should eat his
true body, but in another forme of bread
and wyne.

13.   And yet that yt is the selfe-same body &
the selfe-same bloud, the same Doctor and
Father affirmeth expressely, both in this and
many other places. *Verè magnus Dominus, &c.* he
is in deed a great God, that hath giuen to eat
his owne body, in which he suffered so many,
and great thinges for vs. And againe talkinge
of his

*S. Augu-
stines* sen-
tence of
drinkinge
Chrifts
bloud.
,,
,,

*Aug. in
expofit.
Pfalm. 33.*
,,

of his tormentors : *Ipsum sanguinem quem per in-*
saniam fuderant, per gratiam biberunt. The selfe-
same bloud which by fury they sheed, by
grace they dronke. And yet further of the

same : *Quousâ biberent sanguinem quem fuderunt;*
mercy left them not, vntill they beleeuinge
him, came to drinke the bloud, which they
had shedd. And finally in another place: *Vt eius*

iam sanguinem nossent bibere credentes, quem fuderant
seuientes; that comminge to beleeue in him,
they might learne to drinke that bloud, which
in their cruelty they sheed. And last of all, in
another place explaninge his owne faith, and
the beleefe of all Christians in this behalfe, he

saith against heretiks of his tyme ; *Mediatorem*
Dei, &c. We do with faithfull hart and mouth,
receaue the mediator of God and man Christ
Iesus, giuing vnto vs his flesh to be eaten, and
bloud to be dronken, *though yt may seeme more*
horrible to eate mans flesh, then to slea the same, and to
drinke mans bloud, then to shedd the same. Consider
heere the speach of *Saint Augustine*, whether it
may agree to the eatinge of a signe of Christs
body or bloud ; what horror is there in that?
And thus much to this first argument.

2.   *Argument.*

a VVith-
out all
quantity.
b Not
vvithout
all quan-
tity.

Fe-

ri-

a Bodyes organicall without quantity,
    be no bodyes.

b The Popes doctrine maketh the body
    of Christ in the Sacrament to be
    without quantity.

¶ Ergo:

9.   Ergo : the Popes doctrine maketh the
     body of Christ in the Sacrament to be
     no body.

Aunswere.

14. We graunt that bodyes organicall, without all quantity are no bodyes; but Catholike
doctrine doth not teach, that Chrifts body in
the Sacrament, is without all quantity, but
only without externall quantity, aunfwering
to locall extenfion, and commenfuration of
place, which repugneth not to the nature of
quantity, as before is declared at large, in the
fourth obferuation of the precedent Chapter;
wherby yow may fee both the vanity of this
argument, as alfo the notorious folly & ignorance of Fox, who by occafion of this argument of an organicall body vrged, by *Cranmer*
in *Oxford*, againft *Maifter Harpesfield* when he
proceeded Bachler of diuinity, bringeth in a
whole commedy of vayne diuifes, how all
the learned Catholike men of that vniuerfity,
were aftonifhed at the very propoundinge of
this graue doubt, to witt ; *VVhether Chrift hath*   Fox *pag.*
his quantity, quality, forme, figure, and fuch like pro-   1327.
pertyes in the Sacrament. All the Doctors (faith Fox)
fell in a buzzinge, vncertayne what to aunfwere, fome
thought one way, fome another, and thus Maifter Do-
ctors could not agree. And in the margent he hath
this note: *The Rabbyns could not agree amongft them-*
felues: and then he profecuteth the matter for
a whole column or page togeather, makinge
                                        Doctor

A Comi-
call diuise
of Iohn
Fox.

Fox *ibid.*

Doctor *Tressam* , to say one thinge , *Doctor Smith*
another, *Harpesfield* another , *VVeston* another,
M. *VVard* philosophy-reader another, whose
philosophicall discourse about the nature of
quantity, Fox not vnderstandinge, neyther
the other that were present, as he affirmeth,
concludeth thus: *Maister VVard amplified so largely his words, & so high he clymed into the heauens with
Duns ladder, and not with the scriptures, that yt is to be
maruayled , how he could come downe againe without
falling.* So Iohn according to his skill; but *Maister VVard* and the rest, that vnderstood philosophy, knew well inough what he said , and
yow may easily conceaue his meaninge, as also the truth of the thinge yt selfe, by readinge
my former obseruation ; for I thinke yt not
conuenient to repeate the same againe heere.

3 . *Argument* .

Da-

a False &
foolish.

ri-

j.

All thinges which may be diuided haue
　quantity .
a The body in the Popes Sacrament is
　diuided into three parts.
Ergo: the body in the Popes Sacrament
　hath quantity, which is against their
　owne doctrine.

Aunswere .

15.　We deny that it is against our doctrine,
that Christs body in the Sacrament hath inward quantity , but only externall and locall.
　　　　　　　　　　　　　　　　　　We

We deny alſo, that Chriſts body is diuided into three parts in the Sacrament, or into any part at all,for it is indiuiſible; only the formes of bread are diuided. And this is the ignorance of the framer of this argument, that vnderſtandeth not what he ſaith; for it is ridiculous to affirme, that when the conſecrated hoſt is diuided into three partes, that Chriſts body is diuided alſo, which is no more true, then when a mans fingar is cutt of wherin the ſoule was wholy before, that ſhe is alſo diuided therwith.

4. *Argument.*

Ee-   No naturall body can receaue in yt ſelfe at one tyme contrary or diuers qualityes. *Vigil. cont. Eutich. lib. 4.*

ri-   ᵃ To be in one place locall, and in another place not locall, in one place with quantity, and in another place without quantity, in one place circumſcript, in another place incircumſcript, is for a naturall body to receaue contrary qualityes.

ᵃ Falſe, nor are theſe properly qualityes.

ꝛ.   Ergo: they cannot be ſaid to be in Chriſts body.

Aunſwere.

16.   To the firſt propoſition of this argument, I ſay, that the ſentence of *Vigilius,* alleaged by Fox in this place, is nothinge to his purpoſe:

purpose: For that *Vigilius* dealinge againſt the heretike *Eutiches,* that would haue Chriſts humanity confounded with his diuinity, ſaith, as Fox alleageth him: *Theſe two things are diuers, and farre vnlike, that is to ſay, to be conteyned in a place, and to be euery where, for the word is euery-where, but the fleſh is not euery-where.* Which ſentence of *Vigilius* maketh, againſt Iohn Fox his frends, and ſome of his Saints alſo the *vbiquitaryes,* that hold Chriſts body to be euery where, as his diuinity is, of which hereſie yow haue heard before * *Melancthon* to be accuſed by *Coliander* one of his owne ſect, but Catholiks do not hold this vbiquity of Chriſts body, but that yt may be circumſcribed in a certayne place, and ſo yt is *de facto* in heauen, though otherwiſe by Gods omnipotency, the ſame body may be and is in diuers places; which this ſentence of *Vigilius* nothing impugneth, and conſequently is nothing to the purpoſe.

* Supra menſe de-vembri.

17.   To the ſecond or minor propoſition, I ſay that Fox is a ſimple fellow, when he calleth contrary qualityes to haue quantity locall and not locall, circumſcript and vncircumſcript, wheras theſe do appertayne to the predicaments of quantity and *vbi,* rather then to quality, and are not ſo contrary or oppoſite to themſelues; but that in diuers reſpects they may be in one, and the ſelfe-ſame thinge, as Chriſt is locally in heauen, and not locally in the Sacrament; with viſible and externall quantity in heauen, but with internall and inuiſible in the Sacrament.

The

The third head or ground of Sacramentary arguments, concerninge the receauinge and receauers of the Sacrament. §. 3.

18. Another company or squadron of arguments against the reall-presence, though lesse then the former, is framed by our Sacramentaryes against the reall-presence, concerning the receauers, or manner of receauinge the same. Yow shall heare them as Fox layeth them downe.

1. *Argument.*

Fe- " The wicked receaue not the body of Christ.

a It is denyed.

ti- *b* The wicked do receaue the body of Christ, yf Transubstantiation be graunted.

b And the like followveth of the reall presence vvithout Transubstantiatiō.

son. Ergo. Transubstantiation is not to be graunted in the Sacrament.

Aunswere.

19. Do yow see a wise argument? and why leapeth Fox (thinke yow) from the reall presence to Transubstantiation, but that he is weary of the former controuersie, for that

Tran-

Tranfubftantiation hath a proper place very largely afterward, fo as heere yt is wholy impertinent. And further, yf yow confider the matter rightly, yow will fee that the fame followeth as well of the reall-prefence, as of Tranfubftantiation; for yf Chrift be truly and really in the Sacrament, eyther with bread, or without bread, then whofoeuer receaueth the faid Sacramét, muft needs receaue alfo Chrifts body. Wherfore this fkipp of Fox from _reall prefence_ to _Trausubftantiation_ was needles, and helpeth him nothinge; befides that, the whole argument is foolifh; for that his _Maior_ or firft propofition; _that wicked men receaue not the body of Chrift_, is wholy denyed by vs, and not proued by him, but prefumed; and how fondly yt is done, fhall appeare prefently in our aunfwere to his other arguments of this kind, and the whole matter is difcuffed more at large in our ninth precedent obferuation.

2. _Argument._

_a_ True, fruitfully.	Ca-	_a_ To eat Chrift is for a man to haue Chrift dwelling and abiding in him. _Cyprian. de Cœna, Domini & Aug. lib. de ciuit. Dei 21. cap. 15._
_b_ Fruitefully they haue not.	mef-	_b_ The wicked haue not Chrift dwellinge in them.
	tres.	Ergo the wicked eat not the body of Chrift.

Aunfwer

Aunswere.

20. The whole aunswere of this argument is sett downe more at large in our foresaid ninth obseruation, where yt is shewed, that there are three manners of receauinge Christ *sacramentally only*, *spiritually only*, and both *sacramentally* and *spiritually*, and that euill men do receaue him after the first manner *only*, that is to say, they receaue Christs true body in the Sacrament, but not the spirituall fruite therof, which *S. Paul* expresseth most cleerly, when he saith; that an euill-man, receauinge the Sacrament, *Iudicium sibi manducat, non dijudi-* 1. Cor. 11. *cans corpus Domini,* Doth eat his owne iudgement and condemnation, not discerninge, or respectinge the body of Christ which he eateth. And this is the assertion of all holy Fathers after him, to witt, *that vvicked-men do eate the body of Christ but not the fruite,* and namely the two heere cited by Fox to the contrary, *S. Cyprian* and *S. Augustine* do expressely hold the same : For that *S. Cyprian* vpon these words of th' Apostle, making an inuectiue against them that receaue Christs body vnworthily, saith: *Antequam expiantur delicta, ante exhomologesin fa-* Cypr. serm. *ctam criminis, ante purgatam conscientiam sacrificio,* de lapsis. *& manu sacerdotis, &c.* Before their sinnes be „ clensed, before they haue made confession of „ their faults, and before their conscience be „ purged by the sacrifice and hand of the Priest „ (this was the preparation to receaue worthily „

in *S. Cyprians* tyme) they do presume to receaue
,, the body of Christ. Wherof the holy Father
,, inferred: *Spretis his omnibus atque contemptis, vis in-*
fertur corpori eius & sanguini. These due prepara-
tions being contemned, violence is offered by
them to the body and bloud of Christ, which
he would neuer haue said, yf those wicked-
men had not receaued the body and bloud of
Christ at all, as Protestants do hould.

Aug. l. cont. S. *Augustine* is frequent also and earnest in
Fulgent. this matter: *Corpus Domini* (saith he) *& sanguis*
Donatist. *Domini, nihilominùs erat illis quibus, &c.* It was no
cap 6. lib. 2. lesse the body and bloud of Christ vnto those
cont. Petti-
lian. cap. 11. (wicked-men) to whome the Apostle said:
& in psalm. *he that eateth vnworthily, eateth & drinketh his iudge-*
10. & serm. *ment,* then yt was to the good. And the same
11 de verbis
Domini & Father in diuers places affirmeth, that aswell
l. de adulter. *Iudas* receaued the true body of Christ, as the
consug c. 17.
& tract. 50. rest of the Apostles, though yt were to his
in Ioan. owne damnation: *Nam & Iudas proditor bonum*
corpus (saith he) *& Symon magus bonum baptisma à*
Christo accepit, sed quia bono benè non sunt vsi, mali
malè vtendo deleti sunt. For that *Iudas* the Tray-
,, tor also receaued the good body of Christ, and
,, *Symon Magus* the good baptisme of Christ, but
,, for that they vsed not well that which was
,, good, they being euill-men perished accor-
,, dingly.

22.   The other places cyted in the margent,
I pretermitt for breuity sake to sett downe at
large, this being knowne to be the generall
Catholike sentence of all auncient holy Fathers, concerninge *Iudas* and other euill-men,
that

that they receaue Chriſt, but to their owne
damnation, and the ſentence of S. *Paul* before
cyted is ſo cleere, and euident, as no reaſonable doubt can be made therof. And when
Fox doth heere alleage certayne places of
S. *Cyprian* and S. *Auguſtine*, affirminge that the
eatinge of Chriſt *is dwellinge in him* and he in vs,
and that thoſe that dwell not in him, do not
eat him, yt is to be vnderſtood of ſpirituall
and fruitfull eatinge of Chriſts body, which
agreeth only to good men and not to euill,
which euill do only receaue ſacramentally
the body and bloud of Chriſt, as before we
haue ſaid, and more at large is declared in our
ninth obſeruation; yea the very words alleaged heere of S. *Auguſtine* by ſimple *Iohn Fox*, that
diſcerneth not what maketh for him, & what
againſt him, do plainly teach vs this diſtinction. For that S. *Auguſtine* vpon thoſe words
of Chriſt in S. *Iohns* ghoſpell; *he that eateth my
fleſh, and drinketh my bloud, dwelleth in me, and I in
him,* inferreth preſently theſe words: *Chriſt
ſheweth what yt is, not* ＊ *ſacramentally, but indeede to
eat his body and drinke his bloud, vvhich is when a man
ſo dwelleth in Chriſt, that Chriſt dwelleth in him.*
23. So he. Which words are euidently meant
by S. *Auguſtine* of the fruitfull eating of Chriſts
body to our Saluation, which may be ſaid in
effect the only true eatinge therof, as he may
be ſaid truly to eat and feed of his meate, that
profiteth and nouriſheth therby: but he that
taketh no good but rather hurt by that he eateth, may be ſaid truly and in effect not to

feed

*Aug. l. 21.
de Ciuit. dei
cap. 25.*

Ioan. 6.

＊ *Non Sa-
cramento
tenus.*

feed in comparison of the other that profiteth
by eatinge, though he deuoure the meate sett
before him ; and so yt is in the blessed Sacrament, where the euill doe eat *Sacramento tenus*,
as *S. Augustine* saith, that is sacramentally only,
and without fruite; not that they receaue not
Christs body , but that they receaue yt without fruite to their damnation ; which distinction is founded in the scriptures , not only
out of the place of *S. Paul* before alleaged to
the *Corinthians*, but out of Christs owne words
in sundry places of the ghospell , as that of
Math. 20. S. Mathew: *Venit filius hominis dare animam suam re-*
demptionem pro multis. The sonne of man came
to giue his life for the redemption of many,
wheras indeed he gaue yt for all , but for that
not all, but many should receaue fruite therby,
yt is said to haue byn giuen fruitfully only for
Math. ibid. many and not all. And againe in the same
Euangelist : *This is my bloud of the new Testament*
that shalbe shedd for many, that is to say fruitfully,
and to their saluation , but sufficiently for all,
and so in like manner all men good and badd,
do eate Christ in the Sacrament , but euill-
men sacramentally only, without the spirituall effect therof, but good men both spiritually and sacramentally togeather.

24.   And to this end appertayne also those
words of *S. Augustine*, alleaged by *Bradford*, *Rid-*
Fox pag. *ley* and others, that wicked-men *edunt panem*
1466. *Domini & non panem Domini*, they eat the Lords
bread , but not the bread that is the Lords;
that is to say, they eat not the bread, that bringeth

geth vnto them the true effect and fruite of
the Lords body, which is grace, spirit, and life
euerlasting, though they eat the body it selfe,
which is called the bread of our Lord only in
this sense, that it hath no fruite nor vitall operation, but rather the contrary.

3. *Argument*

Sa- Yf the wicked and infidells do receaue
the body of Christ, they receaue him
by sense, reason, or faith.

ro- But they receaue him neyther with
sense, reason, or faith, for that the body of Christ is not sensible, nor the
mystery is accordinge to reason, nor
do infidells beleeue.

co. Ergo. Wicked-men receaue in no wise
the body of Christ.

Aunswere.

25. This argument is as wise as the maker;
for first we do not alwayes ioyne wicked-
men and infidels togeather, as he seemeth to
suppose, for that an infidell (their case in receauinge being different) when he receaueth
the Sacrament, not knowinge or beleeuinge
yt to be the body of Christ, he receaueth yt
only materially, no otherwise then doth a
beast or senseless-man, without incurringe
new sinne therby: wicked-men receaue yt to
their damnation, for that knowinge and be-

P 4   leeuing

leeuinge yt to be the body of Chriſt (or at leaſtwiſe ought to do) they do not diſcerne or receaue yt with the worthyneſſe of preparation, which they ſhould do: and as for ſenſe & reaſon, though Chriſts body be not ſenſible, yet are the formes of bread, vnder which yt is preſent and receaued, ſenſible, for that they haue their ſenſible taſt, coulour, ſmell, and other like accidents, and though the myſtery yt ſelfe ſtand not vpon humayne reaſon, yet are there many reaſons both humayne and diuyne, which may induce Chriſtians to beleeue the truth therof, euen accordinge to the rule of reaſon yt ſelfe, which reaſons we call arguments of credibility: So as in this Sacrament, though yt ſtand not vpon ſenſe or reaſon, yet in receauinge therof is there fraude both in ſenſe and reaſon, which is ſufficient to ſhew the vanity of him that vrgeth it: now ſhall we paſſe to the laſt argument of *Peter Martyr* though drawen from another ground.

4. *Argument.*

See this argument vrged by *Cauſon, Higbed,* and other Foxian Martyrs. *pag.* 1400. &c.

Ba-   The holy Ghoſt could not come yf the body of Chriſt were really preſent, for that he ſaith: *Ioan.* 16. *vnleſſe I go from yow the holy ghoſt ſhall not come.*

car-   But that the holy-ghoſt is come, yt is moſt certayne.

do.   Ergo: yt cannot be that Chriſt himſelfe ſhould be heere really preſent.

Aunſwere.

Aunſwere.

26.   Firſt neyther Fox, nor his *Martyr* can deny but that the holy-ghoſt was alſo in the world, whilſt Chriſt was bodyly preſent, for that yt deſcended viſibly vpon him in the forme of a doue, and after he gaue the ſame to his diſciples ſayinge: *accipite ſpiritum ſanctum*;re- ceaue ye the holy-ghoſt; wherby is manifeſt, that there is no repugnance, why Chriſts bo-dyly preſence may not ſtand togeather, with the preſence of the holy-ghoſt. Wherfore the meaninge of thoſe other words *Ioan.* 16. that *except Chriſt departed, the holy-ghoſt ſhould not come,* muſt needs be, that ſo long as Chriſt remay-ned vpon earth viſibly, as a Doctor, teacher, & externall guide of his diſciples & Church;ſo longe the holy-ghoſt ſhould not come in ſuch aboundance of grace, to direct the Church, eyther viſibly, as he did at pentecoſt or inui-ſibly, as after he did. But this impugneth no-thing the preſence of Chriſt in the Sacramet, where he is inuiſibly,& to feed our ſoules, not as a Doctor to teach & preach,as in his bodiiy conuerſation vpon earth he was;for this he aſ-cribeth to the holy-ghoſt after his aſcenſion: *Ille ſpiritus veritatis docebit vos omnem veritatem,*that ſpirit of truth ſhall teach you all truth.

Ioan. 20.

Ioan. 16.

27.   And theſe be all the arguments of *Peter Martyr* regiſtred by Fox, who concludeth in theſe words: *And thus briefely we haue runne ouer all the arguments, and authorityes of Peter Martyr in*
that

that *difputation at* Oxford vvith Doctor Tre-
fham, Chedfey *and* Morgan, *before the Kings vifitours aboue named, anno* 1549. So he. And for fo
much as he fetteth downe no folution vnto
thefe arguments; we may imagine that he
held them for infoluble: and then yf you confider how weake and vayne they haue byn,
and how eafy to aunfwere; yow will therby
fee how fure grounds, this poore Apoftata-
friar *Martyr* had to become a facramentary, &
to leaue his former Religion, which had endured in Chrifts Church for fo many ages before; yea and to oppofe himfelfe againft *Docter
Luther* in this point of the reall-prefence, who
was their Prophet, and had firft of all opened
vnto him & others the gapp to his Apoftafie.
And finally what good affurance a man may
haue, to aduenture his foule with thefe companions in fuch a quarrell, as *Cranmer*, *Ridley*,
Latymer, *Rogers*, *Hooper*, and others did, who
hauing byn Cath. Priefts for many yeares, did
firft of all others imbrace in England thefe
new opinions of *Peter Martyr*, which yet were
fo yonge and greene, as himfelfe was fcarfely
fettled in them, when he firft entred into that
Iland, as in his * ftory more particularly we
haue declared. Wherfore to leaue him, we
fhall now examine fome other arguments, alleaged by others after him, efpecially by thofe
that were actors in the former ten difputations at *Oxford*, *Cambridge* and *London*, which
are not much fewer in number, then thefe alleaged already of *Peter Martyr*.

The

The fourth sort of arguments alleaged by others after Peter Martyr. §. 4.

28. And of these the first shalbe that of *Cau-*
ston and *Higbed*, in their confession to *B. Bonner*
anno Domini 1555. *The flesh profiteth nothinge* (saith
Christ) *Ioan.* 6. Ergo *Christ hath not giuen his flesh*
to be eaten in the Sacrament; and diuers others do
obiect the same, as a great argument ; yea
Zuinglius himselfe calleth this argument: *A bra-*
sen vvall , and a most stronge adamant , that cannot be
broken. But the auncient Fathers, that knew
more then *Zuinglius,* did easily breake this adamant , and brasen-wall, giuinge diuers solu-
tions therof : as first, that yf we take these
words of our Sauiour to be spoken properly
of his flesh ; then must the sense be , that his
only flesh, without his soule & diuinity, profiteth not to our saluation: and so do expound
the place both *S. Augustine* and *S. Cyrill,* for that
otherwise no man can deny, but that Christs
flesh with his soule and diuinity, doth profitt
greatly euen in the Sacrament yt selfe; for that
Christ in the selfe-same Chapter of *Saint Iohn*
saith : *he that eateth my flesh hath life euerlastinge.*
Secondly, other Fathers more to the literall
sense do interpret those words: (*the flesh profi-*
teth nothinge) not that Christs flesh doth not
profitt, but that the carnall vnderstandinge of
that speach of Christ, about his flesh, to be eaten

First obie-
ction.
Fox pag.
1400.

Zuingl.l.de
vera &
fals. Relig.
cap. de Eu-
char.

The an-
svvere.

Aug. &
Cyril. in
Ioan.

Ioan. 6.

ten in the Sacrament (such as the *Capharnaites*
had, whome he refuteth) profiteth not to our
saluation, but requireth a more spirituall and
high vnderstandinge, to witt, that yt is to be
eaten in another manner vnder the formes of
bread and wyne. And this is the exposition
both of a *Origen*, b *S. Cyprian*, c *S. Chrysostome*,
d *Theophilact*, e *Euthimius*, and others, and is the
more playne and manifest sense of that place.

29. *Maister Guest* (one of the Protestant opponents) in the first Cambridge disputation
against *Doctor Glyn*, vrgeth againe and againe
this argument: *That vvhich Christ tooke, he blessed:
that vvhich he blessed, he brake: that vvhich he brake,
he gaue: but he tooke bread: ergò he gaue bread:* To
which argumēt *Doctor Glyn* answered by a like
Collection out of the scripture: *That which God
tooke out of Adams side, vvas a ribbe: but what he tooke,
that he brought and deliuered to Adam for his vvife:
ergò he deliuered him a ribbe for his vvife.* Which
aunswere, though yt made the auditory to
laugh: yet *Maister Perne* comminge to answere
for the Protestant party, vpon the third day of
disputation, would needs vrge the same argument againe in his preface; which *Maister Va-
uisour*, that disputed against him, repeating publikely, gaue the like answere about the ribbe
out of *Genesis*: vvherwith Fox being angry
maketh this note in the margent: *An vnsauery
comparison:* perhaps for that he holdeth the
ribbe for rotten, which so longe agoe was taken out of Adams side: for that otherwise I do
not see what euill sauour Fox can find therin:
but

Marginal notes:

a *Lib. 3. in ep. ad Rom. cap. 1.*
b *Serm. de Cana Dom.*
c { *Omnes*
d { *in hunc*
e { *locum*
  { *6. Ioan.*

M. Guests argument against the reall presence.
Fox *pag.* 1258. *col.* 2. *num.* 80.

Gen. 2.

D. Perne.

Fox *pag.* 1261. *col.* 1. *num.* 8.

but the effect of the aunfwere ftands in this:
that as God tooke a ribbe, and made therof
our mother *Eua:* fo Chrift tooke bread, and
therof made his body, though in a different
manner, the matter or fubftance remayninge
in the one change, but not in the other.

30. The fame *Gueft* in the fame difputation
maketh this other argument againft the reall-
prefence. *The body of Chrift is not generate, or be-*
gotten in the Sacrament; ergò, *yt is not in the Sacra-*
ment. Whervnto *Doctor Glyn* anfwered: Yow
impugne a thinge yow know not: what call
yow generation? *Gueft.* Generation is the
production of accidents. *Glyn.* A new definition of a new philofopher. Thus they two,
and no one word more about this argument:
nor did *Gueft* reply, either in ieft or earneft, but
leapt prefently to his former argumēt againe:
That which he tooke he bleffed; that which he bleffed he
brake; that vvhich he brake, he gaue, &c. Wherfore
to aunfwere *Guefts* obiection we fay: firft that
generation is *not the production of accidents,* as
fondly he affirmeth, which production of accidents appertaineth rather to alteration, aug-
mentation and locall motion, as *Ariftotle* teacheth; wheras generation is the production
of a fubftance and not of accidents: Secondly
we fay that Chrifts body in the Sacrament is
there, not by generation nor creation, but by
another miraculous operation of God called
Tranfubftantion, which is a conuerfion of the
bread & wine into the true body & bloud of
Chrift. And thus much in earneft to *M. Gueft.*

31. After

Guefts fe-
cond ar-
gument.
Fox pag.
1259.

Lib. primo
Generat. &
lib.3. Phyf.

31.   After *Guest* there commeth *Maister Pilkinton*, as wise as the other in matter of disputation, though afterward by the creditt of his manhood therin, he gott the Bishoppricke of *Durham*. He began thus against *Doctor Glyn*. This one thinge I desire of yow most worshippfull Maister Doctor, that yow will aunswere me with breuity as I shall propound, and thus I reason:

> The body of *Christ* that vvas broken on the Crosse, is a full satisfaction for the sinnes of the vvhole vvorld.
>
> But the *Sacrament* is not the satisfaction of the vvhole vvorld.
>
> Ergo, the *Sacrament* is not the body of Christ.

To this argument *Doctor Glyn* answered, that he vsed an equiuocation in the word *Sacrament*: for that yf the word *Sacrament* in this place, be taken for that which it conteyneth, to witt the body of Christ; then is the minor proposition false; for that the body of Christ, as yt was giuen on the Crosse, is the satisfaction for the world: But yf he take the Sacrament for the outward signes only of bread & wyne, them he graunteth both the conclusion and the whole sillogisme to be true, that the Sacrament is not the body of Christ. Whervnto *Pilkinton* maketh one only reply, and that most fondly, out of the same equiuocation, sayinge: that the Sacrament hath not satisfied for the world, and that men may be saued without the Sacrament, as many were before yt was instituted: Whervnto *Doctor Glyn* very
learnedly

learnedly aunfwered: that yf he tooke the *Sacrament*, as before he had diftinguifhed, for Chrift conteyned in the Sacrament, then had the *Sacrament*, that is to fay Chrift therin conteyned, both fatisfied for the whole world, and none were euer faued without him, for that all were faued by faith in him to come.

32. The fame *Pilkinton* leaping from his former argument, without takinge his leaue, falleth vpon another *medium* in thefe words:

The body of Chrift is refiant in heauen.
And the body of Chrift is in the Sacrament.
Ergo: the Sacrament is in heauen.

Pilkintons fecond argument.

This argument yow fee is as good and no better, then yf we fhould fay:

The foule of a man is in the fingar.
And the foule of a man is in the foote.
Ergo, the foote is in the fingar.

But yet *Doctor Glyn* declared there further, after he had iefted at the argument, that Chrift was in one fort in heauen, and after another fort in the Sacrament; in heauen locally, vifibly & circumfcriptiuely, but in the Sacrament inuifibly and facramentally : which differences being not found in the foule, being in the foote and fingar, maketh our argument more heard to anfwere, then that of *Pilkinton*.

33. There followeth a third argument of *Pilkinton* thus:

In the body of Chrift there be no accidents of bread.
But in the Sacrament there be accidents of bread.
Ergo: the Sacrament is not the body of Chrift.

Pilkintons third argument.

Heere yow fee is the fame fond equiuocation

and

and doubtfull sense of the word Sacrament
before expounded, and poore *Pilkinton* can not
gett out of yt: For yf he take the word *Sacra-*
ment, for the only body of Christ conteyned
therin, then is the minor proposition false; for
that the Sacrament in this sense hath no accidents of bread in yt. But yf he take the Sacrament for externall signes, then we graunt both
his minor and conclusion to be true, and nothinge against vs, to witt, that the Sacrament
in this sense is not the body of Christ, though
comonly in our sense the Sacrament comprehendeth both the one and the other.

3.4. But further *Maister Pilkinton* had a fourth
argument, & with that he was briefly dispa-
tched: he proposed the same in these words.

Pilkintons
fourth ar-
gument.

> *VVhersoeuer Christ is, there be his ministers also, for*
> *so he promiseth.*
>
> *But Christ, as yow hould is in the Sacrament;*
> *Ergo: his ministers are there also:*

This argument is worthy of *Maister Pilkinton*,
and his ministers, for yt proueth by like consequence, that they should haue byn in Pilatts
pallace with him, and on the Crosse. And yt
may be argued also, *that for so much as they are not*
with him now in heauen, ergo: *he is not there.* Wher-

Ioan. 12.

fore the meaninge of that place in S. Iohns
ghospell: *VVhere I am there shall my minister be;* (he
saith not *vvheresoeuer* as *Maister Pilkinton* putteth
yt downe) is to be vnderstood of the participation of Christs glory in the next life, as

Ioan. 17.

himselfe expoundeth in the 17. of *S. Iohn,* where
he saith to his Father, that he will haue them,
to be

to be with him, to see his glory. And in the meane space we see how these fellowes, that glory so much of scripture, do abuse the true sense of scripture, in euery thinge they handle. And thus much do I find obiected againſt the *reall-presence* in the *Cambridge* diſputations.

35. There ensueth another diſputation houlden in the *Conuocation-houſe*, in the beginninge of *Q. Maryes* raigne, which in our former order or Catalogue of diſputations is the ſeauenth; wherin *Maiſter Phillips* Deane of *Rocheſter*, did argue againſt the *reall-preſence* in this ſort.

Chriſt saith, yow ſhall haue poore people with yow.

But me yow ſhall not haue.

Ergo. Chriſt is not preſent in the Sacrament.

Wherynto *Doctor VVeston* prolocutor in that conference anſwered, that Chriſt is not preſent in that manner of bodyly preſence, as then he was, ſo that good people may vſe works of deuotion and piety towards himſelfe, as then *S. Mary Magdalen* did, in whoſe defence he ſpoke thoſe words: But *Phillips* not contenting himſelfe with this anſwere, alleaged a longe diſcourſe out of *S. Auguſtine* in his commentary vpon *S. Iohns* ghoſpell, where the holy-father ſaith; *that Chriſt is preſent with vs in Maieſtie, prouidence, grace, and loue now, but not in corporall preſence.* Wherynto anſwered *D. VVatſon* afterward B. of *Lincolne*, expoundinge that place by another of the ſame Father vpon the ſame Euangeliſt, where he ſaith: *that Chriſt is not now preſent after that mortall condition, which then he was, &c.* Which nothinge letteth his being

M. Philips his argument.
Fox pag. 1283.
Matth. 13.
Ioan. 12.

Aug. tract. 50. in Ioan.

Tract. 70. in Ioan.

Q   after

after another manner in the Sacrament. **Nay**
S. *Augustine* in the very same Treatise, not ten
lynes before the words alleaged by M. *Philipps,*

Aug. ibid. hath these words: *Habes Chriſtum praſentem, per
altaris cibum & potum.* Thou haſt Chriſt preſent
in this life, by the foode and drinke of the Altar: which is another diſtinct way of preſence
from thoſe two, named by him in the former
place, of *grace* and *corporall conuerſation.* And yt
may ſeeme that this *Philipps* was not only ſatisfied by this anſwere, for that he replied not;
but further alſo was conuerted vpon this
conference, or diſputation in the conuoca-
Pag. 1213. tion-houſe, or very ſoone after: For that Fox
in margine. affirmeth that he continued Deane of *Rocheſter,*
all *Q. Maryes* dayes, which no doubt he ſhould
not haue done, yf he had not ſubſcribed, as all
the reſt did, to this article of the *reall-preſence.*

36.   Next after *Philips* Deane of *Rocheſter,* ſtep-
ped vp *Philpott* Archdeacon of *VVincheſter*
Fox pag. with great vehemency, and tooke vpon him
1254. col. 2. to proue, that Chriſt in his laſt ſupper did not
num. 10. eat his owne body by this argument: *that for ſo*
Philpotts *much as remiſſion of ſinnes was promiſed vnto the re-*
firſt argu- *ceauinge of Chriſts body, and that Chriſt did not receaue*
ment. *remiſſion of ſinnes, ergò, Chriſt did not receaue his owne*
body. Whervnto *Maiſter More-man* who, *extem-*
pore was appointed to anſwere him, and *Doctor*
VVeſton the prolocutor, gaue this anſwere; that
as weil he might proue that Chriſt was not
baptized, for that he receaued no remiſſion of
ſinnes therin: but as he receaued that Sacramēt
for our inſtruction and imitation only; ſo did
                                              he

he this other. Wherabout though *Philpot* made
a great ftyrre, as not content with the aunfwere, yet could he reply nothing of any moment, and fo ended that dayes difputation.
The next day he returned againe, and would
haue made a longe declamation againft the
reall prefence, but being reftrayned he fell into
fuch a rage and pafsicn, as twife the prolocutor faid, he was fitter for Bedlam, then for difputation.

37. After *Philpott*, ftood vp *Maifter Cheney*
Archdeacon of *Hereford*, another of the fix
which did contradict the *maffe* and *reall prefence*
in the *Conuocation-houfe*, who was after made
B. of *Glocefter*, being that tyme perhapps inclyned to Zuinglianifme, though afterward he
turned, and became a Lutheran and fo lyued
and died in the late Queenes dayes. There is
extant to this man an eloquent epiftle in Latyn of F. *Edmund Campian*, who vnhappily had
byn made Deacon by him, but now being
made a Catholike, exhorted the Bifhopp to
leaue that whole miniftry: This mans argument againft the *reall prefence*, being taken out
of the common obiections of Catholike wryters and fchoole-men, was this, that for fo
much as it is cleare by experience, that by eatinge confecrated hofts for example, a man
may be nourifhed, and that neyther Chrifts
body, nor the accidents and formes alone, can
be faid to norifh, ergo befides thefe two there
muft be fome other fubftance, that nourifheth,
which feemeth can be no other but bread:

And

And the like argument may be made of confecrated wyne that alfo nourifheth . And further in like manner he argued , concerninge
confecrated bread burned to afhes , demaun-
dinge wherof,that is to fay, of what fubftance
thefe afhes were made , for fo much as we
hould no fubftance of bread to be therin : and
Fox would make vs beleeue, that all the Catholiks there prefent could not aunfwere that
doubt , and amongeft others he faith of *Doctor*

Fox pag.
1287. &
1288.
*Harpesfield: Then vvas Maifter Harpesfield called in to
fee vvhat he could fay in the matter, vvho tould a fayre
tale of the omnipotency of almighty God.* But Fox
vnderftood not what *Doctor Harpesfield* faid in
that behalfe, as may eafily appeare by his fond
relatinge therof: We haue fett downe the
aunfwere to thefe and like obiections, before

The aun-
fvvere to
M. Che-
neyes ar-
gument
about mi-
trition &
generatiō.
in the 7. and 10. Obferuations , and yt confifteth in this; that in thefe naturall actions,and
fubftantiall changes of nutrition and generation , wherin not only accidents are altered,
but new fubftances alfo are produced,& confequently according to nature that operation
doth require not only accidents, but alfo fubftantiall matter wherof to be produced ; God
by his omnipotency doth fupply that matter,
which is neceffary to the new production
of that fubftance, eyther by nutrition or generation .

38.   And albeit the vnbeleefe of heretiks doth
not reach to comprehend and acknowledge,
that God fhould do a myracle or action aboue
nature euery tyme that this happeneth our,
yet

yet can they not deny yt in other things : As
for example, that euery tyme, when any children are begotten throughout the world,
God immediatly createth new ſoules for
them, which needs muſt be thouſands euery
day, yet none of our ſectaryes will deny or
ſcoffe at this, or hold yt for abſurd, the like
may be ſaid of all the ſupernaturall effectes &
benefites which God beſtoeth dayly & hour-
ly vpon vs in the Sacraments or otherwiſe.

39.　There remayne only ſome few places
out of the Fathers to be explaned, which
were obiected in this article, partly by *Maiſter*
Grindall againſt *Doctor Glyn* , and partly alſo by
Peter Martyr in the end of his Oxford-diſputation, but related by Fox in the queſtion of
Tranſubſtantiation,& not of the *reall-preſence,*
though properly they appertayne to this , as
now yow will ſee. The firſt place is out of
Tertullian againſt *Marcion* the heretike , where
he hath theſe words (ſaith Fox): *This is my body,*
that is to ſay, this is the ſigne of my body. Whervnto
I anſwere , that Fox dealeth heere like a Fox
in cytinge theſe words ſo cuttedly , for that
Tertullian in this very place (as in many others)
doth moſt effectually, not only ſay, but proue
alſo, that bread is turned into Chriſts true body after the words of conſecration; and ſo do
the *Magdeburgians* affirme expreſſely of him:
his words are theſe: *Chriſt takinge bread, and di-*
ſtributinge the ſame vnto his diſciples, made yt his body;
ſayinge this is my body , that is the figure of my body,
and immediatly followeth : *Figura autem non*

Certayne places of Fathers explaned.

Fox pag. 1250.col.2.

Tert. lib. 4. cont. Mar- cion. c. 40. Magd. cent. 2. cap. 4.

　　　　　fuiſſet,

fuiffet, *nifi veritatis effet corpus: but yt had not byn the figure of Chrifts body, yf his body had not byn a true body or truly their prefent.* In which words *Tertullian* affirmeth two things, yf yow marke him; First that Chrift made bread his true body; & then that bread had byn a figure of his body in the old Teftament, which could not be, yf his body were not a true body, but a phantafticall body as *Marcion* did wickedly teach: for that a phantafticall body hath no figure. And this much for the true literall fenfe of *Tertullian* in this place; who goinge about to fhew that Chrift did fullfill all the figures of the old Teftament (& confequently was fonne of the God of the old Teftament, which *Marcionifts* did deny) fullfilled alfo the figure wherin bread prefignified his true body to come, by makinge bread his body : fayinge, this bread that was the figure of my body, in the old Teftament, is now my true body in the new, and fo doth the truth fucceed the figure. And this to be the true literall fenfe and fcope of *Tertullian* in this place (as before I haue faid) euery man may fee plainly, that will read the place.

40.   The other places are taken out of diuers other Fathers, who fome tymes do call the Sacrament, *a figure* or figne, reprefentation, or fimilitude of Chrifts body, death, paffion, & bloud, as S. *Auguftine in Pfalm. 3. Chrift gaue a figure of his body*, and *lib. cont. Adamant. cap. 12. he did not doubt to fay this is my body, when he gaue a figure of his body.* And S. *Hierome: Chrift reprefented*

vnto

vnto vs his body. And *S. Ambrose lib. 4. de Sacram.*
cap. 4. As thou hast receaued the similitude of his death,
so drinkest thou the similitude of his pretious bloud:
These places I say, and some other the like,
that may be obiected, are to be vnderstood in
the like sense, as those places of *Saint Paul* are,
wherin Christ is called by him *a figure, Figura*
substantiæ Patris: A figure of the substance of his
Father. *Heb.1.* And againe; *Imago Dei.* An Image
of God. *Colloß.1.* And further yet: *Habitu inuen-*
tus vt homo. Appearinge in the likenes of a man.
Philipp. 2. All which places, as they do not take
from Christ, that he was the true substance of
his Father or true God, or true man in deed
(though out of euery one of these places some
particular heresies haue byn framed by auncient heretiks, against his diuinity or humanity) so do not the forsaid phrases, some tymes
vsed by the auncient Fathers, callinge the Sacrament a figure, signe, representation or similitude of Christs body, exclude the truth or
reality therof, for that there is as well, *signum*
& figura rei præsentis quam absentis, A signe or figure of things present, as well as of things absent, as for an example, a firkyn of wyne hanged vp for a signe at a Tauerne dore, that there
is wyne to be sould, is both a sygne of wyne,
and yet conteyneth and exhibiteth the thinge
yt selfe: And so yt is in the Sacrament, which
by his nature being a signe, figure, or representation, doth both represent and exhibitt, signifieth and conteyneth the body of our Sauiour.

Ould he-
tetikes
haue fra-
med some
particular
heresies
out of the
Fathers
by their
misvnder-
standinge
their
meaning.

4t. And

41. And as it should be an hereticall cauill to argue out of the said places of *S. Paul*, as the old heretiks did, that Christ is called *a figure of the substance of his Father, and the Image of God, or the similitude of man*: ergo, he is not of the reall substance with his Father, nor really God, nor truly man: so is it as hereticall to argue as our Sacramentaryes do; that *Tertullian, Augustine*, & some other Fathers do sometymes call the Sacrament *a similitude, figure, signe or remembrance* of Christs body, his death and passion, as in deed yt is; (for that otherwise yt should not be a Sacrament) *ergo*: yt is not his true body, that is conteyned therin, especially seing the same Fathers, do in the selfe-same places, whence these obiections are deduced, expresfely & cleerly expound themselues, affirming Christs true reall body to be in the Sacrament vnder the formes of bread and wyne: as for *Ambr. l. 4. de Sacram. cap. 4.* example *Saint Ambrose* heere obiected in the fourth booke *de Sacramentis cap. 4.* doth exprefely and at large proue the *reall-presence*, as exactly as any Catholike can wryte at this day: sayinge: *that before the words of consecration, yt is bread, but after yt is the body of Christ.* And againe. *S. Ambrose expoundeth himselfe against the Protestāts. Before the words of Christ be vttered, the chalice is full of vyne and water, but when the words of Christ haue wrought their effect, then is made that bloud which redeemed the people.* And yet further. *Christ Iesus doth testifie vnto vs, that we receaue his body & bloud, and shall we doubt of his testimony?* Which words being so plaine and euident for the truth of Catholike beleefe, lett the reader consider,

how

how vaine and fond a thing yt is for the Protestants to obiect out of the selfe-same place, *that vve receaue the similitude of his death, and drinke the similitude of his pretious bloud,* for that we deny not, but the body of Christ in the Sacrament is a representation and similitude of his death on the Crosse, and that the bloud which we drinke in the Sacrament, vnder the forme of wine, is a representation and similitude of the sheddinge of Christs bloud in his passion. But this letteth not, but that it is the selfe-same body & bloud, though yt be receaued in a different manner, as it letteth not, but that Christ is true God, though he be said, to be the Image of God, as before yow haue heard.

42. There remayneth then only to be auuswered, that speach of *S. Augustine* obiected in these disputations. *Quid paras dentes & ventrem? crede & manducasti:* Why dost thou prepare thy teeth and thy belly? beleeue and thou hast eaten. Whervnto I answere, that this speach of *S. Augustine* and some other like, that are found in him, and some other Fathers, of the spirituall eatinge of Christ by faith, do not exclude the *reall-presence,* as we haue shewed before in our nynth obseruation. It is spoken against them, that come with a base and grosse imagination to receaue this diuine foode, as if yt were a corporall refection, and not spirituall; wheras indeed faith & charity are those vertues, that giue the life vnto this eatinge: faith in beleeuinge Christs words to be true, as *S. Ambrose* in the place before cyted saith, and

Aug. tract. 25. in Ioan.

and therby assuringe our selues, Chrifts true
body to be there: and charity in preparing our
felues worthily, by examinations of our confcience, that we do not receaue our owne
damnation, as *S. Paul* doth threat. And this
is the true fpirituall eatinge of Chrifts body
by faith, but yet truly and really, as the faid
Fathers do expound vnto vs, whofe fentences
more at large yow fhall fee examined in the
Chapter followinge.

The con-
clufion of
this chap-
ter. 43.   Thefe then being all in effect, or at leaft
wayes the moft principall arguments, that I
find obiected by our Englifh *Sacramentaryes* in
the forfaid ten difputations, againft the article
of Chrifts true & reall being in the *Sacrament*,
you may confider with admiration and pitty,
how feeble grounds thofe vnfortunate men
had, that vvere firft dealers in that affaire,
wheron to change their faith and religion,
from that of the Chriftian world, from tyme
out of mynd before them : and to enter into
a new fect and labyrinth of opinions contradicted amonge themfelues, and accurfed by
him that was their firft guide to lead them
into new pathes, to witt, *Luther* himfelfe, and
yet to ftand fo obftinately & with fuch immoueable pertinacy therin, as to offer their bodyes to temporall fire, and their foules to the
euident perill of eternall damnation for the
fame; but this is the ordinary enchauntement
of herefie founded on pride, felfe-iudgement,
and felfe-will, as both by holy fcriptures and
auncient Fathers we are admonifhed.

44. One

44. One thinge alſo is greatly heere to be
noted by the carefull reader, vpon conſideration of theſe arguments to and fro, how vncertayne a thing yt is for particular men, whether learned or vnlearned (but eſpecially the
ignorant) to ground themſelues & their faith
ypon their owne or other mens diſputations,
which with euery little ſhew of reaſon to and
fro, may alter theire iudgement or apprehenſion, and in how miſerable a caſe Chriſtian
men were, yf their faith (wherof dependeth
their ſaluation or damnation) ſhould hange
ypon ſuch vncertayne meanes as theſe are, &
that God had left no other more ſure or certaine way then this for men to be reſolued of
the truth, as we ſee he hath, by his viſible
Church, that cannot erre ; yet thought we
good to examine this way of diſputatiõs alſo,
and the arguments therof vſed by Proteſtants
againſt the truth. But now followeth a larger
& more important examen, of the Catholike
arguments alleaged by our men againſt them,
in this article of the *reall-preſence*. And what
kind of aunſwers they framed to the ſame,
wherby thou wilt be greatly confirmed (good
reader) yf I be not much deceaued, in the opinion of their weakneſſe, and vntruth of their
cauſe.

The miſe-
rable caſe
of ſecta-
ryes, vvith
out any
ſure
ground to
leane vn-
to.

WHAT

VVHAT CATHOLIKE

A R G V M E N T S

*VVere alleaged in thefe difputations for
the* reall-prefence; *and how they
were aunfwered or fhifted of
by the Proteftants.*

C H A P. V.

A s I haue briefly touched in the former
Chapter, the reafons and arguments alleaged for the Sacramentary opinions, againft
the *reall-prefence*; fo now I do not deeme yt
amiffe, to runne ouer in like manner, fome of
the Catholike arguments that were alleaged
againft them, though neyther tyme nor place
will permitt to recyte them all, which the
difcreett reader may eafily imagine by the
grounds and heads therof, fett downe in the
fecond Chapter of this Treatife, though many & waighty they were or might be. Wherfore to fpeake breifely fomewhat therof, and
for more breuity and perfpicuity, to draw the
matter to fome kind of order and methode:
yow muft note, that of thefe ten difputations,
only foure were in tyme of Catholike gouernement, as before I fignified, that is to fay;
the fix-dayes conference in the *Conuocation-
houfe,*

houfe, in the beginninge of *Q. Maryes* raigne, & the three-dayes feuerall difputation at *Oxford* with *Cranmer, Ridley,* and *Latymer,* fome monethes after. And as for the firſt in the *Conuocation houfe,* the Proteſtants only did difpute, for three continuall dayes togeather, to witt, *Phillips, Haddon, Cheyney, Elmour,* and *Philpott,* and feuerall Catholike men were appointed to aunfweré them. And when in the end the Proteſtants were required to aunfwere according to promife, in their turnes, the Catholike opponents for other three dayes, they refufed yt all, fauing *Philpott,* vpon certayne conditions to be heard yet further, but *Doctor VVeſton* the prolocutor reiected him, *as a man fitter to be fent to bedlam* (faith Fox) *then to be admitted to difputation, &c.* For that he both was vnlearned, and a very madd man in deed. Wherfore out of this difputation, little or nothinge is offered about this article of reall-prefence, for that the Catholike party difputed not at all.

Difputation in the conuocatió houfe,

Fox *pag.* 1287.*col.*2. *num.* 30.

Philpott.

2. And as for the other three dayes difputation in *Oxford,* the laſt, which was with *Latymer,* was very little, for that he fledd difputation, as there yow fhall fee; and the few arguments that were made againſt him, were rather in proofe of the facrifice of the maſſe: fo as moſt arguments were alleaged in the former two-dayes conflict againſt *Cranmer* and *Ridley,* which prefently we fhall examine, though vnder *K. Edward* alfo, one day of the *Cambridge* difputations was allowed to Catholike opponents, to propofe their arguméts.

Doctor

Doctor Madew being defendant for the Protestants, and *Doctor Glyn, Maister Langdall*, & *Maister
Sedg-wicke* opponents for the Catholiks : so as
out of these foure disputations, we shall note
breifely some Catholike arguments, that
were alleaged, aduertisinge the reader first
to consider with some attention the points
ensuinge.

First
point to
be obser-
tied.

3. First that we haue nothinge of these disputations, their arguments or aunswers, but
only such as pleaseth Iohn Fox to deliuer and
impart with vs, which most euidently do appeare to be mangled and vnperfect in many
places, without head or foote, coherence or
consequence, which must proceed eyther of
purpose to make matters obscure, and therby
to bring the reader into doubt and confusion,
or of lacke of good information; and that the
former is more credible then the second, may
be ghessed by the variety of impertinent notes
in the margent, scoffes, and iests in the text yt
selfe, often tymes putt in to deface the Catholike party, and to giue creditt to his sectaryes:
And consequently what faith may be giuen
to his narrations (but only where they make
againtt himselfe) is easy to be seene, especially
in that himselfe cõfesseth, that *Ridley* wrote in
prison his owne disputations after they were
past, & the same we may presume of the rest,
and then no man can doubt, but that they
would putt downe their owne parts to their
vttermost aduantage, or at least-wise with the
smallest losse, that they could diuise.

4. Se-

4. Secondly yt is to be confidered of the precedent reader , that muft aduenture his foule euerlaftingely by takinge one part or other in this controuerfie heere in hand, how much yt may import him to ftand attent to the places and authorityes, alleaged out of fcriptures & Fathers for the truth,& to confider them well, reading them ouer againe, and againe & weighing the true meaning & fenfe of the wryter, and not how fleightly or cunningly they are, or may be fhifted of by any witty wrangler, for fo much as this may be done with any wrytinge or euidence neuer fo manifeft, yf the defendant will lift to cauill,& the reader be fo inconfiderate or careleffe of his owne perill , as to be delighted or abufed therwith .

The fecõd point to be obfer-ued.

5, Thirdly in the allegation of Fathers teftimonyes, which heere are to enfue, yt is to be weighed , not only what they fay, but alfo how they fay, what phrafes and fpeaches they vfe, and to what end , and whether yf they had byn of the Proteftants Religion, they would haue vfed thofe phrafes or no , more then Proteftant wryters do themfelues at this day , efpecially fo ordinarily and commonly as the faid Fathers do , they being men both learned, wife , and religious, that well knew how to vtter their owne mynds & meaning, what is proper & improper fpeach,& withall not being ignorãt, how great inconueniences muft enfue of improper fpeaches in matters of faith, where men are bound to fpeake precifely

The third point confiderable.

cifely and warily: and on the other fide is to be confidered alfo , yf they were of contrary opinions to the Proteftants , and of that faith which we affirme them to be in this point of the *reall prefence*, what more effectuall fpeaches could they haue vfed to expreffe yt, then they do, callinge yt *the true body, the reall body, the naturall body of our Sauiour, the fame body that he tooke of the bleffed Virgin, and gaue vpon the Croffe, the body vvherby he is vnited vnto vs in humanity* ; and denyinge it expreffely *to be bread after the vvords of confecration, though yt feeme to be bread to our eyes & taft , and that we muft not truft our fenfes therin , but yeld to Gods omnipotency , and beleeue, that as he hath vvrought infinite other miracles , fo hath he done this; that we muft adore yt, vvith the higheft adoration;* and other like phrafes, which neyther Proteftants can abide , or euer do vfe in their wrytinges; nor could the Fathers, yf they had byn expreffely of our Religion (as we fay they were) diuife words more fignificant, proper , or effectuall to expreffe the truth of our Catholike faith, then yf of purpofe they had ftudyed for yt, as no doubt they did; So as yf the auncient Fathers did vnderftand what they fpake, and that they fpake as they meant ; then are the Proteftants in a pittifull plight , whofe faluation or damnation dependeth in this, whether we muft vnderftand them , *S. Paul*, and Chrift himfelfe literally, as they fpake, or by a figure only ; fo as yf they vfed no figure, then is the Sacramentary opinion to be held for herefie.

                6. Fourthly

6. Fourthly is to be conſidered alſo in this The 4. matter, as elſ-where we haue noted, that point of when any one of theſe auncient Fathers, in what age ſoeuer, is found to vſe theſe effe-ctuall words, for vttering his meaning about this high myſtery, of Chriſts being preſent in the Sacrament, he is to be vnderſtood to ex-preſſe not only his owne iudgement, and be-leefe therin, but the iudgement alſo and be-leefe of the whole Church of Chriſtendome in that age, for ſo much as any Doctor, neither then nor after, did note him for error, or teme-rity in ſpeakinge & wrytinge as he did, which no doubt would haue happened, as in all other occaſions of errors or hereſies yt did, yſ his ſpeach had bin vnſound, vnproper, or dan-gerous; ſo as when we find but one Father vncontroulled in theſe aſſertions, we are iuſt-ly to preſume, that we heare the whole age and Chriſtian Church of his tyme ſpeake to-geather, and much more when we ſee diuers Fathers agree in the ſelfe-ſame manner of ſpeach, and vtteringe their meaninge. And whoſoeuer is carefull of his ſoule in theſe dan-gerous tymes of controuerſies, ought to be mindfull of this obſeruation, and ſo ſhall we paſſe to the diſputations themſelues.

R   *Out*

Out of the firſt Cambridge-diſputa-
tion *in* K. Edvvardes *dayes, wherin
the defendantes were* D. Madevv,
and B. Ridley *highe Comiſſioner.*
20. *Iunij.* 1549. §. 1.

7. Albeit in this diſputation matters were
but ſleightly handled, and no argument vrged
to any important iſſue, by reaſon of the often
interruptions of the Cambridge-proctors and
ſleights vſed by *Ridley* himſeife; yet do I find
that *Doctor Glyn*, being a very learned man indeed, did touch diuers matters of moment,
though he proſecuted not the ſame, yf Fox his
relation be true, and much leiſe receaued he
any ſubſtantiall ſolution therof. As for example, in the beginninge he made a very effectuall diſcourſe how this diuine Sacrament,
conteyninge Chriſts reall body, was not only
prefigured by diuers figures in the old Teſtament, as namely the *Paſchall-lambe*, the *manna*

D. *Glynne*
his firſt
diſcourſe.

and *ſhew-bread* (which ſignifyed the great importance and moment therof when yt ſhould
be performed) but alſo was ſo peculiarly and
diligently promiſed by our Sauiour, in the ſixt
of *S. Iohn*, comparinge yt with the ſaid figures,
and ſhewing how much yt was to exceed the
ſame, and namely the *manna* that came from
heauen, and finally expoundinge yt to be his
owne

@wne fleſh which he would giue vs to eate in fullfillinge thoſe figures: *Panis quem ego dabo ca-* *Ioan. 6.* *ro mea eſt*, the bread that I will giue you ſhalbe my fleſh, and that truly and indeed : *caro enim* *Ibidem.* *mea verè eſt cibus*; for my fleſh is truly meate, *&c.*

8. This promiſe then, and this prefiguration was not (quoth he) performed by Chriſt, but in his laſt ſupper when he tooke bread and de-liuered it ſayinge: *this is my body*: which perfor-mance, yf yt muſt aunſwere eyther to Chriſts promiſe in the ghoſpell, or to the figures in the old Teſtament, muſt needs be more then bread, for that otherwiſe yt ſhould not be better then the *manna*, that was bread from heauen, which Chriſt in *S. Iohns* ghoſpell ex-preſſely promiſed, ſhould be changed into his fleſh. And yf Chriſt in his laſt ſupper, had but giuen a figure of his true body; then had he fullfilled the figures of th'old Teſtament with a figure in the new, and ſo all had byn figures contrary to that of *S. Iohn : Lex per Moyſen data* *Ioan. 2.* *eſt, veritas autem per Ieſum Chriſtum facta eſt.* The law was giuen by Moyſes (in figures) but the truth thereof was performed by Ieſus Chriſt, *&c.*

9. Thus began *Doctor Glyn*, but I find no ſo-lution giuen thervnto, but that *Doctor Madew* being asked whether the Sacraments of the old law, and new were all one? he ſaid: *yea in* *deed & effect: Doctor Glyn* inferred, that then they were not inferiour to vs; for that they had bread that ſignified Chriſts body as well as ours, and they by eating that bread with faith

The Ievves equall to vs by the ſacramen-tary do-ctrine.

R 2   in

in Chrift to come, did eat Chrifts body, and
participate his grace therby, no leffe then we,
which is a great abfurdity, and contrary to the
whole drift of *S. Paul* fpeaking of that matter,
and extollinge the dignity of this Sacrament,
yea cōtrary to the expreffe difcourfe of Chrift

Ioan. 6.   himfelfe, fayinge: *not Moyfes gaue yow bread from
heauen* (meaning the Manna) *but my Father giueth
yow true bread from heauen.* And to this difcourfe
alfo yow fhall find nothinge aunfwered in
effect.

10.   From this *Docter Glyn* paffeth to fhew
Fox pag.   out of *S. Auguftine, S. Ambrofe,* and *S. Bafill,* that
1253.   the body of Chrift muft be adored before yt
be receaued; whervnto was aunfwered: *that*
Adoratiō   *only a certayne reuerent manner of receauinge was*
of the Sa-   *therby meant, but no adoration;* but the other re-
crament.   plyed, that the Fathers fpake of proper adoration; yea *S. Auften* went fo farre therin in his
books *De ciuitate Dei,* that he affirmeth the
heathens to haue efteemed the Chriftians, to
haue adored *Ceres* and *Bacchus,* Gods of bread
and wyne, by the adoration which they vfed
to this Sacrament of bread and wyne, which
they would neuer haue fufpected of the Proteftants, by their behauiour towards their
fupper of bread and wyne. Whervnto another aunfwere was framed, that *Saint Auguftine*
meant only of adoringe Chrifts body in heauen, and not in the Sacrament; and this aunfwere was confirmed by *Ridley* very follemne-
ly, fayinge for his preface: *For becaufe I am one
that doth loue the truth, I will heere declare what
I thinke*

I thinke in this point, &c. *I do graunt a certayne honour and adoration to be done vnto Chrifts body, but then the Fathers speake not of yt in the Sacrament, but of yt in heauen,* &c. Neyther is there any other aunfwere giuen. And yet who feeth not, that this is but a playne fhift? For when *S. Auguftine* for example faith: *Nemo illam carnem manducat, niſi prius adorauerit:* No man eateth that flefh (in the Sacrament) but firft adoreth yt. And Saint *Chryſoftome: Adora & communica, dum proferatur ſacrificium,* adore and communicate, whilft the facrifice is brought forth; yt is euident by common fenfe, that the adoration is appointed to that body, which there prefently is eaten, and not to Chrifts body abfent in heauen; for by this kind of their adoration, we adore alfo our ordinary dinners, to witt by adoringe God in heauen, and fayinge grace &c. And he that fhall read the place of the Fathers themfelues, will wonder at this impudency, for *Saint Auften* doth expound thofe words of the Pfalme *Adorate ſcabellum pedum eius,* and applieth yt to his flefh in the Sacrament, and *S. Chryſoftome* fpeaketh expreffely of Chrifts flefh, as yt is in the Sacrament, and offered as a facrifice.

Aug. in Pſalm. 98.

Chryſoft. hom. 60. ad Pop. Antioch.

Pſalm. 98.

11. And yet doth Fox make *Doctor Glyn* to haue replyed neuer a word, nor fo much as produced the textes themfelues of the Fathers named by him, but giuinge yt ouer paffed to another argument, fayinge: *Yf yt pleaſe your good Lordſhipp,* S. *Ambroſe* and S. *Auguftine do ſay, that before the conſecration yt is but bread, and after the con-*

S. Ambrose
and S. Au-
ſten hand-
ſomely
ſhifted of.

ſecration yt is called the body of Chriſt; Wherto was aunſwered: *Indeed yt is the very body of Chriſt Sacramentally after the conſecration, vvheras before yt is nothinge but common bread, and yet after that yt is the Lords bread, and thus muſt S. Ambroſe and S. Auguſtine be vnderſtood.* So ſaid the aunſwerers, and Doctor *Glyn* vvas by the procters commaunded to ceaſe, and paſſe to the ſecond queſtion; but he

D. Glyns
reply.

obtayned by intreaty to go foreward an inſtance or two more, ſhewing out of the words of *S. Ambroſe*, that *Ridleyes* aunſwere could not

Fox pag.
1254.

be true ; for that *S. Ambroſe* ſaid ; *that after the conſecration, there is not the thinge that nature did forme, but that which the bleſſing doth conſecrate.* And that yf the benediction of *Elias* the Prophett, could turne the nature of water , how much more the benediction of Chriſt, God & man can do the ſame, *ergò* there is a greater change in the natures then of common bread, to become the Lords bread.

12. To this reply there was no other aunſwere giuen, but that *S. Ambroſe* his booke *de Sacramentis* was not his, & *Ridley* affirmed that all the Fathers did ſay ſo: which was a ſhameleſſe lye in ſo great an auditory , nor could he bringe forth ſo much as one Father that ſaid ſo, nor alleaged he any one argument to proue yt to be ſo; and yf he had, yet *S. Ambroſe* repeatinge againe the very ſame ſentence in his booke *de initiandis* is ſufficient for the authority of the place, but *Glyn* is made to paſſe away the matter with ſylence, ſayinge: *VVell lett this paſſe, &c.* And then goinge to other authorityes

tyes of Fathers, ys wyped of with like fhif.s;
as when he cyteth *S. Cyprians* words : *Panis non* A ftrange fhittinge of the au-thorityes of Fa-thers.
effigie, fed natura mutatus, omnipotentia Dei fit caro:
the bread by confecration being chang.d not
in fhape, but in nature, is by the omnipotency
of God made flefh; they aunfwere that by nature is vnderftood a naturall property or quality, and by flefh, a flefhly thinge or quality,
and not the fubftance, fo as the fenfe muft be,
that bread is changed not in outward fhape,
but into a naturall property of a flefhly thing,
&c. And when *Doctor Glyn* replyed to ouerthrow this inuention out of *S. Ambrofe*, who
affirmeth this cháge of bread to be made into
the flefh, that was taken of the Virgin Mary,
ergò yt was not only into a flefhly thinge, quality, or property, but into the true flefh of
Chrift; *Ridly* gaue an aunfwere, that I vnderftand not, nor himfelfe I thinke, but only that
he muft fay fomwhat in fo great an audience,
and expectation; or Fox vnderftood yt not
that fetteth it downe: for thefe are his words:

13.   *VVhen Doctor Glyn vrged the fayinge of S. Am-*
brofe, that bread is changed into the body taken from the Fox pag. 1154 col. 3. num. 3.
virgin Mary, that is to fay (faith he) *that by the word*
of God, the thinge hath a being that yt had not before,
and we do confecrate the body, that we may receaue the
grace and power of the body of Chrift in heauen by this
Sacramentall body. So he. And doth any man vnderftand him? or is his aunfwere any thinge
to the purpofe for fatisfyinge the Fathers?
S. Cyprian faith: that the bread by the omnipotency of God is changed in nature, and made

flesh and *S. Ambrose* faith : *yt is the flesh taken from the Virgin*; and *Ridley* faith heere ; *that yt hath a being, vvhich yt had not before*, and that, *they do confecrate a sacramentall body of Chrift, therby to receaue the grace and power of Chrifts body in heauen*; but howfoeuer they do *confecrate* that body: (which is a ftrange word for Sacramenraryes to vfe)yet do they graunt that this Sacramentall body is but bread; and how then can yt be flefh, and flefh of the Virgin; were not the Fathers ridiculous, yf they vfed thefe equiuocations, yea falfe and improper fpeaches?

14.   Well *Doctor Glyn* goeth foreward, and alleageth *S. Chryfoftome* vpon *S. Mathewes* ghofpell, where to perfuade vs the truth of Chrifts body in the Sacrament, he faith : *that we muft beleeue Chrifts words in thefe myfteryes, and not our fenfes, for that our fenfes may be deceaued*; *but Chrift fayinge this is my body cannot deceaue vs*; *and that he made vs one body with himfelfe, not through faith only, but in very deed: and further, that the miracle which he wrought in his laft fupper, he vvorketh dayly by his minifters, &c.* Wheruuto *Ridley* aunfwered nothinge but thefe words: *Maifter Doctor, yow muft vnderftand, that in that place S. Chryfoftome fhewed, that Chrift deliuered vnto vs no fenfible thinge in that fupper.* So he. Which notwithftanding is euidently falfe, for he deliuered fenfible bread & wyne, according to the Proteftants faith, and accordinge to ours , the formes of bread and wyne , which are alfo fenfible : and yf there were no fenfible thinge , then could there be no Sacrament, which muft conteyne a fenfible

sible signe. And to refute this shift of *Ridley*, *Doctor Glyn* obiected *Theophilact*, expoundinge *S. Chrysostome*, and vsinge the same words that he did, to witt, that the bread is *transelemented*, and *transformed*. He alleageth another place or two of *S. Augustine* togeather with *S. Irenæus*: *Matth. 11.* To all which *Rochester* aunswereth resolutely: *Well say what yow list; yt is but a figuratiue speach, as S. Iohn Baptist was said to be Elias for a property, &c.* *Howv S. Iohn Baptist vvas Elyas.* But who doth not see the absurdity of this euasion; for so much as the meaning of Christ, about *Elias* his spiritt in *S. Iohn Baptist*, is euident, nor euer went any auncient Fathers about to affirme or proue by arguments, that *S. Iohn Baptist* was truly *Elias* in person (him- *Ioan. 1.* selfe expressely denyinge yt) or that yt was meant literally, as they do of the words of Christ in the Sacrament: And this could not *Ridley* but see, but that he was blinded in pride and passion, for that otherwise he would ne-uer haue gone about to aunswere the Fathers by euident wranglinge, so contrary to their owne sense and meaninge.

15. After *Doctor Glyn* was putt to silence in *Langdale disputeth* this order, succeded *Maister Langdale*, *Maister Sedgewicke* and *Maister Yonge*, but very breefely concerninge this article of the reall-presence, not being permitted to speake more, and the most part of the tyme trifled out also, with courtesyes of speach, the one to the other; *My good Lord; good Maister Doctor; pleaseth yt your good Lordshipp; liketh yt your good Fathershipp; honourable Father,* and the like ceremonyes, for they durst

do

do no other, *Ridley* being then high commiſ-
ſionar; yet *Maiſter Langdale* vrged a place of *S.
Chryſoſtome*, where he bringeth Chriſt, ſayinge

Fox pag.
1256. col. 1.
num. 43.

theſe words: *I vvould be your brother, I tooke vpon
me common fleſh and bloud for your ſakes ; and euen by
the ſame things that I am ioyned to yow, the very ſame
I haue exhibited to yow againe*; meaninge in the
Sacrament. Wherof *Maiſter Langdale* inferred,
that ſeing Chriſt tooke vpon him true naturall fleſh, and not a figure of fleſh only , or remembrance therof, therfore he gaue vs his
true naturall fleſh like man in the Sacrament,
and not a figure. Wherto *Ridley* aunſwereth

Fox ibid.

in theſe words and no more: *VVe are not ioyned
by naturall fleſh; but do receaue his fleſh ſpiritually from
aboue.* Which aunſwere is not only contrary
to the expreſſe words and meaning of *S. Chryſoſtome* in this place, but of Chriſt himſelfe alſo
brought in heere by *S. Chryſoſtome* to vtter his
meaninge, as yow haue heard. *I tooke vpon me
common fleſh for your ſakes; and by the ſame things that
I am ioyned to yow, the very ſame I haue exhibited vnto yow againe.* Where yow ſee that he ſaith, he
gaue the very ſame in the Sacrament , which
he had taken vpon him for our ſakes, and that
by the ſame he was ioyned to vs againe ; and
now *Maiſter Ridley* ſaith; *that vve are not ioyned to
him by naturall fleſh.* Theſe be contraryes, which
of two ſhall we beleeue? *Chriſt*, and *S. Chryſoſtome* expoundinge him, or *Ridley* againſt them
both ?

M Sedg-
vvicke his
diſputa-
tion.

16. *Maiſter Sedg-wicke* diſputed next, but hath
not halfe a columne or page allowed to the
setting

ſettinge downe of his whole diſputation; yet
he vrginge diuers reaſons in that little tyme
out of the ſcriptures, why the Sacrament of
the Altar cannot be in the new law by a figure, but muſt needs be the fullfillinge of old
figures, and conſequently the true and reall
body of Chriſt; he brought *Maiſter Ridley* within the compaſſe of a dozen lines, to giue two
aunſwers one plaine contrary to another, as
his words do import: for this is the firſt: *I do*
graunt yt to be Chriſts true body and fleſh, by a property M. Ridley
of the nature aſſumpted to the God head, and we do his owne
really eate and drinke his fleſh and bloud, after a cer- ction.
taine reall property. His ſecond aunſwere is in
theſe words: *It is nothinge but a figure or token of* Fox ibid,
the true body of Chriſt, as it is ſaid of S. Iohn Baptiſt,
he is Elias, *not that he vvas ſo indeed or in perſon, but*
in property and vertue he repreſented Elias. So he.
And now lett any man with iudgement examine theſe two aunſwers: For in the firſt he
graunteth at leaſt wayes a true reall property
of Chriſts fleſh, aſſumpted to his Godhead, to
be in their bread, wherby we do really eate
his fleſh, and drinke his bloud. And in the ſecond he ſaith, yt is nothinge but a figure, and
conſequently excludeth all reall property; for
that a figure hath no reallity or reall property,
but only repreſenteth and is a token of the body, as himſelfe ſaith; which is euident alſo by
his owne example, for that *S. Iohn Baptiſt* had
no reall property of *Elias* in him, but only a ſi-
militude of his ſpiritt and vertue. And ſo theſe
people, whilſt they would ſeeme to ſay ſomewhat,

what , do speake contradictoryes amonge
themselues.

17.　There followed *Maister Yonge* , who as
breefly as the other, touched some few places
of the Fathers (though they be not quoted)
where they say that our bodyes are nourished
,, in the Sacrament by Chrits flesh, and that
,, truly we drinke his bloud therin, and that for
,, auoyding the horror of drinking mans bloud,
,, Christ had condescended to our infirmityes,
,, and giuen yt to vs vnder the formes of wyne;
and other like speaches , which in any reasonable mans sense , must needs import more
then a figure of his body and bloud, or a spirituall being there only by grace, for so much as
by grace he is also in Baptisme and other Sacraments: & finally he vrged againe the place
of *S. Cyprian* : *That the bread being changed not in
shape but in nature , vvas by the omnipotency of the
vvord, made flesh*. Wherto *Ridley* aunswered
againe in these words : *Cyprian there doth take
this vvord nature for a property of nature, and not for
the naturall substance*. To which euasion *Maister
Yonge* replyeth: *this is a strange acception,that I haue
not read in any authors before this tyme*. And so
with this he was glad to giue ouer (saith Fox)
and askinge pardon for that he had done, said:
*I am contented , and do most humbly beseech your good
Lordshipp to pardon me of my great rudenesse , &c.*
Belike this rudenesse was for that he had said,
that vt was a strange acception of *S. Cyprians*
words, to take *change in nature* , for *change into a
property of nature* , and flesh for a fleshely thinge

*M. Yonges
disputa-
tion.*

ᵒr quality, as before yow haue heard, and that this ſhould aunſwere *S. Cyprians* intention: for lett vs heare the application: *Bread* (in the Sacrament) *being changed not in ſhape but in nature* (ſaith S. Cyprian) *by the omnipotency of the word is made fleſh*; that is to ſay, as *Ridley* will haue yᵗ bread, *being changed not in ſhape, but in a property of nature, is made a fleſhely thinge, or fleſhely quality:* What is this? or what ſenſe can it haue? what property of fleſhely nature doth your communion bread receaue? or what reall property of bread doth it leeſe by this change mencyoned by *S. Cyprian?* We ſay, (to witt *S. Cyprian*) that our bread retayning the outward ſhape, doth leeſe his naturall ſubſtance, and becommeth Chriſts fleſh, what naturall property of bread doth yours leeſe? And againe. What fleſhely thinge or quality doth yᵗ receaue by the omnipotency of the word in conſecration? And is not this ridiculous, or doth *Ridley* vnderſtand this his riddle? But lett vs paſſe to the next diſputation vnder *Q. Mary*, where we ſhall ſee matters handled otherwiſe, and arguments followed to better effect and iſſue.

The conſutation of Maiſter Ridleyes euaſion about *Saint Cyprian.*

Out

Out of the first Oxford-disputation in the beginninge of Q. Maryes *raigne*, *wherin* D. Cranmer, *late Archbishopp of Canterbury, was defendant for the Protestant party, vpon the 16. of Aprill anno* 1554. §. 2.

18.   When as the Doctors were sett in the diuinity schoole, and foure appointed, to be *exceptores argumentorum* (saith Fox) sett at a Table in the middest therof, togeather with foure other notaryes sitting with them, and certayne other appointed for iudges (another manner of indifferency, then was vsed in *King Edwards* dayes vnder *B. Ridley*, in that disputation at *Cambridge*) *Doctor Cranmer* was brought in, and placed before them all to answere, and defend his Sacramentary opinion, giuen vp the day before in wrytinge, concerninge the article of the *reall presence.* Fox according to his custome noteth diuers graue circumstances,

Fox *pag.* 1300. as amonge others, *that the beedle had prouided drinke, and offered the aunswerer, but he refused with thanks.* He telleth in like manner, that *Doctor VVeston* the prolocutor offered him diuers courtesyes for his body, yf he should need, which I omitt for that they are homely: against which *Doctor VVeston* notwithstanding he afterwards stormeth, and maketh a great

inuectiue

inuectiue for his rudenes, and in particular for
that he had (as Fox saith) his *Theseus* by him,
that is to say a cuppe of wyne at his elbow,
whervnto Fox ascribeth the gayninge of the
victory, sayinge; *yt vvas no maruayle though he gott*   Fox pag.
the victory in this disputation, he disputinge as he did,   1326.
non sine suo Theseo, *that is not without his tiplir g-*
cupp. So Fox. And yet further, that he holding
the said cuppe at one tyme in his hand, and
hearinge an argument made by another that
liked him, said : *vrge hoc, nam hoc facit pro nobis:*
vrge this, vrge this, for this maketh for vs.
Thus pleased it Iohn Fox to be pleasant with
Doctor VVeston; but when yow shall see, as presently yow shall, how he vrged Iohn Fox his
three Martyrs, *and rammes of his flocke* (for so
els-where he calleth them) in these disputations, not with the cuppe, but with substantiall, graue, and learned arguments, yow will
not maruaile that he is so angry with him : for
in very deed he brought them alwayes to the
greatest exigents of any other, and more then
all the rest togeather : Now then lett vs passe
to the disputation.

19.   *Doctor Chadsay* was the first that disputed
against *Cranmer*, beginninge with the institution of Chrilts Sacrament, recorded by S. Ma-   Matth. 26.
thew, *Marke*, and *Luke*, shewinge out of them   Mate 14.
by diuers plaine clauses and circumstances,   Luc. 22.
that Christ in his last supper, gaue vnto his
disciples, not bread, but his true naturall
body, which was giuen the next day on the
Crosse, to all which *Cranmer* aunswered thus:

If

Yf yow vnderstand by the body naturall, Organicum,

Fox pag.
1302.col.1.
num.70.

*that is hauing such proportion of members, as he had li-
uinge heere, then I aunswere negatiuely.* By which
aunswere we may perceaue, that this great
Doctor, who had wrytten a great booke a-
gainst the *reall-presence*, by which *Latymer* a-
mongst others was made a Sacramentary, and
stood therin vnto death vpon the creditt of

D. Chadseys
first argu-
ment.

this booke (as after yow shall heare him often
professe) vnderstandeth not the very state of
the question betweene vs, for that we hould
not Chrifts body in the Sacrament to be *Organicall*, in that manner as *Cranmer* heere imagineth, with externall dimensions & propor-

Sup. cap. 3.

tions of members as he liued vpon earth,
though truly organicall, in another manner,
without extension to place, as in our fourth
and fifth obseruations before sett downe we
haue declared; so as he erringe in the very
grounds and first principles of the controuersie, yow may imagine how he will proceed in
the rest.

The secōd
argumēt.

20.   It was obiected vnto him next after
this, that as a wise-man lyinge on his death-
bedd, and hauing care that his heyres after his
departure do liue in quiett, and not contend
about his Testament, doth not vse tropes and
figures, but cleare and plaine speach in the said

Fox pag.
1302.

Testament; so must we presume of Christ, &
for the confirmation of this, *Doctor VVeston* alleaged a place out of *S. Augustine, De vnitate Ecclesiæ* vrginge this very same similitude; that
yf the last words of any graue or honest man
lyinge

Aug. l. de vnitat. Eccl. cap. 10.

lyinge on his death-bedd, are to be beleeued, much more the laſt words of our Sauiour Chriſt in his ſupper, to which argument I find no effectuall aunſwere giuen at all, but only that *Cranmer* ſaith: *that he vvhich ſpeaketh by tropes and figures, doth not lie;* but he aunſwereth not to the other inconuenience, that his heyres may fall out about his Teſtament, the one vnder-ſtandinge them literally, the other figuratiue-ly, as we & they do the words of Chriſt about this Sacrament.

3. Argument.

Chryſoſt. hom. 61. ad Pop. An-tioch.

21. Next to this is brought in a large teſti-mony of *S. Chryſoſtome,* out of his homily vnto the people of *Antioch,* which beginneth: *Neceſ-ſarium eſt, dilectiſſimi, myſteriorum diſcere miracu-lum, quid tandem ſit, & quare ſit datum, & quæ rei vtilitas, &c.* It is neceſſary, moſt dearely be-loued, to know this myracle of myſteryes, what yt is, and why yt was giuen, and what profitt cometh to vs therby, &c. And then *S. Chryſoſtome* declareth at large, how Chriſt moſt myraculouſly aboue all humaine power, giueth his body to be handled and eaten by vs in the Sacrament; ſo as we faſten our teeth in his fleſh, and that he did more then euer any parents did, who many tymes giue their chil-dren to others to be fed, but Chriſt feedeth vs with his owne fleſh, and with that very fleſh by which he is our brother, and vnited vnto vs in fleſh. Out of which diſcourſe D. *VVeſton* vrged, that for ſo much as Chriſt is made our brother and kinſ-man, by his true, naturall & organicall fleſh; *ergo* he gaue the ſame his true

S   naturall

naturall and organicall flesh to vs to be eaten
in the Sacrament. Wherto *Cranmer* aunswe-

Fox *pag.*
1303 *col.* 2.
num. 2.

red: *I graunt the consequence, and the consequent:*
Which is contrary to that he said a little before, (yf yow marke yt) that his organicall body was not there.

22. But *Doctor VVeston* went further, that seing
he graunted this, then did yt follow also, that
his true organicall flesh was receaued in our
mouth, which *S. Chrysostome* calleth our teeth.
But this *Cranmer* denyed, and said, *he vvas eaten
only by faith:* Whervpon *VVeston* came on him
againe sayinge, that for so much as he gaue vs
the selfe-same flesh to eate in the Sacrament
(and this with our teeth, as *S.Chrysostome* saith)
wherby he became our brother & kins-man,
yt must needs import a reall eatinge: Wherto
Cranmer aunswered: *I graunt he tooke and gaue*
(in the Sacrament) *the same true naturall and organicall flesh, vvherin he suffered, but feedeth vs spiritually, and his flesh is receaued spiritually.* This was
his aunswere, and this he repeateth often, and
from this he could not be drawne: And heere
now yow see, the practise of that shift, wherof we haue spoken before in our eyght and
nynth obseruation , whereby these willfull
people , vnder the tearmes of spiritually and
sacramentally, do delude them-selues, & their
readers , as though they said somewhat to
auoid Catholike arguments, taken out of auncient Fathers plaine and perspicuous authorityes, wheras indeed they say nothinge in
substance at all , but do turne and wynd and
hide

hide themſelues vnder the ſound of different
words without ſenſe. For yf yt be true as
Cranmer heere graunted, that Chriſt gaue his
true naturall and organicall fleſh to be eaten
in the Sacrament, and that with our teeth or
corporall mouth, as *S. Chryſoſtome* ſaith, how
can yt be denyed, but that we eat his fleſh
really, and not ſpiritually only, yf ſpiritually
be oppoſite to really, as in *Cranmers* ſenſe yt is,
which vnderſtandeth, *ſpiritually* and *figuratiuely*
to be all one: but in our ſenſe *ſpiritually* ſtandeth with *really*, for that we hould Chriſts
body to be receaued really and ſubſtantially in
the Sacrament, but yet after a ſpirituall manner, different from that which the *Caphatnaits*
did imagine of a groſſe carnall eatinge of
Chriſts fleſh, as other fleſh is accuſtomed to be
eaten, wherfore to imagine that Chriſts true
naturall or organicall fleſh is eaten truly in the
Sacrament, and yet only abſent, by faith, ſpiritually and in a figure, is to ſpeake contradictoryes with one breath.

23.   Diuers other texts and teſtimonyes of
S. Chryſoſtome were alleaged by *Doctor VVeſton*
to confute this ideacall fiction of *Doctor Cran-*
mer, as that for example *homilia* 83. *in cap.* 26.
Matth. Where he ſaith amonge other thinges:
Veniat tibi in mentem, &c. Lett yt come into thy „
remembrance with what honour thou art „
honoured, (in the Sacrament) what table „
thou doſt inioy, for that we are nouriſhed „
therin with the ſelfe-ſame thinge, which the „
Angells do behould and tremble at, *&c.* VVho

4. Argu-
ment or
reply.

S 2   ſhall

shall speake the powers of thy Lord ? VVho shall declare
forth all his praises ? VVhat pastor hath euer nourished
his sheepe vvith his owne flesh, &c. *Chrift feedeth vs
vvith his owne body, and conioyneth & vniteth vs to him*
In Psal. 50. *therby* . And againe vpon the 50. Psalme : Pro
cibo carne propria nos pascit, pro potu sanguinem suum
nobis propinat. In steed of meat, he feedeth vs
with his owne flesh, and in steed of drinke he
giueth vnto vs to drinke his owne bloud. And
Chrysost. againe, *homil. 83. in Matth. Non fide tantum , fed*
hom. 38. in
Matth. · *reipsa nos corpus suum effecit , &c.* Not only by
faith , but in deed he hath made vs his body.
And finally for that yt was denyed expreffely,
Fox pag. *Saint Chrysostome* to meane that we receaued
1303. Chrifts body, with our corporall mouth, *Doctor*
Chrysost. *VVeston* vrged thefe words of *Saint Chrysostome:*
hom. 29. in
2. Cor. 13. *Non vulgarem honorem confecutum eft os nostrum ex-*
*cipiens corpus dominicum.*Our mouth hath gotten
no fmall honour in that yt receaueth the body
of our Lord .

24.   But all this will not ferue, for ftill *Cranmer.* aunfwered by his former fleight thus:
*VVith our mouth , vve receaue the body of Chrift , and
teare it vvith our teeth , that is to fay the Sacrament of
the body of Chrift.* Do yow fee the euafion? And
what may not be fhifted of in this order, doth
any minifter in England vfe to fpeake thus of
his communion-bread, as *S. Chrysostome* in the
place alleaged of the Sacrament , after the
words of confecration? or do any of the aun-
Fox pag. cient Fathers wryte fo reuerently of the wa-
1233. col. 1. ter of baptifme, which they would haue done,
com. 74. and ought to haue done, yf Chrifts body be no
other-

otherwise present in this Sacrament, then the
holy-Ghost is in that water, as *Cranmer* oftentymes affirmeth, and namely some few lynes
after the foresaid places alleaged? But *Doctor*   5. Argu-
VVeston seing him to decline all the forsaid au-   ment.
thorityes by this ordinary shift, of the words
spiritually and *sacramentally*, vrged him by another way out of the same *Chrysostome*, concerninge the honour due to Christs body vpon
earth, *quod summo honore dignum est id tibi in terra*   *Chrysost.*
ostendo, &c. I do shew thee vpon earth, that   *hom.* 34.
which is worthy of highest honour, not An-
gells, not Archangells, nor the highest heauens, but I shew vnto thee the Lord of all
these things himselfe. Consider how thou dost
not only behould heere on earth, that which
is the greatest and highest of all things, but
dost touch the same also, & not only touchest
him, but dost eat the same, and hauing receaued him, returnest home.

25. Thus *S. Chrysostome.* Out of which place
Doctor VVeston vrged him eagerly, excludinge
all figures, and eatinge of Christs body absent
by faith; for that *S. Chrysostome* saith not only
Ostendo tibi, I do shew vnto thee, that which is   *D. VVeston*
worthy of highest honour aboue Angells, and   doth vrge
Archangells, but *ostendo tibi in terra,* I shew yt to   eagerly.
thee heere vpon earth, which signifieth the   *vrge hoc,*
   vrge hoc.
presence of a substance, wherto this highest
honour is to be done, and that this thinge is
seene, touched, & eaten, in the Church, which
cannot be a figure, nor the sacramentall bread,
for that highest honour is not due to them;

nor

nor can yt be Chriſt abſent only in heauen, for
S. *Chryſoſtome* ſaith, I *ſhew it thee heere on earth, &c.*
To all which preſſinges when *Doctor Cranmer*
had no other thing in effect to aunſwere, but
theſe phraſes often repeated ; *that it is to be vnderſtood ſacramentally,* and, I *aunſwere that it is true
ſacramentally, &c.* The hearers fell to cry out,
and hiſſe at him, *clappinge their hands* (ſaith Fox)
and callinge him , indoctum, imperitum, impudentem,
vnlearned, vnſkillfull & impudent. And Fox
to help out *Cranmer* in this matter, beſides all
other excuſes, maketh this learned gloſſe in
the margent vpon *S. Chryſoſtomes* words: *Oſten-
do tibi in terra, &c.* I do ſhew vnto thee vpon
earth, what is worthieſt of higheſt honour, to
witt, Chriſts body. *The body of Chriſt* (ſaith Fox)
*is ſhewed forth vnto vs heere on earth diuers vvayes , as
in readinge ſcriptures , hearinge ſermons , and Sacraments, and yet neyther ſcriptures, nor ſermons, nor Sacraments are to be worſhipped, &c.* So he, which is
as iuſt as Germans lippes. And I would aske
this poore gloſſiſt, what maketh this note to
the purpoſe of *S. Chryſoſtome?* for neyther doth
he ſpeake of the different wayes , wherby
Chriſts body may be ſhewed forth vpon
earth, but ſaith that himſelfe did ſhew yt in
the Sacrament vpon the Altar , to all that
would ſee it. Nor doth he ſay that the meanes
or wayes, wherby Chriſts body is ſhewed, are
worthy greateſt honour or worſhipp, but that
the thinge that is ſhewed forth , is worthy of
higheſt honour. And how then ſtandeth Fox
his gloſſe with this ſenſe, or wheryunto ſerueth

Fox pag.
1233.

ueth it, but only to shew these wreched-mens
obstinacy, that one way or other will breake
through, when they are hedged in by the Fathers authorityes most plaine and manifest.

26. After this assault giuen by *Doctor VVeston*,
the first opponent *Doctor Chadsey* returned to
deale with *Cranmer* againe, & by issue of talke,
came to vrge these words of *Tertullian*; *Caro
corpore & sanguine Christi vescitur, vt anima de deo
saginetur*. Our flesh is fedd with the body and
bloud of Christ, to the end that our soule may
be fatted with God, which is as much to say,
that our mouth doth eate the body of Christ,
and our mynd therby receaueth the spirituall
fruite therof. Out of which words *D. VVeston*
vrged, that seing our flesh eateth the body of
Christ (which cannot eat, but by the mouth)
Christs body is really eaten and receaued by
our mouth, which so often by *Cranmer* hath
byn denyed, but now his words are: *Vnto Tertullian I aunswere, that he calleth that the flesh, which
is the Sacrament.* Of which aunswere I cannot
vnderstand what meaninge yt hath, except
Fox do erre in settinge yt downe; for yf the
flesh be the Sacrament, then must the Sacrament feed on the body and bloud of Christ,
accordinge to *Tertullian* which is absurd. But
I suspect that *Cranmers* meaninge was, that
the body of Christ was called the Sacrament,
for so he expoundeth himselfe afterward,
when he saith: *The flesh liueth by the bread, but the
soule is inwardly fedd by Christ*: so as when *Tertullian* saith ; *our flesh is fedd by Christs body and bloud*.

6. Argu-
ment.
D. Chadsey.

*Tertull. l. de
resurrect
carnis. c. 8.*

*Cranmers
shifting of
Tertullian.*

he

he would haue him to meane, that our flesh
eateth the Sacramentall bread and wyne, that
signifieth or figureth Chrifts body and bloud,
& our foule feedeth on the true body of Chrift
by faith: but both *Doctor Chadfey* & *Doctor VVe-*
fton refuted this shift prefently by the words

Tert. ibid.   immediatly enfuinge in *Tertullian : Non poffunt*
ergo feparari in mercede, quas opera coniungit : Our
body and foule cannot be feparated in the reward, whome the fame worke doth conioyne
togeather ; and he meaneth euidently by the
fame worke or operation, the fame eatinge of
Chrifts body. Wherfore yf the one, that is the
foule, doth eat Chrifts true body, as *Cranmer*
confeffeth, then the other, which is our flesh,
eateth alfo the fame body as *Tertullian* faith;
and for that *Doctor VVefton* liked well this ar-

Fox pag.   gument out of *Tertullian*, and faid to *Doctor*
1306.   *Chadfey, fticke to thofe words of Tertullian*, as Fox
affirmeth, yt is like that the forefaid tale of
vrge, vrge, feigned of him was meant at this
tyme. But yf yt were, the reader may eafily
fee that he had more to vrge againft his aduerfary, than a port at his elbow ; and fo fhall
yow fee by that which is to enfue ; wherfore lett vs paffe yet fomewhat further in this
combatt.

7. Argu-   27.   *Doctor Cranmer* hauinge breathed a little
ment out   vpon the former fharp on-fett of *Chadfey* and
of S. Hi-
lary.   *VVefton,* one *Doctor Treffam* began very grauely
and moderately to vrge a new argument and
difcourfe, which feemed very important, and
after yt was vrged, did more ftraine and preffe
the

the defendant, then any thinge before disputed. The argument was founded vpon a place *D. Treſſam.*
of *S. Hilary,* in his eight booke *de trinitate* againſt
the *Arrians*, which both for the great authority and antiquity of the Father, and cleernes
of his words and reaſon, ſeemed to all there
preſent to conuince; nor could *Doctor Cranmer*
any way handſomely ridd himſelfe of this
place, but by his ordinary ſhiftinge interpretation, as preſently ſhalbe ſeene. *Doctor Treſſam*
his diſcourſe was this, that wheras the like
controuerſie for diuers points, had byn betweene the old Catholiks and *Arrians* in *Saint
Hillaryes* tyme, as now is betweene vs and *Doctor Cranmer*, and his fellowes, the Catholiks
houldinge in that controuerſie, the vnion of
Chriſt with his Father to be in nature and
ſubſtance, and the *Arrians* in will only and
affection: Whatſoeuer authorityes the ſaid
Catholiks alleaged out of ſcriptures or auncient Fathers, for the naturall vnion betweene Chriſt and his Father; *I and my Father are one*. Such other places: the *Arrians*
ſhifted of by ſayinge: *that is true in vvill, but not in
nature, yt is true in loue and affection, but not in ſubſtance*; euen as our Sacramentaryes do now,
when we alleage neuer ſo cleere authorityes,
for the true reall nature and ſubſtantiall preſence of Chriſt in the Sacrament, and therby
of his reall vnion alſo with vs by eatinge the
ſame; they delude all with ſayinge only; *yt is
true by grace and not by nature; yt is true by faith, but
not in ſubſtance; yt is true figuratiuely and ſacramentally,*

rally, but not really; yt is true in a signe, by a trope; after
a certaine manner of speach; yt is true spiritually , and
by a naturall property, but not indeed substantially: and
such aunswers; but all these shifts (saith *Doctor
Tressam*) did *S. Hilary* cutt of so longe agoe, for
that he proueth the true naturall coniunction
of Christ with his Father, by our true naturall
coniunction with him, by eatinge his flesh in
the Sacrament; so as except we deny the true
essentiall, reall and substantiall vnity of Christ
with his Father , we cannot accordinge to *S.
Hilary* deny the true, reall and substantiall vnity of vs with Christ, by receauing his true naturall flesh in the Sacrament.

28.   The place of *S. Hilary* is in his 8. booke
of the *blessed Trinity* against the *Arrians* , as hath
byn said , where he expoundeth these words
of Christ in *S. Iohns* ghospell: *As the liuing Father
sent me, so do I also liue by the Father, and he that eateth my flesh, shall also liue throw me* : vpon which
words of our Sauiour *S. Hilary* saith : *This truly
is the cause of our life, that vve haue Christ dwellinge
by his flesh in vs , that are fleshye , vvhich also by him
shall liue in such sort , as he liueth by his Father.* Of
which was inferred, that Christ dwelled in vs
in flesh by the Sacrament, and not only in spiritt. For better declaration wherof D. *Tressam,*
before the allegation of these words, alleageth
a larger discourse of the same *S. Hilary,* against
the said *Arrians* vpon this point in these words:
I demaund of them now (saith *Hillary*) *who will needs
haue the vnity of will only betweene the Father, and the
Sonne, vvhether Christ be now in vs truly by nature , or
only*

Ioan. 6.

For pag.
1306.

Hilar. l. 8.
de Trinit.

only by the agreement of vvilles? yf the vvord be incarnate in very deed, and vve receaue at the Lords table the vvord made flesh, how then is he to be thought not to dwell in vs naturally, &c. Out of which words of S. *Hilary Doctor Treſſam* vrged, that Chriſts fleſh was not only imparted vnto vs in faith and ſpiritt, but alſo really and naturally, according to S. *Hilary*, and that as his coniunction was naturall with his Father, and not in will and loue only: ſo is his coniunction with vs in fleſh truly naturall, ſubſtantiall, and reall, and not only in ſpiritt and faith. For more confirmation wherof, *Doctor Treſſam* alleaged alſo the words of *Martyn Bucer*, their late Proteſtant-reader in *Cambridge*, who wryteth that according to the holy Fathers meaning, *Chriſt dwelleth in vs (by the body giuen in the Sacrament) not only by faith and loue, as abſent, but naturally, corporally, and carnally, &c.* To which authority of *Bucer Doctor Cranmer* gaue no other anſwere but this ieſt. *I know that Maiſter Bucer* (ſaith he) *was a learned man, but your faith is in good caſe which leaneth vpon Bucer, &c.*

Bucer. t. cont. A-brincenſem

29.   But he could not ſo eaſily ſhake of the autority of *Hilary*, but was hardly preſſed therwith, as yow may ſee readinge ouer the place yt ſelfe of this diſputation, as alſo by that his aduocate *Iohn Eox* is conſtrayned to make ſundry large notes, and gloſſes in the margent to help him out: For *Doctor Treſſam* vrged, that we are not only vnited to Chriſt by faith and ſpiritt, but carnally alſo: Whervnto *Cranmer* ſeekinge an euaſion anſwereth: *I ſay that Chriſt*

Fox p.
1396.

was

was communicated vnto vs not only by faith, but in very deed alſo, vvhen he vvas borne of the Virgin. Behould the ſhift, we talke of Chriſt imparted to vs in the Sacrament, and ſo doth *Hillary*; he anſwereth, that Chriſt was imparted to vs in the incarnation; and yet yf yow conſider, our fleſh was then rather imparted to him, then his to vs. And againe, Turks and Infidells haue as much coniunction with him by the incarnation as we, for that they are men, & the fleſh that he tooke, was common to all; So as heere yow ſee nothing but euaſions ſought for; and *Doctor Treſſam* perceauing that he could gett no more of him to the purpoſe, fell to pray for him; but *Doctor VVeſton* followed the argument much further, as there yow may ſee, for yt is ouerlonge to be alleaged heere. The principall point is, that *S. Hilary* auoweth: That our coniunction with Chriſt is not only by will, affection, and faith: but naturall alſo and reall, by eatinge his fleſh in the Sacrament, as himſelfe is naturally vnited to his Father and not only by will. And when *Doctor Cranmer* ſought many holes to runne out at, *VVeſton* preſſeth him againe with other words of *S. Hilary* explicatinge himſelfe, which are theſe.

Hilar. ibid. 30.   *Theſe things* (ſaith he) *are recited of vs to this end, becauſe heretiks feiginge a vnity of vvill only, betweene the Father, and the ſonne, did vſe the example of our vnity vvith God, as though we being vnited to the ſonne, and by the ſonne to the Father only by obedience, and vvill of Religion, had no propriety of the naturall coniunction by the Sacrament of the body and bloud.*

Lo.

Lo heere yt is accoumpted a point of Arrianisme by *S.Hilary*, to hould that we are vnited
to Chrift only by obedience and will of Reli-
lion, and not by propriety of naturall communion with him, by eatinge his flefh in the
Sacrament of his body and bloud. Whervpon
Doctor VVefton vrged often and earneftly, that
not only by faith, but by the nature of his flefh
in the Sacrament, we are conioyned not fpiritually only, and by grace, but naturally and
corporally; Whervnto *Cranmers* aunfwere was
in thefe words : *I graunt that Cyrill and Hilary do
fay that Chrift is vnited to vs, not only by vvill, but alfo
by nature, he is made one with vs carnally and corporally, becaufe he tooke our nature of the Virgin Mary, &c.*
Do yow fee his runninge from the Sacrament
to the natiuity; but heare out the end.

VVeft. Hilary, where he faith Chrift commu- ,,
nicated to vs his nature, meaneth not by his ,,
natiuity, but by the Sacrament. *Cran.* Nay he ,,
communicated to vs his flefh by his natiuity. ,,
VVeft. We communicated to him our flefh, ^Fox *ibid.*
when he was borne. *Cran.* Nay he commu- ,,
nicated to vs his flefh when he was borne, & ,,
that I will fhew yow out of *Cyrill. VVeft. ergò,* ,,
Chrift being borne gaue vs his flefh. *Cran.* In ,,
his natiuity he made vs partakers of his flefh. ,,
VVeft. Wryte fyrs. *Cranm.* Yea wryte. And
fo ended this Encounter, brought (as yow
fee) to two abfurdityes on *Cranmers* fide; the
one, that where *S. Hilary* fpeaketh of the Sacrament of the body and bloud of Chrift, he
flyeth ftill to the incarnation: the other, that
　　　　　　　　　　　　　　　　　　　　　he

he faith; Chriſt to haue imparted his fleſh to
vs in the incarnation, wherin he tooke ours.
Wherfore *Doctor Chadſey* ſeing the matter in
this ſtate, interrupted them by accuſing *Cranmer* to haue corrupted this place of S. *Hilary*, in
his booke againſt the reall preſence tranſlatinge theſe words: *Nos verè ſub myſterio carnem
corporis ſui ſumimus*, we receaue vnder the true
myſtery the fleſh of his body ; wheras he
ſhould haue ſaid: *VVe do receaue truly vnder a myſtery* (or Sacrament) *the fleſh of his body*; vvhich
fraud *Cranmer* could by no other wayes auoid,
but by ſayinge, that his booke had *Vero* and
not *verè*, which *Iohn Fox* faith was a ſmall fault;
and yet yow ſee yt altereth all the ſenſe, as yf
a man ſhauld ſay *Piſtor* for *Paſtor*.

31.   The next conflict to this was betweene
Doctor Tonge, and *Doctor Cranmer*, wherin *Tonge*
accuſinge him firſt for denyinge of principles,
and conſequently, that they could hardly go
forward with any fruitfull diſputation, except
they agreed vpon certayne grounds, he made
ſundry demaunds vnto him, as firſt, whether
there were any other naturally true body of
Chriſt, but his organicall or inſtrumentall body? *Item* whether ſenſe and reaſon, ought not
to giue place in this myſtery to faith ? *Further*,
whether Chriſt be true in his words, & whether he mynded to do that, which he ſpake at
his laſt ſupper? And finally, whether his words
were effectuall, and wrought any thinge or
noe ? To all which *Doctor Cranmer* aunſwered
affirmatiuely, graunting that the ſaid words of
Chriſt

*D. Tonge
diſputeth.*

Christ did worke the institution of the Sacrament, wheruntó *Doctor Tonge* replyéd, that a figuratiue speach wrought nothinge, *ergò* yt was not a figuratiue speach when he said: *Hoc est corpus meum.* And albeit D. *Cranmer* sought by two or three struglinges to slipp from this inference, sayinge that yt was sophistry, yet both *Doctor Tonge* and *Doctor VVeston*, who came in still at his turne, said; *sticke to this argument. It is a figuratiue speach, ergo yt vvorketh nothinge*, that quickely they brought *Doctor Cranmer* in plaine words to graunt, *that a figuratiue speach vvorketh nothinge* : Wherof they inferred the contrary againe on the other side : *A figuratiue speach* (say they) *vvorketh nothing by your confession, but the speach of Christ in the supper, as yow now graunted, vvrought somewhat*, to witt the institution of the Sacrament, *ergo the speach of Christ in the supper vvas not figuratiue*, which is the ouerthrow of the foundation of all sacramentall buildinge.

Fox pag. 1307. col. 2. num. 30.

32. And heere yow must note by the way, that Fox doth not crowne the head of this syllogisme with any *Baroco*, or *Bocardo* in the margent, as he is commonly wont to do with the rest, for that yt pleased him not. Wherfore to leaue him, we shall passe to *Doctor Cranmer* himselfe, whose aunswere yow shall heare in his owne words: *I aunswere* (saith he) *that these are meere sophismes, for speach doth not vvorke, but Christ by speach doth worke the Sacrament, I looke for scriptures at your hands for they are the foundation of disputations.* So he. And yow may see by this

Fox angry vvith a syllogisme.

his

his speach, that he was entangled, and would
gladly be ridde of that he had graunted, for
that both the *maior* and *minor* propositions
were of his owne grauntinge, and the fillo-
gisme good both in moode and forme, though
the conclusion troubled both him and Fox,
and the refuge wherunto both of them do
runne in this necefsity, the one in the text, the
other in the margent, is very fond, fayinge:
that not the speach of Ghrist, but Christ did vvorke, as
though any man would fay, that a fpeach
worketh, but by the vertue of the fpeaker: and
confequently yf Christ do worke by a figuratiue fpeach, then doth a figuratiue fpeach
worke by his power and vertue, and fo was
yt fondy grannted by *Cranmer* before, that the
figuratiue fpeach of Christ, in instinutinge the
Sacrament (for of that was the queftion) did
not worke; and yt is a fimple euafion now, to
runne from Christs fpeach to Christ himfelfe,
as though there could be a diuerfity; euery
man may fee thefe are but euafions.

33.   But now further *Doctor Yonge* refuted largely this affertion, *that Christs fpeach worketh not*,
out of diuers and fundry plaine teftimonyes of
the Fathers, which there openly he caufed to
be read and namely *S. Ambrofe*, as well in his
booke *de initiandis*, as *de Sacramentis*, where he
handleth this matter of purpofe, to proue that
the fpeach of Christ in the Sacrament, to wit,
hoc eft corpus meum, did worke & conuert bread
and wyne into flefh and bloud, and proueth
the fame by many other exáples of fcriptures:

Sermo

Sermo Christi (faith he) *qui potuit ex nihilo facere,*   *Amb. de eis*
quod non erat, non potest ea, quæ sunt in id mutare, quæ   *qui initiantur.*
non erant? The speach of Christ which was   „
able to make of nothing that, which was not   „
before, shall yt not be able to change those   „
things that were before, into things that are   „
not? And to the same effect in his booke *de Sa-*   *Ambr. l.4.*
cramentis : Ergo sermo Christi hoc conficit Sacramen-   *de Sacram.*
tum, Qui sermo? nempe is, &c. Therfore the speach   *cap. 4.*
of Christ doth make this Sacrament; but what   „
speach? to witt, that wherby all things were   „
created : the Lord commaunded and heauen   „
was made, the Lord commaunded & earth was   „
made, the Lord commaunded & the seas were
made, *&c. Vides ergo quàm operatorius sit sermo*
Christi: si ergo tanta vis est in sermone Domini, vt inci-
perent esse quæ non erant; quanto magis operatorius erit,
vt sint quæ erant, & in aliud commutentur? Yow see   *S. Ambrose*
therfore how working the speach of Christ is;   most
& yf then there be so much force in the speach   cleere
of our Lord, as that those things which were   *Cranmer*
not, tooke their beginning therby; how much   and *Fox.*
more potent is the same speach in workinge,
that those things which were before, be changed into another? And presently he addeth:
the heauen was not, the sea was not, the earth   „
was not, but heare him speake: *he said the word,*   „
and they were done, he commaunded and they were
created; Wherfore to answere yow I say, that
it was not the body of Christ before consecration, but after consecration, I say vnto thee, that
now yt is the body of Christ. So *S. Ambrose.*

34. And heere now (good reader) I doubt

T   not,

not, but yow see the fond euasion of *Cranmer*
and Fox his aduocate, cleerly refuted by *S. Am-*
brose; where they say, *that the speach or words of*
Christ worke not, but Christ by the words; as though
there were a great diuersity in that point. But
now lett vs see, how they will scamble ouer
this authority of *S. Ambrose,* that saith expressely, both that the speach of Christ did worke
potently, and worke the conuersion of bread
and wyne into flesh and bloud: first Fox hath
this note in the margent against *S. Ambrose*, as
though he had miscompared the words of
creation, with the words of the institution of

S. Ambrose the Sacrament. The *Lord Iesus* (saith Fox) *vsed*
corrected *not heere commaundement in the Sacrament, as in*
by Fox. *creation, for we read not Fiat hoc corpus meum, as vve*
read Fiat lux, &c. Do yow see the mans subtile
obseruation, or rather simple & sottish cauillation against so graue a Father? The words:
Hoc est corpus meum, this is my body, imployeth
somewhat more then *Fiat corpus meum:* lett yt
be my body; for that yt signifieth the thinge
done already, which the other willeth to be
done. And so for this we will leaue *Iohn Fox* to
striue with *S. Ambrose,* about the vsinge or abu-
singe of scriptures alleaged by him. And so
much of Fox.

35.   But how doth *Cranmer* himselfe auoyd
this plaine authority of *S. Ambrose,* thinke yow?
Yow shall heare yt in his owne words, for
they are very few to so large an authority. *All*
these thinges (saith he) *are common, I say that God*
doth chiefly vvorke in the Sacraments. Do yow see
his

his breuity and obscurity? but his meaning is, that wheras before he had denyed, for a shift, that Christs words did worke, but only Christ by his words (a difference without a diuersity) now seing *S. Ambrose* so plaine to the contrary, in setting forth the workinge of Christs words, he seeketh another shift in this aunswere, which is, *that albeit Christs words do worke in the Sacraments, yet Christ chiefly*; as though any controuersy were in this, or any man had denyed yt. But what saith he to the mayne point, wherin *S. Ambrose* affirmeth not only Christs vvords to be *Operatoria*, vvorkinge-words, but that their worke is to make bread, the true and naturall body of Christ after they be vttered by the Priest? nothing truly in substance doth he aunswere herevnto, but after his shifts he saith only, *that yt vvas called the body of Christ, as the holy-ghost vvas called the doue, and S. Iohn Baptist was called Elias* (which are but bare signes & representations, as euery one seeth) nay he goeth againe presently from this, which heere he had graunted, *that God worketh in the Sacraments:* For when *Doctor Yonge* vrged him thus: *If God worke in the Sacraments, he worketh in this Sacrament* (of the Eucharist) *Cranmer* aunswereth: *God worketh in his faithfull, not in the Sacraments.* And thus he goeth forward graunting and denyinge, turninge and wyndinge, and yet poore miserable man he would not turne to the truth, nor had grace to acknowledge the same laid before him, but toyled himselfe in contradictions, endeauouring

Hovv *Cranmer* shifteth of *Saint Ambrose.*

Fox pag. 1308 col. 1. num. 70.

T 2   to

to fhift of moft euident authorityes of ancient
Fathers, by impertinent interpretations. As
when *Doctor Yonge* vrged him with thofe cleere

words of *S. Ambrofe*: *Before the words of Chrift be*
fpoken, the chalice is full of wyne and water, but when
the vvords of Chrift haue vvrought their effect, then is
there made the bloud that redeemed the people. Cran-
mer aunfwered: that the words of Chrift
wrought no otherwife in this Sacramēt, then
in baptifme. *Ambrofe faid* (quoth he) *that the*
bloud is made, that is, the Sacrament of the bloud is
made, fit. fanguis the bloud is made, that is to fay
oftenditur fanguis; the bloud is fhewed forth
there.

36.   Thefe and fuch like vvere *Cranmers*
fleights to ridd himfelfe that day, and yet did
not *Doctor Chadfey* and *VVefton* leaue him for
thefe ftarts, but followed him clofe with other
cleere places of *S. Ambrofe,* the one expounding

the other. As for example, *Fortè dicas, &c. Per-*
haps yow may fay, how are thefe things true? I vvhich
fee the fimilitude, do not fee the truth of the bloud: Firft
of all I tould thee of the word of Chrift, vvhich fo vvor-
keth, that yt can change and turne the kinds ordayned
of nature, &c. And againe in another place.
Ergo didicifti, &c. Therfore thou haft learned that of
bread is made the body of Chrift, and that vvyne and
vvater is putt into the cupp, but by confecration of the
heauenly vvord it is made bloud. Sed fortè dices fpeciem
fanguinis non videri, fed habet fimilitudinem: But
perhaps yow will fay, that the fhape or forme
of bloud is not feene; but yet it hath the fimilitude. So *S. Ambrofe,* and for that he faith, as

yow

yow fee, that albeit the bloud after confecration, hath not the fhew or forme of true
bloud; yet hath yt fimilitude, (for that the
forme of wyne commeth neereft to the likeneffe of bloud) heerof *Cranmer* layinge hands,
could not be drawne from affirminge that
S. Ambrofe meaninge is, that it is not true naturall bloud after the confecration, but beareth
a fimilitude only, reprefentation, or tipe therof, which is quite contrary to *S. Ambrofe* his
whole drift and difcourfe, yf yow confider ye
out of paffion.

37.   After thefe bickerings about *S. Ambrofe*,
were vrged againft him, by the two Doctors,
Chadfey and *VVefton*, diuers other Fathers, as
Iuftinus Martyr aboue 14. hundred yeares gone,
whoe in his Apology for Chriftians writeth:
that as by the word of God, Iefus Chrift our Sauiour
being made flefh, had both flefh, and bloud for our falua-
tion: fo are we taught, that the meate confecrated by
the vvord of prayer inftituted by him (vvherby our bloud
and flefh are nourifhed by communion) is the flefh and
bloud of the fame Iefus, that was made flefh. Out of
which place they vrged, that as Chrift is truly
and really incarnate, fo is he truly and really
in the Sacrament, accordinge to *S. Iuftinus*, and
that our flefh and bloud is nourifhed by that
communion, and confequently in *Saint Iuftinus*
tyme, yt was not held that Chrifts body was
receaued only by faith.

The tefti-
mony of
S. Iuftine
examined

Iuftin.
Apol.

38.   The words of *Saint Irenaeus* were vrged in
like manner, he being another Martyr of the
fame age with *S. Iuftine*, who wryteth thus:

Eum

Eum calicem, qui eft ex creatura, fuum corpus confir-
mauit, ex quo noftra auget corpora, &c. This is the
cupp, which being a creature, he confirmed to
be his body, by which he encreaseth our bodyes, when both the cupp mixed & the bread
broken, hath ioyned to yt the word of God,
vt is made the Euchariſt of the body & bloud
of Chriſt, of which the ſubſtance of our fleſh
is encreaſed and conſiſteth. By which words
the ſaid Doctors proued, that the fleſh and
bloud of Chriſt was otherwiſe held by *S. Ire-*
næus to be in the Sacrament, and receaued by
vs, than only by faith, ſeing our bodyes alſo
are nouriſhed therwith;yea the very ſubſtance
of our fleſh is encreaſed and conſiſteth therby,
as his words are. To all which *Cranmer* had
no other aunſwere, but his old ſhift, *that the*
Sacrament of the body and bloud, vvas called the fleſh
and bloud of Chriſt, though really yt be not. And from

this he could not be drawne: And ſo finally
the tyme drawinge late,they vrged him there
publikely with certayne falſityes, vſed in his
booke againſt the reall preſence, and beſides
thoſe that had byn obiected before, as for example. *Doctor Chadſey* obiected a manifeſt corruption in tranſlatinge the foreſaid place of

S. Iuſtine, which *Cranmer* excuſed no otherwiſe, but that he tranſlated not *Iuſtine* word
for word, but only gaue the meaninge; but
the other,as alſo *Doctor Harpesfield,* ſhewed that
he peruerted the whole meaninge,and ſo yt is
euident to him that readeth *Iuſtine.*

39.   *Doctor VVeſton* obiected a place corrupted
in

in *Emissenus* by putting in the word *spiritualibus*, *Cranmer* aunswered, that yt was so in the decrees, *Doctor VVeston* replyed, that he had left out diuers lynes of purpose, vvhich made against him in *Emissenus* for the *reall-presence*, *Cranmer* aunswereth: *this booke hath not that.* *VVeston* obiected another place falsified, where for *Honora corpus Dei tui*, honour the body of thy God, to witt of Christ, *Cranmer* had translated yt thus: *honour him vvhich is thy God.* Wherto he answered, that he did it not without a weighty cause, that men should not thinke that God had a body. *Doctor VVeston* obiected also, that alleaginge a sentence out of *Scotus*, he had left out a clause, that made much to the purpose in the matter handled, to witt *secundum apparentiam*, as may appeare. *Cranmer* answered iestingly: *that is a great offence I promise yow.* Another place in like manner was obiected, as peruerted by him in *Scotus* words, as also one or two in *S. Thomas Aquinas*, wherto I find no aunswere; but disputation is broken vp with this cry of the auditory, in fauour of the Catholike party, *vicit veritas*, the truth hath had the victory; and with this we shall also end this first disputation against *Cranmer*, hauinge byn forced to be longer then we purposed at the beginninge, & therfore we shalbe so much the shorter, yf it may be, in that which ensueth with *Ridley* and *Latymer*.

Out of the Diſputation with D.Ridley
in the ſame dininity-ſchoole at Oxford, *the next day after* Cranmer,
to witt, the 17. *of* Aprill 1554. §. 3.

40. The next day followinge (ſaith Fox)
was brought forth *Doctor Ridley* to defend in
the ſame queſtions of the *reall-preſence*, *Tranſubſtantiation*, and *Sacrifice*; againſt whome *Doctor Smith* was the firſt and principall opponent, for which cauſe Fox, before he beginneth to relate the combatt, maketh a particular inuective againſt him, for that he had byn
vnconſtant in Religion, the ſimple fellow not
conſideringe that yf yt had byn true; yet that
the ſame might be obiected with much more
reaſon, againſt theſe his cheefe champions,
Cranmer, *Ridley* and *Latymer*, that had byn Catholike Prieſts for many yeares togeather; But
Fox his great anger againſt *Doctor Smith* was,
for that he preſſed hardly *B. Ridley* in his diſputation, and ſo did *Doctor V. Veſton* alſo, as after
yow ſhall ſee, for that vpon all occaſions he
came in with *Vrge hoc, vrge hoc*; but for the reſt
Ridley was moſt courteouſly vſed by them
both, and offered to haue his opinions taken
in wrytinge, and that he ſhould haue ſpace till
ſaturday after to conſider of them, and that
what bookes ſoeuer he vvould demaund,
ſhould

D. Smith
Opponent.

should be deliuered to him, and that he might
choofe any two of the whole company to be
his feuerall notaryes, and he tooke *Maifter Iohn*
Iewell afterward made B. of *Salisbury* by Q. *Eli-*
zabeth, and *Maifter Gilbert Monfon*, that had byn
notaryes vnto B. *Cranmer* the day before.

Tvvo no-
taryes
chofen.

Fox *pag.*
1311.

41.   But the greateft difference, and difficulty fell out, for that *Ridley* hauing brought thither with him his opinion, and large explication thereof already wrytten, would needs
read the fame openly to rhe whole auditory,
which was penned in fuch bitter, fpitefull &
blafphemous termes, with fuch abhominable
fcoffes, and raylinge contemptuous fpeach,
againft the facred myfteryes, and the vfe therof, as the commiffionars were often-tymes
forced to interrupt him, and commaund him
to fylence, or to begin difputation, neyther
wherof would he do, but with an obftinate
face go foreward in readinge his declarations,
wheruppon, *Doctor VVeſton* callinge vnto him
faid, as Fox relateth: *Yow vtter blafphemyes vvith*
an impudent face. Wherfore finally they made
him breake of, promifinge that they would
read & ponder all themfelues, not being conuenient to infect mens eares with publike
readinge therof, but that he might defend the
fame, as occafion fhould be offered in his anfwers and difputations.

Fox *pag.*
1312.

42.   The firft argument brought againft him
by *Doctor Smith* was, for ouerthrowinge that
principall foundation of the Sacramentary
herefie: *Chriſts body is inheauen, ergo yt is not in the*
Sacra-

Sacrament. Wherof yow haue heard often before, for that both *Peter Martyr* alleaged yt, as a
cheefe fortresse of their faith, though *Philipp
Melancthon*, that is a Calendar-saint togeather
with *Peter Martyr*, as before yow haue heard,
did say, *that he had rather offer himselfe vp to death,
then to affirme vvith the Sacramentaryes, that Christs
body cannot be but in one place at once.* And this was
a principall ground also of *Iohn Lambert*, burned for Sacramentary opinions vnder *K. Henry* the eyght, against whome *Doctor Cranmer,*
then Archbishopp of *Canterbury*, was the first
and cheefest disputer after the King, and specially tooke vpon him to confute this reason
of *Lambert* as vayne and false, and contrary to
scripture, as before yow haue heard in the story of *Lambert.* And the same reasons, and arguments, which *Cranmer* vsed against *Lambert*
out of the scriptures, doth *Doctor Smith* vse now
against *Ridley*, to witt *that Christ appeared corporally and really on earth, after his assension, to S. Paul
and others, ergò, his being in heauen is no let to his reall
presence in the Sacrament.* The antecedent he
proued out of the Acts of the Apostles, and
S. Paules Epistles, where yt is shewed, that
Christ appeared vnto him after his assension;
but *Ridley* did not aunswere this argument, as
Lambert, and other Sacramentaryes before
him had done, denyinge that Christ appeared
corporally and really vpon earth, but rather
that his voyce was heard from heauen, but he
said, *that Christ* left heauen for a tyme, and
came downe. *I do not* (saith he) *so straitly tye
Christ*

Chrift vp to heauen, that he may not come into earth at   Fox pag. 1314. col. 2. num. 28.
his pleafure, howbeit I do affirme, that yt is not pofsible
for him to be in earth and heauen at one tyme. So hee,
whervnto *Doctor Smith* replyed: *ergò yt is lawfull*
for Chrift to be heere prefent on earth vvhen he will.
Ridley. Yea when he will yt is lawfull. *Smith.*   ,,
Ergò his afcendinge to heauen, doth not re-   ,,
ftrayne his reall prefence in the Sacrament.   ,,
Ridley. I do not gainfay, but that yt is lawfull   ,,
for him to appeare on earth, when he will,   ,,
but proue yow that he will.

43. Lo heere another ftarting-hole: but yet
firft yow fee the great Sacramentary bull-
warke, fo much ftood vpon by others, that   Matth. 14. Act. 3. Coloff. 3.
Chrift is in heauen at the right hand of God, and that
the heauens muft receaue him, vntill the day of iudge-
ment, and confequently cannot be vpon earth or in the
Sacrament; is quite forfaken by *Ridley*, grauntinge that this argument proueth nothinge:
he is afcended to heauen, ergò, *he is not on earth;* for
he may leaue heauen and come downe, accor-
dinge to *Ridley.* Yea *Ridleyes* owne principall
ground is forfaken by him, for that among his
fiue principall grounds and headfprings (for fo he calleth them) fett downe by him in his *Cambridge*
difputation, * *vvhy he did inclyne to this fentence*   * Fox pag. 1261.
and iudgement, (for then he was but inclininge)
the laft was (yf yow remember) *the moft fure*
beleefe of the article of our faith, he afcended into hea-
uen, which now yow fee may ftand without
this doctrine. Secondly, wheras he denyeth
that Chrift will depart from heauen at any
tyme, fayinge: *proue yow yf he vvill,* yet very
                                                    foone

foone after being preſſed by *Doctor Smith* out of the ſcriptures, that *Chriſt after his aſſenſion vvas ſeene viſibly, really, and corporally vpon earth*, he anſwered in theſe words: *I graunt the antecedent*; (that is Chriſt did appeare on earth). Smith. *Do yow graunt the antecedent?* Ridley. *Yea I graunt the antecedent, becauſe I know that there be certayne ancient Fathers of that opinion.* Heere yow ſee that *Ridley*, by grauntinge this antecedent, to witt, *that Chriſt after his aſſenſion, did appeare really and corporally vpon earth*, eyther doth contradict hinſelfe, when he denyed before, that Chriſt would euer come out of heauen (notwithſtandinge he could) or els he muſt graunt, that Chriſt appeared vpon earth againſt his will, or without his owne will, which were a greater abſurdity, then any of the other.

44. And furthermore he contradicteth himſelfe againe, in that he ſaid a little before, *that Chriſt may leaue heauen, and come downe into earth vvhen he vvill:* For being asked by *Doctor Smith* this queſtion: *Doth Chriſt ſo ſitt at the right hand of his Father, that he doth neuer foreſake the ſame?* *Ridley* anſwereth in theſe words: *If yow vnderſtand his ſitting to be after a corporall manner of ſitting,*

Fox pag.
1315 col. 1.
num. 40.

ſo is he alwayes permanent in heauen: Which yf yt be true, then is that falſe which before he ſaid, *that Chriſts body is not ſo tyed to heauen, but that he may come downe into the earth vvhen he vvill.* And much more falſe is yt, that Chriſt did really and corporally appeare vpon earth to *Saint Paul*, and others as a little before he graunted; ſo as by theſe yow may ſee the briars
wherinto

wherinto *Ridley* was driuen about this argument.

45. The third point to be noted in these inconstant speaches of *Ridley*, is, that yt is not possible for Chrifts body to be in heauen and earth at one tyme; and yet when we vrge them with impiety for laying impossibilityes to Gods omnipotency, they will presently runne to that answere, as *Ridley* also afterward doth: *that they dispute not what God can do, but what he will do.* Wherfore to returne to our disputation; when *Doctor VVeston* heard him talke of this impossibility, & that Christ yf he would appeare in earth, must leaue heauen, he tooke vpon him to conuince this falsity, out of two authorityes, the one of S. *Chrysostome*, the other of S. *Bernard. S. Chrysostome* his place, is vpon the Epistle to the *Hebrues*, talkinge of the dayly externall sacrifice of Christians, offered throughout the world in many churches at once, saith thus; *vna est hæc oblatio, non multa, &c.* this oblation we offer is one and not many; ,, and how is it one and not many, which being ,, once offered vp in *sancto sanctorum* (to witt, ,, vpon the Crosse) notwithstandinge is offered ,, by vs dayly ? This sacrifice (which dayly we ,, offer) is a paterne of that (once offered on the ,, Crosse) and alwayes we offer the selfe-same, ,, not offeringe now one lambe, and to morrow ,, another, but alwayes the selfe-same; wherfore heere is but one sacrifice, for that otherwayes by this meanes, yf there be many sacrifices in many places, there should be many ,,

Chrysost. hom. 17. in ep. ad Hebr.

Chrlfts,

Chrifts, which is not fo, but one Chrift in all places; *qui & hic plenus, & illic plenus, vnum corpus,* which Chrift is fully heere, and fully there, being but one body, *&c.*

46.   Out of which place *Doctor VVefton* did vrge *B. Ridley* very ftraitly, who firft, would feeme to make light of the place, fayinge: *thefe things make nothinge againft me:* but *VVefton* vrged: how fay vow then, *one Chrift is in all places, heere fully, and there fully.* Ridley. *One Chrift is in all places, but not one body is in all places, &c.* And this euafion pleafeth fo much *Iohn Fox,* as he wry-tech in the margent, *one Chrift, but not one body in all places,* as though Chrift could be feparated from his body, or as though *S. Chryfoftome* did not expreffely talke of one body: *Heere Chrift fully, and there Chrift fully one body*; and the very next words of *Chryfoftome* immediatly fol-lowinge are thefe; *euen as then Chrift offered in many places, is one body, and not many bodyes, fo is the facrifice alfo but one.* But lett vs heare *Doctor VVe-fton* vrge the fame: Wefton. *One body faith Chry-foftome.* Ridley. *But not after the maner of bodily fubftance he is in all places, not by circumfcription of places: for* hic & illic, *heere and there in Chryfoftome do affigne no place as Auguftine faith: Surfum eft Do-minus, & vbique eft veritas Domini.* The Lord is aboue, but the truth of the Lord is in all places.   Wefton. *Yow cannot fo efcape, Saint Chryfoftome faith, not the verity of Chrift is one, but one Chrift is in all places both heere and there.* Ridley. *One facrifice is in all places, becaufe of the vnity of him, vvhome the facrifice doth fignifie,*

not

not that the sacrifices be all one and the same.

47. Marke now heere gentle reader, what yt is to dispute with these people, that seeke after nothinge but shifts & holes to runne out at, or slipp away? Consider how many they be vpon this only place. For first when *Ridley* was pressed with *S. Chrysostomes* authority, as yow haue heard, prouinge euidently, that Christ could be at one tyme in diuers places, his first shift was, that yt maketh nothinge against him; and then, that albeit Christ be in many places, yet his body cannot be in many places, as though Christ were in any place without his body: And then againe yt being shewed, that *S. Chrysostome* speaketh expressely of Christs body, the next shift was, that his body is not there after the ordinary manner of bodily presence, to witt, by circumscription of place, which is quite from the purpose, for that we hould this also, as before you haue heard in the fifth & sixt obseruations, to witt, that Christ is not circumscriptiuely in the Sacrament. And further yt is another absurd shift, or rather ignorance in *Ridley* (and may be the fift or sixt about this matter) to affirme as heere he doth, that Christs body is not by circumscription euery-where, or in all places: for we hould also, not only, that which he saith, by circumscriptió, but that no wayes, either circumscriptiuely, or definitiuely, or sacramentally is Christs body euery-where, but only in many distinct places, by Gods omnipotent will. The other of vbiquity being a pro-

próperty of Gods diuinity only, to be in euery place at óne tyme, as before we haue shewed. And lastly to follow *Ridley* and his riddles no further about this matter, the words of *S. Augustine* are foolishely alleaged by him; *that the Lord is aboue , but the truth of the Lord is in all places:* for as *Doctor VVeston* well noteth and telleth him, *vve talke not heere, how the Lords truth is eueryvvhere* , but whether Christs body be in diuers places or noe : for Christs truth is euerywhere, where his faith grace or power is, but not his body. And albeit his truth admitt not the circumstances or proprietyes of places *sursum* and *deorsum*, yet his body doth: which *Ridley* considered not, when he brought this example , but only desyred to say some-what, though neuer so much from the purpose.

48.   And the like shiftes he sheweth in his last answere about this place of *S. Chrysostome*, when *Doctor VVeston* vrginge, *that one Christ and one body is in all places wherfoeuer his facrifices are offered,* he aunswereth not to the words of *Saint Chrysostome* at all , but saith only at randome, *that one facrifice is in all places (S. Chrysostome* saith one body) *because of the vnity of him vvhome the facrifice doth fignifie,* which is as much to say in his sense, as the facrifice being but a signe or signification of Christ that is one, is multiplyed in diuers places. And what great miracle is this I pray yow , to multiply many figures in diuers places of one thinge, who may not do fo? and yet *Saint Chrysostome* setteth yt downe for a wonderfull strange and admirable matter,

that

that one Chrift the felfe-fame lambe, one body, fully
heere and fully there, fhould be offered at one
tyme in many places, which miracle in *Doctor
Ridleyes* fenfe is both eafy and no miracle at all,
and fo much about this place of *Saint Chryfoftome.*

49. The fecond authority out of *S. Bernard*
is in thefe words: *Vnde hoc nobis pyſsime Iefu, &c.*   *Bern. ſerm. de Cœna Dom.*
How cometh this vnto vs, ô moſt pious Iefu,
that we feely wormes creepinge on the face ,,
of the earth, that are but duſt and aſhes, fhould ,,
deferue to haue thee prefent in our hands, & ,,
before our eyes, who fitteth both whole and ,,
full at the right hand of the Father, and who ,,
in the moment of one houre, from the rifinge ,,
of the funne, vnto the goinge downe thereof, ,,
art prefent one and the felfe-fame in many ,,
and diuers places, *&c.* To this place D. *Ridley*
gaue diuers anfwers: *Firſt* (faith he) *thefe words
of Bernard make nothing for yow at all.* This is very
confidently fpoken as yow fee, no leffe then
to the place of *S. Chryfoſtome* before; and I beleeue he will not ſtand longe vnto yt: For yf
Saint Bernard doth meane as he faith, he muſt
needs make much for vs in the words now recyted, wherin I referre me to the iudgement
of the reader. Wherfore *Maiſter Ridley* not tru-
ſtinge much to this anfwere, paffeth to his fecond fayinge: *I know that Bernard vvas in ſuch a* *Fox pag.*
tyme, that in this matter he may vvorthily be ſuſpected. *1315.*
So he. And yet leaſt he might feeme to leefe
fome creditt in reiectinge *S. Bernard,* he hath
a third anfwere thus: *notwithſtanding* (faith he)
              V   *I will*

*I will so expound him rather then reiect him , that he
shall make nothinge for yow at all.* Lo heere his last
cast; and this he learned of his *Maister Caluyn*,
not so much to reiect in words the Fathers, as
Luther did, but rather by false and crafty interpretation, sleightly to auoyd them, which indeed is not humility but double impiety; and
more impious to the Fathers themselues, then
to be vtterly denyed , for by this meanes they
are made coadiutors of heretiks : lett vs heare
then *S. Bernard* expounded by *Ridley* to his purpose : *S. Bernard* (quoth he) *saith , that we haue
Christ in a mystery , in a Sacrament, vnder a veyle or
couer; in the meane tyme heere now he saith , that the
verity of Christ is euery-vvhere.* So he. And is not
Ridley ridiculous heere ? let the reader compare *S. Bernards* words before alleaged, with
this exposition of *Ridley* , and he will say that
the commentary hitteth as right the text , as
the blynd-fold-man doth hitt the hennes
head on the ground, when his face is another
way from her. And thus much of *Doctor Ridleyes* three aunswers to this place of *Saint
Bernard* .

50.   After this *Doctor Smith* vrged him againe
Another
place of
S. Chryso-
stome vr-
ged about
Elias.
with another place of *S. Chrysostome*, where he
makinge a comparison , betweene *Elias* the
Prophett and *Christ* , saith , that *Elias* left his
cloake to *Elizeus* with his double spiritt, when
he went vp to heauen ; but *Christ* did much
Chrysost.
hom 2. ad
Pop. An-
tioch.
more miraculously, for that he left vs his flesh
in the Sacrament , and yet tooke the same vp
with him: *Helias quidem melotem discipulo reliquit;*
filius

filius autem Dei ascendens, suam nobis carnem dimisit;
Helias quidem exiuit, Christus autem & nobis reliquit,
& ipsam habens ascendit. *Elias* indeed at his departure, left his cloke or hearcloth vnto his
disciple *Elizeus*; but the sonne of God ascen-
dinge vp to heauen left his owne flesh vnto
vs: *Elias* left his cloake, but Christ both left
vnto his his flesh & yet carryed the same with
him. Which plaine place when *Ridley* went
about to delude, as he had done other former
places, by sayinge that *Chrysostomes* meaninge
was; that he left his flesh vpon earth not really and substantially, but to be receaued after a
spirituall communication, by grace, addinge
this example: *as we also* (quoth he) *by hearing the*
ghospell, and by faith: So as by this aunswere we
haue Christs flesh no otherwise present by
meanes of the Sacrament, then we haue him
present by hearinge the ghospell, or by beleeuinge in him, which is to euacuate wholy the
speach & comparison of *S. Chrysostome.* Wherfore to ouerthrow this shift, *Doctor Smith* alleaged another plaine place of the same *Chryso-*
stome in confirmation of this where he saith:
O miraculum! ô Dei benignitatem! qui sursum sedet,
tempore sacrificij hominum manibus continetur, &c.
O miracle! o goodnesse of God! that he
which sitteth aboue, is conteyned in mens
hands in the tyme of the sacrifice. But all this
would not serue, for he auoyded this as he
had done the other, sayinge: *he that sitteth there*
(to witt in heauen) *is heere present in mystery and*
by grace, and is holden of the godly, &c. And finally

Chrysost.
l. 3. de Sa-
cerdotio.

V 2   though

though there were diuers boutes in this matter, yet could nothinge be gotten more.

51.   But ro this fenfe, *Doctor Smith*, *Doctor Seton*,
Doctor Harpesfield and *Doctor VVeston*, vrged him
much about the place, asking him where was
the miracle, yf Chrift left his flefh heere only
in myftery and by faith; how could the comparifon ftand betweene *Helias* and *Chrift* ? for
Chrift muft do more then *Elias*; *Elias* left his
mantle and could not carry yt vp with him,
Chrift not only left his flefh, but carryed vp
the fame, *ergò* he left the fame that he carryed
vp, *&c.* But he carryed vp his true and naturall flefh, *ergò* he left the fame; to all which he
aunfwered againe : *He tooke vp his flesh vvith him
to heauen, and left heere the communion of his flesh on
earth.* With which fhiftinge aunfwere *Doctor
VVeston* being moued, began after his fafhion
to vrge the matter earneftly fayinge: yow vnderftand in the firft place his flefh for very true
flefh, and in the fecond place for grace and
communion of his flefh, I will make yt euident how blockifh and groffe your aunfwere
is: *As Elias left his cloke* (faith S. *Chryfoftome*) *fo the
sonne of God left his flesh*; *but Elias left his true substantiall cloke, ergò Chrift left his true substantiall flesh:*
and heerin he fpake in Englifh. *Ridly. I am glad
yow speake in English, and surely I vvould vvish all the
vvorld might vnderstand your reasons and my answers:
Reliquit nobis carnem,* Chrift left vnto vs his flefh.
*This yow vnderstand of flesh, and I vnderstand of grace:
he carryed his flesh to heauen, and left behind him the
communion of his flesh vnto vs.* Wefton. *Yee iudges
what*

*Chryfoft.
hom. 2. ad
Pop. An-
tioch.*

vvhat thinke yow of this, aunsvvere Iudges. Iudges.
It is a ridiculous, and very fond aunsvvere. Ridley.
vvell I vvill take your vvords patiently for Christs sake.
52.   And this was the end of the controuer-
sy about this place of *S. Chrysostome,* to witt,
that we must take grace for flesh, and when
Christ is said to haue left his flesh heere with
vs, we must vnderstand his grace : Yet *Doctor
VVeston* alleaged also another place out of the
same Father, where he saith : *Spargimur, &c.*
VVe are sprinkeled vvith the very selfe-same bloud, Fox pag.
1317. col.1.
that Christ carryed vp vvith him, &c. Whervnto num. 80.
Ridley answered after his fashion : *yt is the same
bloud, but spiritually receaued.* Then vrged he *Saint
Bernards* words againe; *the selfe-same Christ is present vvholy in diuers places, euen from the vvest to the
east, from the north to the south, &c.* Wherto *Ridley*
aunswered ; *that God accordinge to his Maiestie and
prouidence, as S. Augustine saith, is euery-where with
the faithfull, and so must Bernard be expounded.* Do
yow see this exposition? Read *Saint Bernards*
words before sett downe, and yow shall see,
that he speaketh of Christ, *as sittinge in heauen,
and yet present vvholy in the Priests hands, &c.*
And not of his Maiestie & prouidence, wherby he is euery-where, as before hath byn declared : So as this is not to expound, but to
confound the Fathers, and I thinke verily that
Ridley was much troubled, when he gaue such
impertinent aunswers and expositions.
53.   And with this would I passe ouer this
whole strife about *Saint Chrysostomes* places of
Elias, but that I must let yow know, that there
V 3   had

had byn some yeares before, a great styrre and altercation in the conuocation-house about the same, for that *Philpott* hearinge that place alleaged against him, as his fashion was, vaunted wounderfully, that this being the Papists cheefe and principall foundation, he would so beat them from yt, *and (as Fox addeth) giue such a plucke at yt, as yt should neuer serue their turne more*: and when yt came to the triall, he said that he had two wayes to beate them from it: The first was, that Christ goinge vp to heauen carryed his owne flesh with him, and left

Tvvo pluckes of *Philpott* praysed by *Fox*.

the same behind him, *in that he left vs behind him, that are flesh of his flesh and bones of his bones.* This is the first blow and *plucke*, wherby yow see, that Christs progatiue is plucked also; for *Helias* as well as he left his flesh behind him in this sense, for he was of our flesh: and *Philpott* also left his flesh behind him in vs, though his owne were burned in Smith-field. And finally *S. Chrysostome* speaketh expressely of the Sacrament of the Altar, sayinge: that therein Christ left his flesh, but he did not leaue all mankynd in that Sacrament; wherfore this first plucke is to small purpose. But lett vs see his second.

54.   The second is, *that Christ* (saith he) *left his flesh in the mysteryes, that is sacramentally; and that this mysticall flesh, Christ leaueth as well in the Sacrament of baptisme, as in the sacramentall bread & wine.* So he. Wherin (yf yow marke) he giueth not only the ordinary old plucke of other Sacramentaryes, to the verity of Christs flesh, ma-

kinge

kinge that myfticall, which *S. Chryfoftome* fpeaketh expreſſely of the naturall fleſh left by
him, and therby plucketh out of ioint all *Saint* The abfurdityes
of *Philpott.*
Chryfoftomes whole meaninge and difcourfe,
but giueth a new plucke alfo to the whole
Sacrament of the *Euchariſt*, affirminge Chriſts
fleſh to be as much in baptifme , as in the
other, & confequently that both *Saint Chryfoſtome*, and other Fathers , do in vayne trouble
themfelues, with fo much extollinge the excellency of the *Euchariſt* for hauinge Chriſts
fleſh in yt, for that the water of baptifme hath
the fame, & fo yow fee the whole Sacrament
plucked vp by thefe pluckes of *Philpott* , *and yet*
(faith Fox) *that he did ſhrewdly ſhake our reall pre-* Fox *pag.*
1294.
fence, by giuinge ſuch a plucke to one of our cheefe foun-
dations. Yow fee how one of thefe men do
flatter the other.

55.   Next to this entred one *Maiſter VVard* to *M. VVard*
difputeth.
difpute that had byn *Philpotts* reader, and feing
D. *Ridley* to haue doubted fo much in grauntinge and denyinge Chriſts body to haue appeared vpon earth , as in the former difputations of *Doctor Smith* , yow haue partly heard,
though much be omitted for breuityes fake,
he began to vrge him againe in that point, al- Fox *pag.*
1317.
leaginge againſt him the authority of a Ca-
techifme fett forth by himfelfe , in the name
of the whole conuocation-houfe in *K. Edwards*
dayes, where the felfe-fame point is graunted,
which heere he denyed ; but *Ridley* for two or
three about, would not yeld that the Cate-
chifme was his, though the iudges faid that

Cranmer

Cranmer had confessed the matter the day before, and *Maister VVard* auouched to his face, that he being Bishop of *London*, & in his ruffe, compelled him to subscribe therunto; yet at length he confessed, that both he and *Cranmer* had approued the same vnder their hands, & that the place alleaged against him, might easily be expounded without any incōuenience; and so they slydd away from that matter, and a place of *Theophilact* came in question, where he wryteth, that Christ in the institution of the Sacrament of the Altar *non dixit, hoc est figu-*

Theoph.
comment. in
26. Matth.

ra corporis mei, sed hoc est corpus meum: he said not, that this is the figure of my body, but this is my body: which authority *Ridley* wiped of by sayinge his meaninge to be, that yt was *not only a figure of his body*. Wherevnto *Doctor VVesson* replyed, that this *only* was *one lye* put in by him, for that *Theophilact* had no such word, nor could yt stand with his sense, for that he did not make the opposition betweene *figure*, and *only*, but betweene the *body* and *figure*, sayinge; *yt vvas his body, and not a figure of his body*. And for proofe of this, another place of *Theophilact* was

Theoph. in
cap. 6. Ioan.

alleaged vpon *Saint Iohn*, where his words are: *quoniam infirmi sumus, &c. for that vve are infirme, and abhorre to eate raw-flesh especially the flesh of man, therefore yt appeared bread, but is flesh*: what can be more plaine, and perspicuous then this? and yet do I not find any annswere to haue byn giuen by *Doctor Ridley* to this place, but that he passed to another matter, to expound the word *Transelemented* vsed by *Theophilact*. And I

passe

paſſe ouer diuers other places, as that of *Ter-* *Tert. lib. 4.*
tullian, *acceptum panem corpus ſuum illud fecit:* he *cont. Mar-*
takinge bread made yt his body; and that of *cion.*
Iuſtinu Martyr, ſayinge: *That Chriſts fleſh in the Sa-* *Iuſt. Mart.*
crament, is the ſame that vvas taken of the bleſſed Vir- *in Apol. 2.*
gin. And that of *S. Auguſtine* vpon the Pſalme; *Aug. in*
that he gaue vs to eat the ſelfe ſame fleſh, wherin he *Pſalm. 96.*
vvalked vpon earth. All which places being ob-
iected before to *Cranmer*, and read both then
& now out of the authors themſelues, by *Do-*
ctor VVeſton that had the books by him, were
no otherwiſe aunſwered heere, then by the
ſame ſhifts which *Cranmer* had auoyded them
before, yt appearinge euidently that they had
agreed vpon certayne diſtinctions, and common euaſions, wherby to delude all the Fathers authorityes that might be brought a-
gainſt them, though they were neuer ſo cleere
or pregnant for the purpoſe.

56. It followeth, that by order of diſputation
the turne came to *Doctor Glyn* to diſpute againſt
Doctor Ridley, who made (ſaith Fox) a very contumelious preface againſt him, vvhich Ridley D. Glyns
tooke the more to heart, for that he had allwayes taken argument
him to be his friend. And albeit Fox doth not ſett about
vvorſhip-
downe the ſame preface, yet by *Doctor Glyns* pinge the
entrance to his argument, a man may ſee, that Sacramēt.
the cheefe point was in reprehendinge him,
for deludinge and ſhiftinge of both ſcriptures
and fathers ſo ſhamfully, as he had heard him
do, for he ſaith: *I ſee that yow euade or ſhift away* Fox pag.
all ſcriptures & fathers. And *Ridley* anſwered: *this* 1319.
is a greeuous contumely, that yow call me a ſhifter, &c.

And

And finally *Doctor Glyn* endeauored to draw
him to yeld to the Catholike Church, which
being the piller of truth, could not be thought
to haue fallen to such Idolatry, as for many
ages to haue worshipped erroneously bread
and wyne, for the flesh and bloud of Christ in
the Eucharist, and for proofe therof he alleaged *Saint Augustine* against *Faustin* the *Manichee*,
where he saith, that this vse of adoring Christs
body in the Sacrament, was so auncient and
publike, as some pagans did thinke that Christians did adore *Ceres* and *Bacchus* the Gods of
bread and wyne. He alleaged also *Erasmus* authority, who affirmeth that this worshipping,
and adoration of the Sacrament of the Altar,
was in vse before the tyme of *S. Augustine* and
S. Cyprian; which is not so in the Sacrament of
Baptisme, though *Ridley* affirme there is as
much the flesh of Christ, as in the other, and
consequently, there is some speciall cause in
the *Eucharist* aboue other Sacraments. To
which two authorityes I find nothinge aunswered particularly; (as neyther to *Erasmus*)
but to the thing it selfe *Ridley* aunswered: *VVe
do handle the signes reuerently, &c.* And againe:
There is a deceyt in this word Adoramus, we adore,
*for vve vvorshipp the symbolls, vvhen reuerently vve
handle them: vve vvorshipp vvherseeuer vve perceaue
benefitts.* Whervnto *Doctor Glyn* aunswered: *So
I might fall downe before the bench heere, and worshipp
Christ therin, &c.* For a bench also is a beneficiall creature to them that sitt on yt. But for
all this no further satisfaction could be had,
but

*Aug. cont.
Faust. Ma-
nich. l. 20.
cap. 13.*

*Erasm. in
ep. ad frat.
Infer.
Germ.*

but that all the adoe which the Fathers do make, *about the highest honour in earth to be giuen to the Sacrament of the Altar* , comes to no more by these mens interpretations ; *but that the signes of bread and vvyne must be reuerently handled, & Christ absent must be vvorshipped therein, as in other thinges, vvherin vve perceaue or receaue his benefitts :* vvhich indeed are all his creatures made & ordayned for our profitt, for by them all, we perceaue & receaue Chrifts benefitts : So as all these great admirations of the Fathers, about the honour, worshipp & adoration due to this Sacrament, come to no more in effect, *but that vve must reuerence Christ therin, as in other his beneficiall creatures, and vvorshipp the symboll of bread and wyne, as much as yow do the water in baptisme :* vvhich yet neuer any of the Fathers said was to be adored by vs (as they do of the Eucharist) though Baptisme be a most necessary and profitable Sacrament.

57. Then disputed one *Doctor Curtopp,* alleaginge a place out of *S. Chrysostome,* affirminge: *that which is in the cupp, or chalice, to be the same bloud* (after the words of consecration) *that flowed from the side of Christ* , wherof he inferred, that true and naturall bloud did flow from the side of Christ, *ergò* true and naturall bloud was in the chalice. To this *Ridley* answered in effect after his ould fashion, that yt was true bloud, that is to say, *the Sacrament of his bloud.* Curtopp. *The Sacrament of the bloud is not the bloud.* Ridley. *The Sacrament of the bloud, is the bloud, and that is attributed to the Sacrament, vvhich is spoken of the thing*
of the

D. Curtopp argued.

Chrysost. hom. 24. in 1. Cor. 10.

Fox pag. 1319.

of the Sacrament. At which aunſwere Ɖ. *VVeſton*
being moued, as yt ſeemed, argued in Engliſh
(ſaith Fox) thus: *That vvhich is in the chalice is the*
ſame that flowed out of Chriſts ſide, but there came out
very true bloud , ergò there is very true bloud in the
chalice. Ridley. *The bloud of Chriſt is in the chalice*
in deed, but not in the reall preſence, but by grace and in
a Sacrament. Weſton. *That is very vvell ; then vve*
haue bloud in the chalice. Ridley. *It is true , but by*
grace , and in a Sacrament ; and heere the people
hiſſed at him , (ſaith Fox) wherat *Ridley* ſaid:
O my maiſters I take this for no iudgement, I will ſtand
to Gods iudgement. This was his laſt refuge and
further then this, nothinge could be had at his
hands.

58.   There roſe vp after this *Doctor VVatſon*,
who after a long altercation with *Ridley*, whether after conſecration the Sacrament might
be called true bread : *Ridley* alleaged this place
of *S. Paul. The bread which we breake, is yt not a com-*
munication of the body of Chriſt? As though yt had
made for him. But *VVatſon* brought *S. Chryſo-*
ſtomes expoſitiō: *Quare non dixit participatione, &c.*
VVherfore did not S. Paul ſay heere, that yt is the par-
ticipation (of Chriſts body) *but the communication?*
becauſe he would ſignify ſome greater matter, & that he
vvould declare a great conuenience betwene the ſame,
for that vve do not communicate by participation only
& receauing, but by co- vniting or vnion; for euen as the
body is co-vnited to Chriſt ; ſo alſo are we by the ſame
bread conioyned and vnited to him. Out of which
place of *S. Chryſoſtome,* yt appeareth euidently,
that his beleefe was; that as his body and fleſh

was

was really vnited to his person, so are we vnto him in flesh, by eatinge the same in the Sacrament, which is another manner of vnion then by faith and generall only. But to this lett vs heare *Ridleyes* aunswere in his owne words: Ridleye. *Let Chrysostome haue his manner of speakinge, and his sentence, yf yt be true, I reiect yt not, but lett yt not be preiudiciall to me, to name yt bread.* So he. And thus was *S. Chrysostome* shifted of, neyther admitted, nor fully reiected; but if he spake truly, then was he to be credited, which was a courteous kind of reiection; for *Ridley* would haue the reader beleeue, that he spake not truly. And so much for him.

Fox *pag.* 1320.

59. And so when nothinge more could be gotten by *Doctor VVatson* from *Maister Ridley* in this argument, *Doctor Smith* stepped in to him againe, and vrged a place of *S. Augustine* vpon the thirty and third Psalme: *Ferebatur in manibus suis, &c.* He was carryed in his owne hands, applyed by *S. Austen* to Christ: his words are: *Hoc quo modo fieri possit in homine, quis intelligat?* Who can vnderstand how this can be done by a man? *for that no man is borne by his owne hands, but by other mens hands, neyther can vve find how this was fullfilled literally in K. Dauid, but by Christ we find it fullfilled, for that Christ was borne in his owne hands, when he said this is my body, for he did become that body in his owne hands, &c.* And againe in another sermon vpon the same place, he repeateth againe the very same thinge sayinge: *How vvas Christ borne in his owne hands? for that vvhen he did commend vnto vs his body and blood, he tooke into his hands*

1. *Reg.* 21.

Aug. in Psalm. 33. *concion.* 1.

Aug. ibid. conc. 2.

hands that vvhich the faithfull know, and so he bare himselfe after a certayne manner, vvhen he said this is my body. Out of which places appeareth euidently, that *S. Augustine* beleeued, that Christ after the words of consecration vttered, did beare his owne body in his hands, and that this in his iudgement was so miraculous a thinge, as neyther King *Dauid*, nor any other mortall man could do yt, but only Chirst, which yet is not so in a figure (for euery man may beare a figure of his owne body in his hands) and furthermore yt is cleere by these authorityes, and by those words *(norunt fideles)* that this was the beleefe by all faithfull people of *S. Austens* tyme. Which argument being much vrged against *Maister Ridley*, both by *Doctor Smith* and others, he sought to declyne the force therof dyuers-wayes, as saying first; *that S. Augustine vvent from others in this exposition,* (but yet named none) and then, *that this place of scripture vvas read othervvise of other men, accordinge to the hebrew text,* & other like euasions, which yet proue not (as yow see) but that *Saint Austen* was of this opinion and beleefe himselfe, (which is the question in this place) and after all this he passed to his ordinary refuge, *that Chrst bare himselfe sacramentally only, and not othervvise*; layinge hands, for some shew of reason, vpon the word *quodammodo,* vsed in the second place by *S. Austen,* that is, *after a certayne manner.* And when it was replied to him, that *S. Austen* vsed that word, to shew the different manner of his being in the Sacrament, and out of the

Sacra-

Sacrament, but that otherwayes all parts and circumstances of *S. Austens* speach do shew, that he beleeued Christ to haue holden really, and truly his owne body and flesh in his hands, they could gett no other aunswere from him but this: *He did beare himselfe, but in a Sacrament.* Wherat men maruaylinge, *Doctor Smith* said: *Yow are holden fast, nor are ye able to escape out of this labyrinth.* And then began *Doctor Tressam* to pray for him with a sollemne prayer, which being ended he said: *If there were an Arrian heere that had this subtile witt, that yow haue, he might soone shift of the scriptures, and Fathers as yow doe.* Wherat *Doctor VVeston,* seeming vnwilling that tyme should be spent in prayinge and not in disputinge, said: *eyther dispute, or hould your peace I pray yow.* And with this they passed to another disputation, *vvhether euill men do receaue the true body of Christ or not:* But *S. Austens* authority of bearinge himselfe in his hands, gatt no other solution, but that Christ bare himselfe in his hands, that is the figure or representation of himselfe, which neither *Dauid,* nor other mortall man could do: At which absurdity most of the audience did laugh.

60.   But concerninge the other questions, *vvhether euill men do receaue Christ,* *Doctor Tressam* brought two or three places out of *S. Austen* concerninge *Iudas,* that he eat the true body of Christ, as the other Apostles did, and then againe of wicked men in generall: *Quia aliquis non ad salutem manducat, non ideò non est corpus:* because some do not eate to saluation, yt followeth

Fox pag. 1321.

D. Tressam disputeth.

Aug. lib 5. cont Donat. cap. 8.

loweth not therfore, that yt is not his body:
but to all this *Maister Ridley* aunswered by his
former shift, *that yt is the body to them,* that is, *the
Sacrament of the body.* Do yow see the fond euasion? there was no doubt or question whether
euill men did eat the Sacrament, or externall
forme, (for euery man doth eat that, when
they receaue) but the question was and is of
the true body : and therfore when *Saint Austen*
speaketh of this body, yt is madnes to vnderstand yt of any other thinge, then the reall
body. But lett vs heare what was replyed:
Doctor VVeston said: I bringe *Theophilact* against
yow: *Iudas* (saith he) *gustauit carnem Domini:*
Iudas did eate or tast the flesh of Christ. Ridley. *That is the Sacrament of the Lords flesh.* Doctor
VVatson replyed out of the Councell of *Nice:*
*Exaltata mente fideliter credamus, iacere in illa sacra
mensa agnum Dei tollentem peccata mundi, a sacerdotibus sacrificatum.* Let vs faithfully beleeue with
an exalted mynd , that there lyeth in the holy
,, table the lambe of God, that taketh away the
,, sinnes of the world, which is sacrifieed by the
,, Priests. Ridley. *That Councell vvas collected out of
auncient Fathers, and is to me of great authority,* &c.
*the vvords make for me : the lambe of God is in heauen
accordinge to the verity of the body, and heere he is with
vs in a mystery accordinge to his power , not corporally.*
Watson. *But the lambe of God lyeth on the table.*
Ridley. *Yt is a figuratiue speach, for in our mynd vve
vnderstand him vvhich is in heauen.* Watson. *But he
lyeth there, the Greeke vvord is* ΚΕῖΤΑ. Ridley.
He lyeth there, that is, he is there present, not corporally,
                                                              but

*Fox ibid.
num. 49.*

*Concil Nicen primum
int. de diuina mensa,
&c ultim.
editionis.*

Fox ibid.

but he lyeth there in his operation, &c. And by this
yow may see, to what purpose yt was to dispute with this man; for that God by his
power and operation is euery where, and in
euery creature. And yf Christ be no otherwise heere, but by his power and operation,
as in baptisme, what an impertinency is this
of the Councell of *Nice*, to vse so many and significant words, *that vve must faithfully beleeue
vvith a high mynd and courage*, against sense and
reason, *that the lambe of God lyeth on the table sacri-
ficed by Priests*, and the like; Is there any Protestant that speaketh thus, or can the like words
be verified in the Protestants communion, of
signes, figures, representations and symbolls?

61. Lastly to skipp ouer diuers other things,
Doctor VVeston pressed him with two other
places of S. *Chrysostome*, so cleere, as nothinge
can be spoken more cleerer. The first is in
these words: *vve vvorshipp the selfe same body in
the Eucharist, vvhich the vvise men did vvorshipp in the
manger.* And then againe: *vve haue not heere the
Lord in the manger, but on the Altar; heere a vvroman
holdeth him not in her hands, but a Priest.* These are
the words. Let vs heare his answere. Ridley.
*I graunt the Priest holdeth the same thinge, but after
another manner. She did hold the naturall body, the
Priest holdeth the mystery of the body.* So hee. And
Fox wryteth in the margent. *The same thinge,
but the manner diuerse.* But who seeth not, that
our contention is about the thing, and not the
manner; for we teach also that the manner of
Christs being in the Sacrament, is different

Fox *pag.* 1321.

Chrysost. hom. 24. *in* 1. *ad Cor.*

Fox *pag.* 1322.

X   from

from the manner of his being in heauen, but the thinge really is all one. And so yf *Ridley* do graunt the same thinge to be holden by the **Priest** hands, which the blessed virgin held in her hands, as heere yow see him graunt in words, then the controuersie betweene vs and him is ended. But presently he leapeth from his graunt againe, sayinge she did hold the naturall body, and the Priest holdeth the mystery of the body, which are different things, and not only different manners of holdinge. Wherefore *Doctor VVeston* repeatinge againe this argument out of *S. Chrysostome* to the multitude in English (saith Iohn Fox) and consideringe the manner of *Ridleyes* aunsweringe, and that nothinge more could be had of him, he dissolued the disputation in these words: *Videtis præfracti hominis animum, gloriosum, vasrum, inconstantem, &c.* Yow see the stubborne, vauntinge, deceytfull, and inconstant mynd of this man. And with this Encomion departed *Doctor Ridley* to his prison againe, and the other Doctors each man to their owne lodginges.

Out of the Disputations with M. Hugh
Latimer, *togeather with the con-*
clusion of the whole triall
in this article. §. 4.

64. Vpon the third day being wednesday
the

the 18. of Aprill, was brought forth *Maiſter Hugh Latymer* to aunſwere as the former had done, but the diſputation was much more ſhorter then the other, and in Engliſh, *for Maiſter Latymer* (ſaith Fox) *alleaged that he vvas out of vſe vvith Latyn, and vnſitt for that place.* He gaue vp his confeſſion about the three articles in wrytinge, after the imitation of *Cranmer* and *Ridley*, full of ſcoffes and bitter taunts, as his veyne was, and reſted moſt vpon the maſſe, and the *foure marrow-bones therof* (for ſo blaſphemouſly he called them) which were (forſooth) *conſecration, tranſubſtantiation, oblation,* and *adoration,* of all which yow haue heard the ancient Fathers ſpeaches before, how different they are from theſe of *Latymer*, as was alſo their ſpiritt.

Fox pag. 1322.

Latymers 4. morrovv-bones of the maſſe.

63. The firſt entrance to talke betwene *Maiſter Latymer,* and the Doctors was, for that he ſayinge in his wrytinge, that nothinge was to be receaued concerning the Sacramet, which was not expreſſely ſett downe in the inſtitution of Chriſt, *Doctor VVeſton* inferred, that then weomen muſt not receaue the communion, for that no expreſſe mention is made in ſcripture of their receauinge; and when *Latymer* aunſwered, that S. *Paal* ſaid: *Probet autem ſeipſum homo,* which ſignifieth ſaid he both men and weomen, yt was replyed, that in Greeke yt was *anthropos* that was proper to man, *&c.* Then *Doctor VVeſton* asked him, how longe he had byn of this opinion? he ſaid about ſome ſeauen yeares (he being more then ſeauenty

X 2

of

of age)and that my L. of Canterburyes booke had specially confirmed his iudgement therin. *And yf* (quoth he) *I could remember all therin conteyned, I vvould not feare to aunsvvere any man in this matter.* So he. And many tymes after he ran still to this booke of *Cranmer.* *My Lord of Canterburyes booke* (saith he to an argument of *Doctor*

Fox *pag.*
1325.

Cartwright) handleth this very vvell, and by him could I aunsvvere yow, yf I had him. And againe in another place to another argument. *The solution of this* (saith he) *is in my Lord of Canterbury his booke.*

Latymer
foundeth
himselfe
on *Cranmers*
booke.

And yet further to another. *I remember I haue read this in my Lord of Canterburyes booke.* Wherto *Doctor Tressam* aunsvvered, *that there are in that booke six hundred lyes*, but *Latymer* replyed nothinge, *&c.*

64.	Then said *Doctor VVeston: Yow vvere once a Lutheran.* Latimer. *No I vvas a Papist, for I could neuer perceaue how Luther could defend his opinion, vvithout transubstantiation. The Tygurines once did vvryte a booke againsi Luther, and I oft desired God that he might liue so longe as to make them aunsvvere.* So he, wherby is seene, that he fauoured *Luther* more then the *Tygurines* at that tyme, for that he would haue had them aunsvvered. But

Luth. l. de
missa Priua-
ta fol. 4.
Contigit

Doctor VVeston said further: *Luther in his booke de priuata missa, testifieth that the diuell reasoned vvith him, and persuaded him that the masse vvas not good, vvherby yt appeareth that Luther said masse, and the diuell dissuaded him from yt.* Latimer. *I do not take in hand heere to defend Luthers sayings or doings: yf he vvere heere, he vvould defend himselfe vvell inough I trow.* So Latymer, leauinge Luther to himselfe,

selfe, but Fox will needs defend him with this
marginall note sayinge : *In that booke, the diuell* Fox *pag.*
doth not diffuade him so much from sayinge masse, as to 1324.
bring him to desperation for sayinge masse, such tempta-
tions many tymes happen to good men.

65. And will yow consider the grauity and
verity of this note ; first he saith that the diuell did not so much dissuade him from sayinge masse, as to bringe him to desperation:
then somewhat he did dissuade him , though Iohn Fox
not so much as to the other; which I beleeue, excuseth
for that the one was his damnation, and his and accu-
leauinge of masse was but the way to yt . Se- seth Lu-
condly yf the diuell did endeauour to bringe ther.
Luther to desperation for sayinge of masse,
he must needs persuade him first , that the
masse was naught, as yf he would draw a man
to desperation for vsing almes deeds, he must
first persuade him , that almes-deeds are
naught and wicked, and as wise a man as he
should shew himselfe , that at the diuells persuasion will beleeue that almes-deeds were
naught, and leaue the same; so were *Luther* &
Latymer as wise to beleeue this suggestion of
the diuell against the masse. And where Fox The di-
saith , *that such temptations of the diuell do happen* uells im-
many tymes to good-men. I graunt yt, but not that pugninge
euer any good man did yeld therevnto, or masse as
iudge a thinge euill, for that the diuell did say euill, pro-
yt was naught, but rather to the contrary, his ueth yt to
impugnation of yt is always a signe, that the be God.
thing is good and pleasinge to almighty God,
whose aduersary the diuell is; yea the greater
his

his impugnation is, the better muſt we preſume the thing to be, and conſequently when he would make the maſſe to ſeeme ſo heynous a thinge to Luther, as that he ſhould be damned for ſayinge the ſame, yt is a good proofe that the maſſe is an excellent thing, & diſpleaſeth the diuell, and that *Luther* and his followers leauing to ſay maſſe, do pleaſe much the diuell in followinge his ſuggeſtion therin, as good and obedient children, to ſo holy a ghoſtly Father, and ſo to him we leaue them.

66.   There followeth, that albeit *Latymer* was loath to diſpute, yet ſome few arguments were caſt forth againſt him, but all in Engliſh, for ſo he would haue yt. And firſt *Maiſter Doctor Treſſam* alleaged an authority of *Saint Hilary*, affirminge *a naturall vnity to be in vs with Chriſt by eatinge his fleſh*. Which place, for that yt was alleaged before againſt his fellowes, I will not ſtand much vpon yt, but only note this mans euaſion: Latymer. *I can not ſpeake Latyn ſo longe, &c. But as for the words* (ſaith he) *of Hilary, I thinke they make not ſo much for yow: but he that ſhould anſwere the Doctors, had not neede to be in my caſe, but ſhould haue them in a readyneſſe, and know their purpoſe: Melancthon ſaith, that yf the Doctors had forſeene, that they ſhould haue byn ſo taken in this controuerſie, they vvould haue vvrytten more plainly.* This was his anſwere, and more then this yow ſhall not find, and in this, there is a notable impoſture of an old deceauer, for that *Melancthon* being of oppoſite opinion to him in this article, and wrytinge a whole worke of the Doctors ſentences

tences for proofe of the *reall-presence*, againſt
the Sacramentaryes, as in his ★ life we haue
ſhewed, what he ſpeaketh of this myſtakinge
the Fathers and Doctors, he ſpeaketh expreſſely of the Sacramentaryes, and not of thoſe
that defend the *reall-preſence*, which he alſo,
being a Lutheran, defended, and affirmeth
plainly that all the Fathers are of the ſame
opinion, though yf they had foreſeene, that
ſuch heretiks, as are the Sacramentaryes,
would haue riſen vp, and haue wreſted their
words and meaning (as yow haue heard both
Cranmer, Ridley, and *Latymer* to haue done) they
would haue ſpoken more plainly in the controuerſie, though hardly they could haue ſpoken more cleerly againſt them. And by this
firſt entrance, yow may marke the plaine dealinge of old Father *Latymer.*

67.   Doctor *Seaton* Vice-chauncelour of *Cambridge,* ſeing theſe ſleights of the old fellow, beginneth thus with him: *I know your learninge
vvoll inough, and how ſubtile yow be: I will vſe a few
vvords vvith yow out of S. Cyprian, vvho ſaith, that the
old Teſtament doth forbidd the drinkinge of bloud, and
the new Teſtament doth commaund the drinkinge of
bloud.* Out of which words he framed this argument. *That yt vvas true and reall bloud, vvhich the
old Teſtament forbadd to drinke, ergò yt is true and
reall bloud vvhich the new Teſtament commaundeth to
drinke;* for that otherwiſe the *antitheſis* or oppo-
ſition of the two Teſtaméts in this point can
not hold, yf the one forbidd the true drinking
of true and reall bloud, and the other com-

maun-

*★ Menſe
Decembri.*

Fox pag.
1325.

D. Seatons
argument
*Cypr. de
Cœn. Dom.*

maundeth the figuratiue drinking of spirituall bloud by faith, for that these things are oppo-site, and that the Iewes alfo in the old Testa-ment did drinke Chrifts bloud by faith , *&c.*
To which argument *Latymer* aunfwered no-thinge in effect , but this ; *vve do taft true bloud, but fpiritually, and this is inough.* Aud then proueth he the fame by thofe words of *S. Auguftine* be-fore aunfwered by vs ; *crede & manducafti* ; be-leeue, & thou haft eaten, as though the words *credere* and *edere*, were all one in the fcriptures. Whervpon *Doctor VVefton* recyted a ftory that paffed betwene *Maifter Hooper* and *B. Gardener*; for when *Hooper* would needs hould , that *to eate* was *to beleue* , and that an *Altar* fignified Chrift in the fcriptures, *B. Gardener* inferred, ergò, when *S. Paul* faith to the Hebrewes, *that vve haue an Altar, vvherof the Iewes muft not eat: the fenfe is, vve haue Chrift, in whome the Iewes muft not beleeue.* And after this he retourned to preffe *Latymer* ftrongly againe vpon this place of *S. Cyprian*; fayinge : *that is commaunded in the new Teftament, vvhich is forbidden in the ould , but true bloud vvas forbidden in the old, ergò true bloud alfo is commaunded to be drunken in the new.* Whervnto *Latymer* aunfweringe twife, vttered two con-traryes: for firft his words are : *It is true as tou-chinge the matter ; but not as touchinge the manner of the thinge,* where he graunteth (as yow fee) that true bloud is meant in both Teftaments, but the manner of drinkinge is different , which alfo we graunt & teach : but heare his fecond aunfwere vpon the other inftance.

68. We-

Fox pag. 1325.

Aug. tract. 25. in Ioan.

Heb. 13.

S. Cyprians place vr-ged by D. VVefton.

Fox pag. 1325. col. 1. num. 27.

98.   Weſton. *The old Teſtament doth forbidd the*
taſtinge of bloud, but the new doth commaund yt. Latymer. *It is true, not as touchinge the thinge , but as*
touchinge the manner therof. Before he ſaid: yt is
true touchinge the matter, but not touchinge
the manner; now he ſaith; yt is true touching
the manner and not touchinge the thinge: ſo
as yf the *thinge and matter* be all one, as yt is, he
ſpeaketh contraryes. Whervpon *Doctor VVeſton*
opened the whole argument to the people in
Engliſh, and the abſurdity of his anſwere. but
Latymer replyed againe and againe : *that true*
bloud vvas commaunded ſpiritually to be dronken in the
new Teſtament . Whervnto one *Doctor Pye* replyed , and obiected , that yt was not forbidden to be dronken ſpiritually in the old law:
for that (ſaith he) *they drinke ſpiritually Chriſts bloud*
in the old law, ergò , *the drinkinge therof in the new*
muſt be more then only ſpirituall. To this *Latymer*
aunſwered, *the ſubſtance of bloud is dronken, but not*
in one manner. So as heere yow ſee , he graunteth alſo the ſubſtance of bloud to be dronken, though in a different manner from that
of the old Teſtament. But being preſſed by
the ſaid *Doctor Pye* , that we require not the
ſame manner of drinkinge bloud in the new
law, which was forbidden in the old; but only that yt is as really and truly bloud , as the
other was; his finall aunſwere and reſolution
is this, *It is the ſame thinge, but not the ſame manner,*
I haue no more to ſay. Heere then is his laſt deter-
termination, and conſider I pray yow the ſubſtance therof ; yf yt be the ſame thinge , then
must

Fox *ibid.*
num. 70.

D. *Pye*
diſputeth.

muſt yt needs be really and truly bloud; for
this is the thinge or matter wherof the queſtion is, for that otherwayes we know that
the bloud forbidden in the old Teſtament, is
meant the bloud of beaſts, and the bloud commaunded in the new, is meant of the bloud of
Chriſt; So as in this, *Latymer* cannot graunt
them to be one thinge, but only in the reallity and truth of bloud, that is, as the one is true
and reall bloud of beaſts: ſo is the other true
and reall bloud of Chriſt; which yf he graunt
(as heere in words he doth) then cannot the
different manner of drinkinge the ſame alter
the ſubſtance of the thinge yt ſelfe; or yf yt do,
then is yt falſe, that yt is the ſame thinge; and
ſo euery way is ould *Latymer* taken, but lett vs
paſſe forewatd.

69.　Doctor *VVeſton* to confirme the reallity of
Chriſts bloud, receaued in the Sacrament, al-

leaged another place of S. *Chryſoſtome*, where
talkinge of *Iudas* he ſaith, *Chriſtus ei ſangninem
quem vendidit offerebat.* Chriſt gaue him (in the
Sacrament, to witt, to *Iudas*) the bloud which
he had ſould. Can any thinge be playner ſpoken. *Latymer* anſwered: *he gaue to Iudas his bloud,
in a Sacrament*, and by this thinketh he hath
ſaid ſomewhat to the purpoſe, wheras indeed
he ſaith nothinge. For we ſay alſo, that he
gaue him his bloud in a Sacrament, as we ſay,
that we giue wyne in a cuppe, but this excludeth not the reality of the bloud, no more then
the giuinge in a cupp, or vnder a veyle, taketh
away the true reality of the wyne; yet is this
the

the common hole for Sacramentaryes to
runne out at, when they are preſſed; for both
they and we do agree, that Chriſts bloud is
giuen in the Sacrament vnder a ſigne ſacramentally, and the like phraſes; but the difference betweene vs is, that we by this do not
exclude the truth & reality of the thing therin
conteyned, as they do, & therby delude both
themſelues and others, ſpeakinge in ſuch ſort,
as they cannot be vnderſtood, but only that
a man may eaſily vnderſtand, that they ſeeke
therby euaſions, and wayes to ſlipp out at.

70.   I paſſe ouer diuers other authorityes of
Fathers alleaged by the Doctors, as thoſe
words of *S. Cyrill: Per communionem corporis Chri-*   *Cyrill. l. 10,
in cap. 13.
Ioan.*
ſti, habitat in nobis Chriſtus corporaliter. By the
communion of Chriſts body, he dwelleth in
vs corporally, *ergò,* not ſpiritually only and by
faith. *Latymer* aunſwered; *firſt that (corporally)*   *Fox pag.
1325.*
hath another vnderſtandinge, then yow do groſſely take
yt. And then being preſſed againe, he ſaid: *The*
ſolution of this is in my Lord of Canterburyes booke.
So he. But Fox not contented, (as it ſeemeth)
with this aunſwere, putteth downe a larger,
though without an author, wherby we may
conceaue yt to be his owne. *Corporally* (ſaith
he) *is to be taken heere in the ſame ſenſe, that S. Paul*
ſaith, the fullnes of diuinity to duuell corporally in
Chriſt, that is, not lighty, nor accidentally, but perfectly
& ſubſtantially, &c. Which anſwere yf Fox will
ſtand vnto we are agreed; for we require no
more but that Chriſt by the commnnion of
his body in the Sacrament, doth dwell perfectly

fectly aud substantially in vs, for that importeth also really, as the fullnesse of diuinity is
really in Christ incarnate, and not by vnion
only of will, as the *Arrians* said, and as our Sacramentaryes do talke of Christs vnion only
by faith in vs. And lett the reader note by the
way *Iohn Fox* his witt, & deepe diuinity, who
knowinge not what he saith, graunteth by
this example more then we require; for he
graunteth the same substantiall vnity to be
betweene Christ and our soule, which is betweene Christs diuinity, and his humanity;
which is false; ours being accidentall and separable; the other substantiall & inseparable,
for that yt is hypostaticall. But these thinges
Iohn had not learned, and so we pardon him,
and do returne to *Latymer* againe, who being
vrged hardly by *Doctor Smith* about *Saint Cyrills*
words; that Christ by communion of his body in the Sacrament *dwelleth corporally in vs*, ergò, *not only spiritually by faith*;he aunswered: *I say
both that he dwelleth in vs spiritually, and corporally,
spiritually by faith, and corporally by takinge our flesh
vpon him; for I remember that I haue read this in my
Lord of Canterburyes booke.* Heere now yow see
another shift different from that of Fox, au-
thorised by my L. of *Canterburyes* booke, but
shaken of by *S. Cyrills* booke, which saith expressely as vow haue heard, *that Christ dwelleth
in vs corporally by the communion of his body in the Sacrament*, and talketh not of the incarnation.

71. Wherfore *Doctor VVeston* seing that more
could not be had of *Latymer* in this point, he
passed

paffed to another matter, which was to deale
with him about *the Sacrifice of che maſſe*. In ſcoffinge againſt which, *Latymers* grace, or diſgrace rather and ſinne, did principally con-
ſiſt; and ſo alleaginge many auncient Fathers
authorityes againſt him for this purpoſe, and
reading the places at length, hauing the books
there preſent, *Latymer* was quickly dryuen to
a *non-plus*, as may appeare by Fox his owne
narration, though he ſetteth yt downe like a
Fox indeed, ſuppreſsinge all the particulars of
the ſaid places, but only the names of the authors, and the firſt words of the texts, and not
them alſo in all. And then toucheth he the
aunſwers of *Latymer*, and the Catholike Doctors replyes ſo brokenly and confuſedly, as
may eaſily ſhew that he would declyne the
tempeſt of that combatt from *Latymers* ſhoul-
ders, and not haue the matter vnderſtood, in-
ſinuatinge only ſome 8. or 9. authorityes alleaged for proofe of the propitiatory ſacrifice,
whetas more then 8. or 9. ſcore might haue
byn cyted to that effect. And finally though
Laiymer muttered out two or three particular
aunſwers heere and there, ſayinge; *that S. Chryſoſtome had Emphaticall locutions*, and the like; yet
his laſt reſt was ſett vpon this; *that the Doctors
might be deceaued in ſome points, though not in all
things:* Wherof Fox well allowinge, maketh
this ſcoffinge comment in the margent, *Docto-
res legendi ſunt cum venia*; the Doctors are to be
read with pardon, which can haue no other
ſenſe, but that eyther we muſt pardon them
when

when they speake not truth, or we must aske
pardon of them, not to beleeue them when
we mislike them; for other sense I cannot
make of this comentary.

27. *Doctor* Cole replyed; *is it not a shame for an
old man to lye? yow say yow are of the old Fathers faith.*
Latymer. *I am of their faith vvhen they say vvell, I
referre my selfe to my Lord of Caterburyes booke wholy
herin.* Doctor Smith. *Then yow are not of S. Chrysostomes faith, nor S. Augustines faith.* Latymer. *I
haue said, vvhen they say vvell, and bring scriptures for
them, I am of their faith, and further Augustine requireth not to be beleeued, &c.* Weston. *Forty yeares
gone, vvhether could yow haue gone to haue found your
doctrine?* Latym. *The more cause we haue to thanke
God now, that hath sent the light into the vvorld.*
Weston. *The light? ney light and lewd preachers, &c.
remember vvhat they haue bin, that haue bin the be-
ginners of your doctrine, none but a few flyinge Aposta-
taes, runninge out of Germany, &c. remember vvhat
they haue bin, that haue sett forth the same in this
realme, a sort of flyinge braines, and light heads, wbich
vvere neuer constant in any one thinge, vvhich vvas well
seene in the often alteringe of their communion-booke,
and turninge their table one day vvest, and another day
east, they gott them a tankerd, and one saith I drinke
and am thankefull, the more ioy of thee, saith another,
&c. Yow neuer agreed vvith the Tigurynes of Germa-
nie, or vvith your selues, your stubburnesse is of vaine
glory, and vve all see by your owne confession, how little
cause yow haue to be stubburne, your learninge is in
feoffers hold, the Queenes grace is mercifull, if yow
vvill returne.* Latymer. *Yow shall haue no hope in
me*

me to returne. And thus ended that difputation.

74. And heere Iohn Fox is very angry with
Doctor VVeſton for this fpeach, and for reuenge
therof, maketh this note in the margent: *Blaſ-*
phemous lyes of Doctor VVeſton ſittinge in the chaire of
peſtilence, and then prefently he maketh the
narration of him, which before we haue related about *Vrge hoc, vrge hoc,* and in the margent
he hath this other *Notandum, vrge hoc quod VVe-*
ſton, vvith his beere-pott in his hand: which notwithſtandinge is more modeſt, then yf yt had
byn a wyne-pott. And I maruayle much why
the wifdome of Fox fhould obiect this beer-
pott fo often & eagerly againſt *Doctor VVeſton,*
feeing his owne great chaire, which is yet
kept for a relique of his holines in London by
the fiſters, hath two places made on both fides
therof, the one for the Candleſticke, the other
for the ale-pott and nutmegges, which *Father*
Fox is faid to haue loued well, and fo do his
wrytings alfo fhew, & yet no Catholike man
I thinke hath euer obiected the fame vnto
him before this, as he doth the beer-pott to
Doctor VVeſton. But thefe are trifles. Lett vs
paffe to more ferious confiderations.

The Concluſion, with ſome Conſide-
rations theron. §. 5.

75. By the re-view then of thefe three dayes
difputations, a coniecture may be made, how

matters did passe then, and how they stand at
this day betwixt vs and Protestants in these
articles of controuersie: Yow haue heard before the great vaunts that *Doctor Ridley* made
in his disputations at *Cambridge* vnder K. *Edward*, how euidently forsooth and apparently
the truth stood with him and his fellowes, &

Fox *pag.*
1161.

this vpon *fiue principall grounds* and head-springs
as he calleth them; *vvhich are the Maiestie and verity of scriptures; the most certaine testimony of the ancient Fathers; the definition of a Sacrament; the abhominable heresie of Eutiches, and the most sure beleefe of
the article of our faith;* He *ascended vp to heauen.*

The vaūts
of *Ridley*
& *Cranmer*
hovv vvell
perfor-
med.

B. *Cranmer* also after that againe in the beginninge of *Q. Maryes* raigne, setting forth a certayne vauntinge schedell, which Fox called a
Purgation of Thomas Archbishopp Cranmer, hath
this chalenge therin: *I vvith Peter Martyr* (saith

Fox *pag.*
1261.

he) *and other foure or fiue vvhich I shall choose, vvill by
Gods grace take vpon vs to defend all the doctrine and
Religion, sett forth by our soueraigne Lord K. Edward
the sixth to be more pure, and accordinge to Gods word,
then any other that hath bin vsed in England these
thousand yeares, so that Gods vvord may be iudge, and
that the reasons and proofes of both parts may be sett
out in vvrytinge, to the entent as vvell, that all the world
may examine and iudge theron, as that no man shall
start backe from his vvrytinge.*

76. Thus he. And now yow haue seene
more or lesse by the former disputation, how
he, & his fellow *Ridley* were able to performe
their bragges, and though yow haue seene
them brought to the exigents, which before
hath

hath appeared: yet yf yow will beleeue them
or Iohn Fox their Chronicler, settinge forth
their Acts and Monuments, they were so farre
of from being conquered, as the aduerse part
was rather putt to the foyle, for that they
could say nothinge in effect against them. And
for example, Fox wryteth of *Doctor VVeston* Fox pa.
(who most of all other vrged them with ma- 1326.
ny good arguments as yow haue heard) *that*
not only he had his Theseus there by him to help him out Ibid. pag.
(to witt his beere-pott) but moreouer that he said 1330.
neuer a true word, nor made neuer a true conclusion al-
most in that disputation. Which how true or false Impuden-
yt is, the reader himselfe may be iudge, that cy of Fox,
hath peruſed ouer the same in this our *re view:*
And the very like in effect wryteth *B Cranmer* Fox pag.
in a certayne letter of his to the Councell, 1331.
vpon the 23. of *Aprill* 1554. immediatly after
the disputation ended, complayninge greatly
of the disorder & iniquity therin vſed, which
yet by that we haue examined before out of
their owne words, I meane set downe in Fox,
his penne being bent wholy to their fauour,
there could not be great iniquity or inequality, the combatt consistinge in discussinge authorityes of auncient Fathers; but yt is the nature of this people as alwayes to be conten-
tious, so euer to be clamourous, and neuer satisfied except they haue their will, but especially to wryte and speake both contemptu-
ously and partially: yow shall heare how *Mai-*
ster Ridley relateth the euent of this disputation; for that hauinge sett downe his owne

Y   *dispu-*

difputations and aunfwers in the prifon, and this with the greateft aduantage, yow muft imagine that he could diuife, after much gall vttered in the preface therof againft this difputation, concludeth the fame with thefe pafsionate words, as they are in Fox.

D. *Ridleyes* pafsionate fpeach of the difputation.

77. *Thus vvas ended the moft glorious difputation of the moft holy Fathers, Sacrificers, Doctors and Maiflers, vvho fought moft manfully for their God and Gods, for their faith and felicity, for their countrey and kitchen, for their beuty and belly, vvith triumphant applaufes and famous of the vvhole vniuerfity. So hee.* And by this yow may know the man, and how much his words are to be credited; yow hauing confidered what hath byn laid downe before, by Fox his owne report, touching the fubftance of the difputation and authorityes of Fathers, alleaged and examined and fhifted of, though in the forme of fcholafticall difputation and vrging arguments, yt may be there were fome diforders; yet that maketh not fo much to the purpofe, how arguments were vrged againft them, as how they were aunfwered by them; and yet could not the diforder be fo great, as it was vnder *Ridley* himfelfe in the Cambridge-difputation, as is moft euident to the reader by Fox his owne relation, who as before I haue noted, is always to be prefumed to relate the worft for vs, and the beft for himfelfe in all thefe actions.

Fox *pag.* 1330.

78. Wherfore yt is not a little to be confidered, what was the difference in fubftance or fubftantiall proofes, brought forth in the *Cambridge*

bridge Proteſtant-diſputations vnder *K. Edward*, and theſe *Oxford* Catholike-diſputations vnder *Q. Mary*; and whether *Doctor Ridley* that was moderator of thoſe, or *Doctor VVeſton* prolocutor in theſe, did beſt vrge or ſolue arguments againſt their aduerſaryes; for that this conſideration and compariſon only, will giue a great light to diſcerne alſo the difference of the cauſes therin defended. One thinge alſo more is greatly in my opinion to be weighed in this matter, which is, that the ſaid auncient Fathers hauinge to perſuade ſo high and hard a myſtery as this is, that Chriſts true and naturall fleſh and bloud, are really vnder the formes of bread and wyne, by vertue of the Prieſts conſecration, they were forced to vſe all the manner of moſt ſignificant ſpeaches, which they could diuiſe to expreſſe the ſame, and to beate yt into the peoples heads and mynds, though contrary to their ſenſes and common reaſon, and therby to fly from the oppoſite hereſie and infidelity of our Sacramentaryes; lurkinge naturally in the harts of fleſh and bloud, and of ſenſuall people; but ſynce that tyme by Sathans incytation, broached and brought forth publikely into the world. For meetinge wherwith the holy prouidence of almighty God was, that the forſaid Fathers ſhould by all ſorts of moſt ſignificant ſpeaches & phraſes, as hath byn ſaid, ſo cleerly lay open their meanings in this matter, as no reaſonable man can doubt therof, and not only this, but alſo that they ſhould vſe certaine

Y 2   exag-

exaggerations the better to explane themfelues, fuch as they are wont to do in other
controuerfies alfo, when they would vehemently oppofe themfelues againft any error
or herefie,as by the examples of *Saint Auguftine*
againft the *Pelagians* in behalfe of *Grace*, and
againft the Manichees in the defence of *Freewill*. And of *S. Hierome* againft *Iouinian* for the
priuiledge of *Virginity aboue marriage*. and other
like queftions, wherin the faid Fathers, to
make themfelues the better vnderftood, do
vfe fometymes fuch exaggeratiue fpeaches,as
they may feeme to inclyne fomewhat to the
other extreme, which indeed they do not,but
do fhew therby their feruour in defence of the
truth, and hatred of the herefie which they
impugne.

The Fa-
thers effe-
ctuall
fpeaches
to per-
fuade the
reall-pre-
fence.

79.   And the like may be obferued in this article of the reall-prefence, of Chrifts facred
body in the Sacrament of the Altar, which
being a myftery of moft high importance, and
hardeft to be beleeued, as aboue humayne
fenfe and reafon, and therfore called by them:
the myracle of myfteryes: yt was neceffary for

Chryfoft.
hom. 61. ad
Pop. An-
t·och. &
alij.

them, I fay, to vfe as many effectuall wayes,
as they pofsible could for perfuadinge the faid
truth vnto the people, and for preuenting the
diftruftfull cogitations and fuggeftions both
of humayne infirmity,and diabolicall infidelity againft the receaued faith and truth of this
article; and fo they did, not only vfinge moft
cleere, plaine effectuall and fignificant manner of expounding themfelues,and their meaninge,

ninge, but many such exaggerations also, as
must needs make vs see the desire they had, to
be rightly and fully vnderstood therein. For
better consideration of which point (being of
singular moment as hath byn said) the reader
shall haue a little patience, whilst I detayne
my selfe somewhat longer, then I meant
to haue done, in layinge forth the same before him.

80.   And first of all, concerninge the effectuall speaches for vtteringe the truth of their
beleefe in this article, yow haue heard much
in the former disputation, and heere we shall
repeat some points againe, which in effect are,
that wheras the said Fathers founded themselues ordinaryly vpon those speaches of our
Sauiour: *This is my body vvhich shalbe giuen for yow:*   *Matth.* 26.
my flesh is truly meate, and my bloud is truly drinke.   *Luc.* 14.
The bread vvhich I shall giue yow is my flesh for the life   *Ioan.* 6.
of the vvorld, and other like sentences of our
Sauiour; the Fathers do not only vrge all the
circumstances heere specified or signified, to
proue yt to be the true naturall and substantiall body of Christ (as that yt was to be giuen
for vs the next day, after Christs words were
spoken, that yt was to be giuen for the life of
the whole world, & that yt was truly meate,
and truly Christs flesh) but do adde also diuers
other circumstances of much efficacy to confirme the same, affirminge the same more in
particular; *that it is* the very same body which
was borne of the blessed Virgin, the very
same body that suffered on the Crosse, *corpus*

     affixum,

affixum, verberatum, crucifixum, cruentatum, lancea
vulneratum (ſaith S. *Chryſoſtome*) the ſelfe-ſame
„ body, that was nayled, beaten, crucified, blou-
„ ded, wounded with a ſpeare, is receaued by vs
„ in the Sacrament. Whervnto S. *Auſten* addeth
this particularity, that yt is the ſelfe-ſame body that walked heere amonge vs vpon earth.

Aug. in
Pſalm. 98.

As he vvalked heere in fleſh (ſaith he) *amonge vs* ; ſo
the very ſelfe-ſame fleſh doth he giue to be eaten, and
therfore no man eateth, that fleſh ; *but firſt adoreth it;*
and *Hiſichius* addeth ; *that he gaue the ſeife-ſame*

Heſich. in
cap 12.
Leuit.

body, vvherof the Angell Gabriell ſaid to the Virgin
Mary, that it ſhould be conceaued of the holy Ghoſt.
And yet further ; yt is the ſame body (ſaith
S. *Chryſoſtome*) that the *Magi*, or learned men

Chryſoſt.
hom. 2. in
2. ad Cor.

did adore in the manger. *But thou doſt ſee him*
(ſaith he) *not in the manger, but in the Altar, not in*
the armes of a vvoman, but in the hands of a Prieſt.

Aug. in
Pſalm. 33.
concion, 1.
& 2.

The very ſame fleſh (ſaith S. *Auſten* againe) *that ſate*
at the table in the laſt ſupper, and vvaſhed his diſciples
feet ; *The very ſame* (I ſay) *did Chriſt giue with his*
owne hands to his diſciples, vvhen he ſaid; take eate, this
is my body, &c. *And ſo did he beare himſelfe in his*
owne hands, vvhich vvas propheſied of Dauid, but ful-
filled only by Chriſt in that Supper.

81.   Theſe are the particularityes vſed by the
Fathers for declaring what body they meane;
and can there be any more effectuall ſpeaches
then theſe? but yet harken further. *Thou muſt*

Cyrill. Hie-
roſ. Cathec.
4. myſtagog.

know and hold for moſt certaine (ſaith S. *Cyrill*) *that*
this vvhich ſeemeth to be bread, is not bread but Chriſts
body, though the taſt doth iudge it bread. And againe
the ſame Father; *Vnder the forme or ſhew of bread,*

is giuen

is giuen to thee the body of Christ, & vnder the forme or shape of wine, is giuen to thee the bloud of Christ, &c. And S. *Chrysostome* to the same effect: *VVe must not beleeue our senses eassie to be beguiled,* &c. *VVe must simply, and vvithout all ambyguity beleeue the vvords of Christ sayinge: This is my body,* &c. *O how many say now adayes, I vvould see him, I vvould behould his visage, his vestments,* &c. *But he doth more then this, for he giueth himselfe not only to be seene, but to be touched also, handled and eaten by thee.* Nor only do the Fathers affirme so asseuerantly, that yt is the true naturall body of Christ, though yt appeare bread in forme and shape, and that we must not beleeue our senses heerin; but do deny expressely that yt is bread after the words of consecration, wherof yow heard longe discourses before out of S. *Ambrose* in his books *de sacramentis,* and *de initiandis. Before the words of consecration, it is bread* (saith he) *but after consecration, de pane fit caro Christi,* of bread yt *is made the flesh of Christ;* And note the word *(fit)* yt is made. And againe. *Before the words of Christ be vttered* (in the consecration) *the chalice is full of vvine and vvater; but vvhen the vvords of Christ haue vvrought their effect,* ibi sanguis efficitur qui redemit plebem, *there is made the bloud that redeemed the people.* And marke in like manner the word *efficitur,* is made, and consider whether any thinge can be spoken more plainly.

83.   But yet the Fathers cease not heere, but do passe much further to inculcate the truth of this matter, reprehending sharply all doubt, suspition or ambiguity, which the weaknesse

Chrysost. hom. 60. ad Pop. Antioch.

Ambr. l. 4. de Sacram. cap. 4. & l. de initiand.

All doubts about this matter condemned.

of

of our flesh or infection of heresie may suggest
in this matter. S. *Cyrill* reasoneth thus: *VVheras Christ hath said of the bread, this is my body, vvho vvill dare to doubt therof? and vvheras he hath said of the wine, this is my bloud, vvho vvill doubt or say yt is not his bloud? he once turned vvater into vvine in Cana of Galiley by his only will, which wine is like vnto bloud, and shall vve not thinke him vvorthy to be beleeued, vvhen he saith, that he hath changed vvine into his bloud?* So he. And S. *Ambrose* to the same effect. *Our Lord Iesus Christ doth testifie vnto vs, that we do receaue his body and bloud, and may we doubt of his creditt or testimony?* And the other Saint *Cyrill* of *Alexandria* saith to the same effect; that in this mystery we should not so much as aske *quomodo how yt can be done? Iudaicum enim verbum est* (saith he) *& æterni supplicij causa:* For yt is a Iewish word, and cause of euerlastinge torment. And before them both Saint *Hilary* left wrytten this exhortation: *These things ,saith he) that are wrytten, lett vs read, and those things that vve reade lett vs vnderstand, and so vve shall perfectly performe the duty of true faith; for that these points vvhich vve affirme of the naturall verity of Christs being in vs, except we learne them of Christ himselfe, we affyrme them wickedly and foolishly, &c. VVherfore, vvheras he saith my flesh is truly meat, and my bloud is truly drinke, there is no place left to vs of doubting concerning the truth of Christs body & bloud, for that both by the affirmation of Christ himselfe, and by our owne beleese, there is (in the Sacrament) the flesh truly and the bloud truly of our Sauiour.*

83.   So great S. *Hilary:* and *Eusebius Emissenus*
bringeth

Cyrill Hier. catech. mystagog. 4.

Ambr. l. 4. de Sacerdot. cap. 4.

Cyril. Alex. l. 4. in c. 13. Ioan.

Hilar. l. 8. de trinit. cont. Arrian.

bringeth in Chriſt our Sauiour ſpeakinge in
theſe words: *For ſo much as my fleſh is truly meat,* Euſeb.
and my bloud is truly drinke, lett all doubtfullnes of in Emiſſenus.
fidelity depart ; for ſo much as he vvho is the author of Paſch.
the gift, is vvittneſſe alſo of the truth therof. And S.
Leo to the ſame effect: *Nothinge at all is to be* Leo ſerm.6.
doubted of the truth of Chriſts body , and bloud in the de teiurio
Sacrament, &c. *And thoſe do in vaine aunſwere amen* 7. menſ.
(when they receaue yt) *if they diſpute againſt that*
vvhich is affirmed. And finally S. Epiphanius con- Epiph. in
cludeth thus : *He that beleeueth it not to be the very* Anccr.
body of Chriſt in the Sacrament , is fallen from grace
and ſaluation.

84. And by this we may ſee the earneſt-
neſſe of the Fathers in vrginge the beleefe of
Chriſts true fleſh, and bloud in the Sacrament;
But they ceaſe not heere , but do preuent and
exclude all ſhifts of Sacramentaryes, which by
Gods holy ſpiritt they forſaw , euen in thoſe
auncient dayes, affirminge that not by faith
only, or in figure, or image, or ſpiritually alone
Chriſts fleſh is to be eaten by vs ; but really,
ſubſtantially, and corporally: *Not only by faith*
(ſaith S. Chryſoſtome) *but in very deed he maketh vs* Chryſoſt. in
his body, reducinge vs as yt were into one maſſe or ſub- hom. 87. in
ſtance vvith himſelfe. And Saint Cyrill: *Not only by* Matth.
faith and charity are we ſpiritually conioyned to Chriſt Cyril. Alex.
(*by his fleſh in the Sacrament*) *but corporally alſo* l.10. in cap.
by communication of the ſame fleſh. And S. Chryſo- Chryſoſt. ib.
ſtome againe: *Not only by loue, but in very deed are we*
conuerted into his fleſh by eatinge the ſame. And Saint
Cyrill againe: *VVe receauinge (in the Sacrament* Cyril. Alex.
corporally and ſubſtantially the ſonne of God vnited na- ib. l. 11. in
turally Ioan. c. 27.

*turally to his Father, we are clarified & glorified ther-
by, and made partakers of his supreme nature.* Thus
they. Wheruntofor more explication addeth

Theophil.
Alex. in
cap. 10.
Marc.

Theophilact: *VVhen Christ said: This is my body*; he
*shewed that it vvas his very body in deed, and not any
figure correspondent thervnto, for he said not; this is the
figure of my body; but, this is my body; by vvhich vvords
the bread is transformed by an vnspeakable operation,
though to vs it seeme still bread.* And againe in ano-

Idem in ca.
6. Ioan.

ther place. *Behould that the bread vvhich is eaten by
vs in the mysteryes, is not only a figuration of Christs
flesh, but the very flesh indeed, for Christ said not, that
the bread vvhich I shall giue yow, is the figure of my
flesh, but my very flesh indeed, for that the bread is tranf-
formed by* * *secrett vvords into the flesh.* And ano-

* arcanis
verbis.

ther Father more auncient then he, aboue
twelue hundred yeares past, handlinge those
words of Christ *This is my body*, saith: *It is not the*

Magnes l. 3.
ad Theofti-
nem.

figure of Christs body and bloud; *vt quidam stupida
mente nugati sunt*; as some blockish mynds haue
trifled; *but it is truly the very body and bloud of our
Sauiour indeed.* And finally the whole generall
Councell of Nice the second, aboue 800. yeares

Conc. Ni-
can. 2. act. 6

past, hath these words: *do yow read, as longe as
yow vvill, yow shall neuer find Christ or his Apostles, or
the Fathers to haue called the vnbloudy sacrifice of
Christ offered by the Priest, an image* (or representation) *but the very body and bloud of Christ it selfe.*
And could the auncient Fathers speake more
effectually, properly or cleerly then this?

85.   And yet he that will examine and weigh
their sayings, a man exactly shall find them to
speake, in a certaine manner more effectually:

for

for that they did ftudy, (as we haue faid) how
to vtter their meaninge with emphafie. *S. Hi-*
lary vfeth this kind of argument: *yf the word of*
God were truly made flesh, then do we truly receaue his
flesh in the Lords fupper, and therby he is to be efteemed
to dwell in vs naturally: S. Cyrill proueth, *not only*
a fpirituall, but a naturall and bodily vnion to be be-
tweene vs and Chrift, by eatinge his flesh in the Sacra-
ment. Theodorete doth proue that Chrift tooke
flefh of the bleffed Virgin, and afcended vp
with the fame, and holdeth the fame there,
by that he giueth to vs his true flefh in the Sacrament; for that otherwayes he could not
giue vs his true flefh to eate, yf his owne flefh
were not true, feeing that he gaue the fame
that he carryed vp, and retayneth in heauen.
S. Irenaus, S. Iuftine, & *S. Chryfoftome* do proue not
only this, but the refurrection alfo of our bodyes by the truth of Chrifts flefh in the Sacra-
crament, for that our flefh ioyninge with his
flefh which is immortall, ours fhalbe immortall alfo. And the fame *Saint Irenaus* alfo doth
proue further, that the great God of the ould
Teftament, creator of heauen and earth, was
Chrifts Father; for proofe wherof he alleageth this reafon; that Chrift in the Sacrament
did fullfill the figures of the old Teftament, &
that in particular, wherin bread was a figure
of his flefh, which he fulfilled (faith *Irenaus*)
makinge yt his flefh indeed.

86. I paffe ouer many other formes of
fpeaches no leffe effectuall; which doe eafily
declare the Fathers mynds and meaninges in
this

Emphati-
call & ef-
fectuall
fpeaches
of the fa-
thers.
Hilar. lib. 8.
de Trinit.
Cyril. l. 11.
in Ioan. c. 26

Theod. dial.
2. inconfus.

Iren. lib. 4.
cont. hæref.
cap. 3.
Iuftin apol.
2. ad An-
tonin Piuin
Imp.
Chryfoft.
hom 60. &
61. ad pop.
Antioch.

*Optat. l.6.
contra Do-
natist.* this point, as that of *Optatus Mileuitanus*, who accused the Donatists of sacriledge & horrible wickednesse, for hauing broken downe Catholike Altars, wheron the body, and bloud of Christ had byn borne: *VVhat is so sacrilegious* (saith he) *as to breake downe, scrape and remoue the Altars of God, on vvhich your selues haue sometymes offered, and the members of Christ haue byn borne,* &c.

Chalice-
breakers. *VVhat is an Altar, but the seate of the body and bloud of Christ? and this monstrous villany of yours is doubled, for that yow haue broken also the chalices, vvhich did beare the bloud of Christ himselfe.* So he. And is there any Protestant, that will speake thus at this day? or doth not this reprehension agree fully to Protestants, that haue broken downe more Altars, and chalices, then euer the Do-

*Leo serm.
7. de Pas-
chate.* natists did? Saint *Leo* the first saith: *that the truth of Christs true body and bloud in the Sacrament, was so notorious in his dayes; vt nec ab infantium linguis taceretur.* That very infants did professe the same. And in the same sermon he saith: that the body of Christ is so receaued by vs in the Sacrament; *vt in carnem ipsius, qui caro nostra factus est, transeamus,* that we should passe into his flesh, who by his incarnation is made our flesh. Saint *Chrysostome* in many places of his works, doth vse such deuout, reuerent and significant speaches of that, which is conteyned in the Sacrament vnder the formes of bread, & wyne after consecration, as no doubt can be of his meaninge, whereof yow haue heard diuers points before in the disputations, *as that it deserued the highest honour in earth; that he*

did

did ſhew it lyinge vpon the *Altar*; that the Angeils deſcended at the tyme of conſecration, and did adore *Chriſt*
there preſent vvith tremblinge and feare, and durſt not
looke vpon him for the *Maieſtie of his preſence* . And
other ſuch ſpeaches, which is conforme to
that before cyted in the diſputation out of the
Councell of Nice : *Credamus iacere in illa menſa*
ſacra, agnum Dei à Sacerdotibus ſacrificatum. Let vs
beleeue to lye on that holy table, the lambe of
God ſacrificed by Prieſts. And is there any
Proteſtant that will ſpeake thus?

87. But aboue all the reſt are thoſe ſpeaches,
which before I ſaid to tend to a certeyne exaggeration, as that, *eur fleſh is turned into his fleſh*
by receauinge the bleſſed Sacrament : that our fleſh is
nouriſhed by his ; *and that of two fleſhes there is made*
but one fleſh; Whervnto do appertayne not only thoſe former phraſes, which already yow
haue heard of the naturall and corporall vnity ; which the Fathers do ſo often inculcate ,,
to be betweene Chriſt and vs, by eatinge his ,,
fleſh in the Sacrament, & that we are brought ,,
therby into one maſſe , or ſubſtance of fleſh ,,
with him ; but many other like ſignificant
manners for vtteringe their mynds, as that of
S. *Chryſoſtome* : *he nouriſheth vs vvith his owne body,*
and doth ioyne and conglutinate our fleſh to his. And
againe: That by his body (giuen vs in the Sacrament) *Se nobis commiſcuit, & in vnum nobiſcum*
redegit. He hath mixt himſelfe to vs , and ,,
brought himſelfe and vs into one body and ,,
fleſh. And yet further: he doth permitt him- ,,
ſelfe not only to be handled by vs , but alſo to ,,

be

Chryſoſt.
hom. 61. ad
Pop. An-
tioch. &
hom. 6. de
verbis
Iſaia. &
hom. 3. de
incompre-
hens. Dei
natura.

Exaggera-
tiue ſpea-
ches of
the Fa-
thers to
vtter their
minds the
more
cleerly.

Chryſoſt.
hom. 61. ad
Pop. An-
tioch. &
hom. 45. in
Ioan.

be eaten, and our teeth to be faftened vpon his flefh, and vs to be filled with the fame flefh; which is the greateft point of loue (faith *Saint Chryfoftome*) that pofsible can be imagined. So

Cyrill.
Alex lib.4.
in loan.cap.
17.

he. And conforme to this *S. Cyrill* of *Alexandria* vttereth himfelfe after another fort, for he vfeth the example of leuen, which *Saint Paul* doth touch in his epiftle to the Corinthians,

1.Cor. 5.

when he faith; *that a little leuen doth leuen a whole bach; euen fo* (faith *S. Cyrill*) *the flesh of Chrift ioyned to our flesh, doth leuen or pearfe through it, and conuert*

Idem. l.10.
in loan.cap.
33.

it into it felfe. And in another place he vfeth this fimilitude ; *that as vvhen yow take a peece of vvax melted at the fire , and do droppe the fame vpon another peece of vvax , thefe two vvaxes are made one;* fo by the communication of Chrifts body and bloud vnto vs, he is in vs and we in him.

88.   Another auncient Father alfo vpon the point of 1200. yeares gone had this fimilitude:

Marcus
Anachoreta
in 1.ad Cor.

As wine (faith he) *is mixed vvith him that drinketh the fame, in fuch fort, as the wine is in him , and he in the wine: fo is the bloud of Chrift mixed alfo vvith him that drinketh the fame in the Sacrament.* And *S.Irenaus, Tertullian,* & *S. Iuftinus* Martyr, all of them elder then this man, do vfe commonly this phrafe of nourifhinge , and feedinge our flefh

Iren. lib. 4.
cont. haref.
cap. 34.

by the flefh of Chrift. *How do they affirme* (faith *S. Irenaus* againft certayne heretiks that denied the refurrection' that our flesh fhall come to corruption, and not receaue life againe, vvhich is nourifhed by*

Ibid. lib. 5.
cap. 2.

the body and bloud of Chrift? And againe. *Ex quibus augetur & confiftit carnis noftra fubftantia .* Of which body and bloud of Chrift, the fub-

ftance

ſtance of our fleſh is encreaſed and conſiſteth. And *Tertullian*, *caro*, *corpore & ſanguine Chriſti veſcitur*, *&c.* Our fleſh doth feed on the body and bloud of Chriſt. And marke that he ſaith the fleſh, and not only the ſoule. And *Iuſtine* in his ſecond Apology to the Emperour *Antoninus* talkinge of the Sacrament, ſaith, it is, *cibus quo ſanguis carneſq; noſtra aluntur.* The meat wherwith our bloud and fleſh is fedd; and to this manner of ſpeach appertayne thoſe ſayings of *S. Chryſoſtome*: *Altare meum cruentum ſanguine*, my Altar that is made redd with bloud. Where he ſpeaketh in the perſon of Chriſt. And againe to him that had receaued the Sacrament, *dignus es habitus qui eius carnes lingua tangeres*: Thou are made worthy to touch with thy tongue the fleſh of Chriſt: And yet further in another place: *Thou ſeeſt Chriſt ſacrificed in the Altar, the Prieſt attendinge to his ſacrifice, and powring out prayers; the multitude of people receauinge the Sacrament*, *pratioſo illo ſanguine intingi & rubefieri.* To be died and made read with that pretious bloud. All which ſpeaches and many more, that for breuity I pretermitt, though they tend to a certayne exaggeration (as hath byn ſaid) yet do they plainly declare the ſenſe, iudgement and beleefe of the Fathers in this article, and ſo albeit literally, and in rigour, they be not in all reſpects verified: yet need we no better arguments to certifie vs of the Fathers meaninges then theſe, to witt, how farre they were of, from the Proteſtants opinions in this myſtery.

Tert. lib. de reſurrect. carnis.

Chryſoſt. hom. 24. in 1. Cor. 10.

Hom. 27. in c. 11. ad Cor.

Ibid. l. 3. de Sacerdot.

89. And

89. And truly yt we would now put downe heere on the contrary fide the Proteſtants aſſertions, and their cold manner of ſpeaches in this behalfe, and compare them with this vehemency of the Fathers; we ſhould preſently ſee a wonderfull difference. I will touch ſome few only conteyned in this booke. Firſt they

1. ſay (and yt is a common refuge of *Cranmer* and the reſt in this diſputation as you haue heard) that their communion-bread is Chriſts true body, as *S. Iohn Baptiſt* was true *Elias*.

2. *Item.* That yt is Chriſts body, as the doue was the holy-ghoſt.

3. *Item.* That the body of Chriſt is eaten in the Sacrament of the Altar, no otherwiſe then yt is in baptiſme.

4. *Item.* That infants when they be baptized do eate the body of Chriſt alſo.

5. *Item.* That Chriſts body is in the Sacrament, as when two or three are gathered togeather in his name.

6. *Item.* That the body of Chriſt is eaten in the Sacrament, as yt is eaten, when wee read ſcriptures, or heare ſermons.

7. *Item.* That the breakinge of Chriſts body, is nothinge but the breaking of the ſcriptures to the people. And theſe are the common phraſes of all lightly. For I lett paſſe many particular aſſertions of ſome, much more cold and contemptible then theſe, wherby yow may eaſily ſee the difference of eſtimation, reuerence, reſpect, and beleefe betweene them and the auncient Fathers.

90. And

90.   And on the other side, he that will consider the great care and warynesse, which the
said Fathers did vse in speakinge properly and
exactly, as well in other mysteryes & articles
of our faith, as in this, shall easily see, that they
could not fall into such excesse of speach, with
open reprehension & contradiction of others,
yf their meaninge had not byn euidént, and
the doctrine Catholike and generally receaued, which they endeauoured to inculcate by
these speaches; for so much as we are taught
by all antiquity, that there was such exact rigour vsed in this behalfe in those dayes, that a
word or sillable could not be spoken amisse,
without present note or checke. And *S. Hierome* saith: *that sometymes for one only vvord heretiks haue byn cast out of the Church.* And *Saint Basill*
being intreated and vrged by a Gouernour of
Constantius the *Arrian* Emperour, to accomodate himselfe in manner of speach only about
two words: *homiousion,* and *homousion* (which
are not, said the gouernour, found in scripture) *he answered him noe: & that for one Sillable he
vvould offer his life, yf it vvere need.* And the like ex-
actnesse did the anciét Fathers, of the Coúcell
of *Ephesus,* shew afterwards in standinge so resolutely for the word *Deipara,* mother of God
against *Nestorius,* & refusing the vse of the other
word *Christipara,* mother of Christ, though the
one & the other of the words réfused, to witt,
homiousion & *Christipara* in their senses are true;
but for that some hereticall meaninge might
lurke therin, they were refused.

The great
vvarynesse
of the Fa-
thers in
speakinge
of articles
of faith.

*Hier. lib. 3.
Apol. cont.
Russin.*

*Theodoret.
lib. 2. hist.
c.18. & 19.*

*Concil.
Ephes. act.
1. & 2.*

Z   91. And

91. And to conclude, yf antiquity was so carefull and vigilant, to exclude dangerous & incommodious speaches in other articles, how much more would yt haue byn in this also of the *reall presence*, yf the said Fathers speaches before rehearsed had not byn true, as in the Protestants sense they cannot be, but must needs tend to most dangerous error of misbeleefe and idolatry? And consequently there is no doubt, but that they would haue byn reproued by other Fathers, yf the Protestants opinions had byn then receaued for truth. And this shall suffice for this Chapter.

OF THE TVVO OTHER

ARTICLES ABOVT

Transubstantiation, *and the Sacra-ment, what passed in this Disputation.*

CHAP. VI.

HAVINGE handled more largely, then was purposed at the beginninge, so much as apperteyneth to the first article of the *reall-presence*, as the ground and foundation of the other two; I meane to be very breefe concer-ninge the rest, as well for that in the *Oxford-Disputations* there was scarse any thinge handled therof;

therof; but only some demonstrations out of
the Fathers alleaged to *Latymer* (which he as
yow haue heard could not aunswere) about
the third and last point; as also for that whatsoeuer was treated therof in the disputations
at *Cambridge*, and in the *Conuocation-house*, especially about *Transubstantiation*, hath byn aunswered for the most part in our former treatise about the reall presence. And albeit it was
some art of the Sacramentaryes, in the beginninge of these controuersies vnder *K. Edward*,
to runne from the discussion of the principall
point, as more cleerly against them, vnto the
question of *Transubstantiation*, for that might
seeme to yeld them some more shew of matter
or obiections to cauill at, as before we haue
declared : yet when the matter commeth to
examination, they haue as little for them in
this as in the other, or rather lesse, for that the
other, to witt, the *reall-presence*, or being of
Christ really and substantially present in the
Sacrament, hauinge byn so euidently proued
against them, as before yow haue seene ; this
other of *Transubstantiation*, being but *modus essen-*
di, the manner how Christ is there, little importeth them; nay themselues do graunt, that
yf Christ be there really present, yt cannot be
denyed but that he is there also by *Transubstan-*
tiation of bread into his body: for so *Father La-*
tymer, yf yow remember, affirmed before in his
disputations, when he was said once to haue
byn a Lutheran (which Lutherans do hould
both Christs body and bread to be togeather

in the

Reall pre-
sence can-
not be
graunted
without
Transubstan
tiation ac-
cording to
Latymer.

in the Sacrament) he aunſwered, I ſay, that he
could neuer perceaue, how *Luther* could de-
Fox *pag.*
1324.
fend his opinion without *Tranſubſtantiation*, &
that the Tygurynes, being alſo Sacramentaryes, did write a booke againſt him in this behalfe, prouinge belike that in grauntinge the
reall preſence, as he did; he muſt needs graunt
Tranſubſtantiation alſo, wherin they had great
reaſon: for that in truth the imagination of
Luther, and Lutherans, that Chriſts body and
bread doe ſtand togeather, vnder the ſame
formes and accidents, and be receaued togeather being ſo different ſubſtances, is a moſt
groſſe and fond imagination; ſo as the Lutherans graunting the one, & denying the other,
are condemned of abſurdity euen by the
Zuinglians themſelues, as yow ſee, and as we
ſay alſo iuſtly.

2.   And on the other ſide we ſay in like manner, as before hath byn noted, that the Zuinglians and Caluiniſts, and other Sacramentaryes denyinge wholy the ſaid *reall preſence,* do
in vayne wrangle about *Tranſubſtantiation.* For
as he that ſhould deny (for example ſake) that
any ſubſtance of gould were in a purſe, or any
ſubſtance of wyne in a barrell, ſhould in vaine
diſpute whether the gold were there alone,
or togeather with ſome baſer metall, as ſiluer,
tynne, or copper, or whether the wyne were
there alone, or in company of water; ſo in this
controuerſie yt is an idle diſputation for Sacramentaryes to diſcuſſe, whether the ſubſtance of Chriſts reall fleſh be alone in the Sacrament,

crament, or togeather with the ſubſtance of bread, for ſo much as they deny yt to be there at all.

3.   Yet notwithſtanding, for that their cheefe altercation is about this point, as by their diſputations may appeare, I ſhall breefely examine their grounds, vvhich, according to B. *Ridleyes* oſtentation vttered in *Cambridge* out of the diuinity chayre, vnder *King Edward* the ſixt, as before yow haue heard, are fiue in number ſett forth in theſe vauntinge words: *The principall grounds or rather head-ſprings of this matter are ſpecially fiue.* Firſt, *the authority, maieſtie, & verity of holy ſcriptures:* the ſecond: *the moſt certayne teſtimonyes of the auncient Catholike Fathers:* the third, *The definition of a Sacrament:* the fourth, *The abhominable hereſie of* Eutiches, *that may enſue of Tranſubſtantiation.* The fifth: *the moſt ſure beleefe of the article of our faith:* He aſcended into heauen. And then a little after he concludeth thus: *Theſe be the reaſons vvhich perſuade me to enclyne to this ſentence and iudgement.*

Ridleyes fiue grounds againſt Tranſubſtantiation at Cambridge. anno 1549. Fox *pag.* 1261.

1.
2.

3.
4.
5.

Fox *ibid.*

4.   Heere yow ſee the principall grounds, or rather *head-ſprings,* that perſuaded *Ridley* to inclyne, or rather declyne, for yet he ſeemed not fully ſetled in this article of beleefe. And albeit theſe grounds may ſeeme to conteyne ſomewhat, in ſhew and ſound of words: yet when the ſubſtance thereof commeth to be examined, they are found to be idle, and puffed vp with words indeed. For firſt what authority, maieſty and verity of ſcriptures doth this man bring forth, trow you, for confirma-

tion

tion of this his vaunt? truly nothing in effect,
or of any shew or probability, but only that yt
is called bread and wyne in the scripture, after
the words of consecration: For which purpose he hauinge alleaged the words of Christ:

*Math. 26.
Marc. 14.* *I will not drinke heereafter of this fruite of the vyne,
vntill I do drinke yt new vvith yow in the kingdome of
my Father:* he inferreth that the fruite of the
vyne is wyne, which we graunt vnto him, &
do hould is called wyne by him after the consecration, as his flesh after the words of conse-
₊ 1.Cor.11. cration is called bread by S. ₊ *Paul,* S. *Luke,* and
other Apostles, affirming yt notwithstanding
to be his owne true body and flesh, but retay-
ninge the name of bread, for that yt was made
of bread, and was bread before, as the serpent
Exod. 7. was called the rodd of *Aaron,* for that yt was
made of that rodd, and not because yt was not
a true serpent afterwards, though yt were still
called a rodd, and to signifie this, that bread
conuerted into Christs flesh is not really
bread afterward, but the true flesh of Christ,
though yt retayne the former name of bread,
yt is not simply called bread but with some
Ioan. 6. addition; *as bread of life: bread of heauen, this bread,*
and the like. And finally Christ himselfe doth
expound what bread yt is in S. *Iohns* ghospell
when he saith: *The bread that I shall giue yow, is my
flesh for the life of the vvorld.*

5. Heere then yow see, that *Ridleyes* text of
scripture; *I vvill not drinke hereafter of the fruite
of the vyne, vntill I drinke yt new vvith yow in the
Kingdome of my Father;* doth not proue that yt
was

was materiall wine which he dronke, for that he should then drinke materiall wyne also in heauen: And yet assoone as *Ridley* had brought forth this place, as though he had done a great feate, and fully performed his promise, for proofe of the authority, maiesty, and verity of scripture, he beginneth presently to excuse himselfe, for that he hath no more store, sayinge. *There be not many places of scripture, that do confirme this thinge; neyther is yt greatly materiall, for yt is inough yf there be any one plaine testimony for the same.* Lo wheruvnto this vaunt of the authority, maiesty, and verity of holy scriptures is come, to witt, to one place, vnderstood and interpreted after his owne meaninge alone, against the vnderstandinge of all antiquity. And though he go about afterwards to scrape togeather diuers other parings of scripture, nothinge at all to the purpose, as, *Yow shall not breake any bone of his: Do yow this in my remembrance: labour for the meate that perisheth not: this is the worke of God, that they beleeue in him whome he hath sent: he that eateth my flesh and drinketh my bloud, dwelleth in me and I in him;* and some other like places: yet as yow see by his owne confession, they are not plaine places, and consequently his vauntinge of authority, maiesty and verity of scriptures, commeth to iust nothinge indeed, but only to words and wynde. Lett vs see what he bringeth for his other foure grounds and headsprings.

6. The second is, *the most certayne testimonyes of the auncient Catholike Fathers.* This we shall examine

Z 4   mine

Fox pag. 1161.

Impertinēt places alleaged against *Transubstantiation.*

Exod 12. 1. Cor 11. Ioan. 6.

Ridleyes secōd groūd of fathers.

mine afterwards when we haue considered
of the other three, yet may yow marke by the
way, that he vseth heere also the superlatiue
degree, *of most certayne testimonyes*, which certainty of testimonyes yow shall find afterward, to be like his *maiesty of scriptures*, already
alleaged. Wherfore let vs see his third ground.

Ridleyes 3.
ground.
The na-
ture of a
Sacramēt.

The third ground (saith he) is the nature of
the Sacrament, which consisteth in three
things: *vnity, nutrition* and *conuersion*. And then
he explaneth himselfe thus: *that as in bread one
loafe is made of many graynes, so signifieth this Sacrament, that we are all one mysticall body in Christ.* And
againe. *As bread nourisheth our body, so doth the body
of Christ nourish our soule.* And thirdly. *As bread is
turned into our substance, so are vve turned into Christs
substance. All vvhich three effects cannot be signified*
(saith he) *by this Sacrament, yf there be Transubstantiation, and no nature of bread left, and therfore
there can be no Transubstantiation.*

7. This is *Maister Ridleyes* deepe diuinity about
the nature of this Sacrament: but yf yow
reade that which we haue noted before in our
Sup. cap. 3.
§. 8. eyght obseruation, concerninge the true definition and nature of a Sacrament in deed,
yow will see that this was great simplicity in
him (though accordinge to his hereticall
groūd, that the Sacramēts doe not giue grace)
to leaue out the principall effect signified in
the Sacrament, which is grace, for that a Sacrament is defined: *A visible signe of inuisible grace
receaued therby.* This Sacrament also is a signe
of Christs body there present vnder the
for mes

formes of bread and wyne: yet deny we not
but that thefe other three effects alfo of vnity, nutrition and conuerfion may be fignified
therby, as in like manner the death and paffion of our Sauiour, wherof this Sacrament is
a memoriall and commemoration : neyther
doth the *Tranfubftantiation* of the bread into the
body of Chrift, lett or take away thefe figni-
fications, for fo much as to make this Sacrament, there is taken bread and wyne, which
naturally doth fignifie thefe effects of vnion,
nutrition, and conuerfion, which *Ridley* heere
mentioneth, though yt be not neceffary, that
the fubftance of the faid bread and wyne
fhould ftill remayne, but only there formes
and accidents, which do fignifie and are fignes
to our fenfes, as much as yf the fubftances
themfelues of bread and wyne were prefent.
As for example the brafen ferpent, did as Fox *pag.*
much reprefent, and was a figne of Chrift in ¹²⁶¹.
refpect of the analogie betwene Chrift and a
true ferpent, as yf he had had the fubftance of
a true ferpent, whereof he had but only the *Exod.* 7.
forme and fhape ; and fo are the outward
formes of bread and wyne, after the words of
confecration, fufficient to reprefent vnto vs
the Analogy that is betweene feedinge the
body, and feedinge the foule, vnity of graines,
and vnity of Chrifts myfticall body which is
his Church.

8. And thus much of *Ridleyes* third ground
which impugneth *Tranfubftantiation* ; which
ground (as yow fee) is fo weake and feeble,

as he

as he that shall build theron, is like to come
to a miserable ruyne of his owne saluation.
But much more ridiculous is his fourth
ground, vttered in these words: *The fourth
ground* (saith he) *is the abhominable heresie of Eutiches, that may ensue of Transubstantiation.* Thus
he saith in his position, but lett vs heare him
afterward in his probation, which is not
much larger then his proposition, for thus he
wryteth: *They which say that Christ is carnally present in the Eucharist, do take from him the verity of
mans nature. Eutiches graunted the diuyne nature in
Christ, but his humayne nature he denyed.* And is
not this a goodly proofe of so great a charge?
Nay is not this a goodly ground and head-
springe of proofes? Consider I pray yow how
these matters do hange togeather. *Eutiches* heresy was, as yow may see in the letters of *Saint
Leo* the first, and in the Councell of *Calcedon*,
that Christs flesh being ioyned to his diuinity
was turned into the same, and so not two distinct natures remayned, but one only made
of them both. And how doth this heresie I
pray yow, follow of our doctrine of Transubstantiation! *Eutiches* said that the diuine
and humayne natures in Christ were confounded togeather, and of two made but one:
we say that they remayne distinct, and do
condemne *Eutiches* for his opinion, and by our
Church he was first accursed and anathematized for the same: *Eutiches* said, Christs humayne nature was turned into his diuine; we
say only that bread and wyne is turned into
                                            Chri**s**

Chrifts flefh and bloud: what likeneffe hath
this with *Eutiches* herefie? *But* (faith *Ridley*) *vve
do take from Chrift the verity of mans nature* . This
is a fiction and foolifh calumniation, as before
yow haue heard, and confequently deferueth
no further refutation.

9.　The fifth ground, *is* (faith he) *the moſt ſure* *Ridleyes 5.*
beleefe of the article of our faith: He aſcended into ground
heauen. This ground yf yow remember hath Chrifts
byn ouerthrowne before, and abandoned by affenſion.
Ridley himfelfe in his *Oxford-diſputation*, where
he graunted; *that he did not ſo ſtraitly tye Chriſt vp
in heauen* (to vſe his owne words) *but that he
may come downe on earth at his pleaſure*. And againe Fox pag.
in another place of the ſaid diſputation: *VVhat* 1314. &
letteth but that Chriſt yf yt pleaſe him, and vvhen yt 1515.
pleaſeth him, may be in heauen and in earth? &c.
And yet further to *Doctor Smith* that aſked him
this queſtion: *Doth he ſo ſitt at the right hand of
his Father, that he doth neuer forſake the ſame?
Ridley* aunfwered: *Nay I do not bynd Chriſt in
heauen ſo ſtraitly*. By which aunfweres yow
fee, that this whole principall ground and
head-fpringe of Ridleyes arguments againft
Tranſubſtantiation, is quite ouerthrowne. For yf
Chriſt in fleſh after his afcenſion may be alfo
on earth when he will, as *Ridley* heere graunteth, then is it not againſt the article of our
Creed (*He aſcended into heauen,*) to beleeue, that
not withſtandinge his afcenſion, he may be
alfo on earth in the Sacrament. And albeit
Ridley do cyte heere certayne places of *S. Auguſtine,* that do feeme to ſay: that Chriſt after
his

his afcenfion is no more conuerfant amonge
vs vpon earth;yet that is not to be vnderftood
of his being in the Sacrament, which is a fpirituall manner of being, but of his corporall
manner of conuerfation, as he liued vifibly
among his difciples before his afcenfion. And
this is fufficient for difcuffion of this fifth
ground, wherof the cheefe particulars haue
byn handled in diuers places before.

The dif-
cuffion of
the Fa-
thers au-
thorityes
alleaged
by *Ridley.*
Dionyf.
Areop. in
Ecclef. Hie-
rarch.

p. 3, 8

1. Cor. 11.

Ignat. in
epift. ad
Philadelph.

10. Now then will we returne to his fecond
ground againe, *of the moft certayne teftimonyes of*
the auncient Catholike Fathers. And firft he allea-
gath *Saint Dionyfius Areopagita,* for that in fome
places of his works he callerh yt *bread.* And
the like of *Saint Ignatius* to the *Philadelphians,*
which we deny not, for *S. Paul* alfo calleth yt
fo, as before we haue fhewed: but yet fuch
bread, as in the fame place he declareth to be
the true body of Chrift, fayinge: *that he which*
receaueth yt vnworthily, fhalbe guilty of the body and
bloud of Chrift, addinge for his reafon *non dyudi-*
cans corpus Domini, for not difcerninge the body
of our Lord there prefent. And fo *S. Ignatius*
in the very felfe-fame place faith: *that yt is the*
flefh and bloud of Chrift, as yow may read in
that Epiftle.

11. After thefe he citeth *Irenæus* whofe words
are: *Euchariftia ex duabus rebus conftans, terrena &*
calefti, which *Ridley* tranflateth thus: Sacra-
,, mentall bread confiftinge of two natures
,, earthly and heauenly: But by *Maifter Ridleyes*
leaue *Euchariftia* in this place is fraudulently
tranflated by him *Sacramentall bread,* except he

men a

meane as we do, and as *Ireneus* did, that yᵗ
was the body of Chriſt, but called bread for
that yt was made of bread: For that *Ireneus* in
the very ſame place, wryting againſt heretiks
asketh this queſtion: *Quomodo conſtabit eis, eum* — *Iren. lib. 4:*
panem in quo gratiæ acta ſint, corpus eſſe Domini ſui? — *cont. hareſ.*
How ſhall yt be made euident to theſe here-
tiks, that this bread, in which thanks haue
byn giuen, is the body of their Lord? Wherto he aunſwered, and proueth the ſame by
diuers arguments: ſo as no place of any Father could haue byn alleaged more againſt
himſelfe, then this is by *Ridley*. And as for
that he ſaith, that the Euchariſt conſiſteth of
two natures, *earth-ly* and *heauenly*, he meaneth
euidently, by the heauenly nature, the true body of Chriſt, and by the earthly nature, the
externall ſymbolls, formes, and accidents. And
ſo much of him.

12. And the ſelfe-ſame thinge do meane — *Theod. dial:*
both *Theoderete* and *Gelaſius*, heere alſo by him — *2 Gelaſ. l.*
alleaged, as vſinge the like phraſes; that the — *de duabus*
natures of bread and wyne do remayne, — *naturis*
which they vnderſtand of the externall ſymbolls, formes and accidents. For as for the
reall preſence, they do both of them affirme yt
in the ſame places by *Ridley* alleaged. And ſo
this ſhall ſuffice for this place, there being
nothing els worthy aunſweringe. And now
yf yow conſider, what variety of plaine and
perſpicuous authorityes haue byn alleaged by
vs before, both out of the diſputations and
otherwiſe, for confirmation of the Catholike
beleefe

beleefe of the *reall presence* and *Transubstantia-*
tion, yow will eafily fee what broken wares
thefe bee, which Proteftants bringe forth to
the contrary, and how fondly this fecond
ground of *Ridleyes* proofes is intituled by him;
the most certaine testimonyes of the auncient Catholike
Fathers: vvho after my iudgement (faith he) *do suffi-*
ciently declare this matter. And I will not greatly
ftand againft him, for that the mans iudgement being peruerted by herefie, faction and
ambition of thofe tymes, any thinge would
feeme fufficient to him to draw him to that
byas, whervnto himfelfe inclyned. And thus
much of this article.

Fox pag. 1261.

About the third Article of the Sacrifice of the Maſſe. §. 2.

13.   For that there was little or nothinge difputed of this third article, eyther in *Cambridge,*
Oxford, or *London*, except only a little againft
Latymer, as prefently we fhall fee, I haue
thought beft to betake me only to *Ridleyes* determination in this matter: he beginneth the
fame thus: *Now in the later conclusion, concerninge*
the facrifice, becaufe yt dependeth vpon the firft (to
witt of the *reall-prefence*.) *I will in few vvords de-*
clare vvhat I thinke; for yf we once agree in that, the
vvhole controuerfie in the other vvill foone be at an end.
Marke heere good reader that *Ridley* confeffeth this controuerfie of the facrifice to de-

Fox pag. 1262.

pend

pend of the *reall-presence*, which *reall-presence* being so substantially proued before, as yow haue heard, little doubt can be made of this; yet will *Ridley* tell vs what he thinketh (a goodly ground for vs to hange our soules on) which is, that there is no sacrifice at all, but that of Christ vpon the Crosse, and he will tell vs also his grounds for so thinkinge : *Two things* (saith he) *there be, vvhich do persuade me, to* Fox *ibid. vvitt, certayne places of scripture, and certayne testimonyes of the Fathers.* So he. And as for scriptures, he alleageth no one, but out of the Epistle to the Hebrues; *that Christ entred once for* Heb. 9. *all into the holy-place, and obtayned for vs eternall redemption.* And againe. *That Christ vvas once offered* Heb. 10. *to take away the sinnes of many.* And yet further: *that with one offeringe he made perfect for euer those that are sanctified.* And hauinge cyted these places, he maketh this conclusion . *These scriptures do persuade me to beleeue, that there is no other oblation of Christ (albeit I am not ignorant there are many sacrifices) but that vvhich vvas once made vpon the Crosse.*

14. Heere now yow may see the force of a passionate iudgement, and how little doth suffice to persuade a man to any heresie, that is inclined thervnto of himselfe. I would aske of *Ridley* heere, how chaunceth yt that S. *Chrysostome,* S. *Basill,* S. *Ambrose,* S. *Cyrill,* S. *Hierome,* S. *Augustine* and other Fathers cyted before so aboundantly, and perspicuously affirming the dayly sacrifice of the masse, and distinguishing betweene *Cruentum & incruentum sacrificium,* the

bloudy

bloudy sacrifice of Christ on the Crosse once offered vp for all; And the selfe-same sacrifice dayly reiterated, and offered againe in many places throughout the world, after an vnbloudy manner: how these Fathers, I say, had not byn persuaded, as *Ridley* was, by these places of scripture to deny the Sacrifice of the Masse? had they not read (thinke yow) the Epistle to the Hebrewes; or did they not ynderstand yt as well as *Ridley*? and how then was *Ridley* persuaded, and not they? there reason is, that, which he touched before, when he said: *after my iudgement*, *&c.* For that he followed his owne iudgement, blynded by his owne affection in this point against the masse, and they followed not their owne iudgement, but the vniuersall iudgement and beleefe of the Catholike Church in their dayes, and so must *Ridley* giue vs leaue to follow them, rather then him.

15.   As for his second motiue of certayne testimonyes of the Fathers, yt is so weake and broken a thinge, as he dareth not come forth with yt, but only quoteth certayne places of *Saint Augustine*, wherby he saith that the Christians keepe a memoriall of the sacrifice past; and that *Fulgentius* in his booke *de fide* calleth the same a commemoration. And these be all the Fathers, and their authorityes which he alleageth for his second motiue: wherby yow may see, that he was moued by a little against the masse: For we deny not but that the sacrifice of the masse is a commemoration also of the

the death, pasſion, and Sacrifice of Chriſt
vpon the Croſſe, and he that in ſteed of theſe
impertinent citations out of *S. Auſten* nothing
at all to the purpoſe, would lay downe on the
contrary ſide, all the cleere, euident, and effectuall places, ſentences, diſcourſes and aſſe-
uerations, which this holy Father hath in
profe and confirmation of the viſible externall ſacrifice of the maſſe, wherin Chtiſts ſacred body, the ſame that was offered on the
Croſſe, is offered againe dayly both for quicke
and dead by Chriſtian Catholike Prieſts on
the Altar, might make a whole Treatiſe ther-
of, and I remitt the reader to *Hieronymus Tor-*   *Torrenſ. lib*
renſis his collection, called *Confeßio Auguſtiniana,*   *Confeſſ.*
where throughout a 11. or 12. paragraphes, he   *Auguſt*
lib. 3. cap. 7.
doth ſet downe large authorityes, moſt plaine
and euident out of the ſaid Fathers works.
And yt is inough for vs at this tyme, that *La-*
tymer being preſſed in his diſputations with
diuers of theſe authorityes anſweted: *I am not*   *Fox. pag.*
aſhamed to acknowledge my ignorance, and theſe teſti-   1325.
monyes are more then I can beare away; and after
againe, being further preſſed with the moſt
euident authorityes of *S. Auguſtine,* and *S. Chry-*
ſoſtome in particular, affirminge that the ſacrifice of the maſſe is propitiatory both for
quicke and dead, he aunſwered: *The Doctors*
might be deceaued in ſome points, though not in all
things: I beleeue them when they ſay vvell. And yet
further: *I am of their faith vvhen they ſay vvell. I re-*   *Fox pag.*
ferre my ſelfe to my L. of Canterburyes booke vvholy   1326.
heerin. And yet againe. *I haue ſaid vvhen they ſay*

vvell

vvell and bringe the ſcriptures for them , I am of their faith. And further. *Auguſtine requireth not to be be-leeued.* So he. And by this yow may ſee, what accompt they make both of S. *Auguſtine* and other Fathers, notwithſtandinge for a ſhew, ſometymes they will cyte ſome places out of them little to the purpoſe, but being witting in their owne conſciences, that really and ſubſtantially they make againſt them, they ſhift them of finally in this order as yow haue heard, and will beleeue and teach only as pleaſeth themſelues, which is the peculiar pride and willfullnes of hereſie, from which God deliuer vs. And with this I end this whole Treatiſe.

F I N I S.